In Byron's Shadow

IN BYRON'S SHADOW

MODERN GREECE IN THE

ENGLISH & AMERICAN

IMAGINATION

David Roessel

OXFORD

UNIVERSITY PRESS

2002

OXFORD

UNIVERSITY PRESS

Oxford   New York

Athens   Auckland   Bangkok   Bogotá   Buenos Aires   Cape Town
Chennai   Dar es Salaam   Delhi   Florence   Hong Kong   Istanbul   Karachi
Kolkata   Kuala Lumpur   Madrid   Melbourne   Mexico City   Mumbai   Nairobi
Paris   São Paulo   Shanghai   Singapore   Taipei   Tokyo   Toronto   Warsaw

and associated companies in
Berlin   Ibadan

Published by Oxford University Press, Inc.
198 Madison Avenue, New York, New York 10016

Oxford is a registered trademark of Oxford University Press

Library of Congress Cataloging-in-Publication Data
Roessel, David E. (David Ernest), 1954–
In Byron's shadow : modern Greece in the English and American imagination /
David Roessel.
p.   cm.
Includes bibliographical references and index.
ISBN 0-19-514386-8
1. English literature—History and criticism.   2. Greece—In literature.
3. Byron, George Gordon Byron, Baron, 1788–1824—Knowledge—Greece.
4. Byron, George Gordon Byron, Baron, 1788–1824—Influence.
5. American literature—History and criticism.   6. American literature—Greek influences.
7. English literature—Greek influences.   I. Title.
PR129 .G8 R64   2001
820.9'32495—dc21   00-068454

1 3 5 7 9 8 6 4 2

Printed in the United States of America
on acid-free paper

PREFACE

I first went to Greece in 1979 after receiving an M.A. in classics, driven by a desire to see the places I had studied. All I had at the time was enough for a one-way ticket, and upon arriving I took a job teaching English to the grandchildren of refugees from Smyrna in order to make ends meet. My career in classics did not end there, for I went on to teach in the Classics Department at Howard University in the early 1980s. But that experience repeatedly led me back to the eastern Mediterranean and started me on the road to this book.

I was outside of and somewhat at odds with academia when I began this study more than a decade ago, but three remarkably generous academics helped to make it possible. Carrie Cowherd, with whom I shared an office when I taught at Howard University, functioned as an early mentor and has read almost everything I have written. Eileen Gregory of the University of Dallas, whom I met at a conference on H. D. in 1986, took an interest in my work and urged me to apply for a grant from the National Endowment for the Humanities. When I pointed out that I had no one in the field to write recommendations, she promptly offered to write one. I received the grant for 1990–1991 and did my first research on the present subject at the New York Public Library and the British Library. At the end of the fellowship period, I had a great deal of data, which I had to put together in some coherent way. I went looking for an example and for guidance and found both in one person. I wrote to Arnold Rampersad, who was then at Columbia, to ask if I might become a student of his. It never occurred to me that it was a bit odd for a professor at Columbia to correspond faithfully with an unknown person in Cleveland, who had appeared out of the blue. I am now aware of the number of letters and messages that come into his office, and his generosity and humanity astounds me even more. In 1991, I went to Princeton to work with Arnold. The greatest praise I can give him as a teacher is that he showed me, by setting the highest standard, how to write this book in the proper way. Pam and I continue to value his and Marvina's friendship.

At Princeton I also met Mike Keeley, whose name I had known for years from my reading. Mike shared my passion for Greece and for writing about Greece, and over the years he went from dissertation adviser to close colleague. Mary Keeley added her own keen insight into things literary. Will Howarth has been an untiring source of support. I also owe a great debt to Walt Litz, who read several early versions and offered cogent advice. John Logan helped me with French sources at several points. Dimitri Gondicas, Ian MacNiven, Susan Wolfson, and Nick Moschovakis read and commented on early chapters.

The Gennadius Library of the American School of Classical Studies in Athens has become my second home. Only those who work on Greece in the modern period know the incredible job of book collecting that was done by the intrepid John Gennadius around the turn of the twentieth century. Haris Kalligas, the director of the Gennadius, has been a good friend and staunch supporter. The staff at the library are like family now, so I know that they will not mind me using their first names. Many thanks to Sophie, Anna, Maria, Andreas, Dimitri, Soula, Katerina, Vasso, and Aliki; to Natalia and Maria in the archives; to Saki, Litsa, and Voula in Loring Hall; and to the rest of the staff at the Classical School. I am grateful to College Year in Athens for its interest in this work, especially to Kimon Giocarinis and Mary Lee Coulson. I made extensive use of the British Library, the New York Public Library, the Library of Congress, the Cleveland Public Library, the Firestone Library of Princeton University, the Van Pelt Library of the University of Pennsylvania, and the library at the British School at Athens.

In the early years, I was aided by Frank Toti, Mike and Del DeMauro, Susan Roessel, Pat and Jim Foung, George and Judy Green, and Garo and Rosie Yacoupian, on whose couches I slept during research trips. In recent years, I have been helped in similar ways by Ruth Keshishian, William Packard, Yannis and Joan Moschovakis, Kim Toh and Scott Pike, George Kacandes and Nicolette Trahoulias, Nancy Serwint, Diane Bolger, Gerald L. Vincent, Damla Demizoglu, Ian and Susan MacNiven, and Lawrence and Carolyn Roessel. Nick Moschovakis endured Mount Athos with me more than once; Mike DeMauro was with me during my exploration of the Byronic regions of Epirus; Frank Toti sat with me in Delphi and Missolonghi; and with Jerry Vincent I followed Durrell on Corfu, trailed Rimbaud on Cyprus, and took journeys to Lebanon, Aleppo, Luxor, and Alexandria. Pamela has been a presence παντα καί παντοῦ.

During work on this book, I received support from the National Endowment for the Humanities, the Cyprus Fulbright Commission, the American School of Classical Studies (in the form of the Gennadeion Fellowship), the Princeton Hellenic Studies Program, the American Studies Program at Princeton, the Cyprus American Archaeological Research Institute, the Foundation for Hellenic Culture, and Professor Costas Vayenas and his group at the University of Patras.

My editors at Oxford University Press have truly been a pleasure with which to work. Elissa Morris's commitment to the book raised my own faltering spirits at times. Stacey Hamilton was a great aid. Merryl Sloane, much more than a copy editor, combined remarkable diligence and a graceful intelligence in going through the text. They all contributed in making this a better book. I learned a great deal from each of them. I have been a member of the American School of Classical Studies at Athens (1995–1996), the British School at Athens (spring 1997), and the Cyprus American Archaeological Research Institute (spring 1998).

D. R.

ACKNOWLEDGMENTS

Grateful acknowledgment is made for permission to use the following quotations:

W. H. Auden excerpt from "Letter to Lord Byron" from *W. H. Auden Collected Poems*. Copyright © 1937 by W. H. Auden. Used by permission of Random House, Inc.

Kay Boyle excerpt from "A Poem for the Students of Greece" from *Collected Poems*. Copyright © 1991 by Kay Boyle. Reprinted with permission of Copper Canyon Press, P.O. Box 271, Port Townsend, WA 98366.

Quotations from *The Collected Poems of C. P. Cavafy*, translated by Edmund Keeley and Philip Sherrard, Princeton University Press. Copyright © 1992 by Princeton University Press. Used by permission of Princeton University Press.

The line from "by god i want above fourteenth." Copyright © 1925, 1953, 1991 by the Trustees for the E. E. Cummings Trust. Copyright © 1976 by George James Firmage, from *Complete Poems: 1904–1962*, by E. E. Cummings, edited by George J. Firmage. Used by permission of Liveright Publishing Corporation.

Quotations from *The Collected Poems of Lawrence Durrell*, edited by James Brigham, Faber and Faber. Copyright © 1985 by Estate of Lawrence Durrell. Used by permission of Faber and Faber.

Eight lines from "The Waste Land" from the *Collected Poems 1909–1962*, by T. S. Eliot. Copyright © 1963 by Thomas Stearns Eliot. Used by permission of Faber and Faber and the estate of T. S. Eliot.

Lawrence Ferlinghetti excerpt from "Forty Odd Questions for the Greek Regime and One Cry for Freedom" from *Open Eye, Open Heart*. Copyright © 1973 by Lawrence Ferlinghetti. Used by permission of New Directions Publishing Corporation.

Robert Frost excerpt from "Greece" in Robert Frost's *Collected Poems, Prose, & Plays* (New York: Library of America), 1995. Used by permission of the Library of America.

Excerpt from "America" by Allen Ginsberg from *The Collected Poems, 1947–1980*. Copyright © 1956 by Allen Ginsberg. Used by permission of HarperCollins Publishers.

Rachel Hadas excerpts from "Last Trip to Greece" from *Halfway Down the Hall*. Copyright © 1998 by Rachel Hadas, Wesleyan University Press. Reprinted by permission of the University Press of New England.

Kenneth O. Hanson excerpt from "Take It from Me" from *The Distance Anywhere*, University of Washington Press. Copyright © 1967 by Kenneth O. Hanson. Reprinted by permission of University of Washington Press.

Kenneth O. Hanson excerpts from "Political Poem" and "After the Counter-coup that Failed" from *The Uncorrected Word*. Copyright © 1973 by Kenneth O. Hanson, Wesleyan University Press. Reprinted by permission of the University of New England Press.

Ernest Hemingway's "To the Good Guys Dead" from *88 Poems by Ernest Hemingway*, edited by Nicholas Gerogiannis. Copyright © 1979 by the Ernest Hemingway Foundation and Nicholas Gerogiannis, reprinted by permission of Harcourt, Inc.

Quotation from Israel Horovitz from *The Good Parts*. Copyright © 1983 by Israel Horovitz. All rights reserved. Stock and amateur production rights controlled exclusively by Dramatists Play Service, 440 Park Avenue South, New York, NY 10016. Used by permission of Israel Horovitz.

Excerpt from Rudyard Kipling's translation of the Greek national anthem from *Rudyard Kipling's Verse, 1885–1926*, Doubleday Publishing, 1931. Also used by permission of A. P. Watt Ltd. on behalf of the National Trust for Places of Historical Interest and Natural Beauty.

John Lehmann excerpt from "The Road to Rhamnous" from *The Collected Poems: 1930–1963*. Copyright © 1963 by John Lehmann. Used by permission of David Higham Associates, Limited.

Excerpt from "Hypocrite Auteur" from *Collected Poems 1917–1982* by Archibald MacLeish. Copyright © 1985 by the Estate of Archibald MacLeish. Reprinted by permission of Houghton Mifflin Co. All rights reserved.

Quotations from *The Collected Poems of Louis MacNeice*, edited by E. R. Dodds. Copyright © 1967 by the Estate of Louis MacNeice. Used by permission of David Higham Associates, Limited.

James Merrill excerpts from "After Greece" and "Kostas Tympaniákis" from *Selected Poems*. Copyright © 1992 by James Merrill. Reprinted with permission of Alfred A. Knopf.

Passages from *The Colossus of Maroussi* by Henry Miller. Copyright © 1941 by Henry Miller. Used by permission of New Directions Publishing Corporation.

William Plomer excerpts from "Three Pinks" and "On the Poems of C. P. Cavafy" from *The Five-Fold Screen*, Hogarth Press. Copyright © 1932. Used by permission of Barclays Bank Trust Company as trustee for the Estate of William Plomer.

William Plomer excerpts from "Another Country" and "Three Pinks" from *The Collected Poems*, published by Jonathan Cape, 1973. Used by permission of the Random House Archive and Library, UK.

Excerpt from *Cantos* by Ezra Pound. Copyright © 1948 by Ezra Pound. Used by permission of New Directions Publishing Corporation.

Excerpts from "Birthday on the Acropolis" from *Collected Poems 1930-1993* by May Sarton. Copyright © 1993, 1988, 1984, 1980, 1974 by May Sarton. Used by permission of W. W. Norton & Company.

Quotations from *The Collected Poems of George Seferis*, translated by Edmund Keeley and Philip Sherrard. Copyright © 1967 by Princeton University Press. Used by permission of Princeton University Press.

Bernard Spencer, "Aegean Islands, 1940-1941" from *Collected Poems*, edited by Roger Bowen. Copyright © Oxford University Press, 1981. Used by permission of Oxford University Press.

Bernard Spencer, "Greek Excavations" from *Collected Poems*, edited by Roger Bowen. Copyright © Oxford University Press, 1981. Used by permission of Oxford University Press.

Bernard Spencer, "Salonika (June 1940)" from *Collected Poems*, edited by Roger Bowen. Copyright © Oxford University Press, 1981. Used by permission of Oxford University Press.

John Waller excerpt from "Spring in Athens" from *The Kiss of the Stars* (copyright © John Waller, 1948). Used by permission of A. M. Heath, Limited.

W. B. Yeats excerpts from "September 1913" and "The Man and the Echo" reprinted with the permission of Scribner, a division of Simon and Schuster, from *The Collected Poems of W. B. Yeats*, rev. 2d ed., edited by Richard J. Finneran. Copyright © 1924 by Macmillan Publishing Company, renewed by Berthe Georgie Yeats.

CONTENTS

CONTENTS

ABBREVIATIONS AND CITATIONS

In this work, *CPW* refers to Byron's *The Complete Poetical Works*, 7 vols., edited by Jerome McGann. For poetical citations to longer works, specifically *Childe Harold's Pilgrimage*, *The Giaour*, *The Corsair*, *The Bride of Abydos*, *The Siege of Corinth*, and *Don Juan*, I give the canto, stanza, and/or line numbers as they are relevant for each poem. For shorter works and references to Byron's notes, I provide the volume and page number. To keep these citations distinct, where volume and page numbers are given, they are always preceded by *CPW* and include p. or pp. in front of the page numbers, while the references to canto, stanza, and line numbers never have *CPW* nor p. or pp. References to the poetical works of Shelley also provide stanza and/or line numbers, and stanza numbers are given for Felicia Hemans's long poem *Modern Greece*. *BLJ* refers to *Byron's Letters and Journals*, 12 vols., edited by Leslie Marchand. References are to the volume and page number. Quotations from Winckelmann in chapter 1 are taken from *English Romantic Hellenism*, edited by Timothy Webb. The first citation in the text reads Webb, *English Romantic Hellenism*, but subsequent references contain just Webb and the page number. Other works are cited by the author's name and, where needed, the title, followed by the page number. Full reference information is provided in the bibliography.

CHRONOLOGY

1827: Naval battle of Navarino secures
    Greek independence

1833: Founding of modern Greek
    state and arrival of King Otho from
    Bavaria

1843: Revolution in Greece results in a
    constitutional monarchy

1854–1857: British and French troops
    occupy Athens because of Greek
    sympathy for the Russians during
    the Crimean War

1863: Revolution in Greece; King
    Otho abdicates and is replaced by
    George I (from Denmark)
1866–1867: Revolt in Crete

1870: Greek brigands kidnap four for-
    eigners near Marathon and later
    kill them at Dilessi
1876: Bulgarians fail in a revolt against
    the Turks. Turks massacre thou-
    sands of Bulgarians in response

1881: European powers force Turkey
    to cede Thessaly to Greece

1897: Greco–Turkish War

1831: Disraeli's *Contarini Fleming*
1839: Mary Shelley's "Euphrasia"

1848: Edward Lear's painting
    Marathon

1851: Edward Lear's *Journal of a
    Landscape Painter in Albania and
    Illyria*
    Hiram Powers's statue *The Greek
    Slave* exhibited in London.
1857: Edmond About's *Le roi de
    montagnes*

1867: Swinburne's "Ode on the In-
    surrection in Candia"
1869: Mark Twain's *Innocents
    Abroad*

1876: Gladstone's *The Bulgarian
    Horrors and the Eastern Question*

1881: Swinburne's "Athens: An
    Ode"

1896: E. F. Benson's *Limitations*
1897: E. F. Benson's *The Vintage: A
    Romance of the Greek War of In-
    dependence*
1899: Stephen Crane's *Active Ser-
    vice*

1905: E. M. Forster's "The Road
    from Colonus"
1906: Virginia Woolf's first visit to
    Greece and her story "A Dia-
    logue on Mount Pentelicus"

1912–1913: First and Second Balkan
    Wars
1912: Constantine ascends throne in
    Greece in March after the assassi-
    nation of his father, George I
1914: World War I begins
1915: Gallipoli campaign
1917: Greece joins the war on the side
    of the Allies after the abdication
    and exile of King Constantine
1918: Greece is given eastern Thrace
    and the area around Smyrna by the
    Treaty of Versailles

1911: Demetra Vaka Brown's *In the
    Shadow of Islam*
1916: Julia Dragoumis's *A Man of
    Athens*
1918–1919: Vita Sackville-West
    writes *Challenge*
1919: Demetra Vaka Brown's *In
    Pawn to a Throne*

1920: Elections return Royalist party;
    King Constantine returns
1920–1922: Greco-Turkish War;
    Greece defeated and loses eastern
    Thrace and the area around
    Smyrna; Smyrna burnt; revolution
    deposes King Constantine (leaves
    for second exile) and Royalist gov-
    ernment; six ministers executed
1923: Treaty of Lausanne mandates an
    exchange of populations between
    Greece and Turkey; Greece re-
    ceives more than a million refugees

1923: Hemingway's *in our time*;
    first publication of Asia Minor
    vignettes
1924: Centennial of Byron's death
1929: Susan Glaspell's *Fugitive's
    Return*; Robert Byron's *The
    Byzantine Achievement*

1935: Attempted coup by Venizelist
    party; Venizelos goes into exile; re-
    turn of King George II
1936: Beginning of the dictatorship of
    General Metaxas, which lasts until
    Greece's entry into World War II

1930: Hemingway's "On the Quai at
    Smyrna"
1931: William Plomer goes to
    Greece
1932: Christopher Isherwood
    spends the summer in Greece; he
    later includes an account of the
    trip in *Down There on a Visit*
    (1962)
1935: Lawrence Durrell moves to
    Corfu
1937: Auden's "Letter to Lord
    Byron"
1939: Henry Miller travels to Greece

1940: Greece enters World War II

1941: Miller's *The Colossus of
    Maroussi*

1941–1945: Greece occupied by Axis powers

1945–1949: Greek Civil War

1945: Durrell's *Prospero's Cell*

1948: George Seferis's *The King of Asine and Other Poems*, a volume of verse, is translated and published in London

1957: Francis King's *The Firewalkers*

1958: Patrick Leigh Fermor's *Mani*; Edmund Keeley's *The Libation*

1959: Kevin Andrews's *The Flight of Ikaros*

1967: Coup by a group of colonels preempts elections; military junta is established

1964: *Zorba the Greek* (film)

1965: James Merrill's *The (Diblos) Notebook*

1966: John Fowles's *The Magus* (first version)

1974: Fall of the junta; democracy restored to Greece

1971: Death of the poet George Seferis

1973: Kay Boyle's "A Poem for the Students of Greece"

1977: Mary Lee Settle's *Blood Tie* wins National Book Award

1981: Peter Levi's *The Hill of Kronos*

1982: Don DeLillo's *The Names*

In Byron's Shadow

INTRODUCTION

Almost Impossible to Think Sanely about Greece

On the terrace of the Hotel Cecil in the Greek city of Patras just after the outbreak of World War II in the summer of 1939, Henry Miller tried to dissuade Lawrence Durrell from enlisting in the Greek army. "He knew what I thought about war," Miller related, "and I think in his heart he agrees with me, but being young, being serviceable, being English despite himself, he was in a quandary. It was a bad place in which to discuss a subject of this sort. The atmosphere was charged with memories of Byron. Sitting there, with Missolonghi so near, it was almost impossible to think sanely about war" (*Colossus of Maroussi* 25).

Miller's problem was compounded by the fact that it was equally impossible to think sanely about Greece with Missolonghi so near. In Edward Whittemore's *Jerusalem Poker*, a character in Athens asserts that "the light here *is* different. It's a palpable thing and the effect is inescapable, which is why Greece has always been more of an idea than a place. When the modern nation was founded in the last century, Alexandria and Constantinople were the great Greek cities in the world, and Athens was a lonely plain where a few shepherds grazed their flocks at the foot of the Acropolis. But no matter. An idea doesn't die. It only slumbers and can always be resurrected" (113). The idea continuously resurrected from the late eighteenth century into the twentieth century was the regeneration of Greece and the Greeks, the physical reincarnation of the idea of the ancient past. And it was Byron, the martyr of Missolonghi, who had made the dream that "Greece might still be free" a part of a *literary* tradition. In addition to being young, serviceable, and English, Durrell was also a poet, and that, as Miller certainly knew, was a key element in Durrell's desire to join the Greek army.

It was not the last time that Henry Miller would have trouble thinking sanely about either Greece or war, but the shade of Byron did not trouble him long. Durrell, in the end, did not join the Greek army; he went with Miller to Athens, where they met poet George Seferis and George Katsimbalis, a

3

fellow "out of all proportion," as Durrell called him in his poem "My Theology." With these two Greeks as guides, Miller and Durrell would create a new concept of modern Greece in writing in English, one where young, serviceable, poetic young men no longer debated whether they should join the Greek army. They constructed a Greece where one went to escape from precisely such debates.

As Australian author George Johnston signaled in his novel *Closer to the Sun* (1960), Miller's *Colossus of Maroussi* was the work that replaced the verse of Byron as the canonical text of modern Greece for English and American readers. The protagonist, the fortyish David Meredith, asks a fellow expatriate on the island of Silenus (Hydra), an elderly British woman, how she came to be living in the Aegean. "'Asthma,' she replied. 'That . . . and my own passion for Byron.'" "I feel now," she continues, "it should have been Shelley. . . . But then it would have been Italy instead of here" (33). Some fifteen pages later, David's brother Mark asks him the same question. He responds, "Shall I say I am learning to know something about the light and shadow on rocks against the sky, the true taste of water, the rhythms of the season, the values of simplicity." Mark exclaims, "Oh, for God's sake. . . . All this pseudo-poetic Henry Miller guff" (34). Johnston included these two exchanges to indicate the generational gap between the pre- and postwar generations of expatriates on the island, signified by the two different "books" of Greece they carried with them on their voyage. According to Johnston, after Byron came Miller. There was, he suggests, nothing in between. For more than a hundred years after Byron's death, the Greek land was "haunted, holy ground," as Byron said of Athens. But, with Missolonghi so near, the spirit haunting it was Byron himself.

This book examines the significance of what Victor Hugo called the "Greece of Byron," or modern Greece, in English and American writing. Although ancient Greece, Hugo's "Greece of Homer," and modern Greece occupy the same geographical space on the map, they are two distinct entities in the Western imagination, as demonstrated by Virginia Woolf's comment: "I take pains to put old Greece on my right hand and new Greece on my left & nothing I say of one shall apply to the other" (*Passionate Apprentice* 340). Scholarship has tended to follow Woolf's advice, for while there is a large shelf of books devoted to the position and meaning of old Greece on nineteenth- and twentieth-century literature in English, hardly any attention has been given to new Greece. The Greece of Byron is an interesting case study for several interrelated reasons, including its close connection to a single foreign poet, its persistent politicization, and its survival as a Romantic area long after the age of Romanticism ended.

Few countries have remained in the shadow of a single author for so long. In John Fowles's *The Magus* (1966), Nicholas Urfe says, "My knowledge of modern Greece began and ended with Byron's death at Missolonghi"

(39–40), and most of English and American writing about Greece into the twentieth century was also stuck in the milieu of the Greek War of Independence and Byron's Eastern Tales. For a century after the poet's death, writers tended to replicate rather than revise the Greece found in Byron's poetry. This desire was, to be sure, not simply a homage to a single writer but also an attempt to keep alive the social and political currents of the Romantic age, if only in one small spot on the globe. The literary tradition has, of course, more than one Byron. In addition to the hero of Missolonghi, there is the dandy in London and the introspective Manfred. This book is concerned only with the first. Byron was not always a politicized entity, but "Byron in Greece" was. With Missolonghi so near, one could say with some justice that it was also impossible to think sanely about Byron.

The resurrection of Greece, considered the original font of Western culture, was never an end in itself but rather was connected with a new spiritual, political, or cultural revival. Jerome McGann noted that in *Childe Harold's Pilgrimage* Byron was deeply concerned with "the renewal of the value of the individual person, and the renewal of Greece as a political entity becomes Byron's 'objective correlative' for this idea" (*Beauty of Inflections* 260). Greece, therefore, was a highly politicized place on the map of Europe, since its renewal as a political entity was associated with the social and cultural changes desired by Western authors. In Maria Edgeworth's novel *Helen* (1834), therefore, a young Englishman, who spoke "with enthusiasm of modern Greece, and his hopes that she might recover her ancient character," is cautioned that "Greece is a dangerous field for the political speculator" (175). I argue that the lack of innovative writing about modern Greece from 1833 to 1920 is directly related to the fact that the country was such a dangerous field for writers, a place where one had to tread lightly because of the powerful presence of Byron and his legendary death in Greece. During his conversation with Durrell that day in Patras, Miller himself saw Greece as such a dangerous field.

In the first decade of the last century, Saki (Hector Herbert Munro) called modern Greece and the surrounding Balkans "the last shred of happy hunting-ground for the adventurous, a playground of passions that are fast becoming atrophied for want of exercise. . . . If the Balkan lands are to be finally parceled out between competing Christian kingdoms and the haphazard rule of the Turk banished beyond the Sea of Marmara, the old order, or disorder if you like, will have received its death blow. . . . the old atmosphere will have changed; the glamour will be gone" (528–31). Another way of phrasing Saki's words would be to say that modern Greece and Macedonia in particular was, in 1912, the last remaining Romantic area on earth. Through Byron, modern Greece became, as it were, embalmed in the time of Romanticism, and it suffered the fate of all perceived Romantic or nineteenth-century conceptions and values after the Great War. If before 1914, Byron in Greece was a model for the poet as a man of action, then after 1918 he became an anti-model for the young men sent to fight for the dead values of a botched civilization. After the Great War, novels of the conflict, like Dos Passos's *Three Soldiers* and Hemingway's *A Farewell to Arms*, suggested that the only way to save one's self and one's sanity was to desert. A fitting analogy, or objective correlative, of that act was to desert the cause of the Greeks during the Greco-Turkish War of 1920–1922 and all of the cultural meanings associated with that cause.

With contemporary notions of dancing Zorbas and Shirley Valentines with or without bikini tops, we might forget that before the late 1930s almost no one went to Greece to find their inner selves. This is the Greece that Miller and Durrell began to construct after their close encounter with Missolonghi in 1939. English and Americans in the nineteenth century went for that kind of experience—to discover the self and to be changed within—to Italy. One went to Greece, on the other hand, in imitation of Byron, to help change the Greeks and to assist Greece in its restoration to its ancient splendor. As Edgeworth indicated in *Helen*, discussions of whether Greece would recover its ancient character involved one in dangerous *political* speculations, since, in the eyes of those who pursued such speculations, the revival of the Greeks had to have some effect on the rest of Europe and the world at large. Greek regeneration was not simply a part of nineteenth-century nationalism, it contained within it millennial hopes. Yet while I argue that modern Greece had a particular significance for English and American writers from 1770 to 1967, I also suggest that the depiction of Greece had a symbiotic relation to the perception of Italy, Turkey, and the Mediterranean in general. When the idea of Italy became highly politicized, because of Mussolini and Fascism, the idea of Greece lost political force; conversely, when the idea of late nineteenth-century Italy was not politicized, the conception of Greece was.

From a global perspective, two rather insignificant events frame this study. In 1770, the Greeks rose in revolt against Turkish rule. The revolt failed, but because of an increasing idealization of the Greek past in the eighteenth century and the growing revolutionary sentiment of the age, this uprising caught the attention of Western Europe. In 1967, a group of colonels staged a coup in Greece to prevent elections that the Socialist candidate was poised to win. This event also could have passed unnoticed abroad, but it came at a time of intense worldwide political activism during the late 1960s. After three decades as lotus land, Greece once again became a partisan slogan in the West, as it had been in the time of Byron. If the coup did not put a complete end to the Greece of Miller and Durrell, it forced many writers to reconsider their thinking about modern Greece. My point should be clear—it was not what was happening in Greece that caused England and America to think about a small nation in the eastern Mediterranean. Rather, Greece became an important place in the English and American mind when it fit in with other, already established ideas. A book about modern Greece, or the literature of modern Greece, would be quite different; for one thing, it would have far more to say about the brutal civil war of the late 1940s. While events of Greek history will have a prominent place in the pages that follow, my focus will be on the meaning given to those events in works in England and America, not what they meant to Greeks.

Modern Greece, in history and in literature, has been viewed as a transitory moment squeezed between two larger and more important entities. Viewed chronologically, modern Greece rests between the glory of the classical Greek past and the hope of a resurrected Greek future, which in many Western minds ought to resemble the democracies of Western Europe and America, which were founded on classical Greek models. Modern Greece as an entity did not exist but remained in a state of becoming. In 1909, nearly eighty years after the end of the Greek War of Independence, G. F. Abbott edited a book entitled *Greece in Evolution*, which argued that modern Greece was beginning to show the promise that the world expected of it. In 1977, John Koumoulides edited a book entitled *Greece in Transition: New Essays in the History of Modern Greece, 1821–1977*, as if the entire existence of the Greek state was a preparation for something to come. Viewed geographically, modern Greece sits between Europe and Asia; it is in the process of throwing off the "Orientalism" it acquired during four centuries of Turkish rule and reacquiring a European nature. This perception was reinforced by the fact that nearly every generation of English and American philhellenes from 1833 until 1922 experienced at least one of a series of Greek struggles to free themselves from Turkish oppression. The notion that modern Greece was still in a state of becoming, an idea supported by a continual series of armed confrontations with the Turks, helped to fix the conception of modern Greece in the time of the Greek Revolution, the Greece of Byron. This is why it could appear to Saki as the last shred of happy hunting ground for the adventurous.

A broad synopsis of the argument that follows would read: the Romantic age constructed an image of a politicized, female, modern Greece fit for the temple of Apollo. This image dominated representations of Greece into the twentieth century and was eventually transmuted by writers affiliated with modernism into an apolitical, male Greece in a Dionysian frenzy. The transition is obvious in literary works, but the reasons are not, and it certainly cannot be explained only as a modernist reaction to Romantic Greece. The literary geography of the Mediterranean is equally important. While the story of Italy or Egypt in English and American writing differs greatly from that of Greece, the perception of these three places and the adjoining areas interact and affect one another.

The first part of this book covers the years from 1770 through the end of the Greek War of Independence (1821–1833). I look at the development of philhellenism as a cultural movement that had revolutionary implications within a European context while containing imperialist rhetoric with regard to the Turks and the East. I examine the persistent personification of Greece as a female needing rescue from a Turk by a savior from the West and how Byron employed that scenario in works such as *The Giaour*. I argue that one of the main reasons that so little of the mass of philhellenic writings from the Greek War of Independence has lasted is that the canonical texts of the Greek Revolution were written by Byron before the Greek Revolution had even started. With the "scripture" of the Greek uprising intact, later works functioned more as commentary and interpretation.

The second part investigates the omnipresence of Byronic Greece in writing in English from 1833 to 1913. The Greece of Byron was a radical cause linked to other issues, including the abolition of slavery, the extension of the vote, and the independence movements in Italy, Spain, and Poland. For the liberals and the radicals who espoused these causes, the liberation of the Greeks was part of a sacred heritage. Given that the rhetoric about Greece had been established by Byron, the only real developments were an expansion of that rhetoric by Gladstone and other liberals to include the Balkan Christians generally and, in response to that expansion, a simultaneous narrowing of philhellenic rhetoric to cover only those pure Greeks of unmixed blood who lived on remote islands and mountains. Both of these developments had deleterious effects on the perception of the Greeks. On the one hand, when lumped with the other Christians of the East, they were viewed as Balkan or Levantine; on the other, a preserve of real Greeks was created by disenfranchising the majority of Greece's inhabitants. Philhellenes abroad would eventually apply the "true" versus "false" Greek dichotomy to disputes between political factions within Greece.

The third part of this work deals with the reaction to the Greece of Byron in the years during and after the Great War. The idea of a Greater Greece, including Constantinople and Asia Minor, survived the fighting of World War I. In fact, the Versailles Treaty almost established the desired Greater Greece by granting the Greeks eastern Thrace and the territory around Smyrna. Philhellenic writing was surprisingly deaf to the fact that the Romantic nationalism that lay behind the drive for a Greater Greece had died in the trenches. The Greek defeat in the Greco-Turkish War of 1920–1922 and the subsequent exchange of populations with Turkey, in which a million and a half Greeks were forced to leave their homes on Turkish soil and go to Greece, brought an end to Greater Greece and the dream of a Greek regeneration. I argue that Hemingway and other modern writers employed the Greek defeat of 1922 as a symbol for the death of the prewar values because of the focus upon Greek culture and the desire for a revival of the Greeks in the nineteenth century. The fate of the modern Greeks was simply a foil to invert the world of the old men. In the aftermath of the Greek defeat and the end of the Greek revival as it had been envisioned from 1770, authors had to recreate or reinvent a new modern Greece. The third part ends with a look at the most significant attempts in that direction during the two decades after the Great War and why they failed to gain wide recognition.

The conclusion looks at the Greece brought into existence by Miller and Durrell. These two authors reinvested modern Greece with meaning by stripping it of all political significance; ironically, in the late 1930s, when both Italy and Spain were engulfed by contemporary political questions, Greece offered "the discovery of yourself," to borrow the words of Lawrence Durrell. I show that this occurred when Greece itself was under a dictatorship and under the shadow of the impending war, so that the creation of an idyllic Greece during these years was an act of will by both Miller and Durrell. Those writers who came to Greece in the late 1940s and 1950s carrying the books of Miller and Durrell also persisted in turning their eyes from the internal politics of Greece, despite a bitter civil war between the Left and the Right from 1945 to 1949. Greece became repoliticized in Western eyes by the military coup in 1967, partly because leftist political activism in the West viewed the coup as a cause and partly because the unappealing politics within Greece helped to move lotus land elsewhere.

A study of this scope must, of necessity, attempt to provide a framework rather than a comprehensive account of each period. I hope that my work stimulates further investigations on particular periods, movements, and literary works. Despite numerous studies about the Greece of Homer in English and American literature, the Greece of Byron has been largely overlooked, especially after 1833. Terence Spencer, in his invaluable *Fair Greece, Sad Relic: Literary Philhellenism before Byron*, stops just before the Greek Revolution begins. Raizis and Papas have done important work on the poetry about the Greek Revolution but do not deal with fiction or drama and do not go much beyond 1850. Larrabee and Eisner have written books on travelers' accounts of Greece, but they generally avoid creative works. Karanikas's discussion of modern Greeks in American literature focuses more on twentieth-century works written after the period that I discuss. Even Artemis Leontis, in her recent and useful book *Topographies of Hellenism*, speaks as if most, if not all, Western travelers ignore modern Greece in an attempt to make contact with a sublime and serene classical past. But when Noel Brailsford, Allen Upward, and Stephen MacKenna went to Greece to fight against the Turks in 1897, and when E. F. Benson, Isabella Mayo, and George Horton published philhellenic novels that same year, it was Byron who provided the inspiration. Since this is the first attempt to trace the portrayal of modern Greece from the Romantic period through modernism, rather than focus on a few key works I have chosen to use a wide array of sources and to fill in the cultural background.

"The trouble with Greece," as the main character of DeLillo's *The Names* says, is that it is "strategically located," and it needs to be examined in conjunction with Turkey, the Balkans, and Italy. I originally intended such a comparative study but found that Greece (and then Turkey and the Balkans) had to be investigated first.[1] In the course of this study and in the years of my own involvement with Greece, I have at times felt that I have uncovered new territory. But I have always been brought back to earth by Peter Levi's sane words: "Whoever discovers Greece today can hardly rank with Columbus" (*Hill of Kronos* 9). This is not a voyage into the unknown but an investigation into a spot on the literary map that has been generally neglected in the past because it was perceived to be so well known and traveled. My aim is to challenge that perception and to show that modern Greece is more than a transitory moment in writing in English but a place worth stopping in and pondering over.

I

PAST GREATNESS & PRESENT DEBASEMENT

(1770–1833)

1

I Want to Revive Athens

In early 1770, a small expeditionary force from Russia landed in the southern Peloponnesus to aid local Greeks in a rebellion against Ottoman rule. Russia's motives were not at all altruistic; it wanted to divert Ottoman troops from the Russian border and, if possible, add Mediterranean territory to the empire of Czarina Catherine. Nor were local Greeks overly eager to join in the effort for their "liberation." It took several years of negotiations and promises by Russian agents before any prominent Greek chieftains pledged their support. When the Russians finally arrived with far fewer than the expected army of 10,000, a mutual mistrust quickly developed between the local Greeks and the Russian leader, Count Alexis Orloff. Many Greeks who had listened to the appeals for freedom were reluctant to swear allegiance to the Russian sovereign, an oath upon which Orloff insisted. And the Russians found that it was hard to recruit even 3,000 Greek soldiers and harder still to keep any kind of discipline. Further, incidents of indiscriminate massacre and plunder by the Greek warriors against both Turkish and Greek civilians alienated the local population and prevented the revolt from gaining popular support. The result, as Thomas Hope remarked in in his novel *Anastasius* (1819), was that the Greeks and Russians "each, alike disappointed, threw on the other the blame of every failure" (I.28).

The most ambitious action of the campaign occurred when a force of Greeks and Russians pushed north toward the town of Tripolitza. The advance was so slow that it provided ample time for the Turkish commander to receive reinforcements from Albania. When the Ottoman troops attacked the advancing Greco-Russian force, large numbers of Greeks fled the battlefield, leaving 400 Russian soldiers to their fate. The remaining Russians left on their ships. The Ottoman governor quickly extinguished what was left of the rebellion, and the most enduring result of the uprising was the misery of the local population at the hands of the Albanians, called in contemporary sources the Arnauts, who had arrived to assist the Ottoman army.[1]

The revolt of 1770 appears in history, when it appears at all, as a footnote to the Russo-Turkish Wars of 1768–1774 or the more important Greek rebellion of 1821. While it is true that the Greeks had begun a revival of national consciousness in the middle of the eighteenth century, the events of 1770 were caused more from frustration with Ottoman misgovernment than from a fervor for national liberation. The revolt took its place in a long series of activities by disgruntled subject peoples under Turkish rule. For example, a serious uprising by Greeks on the island of Cyprus had occurred just six years earlier. There was no reason to think that any more notice would be taken of the events of 1770 than the other numerous local rebellions in the empire of the sultan.

Yet 1770 marked a watershed in how Western Europeans perceived the modern Greeks. Across the Ionian sea, the rebellion fired imaginations from the moment Count Orloff and his soldiers set foot on Greek soil. The *Gentleman's Magazine* of London for July 1770 announced: "On the first appearance of the Russian succours, the Greeks, who had long groaned under the tyrannical yoke of the haughty Ottomans, assumed for the moment the appearance of the manly bravery of their renowned ancestors, and fell upon their oppressors with all the violence of vindictive rage" (quoted in Constantine 172).[2] In his "Ode Pindarique à propos la guerre présente en Grèce," written while the revolt was in progress, Voltaire put in the mouth of Pallas Athena his own hopes for the outcome of the struggle:

> Je veux ressusciter Athènes.
> Qu'Homère chante vos combats,
> Que la voix de cent Démosthenes
> Ranime vos coeurs et vos bras.
> Sortez, renaissez, Arts aimables,
> De ces ruines déplorables
> Qui vous cachaient sous leurs débris;
> Reprenez votre éclat antique.
>
> (*Oeuvres Complètes* 8.491–92)

> [I want to revive Athens.
> Let Homer sing your combats,
> Let the voice of a hundred Demosthenes
> Revive your hearts and your arms.
> Come forth, be born again, lovable Arts,
> From these deplorable ruins
> That hid you under their debris;
> Take back again your antique brilliance.]

For Voltaire, as for the rest of Western Europe, a necessary corollary of the resumption by the modern Greeks of the mantle of their famous ancestors would be the revival of the "Arts aimables" of antiquity from the deplorable ruins of the present. The independence of modern Greece was for most Western intellectuals never an end in itself but rather a prelude to the regeneration of "Greece," an artistic, spiritual, and/or political ideal. Olga Augustinos noted that, in the case of Voltaire, Greek liberation meant "not the creation of independent Greece but the victory of reason and human rights" (146). And Jerome McGann described the importance of modern Greece in Byron's first narrative poem in the following terms: "*Childe Harold* (1812) is obsessed with the idea of the renewal of human culture in the west at a moment of its deepest darkness. This means for Byron the renewal of the value of the individual person, and the renewal of Greece as a political entity becomes Byron's 'objective correlative' for this idea" (*Beauty of Inflections* 260).[3] Greece functioned as such an objective correlative for a whole generation of writers; this explains why the revival of the Greeks, unlike that of the Serbs, the Bulgars, or the Arabs, was thought to have the power to transform the lives and art of the world, especially the Western part. For with the regeneration of Greece comes a solution to the cultural malaise of the individual in industrial society.

Philhellenism was from its inception more than a chapter in the story of nineteenth-century nationalism. In terms of cultural inheritance, there was a common belief in Europe and America that, as Shelley claimed in the preface to *Hellas*, "We are all Greeks." So, "the final triumph of the Greek cause" should be viewed, in the words of the poet, "as a portion of the cause of civilisation and social improvement" (*Shelley's Poetry and Prose* 409, 408). In a dialogue published in 1829, Walter Savage Landor had the philhellene Edward Trelawny tell a leader of the Greek Revolution: "But other nations do not interest me like the Greeks, to whom I owe every exalted, every generous, every just sentiment" (*Complete Works* VIII.227). In 1877, Edward Augustus Freeman wrote of the Greek War of Independence: "The uprising of Greece against her oppressors had in it all that could attract a like movement in Italy or Poland, while it had further claims which the cause of Italy or Poland could not claim. The practical wrongs of Greece were greater than those of either Italy or Poland, while the name of Greece appealed to all nobler feelings of men's hearts in a way that Poland, or even Italy, could not do" (*Historical Essays* 308).[4] Supporters of Irish, Polish, or Italian nationalism wanted these various peoples to be free; early philhellenic writers like Voltaire and Hölderlin really hoped that a Greek revolution would free them.

The modern Greeks, whether they desired a new Athens or not, would find that the only way they could influence opinion in the West was by accepting and exploiting the Western construction of their own identity and goals.[5] Here again the revolt of 1770 was the crucial precedent, for one could plausibly argue that no notice would have been taken of that rebellion if not for the participation of the Russians and, more important, the manner in which the Russians, even Empress Catherine in her letters to Voltaire, depicted Russian action in Greece.[6] Certainly one goal of Russian propaganda was to use Greek freedom as a cover for Russian conquest, in the manner that Byron complained about Catherine's son, Alexander: "How fain, if Greeks would be his slaves, free Greece!" (*Age of Bronze* 10.445). But the announced Russian commitment to the regeneration of Greece in the late eighteenth century also seemed an attempt to prove the Westernness of Russia. Greek intellectuals in the decades after 1770 would embrace the Western idea of the regeneration of their own race for the same purpose: to demonstrate to the West that they deserved a place among the "civilized" peoples.[7]

The revolt of 1770 was the crystallizing event in the emergence of phil-hellenism as a significant literary movement,[8] and 1770 continued to echo in European writing for decades. In Friedrich Hölderlin's *Hyperion* (published in two parts in 1797 and 1799), the hero participates in the rebellion, and the failed attack on Tripolitza forms the crux of the novel. The singer who appears in the second canto of Richard Polwhele's *Grecian Prospects* (1799) remarks upon "the din of arms in vain" in 1770 but quickly adds: "Yet in these isles, I nurse the martial fires, / Fires, that ere-long, shall far illumine Greece" (36–37). Sydney Owenson's *Woman; or, Ida of Athens* (1809) is set after the failed revolt, and one of its central themes is the hope of a new and successful attempt to overthrow the Ottoman yoke. Byron's first Turkish Tale, *The Giaour* (1814), takes place "at the time the Seven Islands were possessed by the Republic of Venice, and soon after the Arnauts [Albanians] were beaten back from the Morea, which they had ravaged for some time subsequent to the Russian invasion" (*CPW* III, pp. 39–40). And the first historical event in Thomas Hope's *Anastasius* (1819) is the uprising in the Morea, another name for the Peloponnesus (I.27–28), and the young hero's first success occurs during the campaign against the Albanians in 1779 (I.53–59). Just as important as the specific references to the rebellion in Greece were the language and concepts attached to the event. Hölderlin's modern Greek hero rhetorically asks: "Were we born in the swamp, like a will-o'-wisp, or are we descended from the victors of Salamis?" (119). Owenson in her introduction says that the Russians "found no difficulty in inspiriting the Greeks to defence of their national rights, and for the recovery of their ancient liberties. The same love of freedom, the same vivacity of feeling, and ardor of enthusiasms, was found among many of the oppressed descendants of the heroes of Marathon and Plataea as distinguished their immortal ancestors" (I.xxiv). The restoration of ancient Greece figures as the central "prospect" in Polwhele's *Grecian Prospects*. In the second canto of *Childe Harold's Pilgrimage* (1812), Byron also talked of the modern Greeks as the descendants of the ancients:

> In all save form alone, how chang'd! and who
> That marks the fire still sparkling in each eye,
> Who but would deem their bosoms burn'd anew

With thy unquenched beam, lost Liberty!
And many dream that the hour withal is nigh
That gives them back their father's heritage.
(II.75.711–16)

But Byron remained cautious, indeed almost pessimistic, about the possibility of Greek liberation, which, in the event it should occur, should not be dependent on foreign assistance ("Greece! change thy lords, thy state is still the same," II.76.727). In *Itinéraire de Paris à Jérusalem* (1811) Chateaubriand was equally cautious. Despite his claim that "there is still an abundance of genius in Greece; I even think that our masters in every line still reside there," he concluded, "at the same time, I fear the Greeks are not too well disposed to break their chains. If even they were released from the tyranny which oppresses them, they would not lose in a moment the marks of their fetters. They have not only been crushed beneath the weight of despotism, but for two thousand years they have been a superannuated and degraded nation" (180).[9]

In his novel of 1819, Thomas Hope could poke fun at the great interest in the "revival" of the Greeks. An Italian tells Anastasius that a great opportunity awaits him in France, "All you have to do is to present yourself in the august assembly of the great nation as the representative of oppressed and mourning Greece. Be the eloquent, the pathetic organ of its ardent desire to share the benefits which France confers on the world. Tell of the myriads that to her lift their imploring hands. . . . it will be your own fault if in the convention you are not hailed as the worthy descendant of Harmodius and Aristogeiton" (III.103). Still, Hope himself was interested in the regeneration of the Greeks, for he said in his preface that the author wrote the novel because "in an age when whatever relates to the regions once adorned by the Greeks, and since defaced by the Turks, excites particular attention he thought the narrative might add to our information on so interesting a subject" (I.i).[10]

The connection between modern Greeks and ancient Greeks expressed in these works reveals a changed mental and political geography of the Mediterranean. For if the modern Greeks were descended from the victors of Marathon, then they were also Europeans and siblings of the West. And if they were Europeans, indeed the ancestors of the founders of European civilization, they should not be the subjects of Eastern barbarism. For many the proof of the birthright of the modern Greeks was the revolt of 1770.

The reason that the events of 1770 had such an effect on the Western imagination stemmed from factors that had little to do with modern Greece itself. The most significant development came in the middle of the eighteenth century, when intellectuals began to reject the dominant aesthetics of neoclassicism. As Frank Turner said, the "search for new cultural roots and alternative cultural politics developed out of a need to understand and articulate the disruptive, political, social, and intellectual experience that Europeans confronted in the wake of the enlightenment and of revolution" (2). That for many the response to such cultural malaise resulted in a turn to Hellenism was largely the work of Johann Joachim Winckelmann.[11] The German art historian asserted the aesthetic perfection of the fifth-century BCE Athenians by studying fragments of Roman copies of Greek originals. After Winckelmann, in the words of Walter Pater, "the standard of taste, then, was fixed in Greece, at a definite historical period" (*Renaissance* 196). In the Athens of Pericles, Phidias, and Sophocles Winckelmann found the "noble simplicity and sedate grandeur of Gesture and Expression," which constituted for him the central elements of true beauty. He went on to explain: "As the bottom of the sea lies peaceful beneath a foaming surface, a great soul lies sedate beneath the strife of passions in Greek figures" (Webb, *English Romantic Hellenism* 121). In the cultural upheaval of the late eighteenth century, many would find in the idea of the inner repose of the ancient Greeks an answer to their own personal and cultural turbulence.

Winckelmann claimed that "to the Greek climate we owe the production of *Taste*, and from thence it spread at length over all the politer world" (Webb 116). The importance of environment as an explanation for the Greek achievement can be seen from the following comments of Chateaubriand about his visit to Greece in 1806:

> The climate operates more or less on the taste of nations. In Greece, for instance, a suavity, a softness, a repose pervade all Nature, as well as the works of ancients. You may almost conceive, as it were by intuition, why the architecture of the Parthenon has such exquisite proportions, why ancient sculpture is so un-affected, so tranquil, so simple, when you behold the pure sky, the delicious scenery of Athens, of Corinth, of Ionia. In the native land of the Muses, Nature suggests no wild deviations, she tends, on the contrary, to dispose the mind to love of the uniform and of the harmonious. (59)

It became a convention throughout the nineteenth century for visitors to read the aesthetics of repose, which Winckelmann found in classical Greek art, into the Greek landscape and climate. For example, John Addington Symonds's description of Athens, even though first published in 1874, is thoroughly infused with the spirit of Winckelmann's Hellenism:

> Athens by virtue of scenery and situation, was predestined to be the mother-land of the free reason of mankind, long before the Athenians had won by their great deeds the right to name their city the ornament and the eye of Hellas. Nothing is more obvious to one who has seen many lands and tried to distinguish their essential characters, than the

fact that no one country resembles another, but that, however similar in climate and locality, each presents a peculiar and well-marked property belonging to itself alone. The specific quality of the Athenian landscape is light—not richness or sublimity or romantic loveliness or grandeur of mountain outline, but luminous beauty, serene exposure to the airs of heaven. The harmony and balance of the scenery, so varied in its details and yet so comprehensive, are sympathetic to the temperance of Greek morality, the moderation of Greek art. (III. 339)

After his visit to Athens in February 1857, Melville wrote in his poem "The Attic Landscape":

> Tourist spare the avid glance
>   That greedy roves the sight to see:
> Little here of "Old Romance,"
>   Or Picturesque of Tivoli.
>
> No flushful tint the sense to warm—
> Pure outline pale, a linear charm.
> The clear-cut hills carved temples face,
> Respond, and share their sculptural grace.
>
> 'Tis Art and Nature lodged together,
>   Sister by sister, cheek to cheek;
> Such Art, such Nature, and such weather
>   The All-in-All seems here a Greek.
>
> (245–46)

In 1906, a tourist, Sir Sidney Colvin, still marveled at "the affinity of Greek nature and Greek art" (232).[12]

For the present study, the significance of the link between landscape and artistic prowess lies in the fact that, as the quotation from Symonds suggests, the Greek landscape has remained much the same over the course of 2,000 years. The Greeks who lived there in 1800 should have been able to be affected by it in the same way as the fifth-century Athenians. Further, the emphasis on climate and environment served to discourage an attempt to build a New Athens somewhere else. Winckelmann himself suggested the futility of such an enterprise when he remarked, "This *Taste* was not only original among the Greeks, but seemed also quite peculiar to the country: it seldom went abroad without loss, and it was long ere it imparted its kind influences to more distant climes" (Webb 116). By such logic, "Greece" could only be reproduced in Greece. This did not preclude, however, some attempts to see the formation of a New Greece in other areas; Shelley himself would view the United States as a New Athens in the New World in *Hellas* (see ll. 66–71).

But the contemporary interest in the effect of nature on character made Europeans aware of modern Greece as a place on the map in a way that they had not been earlier.

Owenson drew directly upon ideas about the efficacy of the Greek climate in the preface to her novel *Woman; or, Ida of Athens* (1809). Owenson stated that her object in the book was "to delineate the character of woman in the perfection of her natural state." She chose a modern Greek as the best vehicle for that examination because Ida comes from a "country where the genial influence of climate, the classic interest in scenery, and the sublimity of objects with which it abounds, finely harmonize with that almost innate propensity to physical and moral beauty, that instinctive taste for the fair ideal, and that lively and delicate susceptibility to ardent and tender impressions, which should distinguish the character of women in its purest and highest state of excellence" (I.ix–x). In short, "many a charming Aspasia may still exist in Athens unconscious of the latent powers of their own ardent minds" (I.ix–x). The heroine of Owenson's novel is just such a new Aspasia made conscious or simply the old one brought back to life.[13]

Although *Ida of Athens* is set in the late eighteenth century, in many ways it reads like a historical romance of fifth-century Athens. Ida plays the lyre: "She sung; her voice was scarcely louder than a sigh, and her accompaniment was only an harmonic chord, swept at intervals. It is supposed something of the ancient greek song is still to be traced in the popular airs" (I.65–66). She dresses in tunics. At the end of the first volume there is "the festival of seasons," which Owenson terms "evidently a true festival of Delos," which takes place among the "majestic ruins of the temple of Jupiter" (I.157). The celebration begins when "two choirs of nymphs advance from the dark shade of the grove towards the area of the temple, in the spring of youth, beautiful as a vision of poetic fancy" (I.160). Owenson's descriptions of lyre playing, veiled drapery, and festivals at ancient temples tempt one to dismiss her entire novel as a vision of poetic fancy, except that she offered numerous notes to support her portrayal of modern Greek life.

The interest in things Greek had led to an increase of enterprising travelers eager to discover as much as possible about the ancient Greeks. Some made careful drawings of the monuments and extant sculpture, such as James Stuart and Nicholas Revett in their *Antiquities of Athens* (1762–1816). Others, like Lord Elgin, brought as many antiquities home as they could. Still others would occasionally turn from an examination of ruins to use the customs and character of the modern Greeks to elucidate passages from ancient poetry or prose. The majority of such commentaries came from those so overcome with a mania for Hellenism that they were determined to see it in almost everything around them, for, as Constantine noted, "an *idée fixe* can always be substantiated" (155). Many travel narratives encouraged readers to make the connection between ancient and modern Greeks and fueled hopes of Greek regeneration, despite the fact that the travelers were nearly unanimous in the opinion that the present inhabitants were degenerated or debased versions of the originals. These books provided Owenson the sources for *Ida of Athens*.[14]

Owenson glossed the passage about Ida playing the lyre with a citation to performances heard by the French travelers Olivier and Savary (I.216–17). But Owenson's favorite source was P.-A. Guys's *Voyage littéraire de la Grèce* (1771; trans. in 1772 as *Sentimental Journey through Greece*). For Owenson's dance of Greek nymphs, she quoted the following lines of Guys: "The present greeks often exhibit an exact image of the ancient choir of greek nymphs, when with their arms interlaced they dance through the woods, and recall the memory of those descriptions the poets have left us" (I.220). The note to the sentence "Osmyn loved like a greek" (II.130) reads: "The love of the modern greeks, like that of the ancient is, according to de Guys [*sic*] and other travellers, a frenzy rather than a passion" (II.270).[15] Owenson, who, like Winckelmann, never actually saw Greece, created in her novel a closer connection between the ancient and modern inhabitants of Greece than some of her sources had depicted.[16] But whether travelers observed at least some "exact images" of ancient practices among the modern inhabitants of Greece, like Guys, or whether they might say, "In all save form alone, how chang'd," like Byron (*Childe Harold* II.75.711), most acknowledged the modern Greeks as the heirs of Pericles and Aspasia and helped to create both interest in and sentiment for the regeneration of Greece.

The fact that European views of modern Greece were colored by preconceptions about the classical past is also evident in the paintings of European travelers who visited Greece in the early nineteenth century. As Fani-Maria Tsigakou observed, the artists represented "the scenery of the imagined classical Greek world," which has more in common with the representations of artists who never went to Greece than with the real scenery of the country, for it was "the formalized literary past, not the present, that was the attraction of Greece" (28–29).[17] Many visitors to Greece, both authors and painters, wore a set of ideological blinders that kept them from seeing anything that challenged their preconceived view of "Greece." The poet and artist William Haygarth wore just such a set of ideological blinders, for he said of his journey to Greece in 1810–1811 that there "is nothing in our visit resembling the ceremonious introduction of a new circle of acquaintances; it is the revived delight of the society of long absent and beloved friends" (*Greece* 171). Those writers and artists who desired to depict something other than a reunion with classical "friends" were confronted by the ideological blinders of their audience.

If their contact with the Attic landscape caused the Athenians to be viewed as the arbiters of taste for "the politer world," that same contact also inspired their "noble simplicity," a phrase that made the ancient Greeks resemble late eighteenth-century descriptions of the noble savage.[18] There are great similarities between Winckelmann's depiction of the ancient Greeks and the accounts from travelers of the manners and customs of South Sea islanders, as Hatfield noted (2). For example, Winckelmann said of the ancient Greeks: "In their dress they were professed followers of nature. No modern stiffening habit, no squeezing stays hindered Nature from forming easy beauty" (Webb 119). About a hundred years after Winckelmann's death, Ruskin commented: "The Greek lived in all things, a healthy, and, in a certain degree, a perfect life. He had no morbid or sickly feeling of any kind. He was accustomed to face death without the slightest shirking, and to undergo all kinds of bodily hardship without complaint, and to do whatever he supposed right and honorable, in most cases, as a matter of course" (*Works* 5.230). Ruskin concluded his chapter "Of Classical Landscape" in *Modern Painters* by stating that, at base, the ancient Greek was similar to "a Scotch Presbyterian Border farmer of a century or two back" (245), the difference being "that effect of softer climate and surrounding luxury, inducing the practice of various forms of polished art" (246–47).

The first volume of Owenson's novel related the encounter between a dissolute and jaded aristocratic Englishman, a character much like Byron's Harold and tantalizingly referred to as Lord B., and the simple, natural personality of Ida. At the end of the volume, the English lord, mistaking innocence for gullibility, attempts to persuade Ida to leave Greece and become his mistress since, "considering systematic morals, he believed those of an athenian could not be very rigid" (I.198). She must, therefore, be a kind of "pleasure-loving Ariadne" (I.197). He soon learns otherwise, for Ida dismisses his offer with the comment, "Your arguments carry not a single conviction; they are untrue to nature, and must be false to reason" (II.4). Although Owenson's heroine asserts that "the glory of Greece expired when the influence of nature was abandoned" (I.170), Ida's story begins not with a critique of the degenerated state of Greece but with the debased state of aristocratic England. Even before Greece becomes free, Ida's rustic and primitive world can teach England a lesson in morality and natural living. Lord B., we find out in volume 4 of the novel, has been reformed by his meeting with Ida and has left his rakish life behind him. Although without the moral foundations found in Owenson, Byron also employed the image of a Greek Arcadia in the second canto of *Don Juan*. The natural innocence of Haidée allows her to fall in love with and make love to Juan without pondering the jaundiced compromises between love and marriage common among women in Byron's England: "Haidée was Nature's bride, and knew not this; / Haidée was Passion's child, borne where the sun / Showers triple light and scorches even the kiss / Of gazelle-eyed daughters" (II.202.1609–12).[19] As Marilyn Butler noted, "Haidée inhabits a kind of Eden, but sexuality already exists there, and it is natural and good" (*Romantics, Rebels and Reactionaries* 137).

In the "search for new cultural roots and alternative cultural politics," to use Turner's phrase, Europeans in the eighteenth and nineteenth centuries looked to the inhabitants of primitive lands as well as to a glorious past. The ancient Greeks could be offered as sterling examples of both high civilization and noble savages, since they had reached artistic excellence without the mechanization and urbanization of modern life. Further, the term *Greeks* was used for a conflation of the supposed qualities of Sparta and Athens, which were considered the epitomes of noble simplicity and refined elegance, respectively. The fusion of the primitive and the cultured is most notable in Owenson's *Ida*, but occurs in Hölderlin's *Hyperion* as well. Perhaps it was the welding of two deeply held but conflicting desires—the lure of the simple life and the attraction of the big city—which drew so many European intellectuals to Hellenism. These expectations have also accounted for the disappointment of so many travelers to Greece. One does not go to Paris expecting rusticity nor to Wales or Maine expecting urbanity. But on the same airplane flight from Athens one can still hear complaints that Greece was too rustic or too urbane, depending upon whether the speaker was looking for representations of Pericles and Aspasia or of shepherds of an imagined Arcadia.

In addition to nature and climate, the other element central to the ancient Greek miracle was freedom. Winckelmann asserted: "Art claims liberty: in vain would nature produce her noblest offsprings, in a country where rigid laws would choak [*sic*] her progressive growth, as in Egypt, that pretended parent of sciences and arts; but in Greece, where, from their earliest youth, the happy inhabitants were devoted to mirth and pleasure, where the narrow-spirited formality never restrained the liberty of manners, the artist enjoyed nature without a veil" (Webb 119–120).

Here was the reason that the modern Greeks were only the latent descendants of their ancient ancestors. Claude Adrienne Helvétius wrote in *De l'Ésprit* (1758): "The physical position of the Greeks is still the same: why are the present-day Greeks different from the Greeks of former times? It is because the form of the government changed; it is because, just like the water that takes the form of the vessels in which it is poured, the character of nations is susceptible to all sorts of forms; in all countries the spirit of government makes the spirit of nations" (tr. Augustinos 139). Owenson remarked more succinctly that the Greeks "are only *debased* because they are no longer *free*" (I.3). Once the Greeks regained their liberty, Nature would take its course and mold the Greeks as it had done centuries earlier. When Hölderlin's hero, Hyperion, joins the Greek camp, he announces that he is committing himself "to the goal . . . where the young free state dawns and the pantheon of all Beauty rises from the soil of Greece" (119). Hyperion considers the restoration of Beauty, his ultimate goal, as a natural and necessary consequence of an independent Greece.

Winckelmann never seriously concerned himself with the regeneration of the Greeks. This may be due to the fact that he died in 1768, two years before the revolt that stirred hopes of a Greek renewal. Yet it seems doubtful that the German art historian would think that the Ideal, and the capital letter is appropriate, could so easily be regained in modern times. A key element in Winckelmann's thinking was the belatedness of his era. Just how far humanity had fallen from the golden age can be seen in the end of his description of an artistic masterpiece, a torso of Hercules "without head, arms, breast, or legs" (Webb 124):

> Him art bemoans with me: for this work, which she might have opposed to the greatest discoveries of wit and meditation, and proud of whose superior merits she might even now, as in her golden days, have looked down on the homages of mankind; this very work, and perhaps the last, which the united strength of her forces produced—this work she now sees cruelly mangled, and, with many hundred others, almost destroyed.—But from these melancholy reflections her Genius turns, to teach us, from what remains, the ways that lead to perfection.
> (Webb 127)

The perfection mentioned at the end of this passage has more in common with Platonic contemplation than participation in the events of the world. In fact, one form of Hellenism sought a withdrawal from worldly surroundings into the life of the mind. The goal was not the regeneration of the Greeks or culture generally but rather the salvation of the individual through the contemplation of ancient beauty. This did not necessarily require a voyage to Greek shores, for "one may," as Philip Marden noted in 1907, "learn to appreciate the beautiful in Greek thought without leaving home" (2). But some Hellenists found, or at least thought, that just as the climate of Greece aided the contemplation of the ancients, it could also favor the individual who went there in search of "the ways that lead to perfection." In George Gissing's novel *New Grub Street* (1891), Edwin Reardon, a struggling and impoverished writer, discusses with his fellow author Biffen his life after his separation from his wife: "The best moments of life are those when we contemplate beauty in the purely artistic spirit—objectively. I have had such moments in Italy and Greece; times when I was a free spirit, utterly remote from the temptations and harassing of sexual emotion. What we call love is mere turmoil. Who wouldn't release himself from it for ever, if the possibility offered?" (369).

He then goes onto describe one of those moments, "that marvelous sunset at Athens" when the "Acropolis simply glowed and blazed," revealing a "world which seems to me, when I recall it, beyond the human sphere, bathed in diviner light," and providing a satisfaction "infinitely preferable to sexual emotion" (369, 370). Reardon was a "pure" Hellenist, a direct descendant of Winckelmann. Like Symonds in his description of Athens, Reardon never interrupted his meditations to consider the present inhabitants of Greece. Further, to become involved in the contemporary politics of Greece, or any other country for that matter, would be submitting oneself to an extra dose of the turmoil from which one longed to escape. Greece as the realm of the intellectual ideal, especially as it was expressed in the works of Winckelmann, Schilling, Goethe, Coleridge, and Walter Pater, has a long tradition of its own in later nineteenth-century English and American literature and often serves as the conservative classicist counterpart to the legacy of liberal philhellenism.[20]

Authors with a more radical agenda, on the other hand, were extremely quick to exploit the political dimensions of Winckelmann's Hellenism and to make Athens the centerpiece of a revolutionary ideal. For philhellenes, as Lambropoulos said, "above all, Greece was the symbol of the *general* revival of liberty" (83, my italics). For example, in the first canto of Shelley's *Revolt of Islam* (1818), ancient Athens appears as the apogee of human freedom in the battle against tyranny and evil:

> Then Greece, arose, and to its bards and sages
> In dream, the golden-pinioned Genii came,
> Even where they slept amid the night of ages,
> Steeping their hearts in divinest flame
> Which thy breath kindled, Power of holiest name!
> And oft in cycles since, when darkness gave
> New weapons to thy foe, their sunlike fame
> Upon the combat shone—a light to save,
> Like Paradise spread forth beyond the shadowy grave.
>
> (I.32.406–14)

Athens has a similar place in "Ode to Liberty" (1820), where Shelley said that as "One sun illumines Heaven" (88), so "Athens doth the world with thy [Liberty's] delight renew" (90). The radical weekly the *Examiner*, edited by Shelley's friend Leigh Hunt, challenged the notion that an admiration of classical Greek art could be separated from the modern Greek struggle for liberty: "Will they be enraptured with the Elgin marbles; with the very names of Phidias and Praxiteles . . . and not do what they can towards furnishing their quota of men and money in favor of Greek genius no longer petrified, and against barbarians to whom the old Persians were demigods? Scarcely not, or they can never again take up their Aeschylus and Sophocles with comfort" (Oct. 7, 1821, p. 627). The division between Hellenists and philhellenes throughout the nineteenth century was, in a nutshell, the difference between those who could read their Sophocles with comfort when Greeks were fighting Turks and those who could not.

If for Hölderlin the regeneration of Greece would restore the pantheon of all Beauty and if for Voltaire it would bring back the pantheon of all Reason, for Shelley it meant a return of the pantheon of all Liberty. Discussing Shelley's response to the Greek War of Independence, Michael Scrivener wrote, "There is no question that Shelley wanted the Greeks to defeat the Turks in that revolutionary war; this is the primary reason he wrote *Hellas*. But the Greek side is to be admired only insofar as it is libertarian and democratic, actually a rebirth of the Athenian demos" (293). In a letter explaining the setting of *The Revolt of Islam*, Shelley explained: "The scene is supposed to be laid in Constantinople & modern Greece, but without much attempt at minute delineation of Mahometan manners. It is in fact a tale illustrative of such a Revolution as might be supposed to take place in an European nation" (*Letters of P. B. Shelley* I.563).[21] Shelley undoubtedly chose modern Greece as the scene for his revolutionary epic because the environment of Greece was a natural incubator of liberty. But Greece in the poem stands for any place in Europe or even America, and the renewal of the tradition of Greek liberty anywhere becomes a regeneration of Shelley's imaginary Greece. The lack of local details and color does not matter since Shelley's idealized conception of Greece extends beyond such particulars.

While a contemplative, even mystical, form of Hellenism existed apart from political philhellenism, political philhellenism was deeply imbued with the spiritual dimensions of Hellenism from its beginnings until well into the twentieth century.[22] Both Hölderlin's Hyperion and Shelley's Laon must go through a spiritual withdrawal from the world to renew their souls and find the truth before preparing to take part in their respective revolutions. Shelley described the progression from individual awakening to national regeneration in the preface to *The Revolt of Islam*:

> It is a succession of pictures illustrating the growth and progress of individual mind aspiring after excellence, and devoted to the love of mankind; its influence in refining and making pure the most daring and uncommon impulses of the imagination, the understanding, and the senses; its impatience at "all the oppressions which are done under the sun"; its tendency to awaken public hope, and to enlighten and improve mankind; the rapid effects of the application of that tendency; the awakening of an immense nation from their slavery and degradation to a true sense of moral dignity and freedom, the bloodless dethronement of their oppressors. (*Complete Poetical Works* II.100)

Despite the failure of the revolution due to "the treachery and barbarity of hired soldiers" and "the confederacy of the Rulers of the World," Shelley's final, Platonic message is about "the transient nature of ignorance and error, and the eternity of genius and virtue" (100). Laon's movement must be nonviolent because the renewal and reformation of the individual soul precedes mass action, and violence is anathema to those who have undergone such spiritual transformation. Laon says of the revolution: "If blood be shed, tis but change and choice / Of bonds,—from slavery to cowardice" (4.28.1657–58). Laon's public effort fails because all of humanity was not ready for regeneration, but Laon triumphs personally by holding to his principles and in the end is transported to the realm of the blessed. In Hölderlin's novel, Hyperion's experience is similar to that of Laon. On the battlefield, he was horrified by the atrocities committed by his fellow Greeks and left the cause in disillusionment. Yet Diotima had warned him before he had departed for the Greek camp that his desire to move from private thought to public action was premature and an act of hubris: "This is vain pride . . . not long ago you were more modest, not long ago you said 'I must still go away and learn'" (108). For Hölderlin and Shelley, the liberty of Greece without the consequent change in human understanding and behavior was not worth consideration, let alone effort.[23]

Winckelmann fixed the period of Greek greatness in the fifth century BCE. In literary philhellenism, the moment of the Greek past that was to be regenerated was even more specific, the time of the Persian Wars, precisely 490–480 BCE. Hölderlin's hero says that modern Greeks are "descended from the victors of Salamis." Owenson calls them "descendants of the heroes of Marathon and Plataea" (I.xxiv). Along with Thermopylae, these three places would be the sacred sites of early philhellenism. Shelley's decision to make *Hellas* "a sort of imitation of the Persae of Aeschylus, full of lyric poetry" was made within an already well established literary tradition (*Letters of P. B. Shelley* II.364). The Persian Wars were a remarkably bright spot in ancient Greek history, when the disparate city-states were able to work together and preserve their liberty against a more numerous foe. What happened some hundred years later, when both Athens and Sparta alternately allied themselves with the Persians to defeat their fellow Greeks, was conveniently forgotten. An enduring feature of literary philhellenism was the location of the struggle of the modern Greeks for freedom within a Herodotean framework of the heroics of the Persian Wars to the exclusion of the rest of Greek history.

Yet, once again, ancient Greek history had implications far beyond the modern Greeks. In 1881, Denton Snider noted that Marathon "stands for a thousand battles; all other struggles for freedom, of which our Occident has been full, are merely echoes, repetitions, imitations to a certain extent of that great primitive action" (115). In Snider's view, ancient Greece, which "has created to a large extent what we may call the symbols of our Western world" and has provided "the ideals by which we mould our work and to which we seek, at least partially, to adjust our lives," belongs as much to "us" as to the present inhabitants of Greece (115). Thirty-seven years earlier, John Stuart Mill wrote that "the battle of Marathon, even as an event in English history, is more important than the battle of Hastings" ("Grote's History of Greece" 273). Marathon, in European eyes, is the preeminent symbol of Western freedom, not simply Greek freedom.

The seamier side of Athenian democracy, especially its reputation for demagoguery, never became a serious issue in discussions of the regeneration of Greece. This neglect was not because historians or politicians were unaware or uninterested in the weaknesses of Athenian democracy. As Jennifer Tolbert Roberts has shown in *Athens on Trial* (175–207), in the late eighteenth and early nineteenth centuries Athenian democracy was often equated with mob rule and was anything but admired. Conservative or moderate politicians and political thinkers in England and America formed a master narrative of Greek history with Thucydides, not Herodotus, as the dominant text. With the appearance of the volumes of William Mitford's anti-Athenian *History of Greece* (1784–1810), "Tories and liberals fought over Athens like Greeks and Trojans over the body of Patroclus" (Richard Jenkyns 14).

But the writers who constructed the parameters of the discourse of philhellenism were, for the most part, liberals and radicals. St. Clair described the leaders of the London Greek Committee during the Greek War of Independence: "They were at the extreme left of the political spectrum within which British politics was then conducted" (*That Greece Might Still Be Free* 146). Greek freedom was just one item on their list of activities, which included Catholic emancipation, parliamentary reform, and the abolition of slavery.[24] In fact, support for the Greeks in England in the 1820s suffered because of the character and opinions of their most vigorous supporters. With the possible exceptions of the years of Gladstone and Lloyd George, philhellenism was never officially embraced by the institutional power structures in any country.[25]

Indeed, Western governments had some cause to look upon the philhellenic movement with a skeptical eye, since the desire of many philhellenes was to spread revolution from Greece to Italy, Ireland, and the rest of the world. Daniel Webster pointedly stated that in Europe "the Grecian revolution has been discouraged, discountenanced, and denounced for no other reason but because *it is a* revolution" (36, his italics). Speaking of the attitude of the rulers of Europe toward the possibility of Greek freedom, Shelley remarked in the preface to *Hellas*: "Well do these destroyers of mankind know their enemy, when they impute the insurrection of Greece to the same spirit before which they tremble throughout the rest of Europe, and that enemy well knows the power and cunning of its opponents, and watches the moment of their approaching weakness and inevitable division to wrest the bloody sceptres from their grasp" (*Shelley's Poetry and Prose* 410). Earlier in the preface he said that the "apathy of the rulers of the civilized world" to the Greek revolution "is something perfectly inexplicable to a mere spectator of the shows of this mortal scene" (408–9).[26] But the apathy of those rulers was hardly inexplicable when authors like Shelley announced that victory in Greece would be a step toward the demise of European monarchy. The "revolutionizing" of the Greek insurrection was, to a large extent, itself a misreading, or Europeanization, of the goals and aims of the Greek insurrection by authors with their own agendas.

A fair number of the philhellenes who fought in the Greek War of Independence, especially the French and Italian volunteers, had been involved in revolutionary movements in their own countries and in Spain before they landed in Greece.[27] On July 1, 1821, the *Examiner* noted, "Turkey is now the only theatre of events which excites any immediate interest among the other nations of Europe" (p. 407). Byron wryly summed up the experience of these partisans of liberty in two untitled stanzas written in 1820:

> When a man hath no freedom to fight for at home,
>   Let him combat for that of his neighbors;
> Let him think of the glories of Greece and of Rome,
>   And get knock'd on the head for his labors.
>
> To do good to mankind is the chivalrous plan,
>   And is always as nobly requited;
> So battle for freedom wherever you can,
>   And, if not shot or hang'd, you'll get knighted.
>
> (CPW IV, p. 290)

The debate about liberty in general in the late eighteenth and early nineteenth centuries was often waged by means of classical analogies. The anonymous French drama *Les Thermopyles* (1791) and Nicholas François Guillard's opera *Miltiade à Marathon* (1794) were more directly connected with the French Revolution than with ancient Greek history.[28] One of the most popular plays on the English and American stage in the late eighteenth century was Arthur Murphy's *Grecian Daughter* (first produced in 1772), which recounts the victory of Timoleon and the supporters of liberty over Dionysius, the tyrant of Syracuse, who, fittingly, depended upon Punic mercenaries to maintain his position. The rhetoric about freedom in the drama suits the classical subject and the larger cultural concern with freedom and liberty, which led within a few years to the American Revolution. Murphy never alluded to the rebellion of 1770 nor to the possibility of the regeneration of the Greeks in this work, but his play and similar artistic productions helped to lay the foundation for interest in a modern Greek revival through its portrayal of the heroism of their ancestors in the face of tyranny. The connection of classical places and figures such as Thermopylae, Marathon, Salamis, Themistocles, and Leonidas with the cause of liberty in contemporary France and America helped to fix modern Greece within a discourse of revolution. Before anyone in the West had heard any reasons from the Greeks for their War of Independence in 1821, Western preconceptions had already provided the answer. An uprising in modern Greece was, simply by being in Greece, caught up in the rhetoric of European partisan politics in a unique way. Even the Italian Risorgimento, by the fact that it was called "Italian" and not "Roman," was less burdened by established preconceptions.

A good analogy for philhellenism in the first decades of the nineteenth century is the Spanish Civil War of the 1930s, as Jusdanis observed (14). That struggle also attracted writers to a cause that was larger than the battlefields of Spain. Embracing either the Loyalist side in Spain or liberty in Greece was as much a protest against government at home as it was sympathy for those fighting abroad. Finally, support for these two struggles in literature was as pronounced as the lack of practical support by Western governments, as though the outpouring of writing was an embarrassed response to the realpolitik of politicians. In both cases, few artistic voices were raised against the voluminous pages of the literary Left. In fact, one is even less likely to find a poem in English advocating Turkish rule in Greece (I have not found a single one), than a verse encomium of Franco (see Roy Campbell's "Flowering Rifle"). The numerous philhellenic works written in England and France in the early nineteenth century, like those for the Spanish Loyalists in the 1930s, can give a misleading impression. Woodhouse observed, "Philhellenes were always a minority" in England (152), and while the movement was stronger in France and America, it never had enough public support to sway those in power. Still, from the standpoint of literature, it was a prominent and noisy minority. Philhellenic writers would never wholly forget their radical roots. In 1877, Edward Augustus Freeman still claimed that "philhellenism was one of the most prominent and distinctive signs of liberal sentiment" (*Historical Essays* 308). In 1879, poet William Cory commented that "real old Tory spirit . . . comes out unmistakably in a man who sneers at the Greeks. It is, for once in a way, a thoroughly good test of a Liberal to ask whether he favors or spites that nation" (quoted in Esher 168). Political philhellenism, as Robert Byron observed in 1929, was "an offshoot of the French Revolution," "a bastard sister of Liberty" (*Byzantine Achievement* 44). To be a conservative philhellene would always be an oxymoron, since philhellenism was built on the fact that liberty in Greece was the objective correlative of some kind of transformation in the rest of the Western world.[29]

In his poem "America," Allen Ginsberg composed a "holy litany" of leftist causes of the United States in the twentieth century:

> America free Tom Mooney.
> America save the Spanish Loyalists.
> America Sacco & Vanzetti must not die.
> America I am the Scottsboro boys.
>
> (*Collected Poems* 147)

In the nineteenth century, support for the Greek cause became part of a holy litany in the struggle for the liberty of nations. When Jules Verne wanted to indicate Captain Nemo's political convictions in *Twenty Thousand Leagues under the Sea*, he did so by means of the portraits hanging in the captain's bedroom: "Kociuzko, the hero whose dying words were *Finis Poloniae*; Botzaris, the Leonidas of modern Greece; O'Connell, the defender of Ireland; Washington, the father of the American union; Manin, the Italian patriot; Lincoln, who was shot by a defender of slavery; and finally that martyr of the emancipation of the black race, John Brown hanging from the gibbet, just as Victor Hugo had so gruesomely drawn him" (360). Verne later signaled Nemo's commitment to the cause of "oppressed races" when the captain stops at Crete to support the insurrection of the late 1860s. In his novel about the Greco-Turkish War of 1897, *The Broom of the War God*, Henry Noel Brailsford provided the following portrait of a philhellene in the Foreign Legion: "He cared something for the fate of Greece, yes, he was fighting for the national idea, for the freedom of Crete. He would fight for that cause in Poland, in the Transvaal, wherever a down-trodden race asserted its individuality. He was here in the Legion chiefly that he might learn the use of arms, for some day he hoped to march under the green banner of the Irish republic" (121–22).

But if from an intra-European perspective philhellenism seemed progressive and revolutionary, from an extra-European perspective it looked rather conservative and narrow-minded.[30] The analogy between the Persian and Ottoman empires placed the struggle for liberty in Greece in an East-versus-West framework in which East was evil and West was good. For if the rulers of Europe were the foes of liberty, the terrible despots and bloody tyrants of the East were much worse. In the preface to *Hellas*, Shelley said, "But for Greece, Rome the instructor, the conqueror, or the metropolis of our ancestors, would have spread no illumination with her arms, and we might still have been savages and idolaters; or, what is worse, might have arrived at such a stagnant and miserable state of social institution as China or Japan possess" (*Shelley's Poetry and Prose* 409). He used Othman, the name of the founder of the Ottoman Empire, as the embodiment of tyranny in *The Revolt of Islam*. Winckelmann had said that art could never flourish where rigid laws "would choak her progressive growth, as in Eygpt." And Chateaubriand asserted that the "Turks are no ordinary oppressors, though they have found apologists. A proconsul might be a monster of lust, of avarice, and of cruelty, but all proconsuls did not delight, systematically and from a spirit of religion, in overthrowing monuments of civilisation and of the arts, in cutting down trees, in destroying harvests, nay, even whole generations; and this the Turks have done every day of their lives" (181). During the Greek War of Independence, a British resident in Greece wrote in an open letter to Prime Minister George Canning:

> It has been, also, endeavored to misrepresent the cause of Greece, by confounding her struggles and exertions with the variety of disturbances which so lately have agitated the heart of Europe to its core; to reduce it to the standard of attempted revolutions in the extensive peninsulas of Italy, and Spain. . . . With reference to the countries I have mentioned, a partial advancement of liberty (in comparison I mean to Greece), acts, considered by the Government as precautionary and salutary, by the governed as dangerous and wrong; not wresting from them entirely the privileges whereof they were formerly possessed, but removing from that weight and estimation which they supposed themselves entitled to enjoy, was sufficient to put the multitude at issue with its ruler. . . . With the Greeks it is not so; the obligation which forces that nation to extremes, is so prominently marked . . . as to exhibit them to the universe, a sad and solitary example of the restlessness resulting from power without limits, and passion without rule. ("Greece to the Close of 1825," in Bulwer, *An Autumn in Greece* 311–13)

The author of this letter was a liberal who supported the independence movements in Italy and Spain. Yet he still could not bring himself to see the plight of a northern Italian population under the absolute monarchy of Austria as equivalent to the position of the Greeks under the Turks. European governments might be bad by degrees, but the Turks were ruthlessness incarnate. Some thinkers could not even fit the Turks into the progressive and evolutionary conception of history prevalent in the Victorian age. For example, Edward Augustus Freeman declared: "The Turkish domination of Athens can hardly be called a period of the history of Athens. It is a mere break, a time during which Athens ceased to be" (*Historical Essays* 289).

Within this view of the East lies both fear of the Eastern Other and a dismissal of the East as incapable of progress as it was defined in the West. In his speech in support of the Greeks during the War of Independence, Daniel Webster acknowledged, "In various parts of India, to be sure, the government is bad enough; but there it is a government of barbarians over barbarians, and the *feeling* of oppression, of course, is not so keen" (31). It is significant to note that interest in the idea of the regeneration of Greece increases around 1771, the same period when Raymond Schwab dates the Oriental Renaissance in the West, a movement that looked to texts and beliefs from India, China, and the rest of Asia as an inspiration for Western thinking (7). In the late eighteenth and nineteenth centuries Orientalism was seen as another solution to Western cultural malaise. In Flaubert's novel *Bouvard and Pécuchet*, Bouvard "sees the future of Humanity in a cheerful light. Modern man is progressing. Europe will be regenerated by Asia. The historical law being that civilisation goes from East to West" (345). The regeneration of the West by the East did not, of course, preclude Western colonization of the East. Just as, according to Vergil, the Greeks had educated Rome through the Roman conquest of Greece, so the East would teach civilization to the West by means of Western colonization of the East.

Philhellenism, and to some degree transcendental Hellenism as well, can be viewed as a competing ideology to Orientalism, one that sees the West regenerated by returning to its Western roots. This may partly explain the relentlessly Apollonian nature of the late eighteenth- and early nineteenth-century Hellenism developed by Winckelmann. Dionysus came from Asia bearing Asian mysteries, which challenged the rationality of the West. Intellectuals who wanted a regeneration of the West from Greece may have read *The Bacchae*, but their ur-text was *The Persians* of Aeschylus. Modern Greece might lie on the borders of the East, could even be considered by some to be part of the East, but Greek regeneration was part of a Western ideology.[31] Indeed, the author of the letter to Canning echoed the moral of Aeschylus's *Persians* when he said that in the fifteenth century "the Mahometans were seduced to pass from Asia to Europe, and overleap the boundaries which Nature seemed to give them" (in Bulwer, *Autumn in Greece* 325–26).

At a public meeting of the London Greek Committee on May 15, 1823, Lord John Russell proposed a motion that "the liberation of that unhappy country [Greece] affords the cheering prospects of being able to enlarge the limit of Christianity and civilization" (quoted in St. Clair, *That Greece Might Still Be Free* 143). In 1822, William Wilberforce said of Western policy toward Turkey: "It is a disgrace to all Powers of Europe that, long ere now, they have not made a simultaneous effort and driven back a nation of barbarians, the inveterate enemies of Christianity and freedom into Asia" (quoted in Coupland 446). In his 1809 *Horae Ionicae*, W. R. Wright celebrated the defeat of the Turkish attack on the island of Corfu by the Venetians in 1716, which ended the last attempt by the Ottomans to expand their empire westward:

> Let Europe, with exulting voice, recall
> The final triumph of the Christian sword;
> How, still display'd, the winged lion flew

Victorious o'er the ramparts of Corfu:
While the fierce Saracen, o'erwhelm'd with shame,
Despairing fled, and curs'd the Christian name.

(20)

The "Crusading" opposition between Christian and Muslim had a long history in European letters and, as the above quotations show, might seem a natural extension of the Europe-versus-Asia ideology within which the merits of Greek independence were discussed and argued. There were a few clergymen in England who saw the issue of Greek liberation in overtly religious terms, the most prominent being Thomas S. Hughes. Hughes, who called for the extermination of Turks in Europe, should be viewed as a rabid opponent of Islam rather than as a supporter of the Greeks.[32] Hughes was certainly not motivated by sympathy for the Christianity that he had encountered in Greece during his travels, which he dismissed as the "ridiculous and absurd mummeries of the Greek Church" (*Travels* II.97).

The religious dimension of the struggle between East and West in early English philhellenic literature, although always present, was rarely stressed.[33] For example, in her long poem *Modern Greece* (1817), Felicia Hemans referred to the minaret as the "Landmark of slavery, towering o'er the waste" and said that "Within its precinct not a flower may smile, / Nor dew nor sunshine fertilize the ground; / Nor wild bird's music float o'er zephyr's breath, / But all in silence round, and solitude, and death" (st. 32). But the next stanza made clear that Hemans was not attacking Islam in general but contemporary Ottoman rule in Greece. In medieval Spain and Baghdad, Hemans wrote, Islam was the center of learning:

For other influence poured the Crescent's light
O'er conquered realms, in ages past away;
Full and alone it beamed, intensely bright
While distant climes in midnight darkness lay.

(st. 33)

In Shelley's *Hellas*, the phantom of the conqueror of Constantinople, Mahomet II, returns to tell the present Ottoman ruler that "Islam must fall" (888), but this is presented in terms of natural decline ("A later Empire nods in its decay," 870) rather than because the religion itself is more inherently wrong or misguided than Christianity.[34] Owenson, generally more hostile to Islam, spoke deprecatingly of the self-denial of Ramazan (Ramadan), when "the dogma of puerile superstition holds in subjection the influence of climate, of habit, and of inclination; when nature herself stands checked! ... Such is the influence of a bigoted faith on a people, who, with the exception of the time of this annual fast, are, of all nations, the most devoted to the pleasure of the senses!" (III.119). But her heroine, while nominally Christian, never enters a church nor celebrates a Christian ritual in the course of four volumes. Ida is a modern Athenian, and her conversation is of Epicurus, Demosthenes, and Sophocles, not of saints and martyrs.[35]

Even in its most philosophic and abstruse form, such as in *The Revolt of Islam*, philhellenic literature was anti-Turkish and anti-Eastern and so by extension at times employed anti-Muslim language. Chateaubriand, for example, wrote, "In the book of Mahomet, there is no principle of civilisation, no precept that can impart elevation to the character; that book inculcates neither a hatred of tyranny, nor a love of independence" (180–81). But few philhellenes of the sword or the pen were clergymen or, for that matter, regular Christian believers. In his letter to Thomas Love Peacock describing a visit to Pompeii, which he referred to as a "Greek city," Shelley expressed a common sentiment when he named Christianity as one of the factors that had contributed to mankind's decline: "O, but for that series of wretched wars which terminated in the Roman conquest of the world, but for the Christian religion which put a finishing stroke to the antient system, but for the changes which conducted Athens to its ruins, to what an eminence might not humanity have arrived!" (*Letters of P. B. Shelley* II.75). One of the great attractions of the ancient Greeks was that they had never been touched by the deleterious strictures of Christianity, particularly in matters relating to sex. Greece was connected to subversive social ideas like toleration of homosexuality and the abolition of marriage, as in Wilhelm Heinse's 1785 novel, *Ardinghello und die glückseligen Inseln*, where a New Hellas of free love is established on the island of Naxos.[36] A large number of philhellenic authors would not accept the link between Christianity and civilization or freedom made by Russell and Wilberforce; many hoped that the liberation of Greece would be as much a blow to the Christian faith as it would be to Islam. Those who were inspired by the idea of the regeneration of Greece wanted to challenge the status quo in the social as well as the political realm.

Literary philhellenism, then, inherently contained from its inception serious tensions in language and ideas. The regeneration of Greece was conceived and expressed as a subversion of the dominant culture of Europe both politically and socially. But on another level, the regeneration of Greece was depicted and offered as a demonstration of the superiority of Europe over Asia. The Crusading language of religious difference was often used to underscore the separation of Europe from Asia, even though many philhellenic writers desired to change or undermine the religious foundation that had given rise to a Crusading outlook. Further, within the larger East-versus-West framework, which incorporates a Muslim-versus-Christian opposition, literary philhellenism in general was, as McGann said of Shelley's *Hellas*, "open to a political exploitation by Europe's imperialist power" (*Romantic Ideology* 125). Such exploitation was not a complete misuse of literary philhellenism, for however much philhellenism wanted to change conditions in the West, it held to a belief in the superiority of the West because of its Greek/European heritage.[37]

Yet while literary philhellenism sometimes uses the language and concepts of the contemporary literature of Western imperialist expansion, it does not fit easily into the model of Western imperialist encounters with the East constructed by Edward Said. For in this case, the Greeks were subjugated by the Turks, a people of the East, and if Greece cannot technically be called a colony of the Turks, the inhabitants were certainly colonized and had a colonial mentality. Further, after 1770, the Greeks often appealed to Europe for assistance against what they considered an occupying force. While certain European governments might have desired to incorporate Greece into their own empires, as they had other Ottoman possessions, the great majority of philhellenes of both the pen and the sword were adamant that the only acceptable result was independence for Greece. The cultural ambiguities of early philhellenism can be seen from the following sentence of Nigel Leask's concerning Shelley: "The faith of *The Revolt of Islam, Prometheus Unbound*, and *Hellas*, lies in a *ricorso* of liberty spreading over the world from the revolutionary liberation of the long oppressed East" (108). One could rewrite the end of this statement to read: "the revolutionary liberation of the source of Western culture long oppressed by the East." Both formulations would be correct, since the rediscovered fountain of European civilization was within the oppressed East, but it was a part, according to the Greeks themselves, that was oppressed by other Easterners.

Despite the shared goal of Greek freedom, however, there were serious tensions in the relationship between the philhellenes and the Greeks. For if philhellenes did not want to colonize Greece in a political sense, they certainly intended to colonize it culturally, albeit with what they thought to be its own cultural past. Henry Holland ended his account of his travels through Greece in 1812–1813 with the following thought:

> I certainly am far from believing that the ancient Greeks, with all their peculiarities of natural spirit and usage, will be revived in the people who now inhabit the country. The race has undergone many changes —the condition of the surrounding world still more. But this belief is by no means necessary to the question; and it still remains a matter of interesting speculation, whether a nation may not be created in this part of Europe, either through its own or foreign efforts, which may be capable of bearing a part in the affairs and events of the civilized world. (530–31)

Such a view of the Greek future was, and to some extent remains, rare indeed. Most Westerners, like Voltaire, thought the regeneration of ancient

Greece was indeed "necessary to the question." They had no interest in allowing modern Greeks to be modern Greeks.

Modern Greek culture at the beginning of the nineteenth century owed more to Byzantium than to ancient Athens. Many Greeks desired a restoration of the Greek Empire centered on Constantinople. Byron expressed this yearning during his description of Carnival in Constantinople:

> And whose more rife with merriment than thine,
> Oh Stamboul! once the empress of their reign?
> Though turbans now pollute Sophia's shrine,
> And Greece her very altars eyes in vain:
> (Alas! her woes still pervade my strain!)
> (*Childe Harold* II.79.747–51)

And also in this couplet:

> The city won for Allah from the Giaour,
> The Giaour from Othman's race again may wrest.
> (*Childe Harold* II.77.729–30)

The Greeks might eye the altars of St. Sophia and, as the legend goes, long for the last emperor, Constantine XI, to appear from the walls of the church and lead the Greeks to victory, but for Westerners the centuries of Byzantium were best forgotten. The general opinion was that during the long decline and fall, which Gibbon documented in the last half of the eighteenth century, "Whatever arts and sciences, whatever virtues might have been found in antient times among the Greek republicans, seem to have been obscured, or totally lost, under their emperors. The present Greeks have not a trace of them remaining" (James Porter 326–27). As mentioned above, radical philhellenes were not attracted to the Orthodox faith of the Greeks, and Christians in the West considered it a debased form of Christianity in need of instruction.[38]

The fall of Constantinople in 1453, which for Greeks constitutes the defining moment of their history, was the single event of Byzantine history that had any currency in philhellenic writing. Felicia Hemans described the fall of the city and the death of Constantine XI in *Modern Greece* (1817) and at greater length in "The Last Constantine" (1823). But in both works she made numerous allusions to the Persian Wars. For example, discussing the fall of Constantinople in *Modern Greece*, she wrote: "Who from the dead at Marathon arose / all arm'd" (st. 41), and the sound of the approaching Ottoman army in "The Last Constantine" resembled the noise the wind bore "when, of old, / Dark Asia sent her battle-myriads o'er / Th' indignant wave which would not be contoll'd, / But past the Persian chains, in boundless freedom roll'd" (st. 4). Hemans placed the capture of the city in the context of the Herodotean struggle between Europe and Asia. Like many early phil-hellenic writers, she appropriated the fall of Constantinople and subsumed it into the desire to revive Athens. So did Shelley in *Hellas*, where his vision of the recapture of Constantinople by the Greeks was set within the frame-work of *The Persians*. In *The Siege of Corinth*, Byron repeatedly presented the Venetian loss of Greece in the early eighteenth century against the back-ground of the Persian Wars, as in the lines: "But vain her [Freedom's] voice, till better days / Dawn in those yet unremembered rays / Which shone upon the Persian flying, / And saw the Spartan smile in dying" (14.341–44). Some writers, like Hölderlin and, for the most part, Owenson, simply ig-nored Greece's medieval past altogether and focused only on a revival of the ancient past.

After the Greeks failed to gain their freedom in 1770, a few of the first ardent philhellenic authors, notably Voltaire, gave up their dreams of a New Athens.[39] But for most the hopes raised by the revolt were not so easily extin-guished. Over the next decades, the smallest sign of unrest in Greece would find a resonance in English literature. During the war between Russia and Turkey from 1787 to 1792, the Russians encouraged pirates to disrupt Ot-toman sea traffic in the eastern Mediterranean. In typically acerbic fashion, Finlay remarked, "Few accounts of the scenes of bloodshed enacted by the pirates have been preserved; the wail of the murdered has found no echo, while infatuated *literati* have deemed it patriotic to represent every priva-teersman as a Themistocles and every Klepht as a Leonidas" (5:270).

The most renowned piratical Themistocles was Lambros Katsonis or Canziani. Canziani, whose base was in the southern Peloponnesus, terror-ized shipping for two years until the French assisted the Ottoman navy in ending his career (Finlay 5:272–73). In Owenson's *Woman; or, Ida of Athens*, however, the young hero, Osmyn, goes to Thebes, "where he understood the heroic Lambro Canziani then was" (II.111; see also I.211, where Greek gal-ley slaves sing of the "feats of Lambro Canziani" while at their oars). A note for this sentence said that Canziani joined the Russian navy out of hatred of the Turks and "with the assistance of Greek patriots, fitted out twelve small vessels. But the Russians, obliged to suspend the war against the Turks, found it more expedient to check the French revolution than to restore lib-erty to the oppressed Greeks; and Lambro, after many heroic feats, and im-portant captures, was necessitated to disperse his little fleet" (II.270). In *The Bride of Abydos*, Byron's hero, Selim, plans to join a "lawless brood" among whom are a few who aspire to "higher thoughts":

> The last of Lambro's patriots there
> Anticipated freedom share;

And oft around the cavern fire
On visionary schemes debate,
To snatch the Rayahs from their fate
(II.20.380–84)

Byron attached a note that read: "Lambro Canzani [*sic*], a Greek, famous for his efforts in 1789–90 for the independence of his country; abandoned by the Russians he became a pirate, and the Archipelago was the scene of his enter-prizes. He is said to be still alive in Petersburg. He and Riga are the two most celebrated of the Greek revolutionists" (*CPW* III, p. 441). Canziani's name also appears in Hope's *Anastasius* II.95; Catherine Grace Garnett's *Reine Canziani* (1825), whose heroine, the love interest of a hero based on Byron, is the daughter of the legendary Lambro; and Agnes Strickland's narrative poem of 1833, *Demetrius* (7, 147). The hopes of a Greek revival led Owenson, Byron, and Hobhouse (*Journey* II.48–49) to immortalize the exploits of a simple ruffian. If, as seems likely, the pirate Lambro of *Don Juan* is modeled on the famous corsair Canziani, Byron eventually provided a far more accu-rate picture of this celebrated revolutionist:

A fisher therefore was he,—though of men,
    Like Peter the Apostle,—and he fish'd
For wandering merchant vessels, now and then
    And sometimes caught as many as he wish'd.
The cargoes he confiscated, and gain
    He sought in the slave-market too, and dish'd
Full many a morsel for that Turkish trade,
By which, no doubt, a good deal may be made.
(II.126.1001–8)

In 1790, also in connection with the Russo-Turkish war, the Suliots, an Albanian Christian tribe dwelling in a mountainous region of northwestern Greece, rose in rebellion and plundered the villages in the surrounding plains. Although they received none of the promised assistance from Russia, in 1792 they were able to make a favorable treaty with Ali Pasha of Yanina, the ruler of the region. But in 1797, Ali set out to conquer the Suliots. The mountain tribe managed to hold out for several years. In 1803, when Ali's victorious forces appeared, "six men and twenty-two women threw them-selves over a precipice behind the village to avoid falling into the hands of their inhuman persecutors. Albanian soldiers, on returning to Joannina, de-clared they saw several young women throw their children from the rock, and then spring down themselves" (Finlay 6:51).

This event, which occurred among an obscure people in an obscure area, became another piece of evidence that the spirit of freedom lived on in the modern Greeks. As W. R. Wright described his voyage among the Ionian islands in *Horae Ionicae* (1809):

> Mark on the eastern shore where Parga lies,
> And Sulli's crags in distant prospect rise;
> The last of the ancient Greeks, unknown to fame,
> Her sons preserv'd the unconquerable flame
> That erst on freedom's sacred altar glow'd.
>
> (24)[40]

The Suliots were hardly "unknown to fame." They appear, among other places, in stanza 49 of Felicia Hemans's *Modern Greece*, as the high point of a description of a journey of Freedom through modern Greece:

> But from the hills the radiance of her [Freedom's] smile
> Hath vanished long, her step hath fled afar,
> O'er Suli's frenzied rocks she paused awhile,
> Kindling the watch-fires of mountain-war,
> And brightly glow'd her ardent spirit there.

In the next stanza (50), Hemans tells how a Suliot mother, a fitting rival to a Spartan mother, "in dread delirium" hurled to death "her free-born infant, ne'er to be a slave." Hemans returned to this incident in the 1820s in her poem "The Suliote Mother." Byron referred to the Suliot rebellion in *Childe Harold* II.47.421–23 and added the note: "Five thousand Suliotes, among the rocks and in the castle of Suli, withstood 30,000 Albanians for eighteen years: the castle was at last taken by bribery. In this contest there were several acts performed not unworthy of the better days of Greece" (*CPW* II, p. 195). The leap of the Suliot women was so well known by the middle of the nineteenth century that Edward Lear could evoke the event in the painting *The Rocks of Suli* by having the figures look over a precipice (reproduced in *Edward Lear in the Levant* 133).[41] In the Suliot story, Wright, Hemans, Byron, and Lear saw signs of the survival of the ancient Greek devotion to freedom. Whatever the real ethnic origins of the Suliots, in Western literature they would be Greeks. Since 1770 the literati, as Finlay called them, had been watching for any evidence of the survival and revival of the ancient Hellenes. When the Greek War of Independence began in 1821, the pump of poetic inspiration had been primed for five decades. The subsequent flood of philhellenic verse was only to be expected.

Hölderlin ended his epistolary novel *Hyperion* with the two words *nachstens mehr*, "more soon." In the book, the ending symbolizes the fragmentary and incomplete state of the hero's bildungsroman. Hölderlin wants us to imagine that Hyperion would write another letter to Bellarmin about his search for personal renewal and his desire to revive Greece. He does not intend us to read the ending metatextually, that there would be "more soon" on the same subject from a different writer. Yet when reading the conclusion of one of the most important early philhellenic works, it is hard not to see Byron on the horizon even if, as seems likely, Byron had never read *Hyperion*. For in the history of literary philhellenism, the last two words of *Hyperion* make Hölderlin appear a literary John the Baptist, one who lost his mind if not his head, for the poet-Christ who would die at Easter in Missolonghi. There would be more soon.

2

Greeces of Byron and of Homer

On October 20, 1827, the decisive engagement of the Greek War of Independence was fought in the bay of Navarino in western Greece. A fleet of eighty-two Ottoman and Egyptian ships was all but annihilated by a force of twenty-seven ships from England, France, and Russia. The combatants were not at war. The European squadron had been sent to enforce an armistice between the Greeks and their Muslim opponents. The armistice had been agreed upon by the three European powers, but the Ottoman government had not accepted the proposed settlement. Admiral Edward Codrington, the commander of the Allied force, chose to follow and impede the movement of the Muslim fleet, while Greek ships continued to maneuver without restraint. Tension between the Allied contingent and the Muslims was already high when Codrington decided to take his twenty-seven ships into the two-by-three-mile bay of Navarino, where the Muslim navy was anchored. His provocative action had a predictable result. Shots fired at the Allies were returned; the conflict escalated into a full-scale battle; and four hours later only twenty-four of the eighty-two vessels of the Muslim fleet remained. Despite the superiority of his land forces, the Egyptian general, Ibrahim, son of the Egyptian ruler, Mohammed Ali, could no longer protect his vital routes of supply by sea. In the summer of 1828, French soldiers landed in the Peloponnesus to supervise the withdrawal of the Egyptian army. By October of that year, the Greeks were free, at least from the Turks (Finlay 7:16–21, 27–28).

No Greeks fought at Navarino, an irony that did not check the celebrations of armchair philhellenes in England and France. The Greeks were, in fact, very close to defeat in the fall of 1827 until the providential event at Navarino changed the course of the war.[1] Still, the Greeks had accomplished a remarkable, and unexpected, feat. For more than six years, since 1821, they had sustained their rebellion against enormous odds and were still in the field to benefit from Codrington's action. They had received needed money and volunteers from abroad, but it was the effort and sacrifice of ordinary Greeks in a bitter guerrilla war that had kept the struggle going. Even the acerbic and critical philhellene-turned-historian George Finlay said, "The Greek Revolution was emphatically the work of the people. The leaders generally proved unfit for the position they occupied, but the people never wavered in the contest, from the day they took up arms" (6:144). In the fall of 1828, the Greeks still did not have a country, an effective government, or even a common vision of the future. Few nations have achieved their liberty with so little notion of what to do with it. Even fewer have been confronted with such great expectations of a total transformation of their politics and culture.

The battle of Navarino embarrassed the English government. The king in a speech to Parliament all but apologized to the sultan by referring to the action as "an untoward event," and Codrington was recalled as commander of the Mediterranean squadron for "misapprehending his instructions" (Finlay, 7:21). England was in the awkward position of having helped to free Greece without desiring or approving of the result. France, which had also been embarrassed after the battle, adjusted to circumstances and embraced Greek independence. Only Russia was elated by Navarino and promptly declared war on Turkey to take advantage of the weakness of the Ottoman navy in the Black Sea.

Among the dozens of poems written to celebrate the battle was Victor Hugo's "Navarin," composed in November 1827. In the second section, Hugo addressed the two Greeces, modern and ancient:

> Grèces de Byron et d'Homère
> Toi, notre soeur, toi, notre mère,
> Chantez! si votre voix amère
> Ne s'est pas éteinte à crier.
>
> (II.45–48)

> [Greeces of Byron and of Homer
> You, our sister, you, our mother,
> Sing! If your bitter voice
> Has not been extinguished by crying.]

Hugo defined the two Greeces by their perceived relationship to the rest of Europe and by the two poets whose works form the dominant texts of the country in the Western imagination. Ancient Greece, "our mother," is the "Grèce d'Homère" because it was through ancient Greek poetry, especially the epics of the blind bard, that Hugo and his contemporaries would approach and understand the past. However much Europeans might have misread or misunderstood these ancient sources, they began with the "original" writing of the Greeks and often spent numerous hours laboriously learning classical Greek in order to discover the "real" Athens and Sparta. But when the French author calls modern Greece the "Grèce de Byron," he acknowledges that the medium through which Western Europeans knew the Greece of the present was the verse of a contemporary *English* poet.[2] In the nineteenth-century Western mind, modern Greece, although contemporary, stood at a further remove than the Greece of antiquity. John Gennadius underscored the point when, in the preface to his 1881 translation of D. Bikelas's novel *Loukis Laras*, he acknowledged that the "translation into English of a modern Greek tale is a literary enterprise so unusual, if not to say unprecedented, that it calls for some explanation, if not for apology" (i).

The poets of Hugo's two Greeces help to illustrate the pervasive perceptual dichotomy between ancient/pagan/Westernized Greece and modern/Orthodox Christian/Oriental Greece. As the Western ideal of culture and civilization, antiquity must be carefully studied in order that Europeans can learn how to improve themselves. But modern Greece is known through Western observers, chiefly Byron, who, instead of learning from or even about modern Greece, view themselves as advisers for the reclamation of the lost Greek past. In *Childe Harold's Pilgrimage*, Byron counseled the Greeks as to how they can regenerate themselves:

> Hereditary bondsmen! Know ye not
> Who would be free themselves must strike the blow?
> By their right arms the conquest must be wrought?
> Will Gaul or Muscovite redress ye? no!
> True, they may lay your proud despoilers low,
> But not for you will Freedom's altars flame.
> Shades of the Helots! triumph o'er your foe!
> Greece! change thy lords, thy state is still the same;
> Thy glorious day is over, but not thine years of shame.
>   (II.76.720–28)

Byron assumed that the modern Greek view of liberation was consistent with his own, shaped by the revolutionary tradition of late eighteenth-century Europe and based on a Western liberal/radical concept of freedom. Many Greeks might in fact have preferred to be part of an Orthodox empire, such as Russia, or simply achieve greater autonomy under Ottoman rule. But the narrator of *Childe Harold's Pilgrimage* does not stop to ask what a modern Greek desires, he knows what they should want even if they might disagree: "This must he feel, the true-born son of Greece, / If Greece one true-born patriot still can boast" (II.83.783–84). If a Greek did not feel about the regeneration of his land the way Byron presumed that he should feel, he was not a "true-born" Greek. Of course, Byron and Western observers of Greece placed Greece within *their* cultural expectations because modern Greece was considered part of the same family, "notre soeur." Hugo would have been more precise if he had said "our little sister," since all Western writers considered Greece to be a bit behind its other siblings and in need of instruction from older brothers like Byron; in 1910, Jules Bois said, "l'Athenienne est la petite soeur de la Parisienne" (397). Chateaubriand distinguished the two Greeces a bit differently when he spoke of quitting forever "this sacred soil, my mind filled with its past greatness and present debasement" (174). Western Europe approached ancient Greece with awe but modern Greece with condescension. For in the eyes of many philhellenes, "Old Greece was in fact what Christian Europe and America are now" (Freeman, *Historical Essays* 309).

In his poem "The Man and the Echo," W. B. Yeats mused about the power of words and wondered whether his nationalist play *Cathleen ni Houlihan* (1904) helped to inspire the Easter Rising in Dublin in 1916:

> Did that play of mine send out
> Certain men the English shot?
> (*Poems* 345)

With respect to the influence of Byron's poems on those who went to fight for Greece during the Greek War of Independence, the question mark is unnecessary. Dozens of young men from Germany, France, England, and America went off to serve the cause of Greek freedom with copies of Byron in their pockets. Unlike the men in the Dublin Post Office, they had not even seen the country for which they were fighting except on the printed pages of Byron's books. From 1821 to 1824, philhellenes like the future historian George Finlay or the young Boston doctor Samuel Gridley Howe read Byron on the decks of ships heading east across the Ionian sea.[3] In 1897, dozens more would "dream that Greece might still be free" and participate in another Greco-Turkish War. Byron had created a country that could motivate men to action and dominate the imaginations of powerful intellects like Hugo's. What did the Greece of Byron look like?

In many respects, and this is particularly true for Canto II of *Childe Harold's Pilgrimage*, Byron's Greece differed little from the picture of the country provided by his predecessors and contemporaries. Terence Spencer, in his admirable study of literary philhellenism before Byron, said, "One important source of his [Byron's] success was the fact that the feelings he described, and aroused, were authentic. . . . The land which had gained a stronger and stronger romantic appeal during the eighteenth century was present in Byron's poetry amid all its sorrows and humiliations, never forgetting the splendours and glories of its past, and therefore making memory, indignation, and sympathy more poignant" (293). The Grèce de Byron was already familiar ground to his readers; for forty years they had pondered, like Chateaubriand had in 1806, Greece's glorious past, its degraded present, and its possible future.

That same Western construction of Greece helped to draw Byron to Grecian shores. Edward Trelawny recorded Byron saying:

> Travelling in Greece, Hobhouse and I wrangled everyday. His guide was Mitford's fabulous history. He had a greed for legendary lore, topography, inscriptions; gabbled in lingua franca to the Ephori of the villages, goatherds, and our dragomen. He would potter with map and compass at the foot of Pindus, Parnes, and Parnassus, to ascertain the site of some ancient temple or city. I rode my mule up them. They had haunted my dreams since boyhood; the pines, eagles, vultures, and owls were descended from those Themistocles and Alexander had seen, and were not degenerated like the humans; the rocks and torrents the same. John Cam's dogged perseverance in pursuit of his hobby is to be envied; I have no hobby and no perseverance. I gazed at the stars and ruminated; took no notes, asked no questions. (*Records* 82–83)

Trelawny is not the most accurate source,[4] yet Byron himself indicated that, on this occasion, his friend may not have been far from the truth. The poet wrote to Francis Hodgson from Athens on January 20, 1811: "I am living in the Capuchin Convent, Hymettus before me, the Akropolis behind me, the temple of Jove to my right, the stadium in front, the town to the left, eh, Sir, there's a situation, there's your picturesque!" (*BLJ* II.37). Byron's poetic account of a journey through Greece is strikingly different from the antiquarian pursuits and fascination with minutiae so apparent in John Cam Hobhouse's *Journey through Albania and Other Provinces of Turkey*.[5]

But whether or not it reflected Byron's own emotional response, the description of the "haunted, holy ground" of Athens and Greece in *Childe Harold* was decisively shaped by the tradition of literary philhellenism that had been established in the previous four decades (II.88.828).[6] Byron's use of a Greek temple, in this case the Parthenon, to lament the past greatness of Greece was, by the time he composed it, a literary convention:

> Look on its broken arch, its ruin'd wall
> Its chambers desolate, and portals foul;
> Yes, this was once Ambition's airy hall,
> The dome of Thought, the palace of the Soul,
> Behold each lack-lustre, eyeless hole.
> (II.6.46–50)

His encomium of the natural beauty of Greece and the musing on Greece's lost liberty and its possible recovery were also standard fare:

And yet how lovely in thine age of woe,
Land of lost gods and godlike men! art thou!
Thy vales of ever-green, thy hills of snow,
Proclaim thee Nature's varied favorite now.
                    (II.85.801–4)

Fair Greece! sad relic of departed worth!
Immortal, though no more! though fallen, great!
Who now shall lead the scatter'd children forth,
And long accustom'd bondage uncreate?
Not such thy sons who whilome did await,
The hopeless warriors of a willing doom,
In bleak Thermopylae's sepulchral strait—
Oh! who that gallant spirit shall resume,
Leap from Eurotas's banks, and call thee from the tomb?
                    (II.73.693–701)

Byron's version of what were commonplaces became canonical because, as Spencer noted, "Byron could express these opinions and emotions with an intensity hitherto unknown" (290).

The dominance of Byron's poetical skill can be illustrated by comparing a couplet of *Childe Harold* to two similar passages by other poets.[7] The lines of Byron read:

Cold is the heart, fair Greece! that looks on thee
Nor feels as lovers o'er the dust they lov'd.
                    (II.15.127–28)

William Haygarth's *Greece: A Poem in Three Parts* (1814) was, according to the author in the preface, "designed in the country which it attempts to delineate and a part of it was written in Athens in the middle of 1811" (v). Byron and Haygarth had met in Athens in 1811 (see *BLJ* 2.33), where they could have discussed their poetic projects. The following couplet, despite the obvious similarity to the lines of Byron above, might have been written before Haygarth had read *Childe Harold*:

Hard is the heart, O Corinth! who beholds
Thee bow'd to dust, nor sheds one pitying tear.
                    (III.626–27)

These lines, and numerous other passages of Haygarth, sound eerily like paraphrases of Byron, but at least some of the resonances resulted from the

fact that Byron and Haygarth were operating in what had become an established genre. Indeed, from the standpoint of literary history, Haygarth's importance is to demonstrate just how conventional the stirring lines of *Childe
Harold* really were.

Felicia Hemans's long poem *Modern Greece* (1817), on the other hand,
was inspired by and written in imitation of the second canto of *Childe
Harold*. It includes the following passage:

> Is there one who views with cold, unaltered mien
> His frozen heart with proud indifference fraught,
> Each sacred haunt, each unforgotten scene
> Where Freedom triumphed or where Wisdom taught?
>
> (st. 2.1–4)

Hemans's effort is a good example of the fate of poems about Greece in
the decade after *Childe Harold* and Byron's Tales. There are only so many
ways one can say that a person must be hardhearted not to be distressed at
Greece's present state. When the idea had been said simply and well, as in
"Cold is the heart fair Greece! that looks on thee," then the poets who came
later often had to stretch words or syntax, as Hemans does in the lines above.
Hemans, an extremely popular author in her day, was a better poet than this
passage suggests. But by the time of *Modern Greece*, Byron had fixed an
image of Greece and the ways to describe it in the English imagination. With
little room to maneuver, Hemans could only provide pale echoes of the sentiments expressed in *Childe Harold*.

In a letter to Lord Holland after the publication of *The Bride of Abydos*
(1813), Byron wrote: "My head is full of Oriental names and scenes" and
added that "the whole of the Bride cost me *four* nights—and you can very
easily suppose that I have no great esteem for lines that can be strung together as fast as minutes: . . . but it is my story and my East—(& here I am
venturing with no one to contend against—from having *seen* what my contemporaries must copy from the drawings of others only)" (*BLJ* 3.168).
Byron claims for his Tales, and one supposes by extension *Childe Harold* as
well, an authenticity based on firsthand knowledge. And he had in fact traveled to places where Owenson had not been. But there were others who had
seen the East, or at least Greece, with their own eyes, like W. R. Wright, John
Cam Hobhouse, William Haygarth, and Charles Kelsall. In *Childe Harold*,
Byron eclipsed his contemporaries not, as he suggested, because his descriptions of Greece were more authentic than those in the verse of Wright, Haygarth, or Kelsall, but rather because, as Spencer indicated, he more readily
aroused authentic feelings about a shared ideal construction of Greece in his
English readers.

Byron was, however, one of the first to attempt to substantiate the Greek revival with evidence from the modern Greeks in their own words. He translated Romaic (modern Greek) songs and attached an appendix of Romaic authors at the end of *Childe Harold* (*CPW* II, pp. 211–17). The most important of the translations was the "War Song" of Rhigas, which appeared in the first edition of *Childe Harold* and in subsequent collections of Byron's verse. Rhigas was a Greek patriot inspired by the French Revolution; he had even hoped for French aid in setting up a republic in Greece. He established himself in 1796 in Vienna, where he wrote prose and poetry to prepare his countrymen for the future rebellion. In 1797, spurred by French victories in Italy and the French occupation of the Ionian islands, he left Vienna to ask Napoleon for assistance in Greece. Rhigas was arrested by the Austrians in Trieste and turned over to the Turks. He was executed in Belgrade in June 1798.[8]

In 1809, Byron and Hobhouse had heard Rhigas's "War Song" sung by a young Greek nobleman, Andreas Lontos, who later fought in the War of Independence (Hobhouse, *Journey* II:586). Both Englishmen were impressed by the sentiments of the song and the singer, and both translated it for English readers. In Byron's more famous version, the third stanza begins:

> Sparta, Sparta, why in slumbers,
>   Lethargic dost thou lie?
> Awake, and join thy numbers
>   With Athens, old ally!
> Leonidas recalling,
>   That chief of ancient song,
> Who sav'd ye once from falling,
>   The terrible! The strong!
> Who made that bold diversion
>   In old Thermopylae.
>   (*CPW* I, pp. 331–32)

Byron and Hobhouse may have believed that they were providing an authentic Greek yearning for the regeneration of Greece. In fact, what they had done was to translate back into English Rhigas's own "translation" of Western nostalgia into modern Greek. For Rhigas, who had assisted in a translation into Greek of Abbé Barthélemy's popular historical novel of ancient Greece, *Voyages du jeune Anacharsis* (1789), had modeled his "War Song" on the French national anthem, *La Marseillaise*.[9] If Byron's translation of Rhigas's poem made an English audience think that the Greeks held the same views about the revival of Greece as readers in London, it was because Rhigas had sought to propagate those ideas in his native land. As Byron himself must have realized, the great majority of Greeks who he met in the Levant would not have known who Leonidas was. Byron's use of the translation of a "translated" modern Greek text to support the cause of Greece would be imitated by others.[10]

Harold Spender, father of the poet Stephen Spender and a member of the last generation to mature while the Grèce de Byron still reigned supreme, asserted of the second canto of *Childe Harold* in 1924: "It contains his sublimest presentation of the case for modern Greece, as the cradle of freedom and the treasure-house of our art. It produced on Europe something of that same magical awakening, which came, six centuries before, from Peter the Hermit's appeals for the enslaved Holy Land" (*Byron and Greece* 10). This is a colossal misreading of Byron's poem, although Spender's comment about reader response appears accurate. Unlike Owenson, Byron never unambiguously advocated the liberation of modern Greece. When the poet discussed the regeneration of Greece in stanza 73 of *Childe Harold* (quoted earlier), he ended in a question mark. It is not certain that the author intended the resounding affirmative answer that Spender reads. The opening of *The Giaour* also contained stirring lines about Greek regeneration: "For Freedom's battle once begun, / Bequeathed by bleeding Sire to Son, / Though baffled oft is ever won. / Bear witness Greece, thy living page, / Attest it many a deathless age" (123–26). But again the ending of the passage undercut Byron's stirring exhortation: "Enough!—no foreign foe could quell / Thy soul, till from itself it fell, / Yes! Self-abasement pav'd the way / To villain-bonds and despot-sway" (138–41). In neither *Childe Harold* nor *The Giaour* did Byron ever clearly claim that the Greeks would, or could, overcome their self-abasement. The desire and hope for their regeneration is expressed but not the expectation.

Indeed, in the notes to *Childe Harold*, which apparently went unread by Spender, Byron appeared skeptical about the probability of a revival of the Greeks and suggested a future for the country as a colony of Europe:[11]

> The Greeks will never be independent; they will never be sovereigns as heretofore, and God forbid they ever should! but they may be subjects without being slaves. Our colonies are not independent, but they are free and industrious and such may Greece be hereafter. (*CPW* II, p. 201)

> To talk, as the Greeks themselves do, of their rising again to their pristine superiority, would be ridiculous; as the rest of the world must resume its barbarism, after re-asserting the sovereignty of Greece;— but there seems to be no very great obstacle, except in the apathy of the Franks, to their becoming an useful dependency, or even a free state with a proper Guarantee;—under correction, however, be it spoken, for many, and well-informed men doubt the practicability even of this. (*CPW* II, p. 202)

Byron was never quite sure what to make of the Greeks, as his private letters to Hobhouse demonstrate. After his return from a year and a half stay in the Levant (1809–1811) and not long before the publication of the first two cantos of *Childe Harold's Pilgrimage*, Byron wrote his former traveling companion, "My mind is not very well made up as to ye. Greeks, but I have no patience with the absurd extremes into which their panegyrists & detractors have equally run" (*BLJ* 2.125). Yet within months after the publication of the first two cantos of *Childe Harold*, Byron would be read as the foremost panegyrist of the Greeks.

In an intriguing note to *Greece*, William Haygarth explained: "I have ventured to predict in poetry what I certainly should not be so hardy as to foretell in prose—the moral regeneration of Greece" (276). The same dichotomy entered into the writing of Byron. In his letters and notes he was never "so hardy" as to talk seriously about Greek regeneration. But in his poetry, Byron, like Haygarth, drew as much on Western feelings about Greece as on what he actually saw on his journey. So while he did not go so far as to predict a regeneration of the Greeks, he certainly considered the possibility fondly. And Byron's passages about a Greek revival are easily taken out of their ambiguous context. The most striking example is "The Isles of Greece" from *Don Juan*, Canto III (1820), which became the single most important philhellenic text, particularly stanzas 3 and 7:

> The mountains look on Marathon—
>   And Marathon looks on the sea;
> And musing there an hour alone,
>   I dreamed that Greece might still be free;
> For standing on the Persian's grave,
>   I could not deem myself a slave . . .
>
> Must *we* weep o'er days more blest?
>   Must *we* blush?—Our fathers bled.
> Earth! Render back from out thy breast
>   A remnant of our Spartan dead!
> Of the three hundred grant but three,
>   To make a new Thermopylae!
>   (*CPW* V, pp. 189–90)

Within the context of *Don Juan*, this lyric is sung by a "sad trimmer," a bard who has learned to give the audience what it wants: "Thus usually, when he was ask'd to sing, / He gave the different nations something national; / Twas all the same to him—'God save the king' / or 'Ça Ira,' according to the fashion all. / . . . In Greece, he'd sing some sort of hymn like this t'ye" (85.1–4, 86.8). In an earlier stanza, Byron said of the poet:

> He deemed, being on a lone isle, among friends,
> That without any danger of a riot, he
>   Might for long lying make himself amends;
> And singing as he sung in his warm youth,
> Agree to a short armistice with the truth.

(III.83.4–8)

This passage suggests that he is not "trimming" when he sings "The Isles of Greece." Yet the line just before the trimmer sings, "In Greece, he'd sing some sort of hymn like this t'ye," equally hints that he might be singing according to fashion.[12] Like nearly all of Byron's calls for Greek regeneration, the text here is ambiguous; McGann said that it "concludes in a typical Byronic gesture of resolute irresolution" (*Beauty of Inflections* 285). There was not, however, much ambiguity perceived by Byron's audience. The song of a sad trimmer became the anthem of Greek renewal for Western readers.

If in *Childe Harold* II and "The Isles of Greece" Byron reproduced the canonical expressions of philhellenic ideas about the fallen state of Greece and the hope for its regeneration in the early nineteenth century, in *The Giaour* and his other Tales Byron made his own original contribution to the idea of modern Greece—it was indeed, as the poet had told Lord Holland, his story and his East.[13] For where *Childe Harold* focused on the revival of an idealized Westernized Greece, *The Giaour* introduced an exotic Eastern conception of Greece.[14] This is strikingly apparent in the illustrations for Byron's first Turkish Tale, in which Byron's Giaour dresses "in Arnaut garb" (615) and is indistinguishable from the Turk he kills.[15] When some philhellenes, enamored of Byron's Tales, arrived in Greece during the War of Independence, they refused to support Byron's own choice as the Greek leader, Alexander Mavrocordato, to whom Shelley had dedicated *Hellas*. No other Greek had such a close connection to the foremost English authors of literary philhellenism. But the educated Mavrocordato in his European clothes did not fit the images of a Giaour or a Conrad, which Byron's Tales had made popular. The philhellenes preferred the heavily mustachioed chieftains in local dress, such as Theodore Kolokotronis or Odysseus Androutsos, to whom Edward Trelawny attached himself.[16] These men, basically brigands, were certainly colorful, but they were hardly the proper leaders for a new country that hoped to take its place among the nations of Europe. Byron's Tales laid the foundation for an enduring paradox of philhellenism: the desire for Greece to become Western and the simultaneous rejection of Westernization in Greece as inauthentic.

The Giaour takes the reader out of the world of morally rigorous and philosophical noble savages inhabiting a benign natural environment into the world of the klephts, brigands who lived in rugged mountains with a social code based on honor and backed by primal violence. The klephts became heroes in Greek folk songs because they lived beyond the control of the Ottomans. Finlay explained that a "life of independence, even when stained with crime, has always been found to throw a spell over the minds of oppressed nations. The Greeks make Robin Hoods, or demi-heroes, of their leading klephts" (6:22–23). In a passage that Byron had written for *The Siege of Corinth* but had not included in the poem, he linked the klephts to the struggle to liberate Greece:

> And some are rebels on the hills
> That look upon Epirus's valleys
> Where Freedom still at moments rallies,
> And pays in blood Oppression's ills.
> (*CPW* III, p. 357)

A note by Byron reads: "The last tidings recently heard of Dervish (one of the Arnaouts [*sic*] who followed me), state him to be in revolt in the mountains, at the head of some of the bands common in that country in times of trouble" (*CPW* III, p. 488). The true character of these bands, according to Finlay, was hardly patriotic: "The ordinary life of the klepht was as little distinguished by mercy to the poor as it was ennobled by national patriotism. There is very little to eulogize in the conduct of criminals" (6:23). Hölderlin's Hyperion wryly comments: "Yes, it was indeed a remarkable undertaking to establish my Elysium with the help of a robber band" (129). But after *The Giaour*, many Westerners dreamed that their Elysiums could be established with the help of robber bands.

The original klephtic act in Western literature is the killing of Hassan by the Giaour, a death required by Hassan's murder of the Circassian woman Leila. Finlay acknowledged the canonical status of Byron's Tale when he mentioned the death of Hassan in his discussion of klephts in his monumental *History of Greece*: "Their [the klephts'] most glorious exploits were to murder Turkish agas in mountain passes, as Lord Byron describes the scene in his 'Giaour'" (6:23).[17] The Giaour, along with a "robber-clan" (590) that he seems to lead, ambushes Hassan's party while it "wind[s] slowly through a long defile" (552) in the mountains. The landscape is quite different from "the congenial earth" of the Greece portrayed in the second canto of *Childe Harold* or other works of nineteenth-century philhellenism:

> Above, the mountain rears a peak,
> Where vultures whet their thirsty beak,
> And theirs may be a feast tonight,
> Shall tempt them down ere morrow's light.
> Beneath, a river's wintry stream

Has shrunk before the summer beam,
And left a channel bleak and bare,
Save shrubs that spring to perish there.
Each side the midway path there lay
Small broken crags of granite gray,
By time or mountain lightning riven,
From summits clad in mists of heaven;
For where is he that hath beheld
The peak of Liakura unveil'd?

(553–66)

This is a Greece that Byron knew from personal observation, the forbidding mountains familiar to most travelers in mainland Greece and Crete where, as Patrick Leigh Fermor remarked, "all is violent and extreme" (*Roumeli* 140). But in *The Giaour* Greece remains a romanticized world in which "True foes, once met, are joined till death!" (654).

The pirates of *The Bride of Abydos* and *The Corsair* also come from a world of lawlessness, which is justified, even ennobled, by the fact that the established authority is despotic, both in the form of the local pasha and in the rule of the sultan. Modern Greek society did tolerate, and even romanticize, klephtic and piratical lawlessness, but that view was balanced by the reality that the klephts were as likely to rob or kill fellow Greeks as the common enemy. Byron knew and provided a glimpse of that reality in the note to line 1077 of *The Giaour*. In the text, Taheer warns Hassan of the attack moments before it occurs. As an explanation of "second hearing," which Byron says is more prevalent in the East than "second sight," the poet recounts how he was almost attacked by pirates during an excursion to Cape Colonna (Sounion): "I observed the Dervish Tahiri riding rather far out of the path, and leaning his head upon his hand, as if in pain.—I rode up and enquired. 'We are in peril,' he answered" (*CPW* III, p. 421). Nothing occurred, but on his return to Athens, Byron learned that pirates intended to attack his party and had only refrained because they thought the group was accompanied by a larger company of Albanian guards than was the case.[18] The ambush in *The Giaour* recreates the near-ambush of Byron at Cape Colonna, as the names Taheer/Tahiri suggest. When Byron has the narrator of *The Giaour* look down from "Colonna's height" to the shore, which has "many a grotto, meant for rest, / That holds the pirate for a guest" (36–37) and end with a lament that man has turned the lovely land of Greece into a place where "lust and rapine wildly reign" (60), he alludes to the personal threat he encountered traveling in Greece.

But despite the allusion to his own danger from Greek brigands, Byron romanticizes the foreigner and his robber clan and positions them on the side of Greek liberation and, by extension, the West. The "Advertisement" attached at the beginning of the Tale states that the story takes place "soon after the Arnauts were beaten back from the Morea, which they had ravaged for some time subsequent to the Russian invasion. The desertion of the Maniotes, on being refused the plunder of Misitra [Mistra], led to the abandonment of that enterprise, and to the desolation of the Morea, during which the cruelty exercised on all sides was unparalleled even in the annals of the faithful" (*CPW* III, p. 40). As chapter 1 has shown, not only would Byron's audience be familiar with the historical benchmark given in the advertisement (the revolt of 1770), they would instantly place that event and Byron's Tale in the context of Greek regeneration. Byron offers a rather bleak view about a Greek revival, for in his account the Maniotes were motivated solely by personal gain and plunged the country into complete ruin. The discouraging picture of modern Greece offered in the advertisement is balanced immediately by the first six lines of the poem, which invoke Themistocles, a hero from the golden past of the Persian Wars:

> No breath of air to break the wave
> That rolls below the Athenian's grave,
> That tomb which, gleaming o'er the cliff,
> First greets the homeward-veering skiff,
> High o'er the land he sav'd in vain—
> When shall such a hero live again?

Themistocles helped to free Greece from the threat of the Persian invasion. He was a man who saved the land as opposed to the present inhabitants who "mar it into a wilderness" (51).[19] Not until Greece once again had such heroes would both the land and the Greeks flourish.

The hero of *The Giaour*, like the pirates, acts for personal reasons: "And in the field it had been sweet / Had danger wooed me on to move / a slave of glory, not of love" (1010–11). Since, as McGann noted, lines 1–167 have "a point of view" that is, "like B[yron]'s, contemporary and English," it is tempting to read into the poem a distinction between what Westerners thought about Greece (1–167) and what it was really like (*CPW* III, p. 415).[20] Still, the reader, already conditioned by the allusions to 1770, properly sides with the Giaour against Hassan because Byron employs political language to describe the love of Leila:

> To me she gave her heart, that all
> Which tyranny can ne'er enthrall.
>   (1068–69)

Although the Giaour acknowledges, "Yet did he [Hassan] but what I had done / Had she been false to more than one" (1062–63), Byron does not present the two situations as equal. Leila was a slave of Hassan and, whatever the aga may have felt for her, was not a willing partner. Leila chose the foreigner; even Hassan calls him "lost Leila's love" (619). Our sympathies are not with Hassan.[21] The use of the loaded word *tyranny*, which could be used almost as a synonym for Ottoman rule,[22] links the personal freedom of Leila to the political freedom of Greece implied in the historical setting of the poem (sometime after 1770).

The connection between personal and political liberty is made stronger by lines 68–102, added to the second edition of the poem, in which the narrator expounds on the political situation of modern Greece. The narrator speaks of an expired Greece: "'Tis Greece—But living Greece no more! / So coldly sweet, so deadly fair, / We start—for soul is wanting there" (91–93). These lines balance a passage in which the Giaour talks of the appearance of a vision of his dead love: "No breathing form within my grasp, / No heart that beats reply to mine, / Yet Leila! yet the form is thine!" (1288–90). In *The Giaour*, especially after the first edition, the love of the Giaour is balanced by, and equated to, the love of the narrator for Greece as a political ideal.[23] The two themes run parallel and employ the same words and imagery, but they never intersect. It is as if, as McGann said of *Childe Harold's Pilgrimage*, the political regeneration of Greece is the objective correlative of a renewal of the personal integrity of the individual. Still, as the lines once intended for *The Siege of Corinth* show, Byron viewed groups like the Giaour and his robber clan as the keepers of the spark of Freedom, who "pay in blood Oppression's ills."[24]

The attitude of a number of philhellenes demonstrates that the brigands of *The Giaour* and the other Tales became an integral and admired part of the Grèce de Byron. Just how integral can be seen from Charles Brinsley Sheridan's preface to *Songs of the Modern Greeks*, his translation of a collection of Greek songs published in 1825.[25] Sheridan was a member of the literary subcommittee of the London Greek Committee, and the book, whose major sections were klephtic songs, historical ballads, and romantic ballads, was intended to increase support for the cause of Greek independence. The klephtic songs, according to the author, are "valuable as a collection, not so much of beautiful poems, as of historical documents, which prove the capacity of the Greeks to defend and govern their country, and, consequently, the injustice of the shackling of their freedom with the condition of receiving a foreign sovereign" (xviii). Indeed these songs stand as proof, from the horse's mouth as it were, that "the accounts of their [Greek] national character, as presented to us by a long succession of travelers, have been mainly erroneous" (xix). How could so many Western observers have been so consistently mistaken?

Tourists naturally resorted to those parts of Greece which were the most accessible, and the most worth visiting. But the fertility and the exposure of these very spots had long ensured on the part of the

Turks, both the will and the power to seize them. Thus, their Greek inhabitants became debased by patient submission to a barbarous yoke; while those, who really deserved the glorious title of Greeks, abandon'd such polluted spots, and took refuge among barren and inaccessible mountains. Hence arose a considerable portion of that gallant class term'd by the invaders Klephtai, or robbers, a title they afterwards bore with pride and exultation, much in the same way that "whig," originally a term of abuse, was afterwards complacently assumed by those to whom it was hostilely applied. (xix–xx)

For Sheridan, the klephts are the true descendants of the ancient Greeks, although, with regard to culture and civilization, they are even further from the ancient model than their debased kinsmen in the plains. While it is certainly true that there was a degree of national feeling in the klephts, they hardly formed the Greek equivalent of the Whig party. The songs themselves make this clear. The majority of them speak of fighting the Turks, but none of them talk of Greek liberation, still less of a Greek nation. The following song, "The Summons to the Klephtai of Mount Olympus," chosen for its brevity, will provide a flavor of the genre:

> This summer came the Pasha's threat;
> Its seal was hot, its ink was wet:
> "Ye Klephts, who hold each mountain height,
> Descend and bow to Ali's might."
> But two, the boldest sons of Greece,
> Will never pay that price of peace;
> These grasp their guns and glittering swords,
> And seek what cheer the wild affords.
>
> (41)

Such lyrics are proof of resistance to Ottoman authority but do not provide clear evidence that the Greeks were ready to defend and govern their own country. A poem at the end of the book offered some indication that the Greeks had thought of their struggle in national and libertarian terms:

> Kindle from our country's ashes,
>   Liberty! thy sacred fire—
> Many a *Spartan* sabre clashes,
>   Breathe on one *Tyrtaean* lyre! . . .
>
> Though our father's glorious deeds
>   Form'd a sadly pleasing theme,
> Yet a heart which really bleeds,
>   Is mock'd by memory's dream.
>
> (249–50)

It is no surprise that these lines echo Western sentiments about the revival of Greek freedom, including mention of Tyrtaeus, the poet of ancient Sparta, for they come from a section subtitled "Recent Odes of Greek Literati." The unnamed literati had translated Western notions about the regeneration of Greece into modern Greek just as Rhigas had done in his "War Song." Sheridan's retranslation was meant to convince the English public that modern Greece was really like the modern Greece that existed in the mind of the West.

The Greek literati were the natural allies of philhellenic supporters in the West. But, as St. Clair noted, they were just as likely to be scorned for their Western attitudes and dress. Edward Trelawny wrote: "When the Muses deserted Parnassus, the Klephtes, i.e. outlaws, took possession of their haunts, and kept alive the love of freedom and the use of arms. They were the only Greeks I found with any sense of honour. . . . The Klephtes were the only efficient soldiers at the commencement of the insurrection; and their leaders maintained the war for three years so successfully that the Greek government were enabled to borrow money" (*Records* 289).

At that point, Trelawny asserted, the political leaders of the elite class, and he meant men like Mavrocordato, appointed their own generals, embezzled the loan money, and almost lost the war. Later in the same chapter, Trelawny said: "It was particularly revolting to the mind as well as the feelings of [Colonel Charles J.] Napier, to witness the war as waged in Greece— without a plan, combination, system, or leader; every man frantic with excitement to kill and plunder on his own account" (291). According to Trelawny, Napier would have agreed to become the commander of the Greek forces only if he were given the authority to instill some discipline and structure. Yet it was the klephts who killed and plundered on their own account and resisted any effort to form a regular army. Trelawny himself, after he joined the band of Odysseus Androutsos, would become part of the problem. While he was Odysseus's confederate and brother-in-law, for Trelawny married Odysseus's teenage sister in 1824, the brigand chief switched sides and made an agreement with the Turks. Finlay called the act "the most celebrated instance of treachery among the Greeks during their Revolution" (6:380). Yet Trelawny, in his own eyes, had "taken Byron's fictions and turned them into facts" (St. Clair, *Trelawny* 119). In 1824–1825, he lived the life of a "Giaour," striving for Greek freedom with his own "maid of Athens" as a wife. For the rest of his long life, he would exploit that past in print and speech. Indeed, through his connection to Trelawny, the traitor Odysseus became in England a hero of the Greek revolution.[26]

Many philhellenes with more personal integrity than Trelawny became fond of the klephts during the war. Samuel Gridley Howe, a doctor with a Boston Brahmin background, wrote a sketch about the life of a klepht called "A Modern Greek," which was published in 1831. His subject began his career as a slave in Constantinople but escaped to become first a pirate and later a mountain brigand. Howe concluded: "A fine man, indeed, you have for an attendant, says the reader;—a murderer, robber, and brigand. . . . but be this as it may, Francesco had his redeeming qualities, for he was brave, and gener-ous, and warm-hearted; and he loved his country with a zeal equaled only by his deadly hatred of the Turks" (241–42).

In the West, as in Greece, the klephts became the keepers of the flame of liberty. And it was Byron who in *The Giaour* and the other Tales created the image of the klepht for Western readers. A newspaper article printed in Bal-timore in 1816, five years before the War of Independence, testified to the im-portance of Byron's Tales in the myth making of Greek brigands at the same time as it exposed the romanticism of the genre: "This Romance of the East is a thing better enjoyed at home, by your fire side, than in sailing a solitary caique, among the lonely islands of the Archipelago. The roar of the Helle-spont is harmonious only in the verse of Homer; and in spite of the enchant-ment of Lord Byron's poetry, a Greek pirate is a figure that must be placed at a distance to be pleasing" (quoted in Larrabee 42).

The failure of the revolt of 1770 almost immediately produced a curious dis-crepancy in the depiction of modern Greece. The revolt was supposed to show that the modern Greeks had reclaimed "the manly bravery of their renowned ancestors," that they were the descendants of the heroes of Marathon and Plataea. But modern Greece was more commonly portrayed, in both art and literature, as a woman. The most famous picture of modern Greece in the late eighteenth century was the frontispiece to Marie G. A. F. Choiseul-Gouffier's *Voyage pittoresque de la Grèce* (1782).[27] The text that ac-companies the illustration reads:

> Greece, depicted as a woman in chains, is surrounded by sepulchral monuments erected in honour of the great men of Greece who have championed her liberty, as for example Lycurgus, Miltiades, Themis-tocles, Aristides, Epaminondas, Pelopidas, Timoleon, Demosthenes, Phocion, and Philopoemen. She leans on the tomb of Leonidas, and behind her stands the column on which were engraved Simonides' lines for the three hundred Spartans who died at Thermopylae.

> > Traveler, tell them in Lacedaeomon
> > We lie here in obedience to her laws . . .

> Greece seems to be calling up the shades of these great men, and on the rock nearby these words are inscribed:

> > "*Let someone arise . . .*"
> > (tr. Constantine 175)

The picture of a chained Greek woman who, it is implied, is at the mercy of a Turkish man was one of the most effective and pervasive means of evoking sympathy for the Greek cause. It played upon the fears of a European woman, however degenerated and debased, trapped in an Oriental harem, as if Europe were suffering the ravishment of its eponymous ancestor, Europa. This particular form of the feminization of modern Greece, which had begun decades before Byron's Tales, ensured that the struggle for Greek freedom would almost always be portrayed or discussed in terms of the threat of sexual domination by the Turks and the romantic attraction of the Greek woman for the West. In Demetra Vaka Brown's *In Pawn to a Throne* (1919), the American hero mused, "What other girl in the world would reply to a declaration of love with politics?" (179). For almost 150 years, the answer was "a Greek girl."

One way to show how 1770 politicized the depiction of the Greek woman in the harem is to look at a novel written thirty years before the revolt. In Antoine-François Prévost's *Un Histoire d'une grecque moderne*, translated in 1741 as *The Story of Fair Greek of Yester-Year*, the narrator, a Frenchman, buys a Greek girl from a pasha's harem and eventually takes her back to France.[28] The bulk of the work consists of the narrator's discovery that the girl is accomplished in both painting and music, his acquisition of her, and his attempts to ward off competitors for her sexual favors, which, as a Christian, he does not compel even as her owner. Although the heroine is Greek and a number of the minor characters are Greeks and Turks, the author never raises the question of Greek liberation nor uses the girl's position to evoke, along with the sexual politics of gender, the political situation of modern Greece. This is a harem story, with the narrator a Western voyeur both fascinated and repelled by Eastern customs. Forty years later, the book could not have been written without engaging the interest in Greek regeneration and the place of Greece on the map of Europe, concerns that Prévost blithely ignores. Indeed, it is hard to read the book now without injecting some of these conceptions back onto the text. For after 1770, any narrative entitled *un histoire d'une grecque moderne* operated in a charged political context.

Choiseul-Gouffier's frontispiece looks to the ancient heroes of the past for help, hinting that modern Greek men are too debased to come to their country's aid. Many Westerners as well as Greeks thought that, even with the valiant efforts of Greek men, freedom could only be achieved with assistance from the West and not assistance from dead heroes. Some writers would directly call for their countries to assist Greek independence. Charles Kelsall, in his poem *A Letter from Athens* (1812), wrote such an appeal with language that included Choiseul-Gouffier's image of sexual domination:

> Rise Britain, rise! (for to thy sons is giv'n
> That high prerogative of fav'ring heav'n

> To rescue nations from the tyrant's lust,
> To scourge the guilty, and avenge the just,)
> Pour forth thy dauntless legions, and release
> The fettered Hellespont—ah! rescue Greece!
>
> (37)

In *Greece*, William Haygarth said:

> Yes, wretched Greece! beneath my country's shield
> Thou mayst vanquish and be free again.
>
> (III.703–4; see also III.662–73)

In the preface to *Hellas*, Shelley chastised the governments of Europe: "The apathy of the rulers of the civilized world to the astonishing circumstance of the descendants of that nation to which they owe their civilization, rising as it were from the ashes of their ruin, is something perfectly inexplicable to a mere spectator to the shows of this mortal scene. We are all Greeks" (*Shelley's Poetry and Prose* 408–9).

In these passages, the "someone" who was to arise and unchain the female Greece was not an ancient Greek male but a European man. Byron reacted to such thinking when he told the Greeks:

> Hereditary bondsmen! know ye not
> Who would be free themselves must strike the blow?
>
> (*Childe Harold* II.76.720–21)

Still, in the notes to that poem, Byron forthrightly said, "The English have at last compassionated their Negroes, and under a less bigoted government may probably one day release their Catholic brethren: but the interposition of foreigners alone can emancipate the Greeks, who, otherwise, appear to have as small a chance of redemption from the Turks, as the Jews from the rest of mankind in general" (*CPW* II, p. 202). He went on to talk of Greek attitudes to their "probable deliverers," the Russians, French, and English. He concluded, echoing the end of Choiseul-Gouffier's text, "But whoever shall appear with arms in their hands will be welcome; and when that day arrives, heaven have mercy on the Ottomans, they cannot expect it from the Giaours." It is surely not a coincidence that a work entitled *The Giaour* followed shortly thereafter.

The romance of Greek liberation can succinctly be summed up as a white man saving a lapsed white woman from the Turk, a brown man.[29] The white woman is a Greek or, like Byron's Leila, stands for Greece, but the white man is often English, French, or American, depending on the nationality of the writer. In Owenson's novel, Ida does marry a Greek hero who has devoted himself to Greek liberation. But at the end of the novel he joins the Russian army so that he can be a member of the Russian force that will liberate the Greeks. Only as a Russian can Owenson envision Osmyn freeing Greece.

Although other versions of the romance of Greek liberation appeared in words and pictures after 1770, it was Byron, once again, who supplied the canonical text. In the poem, the Giaour's "race and faith" are "alike unknown" (807), but in a note Byron said that the story "is one told of a young Venetian many years ago" (*CPW* III, p. 423). Leila, a Circassian, is referred to as a swan, and her whiteness is stressed elsewhere (e.g., "thus rose fair Leila's whiter neck," p. 511). The last of the principal characters is the dark Hassan ("black Hassan from the Haram flies," p. 439). This triangle will be recreated numerous times in the course of the next one hundred years; for example, see the continual contrast between the "lovely Greek" Ismene and her Ottoman pursuer "dark Amurath" in Agnes Strickland's *Demetrius* of 1833 (92, 95). A visual representation of the motif occurs in Delacroix's painting *Greece Expiring on the Ruins of Missolonghi* (1827), where the barebreasted Greece, depicted as a white female, stands amidst the ruins of a town with her hands out. Behind her is a dark-skinned, turbaned soldier representing the Muslim attackers, who now pose the familiar sexual threat to the feminized Greece. Below Greece a white male arm extends from the ruins in Western dress—the arm of Byron.

In *The Giaour*, it must be stressed, Byron varied and manipulated the romance of Greek liberation by separating the yearning for freedom from the love story. In fact, in none of Byron's Tales does the romance of liberation appear in its simple, didactic form. In *The Bride of Abydos*, all of the principals—Selim, Zuleika, and her father, Giaffir—are Turks, although they differ in character. Zuleika's father takes the part of the Eastern tyrant (see 16.297–98) and the hero, Selim, is "Greek in soul, if not in creed" (4.87). In *The Corsair*, Byron inverted the romance and presented the triangle of a Western man between Greek and Turkish women. In *The Siege of Corinth*, all the principals are Venetian. Only in this last poem is the struggle for Greek freedom forcefully entwined within the romantic narrative. The setting is the Ottoman recapture of Corinth and the Peloponnesus in 1715. Byron offered the struggle between the two foreign occupiers of Greece as one of "freedom and the West" against "tyranny and the East" in such lines as "Till Christian hands to Greece restore / the freedom Venice gave of yore" (5.104–5) and the allusion to the Persian Wars, that quintessential East/West conflict (14.341–44). The triangle consists of the Venetian commander Minotti, his daughter Francesca, and her lover Alp, who joined the Ottoman army after a false accusation was made against him in Venice. Further, in none of Byron's Turkish Tales is there a successful conclusion, either for the lovers or for captive Greece. Byron's variations on the romance of Greek liberation can be read as subversions of the generic formula.[30] At the very least they are complex investigations of widely held notions.

It is ironic, therefore, that because of their artistry and popularity, Byron's manipulations of the standard romance of Greek liberation as it appears in, for example, Choiseul-Gouffier's frontispiece, became accepted as the new norm of that same romance. As with the passages about a Greek revival in *Childe Harold*, Byron's ambiguous and questioning formulations were read without ambiguity and questions. So, for example, the careful separation in *The Giaour* between the themes of Greek liberation and the romance of the Giaour and Leila would collapse, and some philhellenes would view chieftains dressed as the Giaour as Greek patriots. Literary philhellenes would often exhibit the same lack of discernment and generate reductive versions of the romance of liberation based on Byron but without his probing language or equivocal endings.

One scene from *The Siege of Corinth* would be especially important for later philhellenic writing. It occurs when, on the eve of the final assault on Corinth, Alp walks to the site of an ancient ruin:

> There a temple in ruin stands,
> Fashioned by long forgotten hands;
> Two or three columns, and many a stone,
> Marble and granite, with grass o'ergrown.
>   (18.450–53)

On this "haunted, holy ground" Alp has an encounter with either Francesca or a vision of Francesca. The setting is reminiscent of Choiseul-Gouffier's frontispiece, although Francesca does not appear in chains. Byron's fusion of the two Greeces—ancient Greece personified in the ruined temple and modern Greece personified in Francesca—is subtle and provocative. In his description of the temple, Byron laments the effects of Time on the present, past, and future but does not mention the "lost" greatness of Greece in a context where, especially after *Childe Harold* II, the reader would expect it. Nor does Francesca, whose appearance might simply be Alp's imagination running wild, directly address the issue of freedom in her exhortation to Alp to return to the Christian faith. The scene effectively builds upon literary and artistic precedents without reductively following the established model. The numerous imitations of this scene rarely have the same degree of understatement and suggestion.

In the romance of Greek liberation in literature, the perils of the harem implied in Choiseul-Gouffier's illustration quickly became a permanent fixture. Owenson's Ida, whose conversation and customs are drawn from antiquity, undergoes the threat of sexual domination in volume 3. During a skirmish between Greek rebels and the aga's soldiers, Ida, who had gone out to lend moral support to her compatriots, faints and is carried to the Turkish leader's harem. The aga desires Ida but fears repercussions if he rapes her. He exchanges the life of the captured Greek leader, Ida's love, Osmyn, for her promise of marriage. After the ceremony, at the very moment when the aga intends to consummate the union, the news arrives that Osmyn has escaped. In the confusion, Ida is able to flee the aga's apartments.

Shelley uses the depiction of Greek women in the sultan's harem to encourage readers of *Hellas* to support the struggle for freedom in Greece. One of the key alterations made in adapting the structure of Aeschylus's *Persians* for *Hellas* was the identity of the chorus. In Aeschylus, the chorus is made up of noble Persian ladies who break into mournful laments as they learn that their sons and husbands have been destroyed by the Greeks. In Shelley, however, the chorus consists of "Greek captive women" who are found within the seraglio of the sultan. Shelley's change from his professed model brings his text in line with the romance of Greek liberation and is calculated to provoke a Western European audience to assist the Greeks.

In *The Revolt of Islam*, in which Shelley said that he made little attempt to "delineate Mahommedan customs," one of the few genuinely "Eastern" motifs was the harem rape of the heroine. Cythna is carried off by soldiers and taken to Othman's harem: "One was she among many there, the thralls / Of the cold Tyrant's cruel lust" (7.4.2857–58). Othman sees her "wondrous loveliness" and

> bade her to his secret bower
> be borne, a loveless victim, and she tore
> Her locks in agony, and her words of flame
> And mightier looks availed not; then he bore
> Again his load of slavery, and became
> A king, a heartless beast, a pageant and a name.
>
> (7.5.2869–74)

The rape sends Cythna into madness, which is "a power / Which dawned through the rent soul" (7.7.2884–85). The fear of Cythna's mad power leads Othman to send her to be bound in an undersea cave, a fate similar to that of Byron's Leila in *The Giaour*.[31]

Even though the analogy of Greece-in-chains/woman-in-bondage had become a literary topos by 1813, the year *The Giaour* appeared, the immense popularity of Byron's poem ensured that his version heavily influenced later writers. Byron's Tales became so pervasive in the West that, along with *Childe Harold* and "The Isles of Greece," they have been the lenses, as it were, through which much of Greek history and politics have been read. The feminization of Greece was an integral part of the depiction of the country as a politicized space.

In 1851, Gérard de Nerval said of the women he saw on the island of Syros, "Il n'y avait rien là du charme dangereux d l'antique hétaïre" (II.257), and the same is true of most contemporary Greek women in nineteenth-century Western literature. Although consistently threatened by the harem, the modern Greek female was not portrayed with the exotic sexuality attributed to truly Oriental women but rather with the pure, austere, "classical" character of Owenson's Ida, who was a modern Aspasia but one "innocent as beautiful, and virtuous as intelligent" (II.43). This construction of the Greek female continued in later philhellenic literature for more than a hundred years. In Lynch's novel *Glamour: A Tale of Modern Greece* (1912), the rural Greek heroine is a pagan, "a child of the Earth, deep down in whose nature lovingly reposes the desire for Beauty, who does not wear it as a would-be fashionable cloak. . . . She is natural" (246, 249). Chrysoula's paganism, like the simplicity of Owenson's Ida, is in no way linked to sexual licentiousness or even to immodest behavior. Instead, it stands as a corrective to the decadent manners of Western Europe, since "conduct for her bears two species—right and wrong" (248). Byron presents the contrast in contemporary perceptions between the Greek and Eastern female in the characters of Medora and Gulnare in *The Corsair*. The former, "in life itself . . . so still and fair" (III.603), has been described as "sociable, domestic, civilized, and beautiful" (Elfenbein 23). Gulnare, the Turk who possesses "the fire that lights an Eastern heart" (III.53), can both intrigue and emasculate the male. R. S. Hichens employed and expanded on these perceptions in his novel *In the Wilderness* (1917). The hero becomes involved with two different Englishwomen, one who represents Athens and the other Constantinople. With his wife, Rosamund, a beautiful blonde who, like an Athene Nike, embodies simplicity, endurance, and calmness, he travels to Greece. At one point he tells Rosamund: "You reminded me of the maidens of the porch on the Acropolis. I connected you with Greece—and all my dreams of Greece" (10). But after a tragic accident in which he kills his son, he is ensnared by dark Mrs. Clarke, who personifies the "umber mystery of Stamboul, . . . with its promiscuous degradation" (209, 509). Rosamund returns at the end to save him from his emasculating loss of self-respect in the East. His salvation fittingly occurs at Olympia in front of the Hermes of Praxiteles. Hichens avoids actual Greek and Turkish politics in the book, but the sexual politics of his story obviously build on the notion of the Greeks as the Western ideal and the Turks as the erotic and dangerous Eastern Other.[32]

The construction of the romance of Greek liberation in Byron and others certainly implies the emasculation and consequent disappearance of the Greek male. As Marilyn Butler said of Byron's *The Giaour*, "In this story of

Athens, the native Greeks are virtually invisible" ("Orientalism of Byron's *Giaour*" 87). In Hichens's *In the Wilderness*, Rosamund comments that Greece is "strangely bare of men" (46). The seeming invisibility of the Greek male reflects the uneasiness even of supporters of the modern Greeks about their place among Western nations. The *Examiner* for April 15, 1821, spoke of the modern Greeks as "that mixed and depraved race, the descendants of the effeminate race of the Later Roman Empire," who have finally "risen up from their burdens and contumelies" (231). Freeman called the Byzantines "effete . . . given up only to luxury and sloth" (*Historical Essays* 237).[33] European men will rescue and indeed marry the female Greece in numerous rewritings of the romance by English or American authors over the next century and a half. Greek males will sometimes marry and have a "happy ending" with Greek women, although more often one of the lovers will die. But Greek men will almost never become involved with European or American women until after the Second World War, when modern Greece becomes less of a political and more of a primitive, sexual space in Western literature.[34] There was a racial factor in the squeamish reticence to pair Greek men and Western women, as if the West could only recognize Greek women as European. This may have arisen from the fact that Greek men, at least "real" Greek men, that is, klephts, were not thought to be effeminate but, if not completely Eastern, they were still considered "exotic" primitives. In other words, literature resolved the perceived dichotomy between ancient/West and modern/East in Greece by making the first female and the second male. The former can be fully integrated, even "married," into the European family. Byron suggested such a division in *The Corsair* for, as Elfenbein observed, "Medora is entirely different from Conrad, while Gulnare is his double" (23). One explanation for this construction is that Conrad, as a corsair with the Greek pirates, has become Eastern like Gulnare, whereas Medora remains Western.

A number of nineteenth-century English novels have a woman of Greek descent living in England, among them Geraldine Jewsbury's *Zoe* (1845), Edward Collins's *Vivien Romance* (1870), Henry Creswell's *Modern Greek Heroine* (1880), and William Black's *Briseis* (1896).[35] Greek men, on the other hand, were tacitly kept out of the European family. As late as 1926, the Greek protagonist of Anthony Gibbs's *Enter the Greek* conceals his ethnic background from his English friends and, of course, from the Englishwoman he loves—the first part of the book is really a novel of a Greek man "passing" as a European. Near the end of Dora Bradford's novel *Greek Fire* (1935), the English heroine, Angel, has the following exchange with a young countryman:

"But, my dear child, you can't possibly marry a Greek."
"Why not?"

"It absolutely isn't done."

"Dr. Cameron is doing it anyway. He's going to marry Haidée."

"That's quite different." (350)

It was indeed considered quite different in English and American writing, although the reasons, as in this case, were left rather vague.

While this explanation of the perceived dual nature of Greece certainly underlies both the Tales of Byron and much of the Western writing about Greece, it remains below the surface and is rarely openly stated. For the klephts, and with them the pirates, were the deadly foes of the Turks and kept the flame of freedom burning in their inaccessible hideaways. But they were not, at least in the Western imagination, men with homes and families but rather a group of men without women, joined in a special bond, depicted as homosocial if not homosexual, such as the robber clan in *The Giaour* or the last of Lambro's men in *The Bride of Abydos*. George Francis Savage-Armstrong emphasized this point in his poem "The Klepht's Flight" (1882), written a full fifty years after the War of Independence, in which a klephtic leader explains to his new wife why they must leave their native land and seek a new home elsewhere:

> I am—I *was* a robber-chief.
>   I've fought for Greece and Liberty,
> I've fought for Greece, for love, for thee—
>   A chief of Klephts, no vulgar thief.
>
> No murderer for *only* gain,
>   But Freedom's soldier I have been. . . .
> Alas, the chief of Klephtic band
>   Owns *one* allegiance, only one . . .
> True to his band in rain or sun,
>   To them he yields his heart, his hand,
> His strength, his liberty, his life;
>   No deadlier treason can he speak
> Than in the ear of robber-Greek
>   To breathe the name of *wife*.
>   (*Garland from Greece* 172–73)

His love for the woman won out over his commitment to his fellow klephts, and now "every musket of my band / Is levelled with relentless hand / At this poor heart that at thy feet / Has found an unimagined rest" (174–75). The newly married couple is barely able to escape from the pursuing band and leave for the Ionian islands. Savage-Armstrong was an admirer of the klephts and their role in the fight against the Turks, as his poems "War-Song of the Greeks" and "The Brigand of Parnassus" demonstrate.

"The Klepht's Flight" shows the ambiguous place of the klephts in the English and American imagination, for the captain, by the code of the bands, would never be allowed to integrate himself into ordinary society.[36] In Demetra Vaka Brown's novel *Grasp of the Sultan* (1917), a Greek patriot tells the young English hero:

> I shall never marry. You will find many Greeks of wealth all over the world who will not marry so long as Constantinople is enslaved. It is not an easy thing, because we Greeks love to be fathers, to have sons, and to see them grow up in our traditions. But we, who belong to the Brotherhood in ships, must have no descendants when we die. All our money must go to the buying of dreadnoughts—to the building of the great Greek navy which may some day reconquer Constantinople, may free the Greek spirit, and permit priests to enter St. Sophia again. (195)

In Greece, of course, the klephts married. It was only against the rules in English and American literature.

In William Cullen Bryant's "Song of the Greek Amazon," a poem about a female klepht, the speaker goes to the mountains after the Turks have killed the man that she loved:

> They slew him—and my virgin years
>   Are vowed to Greece and vengeance now,
> And many an Othman dame, in tears,
>   Shall rue the Grecian maiden's vow.
>   (*Poetical Works* I.117)

It is not at all surprising to find that the Greek amazon of this poem, as in many depictions of woman warriors, renounces her accustomed place in society when she takes on a "male" role nor that this choice also entails a renunciation of her sexuality. What must be stressed is that the position of the male klepht acting in the male role differs little from that of Bryant's Greek amazon—as Armstrong's poem indicates, he too was placed outside of human society and his virgin years were "vowed to Greece and vengeance." If klephtic life prevented a klepht's incorporation into the Greek state, and educated Greeks were considered inauthentic, then it is no wonder that English and American writers, like Europeans generally, thought of a regenerated Greece as a female space.

The workings of the romance of liberation were an integral part of literary philhellenism during the Greek Revolution and beyond, so it might be useful to give another example at this time. In Demetra Vaka Brown's *In Pawn to a Throne* (1919), written with her husband, Kenneth Brown, the heroine is

Artemis Byzas, the last of a Greek noble family from Constantinople. Her great-grandfather tells her: "The great sire of all your sires was Constantine Byzas, who with a notable group of Greeks, emigrated from Megara, came here and found the first Greek city, which was named after him, Byzantium" (17). The old man trains the girl to sacrifice herself for her country by making her learn Iphigeneia's final speech at Aulis (38–39). Artemis is chosen as the bride of the half-German crown prince of Greece so that there will be a Greek presence in the royal family at Athens. Unfortunately, with the coming of World War I, Artemis and Greece face a new threat as dangerous as the Turks: "Yet a more sinister influence now hovered over Greece, an influence to whom the killing of a few thousand men, to further their own schemes, was indeed only of academic interest. As the heavy clouds in the sky blotted out the moon, so Teutonism was blotting out Attic gentleness and cultivation" (113).

On the Acropolis, Artemis meets Elihu Peabody, a member of the American legation. To the young diplomat, Artemis "seemed the very embodiment of eternally young Greece, whom the world loves. . . . And there in an instant, ancient Greece receded and gave place to one person alone, a young girl. As he thought of her, she changed: she was no longer the reincarnation of the spirit of old Greece; she became the personification of a New Greece, a Greece alive and forward looking, a Greece of the future" (95, 98). The royal family plans an attack on the republican Greek forces, which have broken away from the threat of Teutonism and are fighting beside the Allies in Salonica. Artemis, who as the prince's betrothed is living in the palace, becomes for all intents and purposes a captive with the sexual threat of earlier Greek heroines hovering over her. She attempts to stop the impending German takeover of Greece by sending Elihu Peabody to intercept a German messenger. He succeeds, and the threat of Teutonism recedes from Greece. Of course, the "last of the Byzas," that very "embodiment of young Greece," promises to become Mrs. Peabody and move to Connecticut. The romance of liberation, then, replicates the cultural colonialism implicit in the removal of antiquities from Greece by men like Elgin, a point made clear by Owenson in 1809 when Lord B. tells Ida: "Let others ravish from your country the ruined fragments of its former glory, but for me, oh! be it still reserved to bear away a nobler prize, and shew the lovely inspiration from which athenian genius drew its splendour" (I.196).[37]

A Greek hero does appear in the novel, Spiro Mellioti. Artemis says that "since 1765 his ancestors fought side by side with mine—and have died and rotted unburied on the battlefields of Greece" (182). Spiro's whole life is devoted to the cause of Greece and the family Byzas, which, given the fact that the present representative is the "personification of Greece," amount to the same thing. It is not surprising that Spiro is the only member of Artemis's group of patriots who dies in the novel. The wife of an American lawyer named Elihu Peabody would not have fierce klephts guarding her doors.

In Pawn to a Throne, with the adjustment of the Germans for the Turks, reprises in a reductive form the romance of Greek liberation inherited from the nineteenth century. In 1919, as in 1770, the best way to gain support for Greece abroad was, in the opinion of the author, not to portray a group of heroic young men in the pass of Thermopylae but rather to depict a beautiful young woman as the captive of brutal forces. There is, of course, a central difficulty with Vaka Brown's novel, as with the romance of liberation in general. After the woman who is the embodiment of Greece has been rescued and agrees to become Mrs. Peabody and live in Connecticut after the war, what is the future of "young Greece"? Vaka Brown, like most philhellenic authors, is too busy attempting to inspire the rescue to worry about the consequences.

The romance of Greek liberation was such a convention by the late nineteenth century that the classical scholar Gilbert Murray provided a caricature of the theme in his early novel *Gobi; or, Shamo* (1889). The heroine is Clearista Botzares, whose "beauty was only a tenth of her charm. Every well-informed person in Arganthos [the fictional island on which the novel begins] or Athens too, for that matter, knew of her learning and patriotism, had heard of her journey to the North of Greece, to nurse wounded insurgents on the Macedonian frontier; and had read that eloquent pamphlet about the same insurrection which appeared in Athens with the signature 'Clearista.' For it was part of her system to discard her second name and bear only one, like the great Greeks of old—a small piece of pedantry" (7). It might be surprising that someone should discard so famous a surname, but it turns out that the name was borrowed from the Suliot Nothi Botzares, whose life was accidentally saved by Clearista's grandfather during the War of Independence. Clearista learns that an old schoolmate has married a wealthy English nobleman in order to use his money and position to redeem Macedonia: "Sophia was a real patriot, and this, Clearista saw, combined with moderate beauty and Greek birth, had fascinated the romantic young philhellene" (32). She resolves to do her patriotic duty as well and sets her sights on the more noble and more wealthy Lord Strathburne, a weak, pale, and insipid Englishman with a lisp. In Murray's novel, rich philhellenic foreigners are now the prey of designing young Greek women. But at the end of the novel, Clearista, like Artemis Byzas, no longer lives in Greece.

The Grèce de Byron had become the norm even before the poet left to join the cause of Greek independence in 1823, so much so that Thomas Hughes in his *Travels in Greece and Albania* (1830) included the following diary entry for the year 1813:

> September 9th—Vain would be the attempt, if I endeavored to express my sensations at first setting foot upon the shores of Greece; that

> *Clime of the unforgotten brave!*
> *Whose land from plain to mountain-cave,*
> *Was freedom's home, or glory's grave!*

The impression is still vivid, but it defies description. (I.168)

Hughes quotes lines from *The Giaour*, which were added to the fifth edition of the poem that appeared, according to McGann (*CPW* III, p. 413), in early September 1813. Hughes has rewritten his "first impressions" of Greece between 1813 and the publication of his book to include a quotation from a poem of Byron that he could not have read at the time of his first visit to the country. Even after the fact, Hughes wants the public to believe that he first saw Greece with the poems of Byron in his head.

Those who came after Hughes did not have to pretend that Byron was in their heads as they disembarked at Piraeus or Patras. The young Edward Everett, who would go on to be a professor of Greek at Harvard and a famous orator, stopped in London to visit Byron in preparation for a visit to Greece. The poet provided advice and some letters of introduction (Larrabee 30–31).

Those who did not journey to Greece also felt the impact of Byron's poetry. Felicia Hemans's *Modern Greece* can best be described as a *Childe Harold's Pilgrimage* without the persona of Harold. And Mrs. Vaughan's *Grecians* (1824), one of the first plays written about the Greek War of Independence, has the Byronic epigraph, "Of the three hundred grant but three / To make a new Thermopylae."

Near the end of "Navarin," Hugo wrote:

> Grèce est libre, et dans sa tombe
> Byron applaudit Navarin.

Hugo and the rest of Europe believed that Byron had died "that Greece might still be free." Byron did not end, however much he might have wished it, as one of "certain men the Turkish shot." He was bled to death by European doctors after he had accomplished very little during four months in the real Greece. But when he stepped into the Grèce de Byron as an actor, he became for all eternity the hero of his own script.

3

On the Ruins of Missolonghi

The Greeks in Missolonghi, alternately spelled as Mesolonghi or Missalonghi in philhellenic literature, were in desperate straits by the middle of April 1826. The town, situated in a salt marsh in western Greece just north of the Corinthian Gulf, had been under siege since April 27, 1825. Food was scarce and ammunition low. Rather than surrender to the attacking Ottoman and Egyptian armies, the defenders of Missolonghi decided to attempt to break through the Turkish lines on the night of April 22, 1826. Out of 9,000 men, women, and children who took part in the sortie, only about 2,000 would eventually reach safety. On April 24, the last remaining Greek soldiers blew themselves up in the town's powder magazine (Finlay 6:391–97). It is most unlikely that any of those soldiers were aware that Byron's Minotti had expired exactly the same way at the end of *The Siege of Corinth* and that, in Western European eyes, they had also lived and died a Byronic fiction.

The War of Independence would not have a new Marathon, but, as George Croly pronounced in his poem "On the Ruins of Mesolonghi," written soon after the fall of the town, it did have a new Thermopylae:

> Glorious spirits! ye have past;
> On the ground your blood is cast,
> Tower and bastion, all are won,
> Round the new Thermopylae
> Lies the gore, and lies the clay,
> To high heaven the soul is gone.
> (*Poetical Works* 2:303)

In his powerful "Les Têtes du Serail," with the haunting line "Missalonghi n'est plus," Victor Hugo would go even further: "Voici votre Calvaire après vos Thermopyles."

The heroic end of the year-long defense of Missolonghi was, in the words of Finlay, "the most glorious military operation of the Greek Revolution. . . . Greek patriotism seemed to have concentrated itself within the walls of

Mesolonghi" (6:373). Unfortunately, the valiant behavior of the defenders of the town did not inspire their fellow Greeks to put aside their differences and strike hard at the enemy. Finlay, who was actively involved in the War of Independence at the time, lamented that the garrison that surrendered the Acropolis to the Turks in May 1827 lacked "the devoted patriotism of the men of Mesolonghi" (6:433).

When news of the fall of Missolonghi reached Western Europe and America, however, supporters of Greek independence redoubled their efforts. As St. Clair said, the Turks found it "totally incomprehensible that the capture of a small fishing village should have ideological significance. Missolonghi had no classical associations" (*That Greece Might Still Be Free* 243). Yet one of the physicians accompanying the Muslim army saw a message scribbled on a house—*hic e vita decessit Lord Byron*. "Here was a clue to a factor that no Turk could have been expected to understand. In the two years since the death of Lord Byron, Missolonghi had become the most famous town in modern Greece, the symbol of the War of Independence, the focus of all philhellenic feeling" (*That Greece Might Still Be Free* 243). In Western literature, only one location from the Greek Revolution would join Marathon, Salamis, and Thermopylae in the pantheon of liberty. Modern Greeks would venerate such locations as Kalavryta, where the flag of the revolution was raised for the first time. The rest of the world revered Missolonghi. And it was Byron, not "the most glorious military operation of the Greek Revolution," who was primarily responsible for placing one of the more obscure and unappealing locations in Greece on the map of the world. The English poet Aubrey de Vere wrote in 1850, Byron's "fate will long impart interest to a place which would otherwise not possess much to attract notice" (*Picturesque Sketches in Greece and Turkey* I.30–31). Without the poet's death, Missolonghi might have been remembered only by Greeks.

Byron arrived in Missolonghi on January 4, 1824. From August 3, 1823, until December 29, the poet had stayed on the Ionian island of Cephalonia, which was then under British control. Some philhellenes and members of the London Greek Committee almost despaired of Byron's ever setting foot in liberated Greece.[1] Even after his arrival in Missolonghi, they continued to be frustrated by what they perceived to be the poet's indecision and inactivity. Byron's inaction, however, stemmed from the enormous confusion and serious conflicts among various Greek leaders. On September 27, 1823, Byron wrote Hobhouse from Cephalonia: "The fact is that matters are in great disorder.—No less than three parties—and one conspiracy going on at this moment among them—a few steps further and a civil war may ensue.—On all sides they are (as you perceive) trying to enlist me as a partizan. . . . I have not yet gone to the Main[a]—because to say the truth—it does not appear that I could avoid being considered as a favourer of one party or another—but the moment I can be of any real service I am willing to go amongst them" (*BLJ* 11.27–28). In the end, as Byron himself must have realized, he could never be of real service to the Greeks.[2] John Cam Hobhouse, after reading accounts of Byron's last days from Leicester Stanhope, the Benthamite who was sent out to establish a free press in Greece, concluded: "Had he lived I am not sure that he could not one day or the other have had cause to regret that he had not fallen by the fevers of Mesolonghi, just as Pompey grieved he had not fallen in Campania" (Marchand III.1239).[3] Whether Byron would have ever regretted escaping the fevers of Missolonghi, it was readily apparent to Hobhouse that Byron had accomplished more by dying than he ever could have by living.

Dr. Julius Millingen, who accompanied Byron to Missolonghi and, in the eyes of some, had a hand in killing the poet, expressed amazement at the discrepancy between the optimistic opinion of the modern Greeks prevalent in Europe and Byron's pessimistic view of the descendants of Miltiades. Millingen recorded Byron's response: "This should not surprise you, for I know this nation by long and attentive experience, while in Europe they judge it by inspiration. The Greeks are perhaps the most depraved and degraded people under the sun, uniting to their original vices both those of their oppressors, and those inherent in slaves" (6).[4] In an essay entitled "The Present State of Greece," dated February 24, 1824, and not published during the poet's lifetime, Byron commented on the almost complete disorganization of the Greeks:

> The Greeks have been downright slaves for five centuries and there is no tyrant like a slave. The Delegate of a Despot is still a bondsman, and men whose fathers' fathers, farther than they can reckon, were absolute vileins, without property, even of their own persons, still move as if they were in fetters, or, in many instances, may seem only to have exchanged the chains of the prisoner for the freedom of the jailor. This is a hard truth; but we fear it *is* one. We are not here to flatter, but to aid, as far as in our power, to a better order of things, and, whether *of* the Greeks or *to* the Greeks, let the truth be spoken. (*Complete Miscellaneous Prose* 193)

Anyone familiar with the notes to *Childe Harold's Pilgrimage* would not find such sentiments about the Greeks at all surprising; Byron had been saying the same sort of thing for more than a decade. Finlay suggested that Byron "did not overlook the vices of the Greek leaders, but at the same time he did not underrate the virtues of the people. The determined spirit with which they asserted their independence received his sincere praise, even while the rapacity, cruelty, and dissensions in the military weighed heavily on his mind" (6:326). Yet, as Finlay acknowledged, Byron was often as disgusted with the Suliot soldiers in his employ as he was with the Greek leaders (6:326–27). Still, Byron remained committed to the establishment of "a better order of things" in Greece even as he increasingly despaired of its probability.

If Europe, as Byron reportedly told Millingen, judged Greece by inspiration rather than experience, it was an inspiration founded in large measure on the poetry that Byron had written. And Byron continued to produce verse that seems at odds with the insightful and searching criticism of the Greeks found in his letters and other prose. In the poem "On this day I complete my thirty sixth year," composed for his birthday on January 22, 1824, he said:

> Thy Sword—the banner—and the Field,
>   Glory and Greece, around me see!
> The Spartan borne upon his shield,
>   Was not more free!
>
> Awake! (*not* Greece—she *is* awake!)
>   Awake my spirit—Think through *whom*
> Thy Life-blood trickles its parent lake,
>   And then strike home! . . .
>
> If thou regret'st thy youth, why *live*?
>   The Land of honorable Death
> Is here—up to the field! and give
>   Away thy breath:
>
> Seek out—less often sought than found,
>   A Soldier's Grave—for thee the best,
> Then look around and choose thy ground
>   And take thy Rest.
>   (*CPW* VII, pp. 80–81)

Byron had seen little around him to connect the glory of Greece and valor of the Spartans with the present inhabitants of Greece. Yet, when this poem was published posthumously, it would, like the purple passages of *Childe Harold* and "The Isles of Greece," encourage its audience to judge Greece by inspiration rather than by close observation of the real situation. To the end of his life, the Greece of Byron's poetry differed greatly from the Greece of his prose. And, as Byron surely knew by the year 1823, it was through his poetry and not his prose that Greece was known abroad. After all, many of the active English and American philhellenes whom Byron met in Greece had been inspired to join the cause by his verse.[5]

Byron's poetic statements about Greece do not appear to be the pose of the bard but rather an indication that, despite his long and attentive experience, he too was moved to judge Greece by inspiration. An unpublished poetic fragment dated June 19, 1823, a few months before he left for Greece, began: "The Dead have awakened—shall I sleep? / The World's at war with tyrants—shall I crouch?" (*BLJ* 11.29). However much he might have railed against the Greeks, a part of Byron wanted to see the War of Independence as a sign of regeneration of the classical dead and a blow to tyranny both abroad and at home. In this fragment, as in "On this day," the problem is not Greece ("she is awake"), but the self-perceived inactivity of the poet. Finlay said of Byron: "It seemed as if two different souls occupied his body alternately" (6:325). If so, then one of these souls wrote his verse, the other his prose. But the reading public, as I have already suggested, seems to have paid attention only to Byron's poetic soul and even then not to its complete output and shaded nuances.

As St. Clair observed, Byron's death and the heroic defense of Missolonghi quickly became conflated. "The name of Missolonghi became one of the great rallying cries of the nineteenth century and not a few who responded to it believed that Lord Byron had died in the destruction of the town" (*That Greece Might Still Be Free* 269). Henry J. Bradfield wrote in his poem "Leandro" (1830), "A warrior from the West shall come, / To aid thy cause, to share thy doom!" (*Tales of the Cyclades* 21). It was, after all, a natural assumption for readers who judge by inspiration; had not the poet himself in one of his last poems said that he wanted to "Seek out . . . / A soldier's grave"? What better ground to choose for him than a place in the new Thermopylae? Years later, Isadora Duncan would ask if there were "anything more touching than Byron's death in the brave town of Missolonghi?" (*My Life* 121).

In Thomas Moore's *Evenings in Greece* (1826), the women of the island of Zea (Kea) gather to sing songs while they await word about their loved ones fighting for freedom on the mainland. Some passing mariners inform them about the news of Missolonghi:

> Twas from an isle of mournful name,
> From Missolonghi, last they came—
> Sad Missolonghi, sorrowing yet
> O'er him, the noblest Star of Fame
>   That e'er in life's young glory set!—
> And now were on their mournful way,
>   Wafting the news through Helle's isles;—
> News that would cloud ev'n Freedom's ray,
>   And sadden Victory 'mid her smile.
> Their tale thus told, and heard, with pain,
> Out spread the galliot's wings again;

> And, as she sped her swift career,
> Again that Hymn rose on the ear—
> "Thou art not dead—thou art not dead"
> As oft 'twas sung in ages flown,
> Of him, the Athenian, who, to shed
> A tyrant's blood, pour'd out his own.
>
> (*Poetical Works* 290)

The chorus then breaks into a lyric about Harmodius, a tyrannicide of the sixth century BCE, whose deed is presented as a classical analogy for Byron's illustrious end.

Moore was working on *Evenings in Greece* in the spring of 1825, well before he learned of the fall of Missolonghi. But few readers in the years after 1826 could look at the phrase "Sad Missolonghi, sorrowing yet" or the following couplet from W. G. Thompson's 1824 "Lines on the Death of Lord Byron": "Yea, on the battlefield expired, / With thy ancestral glories fired" (Chew 197) and not link Byron's heroism and the new Thermopylae.

While Byron is not specifically mentioned in Croly's "On the Ruins of Mesolonghi," Hugo's "Les Têtes du Serail," or a number of other poems about the fall of Missolonghi (e.g., Felicia Skene's "On Missalonghi," 1843), he is unquestionably present in all of these works. One could argue that in the most important of the pieces honoring Missolonghi, "Les Têtes du Serail," Byron's presence is felt even more strongly because, unlike Canaris, Bozzaris, Miaoulis, or even Fabvier, he does not need to be named.

Byron's death and the fall of Missolonghi were quickly taken up into the romance of Greek liberation. One of the most famous and influential examples was Ferdinand Victor Eugène Delacroix's painting *Greece Expiring on the Ruins of Missolonghi* (1827; see chap. 2), from which George Croly took the title of the poem quoted above.[6] The poet who had been instrumental in creating the romance of Greek liberation had become a principal in that same romance.

Byron's entrance into the romance of Greek liberation would politicize many readings of an earlier work written in 1810, during his first stay in Athens. The poem is titled "Song" and begins:

> Maid of Athens, ere we part,
> Give, oh, give me back my heart!
> Or, since that has left my breast,
> Keep it now, and take the rest!
> Hear my vow before I go,
> Ζώη μοῦ σάς αγαπῶ
>
> (*CPW* I, p. 280)

Teresa Macri, later Mrs. John Black, for whom the poem was thought to have been written, became as much a shrine for many Western visitors to Greece in the decades after the War of Independence as the plain of Marathon because, through the conflation of Byron's expression of love for a Greek woman and his commitment to a feminized Greece, she too became a part of the romance of Greek liberation.[7] As late as 1867, C. C. Felton commented that "it is a common thing for travellers to call on Mrs. Black, with no more introduction than *zoe mou, sas agapo*" (*Greece, Ancient and Modern* 515).

After a description of his visit to Teresa Black in 1832, the American Walter Colton discussed Byron's relationship with "the Maid" in what amounted to a free-associative gloss on Byron's text in the romantic light of the poet's death:

> I have ever lamented the blind necessity which so early separated the minstrel and her who drew forth his most passionate and tender lays. Beings so congenial in their sympathies, impulses, desires; so alike in their tastes, pleasures, and susceptibilities, should have met but once, and then never parted. . . . But they were not thus to be united; it was for him to wander on, to encounter strange and familiar faces, to be falsely allied, to seek again the scene of his former exile, to bind the wreath of the lyre upon his sword, and flashing it in the eye of an ex-ulting Greece, drop into an untimely grave! He sunk alone; but like a resplendent star, that kindles with its own effulgence the clouds that would darken its descent. She, that was the object of his early fond-ness, was not there to witness his departure; but she heard, through the tops of her distant isle, the moaning winds conveying onward the sighs of a dismayed nation, the regrets of a bereaved world! (221–22)

While all visitors were not so effusive, many were as prone to view the relations of Byron and the Maid of Athens in terms of the poet's later involvement in Greek politics.

Numerous instances of the politicization of Byron's "Song" appeared in the nineteenth century. As early as June 1824, Byron's little love poem was put to political use when the New Royal Theatre in Drury Lane presented John Baldwin Buckstone's *Revolt of the Greeks; or, The Maid of Athens,* which was followed in June 1828 by the melodrama *Maid of Athens; or, Greece and Liberty* at the Caledonian Theatre.[8] The two most reductive political uses of the poem are Catherine Grace Garnett's *Reine Canziani* (1825), in which a Lord Byron persona named Lord Monthermer falls in love with the daughter of the Greek patriot Canziani and proclaims, "*Zoe mou sas agapo* . . . will be my motto," and a novel fittingly entitled *Maid of Athens* by Lafayette McLaws (Emily Lafayette) published in 1906. In the latter book, on his first journey to Athens, Byron falls in love with Thyrza Rhigas, the daughter of the Greek patriot executed in 1798. McLaws's novel opens on the day of Rhigas's death with the hero's wife singing Byron's 1809 translation of Rhigas's "War Song." In the novel, Thyrza's mother herself constructs the romance of liberation by calling her daughter the "Maid of Athens" and prophesying that "she will become a beautiful woman, and another man will lay down his life for her sake and accomplish what her father began" (9). The book inventively weaves a fictitious connection between the Maid of Athens, Byron's Thyrza poems, and his philhellenism. But it is important to make clear that, while the novel's premise stretches the truth, it would not necessarily strain the credulity of its readers. McLaws's audience had already been conditioned to link the Maid of Athens and Byron's love of Greece.[9] An updated Maid of Athens caught the eye of a young philhellene in a number of novels with that phrase in the title, such as Justin McCarthy's *Maid of Athens* (1883), Joseph Hocking's *Tommy and the Maid of Athens* (1917), French Strother's *Maid of Athens* (1932), and Mary Richmond's *Maid of Athens* (1948).

The canonization of Byron as the hero of Greece was rapid and enduring in European literature. In his poem "To the Shade of Byron" (1827), Henry Bradfield exclaimed "with the fame of thy country, thy name shall be wreathed." For Bradfield, as probably for many of his readers, "Byron's country" was Greece as much as, if not even more than, England. Taking a page from Byron himself, Bradfield did not hesitate to tell the Greeks how they should feel about their hero: "When the Greek thinks of thee, / Shall the tear dim his eye, / For thy genius hath taught him, / Undaunted to die!" (*Tales of the Cyclades* 157). In "The Last of the Klephts: A Glimpse of the Greek War of Independence," written during the Greco-Turkish War of 1897, Isabella Mayo said of the progress of the Greek state: "It has been his [Byron's] hopes which have come true—his endeavors which have been justified" (368). The modern Greeks have certainly honored Byron's effort, but they might legitimately balk at accepting the notion that Byron's poems taught them dedication to the cause of Greek freedom or that modern Greece had to justify his hopes and endeavors.

As William Ruddick noted, from the time of his death "a distinction form[ed] in the opinion of his contemporaries between Byron, the hero of Greece, a man of action, politically and militarily effective, and the slapdash, self-regarding and self-dramatizing poet of earlier days" (27). Even those who found fault with his poetry could, although sometimes grudgingly, acknowledge his courage. For example, in "Courage," Matthew Arnold, who reservedly praised the earlier poet's verse in his essay "Byron," wrote:

> And Byron! Let us dare admire
> If not thy fierce and turbid song,

Yet that in anguish, doubt, desire,
Thy fiery courage still was strong.

(148)

The conception of Byron as a "man of action" was, to a large degree, based on reports of Byron's last days by those who were there, who arrived soon after, or who were in the area. The earliest and most important of them were Count Peter Gamba's *Narrative of Lord Byron's Last Journey to Greece* (1825), William Parry's *Last Days of Lord Byron* (1825), Edward Blacquiere's *Narrative of a Second Visit to Greece, Including Facts Connected with the Last Days of Lord Byron* (1825), and Leicester Stanhope's *Greece in 1823 and 1824, Being a Series of Letters and Other Documents on the Greek Revolution . . . to Which Are Added, Reminiscences of Lord Byron* (1825).[10] Samuel Chew in his useful *Byron in England* rather naively reported: "It is evident, then, that the testimony of Byron's fellow-workers for the cause of independence was entirely, or almost entirely, favorable to him; without doubt this group of disinterested witnesses did much to rehabilitate the reputation which the last years in Italy had somewhat tarnished" (207). Since the writers were all "fellow workers" in the cause of Greece and that cause was still very much in doubt in 1825, how "disinterested" would their accounts really be? Did Byron in his death throes mutter, as Gamba reported, "Poor Greece! . . . I have given her my time, my means, my health—and now I give her my life!— could I do more"? (265). Both before and after Byron's death at Missolonghi, the Western idea of modern Greece was attached to his star.[11]

In the words of Finlay, Byron's arrival in Greece "directed the attention of all Europe to the affairs of Greece by joining the cause" (6:323). Finlay was one of those whose attention was captured, and he left for Greece soon after he heard of Byron's departure. Byron's public fame, or infamy, depending on one's viewpoint, would have attracted notice no matter what cause the poet embraced. But the commitment of the poet of "The Isles of Greece" to the struggle for Greek freedom struck a strong emotional chord throughout Europe and America.[12] Even before Byron's arrival in Greece in 1823, the prominence of the Grèce de Byron had linked the poet and the place in a close association. Byron's death in Missolonghi, especially as it was reported by those with him, solidified that connection into an unbreakable bond. In the eyes of the West, the poet created Greece twice—first when he put the Grèce de Byron down on paper and later when he played a major role in the liberation of the country. Or, as Casimir Delavigne put it in *Messénienne sur Lord Byron*, "Childe Harold sur vos bords revient pour succomber" (13). The French poet went on to call Byron Greece's Homer and Achilles combined ("Il chantait comme Homère, il fut mort comme Achille," 14).

Yet if Byron "saved" Greece, then Greece in turn redeemed Byron. By the early 1820s Byron's verse had declined in popularity, a trend helped by the scandals connected with his personal life and the hostile reception to such works as *Cain* and *Don Juan*. The poet's death, in the words of Ruddick, "rescued his personal reputation" (27). The story of Missolonghi is equally about the redemption of the personal integrity of the poet as it is about the regeneration of Greece. Flaubert said, "In Greece, he [Byron] preferred to die rather than be bled. He went there to fight for the rebirth of a country that had been strangled by servitude. He went there to lift the chariot of freedom out of the mire where tyrants had plunged it. But the mire had an ennobling effect. It immortalized Byron, the son of the century" ("Portrait of Lord Byron" 4). In 1912, Emilie Barrington claimed, "Whatever Byron was elsewhere, the Byron of that Missolonghi I am staring at across the sea was noble-hearted and tender-hearted" (32).

After 1824, the fortunes of Byron and Greece were irrevocably joined, and they would rise and fall together. In the 1850s, when Byron's reputation hit "its lowest ebb" in England (Chew 263), Freeman stated that "dislike towards Greece on the part of Englishmen naturally reached its height during the frenzy of the Russian war." He added: "In all matters relating to Greeks and Turks we reversed the rules by which our sympathies were guided in other parts of the world" (*Historical Essays* 312). When interest in Byron revived around 1880, so did English philhellenism. In America, where Byron and Byronism did not experience as large a midcentury lull, philhellenic feeling remained strong.[13] There were, without question, important political considerations that help explain the different attitudes toward modern Greece in nineteenth-century England and America, yet these same factors also affected opinions about Byron. And Greece was not always the cart behind the Byronic horse, since a revolt in Crete or Macedonia would inevitably call attention to Byron's heroism. But Byron's literary and cultural importance went beyond and, for many British and Americans, could be separated from his philhellenism. Supporters of modern Greece, on the other hand, would invoke Byron, as they would the classical past, whenever Greece was involved in territorial disputes with the Turks.[14] In "Byron in Greece" in the *Temple Bar* of 1881, written at a time when Greece and Turkey were on the verge of war, the anonymous author stated at the outset that "no political virus will find their expression here" but added: "At a time when Greece is once more in everyone's thoughts and on nearly everyone's lips, it may be interesting to revert to what were more familiar to the preceding generation of Englishmen than they are to the present one, the experiences of Byron in Hellas" (100). The final crescendo carries an unsubtle message about contemporary events. "[Byron] died for Greece, which to this hour finds in his name, his Muse, and his sword, one of the strongest claims to the sympathies of mankind" (108).

But since Byron was perceived to be "Freedom's laureate," as Robert Underwood Johnson proclaimed in "To the Spirit of Byron," he could be invoked during rebellions in Italy or Poland, as well as for agitation for domestic reform in Britain.[15] For Europeans and Americans, Byron, "the son of the century," was larger than Greece in the political as well as the cultural realm.[16] Modern Greece was subsumed into Byronism in a way that Byron was never contained by philhellenism. As Carlisle phrased it in the prologue to his play *The Last of the Greeks; or, The Fall of Constantinople* (1828): "Honour to Byron, when the theme is Greece" (v). When the theme was Byron, Greece might not be involved at all.

Modern Greece was associated with a political Byronism of a certain kind.[17] Twenty years after Byron's death, Joseph Mazzini wrote:

> I know of no more beautiful symbol of the future destiny and mission of art than the death of Byron in Greece. The holy alliance of poetry with the cause of peoples; the union—still so rare—of thought and action—which alone completes the human Word, and is destined to emancipate the world; the grand solidarity of all nations in the conquest of rights ordained by God for all his children, and in the accomplishment of that mission for which such rights exist;—all that is now the religion and hope of the party of progress throughout Europe, is so gloriously typified in this image. ("Byron and Goethe" 93)

Earlier in this essay, the Italian patriot said of the two poets: "Both of these—I am not speaking of their purely literary merits, incontestably and universally acknowledged—... greatly aided the cause of intellectual emancipation, and awakened in men's minds the sentiment of liberty" (84). The political Left did not embrace Byron primarily for his artistic or aesthetic value but as the leading example of both poetry and the poet serving the cause of liberty. In nearly all of Mazzini's comments about Byron, politics takes precedence over art. His attitude helps to explain why modern Greece is central to the Byronism of the politically engaged and a radical/liberal symbol throughout the nineteenth century and beyond. For readers who wanted to privilege, or even separate, the aesthetics or dandyism of the "self regarding and self-dramatizing poet" from the poet's political voice, Byron's role in Greece was overlooked or downplayed.[18]

Mazzini, perhaps the high priest of nationalistic Byronism in the middle of the nineteenth century, noted, "I have, throughout my life, scattered Byrons of mine wherever I have been sojourning" (Mack Smith 181). He referred to actual texts of the poet he had to leave behind during his years of hiding. But Mazzini also left, or attempted to leave, other scattered Byrons in the form of poets and writers who were encouraged to emulate Mazzini's conception of the martyr for Greece. The best known was Swinburne, of whom Mazzini "consented to take intellectual charge" in the hopes that the young English poet might be the literary Byron of the Italian Risorgimento

(Gosse 166). The Byron of Greece, like the Greece of Byron and Shelley, became connected to a radical/liberal ideology.

The fascination of other writers with Byron's fate is quite understandable. Authors, such as Dante, Milton, and Yeats, dreamed of being men of action with the power to affect the course of events, yet they were seldom effective. Indeed, for the nineteenth and twentieth centuries, the myth of Byron became the prime instance of the poet as a man of action against whom other writers had to measure themselves. It was a myth, since the poet was hardly effective politically or militarily in Greece. Further, it instilled a belief that the success of a cause could come from the martyrdom of a single literary figure. In 1937, during the Spanish Civil War, a Communist leader in England told Stephen Spender without jest, "Go and get killed, comrade, we need a Byron in the movement" (Hugh Thomas 348).

The literary construction of modern Greece was fashioned among and within ideological arguments about the artist in politics. Implicitly tied up in the discussion of the role of the poet in the world of politics was the place where an author once was a man of action. The desire of authors to strive for the title of "Byron of Italy" or "Byron of Ireland" would add luster to political Byronism, but such aspirations did little for the cause of Greece. Greece already had the real Byron, a fact that may have encouraged some writers apprehensive of the poet's long shadow to turn their attention elsewhere. Many authors who were unsympathetic to the liberal causes associated with Byron allowed that to color their attitude toward Greece. It is one of the paradoxes of nineteenth-century English intellectual history that the Tories invariably exhibited disdain for a small monarchy dominated by a conservative clergy because of misinformed rhetoric about "revolutionary Greece."

In the wake of the poet, a whole new breed of philhellenes, "the romantic Byronists," made their way to Greece: "They were more Byronic than Byron, trying to find in Greece the exoticism which they loved, thinking they were copying Byron but actually behaving in a way Byron himself never did" (St. Clair, *That Greece Might Still Be Free* 176). Yet no matter how rosy their preconceptions, the experience of Greece would in most cases have a deflating effect. Indeed, some, such as David Urquhart in *The Spirit of the East* (1838) or P. J. Green in *Sketches of the War in Greece* (1827), would sour on the Greeks and publish scathing critiques of their shortcomings.[19] But the armchair Romantic Byronists and philhellenes who remained at home remained almost entirely impervious to what was actually happening in Greece. Accurate information, particularly at the beginning of the war, was rarely available, though this was not the real problem. The major difficulty was that authors could not conceive of modern Greece without seeing it through both ancient Greece and Byron's poetry. The result was that, as St. Clair said, "it seemed impossible to represent any event in Modern Greece as an event in its own right without overwhelming it with misleading allusions" (*That Greece Might Still Be Free* 24).

Of the numerous memoirs of the War of Independence written by English volunteers, none would be as popular as the poems of Felicia Hemans and Walter Savage Landor. The American Samuel Gridley Howe would write several pieces on his experience in Greece, but they never approached the circulation of the verse of William Cullen Bryant, Fitz Halleck, or James Gates Percival. Of course, *Childe Harold* and the Tales continued to be read with fervor. Literary philhellenism had defined its terms and set its parameters before the War of Independence began and would not allow the modern Greeks to disturb its view of Greece.[20]

The public perception of modern Greece would continue to be shaped by misleading allusions. For example, in *An Autumn in Greece*, Henry Bulwer wrote in a letter dated August 31, 1824, from the Italian port of Ancona, where he was awaiting a ship for Greece, that the "most splendid news has been received here of a battle fought at Marathon, in which the Greeks did not forget the spot on which they stood, and showed themselves worthy of their ancient glory. The Turks were defeated with great loss" (38). As Bulwer would discover when he arrived in Greece, such a battle never took place. In a note to his famous poem "Marco Bozzaris," Fitz-Greene Halleck related that the Greek leader was "one of the best and bravest of the modern Greek chieftains. He fell in a night attack upon the Turkish camp at Laspi, the site of ancient Plataea, April 20, 1823, and expired in the moment of victory" (Poetical Writings 369). Bozzaris actually died near Karpenisi in western Greece, which is nowhere near the site of the battle against the Persians. But Halleck's note has been repeatedly republished as it was written in 1824. If Americans today know of Bozzaris at all, it is often from Halleck's poem and its misleading note.

So the Grèce de Byron, not surprisingly, survived the War of Independence basically unchanged. The principal idea throughout the 1820s remained the regeneration of the Greeks, as in Bulwer's comment that "changed as the Greek may be from the portrait of his fathers, a family resemblance still remains; that image of Liberty which forsook his dwelling, was cherished in his heart" (4–5) and in the repeated phrase "we are Greeks once again" in the song that opens canto 2 of Agnes Strickland's *Demetrius* (44). The idea formed the central inspiration for Walter Savage Landor's poem "Regeneration" (1825).[21] In that work, as in *Childe Harold*, the revival of Greece is viewed both as a strike against "the spreading / Of Despotism" (103–4) and as a possible cure for English cultural malaise:

> I, in the land of strangers, and deprest
> With sad and certain presage for my own,

> Exult at hope's fresh dayspring
> (*Poetical Works* III.285, ll. 71–73)

The central analogies still referred to the Persian Wars and, to a lesser extent, to the fall of Constantinople in 1453. In part because of the immense popularity of Byron's "The Isles of Greece," Marathon had pride of place as the most frequent misleading allusion. It appears in Landor's "Regeneration" (55–56) and takes center stage in Felicia Hemans's "The Sleeper on Marathon," in whose first two stanzas, especially the debt to Byron is obvious.[22] The young Elizabeth Barrett Browning's debt to Byron is equally clear in her "Riga's Last Song," since Byron was the medium through which both Rhigas and his anthem were widely known in England. Her own reconstruction of "The mountains look on Marathon / And Marathon looks on the sea" shows which of the two poets, Greek or English, was her prime inspiration:

> I looked on the mountains of proud Souli,
> And the mountains they seemed to look on me;
> I spoke my thought on Marathon's plain,
> And Marathon seemed to speak again.
> (*Poetical Works* 57)

It was so commonplace to locate the modern Greek struggle for independence within historical analogies that authors could simply refer to the ancient event and assume the reader would make the necessary comparison to the contemporary struggle in Greece. George Croly's "The Death of Leonidas" and Hemans's "Ancient Greek Song of Victory" (although in this instance the epigraph to Byron provides a connecting link) are both poems concerning the Greek War of Independence. Indeed it is safe to conclude that, from 1821 to 1833, any poem about or, for that matter, any mention of places or classical figures like Thermopylae, Marathon, Salamis, Leonidas, Themistocles, Miltiades, Rhigas, or the Suliots was written in response to the Greek War of Independence.[23]

The ancient Greek heroes, however, were to be revived in the exotic dress of Byron's Giaour, a point visually presented in Karl Krazeisen's painting *Greeks Fighting among Classical Ruins*.[24] Delacroix's influential 1826 painting *The Giaour and the Pasha* demonstrates how Byron's poem became a key text of the struggle for freedom. The continued interest in the klephts in England was demonstrated by Sheridan's translation of klephtic songs in 1825; Landor's dialogues between Maurocordato and Colocotroni and among Odysseus, Tersitza, Akrive, and Trelawny, as well as the fragment about the Suliot uprising, which all appeared in 1829 (*Complete Works*

VIII.185–202, 204–43, 244–48); and Mary Shelley's short story of the same year, "The Evil Eye."[25]

But this was mild compared to the klephtomania that swept America. Dr. Samuel Gridley Howe observed, "There was something exceedingly wild, romantic, and enticing about the life and conditions of the Klepht" (*Greek Revolution* xxvii), and his countrymen all seemed to agree. A misleading analogy between the guerrilla war of the Greeks and the tactics used by both Indians and settlers on the American frontier was at least partly to blame.[26] English authors tended to "civilize" the klephts; Landor's Odysseus and Colocotroni have fine manners and can talk intelligently about European politics, while in Mrs. Vaughan's *The Grecians* the klephts are portrayed as heroic, even classical figures. The Americans, on the other hand, seemed almost to revel in the unorthodox warfare of the klephts. In William Cullen Bryant's "Greek Partisan," the poet described the exploits of his heroes:

> They go to the slaughter
>   To strike the sudden blow,
> And pour on earth, like water,
>   The best blood of the foe;
> To rush on them from rock and height,
>   And clear the narrow valley,
> Or fire their camp at dead of night,
>   And fly before they rally.
> —Chains are round our country pressed,
>   And cowards have betrayed her,
> And we must make her bleeding breast
>   The grave of the invader.
>   (*Poetical Works* I.144–45)

In the most famous American poem about the Greek War of Independence, Fitz-Greene Halleck celebrated Marco Bozzaris's night attack on the Turkish camp. The Turkish captain was sleeping when the raid began:

> He woke—to die midst flame, and smoke,
> And shout, and groan, and sabre stroke,
>   And death shots falling thick and fast
> As lightnings from the mountain cloud.
> ("Marco Bozzaris," Poetical Writings 14)

Such maneuvers were not the stuff of the armies of Napoleon or Wellington, but, as Halleck knew well, Washington had used the same tactic to take Trenton on Christmas Day 1776.

In "Snow-bound" John Greenleaf Whittier looked back on reading the newspaper on a winter day in the 1820s:

> Before us passed the painted Creeks,
>   And daft McGregor on his raids
>   In Costa Rica's everglades.
> And up Taygetos winding slow
> Rode Ypsilanti's Mainote Greeks,
> A Turk's head on each saddle-bow!
>   (406)

Europe recoiled in horror at the barbarity of the Greeks during the war. It was all well and good for a writer like Hugo to use the placement of Greek heads on the sultan's seraglio to show the barbarism of the Turks, but the Greeks were supposed to be different. Whittier's mention of the decapitation of the Turks is not meant to indicate his disapproval of the Greeks and their cause. It would seem that America's experience with frontier heroes like Daniel Boone allowed it to romanticize the actions of the klephts that embarrassed Europe.

Despite the manly activities of the klephts in the war, the feminization of Greece continued, as shown by the following titles of books in three different languages: *The Maid of Scio: A Tale of Modern Greece* by Snowden (1824), the anonymous German novel *Athanasia die schönen Griechin aus Samos* (1829), *Das Mädchen aus Zante* by Ioannides (1822), *Orpheline d'Argos: Épisode de la révolution grecque* by Heidenstam (1830), and *L'Athénienne; ou, Les Français en Grèce* by Sétier (1826), whose very title signifies the the gender relations between Greece and the West. Tsigakou's comment about painting is equally true of literature: "Romantic artists were moved more by the tragedies of the Revolution than by its achievements. It was the failures of the Greeks they depicted—such as *The Massacre of Scio, The Destruction of Missolonghi*, and *The Sacrifice of the Suliot Women*" (55). Of course, in both visual and poetic works of these events, the focus was often on the suffering of women. The enormous concentration in both Europe and America on the tragedies of the Greek Revolution and the fate of the victims is quite striking. The female figure in need of rescue depicted on the title page of Casimir Delavigne's *Messénienne sur Lord Byron* (1824) is another example both of the feminization of Greece and Byron's entrance into the romance of liberation. The goal of philhellenic artists and poets was, to be sure, to generate interest and support for the Greek cause, but one must still ask why a victimized Greece was routinely viewed as the most effective vehicle for that purpose. The West may have been attracted to the depiction of Greece as the heroine of a Greek tragedy awaiting the deus ex machina because it left Europeans and Americans a noble role in the Greek revival. In her novel *Anthea: A Story of the Greek War of Independence* (1892), Cécile Cassavetes has a Greek character say: "We are like sleeping beauty at present, waiting for Russia, France, or England to send a prince who will rouse us out of Turkish slavery" (277). But it is also difficult to dismiss the notion that the feminization of Greece was related to European and American ideas about modern Greece's place in the European family.

Along with Missolonghi, the event that received the most attention from European and American writers was the terrible slaughter of the Greeks on the island of Chios (Scio). Raizis and Papas suggest that "the massacre of Scio excited the imagination of the American poets more than any other event of the Greek war" (*American Poets* 66). In the spring of 1822, a small Greek force had landed on the island in the eastern Aegean to encourage the inhabitants to join the rebellion. They met with little success. Still, masses of Turks from Asia Minor, having heard of the massacres of Muslims in the Peloponnesus, crossed the small channel separating the island from the mainland. Thousands of Greeks were killed and as many as 41,000 were taken as slaves.[27] The depiction of the destruction of Chios in poetry and painting, as in Delacroix's *Scenes from the Massacres of Scio* and Hemans's "Sisters of Scio," closely followed the feminized portrayal of captive Greece, which had developed since the late eighteenth century.[28] The sad fate of Byron's lovely Leila was, as it were, transposed into what Raizis and Papas called "the tragic fate of that beautiful Greek island" (*American Poets* 66).

The sexual threat to Greek women from the Turks remained a prominent feature of philhellenic verse, as in the beginning of Halleck's "Marco Bozzaris":

> At midnight, in his guarded tent,
>   The Turk was dreaming of the hour
> When Greece, her knee in suppliance bent,
>   Should tremble at his power
>
> (13)

In the poem, Bozzaris's night raid becomes a "rescue" of a captive Greece from the threat of the harem. The theme of the seizure of a Greek for a Turk's harem is most prominent in dramatic works; indeed it was almost a requirement for plays set in the context of the modern Greek struggle for freedom to have a scene in which a Greek woman must be rescued from a lustful Turk by her husband or lover.

Curiously, the enemy in these plays was invariably Ali, the pasha of Ioannina, who had subdued the Suliots in 1803. Ali was actually in rebellion against the sultan in 1821 and was killed by Ottoman forces the following year. But, undoubtedly because of his well-known war with the Suliots and the connection between their resistance and the revival of Greek liberty, Ali was firmly on the Ottoman side in literature if not in history. Further, for English and American audiences his presence on stage recalled the tragic suicide of the Suliot women. By the 1820s, then, the Suliot struggle had become one more misleading reference through which England and America viewed the Greek Revolution. Ali was often transposed in space to Athens and in time to the War of Independence. He became the stage personification of the terrible Turk, whom the Greeks were fighting at the time the plays were performed, even though his headless body was already resting in a grave.

In one of the earliest plays about the Greek Revolution for the English stage, Mrs. Vaughan's *Grecians* (1824), the captured woman is Victoria, the wife of the Greek leader, Ypsilantis. Ali announces that Victoria "must bow to my will, / And minister to my pleasure" (9).[29] The Greeks organize a successful rescue of Victoria, in which a Greek prince named Antrobus, a descendant of Agamemnon, dies. His daughter, Menonia, loses her mind and becomes a symbol for the state of modern Greece. When her betrothed sees her wandering aimlessly around the camp, he says:

> View this, ye minions of despotic power!
> Ye advocates of slavery! behold
> The lovely ruin, beautiful in madness.
> How lov'd, how shelter'd from each chilly blast,
> Was once this lovely rose; now view the change
> Which grief has made!
>
> (49–50)

He ends with a plea to "restore the lovely sufferer." Menonia and her lover both die, but the play ends with the remaining Greeks pledging to "struggle for our country's peace" when "liberty again shall smile on Greece" (56).

The first American play inspired by the revolution, Mordecai Noah's *Captive; or, The Fall of Athens* (1822), has a similar plot. The captive is Zelia, the wife of a Greek patriot, with whom Ali has fallen in love; he wants to make her his wife. The Greek leader, Ypsilanti, appears at Ali's palace in Athens disguised as a painter commissioned to make a portrait of Zelia for the pasha. As he prepares for a sitting with the Acropolis in the background, he muses: "Here as artist, I am to sit, and while tracing the features of a female slave, my eyes must wander to Athens. . . . O Greece! Greece! how lovely art thou even in captivity! how splendid thy ruins! how soft and balsamic thy air! how rich and fruitful thy valleys!" (2). Once again the female captive and the country are merged together. The Greeks capture Athens with the help of an American warship, whose commander, Burrows, appears at the end of the play as a deus ex machina who "essentially contributed to the victory" (47).[30]

Interestingly, nineteenth-century philhellenic drama was the genre in which the romance of Greek liberation almost always had a Greek as a hero—though sometimes, as in the case of Noah's *Captive*, foreign help ensured the ultimate success of the Greek cause. At least on stage, the noble Greek male had a presence, perhaps because the audience wanted the visual effect of seeing characters in the garb of Byron's Giaour.

When we survey the enormous output of philhellenic literature in Europe and America during the Greek War of Independence, now admirably catalogued in the bibliography of philhellenic writing by Droulia, one is immediately struck by the fact that almost none of it has lasted. Delacroix's paintings, Hugo's *Orientales*, and Halleck's "Marco Bozzaris" are about all that stand out. English authors and European writers, who composed in the shadow of the Grèce de Byron, have remained in that shadow ever since. The *New Oxford Book of Romantic Verse* grants extensive space to the work of Felicia Hemans, who has been rediscovered in the last few years, but not one of her numerous poems about modern Greece is included. The editor's decision was completely justifiable; Hemans's Greek efforts do not constitute her best work. What is important to note is that authors appear to have made a conscious decision to stay within the language and concepts of their great predecessor, as if by doing so they were paying homage to the creator of their imaginary Greece. Literary philhellenism was still a world of pale paraphrases of Byron, as witnessed by these lines from Scot Thomas Campbell's "Song of the Greeks" (1822):

> Again to the battle, Achaians!
> Our hearts bid the tyrants defiance;
> Our land, the first garden of Liberty's tree—
> It has been, and shall yet be, the land of the free!
>
> (204)

The philhellenic literature of the 1820s offers a striking contrast to the writing about the Spanish Civil War of the 1930s. The latter conflict, another cause for pens on the Left, engendered numerous works by such artists as Orwell, Hemingway, Malraux, Picasso, Koestler, Auden, and MacNeice that have found a permanent place in European art and literature. But there was no equivalent of the Grèce de Byron with which authors of the Spanish conflict had to contend. The struggle for Greek liberty already had a canonical text before the War of Independence began.

The immense hold of Byron over English and American authors in particular both during the Greek Revolution and in the following decades is illustrated by the almost universal decision to avoid prose fiction in favor of lyric or narrative poetry in the Byronic style.[31] Across the channel, the French produced a plethora of philhellenic novels with, of course, Byronic themes and influences: Ducange's *Thélène*, Doin's *Cornelie*, Sétier's *L'Athénienne; ou, Les Français en Grèce*, Dominois's *Alais; ou, La Vierge de Ténédos* (1826), and Heidenstam's *Orpheline d'Argos* represent just the tip of the iceberg. Neither England nor America would produce a sizable amount of fiction about the Greek revolution until the 1890s.

The Greek struggle for freedom may have been called the "cause of Europe," but Greek fever hit only a part of the English literati. The poet laureate, Robert Southey, wrote to Henry Taylor after he heard of Byron's fate at Missolonghi: "I am sorry Lord Byron is dead, because some harm will come from his death, and there was none to be apprehended while he was living. . . . We shall now hear his praises from every quarter. I dare say he will be held up as a martyr to the cause of Greek liberty, as having sacrificed his life by his exertions on behalf of the Greeks. Upon this score, the liberals would beatify him" (*Life and Correspondence* 5.178).

Southey and Byron had a deep antipathy for each other, which was personal, aesthetic, and political.[32] Given Southey's distaste for Byron's life and work, in addition to Byron's ferocious attacks on the laureate's own compositions, it is hardly surprising that Southey would lament any luster to Byron's reputation. But how can any "harm" come from his rival's death in Greece? Some of that harm, clearly, would be political, as "the liberals" could turn Byron's death to their advantage. The liberal causes in the 1820s, all of them championed at one time by Byron, were Catholic emancipation, parliamentary reform, the abolition of slavery, and the extension of liberty. It was for the latter of these causes that Byron died in Greece, and his death generated interest in Greek freedom in Europe and America. The poet laureate did not view that development with enthusiasm.

As far as I am aware, this is the only place in his published correspondence that Southey mentions the Greek War of Independence (he mentions Byron only two other times). Southey's conservatism regarded Greek independence as a threat to the established order of Europe after Waterloo. Even more important, a Greek victory might weaken Turkey and encourage the Russians to attempt to expand southward, endangering British rule in India. "The Great Game," as it was called, between Russia and Britain had begun in earnest by the 1820s. Conservative poets, like conservative politicians, were more concerned about preserving the empire than striking at the heart of tyranny. But they did not take up their pens against the liberation of the Greeks. As the anonymous author of "Greece to the Close of 1825" wrote, "Nor shall we find any writer hardy enough to aver that if an active interest were taken upon the question, their principles would lead them the other way—to support the Turkish Government against the victims of misrule" (in Bulwer, *An Autumn in Greece* 320). If there were any poets so inclined, like Southey they chose silence.[33]

Greek freedom was and would continue to be a partisan issue in England.[34] The notion that all, or even most, classically educated British gentlemen had an innate sympathy for philhellenism is deeply mistaken. Along with a Whig interpretation of history there is a liberal view about the regeneration of Greece, which was passed down from Byron and Shelley. Just as the membership list of the London Greek Committee reads like a roll call of prominent English liberals and radicals of the day, so the list of authors who wrote in support of Greek freedom includes the foremost pens of what constituted the "literary Left"—Byron, Shelley, Thomas Moore, Leigh Hunt, Jefferson Hogg, Walter Savage Landor, Thomas Campbell, Samuel Rogers, and Jeremy Bentham. They were not a harmonious group; no literary Left has ever been. For instance, Byron had serious differences about politics with Leicester Stanhope and about literature with Landor, who in turn, corresponded amicably with Southey.[35] But the composition of a philhellenic work in the 1820s can be used, though not infallibly, to place an author on the map of literary politics in England. Further, since British policy toward Turkey and Greece was dominated by British colonial interests, the cause of Greece continued to be a form of protest against the English government. For example, in 1897, when Noel Brailsford and Allen Upward went off to fight for Greece in a war their own government was trying to prevent, they were in the same situation as the English philhellenes of 1824. Upward later summed up the position of philhellenism in England: "If Britain gives birth to Byrons, she also gives birth to Elgins; and the Byrons are usually in exile, while the Elgins are in office" (*East End of Europe* 21).

English philhellenism was further complicated by the financial machinations of the leaders of the London Greek Committee. In the middle of the 1820s, the committee raised money on the London Stock Exchange with extremely favorable rates for investors (a promised 59 percent down for 100 percent return). The bonds were backed, on the authority of the London Greek Committee, by "the national property of Greece," a promise that would cause problems for decades to come. As the value of the bonds rose, some of the committee saw an opportunity to profit from their philhellenism. The deputies of the Greek government serving in London joined in. When the stock fell drastically, the speculators tried all sorts of maneuvers to save themselves from ruin.[36] The disgraceful scandal was made public, and the philhellenes of the Greek committee were ridiculed by their fellow liberals as well as by the other side. Although Byron had certainly used satirical elements in his writing about Greece, especially in *Don Juan* and *The Age of Bronze*, this episode marked the real beginning of satire in literary philhellenism, which, it almost goes without saying, was never directed against

Greece but rather toward pseudophilhellenes.[37] In Thomas Moore's "The Ghost of Miltiades," the shade of the ancient hero visits one of the speculators, a follower of Jeremy Bentham:

> The Ghost of Miltiades came once more;—
> His brow, like the night, was lowering o'er,
> And he said, with a look that flash'd dismay,
> "Of Liberty's foes the worst are they,
> Who turn to a trade her cause divine,
> And gamble for gold on Freedom's shrine!"
> Thus saying the Ghost, as he took his flight,
> Gave a Parthian kick to the Benthamite,
> Which sent him, whimpering, off to Jerry—
> And vanish'd away to the Stygian ferry!
> (*Poetical Works* 621)

In the United States, on the other hand, Greek fever raged unabated, free of partisan entanglements and financial scandals. Raizis and Papas remarked that the "unreserved public enthusiasm in America for the Greek movement was quite independent of its purely historical significance and the actual conditions of Balkan politics at that time. The concern for the Greek war derived mainly from American interest in the classical tradition and in the hope for the realization of the dream common among romantics and humanists: the restoration of Greece to her old glory and the return of arts and sciences to the land of the Hellenes" (*American Poets* 9). This restoration was, not surprisingly, to take the form of an American-style republic. Noah's *Grecian Captive* ends with a procession of banners with the names of ancient Greeks mixed with those of "Washington, Kosciusco, Bolivar, and La Fayette": "The queen of the Arts has broken the bonds of tyranny and slavery—and a glorious day succeeds to a long night of peril and calamity—Now to meet freedom by the establishment of just laws—a free and upright government—a liberal, tolerant, and benevolent spirit to all" (48).

The American and Greek revolutions were regarded as kindred events; indeed the Greek rebellion was sometimes seen as a validation and extension of the American experiment as well as a return of the classical past.[38] This view is particularly evident in William Cullen Bryant's "Conjunction of Jupiter and Venus," which moves from the peace and promise brought by the achievement of American liberty to the sad state of Greece after the struggle for freedom. The poet tells Greece: "In yonder mingling lights [from America] / There is an omen of good days for thee" (*Poetical Works* I.183). The central concern of the piece is not the historical significance of Greece nor the actual condition of Balkan politics but rather the historical significance of early nineteenth-century America—especially its example and role on the international level. "The universal public enthusiasm" for the Greek Revolution in America stemmed in large part from the fact that the Greek Revolution was perceived as a validation of the American Revolution and the creation of the American republic. This attitude persisted throughout the nineteenth century. In 1880, for example, Joseph Moore simply told his American compatriots that the Greek War of Independence "progressed in a manner similar to our own Revolutionary struggle" (243).

This may explain why there were no deep divisions about liberty in Greece as there were about the domestic issue of abolition. Many Americans, both southerners and northerners, could embrace the Greeks. Indeed, this enthusiasm over the liberation of Greeks in bondage might well have been a means of deflecting the question of slavery at home.[39]

One of the sad ironies of history is that the end of the Greek War of Independence did not create an independent Greece. England, France, and Russia collectively chose a foreign ruler for Greece, Otho of Bavaria, who arrived on February 6, 1833. According to Finlay, the change in the Greek constitution in 1843, by which Greece became a constitutional monarchy, "put an end to alien rulers, under which the Greeks had lived for two thousand years" (7:178). Other historians might choose as the date of real Greek independence the year 1863, when Otho was forced to abdicate in favor of George of Denmark. Still others might prefer 1974, when, at the end of the military junta that had ruled the country since 1967, the restored democracy under Constantine Karamanlis abolished the monarchy.

Still, after 1833, most Europeans and Americans would agree with Felicia Skene's comment in *The Isles of Greece* (1843) that "Time-honor'd Greece at length is free!" (32). Like Charles Brinsley Sheridan in the introduction to *The Songs of the Greeks* and Alexander Baillie Cochrane in *The Morea* (126–37), many philhellenes argued against the imposition of a foreign monarchy, and after independence a few visitors, such as the American Nathaniel Parker Willis, still objected that Greece had "received a king from a family of despots" (II.20).[40] Yet Byron himself had said something needed to be done *to* the Greeks, and even he might not have opposed the imposition of a ruler from abroad. Henry Bulwer, sent to Greece in 1824 by the London Greek Committee to help administer the Greek loan after Byron's death, stated, "I would wish to see [Greece] free, but free according to her means of being so" (8). Further, the Greeks had escaped from the Ottoman yoke and had rejoined, or were in the process of rejoining, the West. A ruler from Bavaria was, in that sense, just one of the family.

The domestic politics of Greece had almost no place in nineteenth-century literary philhellenism.[41] Few supporters of Greece in the 1820s knew the form of the "official" government, just as few in the 1830s paid attention to the official relations between king and assembly. Philhellenism was a movement founded to save Greece from the Turks, to spread liberty to other places, and to start a new cultural renaissance in the West. Many knowledgeable people realized that it would take the Greeks some time to become a political or cultural force; in many reckonings at least one generation would need to pass.[42] Still, for most Europeans and Americans, the formation of the kingdom of Greece was not the event that would give birth to the miracle generation. Instead, philhellenic feeling after the War of Independence was frozen as if its clock had stopped in the destruction of Missolonghi.

The reason lies in the most prescient and neglected work about Greece and its struggle written during the War of Independence, Mary Shelley's *Last Man* (1826). The novel is a roman à clef about the lives and deaths of Shelley and Byron and is best known for its fictional characterization of the two poets. It is set in the future, around the year 2100, but it is not a futuristic or science fiction work. We first meet Lord Raymond, the character based on Lord Byron, after he has just returned from a war between the Greeks and the Turks in which he "became the darling hero of a rising people" (40). Greek independence had been achieved by the time the novel starts, but Shelley never precisely tells us when in the period between 1821 and 2073 it happened.

Later in the book, after Raymond decides to abandon English politics, he asks Adrian (P. B. Shelley) to accompany him to Athens: "You will behold new scenes; see a new people; witness the mighty struggle there going forward between civilization and barbarism; behold, and perhaps direct the efforts of a young and vigorous population, for liberty and order" (153). When they arrive, "a truce was in existence between the Greeks and the Turks; a truce that was like a sleep to the mortal frame, signal of renewed activity on waking" (160–61). The Turks soon attack the Greeks, who had expanded in recent years to take Macedonia and Thrace, "even to the gates of Constantinople" (161). Both Raymond and Adrian join the Greek army.

A year later, Adrian returns to England wounded and disillusioned. He asserts, "I shall not be suspected of being averse to the Greek cause; I know and feel its necessity; it is beyond every other good cause." Yet he objects to the inflated rhetoric that he hears: "But let us not deceive ourselves. The Turks are men; each fibre, each limb is as feeling as our own, and every spasm, be it mental or bodily, is as truly felt in a Turk's heart and being, as in a Greek's" (161). Adrian is wounded when he tries to save a Turkish girl from death as the Greek forces slaughter every Turk in a captured town: "One of the fellows, enraged at my interference, struck me with his bayonet in the side, and I fell senseless" (162). Adrian, while not condemning Raymond's enthusiasm for the Greeks, points out the difference between them: "All this has a different effect on Raymond. He is able to contemplate the ideal of war, while I am sensible only to its realities. . . . I do not sympathize in their dreams of massacre and glory" (162). The passage certainly paints a noble picture of Percy Shelley, one that builds from and points out the problems of the philhellenism of both *The Revolt of Islam* and *Hellas*. Greeks had to be powerless victims to gain P. B. Shelley's sympathy and neither he nor his alter ego, Adrian, knew what to do with Greeks who must compromise fine ideals in a real world.

Raymond, in the meantime, leads the Greeks to a great victory on the river Hebrus in Thrace, but he is captured. The narrator helps effect the ransom and release of Raymond, who stays in Greece to witness the recapture of Constantinople, the finale in "the long drawn history of Greek and Turkish warfare" (175). But when the Greek army arrives in front of the Golden City, they find it eerily undefended. A plague has hit, and all the inhabitants have perished. Only Raymond enters to "plant the Grecian standard on the height of St. Sophia" (194). He catches the plague and dies. The narrator eulogizes him in words echoing the elegies for the real Byron: "Now his death has crowned his life, and to the end of time it will be remembered, that he devoted himself, a willing victim, to the glory of Greece" (204). Constantinople, however, never becomes Greek. The Greek army had fled from the city in fear of the disease, but it quickly spreads and kills them all. Eventually, the narrator of the novel is the last man on earth.

The significance of Constantinople in *The Revolt of Islam* was certainly a key factor in the prime importance of the city in *The Last Man*. Still, Mary Shelley is unique in so clearly assessing the dimensions, goals, and lengths of the Greek struggle. By her account, philhellenism still has another hundred years or so to go, and a future generation of Byrons and Shelleys will still be talking about the need to defeat barbarism and looking forward to the regeneration of the Greeks into a vigorous and free people. Although Shelley reprises nearly all of early philhellenism's central tenets—the magnificence of the Greek climate, the struggle between freedom and tyranny, and the battle between Western civilization and the despotic East—the fact that they do not change in her projected future inevitably tarnishes and deconstructs their value. Just as *The Last Man* critiques Romanticism in general,[43] it also presents, in the midst of the War of Independence and just after the death of Byron, the first anti-Romantic view of philhellenism. Even more strikingly, it predicts the history of Greece and its cause in the West with uncanny accuracy. Unfortunately, *The Last Man* had no literary influence. It received bad reviews when it first appeared and has remained relatively unknown ever since.

The Last Man forcefully impresses upon the reader that the fight for Greek freedom will not really end until Constantinople is taken. If the kingdom of Greece and the Ottoman Empire were not officially at war after 1831, it was, as Mary Shelley put it, simply one of the truces that are like a brief and restful sleep. The overall situation would still be presented, by both Greeks and their supporters, in the same framework and language used since

1770, except that the oppressed Greek was often specified as a Cretan, an Epirot, or a Macedonian. So, for example, William Cullen Bryant ended his poem "Massacre at Scio" by reminding readers that Scio (Chios) and other Greek regions have not been redeemed and that the struggle for Greek freedom is not over: "Stern rites and sad, shall Greece ordain / To keep that day, along her shore, / Till the last link of slavery's chain / Is shivered, to be worn no more" (I.73).

II

THE MAGIC FORCE OF LEGEND
(1833–1913)

4

Dangerous Ground

In Edith Wharton's story "Roman Fever," a character says: "I was just thinking what different things Rome stands for to each generation of travellers. To
our grandmothers, Roman fever; to our mothers, sentimental dangers—how
we used to be guarded!—to our daughters, no more danger than the middle
of Main Street" (*Collected Short Stories* 2.837). In this piece, Wharton is as
concerned with the changes in the Rome of literature as much as the real city,
for she engages and reappraises the portrayal of the place as it appears in
such works as Hawthorne's *Marble Faun* and James's *Daisy Miller*. Ancient
Greece also carried a varied significance for the different generations in the
nineteenth century, from Winckelmann's Apollonian ideal to Nietzsche's
Dionysian ecstasy to the archaeological focus on the objects of daily life. As
with interpretations of Rome, these changes can be charted in notable works
of literature.[1]

In comparison, it is hard to perceive if modern Greece meant different
things to each generation from 1833 to 1913 and harder still to use imaginative writing to map the development. A student of literature in English probably cannot recall a single prominent literary work of the later nineteenth
century that engages and revises the Grèce de Byron in the way that Wharton interacts with James's Rome. Admittedly, more artists and writers visited
Rome than Athens during the Victorian era. Further, interest in Greece was
bound to decline after the surge of attention during the War of Independence, when the events in the country were often front-page news abroad.
But these factors alone cannot explain the lack of literature about modern
Greece, since the opportunity to reinterpret the Greece of Byron would
seem as attractive a subject to an author as a reappraisal of the Rome of
James. Near the beginning of E. F. Benson's *Limitations*, an aspiring sculptor
drawn to Apollonian idealism explained his decision to travel to Athens: "I
don't want to be influenced by any modern art, and if you go to Rome you
must fall in with some modern school or other; there are too many artists at
Rome" (27). There also had been too many novels about artists in Rome for

decades, but it was not until 1896 that Benson's novel about the foreign artist colony in Athens appeared.[2]

The relative neglect of modern Greece by English writers in the century after Byron was observed by Rennell Rodd, the editor of *The Englishman in Greece: Being the Collection of the Verse of Many English Poets* (1910), a volume that appeared just one year after the centenary of Byron's first visit to Greece in 1809. In the introduction to that book, Rodd lamented that the "literary record of the *Englishman in Greece* offers less copious material from which to select than that of the *Englishman in Italy*, to which cherished land, throughout the century but recently closed, our most illustrious singers have dedicated so much of their affection and genius. . . . And now that the highways and waterways [of Greece] are open, that communications easy and secure have unveiled the hidden charms of that storied land, it would almost seem as though the fountains of inspiration had run dry, [even though] no land should appeal more directly to the poet" (5).

The contents of Rodd's collection *The Englishman in Greece* indicate that his title must be read far less literally than that of its companion volume, *The Englishman in Italy*. For where the latter contains mostly English writings that were inspired by trips in Italy, over half of the book about Greece is devoted to works that "reflect the classic spirit" rather than "reveal the living character" of the country (5), which explains the presence of numerous authors who had never set foot in Greece nor expressed the least interest in the modern Greeks, such as William Wordsworth, John Keats, Robert Browning, Alfred Tennyson, and Matthew Arnold. James Elroy Flecker wrote in "Oak and Olive":

> Though I was born a Londoner
>   And bred in Gloucestershire,
> I walked in Hellas years ago
>   With friends in white attire;
> And I remember how my soul
>   Drank wine as pure as fire.
>   (*Collected Poems* 176)

These lines, as the rest of the poem makes clear, look back to the days before Flecker ever visited Athens. Like Flecker, Rodd assumed that one could walk in "Hellas" while in Gloucestershire or other northern parts. In order to walk in Italy, on the other hand, it seems one actually had to go there.

Rodd ended his brief introduction with the forthright statement "From English writers the living Greece has not yet had her due of song" (8). Rodd did not explicitly state that the deficiency exists in both quantity and quality, but that is evident from the poems selected about "living Greece" that were not composed by Byron. Rodd himself offered an explanation for and an example of the pedestrian character of nineteenth-century writing about Greece in his poem "Misolonghi," first published in 1889 and reprinted in 1913. Rodd spoke of traveling through Greece with a copy of Byron to guide him ("Oft with thee since, my poet, where the steep / Of Sunium sees the red evening dye the deep" [Violet Crown 10]), and concluded: "Thou art grown one with these things, and thy fame / Links a new memory to each sacred name" (11). Rodd's volume *The Violet Crown* (1913) stands as a case study for what was wrong with English and American writing about living Greece from 1833 until the Great War. The author was awed and overwhelmed by Byron as shown by the eulogistic "Misolonghi"; the Byronic lament about past glory in ruins in "An Attic Night" and "Delos"; the Byronic echoes of heroic struggles for freedom in poems like "Thermopylae" and "Zalongos: The Flight of the Suliots"; and, of course, the celebration of the quintessential Greek heroes in "The Song of the Klepht." A translation "from the Romaic," a word that by 1889 had a faintly archaic air, is thrown in for good measure. There is not a new perspective in the book.[3]

In *The Marble Faun*, Nathaniel Hawthorne wryly remarked on the mid–nineteenth-century tourists to Rome who made the mandatory visit to the Colosseum at midnight "exalting themselves with raptures that were Byron's, not their own" (*Novels* 981–82). The desire to experience Byron's raptures appears even stronger in the majority of visitors to Greece in the decades after the War of Independence. Instead of searching for new springs of inspiration, the goal was to situate oneself, as Rodd did, within the "haunted, holy ground" constructed by the martyr of Missolonghi.

Byron's poetry became a mantra for entry into the "experience" of Greece with sites where, as late as 1947, Dora Una Ratcliffe claimed that "the temptation to quote tries one sorely" (13). In the same year, standing at Marathon, Osbert Lancaster observed, "'The Mountains look on Marathon, and Marathon looks on the sea': when one has said that one has said everything" (88). The response of Valentine Mott, a Philadelphia physician, could stand as a paradigm for the usual nineteenth-century American or English encounter with Greece. He recounted an excursion he took one afternoon to Plato's Grove and Mars's Hill: "We felt almost as though we were inspired under the world of glorious recollections that pressed upon the memory, as we gazed around us, upon every hallowed temple, rock, and mountain, that spoke to us in mute and sublime eloquence of the past. And could not help but repeat, as we rode along, those magnificent lines of the noble poet, which vividly embodied our exalted feelings" (172). He then quoted not from Homer or Sophocles but from *The Corsair*. The Grèce de Byron had become the medium between the past and the modern traveler.

In 1906, Sir Sidney Colvin remembered his first visit to Athens in lines that call to mind the Greeces of Homer and Byron delineated by Hugo: "You watch and watch, with snatches of Greek and snatches of English poetry ringing in your brain" (227).[4] Byron also was used as the medium for the experience of Greek sites in a number of paintings. For example, Edward Lear's *Marathon* (1848), which Peter Levi called "one of his most Byronic paintings" (113), has a group of figures looking from the mountains onto Marathon, which in turn looks out on the sea, as if the work is as much a gloss on the famous lines from "The Isles of Greece" as a depiction of the landscape of Attica.[5]

Alfred Austin, later poet laureate of Britain, visited Athens in 1881 but wrote no verse honoring the occasion. "The laughter of the gods," he remarked, "would attend the man who attempted to adorn still further what Byron touched on" (*Autobiography* II.143). But British travelers with literary pretensions did provoke the laughter of both gods and men by composing their own Byronic meditations on Greek soil. One such effort was Aubrey de Vere's "Grecian Ode," which ends with a line that recalls and revises Byron's *Age of Bronze* (*CPW* VI, p. 271): "Yes, yes—tis Hellas, Hellas still." No volume of verse entitled *The American in Greece* appeared in 1910, but the results would have been equally meager and disheartening.[6]

No one author dominated writing about Italy or France the way that Byron dominated writing about modern Greece. How static the general perception of the land remained from the War of Independence through the first decade of the twentieth century is indicated by Bohun Lynch's comment about "tourist pilgrims with their traveling editions of Homer and Byron" in his novel of 1912, *Glamour: A Tale of Modern Greece* (28). Unwittingly, Lynch reproduced precisely Hugo's "Grèces de Byron et d'Homère," with exactly the same division between authors and chronological Greeces. Not much had changed since 1827.

The continued prominence of the Grèce de Byron colored modern Greece throughout the nineteenth century with a particular political significance. For all of the recitations of "The Isles of Greece" and evocations or imitations of Byronic verse in poetry and painting recalled not just the Greece of landscape and ruins but also the philhellenic sentiment of the period of the Greek Revolution. About the philhellene from the War of Independence to 1909, R. M. Burrows said in 1916: "His state of mind was that of Byron in his early days, when he wrote the Isles of Greece and dreamed that Greece might still be free" ("Philhellenism in England and France" 162). De Vere's "Grecian Ode" (1850), Felicia Skene's "The Isles of Greece" (1843), and Lear's *Marathon* (1848) were all, by their choice of a Byronic model, politically charged works.

At the end of the Greco-Turkish War of 1897, "Diplomaticus," the author of an article entitled "The Case against Greece" in the *Fortnightly Review*, complained that British public opinion about the Greeks was based upon a sentimental tradition rather than the contemporary facts: "The man in the street has no time . . . and perhaps no opportunity to puzzle out the subtle why and wherefore of the shifting phases of international politics. In this country, and in a less degree France, Italy, and Germany, he is fundamentally Philhellene. The Greek Cause is one of the abiding convictions of his political consciousness. It is founded in memories which, although little more than half a century old, have all the magic force of legend" (772). In the same year, G. W. Steevens protested that the "Greek is what he was—a dishonest, intelligent, chicken-hearted talker, whom nothing will apparently deprive of Britain's sympathy as long as he quotes Byron and lives in the land of Alcibiades" ("What Happened in Thessaly" 160). The idea that the British had been and still were more fundamentally philhellenic than other Europeans was itself part of the legend.

Whether the philhellenic spirit was embraced by the general population or even the majority of writers in nineteenth-century England or America is a matter open to debate. What is demonstrably true is that the novelists and poets who composed works about modern Greece were, almost without exception, supporters of the cause of Greece. Commenting on the cartoons that appeared during the time of the Cretan uprising in 1866, Grand-Carteret observed: "If the official, political and parliamentary world currents were created founded on opinions more favorable to the *status quo* than to the development of Philhellenism, the pencil, disturbing itself little about the Ottoman empire, has seen only the Greeks and their audacious attempt" (Bickford-Smith, *Cretan Sketches* 233). H. D. Traill exclaimed in his 1897 satire "Our Learned Philhellenes": "Oh, the poets! . . . They are now, as they have always been, full of a noble zeal for Hellas and the Hellenes" (506). Philhellenism certainly appeared to be an abiding part of the English and American political consciousness, since it was present in almost every literary effort about modern Greece.

One result of this partisanship, ironically, was that the portrayal of modern Greece lacked depth and development.[7] Although, as Diplomaticus noted, modern Greece was little more than a half century old in 1897, it was already something of a museum piece in the imagination of the West. Terence Spencer concluded his study of literary philhellenism in England up to the time of Byron with a thought about how the changed circumstances after the War of Independence would inaugurate a new view of Greece and the Greeks: "The English poet and traveler since Byron's day had quite other things upon which to meditate" (297). Yet most British and American travelers turned away from those "other things" to reproduce the aura and spirit of the Greek Revolution.

John Pierpont's "A Birthday in Scio," the product of a journey in 1836, remembered the massacre of 1822 with a "tale to freeze a Western freeman's blood" (96). Pliny Earle's "Marathon," written in honor of a visit to the site in 1838, ended with the reawakening of Greece: "She wakens! shout, ye sons of men! / Joy, joy for Greece! she lives again!" (18). To ask what Earle meant by that closing couplet in 1838 would be pointless, for he clearly was thinking in terms of 1821. And Earle was certainly not the last poet to employ the theme of the rebirth of Greece. After the discovery of three female statues on the Acropolis in 1886, Andrew Lang, who thought they represented the daughters of a legendary Athenian king, composed a poem entitled "The Daughters of Cecrops." At the end of the poem, the female statues become a symbol of what modern Greece might become:

> As new arisen they [the statues] stand to-day,
>   Fresh from the hand of Canochus,
> The re-arisen Hellas may
>   Defy the lapse of ages thus;
> In time's despite serenely fair,
>   A marvel in Athenian air!
>
> The laurel of the god of old
>   Was proof against the thunderstroke.
> On laurel'd Hellas Persia rolled
>   In thunder, and in spray she broke;
> Even so this present tyranny
>   Must break, and leave serener sky!
>
> (III.195)

The phrase "this present tyranny" probably referred to the situation on Crete, the site of another rebellion in 1886. But, although no clear allusion to contemporary events on Crete is made, the phrase would not puzzle the English or American reader. In philhellenic poetry, modern Greece was in a permanent state of "arising" or "awaking" throughout the nineteenth century. Greece remained fixed in the English and American imagination in the exact same position that Byron had depicted it some seventy-five years earlier.

The aura of legend that enveloped modern Greece helps to explain the discrepancy between the prevalence of Italy as a site for novels about artists and tourists and the lack of such works set in Greece. During a visit to Athens in 1846, William Makepeace Thackeray was appalled to find that Murray's *Handbook for Travellers in Greece* referred to Byron, not Shakespeare, as "our native bard." Thackeray commenced to criticize Byron but pulled up short: "That man never wrote from the heart. He got up rapture and enthusiasm with an eye for the public; but this is dangerous ground, even more dangerous than to look Athens full in the face, and say your eyes are not dazzled by beauty. The Great Public admires Greece and Byron; the public knows best" (321). Nineteenth-century English authors did not shy away from unfavorable critiques of Byron's literary merit.[8] But, like Thackeray, they avoided the dangerous ground of Greece and Byron taken together. The few who traversed it stayed, for the most part, carefully within the established parameters. It was not the public alone who dictated the course of writing about Greece; Thackeray simply used it as an excuse. A passage from Byron's *Marino Faliero*, which like so many of his lines stands as an eerie epitaph for his end, sheds some light on the hesitancy of other writers to reinterpret Byron's Greece:

> They never fail who die
> In a great cause. . . .
> 　　　Though years
> Elapse, and others share as dark a doom,
> They but augment the deep and sweeping thoughts
> Which o'erpower all others, and conduct
> The World at last to freedom.
>
> 　　　　　　　　　　(*CPW* IV, pp. 356–57)

Not surprisingly, none of the poets and prose writers, however much they might have disparaged Byron's verse, really wanted to be measured against the magic force of legend in which art and action were so blurred.

The paucity of nineteenth-century narrative literature about modern Greece in English is the clearest signal of the general attitude of avoidance. Only a handful of works appeared from 1833 to the Cretan revolt of 1866–1869, including Mary Shelley's short story "Euphrasia" (1839); David Morier's novel *Photo the Suliote* (1857); several narrative poems like C. J. Collins's *Albanian: A Tale of Modern Greece* (1844), Stevenson MacGill's *Nacnud: A Tale of Asia Minor* (1840, about the massacre on Scio), Lucy E. Partridge's *Costanza of Mistra: A Tale of Modern Greece in Four Cantos* (1839), and W. M. Henry's *Corsair's Bride, Scio, and Other Poems* (1840); Willam H. Dixon's play *Azamoglan: An Incident in the Greek Revolution* (1845); and three American dramas about the death of Marco Bozzaris: Nathaniel Deering's *Marco Bozzaris* (1851), O. B. Bunce's *Bozzaris* (1850), and Julius Augustus Requier's *Marco Bozzaris* (1860).[9] None of these works could consider the changes in Greece after 1833, since the central action of each occurs during the Greek struggle for liberty in the decades before independence. Nor do they reexamine the issues of that period in a new way; indeed, each reads as if it had been composed in the 1820s. Most of them rehearse the familiar theme of a young Greek woman who must be rescued from a Turkish harem.[10]

For example, in Mary Shelley's "Euphrasia": "The tale of horror was soon told. Athens was still in the hands of the Turks; the sister of the rebel had become the prey of the oppressor. . . . Her matchless beauty had been seen and marked by the Pasha; she had for two months inhabited his harem"

(303). As in Byron's *Siege of Corinth*, the heroine's personification as the nation of Greece is signaled by her juxtaposition with an ancient temple. Euphrasia's brother tells the narrator that, during the rescue, his sister was shot: "I knew not she was dying; till at last entering a retired valley, where an olive wood afforded shelter, and still better the portico of a fallen ancient temple, I dismounted and bore her to the marble steps, on which I placed her. . . . The lightning showed me her face; pale as the marble which pillowed it. Her dress was dabbled in blood, which soon stained the stones on which she lay" (306).

In Deering's *Marco Bozzaris* the heroine, Bozzaris's sister Eudora—an invention of the author (in Requier's play, the heroine is Bozzaris's imagined daughter)—first appears against "a temple in ruins." Bozzaris himself Byronically muses on the past and present as he seeks his daughter after a successful return from a night raid on the Turkish camp at Carpenisi:

> Surely the traveller, while passing near,
> Must pause and ponder: for it will remind him
> Of Hellas as she was, and—I must speak it!
> Ah, alas, as she is—degraded and in bondage.
> (25)[11]

The heroes in these works are klephts, yet analogies abound between these fierce mountain warriors and their cultured ancient forebears. For example, in *Photo the Suliote*, Morier provided the following description of a band of klephts: "No Homeric heroes ever sat down with keener appetites to their banquet than the redeemed Suliotes; and in imitation of those ancient worthies, it was not until they were fully gorged that they recounted in detail to their friends all that had befallen them" (I.166–67).

The brigands are "these Hellenic Robin Hoods," described as those whose

> divine forms have been transmitted to us in those exquisite sculptures
> —monuments of imperishable glory of the Grecian art—which still
> breathe and move along the stones of the Panathenaic procession of
> the Parthenon. Such were they, too, who strove for the chaplet of pars-
> ley or laurel—the corruptible crown which rewarded the victory in the
> gymnastic struggle of the Olympic games, in the presence of the as-
> sembled nation. These, indeed, appeared in a costume less encum-
> bered by drapery, yet not more picturesquely heroic than the Greek
> Palikari with his short white kilt of many plaits, his embroidered velvet
> vest, his silver greaves, scarlet leggings, and light sandals. (III.132–33)

Morier's klephts may have the soul and form of the ancient Greeks, but they are dressed like Byron's Giaour. These paragons are not above cutting off the ear of a hostage to send as a message to Ali Pasha, an act that the narrator of the tale declines to condemn.

One nineteenth-century book about Greece in English stands out both as a success when it was published in 1851 and as a minor classic of travel writing, Edward Lear's *Journal of a Landscape Painter in Albania and Illyria*. It is an odd fact that this popular and enduring travelogue of Greece does not describe any of the great classical sites or regions but restricts the narrative to the area north of the kingdom of Greece still in Turkish hands at the time of Lear's journey.[12] Lear certainly knew and enjoyed what Richard Monckton Milnes called "Greece proper." In a letter to his sister after three weeks in the Peloponnesus, he wrote: "The beauty of this part of Greece can hardly be imagined" (*Selected Letters* 107). In *Journal of a Landscape Painter*, he remarked, "The further you wander north of Epirus, the less you find that grace and detail which is so attractive in southern Greece, and most especially in Athens and Peloponnesus" (6). Peter Levi, Lear's most recent biographer, says that all of Lear's "wonderful achievements" were made possible by this journey through southern Greece (122). But Lear never published nor prepared for publication a travel journal of the area and, while his trip through the south of Greece may have been crucial for his art, his reputation as a travel writer rests on descriptions of regions with less "grace and detail."[13] It is tempting to see Lear's decision not to include "free" Greece in his travel journal as, at least in part, a desire to avoid the dangerous ground of Greece and Byron. But whether intentional or not, the status of Lear's *Journal of a Landscape Painter* as the preeminent work about "Greece" in English in the middle of the nineteenth century illustrates the lack of any real engagement with or reappraisal of the Grèce de Byron in literature.

The scant production of literature about modern Greece did not mean that there was a dearth of texts about the land in circulation at midcentury. Byron's Tales, as well as the poems about the Greek Revolution by such authors as Hemans, Campbell, Halleck, and Bryant, continued to be anthologized and reprinted through the 1850s and beyond.[14] A youth in 1855, like Swinburne, would encounter Greece with precisely the same books as a young man in 1824. This explains why, unlike Rome, the kingdom of the Hellenes did not acquire a new significance for each generation.

Even the first important conflict between Greeks and Turks since the War of Independence inspired few pens and fewer new thoughts. In May 1866, the Cretans, who had chafed for years under a cruel and inept administration, began a rebellion whose ultimate aim was union with Greece. In November of that year, the Turkish commander, Mustafa Kyrtli Pasha, attacked the Arkadi monastery, which was situated near the northern coast of the island between the towns of Heraklio and Rethymno. An army officer from Greece, Panos Koroneos, had used the monastery as his headquarters, but he withdrew most of his men and equipment before the Turkish advance. Left inside were perhaps 150 armed insurgents, a large part of the religious community, and 400 women and children, who had sought shelter within the church. After the Turks had breached the walls, a priest, in the words of the American consul in Crete at the time, "changed what was before but profitless slaughter into a deed of heroism" by setting fire to the powder magazine (Stillman, *American Consul in a Cretan War* 67). Dakin estimates that 400 Greeks and 450 Turks died in the explosion (*Unification of Greece* 111). With help from Greece, the rebellion continued until 1869, when Turkey threatened to declare war on the Greek state. Ottoman authority was restored on the island with the approval of the Western powers.

The revolt of Crete and the destruction of the Arkadi monastery generated interest in the Cretan struggle abroad. A few philhellenes, most with "no freedom to fight for at home," enlisted beside numerous Greek volunteers in the most recent Greek cause.[15] Another significant American relief effort, headed by the old philhellene Samuel Gridley Howe, was organized for the benefit of Cretan refugees.[16] Public response in America and England replicated the Greek War of Independence. Americans were uniformly supportive of Cretan aspirations; in fact, the American consul on Crete, William Stillman, was one of the most vocal supporters of the rebellion. British public opinion, still dominated by the Russophobia of the Crimean War, was less enthusiastic.[17] Just two years before the revolt, Charles Dickens had cautioned the Greeks on Crete that "they must keep quiet now," since no help would come from Europe (465). Philhellenism remained, as Edward Augustus Freeman noted, "one of the most prominent and distinctive signs of liberal sentiment," and it was the liberal Left, including Freeman, who spoke up for the Cretans. Still, in comparison to the Greek fever of the 1820s, the interest in Crete hardly constituted a mild temperature.

The focus was still on the reclamation of the ancient heritage. For example, in the *Nation* of January 17, 1867, Stillman asserted "These men [the Cretan rebels] are, in my mind, the legitimate successors of Leonidas and Epaminondas, Agesilaus and Themistocles, what wonder would it be if we found some of their vices as well as their virtues?" (*Articles and Despatches* 55–56). S. G. W. Benjamin said, "Crete under Turkish rule is like a prisoner chained to a dead man and struggling for release from the fearful union. Crete under Greek rule will spring to a new existence and develop new energies" (267).

"Crete," a poem by the American Edmund Clarence Stedman, memorialized the tragedy at Arkadi.[18] After two stanzas that recalled the contemporary event, Stedman unskillfully connected the revolt of 1866 to the Greek War of Independence by means of a pale paraphrase of a famous couplet from Byron ("For Freedom's battle once begun / Is handed down from sire to son"):

Though the Cretan eagle fell,
   And the ancient heights were won,
Freedom's light was guarded well,—
   Handed down from sire to son;
Through centuries of shame,
   Ah! it never wholly died,
But was hid, a sacred flame,
   There on topmost Ida's side.

(300)

The poem ends with a plea for the heroes of the ancient epics to appear in Crete and plant the flag of Greece: "Shades of heroes Homer sung—/ . . . Rise with shadowy swords among / Candia's smoking fields and towns." The last two stanzas present, literally and unchanged, the Grèces de Byron et d'Homère of the Greek Revolution.

The destruction of Arkadi also appears in "Ode on the Insurrection of Candia" by Algernon Charles Swinburne. Swinburne was the most famous literary philhellene of his generation, producing a poem on each occasion that the Greeks and Turks found themselves at odds in the second half of the nineteenth century: "Ode on the Insurrection of Candia" in 1867, "Athens: An Ode" in 1881, and "For Greece and Crete" in 1897. Still, it must be conceded that his poetic reputation did not rest upon any of these efforts.

Where Stedman's "Crete" invoked the philhellenic verse of Byron, "Ode on the Insurrection of Candia" resurrected the language, concepts, and even visual structure, with its strophes and antistrophes, of Shelley's *Hellas* and "Ode to Liberty."[19] The struggle in Crete has symbolic significance because, as Greece was the birthplace of freedom, it was part of "the most holy land." Throughout the poem, Swinburne spoke of a return of freedom to Greece (e.g., where freedom must "turn again the beauty of thy brows on Greece," (*Complete works* 2.269). At no time did Swinburne distinguish Crete from free Greece; he never acknowledged that the latter already existed. Rhetoric and reality clearly collide in the lines: "O kings and queens and nations miserable / . . . Ye have one hour, but these [those who died in the pursuit of freedom] the immortal years" (2.264). For Swinburne, as for Shelley, the return of Greek freedom will sound the death knell of monarchs and tyrants. The Cretan insurgents, on the other hand, were fighting to become subjects of the king of Greece.

In his biography of Swinburne, the poet's friend Edmund Gosse said of "Ode on the Insurrection of Candia," "It is a fine performance, learnedly constructed, but it is a little dull and in later years the poet disliked to hear it mentioned. He was conscious, I think, of a slight insincerity in the enthusiasm it expressed, for though he was very deeply concerned for Mentana and Custozza [events in the Italian Risorgimento], he did not really care whether the Cretans insurrected or not" (165). Gosse, in my view, simplified Swinburne's outlook. The poet probably cared little for the Cretans qua Cretans, indeed he almost never refers to them as Cretans. But, like Voltaire, he was interested in the regeneration of the Greeks because he wanted desperately to resuscitate Athens.

Gosse also said, "Swinburne was never tired of reciting, like a thrush singing Greek, and with gestures of ecstasy, the odes in praise of Athenian liberty which break up *The Persians* of Aeschylus. The state of Athens in the fourth [fifth?] century appeared to him [Swinburne] to approach his ideal republic more nearly than any other ancient or modern institution" (229). Swinburne himself wrote in his *Erectheus* one of the finest specimens of Victorian Hellenism:

> A wonder enthroned on hills and seas,
> A maiden crowned with a fourfold glory,
> That none from the pride of her head may rend;
> Violet and olive-leaf purple and hoary,
> Song-wreath and story the fairest of fame,
> Flowers that the winter can blast not or bend;
> A light upon the earth as the sun's own flame,
> > A name as his name,
> > Athens, a praise without end.
> > > (*Complete Works* 7.361)

In "Athens: An Ode," ostensibly written to bolster the Greeks for a confrontation with the Turks in 1881, which almost led to war before the European powers intervened, Swinburne urged "the sons of them that fought the Marathonian field" to return to a time when "Gods were yours yet strange to Turk and Galilean, / Light and Wisdom only then as gods adored: / Pallas was your shield, your comforter was Paean, / From your bright world's navel spoke the Sun your lord" (*Complete Works* 5.81). In a letter, Swinburne said of this poem, "I am writing an anti-Christian and anti-Russian ode on Athens. Watts says that the astute and practical Greeks will laugh at it and me—justly, he seems to think. Let them laugh, in (their) God's name—and so prove that modern Hellas is an annexe [*sic*] of the kingdom of Bulgaria" (*Swinburne Letters* 4:211).

Swinburne was in earnest. His support for the modern Greeks in 1867, 1881, and 1897 was based on the same hopes of Hölderlin and Shelley, the desire for a rebirth of the idealized world of the ancients with its political liberty, its perceived dedication to artistic beauty, and its pagan gods. The kingdom of Greece might have a monarch and practice Orthodox Christianity, but Swinburne was writing for "Greece," the world he depicted so eloquently in his *Erechtheus* and *Atalanta in Calydon*. For him, as for Shelley, that was the real Greece, and nothing that had occurred between the Aegean and Ionian seas in the nineteenth century affected his view of it.

Yet poetry did not need to be written about the Cretan revolt, since it could be borrowed just as easily and, perhaps, more effectively from the past. One of the earliest books published in support of the Cretans, Joseph Cartwright's *Insurrection in Candia and the Public Press* (1866), has an epigraph from Byron on the title page and another at the opening of the first chapter. The Greek Revolution had been misunderstood because of misleading allusions to the classical past and then had itself become a misleading allusion for modern Greek history for the rest of the nineteenth century.

The perception of Greece as geographically indeterminate remained prevalent at the middle of the nineteenth century, although the clear dichotomy of ancient/West and modern/East had begun to break down. Ancient Greece was still culturally and geographically firmly fixed in the West, and the Greek landscape was still perceived as a key to the Greek miracle and the founding of Western culture. In 1900, as in 1800, interest in the modern Greeks stemmed mostly from their perceived connection to the revered past. In 1882, Theodore Cuyler wrote of Greece, "No land on the Continent of Europe has a stronger claim on our hearts, or excites more thrilling hopes for the future, than the land in which Pericles builded [*sic*], and Plato thought, and Phidias carved, and Paul proclaimed the Gospel of eternal life" (170).

After independence, however, modern Greece was viewed as something of a gray area between East and West without being a full or credible member of either region. Monckton Milnes's poem about the Ionian island of Corfu, which appeared in 1834, addressed the place as follows: "Thou art a portal, whence the Orient, / The long-desired, long-dreamt-of Orient / Opens upon us, with its strange forms, Outlines immense and gleaming distances, / And all circumstance of faery land" (8). In 1889, George Gissing noted in a letter from Athens: "The Greeks always talk about 'going to Europe' & indeed this is not Europe but the East. It will be a very long time before Greece rids itself of its orientalism" (*Letters* 4.146). On the other hand, for those seeking the "true" Orient, Greece was already too Western. In 1849, Thackeray remarked on arriving at Smyrna that he was "glad that the Turkish part of Athens was extinct, so that I should not be baulked of the pleasure of entering an Eastern town by an introduction to any garbled or incomplete specimen of one" (325).[20] In his novel *The Bertrams*, Anthony Trollope lamented, "Alexandria is fast becoming a European city; but its Europeans are from Greece and the Levant! . . . Poor Arabs! Poor Turks! giving way on all sides to wretches so much viler than yourselves, what a destiny is before you" (466). Irby and Mackenzie's comment on Greek women in 1866 perhaps best sums up the contemporary attitudes: "The modern Greek woman falls short alike of the softness and fire of the Oriental and the refinement and loftiness of the Western lady" (10).

In 1867, when Mark Twain wondered that "the manly people that performed such miracles as the valor of Marathon are only a tribe of unconsidered slaves to-day" (280), most opinions of the modern Greeks were equally negative.[21] In fact, Twain could only have gotten his information second-hand since he only spent a single night in Greece, when he evaded quarantine to visit the Acropolis. Twain's language, which recalls the discourse about the modern Greeks before the War of Independence, suggests that circumstances were the cause for the low state of the Greeks. What tribe of slaves is not unconsidered, and would that not change if they were no longer slaves? More to the point, perhaps, is to ask "slaves of whom"? Twain was not entirely clear on this point; he suggested that part of the problem had been King Otho, who had abdicated four years earlier in 1863 and been replaced by a new monarch from Denmark, George I.[22] Yet the former king hardly seems the sole reason the Greek kingdom was filled with "confiscators and falsifiers of high repute" (Twain 278). Further, poor opinions of Otho were by no means universal; another American, Walter Colton, said that the Greeks "want a popular, vigorous, and intelligent government, equal laws and freedom from oppression. These they are now beginning to realize under the mild and enlightened policy of Otho" (270). In most minds, if the Greeks were still thought to be unconsidered slaves, both established rhetoric and history indicated that their oppressors continued to be the Turks.

The most famous American artistic effort with a modern Greek theme around the middle of the nineteenth century was titled simply *The Greek Slave*. Hiram Powers's statue, one of the most popular works shown at the Great Exhibition in London in 1851, "represented a Greek girl, naked, her wrists chained, implying that she was destined for a Turkish harem" (Tsigakou 77). The piece is remarkable for its execution not for its innovative conception. The ideology of the statue hardly differs from Choiseul-Gouffier's 1782 frontispiece; even the use of nudity just expanded upon the bared breasts of the Greek female in Delacroix's *Greece Expiring on the Ruins of Missolonghi*. The enormous interest in *The Greek Slave* would in turn strengthen the traditional perception of a feminized Greece made captive by the Turks.

Tsigakou caustically notes that Elizabeth Barrett Browning's sonnet about Powers's statue praises the "passionless perfection" of the work rather than the manifest "erotic implications. Hellenic nudity was capable of purifying any naked figure in the eyes of the prudish Victorians" (77). Browning's response was not, however, simply an instance of Victorian prudery. She saw the work through the established philhellenic lenses of Winckelmann's "grandeur and simplicity" coupled with the aspirations of freedom founded upon ideas about ancient Athens:

They say ideal beauty cannot enter
The house of anguish. On the threshold stands
An alien Image with enshackled hands,
Called the Greek Slave! as if the artist meant her . . .
To confront man's crimes in different lands
With man's ideal sense. Pierce to the centre
Art's fiery finger, and break up ere long
The serfdom of this world. Appeal, fair stone,
From God's pure heights of beauty against man's wrong!

(293)

For Browning, the Greek slave, precisely because she is a Greek, could still symbolize the end of serfdom of this world. When the poet looked at *The Greek Slave*, she did so with the Greek cause as, to use the words of Diplomaticus, an abiding conviction of her political consciousness, one that was preserved and passed down by the liberal Left.

Throughout the nineteenth century the image of the Greek slave endured, in part because of cultural preconceptions and in part because there still were Greeks who were in need of liberation.[23] Monckton Milnes divided his *Memorials* into two parts, "Greece Proper" and "In Turkish Greece," the latter an oxymoronic title that signified the continuing oppression of the region. Charles Dilke, a prominent Liberal politician, asked in Parliament in 1878: "What kind of Greece is a Greece which does not include Lemnos, Lesbos, or Mytilene, Chio, Mount Olympus, Mount Ossa and Mount Athos? Not only the larger part, but the most Greek part of Greece was omitted from the Hellenic Kingdom. Crete, and the islands, and the coast of Thrace, and the Greek colony of Constantinople, are the Greek Greece" (32).

Despite the fact that the modern Greeks had shown little sign of fulfilling the fervent philhellenic hopes for a regeneration of the ancients, Dilke saw the Greeks and the Turks within the ideological framework of the early nineteenth century. He asserted, "I believe in Greece—believe in the ultimate replacement of the Turkish State by powerful and progressive Greece," which would be "an outpost of Western Europe in the East" (32–33). Elsewhere he said that Greece would be "a force of the future instead of a force for the past; a force of trade, rather than a force of war; European instead of Asiatic, intensely independent, democratic, maritime!" (*Eastern Question* 50). In *New Greece* (1878), Lewis Sergeant declared, "The cause of peace and good government in Europe appears to require the establishment of Greece as a Great Power in the Aegean. The interests of Greece and Europe—and particularly Greece and England—are involved together in the accomplishment of this idea" (iv). W. E. Baxter wrote in 1879: "All of the lost deeds of ancient time will again be rivalled by the Greeks of a future age!" (14). Dilke, Baxter, and Sergeant saw the Greeks as a potential bastion of European progressive liberalism not because of the track record of the kingdom of Greece, but rather because as *Greeks* they already occupied that place in a grand ideological scheme.

In 1834, Monckton Milnes had cautioned those who thought that Greece, "having at last attained the means of free action," would quickly develop "anew in all its pristine energy. . . . Until then this generation be extinct, and carry along with it its wild instincts and savage virtues; the atmosphere in which Grecian politics are to work must be turbulent and dark" (151, 154). The future of the country, he predicted, rested with the bright youths whom the revolution had "detacht [*sic*] . . . from Oriental modes and feelings" and who were now "eager to attach themselves to European thoughts and habits" (154). Where the ancient Greeks were the originators of Western culture, the modern Greeks are only "the pensioners of the culture which the rest of Europe has learnt by labor and the fruition of the ages; they [the modern Greeks] have to think with others' thoughts, almost to feel with others' feelings" (155). But the idea that the regeneration of the Greeks would rejuvenate the West died slowly, as the discussion of Swinburne above has demonstrated. Aubrey de Vere, after noting that Sophocles, Homer, and Plato were once again taught in Greek classrooms, concluded, "What then may we not expect when that race, which possesses probably the largest ability of all European races, are, thus, brought into contact at once with the noblest of languages, the noblest of literatures" (*Picturesque Sketches* I.259). De Vere's estimation of the ability of the Greeks was, of course, based on the past, not the present.

Greece's place in the Western imagination explains why, decades after the establishment of a Greek state, the modern Greeks were still discussed in terms of their past and their potentiality while the present was overlooked. The classicist R. C. Jebb wryly noted "Foreign observers of Greek affairs are, broadly speaking, of two classes: those who think that Greece has a future, and those who think that she may be allowed to have a present" (vi). The former were far more numerous than the latter.

Although the general opinion about the modern Greeks was negative, the sentiment of travelers, with their eyes on the glorious past and/or the exciting future, was predominantly philhellenic. Several pro-Turkish books appeared that used the dismal state of modern Greece to argue that the Greeks should never have become independent, such as Sir Grenville Temple's *Travels in Greece and Turkey* (1843) and Adolphus Slade's *Records of Travel in Turkey* (1833) in England or James Ellsworth DeKay's *Sketches of Turkey in 1831 and 1832* (1833) and James Harrison's *Greek Vignettes* (1878) in the United States. In 1830, the German scholar Jacob Fallmerayer published a study that claimed that the modern Greeks were mainly, if not wholly, Slavic in blood. Fallmerayer's book caused an uproar in Greece, but neither his work nor the evidence presented by pro-Turkish travelers had much effect on English or American nineteenth-century literature.[24] A central tenet of philhellenic thought from its inception had been the degeneration and debasement of the modern Greeks, so a catalogue of their faults only proved a point already accepted. Many of the supporters of the Greek cause were as committed as their opponents to the idea of the modern Greeks as an "unconsidered tribe of slaves." It was, after all, precisely the slavery of Greece that, according to Winckelmann and others, had prevented the Greek landscape from producing another Athens like that of the fifth century BCE. Even after independence, it would take time for Greek regeneration to occur. S. G. W. Benjamin wrote in 1874: "Patience must indeed be the motto of the Philhellenist who longs for the restoration of Athens and Greece, his faith in the progress of the Greeks, and in their energy and disposition to overcome obstacles and arise above their present condition, must often be taxed to the uttermost" (216). The heroine's father in Justin McCarthy's *Maid of Athens* (1883) is described as "a Philhellene of the most genuine type; his love for Greece and his faith in her survived the hardest experience and the keenest disappointments. Even the worst failures and meanesses [*sic*] of the worst Greek parties politicians could not cure him of his devotion to the Greek cause" (I.13). The real question for philhellenes was whether a revival of the Greeks were possible, and at a larger philosophical level, ideas of human progress and the transforming qualities of liberty were the crucial issues. Greece and the Greeks were still not of importance in their own right but for their symbolic place in political and cultural battles.

In his *Voyage en Orient* (1835), the French writer Lamartine, employing a pagan-versus-Christian cultural dichotomy, described the Attic landscape as a desiccated wasteland rather than an earthly paradise. "Only God can revivify it. The spirit of liberty will not suffice. To the poet and painter, there is written on these sterile mountains, on these white capes whitened with the ruins of fallen temples, on these marshy and rocky wastes, whereon nothing but sonorous names resound—It is finished" (67–68). The temple of Theseus had "a kind of frigid, dead beauty," which contrasted with the living grandeur of St. Peter's at Rome. Chateaubriand concurred, commenting, "Christianity will prevent modern nations from falling into such deplorable decrepitude" as what he saw in Athens (*Travels in Greece* 160–61).

Benjamin Disraeli's fictional hero Contarini Fleming challenges the philhellenic sentiment from a different cultural standpoint than Lamartine. Fleming concludes a visit to the Acropolis as follows: "These are a few of my meditations amid the ruins of Athens. They will disappoint those who might justly expect an ebullition of rapture from one who gazed upon Marathon at midnight and sailed the free waters of Salamis. I regret the disappointment, but I have arrived at an age when I can think only of the future" (*Contarini Fleming, Works* VI.49). Fleming's chief meditation was on "the absurdity of modern education," which was "confined to the literature of two dead languages" (VI.48). But Fleming does not advocate the study of spoken European languages since "these have been in great part founded upon the classic tongues. . . . Why not study the oriental? Surely in the Persians or the Arabs we might discover new sources of emotion, new modes of expression, new trains of ideas, new principles of invention, and new bursts of fancy" (VI.49). The position advocated by Disraeli's character was hardly a new way of thinking in 1831, the year the novel was published. Romantic Orientalism had been viewed as a means to revive the West for some sixty years. But few real or fictional visitors had espoused the turn to the East while sitting near the Parthenon, the temple of Romantic Hellenism.

The Romantic Orientalism presented in Disraeli's novels *Contarini Fleming* (1831) and *Tancred* (1847) is far more aggressive than the mystical, transcendental version that forms the natural counterpart to the Romantic Hellenism of Winckelmann. Disraeli's Orientalism in these novels appears instead to be an inversion of Romantic philhellenism in which the philosophical concepts have a geographical locus that must be defended from Western intrusions. Fleming's career as a reverse Byron is often signaled in the text. On entering Ioannina he exclaims, "I longed to write an Eastern Tale!" (VI.26), and he enlists in the Ottoman army to help extinguish an insurrection of Albanians. No other character in nineteenth-century English fiction of which I know fights for Turkish rule on European soil. *Tancred* focuses on the regeneration of Arabs and Jews in the Holy Land in order to "bring back the empire of the East" (XVI.121), but Disraeli places it in a rhetorical and conceptual framework that replicates the importance of freedom in philhellenic discourse:

> Asia has been overrun by Turks and Tartars. For nearly five hundred years the true Oriental mind has been enthralled. Arabia alone has remained free and faithful to the divine tradition. From its bosom we shall go forth and sweep away the moulding remnants of the Tartaric system, and then, when the East has resumed its indigenous intelligence, when angels and prophets again mingle with humanity, the sacred quarter of the globe will recover its primeval and divine supremacy, it will act upon the modern empires and the faint-hearted faith of Europe. (XVI.337)

In a review of the novel, Richard Monckton Milnes, a philhellene, complained that in the book the hero "is taught to look on Christendom as an intellectual colony of Arabia" (Blake 208). But *Tancred* actually goes further than that, for it also argues that the East should not be a political colony of Europe. James Buzard said that Disraeli's rejection of philhellenism at the same time that he mimicked Byronic fashion and style stemmed from a desire to be a "Tory Byron" (41). *Contarini Fleming* and *Tancred*, however, suggest the author might also have desired to be an "Oriental Byron."

The degree to which Disraeli's Jewish origin affected his identification with the East and consequent rejection of philhellenism was a matter of some debate.[25] Certainly Disraeli's political opponents fixed on his racial background in the disputes about the Bulgarian atrocities of 1876. As the battle between Disraeli and Gladstone joined in earnest, the Liberal leader wrote his friend the duke of Argyll, "Dizzy's crypto-Judaism has had to do with his policy" (Seton-Watson 78). In 1879, T. P. O'Connor, another philhellene, tried to show that "Disraeli treated the whole Eastern Question from 'the standpoint of the Jew'" (Shannon, *Gladstone and the Bulgarian Agitation* 200). The letters Disraeli wrote during his trip to the East in 1830 do suggest a personal affinity for the Turks. Navarino is called "the scene of Codrington's bloody blunder." Disraeli also announced: "I am quite the Turk, wear a turban, smoke a pipe six feet long, and squat on a divan. . . . In fact, I find the habits of this calm and luxurious people [the Turks] entirely agree with my preconceived opinions of propriety and enjoyment, and I detest the Greeks more than ever" (*Letters* 1:173, 174).

But Disraeli's relation to philhellenism was hardly so simple. In between *Contarini Fleming* and *Tancred*, he wrote *The Rise of Iskander* (1833), as trite a piece of philhellenic writing as any in the decades after Byron. The hero is the fifteenth-century Albanian chieftain Skanderberg, who appears in the novel as an ethnic Greek. The novel opens in Athens, where a "solitary being stands upon the towering crag of the Acropolis, amid the ruins of the Temple of Minerva, and gazed upon the inspired scene. . . . 'Beautiful Greece,' he exclaimed, 'Thou art still my country. A mournful lot is mine, a strange and mournful lot, yet not uncheered by hope. . . . Themistocles saved Greece and died a satrap; I am bred one, let me reverse our lots and die at least a patriot'" (*Works* IV.4–5). In short, *The Rise of Iskander* is simply the Greek War of Independence transported backward in time. If Gladstone had read this novel instead of *Tancred*, admittedly a more innovative and challenging book, he might have come away with an entirely different view of Disraeli's supposed crypto-Judaism.

Contarini Fleming and *Tancred*, with their adaptation of a philhellenic rhetorical style for anti-Western purposes, constitute the most serious assault on the haunted, holy ground of Greece and Byron in mid–nineteenth-century writing in English. Since, however, they amount to a transposition of Romantic philhellenism to the Orient, they do not reappraise or critique the philhellenic tradition in the light of Greek independence.

There is nothing in English around the middle of the nineteenth century comparable to the Greek stories of Arthur de Gobineau (*Souvenirs de Voyage*, 1872) or Edmund About's novel *Le Roi des Montagnes* (1857).[26] Gobineau's two stories, slender as they are, clearly demonstrate the directions British writers failed to take. "Le mouchoir rouge" concerns life on the Ionian island of Cephalonia under British rule. "Akrivie Phrangopoulou" examines the Greek romance after liberation by recounting the experience on Naxos of an English naval officer, whose nationality serves to signal the story's relationship to the Byronic tradition. Both subjects would have been fruitful material for a British writer, but it was a Frenchman who pursued them.

About's book, translated as *The King of the Mountains*, was easily the most famous novel about modern Greece in Europe and America during the second half of the nineteenth century and, not coincidentally, the only work of note to reappraise the romantic klephts of philhellenic legend.[27] The gap between About and English writing can best be demonstrated by the fact that About's book appeared in the same year as one of the first novels in English set in modern Greece written after 1833, Morier's stereotypically philhellenic *Photo the Suliote*.

About's book professes to be a faithful rendering of an account by a German student, Hermann Schultz, of his capture by the famous Greek brigand Hadgi-Stavros, who fought in the war of independence but "never knew exactly whether he was a brigand or an insurgent, whether his men were thieves or patriots. No doubt his hatred of the Turk was great, but it did not blind him to the advantages to be derived from pillaging a Greek village" (26). Abroad, however, they heard only of "the heroic side of his exploits. . . . Byron dedicated an ode to him" (27). About's text describes not only the rampant pillaging of both Greek natives and foreign travelers but also the way it was tolerated and even aided by the authorities. A police captain says, "True, we have among our superiors some madmen who pretend that brigands ought to be treated the same way as Turks," but he assures Schultz that such men are rare and ineffective (164). About also takes aim at philhellenes abroad when the captain tells the young German that publicizing the story of his kidnapping will only make him look foolish: "When you return to Germany, you can do what you like. Speak, write, publish, I shan't care. Works written against us harm no one, unless perhaps their authors. You are free to try the experiment. If you describe faithfully what you have seen, you'll be accused of slandering an illustrious and oppressed race. Our friends, and most men of sixty are of the number, will tax you with levity, caprice, and even ingratitude. . . . But the best of the affair is, no one will believe you" (164–65).

The narrator of Schultz's tale informs the reader that he sent a copy to Athens for comment and dutifully attaches a letter from one Patriotis Pseptis, "author of a volume of dithyrambi on the Regeneration of Greece," which reads: "The history of the King of the Mountains is an invention of some enemy of truth and of—the police. . . . I confess that, formerly, there were brigands in Greece. The most important of these were destroyed by Hercules and Theseus, whom we look upon as the original founder of the

Grecian police. Those who escaped have fallen under the blows of our invincible army" (302–3).

Almost everything in *The King of the Mountains* is delivered in that same lighthearted style; the author makes fun of a German botanist and a French archaeologist as well as the bloodthirsty Greek brigand who banks at Barclay's. Romilly Jenkins correctly noted that About's ironic wit nullified his message: "Yet it is probable that the general effect of the novel in Europe was harmful rather than salutary. Its success was too complete. It presented a state of society so preposterous that, as the gendarme Pericles told Schultz, nobody but a Greek could take it seriously, and in laughing until they cried at the antics of Pericles and Hadgi-Stavros, men forgot the real tyranny and blackmail, the tortures and mutilation, which were the order of the day in that lovely countryside" (12). Still, Greece's friends abroad responded precisely as About predicted, revealing just how dangerous the ground of modern Greece was for a critical and revisionary pen.

The reality of Greek brigands was brought home to the English public in April 1870. An excursion of English and Italian visitors to Marathon ended with the party in the hands of brigands. The outlaws released two women and a child, who were sent to Athens to help arrange the ransom for the four men in the group. The brigands' leader also sought freedom of movement and amnesty. The latter was specifically denied in the new Greek constitution adopted in 1864, a clause that had been approved by the governments of Britain, France, and Russia. When Greek troops caught up to the bandits at the village of Dilessi, all of the hostages were killed. Three of them were English and one was Italian.

Greece reacted with as much horror as Europe, but that did not prevent an outpouring of anti-Greek sentiment in the press. Jenkins said, in "England the public indignation knew no bounds. . . . Greece was a disgrace to civilisation, a nest of robbers and pirates, a country of half-Slav, half-Greek demisavages. . . . The unreasoning prejudice in favour of Greece which had been so strong in 1821 had, after half a century, given way to an equally unreasoning prejudice against her" (79).

A year after the Dilessi murders, the niece of Thomas Wyse, a former British minister to Athens, wrote in the introduction to her late uncle's Greek journals that the Dilessi tragedy had already had a salutary effect on thinking both in Greece and abroad: "a sort of romance still hung around the klephts, and, no matter how much it might be condemned, there was always a poetry surrounding the life, that made one excuse and palliate it." The events at Dilessi, she added, had caused brigandage to lose its luster of "romantic heroism" both in Greece and abroad (19).

Her pronouncement, like Jenkins's comment about the end of "unreasoning prejudice in favour of Greece," is directly at odds with the assertion of

Diplomaticus that the magic force of philhellenic legend was still potent in 1897. And Diplomaticus was right. For, *pace* the younger Wyse, in literature Dilessi had no perceptible effect on English writing about Greece and hardly dented the poetry surrounding klephtic life.

In a book of poems, *A Garland from Greece*, published twelve years after the tragedy at Dilessi, George Francis Savage-Armstrong included a piece called "The Brigand of Parnassus: A.D. 1881." At the opening, an old man asks his son if war has been declared against the Turks:

> War or no war? Iron-fisted shall we fight the Turk and sally,
> Janina be ours, and every Greek and Grecian vale be free,
> Turk and turban roll in ruin from the mountains to the sea?
>
> (276)

The old man is delighted that the decision is for war: "Praise be God!—I'll take my musket, and I'll march to Tempe's vale" (278). He then recalls his youth in 1821:

> I was young, and I was a Captain of a little band of Braves
> Roaming free upon Parnassus' heights above a land of slaves.
> Brigands, robbers, *Klephts*, they called us. Let them call us what they
>   might,
> We were *men*, and we were free, and we were happy day and night.
>
> (282)

The crucial event in his reminiscence is, predictably, the kidnapping of his sister by a pasha and her rescue by the band of klephts. He then returns to the present:

> Greece is not yet free as long as any Greek's a slave—
> That's our watchword now. . . .
> Will not the gallant lads of Greece in freedom born and bred,
> Thinking on the Greece that was, and dreaming of her glorious dead,
> Dare and do to-day if Greece be left to fight the Turk alone?
>
> (300–301)

The poem responded to the political climate of 1881, when Greece and Turkey nearly went to war, a conflict that was avoided when the European powers adjusted Greece's northern borders in its favor. Savage-Armstrong wanted to inspire the spirit of 1821 in his readers, and his composition rehearsed the literary conventions of the Greek Revolution. Even after Dilessi, he had no qualms about calling his hero a brigand nor invoking the romance surrounding the klephts. Savage-Armstrong's sub-Byronic verse may have lost its "poetic element," but his klephts had not.

Justin McCarthy's novel *Maid of Athens* (1883) was also set during the events of 1881. In the book, the heroine makes a spirited defense of Greek brigands, which, given the fact that the author was a member of the British Parliament, amounts to a direct comment about the public uproar over Dilessi:

> English people don't quite understand the hold these brigands some-
> times had on the villagers here. They were robbers to the rich foreign
> traveler; they were very often benefactors to their poor neighbors. A
> brigand chief was often known to give marriage portions to the poor
> girls of the village in which he took shelter now and then. If a poor
> man lost some of his cattle, or his olives had been spoiled or anything
> of the kind happened, the brigand chief was ready to make up the loss
> to him. The villagers regarded him exactly as the Highlanders did
> Rob Roy or the Sherwood people Robin Hood. (II.189)

She tells of the kidnapping of a group of French travelers by klephts that sounds much like Dilessi. The Greek government "would not encourage the giving of ransom; and the friends of the captured were wild with affright lest the delay in payment might make the brigands furious" (II.190). She and her mother, the widow of a respected philhellene, went to negotiate. The bandits instantly agreed to accept half of what was offered. She ends her account: "we had a feast together—the prisoners, the leading brigands, and our-selves." At her departure, the chief gave her a "delightful little dagger, which I hardly need say I cherish as a treasure" (II.192). Although she has never seen the leader of the band again, she knows that he is able to move about the country without interference from the police: "It would be a very unwise thing for the government to rake up old scores against a man like that. . . . He may be their ally one day" (II.194).

George Horton's *Fair Brigand* (1897), an American novel whose plot mir-rors that of About's book, provides a much more benevolent view of Greek brigands than its French precursor. A villager says of the klephtic band, "They do not rob us you see; they rob strangers and give dowries to our daughters and presents to our churches. Who would protect the honest shep-herd that opposed the brigands?" (66). And one of the American captives implicitly criticizes the Greek government for the tragedy at Dilessi: "If there is such a hulla-balloo made that the fool Government sends troops, they will kill us, as they did those Englishmen at Marathon" (79). Clearly, About found no followers in England and America. Even the author who had borrowed About's plot parted company when it came to criticizing klephts.[28]

For Horton, McCarthy, and others, the discourse of modern Greece was fixed in the 1820s. Rather than wanting modern Greece to mean something different for their generation, they insisted on its keeping the same meaning in spite of the facts before them. Like Byron, while in Greece McCarthy and Savage-Armstrong worried about and took precautions against the very brigands whom they romanticized on the page. The kingdom of Greece with its monarchy, its almost feudal regional leading families, its state religion, and its lawless brigands was hardly the paradise of freedom envisioned by Hölderlin or Shelley. But the struggle for Greek freedom had taken on a literary life of its own, which could not be punctured even by events as tragic as Dilessi.

The Greco-Turkish War of 1897 occurred during what was the silver age of literary philhellenism in English, at least in terms of volume. One year earlier, the Cretans had begun another rebellion against Ottoman rule. Men and equipment were sent to the island by the Greek government, which openly declared for annexation. In addition, several klephtic bands crossed Greece's northern border into Turkish territory. In April 1897, Greece and Turkey were officially at war for the first time since the War of Independence. A blockade of Crete by the navies of the European powers prevented major operations on the island by either side. The main campaign in Thessaly ended in a humiliating debacle for the Greeks. Retreat followed retreat until on May 11 the Greek government asked the Western powers to mediate a settlement. Greece lost a small amount of territory and was required to pay an indemnity of 4 million Turkish pounds. The outcome was happier on Crete, where the powers intervened to make the island an autonomous province of the Ottoman Empire with Prince George, the second son of King George of Greece, as governor. As Dakin concluded, "Greece, though defeated, had gained on balance" (*Unification of Greece* 154).

The war occurred at an opportune time. No significant conflicts were in progress elsewhere that diverted attention from events in Greece; as the first European war in a decade, the Greco-Turkish War attracted many of the leading reporters of the time, among them Richard Harding Davis and Stephen Crane. Just one year later, the Spanish-American War would bring the United States onto the world stage as a colonial power, irrevocably complicating American attitudes toward national struggles for liberation. Over the previous decade, Britain had abandoned an Eastern strategy centered on the preservation of the Ottoman Empire as a buffer against Russia. The philhellenism of the British heart was no longer checked by its Russophobic head, and the cause of Greece acquired the kind of mainstream, semiofficial status it had always held in America. Further, Byron's grandchildren, who had no freedom for which to fight at home, rushed to Greece to take part in "these new crusades" for freedom (Brailsford 29).

If active philhellenes were now truly men of the rifle instead of the sword, literary philhellenes also took up a different medium, fiction. Still, a number of poems in the traditional philhellenic strain appeared in 1897, such as Edmond Rostand's "Pour la Grèce," Swinburne's "For Greece and Crete," William Watson's "Hellas, Hail," Andrew Lang's "Member from Crete," and an early offering from Robert Frost entitled simply "Greece," which ends:

> Greece could not let her glory fade!
>   Although peace be in sight,
> The race the Persian wars arrayed
>   Must fight one more good fight.
>
> Greece! in triumph long ago
>   It was you proved to men,
> A few may countless hosts o'erthrow:
>   Now prove it once again!
>   (502)[29]

But philhellenic poems were dwarfed by the pages of prose. Modern Greece had begun to make a sustained appearance in English and American fiction earlier in the decade with the publication of such novels as Elizabeth Edmonds's *Amygdala* (1894), Cécile Cassavetes' *Anthea* (1892), E. F. Benson's *Limitations* (1896), and George Horton's *Constantine: A Tale of Greece under King Otho* (1896), but it was in 1897 that modern Greece gained a significant presence as a fictional space in literature in English.

An air of nostalgia permeates many of the novels of the 1890s. In his history of the Greek War of Independence published in 1897, W. Allison Phillips wrote that the "imagination of Europe is still fired by Byron's dream of a Hellas on whose soil, freed from the blighting rule of the barbarian, the arts and sciences shall once more flourish in their ancient glory" (2). For Phillips, as for many other philhellenes, history appeared to be repeating itself. He opened his volume: "Once more the Greek has measured his strength against the Turk, and once more the passionate cry of the Hellenes for the fulfillment of their national aspirations has, in spite of the unfriendly attitude of the Governments and the warnings of experienced statesmen, awakened sympathetic echoes throughout Europe. The Philhellenic enthusiasm is an instinct rather than a conviction" (1). The war inspired Isabella Mayo to publish her translation of "Patriot Songs of the Greeks," in which she said that the present struggle "carries one's thoughts back to that stirring period, between 1770 and 1830, which closed with the recognition of Greek independence" (275).

The cause of Greece was especially strong in those who felt that they had missed the great struggles for freedom of earlier decades. As the philhellenic hero of Noel Brailsford's *The Broom of the War God* (1898) volunteered to fight for greater Greece, he "thought of his mother's stories of friends of hers who had fought with Garibaldi, and he recalled his boy's sorrow that he had been too late to join them. Was the dream of a great free Italy any fairer than this inspiration of Hellenism?" (33). In *My Life and Times* (1926), Jerome K. Jerome remembered, when the war of 1897 broke out, "Poetical friends of mine went out to fight for Greece" but added that they "spent most of their time looking for the Greek army, and when they found it it didn't know it, and came home again" (274). In Richard Harding Davis's comic play, *The Galloper*, which first appeared on Broadway in 1905, Blanche, a music-hall actress recently arrived in Athens, attempts to take advantage of such emotional reactions: "Well, my story is that little Blanche's father was a volunteer in the *last* Greek war—I come out here to act, my heart bleeds for the Greek soldiers, and I volunteer as a Red Cross nurse—I go to the front— get wounded— . . . Come back by Monday night—and open to two hundred million dollars" (*Farces* 150–51).

Byron's grandchildren of the rifle and the pen sensed that 1897 might be the last opportunity to experience the magic force of philhellenic legend with its ideals of freedom and heroism. And the consensus was that they were already too late. Three years before, in George Bernard Shaw's *Arms and the Man*, the heroine, Raina, wondered: "Perhaps we only had our heroic ideas because we are so fond of reading Byron and Pushkin, and because we were delighted with the opera that season at Bucharest. Real life is so seldom like that! indeed never, as far as I knew it then" (I.392). Philhellenic writers in 1897, all guilty of being too fond of reading Byron, also discovered that real life was different from *Childe Harold* or *The Giaour* and lamented the gap between their world and the golden age of seventy years earlier, when the heroic ideals had, in their eyes, been valid.

While philhellenes of the rifle came from all over Europe, the production of philhellenic fiction in the 1890s was predominantly an English and American phenomenon; the French, who had contributed to the genre so generously in the 1820s and 1830s, offered few additions. French reticence was understandable; the 1897 war could not even point to noble failures, and the Greek Revolution of the 1820s was a well-worn subject in French novels by 1840.[30] For English and American writers, however, it was an opportunity to create the philhellenic fiction that had not been written in the 1820s. For all intents and purposes, that is what they did.

The 1890s generated as much, if not more, writing about the Greek Revolution as about the contemporary situation.[31] In the preface to his 1897 translation of Stefanos Xenos's novel *Andronike: A Heroine of the Greek Revolution*, E. A. Grosvenor stated that, although the characters were from the period of the Greek Revolution of 1821, "They might be reckoned characters of to-day. That revolution, with its mythical heroism and shame, was it-

self an episode in the ceaseless struggle between the Christians and the Mus-
sulmans, the Greeks and the Turks" (vii). The same logic underlies novels
about the Greek Revolution such as Isabella Mayo's *Daughter of the Klephts*
(1897) and E. F. Benson's two volumes *The Vintage* (1898) and *The Capsina*
(1899) or fictional accounts of Byron in Greece such as McClaws's *Maid of
Athens* (1906) and Hallie Ermine Rives's *Castaway* (1904). All of these writings, along with Elizabeth Edmonds's *Amygdala: A Tale of the Greek Revolution* (1894) and Cécile Cassavetes' *Anthea: A Story of the Greek War of Independence* (1892), treat the War of Independence with the same reverence that
authors of the 1820s had given to the Persian Wars. The move to fiction did
not cause a reevaluation of the Grèce de Byron but instead represented the
final apotheosis of Byron's Greece into the pantheon of legend.

Where the Greeks of the revolution had appeared inferior to the warriors
of Salamis and Thermopylae, the Greeks of 1897 were now portrayed as the
degenerated stock of the heroes of 1821. In his memoir *As We Were* (1930),
E. F. Benson recalled his days in Athens in the 1890s. He spoke of how the
modern Greeks were "justly proud of those stubborn ancestors who, seventy
years before, had risen, under the leadership of Petrobey and the Mainats,
and thrown off the damnable yoke of the Turks, kindling by that most heroic
insurrection European sympathy with Hellenism, of which the immortal
mouthpiece was Byron" (134). It was precisely that "most heroic insurrection" that Benson portrayed in *The Vintage* and *The Capsina*, two ponder-
ously hagiographic volumes. He presented the Greeks of 1897, however, as a
people prone to verbal bravado who were "incapable of making any sort of
stand against the enemy" (*As We Were* 145). Benson commented that hardly
a trace of "old Hellenic blood" remained in mainland Greece, and the population was "largely of that mixed blood which by way of a formula we call
Levantine" (134). But he appeared less concerned to show a gap between the
ancients and the Greeks of 1821 than to point out the one between both of
those groups and the Greeks of 1897.

In George Horton's *Like Another Helen* (1900), it is the American philhellene who fails to measure up to the standards of the legendary past. The
novel transposes the romance of Greek liberation to Crete in 1897. The
Turkish commander Kostakes, who desires the beautiful Panayotta for his
harem, appears as the embodiment of the unspeakable Turk of old; in fact,
Horton's novel was published in England with the title *The Unspeakable
Turk*. Panayotta is a true granddaughter of the Greek Revolution; she is captured by Kostakes only after her dress is caught by a branch as she attempts
to commit suicide by leaping off a cliff *a la manière* Suliot. The weak link in
the triangle is John Curtis, a twenty-two-year-old American who "imagined
himself an ancient Greek or Lord Byron" (12) and who whispers the refrain
of Byron's "Maid of Athens" as he rescues Panayotta from a band of Bashi-
Bashouks (187). Later in the novel, Curtis begins to have second thoughts

about Panayotta and his own place in the romance of liberation: "She's grand here in her native mountains, but you can't lug a mountain around with a girl. It would take four years of education to fit her for Boston, or even Lynn. . . . I wonder if Americans wouldn't look askance at a woman who had lived in a Turkish harem. Wouldn't she bring a taint of suspicion with her, no matter how pure she might be?" (305–6). Panayotta's Orthodoxy might seem too much like Catholicism for Curtis's mother, and "a taint of the papacy was as a taint of leprosy" (306). When Curtis discovers that Panayotta was literally tainted by leprosy after she hid in a lepers' colony during her escape from Kostakes's house, he catches the next boat out of Crete. Curtis's failure as a hero is both marked and balanced by the presence of the Swede Peter Lindbohm, a true philhellene of the old stamp, who goes in search of Panayotta as the book closes. *Like Another Helen* is nostalgic not so much for the legendary Greeks of the revolution but rather for the legendary English and American philhellenes of the 1820s.

In Stephen Crane's "Death and the Child," the antihero, the son of an emigrant Greek, has lost his native valor. The principal character, Peza, arrives in Thessaly to cover the war for an Italian newspaper. But after he sees a stream of refugees, he resolves to join the fight: "Ah, this is too cruel, too cruel, too cruel. Is it not? I did not think it would be as bad as this. . . . And yet I am a Greek. Or at least my father was a Greek" (*Works* 5:122). At the front, surrounded by hardy peasant soldiers, the educated expatriate is told to take cartridges off a corpse. Frightened by contact with the dead man, he flees in a manner similar to that of Henry Fleming in *The Red Badge of Courage*. But where Fleming's flight was portrayed as part of an initiation into the world of battle, Peza's is depicted as a complete failure of manhood. At the close of the story, he encounters a lone child of a mountain shepherd, who was left behind by his family. The boy asks the emigrant, "Are you a man?"

> Peza gasped in the manner of a fish. Palsied, windless, and abject, he confronted the primitive courage, the sovereign child, the brother of the mountains, the sky and the sea, and he knew the definition of his misery would be written on a wee grass-blade. (*Works* 5:141)

Crane had an extremely positive view of Greek soldiers; it is somewhat ironic that the great realist still saw legendary klephts all around him in 1897. "In this time of change and surprise," he wrote in a dispatch, "it is good to find something that does not move with either tide. . . . This unchangeable element is the spirit of the Greek people" (*Works* 9:12–13). He added: "There will be a great deal to happen before these people of the mountains care to pause" (*Works* 9:15). After the Greeks had cared to pause more than once, Crane continued to defend their bravery. One of his dispatches, entitled "Greeks Waiting at Thermopylae," noted, "Although the pass has been widened and much changed since Leonidas' fight, it is still an ideal place to hold an enemy in check" (*Works* 9:57). For Crane, the villain was Crown Prince Constantine, who would not allow his troops to engage the Turks. He eulogized General Smolenski, who, according to Crane, wept when ordered to retreat by the prince. For Frederick Palmer, however, Smolenski was himself the problem. As a "European trained Oriental," the general was unsuited for either Western or Eastern modes of warfare (*Going to War in Greece* 120).

Given Crane's positive view of "these mountain people," the confrontation at the end of "Death and the Child" is not simply one between child and man, innocence and the loss of innocence. It also represents a confrontation between a true child of the Greek mountain, one who represents the unchanging spirit of the Greek people, and the son of an emigrant. In "Death and the Child," life abroad took the klepht out of the man.

The works of Benson and Crane point to a curious fact concerning writing about modern Greece before 1920. Benson was justly famous for comedies of bourgeois social manners, from *Dodo* in 1895 to the Lucia and Mapp novels of the 1930s. But his Greek novels, *The Vintage* and *The Capsina*, portray precisely the dry, stereotypical heroic Greeks who would be the perfect targets of Benson's comic wit. Crane, on the other hand, was justly famous for his realistic depiction of Bowery life in *Maggie: A Girl of the Streets* and of warfare in *The Red Badge of Courage*. Yet his novel set in Greece during the war of 1897, *Active Service* (1899), is a flat, uninspired bourgeois romance of the sort that Crane was reacting against in his earlier efforts.[32] Greece had a curious effect; it made otherwise good authors write against themselves, and the result was rather poor work. The satire, criticism, and deconstruction of cherished beliefs that could be done back home somehow were not yet ready for the dangerous ground of Greece and Byron.

Although the writing of Benson, Horton, and Crane all suggest different ways in which the present did not live up to the ideals of philhellenic legend, none of them challenged the worth of those ideals. At the end of his account of the war of 1897 in *A Year from a Reporter's Notebook*, in which he dwelt at length on the ineptitude of the Greek army and its officers, Richard Harding Davis stated:

> There have been many minarets within the last two years standing above burning villages in Asia Minor and Armenia. They have looked down upon the massacre of twenty thousand people through the last two years, and upon the destruction of no one knows how many villages. If the five Powers did not support these minarets, they would crumble away and fall to pieces. Greece tried to uproot them, but she was not brave enough, nor wise enough, nor strong enough, and so they still stand. . . . Some people think that all of them have been standing quite long enough—that it is time they come down forever. (256–57)

For Davis, as for many other writers, the central elements of the Greek cause—the struggle against tyranny, the battle between East and West, the conflict between barbarism and civilization—were still noble and worthy, but a sense of will in Greece, the West, or both, was wanting.[33]

Only in Brailsford's *Broom of the War God* are "the bright aims of Hellenism" rejected. The novel is a fictional account of a philhellene in the Foreign Legion written by a volunteer. Brailsford's hero, Henry Graham, starts out with a head filled with philhellenic rhetoric. When a Greek sergeant thanks Graham for the valiant behavior of the Foreign Legion at the battle of Pharsala, he replies, "It is we who owe everything to Hellas, everything" (279). But Graham has already begun to reject such platitudes. Near the end of the book, he sits at a campfire looking at the mountains: "Liberty and Freedom were there. A bonfire of the vanities. It held all that men loved, home, faith, and fatherland. The war was over, an infinite bitter sadness shrouded all his memories. Patriotism and devotion, all the bright aims of Hellenism,— the words came lightly to his ears mixed with a chatter of frivolity. It seemed better to watch the triumph of a stern and serious barbarism than to dream of the lost ideals of a people too futile to guard them" (329–30).

Yet even Brailsford was not content to part company completely with the legend of the past. For if the Greeks of 1897 had not been too futile to guard the noble ideals, those concepts would not necessarily have been lost. Brailsford's criticism was aimed less at "the bright aims of Hellenism" than at the Greek soldiers who had not been, like his hero, Varatasi, the commander of the Foreign Legion, true descendants of the Hellenes. On his way to the front, Graham meets an old klepht of seventy-three who had gone to Athens at the opening of hostilities because "he wanted to organize a band of irregulars from Domoko to go and fight at the frontier. In '78 he had been captain of such a band, and many a time before he had led revolts against the Turks. They thought he was too old for the work this time" (57). At the end of the book, the aged Alexi dies from wounds received while fighting the Turks one last time. Although the now-disillusioned Graham cannot share Alexi's delight in the death of the Turks who the old klepht had slain, the old warrior stands out as a relic from a nobler, simpler age.

Few literary philhellenes were as critical of the Greeks as Brailsford, but few had had his experience. Crane and Davis spent but a few days at the front and were well paid for their efforts. Brailsford simply got knocked on his head for his labors, like the philhellenes of old. In fact, Brailsford and his fictional alter ego Henry Graham, actually suffered the disillusionment of the volunteers of the 1820s. From Byron down to the simplest private, they had also wondered whether the lost ideals of a people too futile to guard them deserved their sacrifice.

The great public that admired Greece and Byron paid no more attention to Brailsford than it had to earlier refugees from the front lines. After the war,

Henry Norman observed, "Hellas is wrecked today, but let us, for our own sake as well as hers, pray that she remembers who and what were the men whose name she bears—in the words of old George Sandys, 'admirable in the arts, and glorious in arms, famous for government, affectors of freedom, every way noble.' Thus and thus only, and that hardly, shall she fulfill the splendid prophecy of Shelley: 'If Greece must be / A wreck, yet shall its fragments reassemble'" (426). Henry Nevinson chastised the West for not coming to the aid of Greece, concluding: "In the near East, Greece is still what she was of old, the one point of enlightenment and freedom, the one barrier against Oriental darkness and oppression. When greater Powers were hesitating through fear of self interest, she alone had the courage to strike another blow against the barbarian despotism which still holds very many of her race in bondage" (288). Within a year of the defeat in 1897, Samuel Barrows opened his book *The Isles and Shrines of Greece* with the sentence: "There is a Greece of yesterday, a Greece of to-day, and every philhellene believes that there will be a Greece of tomorrow" (3). Barrows did not explicitly say that the Greece of tomorrow would resemble the Greece of yesterday, but that idea was understood by every philhellene.

The lack of impact of the defeat of 1897 on the English and American imagination is perhaps best shown by the conclusion of Richard Harding Davis's play *The Galloper*, a comic romance set during the war of 1897, which opened on Broadway in 1905. The work ends with a Greek advance and an appearance by a triumphant Greek crown prince, who congratulates an American reporter for capturing a Turkish outpost single-handedly. The last stage directions read: "The Crown Prince turns to the soldiers, who wave their muskets and cheer him, as the CURTAIN FALLS" (300). A Broadway hit, Davis's play surfaced again as the musical *The Yankee Tourist*, in which the crown prince and his men sing and dance in celebration at the close. The magic force of legend could, apparently, rewrite the history of actual events. It could not, however, change the fact that recent events had altered the geography of southeastern Europe forever.

5

Pet Balkan People

In April 1876, an insurrection against Ottoman rule broke out in a number of Bulgarian villages in the Rhodope mountains. The Bulgarian nationalists were neither well organized nor well armed. The Ottoman authorities responded quickly, and resistance ended with the death of the Bulgarian leader, Hristo Botjev, on May 19. Ottoman forces, both regular troops and the irregular militia, burned numerous villages and killed thousands of civilians; the number is a matter of some dispute, but a good estimate is between 10,000 and 15,000. The Bulgarian atrocities hardly differed from actions taken by the Ottomans against the Maronite Christians in Lebanon in 1860–1861 or the Cretans in 1866–1869.[1] Yet it was the fate of the Bulgarians that became a cause célèbre in Europe, especially in Britain. Although the last rifle shot was fired in Bulgaria in the spring of 1876, a veritable cannonade of articles and pamphlets continued in Britain throughout the summer. On September 6, William Ewart Gladstone's slight book *The Bulgarian Horrors and the Question of the East* appeared and went on to sell more than 200,000 copies in the first month.[2]

Gladstone entreated the British and the other European governments to obtain "the extinction of Turkish executive power in Bulgaria. Let the Turks now carry away their abuses in the only possible manner, namely by carrying off themselves. Their Zaptiehs and their Mudirs, their Bimbashis and their Yuzbachis, their Kaimakans and their Pachas, one and all, bag and baggage, shall, I hope, clear out from the province they have desolated and profaned" (61–62). And not simply from Bulgaria, for "the five cases of Servia, Bosnia, Herzegovina, Montenegro, and Bulgaria" should be considered "as the connected limbs of one and the same transaction" (48). In short, Gladstone wanted the Turks out of Europe, and his phrase "bag and baggage" was soon appropriated for that goal.

Gladstone's logic was firmly rooted in the perceived differences between Europe and Asia, which had been prevalent in the West since the Enlightenment. His use of Oriental words to enumerate the different Ottoman officials underscored their unsuitability to administer a part of Europe. According to

Gladstone, the Turks had received several opportunities for reform and improvement but, as Muslims of the East, had shown themselves incapable of progress. Gladstone's colleague, Edward Augustus Freeman, forthrightly declared in his pamphlet *The Turks in Europe* (1877) that "the differences between the Turks and the European nations are of a different kind from the differences between one European nation and another. . . . It is a mistake to speak of the Sultan and his ministers as a 'government' and to treat them as such" (46).[3] As K. P. Sandiford noted, Gladstone believed so deeply in the idea of a Europe founded upon the twin poles of Christianity and Hellenism that he was almost "an outright bigot" on the subject of Turkish rule on the western side of the Bosporus (188). Sandiford went on to suggest that Gladstone's negative response to the national aspirations of the Poles and the Magyars stemmed in part from the fact that, in the eyes of the veteran Liberal politician, there was "no sultan to denounce or Graeco-Roman legacy to defend" (189).

How was it that the Bulgarians, about whom little was known in late nineteenth-century Europe, became an integral part of the Greco-Roman legacy? It happened through an extension of the concept of philhellenism to encompass all of the European Christians under Ottoman rule. In his article of 1877, "Medieval and Modern Greece," Freeman forthrightly asserted, "Free Greece must be extended far beyond the present absurd boundary. Wherever Hellenes form the mass of Christian people that land must be Hellas" (*Historical Essays* 382). But he added, "The Greeks must remember that they must claim for themselves no superiority over the Servians or Bulgarians on any ground of past greatness. . . . any narrow philhellenism, grounded on mere classical sentimentalism, will be purely mischievous. . . . They must be satisfied to be first among equals" (315). Freeman, Gladstone, and most other philhellenes of the 1870s embraced what might be called "wider" or, even more problematically, "Balkan" philhellenism, which included but was not limited to the aspirations of the modern Greeks. For, as Freeman also said, the cause of each of the Eastern Christian nations was equally one "of right against wrong, of freedom against oppression, of Christendom against Islam," and were "too great and holy to be affected in any way by the subtleties of ethnology" (338). In large measure, the other Balkan nations entered the consciousness of Europe through Greece.

The extension of the philhellenic outlook was natural not only because an established and effective discourse about the liberation of European Christians from Muslim Turks was already at hand, but also because many of those prominent in the Bulgarian agitation, such as Gladstone and Freeman, had long-standing reputations as philhellenes. For example, William J. Stillman, one of the more vocal American advocates of the liberation of the Slavs in the late 1870s (in his *Herzegovina and the Late Uprising*, 1877), had, as the American consul on Crete, been a strong supporter of Cretan aspirations with *The*

Cretan Insurrection (1874). At the beginning of his account of the rebellion in Herzegovina, Stillman noted, "My Cretan experience hardly left me to conjecture on the immediate causes of discontent" (*Herzegovina* 8). Nor, he could have added, did it leave him to conjecture as to how to present the Slavic uprising to his American audience.[4]

The Greeks and the other Balkan Christians, according to Gladstone, were "sharers in a common religion" and also "sharers in common suffering" (*The Hellenic Factor in the Eastern Question* 25). Through the efforts of Gladstone, Stillman, and others, they would also be sharers in nineteenth-century philhellenic rhetoric. For example, in his essay "Montenegro," published in 1877, Gladstone supported the territorial claims of that small mountain kingdom by stating that in the Middle Ages "Montenegro fought with a valor that rivalled, if it did not surpass, that of Thermopylae and Marathon, with numbers and resources far inferior, against a foe braver and far more terrible" (363). Later he added some remarks about "the resemblances between the characteristic features of Montenegro and of Homeric or Achaian Greece" (370). In a later essay, "The Peace to Come," the Liberal leader quoted two of the most famous philhellenic lines by Byron, "Of the three hundred, grant but three / To make a new Thermopylae," and then added: "Europe did not know then . . . that Montenegro had fought many such a battle, as Thermopylae itself does not surpass" (213). Stillman began his description of the capital city of Montenegro as follows: "The residence of the ruler of Montenegro is worthy of its Lacedaimonian prototype," without explaining why or how Lacedaimonia functioned as a prototype for the Montenegrin city of Cettinja (18). The author and designer William Morris, in a letter to the *Daily News* in 1876 about the Bulgarian atrocities, included a single historical allusion: "those babies murdered in Bulgaria—there were more, I believe, slain in Scio a while ago" (398). The struggles of the Montenegrins and the Bulgarians could be compared to any number of national liberation movements, but the connection was invariably made to the Greeks.

The modern Greeks also served a useful purpose as an example of a European people who had experienced a debasement similar to that of the Bulgarians and their neighbors. Gladstone lamented certain uncivilized customs of the Montenegrins, such as wife beating. Yet he reminded this audience that "this was a practice that did not excite general repugnance one generation back among the Hellenic inhabitants of Cefalonia" ("Montenegro" 376). The implicit message was that the Montenegrins were simply one generation behind the Greeks when measured on the scales of "civilization."

In *The Hellenic Factor in the Eastern Question*, also written in 1876, Gladstone announced, "There are four Christian races under the Porte"—the Slavs, the Wallachs of Romania, the Armenians, and the Greeks (3). He wanted the needs of all four to be addressed equally. Gladstone admitted that, despite their similar cultures and recent histories, the Hellenes and the Slavs "are to some extent rivals in their dreams" (25). From a practical point of view, he perceived this as an advantage for England, since Greece would need allies to balance the power of the more numerous Slavs to the north. But Gladstone expressed the hope that the Eastern Christians would live and work together in harmony. His pamphlet ended with a string of philhellenic quotations from *The Siege of Corinth, The Giaour,* and *The Age of Bronze* of Byron, "whose recollections," he told the reader, "have recently been revived in England by a well meant effort" (27). That effort was, to a degree, closely linked to the new assault on Turkish oppression in Turkey-in-Europe. At the top of page 27, Gladstone wrote that Byron joined the Greek cause "when Greece lay cold and stark in the tomb." But at the bottom of the same page, he subtly shifted the focus: "Lord Byron brought to this Great Cause, the dawn of emancipation, for the East then all in grave-clothes" not only "the enthusiasm of a poet or the reckless daring of a rover" but also "the strongest practical good sense." In the move from "Greece in the tomb" to "the East all in grave-clothes," one can see the appropriation of philhellenic rhetoric and the Byronic mantle for all of the Balkans.

The ideological reasons for such an approach should be evident. The classical past and its "regeneration" at the time of the Greek Revolution had been the means by which Western philhellenes had "legitimized" the place within Europe of the Orthodox Greeks and their seemingly Near Eastern culture. The other Balkan peoples also required such legitimizing, and the logical way to proceed was to tie them, however tangentially, to the only "Western" culture that had existed in Eastern Europe, the glorious ancient Greeks and their regenerated descendants. The Serbs, Bulgarians, and Romanians, Robert Byron observed in 1929, "emerged in emulation of the Greeks" (*Byzantine Achievement* 44), or at least that is the way it appeared to Freeman and others in the West. There was, however, an inherent problem in the "Balkan" philhellenism of the 1870s that was bound to annoy the Greeks. On the one hand, all Eastern Christians were to be treated equally, and the Greeks could claim no superiority over the others on the basis of either the Greece of Byron or the Greece of Homer. On the other hand, because those two Western constructions were the best known *topoi* about the region, they became the very terms used to justify the aspirations of the Bulgarians and other Oriental Christians.[5]

The Bulgarian agitation and its aftermath marked the ideological victory of liberal philhellenism over Russophobia in Britain. In 1876, Disraeli and the Tory government held firm to the traditional British policy of support for Turkey. As for the brutal actions of Turkish troops, Disraeli noted in Parliament on July 10, 1876, "Wars of insurrection are always atrocious," and he cited the severe actions taken by the British government after a recent rebellion in Jamaica.[6] Gladstone and the Liberal party, on the other hand, argued that free Europeans and Christians would provide a better and more secure deterrent to Russia than the decrepit Ottoman Empire. R. W. Seton-Watson's assertion that "the Beaconsfield Government stood or fell by its Eastern policy" in the election of 1880 may overstate the case, but the victory of Gladstone did mark a turning point in British foreign policy (548). It was not, however, simply the victory of altruism for the oppressed over blatant self-interest. One reason for the new direction was that Turkophobia and Islamophobia finally overtook Russophobia in Britain. From a practical point of view, the Russo-Turkish War of 1877–1878 had demonstrated that the Turks were no longer an effective barrier. Disraeli himself recognized the fact when he forced the Ottoman Empire to cede Cyprus in return for British support in 1878.[7]

The anonymous author of the pro-Bulgarian pamphlet *An Appeal for a New Nation* (1876) cried: "Are you a friend of Liberty! If you are, you should be the friends of the struggling Christians of Turkey" (13). The friends of liberty embraced the cause. The link between the Bulgarian agitation and the radical philhellenes of the past is perhaps best exemplified by William Morris, for whom a rally on the Eastern question provided his first public action in a long leftist career.[8] Morris's revolutionary vision, like Shelley's, included the idealization of the ancient Greeks. In Morris's long poem *The Earthly Paradise*, the Arcadian village that the Wanderers finally find is, in the words of E. P. Thompson, "a friendly and fertile land where Greek traditions still linger" (114). The mixture of a contemplative, Platonic Hellenism descended from Winckelmann and the tradition of the Greek love of freedom, which had inspired Shelley and Hölderlin, still functioned as a catalyst for radical ideas. Yet the most prominent public figure of the Bulgarian agitation, Gladstone, was the leader of an established party, a fact that reduced, if it did not entirely undermine, the movement's potential as a vehicle for revolutionary change.[9] If the London Greek Committee of 1824 made up, in the words of St. Clair, "the extreme left of British politics as it was then constructed," the membership of the London Greek Committee of 1879 reads much like the list for a party at Gladstone's house at Hawarden.

An Appeal for a New Nation also asserted that "lightness and darkness are the proper terms for Christianity and Mohammedism" (6). Such rhetoric had been part of philhellenic discourse for decades. For philhellenes, freedom and progress had always been associated with European culture. Yet radical and liberal philhellenes usually had an uneasy, if not hostile, relationship with their fellow Christians at home. The career of William Watson, a man much less controversial both artistically and politically than either Swinburne or Morris, shows this continuing dichotomy. One year after he supported the cause of the Greeks in the 1897 poem "Hellas, Hail," he was severely criticized for his agnostic poems in *The Hope of the World*.[10] And mainstream Christians, among them Gladstone himself, formed the backbone of the leadership of the Bulgarian agitation. The movement succeeded in winning over established Liberal politicians and many influential High Churchmen because it stressed the need to free *Christians* from the Turks. It was, on the whole, fairly satisfied with and confident in its own Western culture and political structures, which caused the Balkan situation to be portrayed primarily in terms of a Muslim/East and Christian/West confrontation. With Gladstone, Robert Byron later lamented, philhellenism "degenerated into that negative and unprofitable emotion, abstract hatred of the Turk" (*Byzantine Achievement* 20).

Gladstone was the most famous English-speaking philhellene in the later nineteenth century and arguably the most famous in all of Europe. He was also the most problematic. For one thing, his reputation for philhellenism exceeded the facts. Contrary to popular belief, he had not advocated the cession of the Ionian islands to the kingdom of Greece during his brief period as high commissioner in Corfu in 1859; he had in fact concluded that "such a union" should not be "an object of immediate or practical desire" (Shannon, *Gladstone* 370).[11] In the late 1870s, he helped to make support for the aspirations of Greece more popular in Britain than ever before and supported the Greek acquisition of Thrace in 1881. But by linking that support with the claims of the Bulgarians, Serbians, and Montenegrins, one effect of his effort was to diminish the special status of the Greeks as the only Western nation in the East. Finally, by altering the social composition of the movement in Britain against Turkish oppression—to put it another way, by institutionalizing philhellenic sentiment within the British political structure—he subverted its effectiveness as a rallying cry for reform both abroad and at home. The nostalgia for the War of Independence that colored so much English philhellenic writing of the 1890s may stem in part from the fact that Gladstone, by making philhellenism "mainstream" and incorporating its radical past into a dominant political discourse, had distanced philhellenism from its revolutionary origins and made it more palatable to a wider public. Bourgeois and middle-class writers, and their readers as well, could be nostalgic for the magic force of legend because it was no longer a threat to them.[12]

The integration of philhellenism into mainstream politics occurred around the same time that the masterpieces of literary philhellenism, Byron's poetry and Shelley's *Hellas*, became accepted as part of an academic literary tradition. Along with Wordsworth, Blake, Coleridge, and Keats, the authors of *The Giaour* and the "Ode to Liberty" emerged as the canonical poets of Romanticism.[13] The political and literary acceptance of philhellenism progressed together, each supporting the other. As Byron and Shelley became recognized as members of England's "great company," their sentiments toward freedom were muted in favor of their poetic style. For example, William Watson, who had ties to the Liberal party, said in "Shelley's Centenary":

> In other shapes than he forecast,
> The world is moulded: his fierce blast,—
> His wild assault upon the Past,—
>   These things are vain;
> Revolt is transient: what must last
>   Is that pure strain,
>
> Which seems the wandering voices blent
> Of every virgin element,—
> A sound from the oceans cavern sent,—
>   An airy call
> From the pavilioned firmament
>   O'erdoming all.
>
> (*Poems* I.55)[14]

Conversely, the new attitude toward the Orient championed by Gladstone, which was much less critical of the West than that of early philhellenism, caused works like *Hellas* to be read in a less threatening way. The result was that, by 1900, literary philhellenism became part of the established tradition not only, or even primarily, a legacy of the Left. Alfred Austin, a poet of the Tories and supporter of Disraeli who had answered Gladstone's *Bulgarian Horrors* with a pamphlet entitled *Tory Horrors*, commemorated a boat trip through the Gulf of Corinth in 1881 with "Off Missalonghi," a celebratory poem about Byron's death in the Greek struggle: "I will not land where He, alas! / Just missed Fame's crown. Enough for me / To gaze and pass" (*Lyrical Poems* 127). In his autobiography, Austin related, "I also visited Marathon and sailed past Sunium's marble steep and repeated the closing couplet of his splendid poem ["The Isles of Greece"]: 'A land of slaves shall ne'er be mine:— / Dash down your cup of Samian wine'" (II.146). Yet a page before reciting lines from the universal anthem of Greek freedom, Austin commented on domestic reforms in Turkey after its defeat by Russia in 1877: "As I write these words, the transformation of Turkey from a despotically and infamously ruled State to a self-governing and self-conscious Nation has taken place, the territorial expansion of Greece seems more remote than ever" (II.145). Where Southey in the 1820s had worried that the beatification of Byron would help a liberal agenda, in the 1880s Austin felt that he could embrace Byron but not the cause for which the poet had given his life. But the authors who supported Turkey, Austin included, refrained from composing celebratory verses about Turkey's victory over Greece in 1897. The Turkish army won on the field of battle, but philhellenic sentiment reigned supreme in English and American verse.

During the late 1870s, the call went out for the new Byrons of the emerging Balkan peoples. Gladstone stated that Montenegro would "long ere this, have risen to world-wide and immortal fame, had there been a Scott to learn and tell the marvels of its history, or a Byron to spend and be spent on its behalf. For want of a *vates sacer*, it has remained in the mute, inglorious condition of Agamemnon's predecessors. . . . I hope that an interpreter between Montenegro and the world has at length been found in the person of my friend Mr. Tennyson, and gladly accept the honour of having been invited to supply a commentary to his text" ("Montenegro" 360). Gladstone referred to Tennyson's sonnet "Montenegro," which preceded the politician's article in the May 1877 issue of *Nineteenth Century*. Just as Mazzini encouraged Swinburne to become a Byron of Italy, it appears that Gladstone approached Tennyson on the subject of the Montenegrins, and the poet sent the piece to the politician for approval before publication (Thorn 445). In the poem, Tennyson depicted an entire nation of klephts:

> They rose to where the sovran eagle sails,
> They kept their faith, their freedom, on the height,
> Chaste, frugal, savage, armed by day and night
> Against the Turk; whose inroad nowhere scales
> Their headlong passes . . .
> O smallest among peoples! rough rock-throne
> Of Freedom! warriors beating back the swarm
> Of Turkish Islam for five hundred years,
> Great Tsernogora! never since thine own
> Black ridges drew the cloud and brake the storm
> Has breathed a race of mightier mountaineers.
>
> (3:24)

If Gladstone hoped that Tennyson would become the "poet of Montenegro" to rival the "poet of Greece," he was soon to be disappointed. When, in 1877, with the Turks pressing upon the Montenegrins and the Serbians, Russia declared war on the Ottomans and advanced to the gates of Constantinople, the proposed poet of Montenegro switched sides. According to Thorn, "despite the sentiments of his poem, Tennyson held on too strongly to the vestiges of the old Crimean spirit not to share the Tory alarm at this Russian victory" (448).

Gladstone did not have to recruit a "poet of Bulgaria"; a young writer applied for the post. Oscar Wilde sent Gladstone his "Sonnet on the Massacre of the Bulgarian Christians," suggesting that the influential politician

"recommend the sonnet to the *Nineteenth Century* or the *Spectator*" (Ell-
mann 82). The poem was composed a short while before Wilde worked on
"Ravenna," in which the major figures are Dante and Byron. Of the latter,
Wilde wrote with a typical philhellenic flourish:

> O Hellas! Hellas! in thine hour of pride,
> Thy day of might, remember him who died,
> To wrest from thy limbs the trammelling chain:
> O Salamis! O lone Plataean plain!
> O tossing waves of wide Eubeoan sea!
> O wind-swept heights of lone Thermopylae!
> He loved you well—ay, not alone in word,
> Who freely gave to thee his lyre and sword,
> Like Aeschylus at well-fought Marathon!
>
> (34)

Contemporaries who understood the expanding spirit of the philhellenism of the late 1870s would read these verses of "Ravenna," Wilde's
membership in the London Greek Committee from 1879 to 1881, and the
Bulgarian sonnet as "the connected limbs of one and the same transaction,"
to use Gladstone's phrase. But, despite his admonition to Greece to remember Byron, Wilde, like Tennyson, composed just one brief offering in support of freedom in the Balkans. The literature of Balkan freedom did not
produce a single work that has entered the English or American canon, in
large part because it originated as a derivative branch of an already ossified
philhellenic language.

William Watson made a more determined effort to become "the poet of
the Armenians" with his two volumes *The Purple East* (1896) and *The Year
of Shame* (1897), works that expressed outrage at the massacre of thousands
of Armenians in the late 1890s.[15] Watson employed a new twist on the theme
of regeneration; in his work it was England that had fallen from its past
greatness. He refers to "this corpse of England's Honour" in "A Hurried
Funeral" (*Year of Shame* 32). In "The Awakening," a poem near the end of
The Year of Shame, he wrote: "Behold, she is risen who lay asleep so long /
Our England, our Beloved!" (65). Watson transposed to an England that
needed to recover its role as a moral agent in the world the rhetoric of an
awakening Greece, which he himself had employed in "Hellas, Hail":
"Fiercely sweet as stormy Springs, / Mighty hopes are blowing wide; / Pas-
sionate prefigurings / Of a world re-vivified" (*Hope of the World* 73).

Watson's transposition of the philhellenic rhetoric of regeneration to
England rather than Armenia points to a central difficulty of the poetry of
wider philhellenism.[16] The public and often the poets themselves had little
knowledge of and slight emotional ties to Oriental Christians other than the

Greeks. In 1915, Noel and Charles Buxton observed, "Serbia, Roumania, and the rest are to most of us mere names" (*War and the Balkans* 34), and the situation was even worse in earlier decades. The Buxtons added, "Many people who have formed no clear conception of the other States are well acquainted with the Kingdom which occupies the territory of ancient Hellas" (61). Even more telling, no one saw the liberation of the Bulgarians or Serbians as an objective correlative for their own condition. At the height of the Bulgarian agitation, George Eliot commented that the "prospects of our western civilization seem more critically involved in the maintenance of the French Republic than in the result of the Bulgarian struggle—momentous as that too is felt to be by prophetic souls" (*Letters* 6.409). Philhellenism, in what Freeman would call the "narrow" sense, survived the attempt at expansion precisely because many intellectuals in the West, still touched by the grandeur and simplicity of Winckelmann's ancients, continued to see in the possible regeneration of the Greeks "passionate prefigurings of a world re-vivified."

One prominent literary philhellene rejected Balkan philhellenism for the pure spirit of pagan and revolutionary Greece. Perhaps Algernon Charles Swinburne refused to take up the cause of the Bulgarians because he thought they had no real connection to the all-important Hellenic heritage. Or perhaps he simply rejected any alliance with High Churchmen. The plain fact is that the man who wrote a series of poems in support of Greek aspirations also wrote, in "The Ballad of Bulgarie," a scathingly satirical picture of the Bulgarian agitation and its principal leaders (although written in 1876, the piece was not privately printed until 1893). Whatever his reason, Swinburne's opinion of the Gladstonian expansion of philhellenic sentiment was perceptive. Radical philhellenism did not completely lose its soul when it was incorporated into the larger, less-focused umbrella of Gladstonian policy in the East; it could still point to a William Morris. But such people were now a small part of a larger landscape. Those philhellenic voices that called for the advance of liberty throughout the West by the same means as were advocated in the East against the Turks and that looked to a regenerated Greece to alter not just aesthetics but political and social life in Europe grew more and more faint.

The events of the late 1870s—the Bulgarian atrocities of 1876, the Serbian and Montenegrin wars against the Ottoman Empire, the Russo-Turkish War of 1877, and the Treaty of Berlin in 1878—did not immediately affect writing about Greece, as the discussion about the response to the war of 1897 has shown. But they significantly changed the map of southeastern Europe in the mind of the West for the first time since the Greek revolt of 1770. The new perspective can be summed up in a single adjective, Balkan. The word is so omnipresent in our current geographical thinking that we often forget that it has only been used to refer to a particular region of Europe for a little more than a century. Before 1876, the term Balkan was rare and almost entirely used to denote a range of mountains, like the words Alps or Rockies. For example, Mackenzie and Irby's well-known account of their journeys in the region between Salonica and Vienna, published in 1866, was entitled *Travels in the Slavonic Provinces of Turkey-in-Europe*. By 1886, however, "Balkan" signified an area extending from Dubrovnik to Constantinople and from the Hungarian border to Crete.[17] By the early twentieth century, it had acquired the further meanings of "fractious" and "unsophisticated," which led to the cognate word *Balkanize* as in Paul Scott Mowrer's *Balkanized Europe* (1921), since these were perceived as the preeminent characteristics of the people living in the region.

Edward Lear's travel book, *Journal of a Landscape Painter in Albania and Illyria*, provides a good example of the unclear picture of the Balkan region prior to 1876 and also illustrates why philhellenic rhetoric was so readily and easily extended beyond the apparent Greek world. Lear stated in his introduction that his book recounts two journeys: "the first, from Saloniki in a north-western direction through ancient Macedonia, to Illyrian Albania, and by the western coast through Epirus to the boundary of modern Greece at the Gulf of Arta;—the second in Epirus and Thessaly" (1). The last sentence of the book reads: "And so, with the last point of Zakynthus and the dim, distant mountains of Kefalonia, ends my journey in the lands of Greece" (428). Are Lear's Albania and Illyria in the title part of the lands of Greece? At least one reader appeared to think so, for Alfred Tennyson entitled his poem honoring the volume "To E. L. on his Travels in Greece."

When Disraeli made the Albanian hero Skanderberg a Greek in his novel *The Rise of Iskander* (1831), he was not attempting to rewrite history nor erase Albanian identity. He just did not view *Greek* and *Albanian* as mutually exclusive terms. Further, the words *Christian* and *Greek* often seem interchangeable when used in opposition to *Turk* in nineteenth-century philhellenic rhetoric. If an area was not Turkish it could, by default, be called Greek.[18] The question of where Greece ended was further complicated by the tendency of nineteenth-century philhellenes to advocate the replacement of the Ottoman Empire with a new Greek or Greco–Slav state. Gladstone had endorsed a new Greek empire centered in Constantinople in the *Gentleman's Magazine* for July 1856. Mazzini put forward the idea of a Greco–Slav republic whose borders resembled those of the Byzantine Empire. In a letter to Jesse White in 1857, he envisioned a federated Europe, one of whose members was to be "Helleneia (Greece) having Epirus, Thessalia, Albania, Macedonia, Rumelia, reaching the Balkan mountains, including Constantinople. Constantinople to be the central town under a Greek presidency of a confederation of races (European and Christian) now constituting the 'Turkish empire'" (Mack Smith 156). The logic behind such thinking was that, as Allen Upward stated, "the Bulgarians have received their religion, and such civilization as they possess, from the Greeks" (*East End of Europe* 10–11). A traveler after 1876 might still, to use the words of a character from Edward Whittemore's novel *Nile Shadows* (1983), never be able "to get the Balkans straight" in his mind (259), but he was now aware of the presence of Serbians, Bulgarians, and Montenegrins. And though conflicting maps might read Albania, Epirus, or Illyria, he had no doubt about where he was—in the Balkans, as the titles of innumerable books attest.[19]

Where Greece had possessed a split personality of ancient/West versus modern/Orient in the mind of the early nineteenth-century West, it now acquired a new schizophrenia of ancient/Western Europe versus modern/Eastern Europe or, more precisely, Balkan Europe.[20] As before, it was the classical past that provided the "Western" half of the construction. Winston Churchill underscored the point when in his famous "iron curtain" speech in Fulton, Missouri, he said that from Stettin on the Baltic to Trieste on the Adriatic, "only Athens—Greece with her immortal glories" had escaped Soviet domination ("The Iron Curtain" 103–4). He could just as well have said, "Greece *because* of her immortal glories." For the West, Greece was "theirs" in a way Poland, Hungary, and Romania were not, and that notion had colored Western Europe's relationship to Greece from 1770.[21] Yet, at the same time that Western Europe acknowledged that connection by including Greece as the only geographically Eastern European nation in "Western Europe," it simultaneously lamented the fact that modern Greece did not really fit into Western Europe because it remained, to a large extent, culturally Balkan.

There is nothing redeeming in a connection with the Balkans. In the early nineteenth century, when Greece was envisioned between East and West, the negative perception of Eastern tyranny and Islamic faith was at least partly balanced by an exotic, "Arabian Nights" image of the Orient. But such exoticism belonged in the Orient, not in Europe. Harry De Windt called his account of a Balkan journey *Through Savage Europe* (1907) and defended his title as follows: "the term [savage] accurately describes the wild and lawless customs between the Adriatic and the Black Seas" (15). De Windt intended his readers to be struck, if not shocked, by his oxymoronic title—no one would question "savage Turkey," "savage Africa," or even "savage China." Europe, by definition, was not savage. The penultimate chapter of James Pettifer's book *The Greeks* (1993) is entitled "A Balkan or European Future," which suggests that "Balkan" and "European" remain conflicting categories.

In literature in English before World War I, the Balkans were usually portrayed as farcical little states or unstable hotbeds of intrigue, as in E. F. Benson's *Princess Sophia* (1900) and Allen Upward's *Prince of Balkistan* (1895).[22] The best-known work set in the region was, of course, Shaw's *Arms and the Man* (1894), which the author later called a "sketch of the theatrical nature of the first apings of Western civilization by spirited races just emerging

from slavery" (*Complete Prefaces* 50). The positive, even heroic, view of the
Bulgarian independence movement in Ivan Turgenev's *On the Eve* (1859)
found no echo in fiction in English nor did the English translation of the
Bulgarian author Ivan Vazov's novel *Under the Yoke: A Romance of the Bulgarian Uprising*, which appeared in 1893 with an introduction by Edmund
Gosse. The lack of effect of the English version of Vazov's novel, the first
great work of Bulgarian fiction, can best be measured by the fact that it was
followed a year later by the depiction of backward Bulgarians in Shaw's
Arms and the Man.

In English and American writing about Greece, *Balkan* is almost always a
term of disparagement. In Henry Miller's *Colossus of Maroussi*, the word
Greek has a universally positive value. He writes of how the "Greek earth
opens to me like the Book of Revelation" (241; see also 40). Yet Miller encountered certain phenomena in Greece that he cannot refer to as "Greek":
"I walked to the edge of the town where as always in the Balkans everything
comes to an end abruptly, as though the monarch who designed this weird
creation had suddenly become demented leaving the gate swinging on one
hinge" (114). The gate swinging on one hinge, the perfect symbol of an inept
civilization, had to be "Balkan." When Miller wrote the phrase "as always in
the Balkans," he might just as well have written "as always in Greece," since
his knowledge of the Balkans was limited to his experience in Greece. But
Miller knew even before he left Paris how to distinguish between what was
Greek and what was *Balkan* in modern Greece.

Benson's *Princess Sophia* illustrates how quickly *Balkan* had come to signify modern Greece's other half, the thing against which Greece had to be
defined even though it shared a common geography and culture. The novel
relates how a fictional Balkan principality called Rhodope, filled with picturesque peasants and an upper class, to paraphrase Shaw, in their first apings of
Western civilization, was turned into a casino by a ruler who became enamored of Monte Carlo. Benson never visited the area where he placed Rhodope, apparently either Albania or Montenegro, but described Greece at the
time of the war of 1897 as "an astonishing little kingdom the like of which,
outside of pure fiction, will never again exist in Europe" (*As We Were* 134).
Princess Sophia is, quite simply, Benson's witty, satirical sketch of modern,
"Balkan" Greece. But, unlike Edmond About in *The King of the Mountains*,
he chose not to set his comic portrait of Greece within Greece. He may have
been checked by his youthful attraction to the Hellenic ideal and his admiration of the Greek Revolution, which he so eulogistically depicted in *The Vintage* and *The Capsina*. *Princess Sophia*, published one year after the second of
Benson's novels about the War of Independence, is a perfect example of how
philhellenic authors attempted to banish the Balkan Other within Greece beyond its boundaries. Rather than finding new springs of inspiration in the
juxtaposition of the old Hellenism and the new geographical configuration

of southeastern Europe, Benson kept Greece as "Greece" by placing Greece's Balkan character north of the border.

Shaw exhibited something of the same impulse. He used the Serbo-Bulgarian conflict of 1885 to deconstruct outdated concepts of romance and heroism in *Arms and the Man*. In *Major Barbara* (1905), however, the Greco-Turkish War of 1897 was invoked in the course of a vastly different lesson. At the end of the play, the Greek professor and soon-to-be munitions manufacturer Cusins says that an artillery shell can destroy "the higher powers just as a tiger can destroy a man: there Man must master that power first. I admitted this when the Turks and Greeks were last at war. My best pupil went out to fight for Hellas. My parting gift to him was not a copy of Plato's Republic, but a revolver and a hundred Undershaft cartridges. The blood of every Turk he killed—if he shot any—is on my head as well as that of Undershaft's" (*Collected Plays* III.182). Cusins does not imply that his student should not have enlisted in the Greek cause nor that he should not have given the young man a revolver. He uses a confrontation of Greeks and Turks as an example of men having to confront evil with evil because his audience, or most of his audience, would agree with Cusins's reasoning in such a circumstance. For Shaw, as for Benson, that significance does not extend to the first apings of Western civilization beyond the northern frontier in Serbia or Bulgaria.

Gladstone's vision of a harmonious Balkan federation soon proved itself to be a utopian fantasy. With the increase in interest in the Balkans in the 1870s, there was the consequent increase in travelers' handbooks about the region. Rebecca West explained: "The problems of India and Africa never produced anything like the jungle of savage pamphlets that sprang up in the footsteps of the liberals who visited Turkey in Europe under the inspiration of Gladstone" (21). She continued:

> English persons, therefore, of humanitarian and reformist disposition constantly went out to the Balkan peninsula to see who was in fact ill-treating whom, and, being by the very nature of their perfectionist faith unable to accept the horrid hypothesis that everybody was ill-treating everybody else, all came back with a pet Balkan people established in their hearts as suffering and innocent, eternally massacree and never massacrer. The same sort of person, devoted to good works and austerities, who is traditionally supposed to keep a cat and a parrot, often set up on their hearth the image of the Albanian or Bulgarian or the Serbian or the Macedonian Greek people which had all the force and blandness of pious fantasy. (20)

One such visitor of humanitarian disposition was Mabel Moore, who remarked: "Possibly the Greeks may be exasperating to their neighbors but I do not believe they are guilty of butchery. . . . the proud, ultimate challenge of the Greek is that he has never, in all the ages of history, raised his hand against defenceless women and children" (137). Clearly, she did not know her Thucydides well. On the Macedonian issue, she said, "I wish they [the Greeks] might have Macedonia all to themselves, for they do want it badly, and wish for it so sincerely and so whole-heartedly" (135).[23] This has all the blandness of the pious fantasies condemned by West.

Those who had championed the freedom of both the Serbians and the Bulgarians in the late 1870s were faced less than a decade later with the Serbo-Bulgarian War of 1885. Shaw undoubtedly chose this conflict as the setting for his critique of "our heroic ideas" in *Arms and the Man* because it revealed some of the conflicts and incoherence of Liberal idealism. But the central battleground of both the Balkan nations and their Western supporters was Macedonia in the last decade of the nineteenth century and the first decade of the twentieth century. Gladstone, still bearing the banner of "wider philhellenism" as late as 1897, found the dissension between the liberated peoples extremely distasteful: "Next to the Ottoman Government nothing can be more deplorable and blameworthy than the jealousies between Greek and Slav, and plans by States already existing for appropriating other territory. Why not Macedonia for the Macedonians, as well as Bulgaria for the Bulgarians and Servia for the Servians. And if they are all small and weak, let them bind themselves together for defence, so they may not be scattered by others, either great or small, which would probably be the effect of their quarreling among themselves" ("Macedonian Question" 4). Allen Upward, a philhellene, asserted that the phrase "Macedonia for the Macedonians" "could not have been used by any man of impartiality or intelligence who possessed first-hand knowledge of the country" (*East End of Europe* 27). G. W. Steevens, a Turkophile with the Ottoman army in 1897, adducing "at least six different kinds of Macedonians," used the absurdity of the phrase to argue that only continued Turkish rule in Macedonia and Thrace could prevent total anarchy (*With the Conquering Turk* 3).

Upward stated that a visitor to Macedonia "may be a Philhellenic or a Bulgarophile, but cannot be both" (*East End of Europe* 104). He then quoted from a reporter in Athens who complained that "it is most disheartening to see the Liberal press, especially the *Tribune*, does not only overlook all Greek grievances or arguments in their favor, but has lately started a systematic counter-campaign against Hellenism in general, reproducing and bringing forward before the eyes of the public all the abuse obviously obtained from Bulgarian sources" (46). Before 1876, philhellenism had been "the foremost sign of liberal sentiment." But by 1906, many Liberals had deserted the cause of the Greeks for that of the Bulgarians.[24] Indeed, the only distinctive sign of liberal sentiment was now opposition to the Turks, whose only apologists were diehard Tories and other conservatives, like novelist Marmaduke Pickthall, who were still wedded to the old policy of Disraeli. Hector Herbert

Munro, a conservative who wrote as Saki, satirized the chasm the Balkans had caused among Liberals in his story "The Oversight." While planning a dinner party, Lady Prowche consults with a friend to ensure that there will be no unpleasantness among the guests. She particularly inquires about two men of whom she knows next to nothing. "They're both of them moderate Liberal, Evangelical, mildly opposed to female suffrage," and, we discover later, both oppose vivisection of animals (515). Relieved, Lady Prowche puts the two men together. But after the party, she reports that they caused a scene. "'Hyenas could not have behaved with greater savagery. . . . They actually came to blows!' 'I thought they agreed on every subject that one could violently disagree about—religion, politics, vivisection, the Derby decision, the Falconer report; what else was left to quarrel about?' 'My dear, we were fools not to have thought of it. One of them was Pro-Greek and the other was Pro-Bulgar'" (517).

In the battle for hearts and minds in Europe and America, the Greeks had an enormous advantage, which could best be summed up by the *PanHellenic Review*'s assertion in 1879 that Greece was "the land where Homer lived, and Epaminondas bled; where Byron breathed his last, and from which he addressed the noblest of his poems as a farewell to the world" (vol. 1, no. 1, p. 2). Writing at the end of the second Balkan War in 1914, J. Irving Manatt asked, "Shall not the civilized world now pay some fraction of its incalculable debt to the old Greece by insisting on historic justice and fair play in settling accounts of a war in which the Greeks of to-day showed themselves the peers of the men who fought at Marathon and died at Thermopylae?" (xi–xii). The civilized world recognized no similar debt to the Bulgarians or Serbs. Indeed, Demetra Vaka Brown quoted a Bulgarian boasting: "When we get to Athens, we shall tear down the Acropolis stone by stone" (*Heart of the Balkans* 201). Neocles Kasasis reminded readers that the Bulgarians had followed the Hunnish horde of Attila and "were not in the least changed since" (13).

The value of the Greek past was clear to the other Balkan nations and their apologists. Since it was impossible to diminish that hold on the Western imagination, the best for which they could strive was to seize upon as much of the glorious heritage as they could. Such a strategy derived naturally from the extension of the philhellenism of the 1870s, which had attempted to legitimize the aspirations of all of the Balkan nations by covering them with the philhellenic mantle. In 1908, Allen Upward protested that the Bulgarians, in order to justify their claims to the region between Epirus and Thrace, seized upon "Macedonia, a name with no more definite signification than Wessex or Languedoc. Unfortunately for themselves [the Bulgarians], the Greeks had been the first to make use of this name, and to give it wide extension to the north in the interests of Hellenism" (*East End of Europe* 26). In *The Shade of the Balkans* (1904), a collection of Bulgarian folk songs made by Henry Bernard, the Bulgarian poet Pencho Slaveikoff wrote: "Our songs of mythology have in them palpable signs showing how close they used to be united to those songs and legends of ancient Greece. It is interesting to know that some of those legends are kept alive by the Bulgars, whereas they have apparently been dropped from the poetic baggage of modern Greece" (54). Edith Durham, the preeminent champion of the Albanians in the English-speaking world, declared that the independence of Greece "had been largely obtained by Albanian aid" (*Burden of the Balkans* 41). In 1941, Rebecca West described the Serbs as "the last legatees of the Byzantine empire in all its law and magnificence," quietly erasing the modern Greeks from any claim to the succession (1149).[25] It was, however, an uphill battle. First, these writers did not challenge the legitimacy of the philhellenic legacy but rather attempted to appropriate it. But by leaving intact the magic force of Greece, they handed an immense advantage to the people who were still called Greeks. Second, when Western readers thought of ancient Greece, they had an image of the Parthenon, and when they thought of modern Greece, they recalled *Childe Harold* and "The Isles of Greece." When they thought of Bulgaria, they might well remember that, according to Shaw, Bulgarians did not wash their hands.

Still, the partisans of the other Balkan nations were, on the whole, rather mild on the subject of the Greeks, especially when one considers that, from 1897 until 1912, a guerrilla war was waged among Greek, Bulgarian, and Serbian bands in Macedonia.[26] Bulgarophiles abroad realized that there was little propaganda value in an attack on the Greeks, toward whom many Westerners still felt a sentimental attraction. The image of the terrible Turk, on the other hand, was still powerful in the West and a far more useful card to play. So, for example, while Arthur Howden Smith made passing remarks about the low character of the Greeks in *Fighting the Turk in the Balkans* (1908), he never mentioned that the Bulgarian band with whom he traveled was also fighting the Greeks in Macedonia. There would, one supposes, have been far less romance in such an endeavor. Further, as Harold Spender succinctly put it, "the bear [Turkey] is not yet slain, and the Balkan states are not likely to divide the bear's skin before the animal is dead" ("Never Again" 30). The appearance of Harold Spender's name, along with that of men like Sir Charles Dilke and William Pember Reeves, on the list of both the pro-Bulgarian Balkan Committee and the Anglo-Hellenic Leagues in the first decade of the twentieth century indicates another reason for the moderation in the attacks on each other by Bulgarophiles and philhellenes. The Gladstonian dream of a Balkan federation survived in important circles of the Liberal party up until 1913, despite the fact that the various Balkan peoples were already engaged in a bloody struggle for Macedonia.

On the other side, philhellenes had little to gain by demonizing the Bulgarians or Albanians.[27] So, even though the Greek bands in Macedonia often worked in collusion with the Turkish authorities against the Bulgarians,[28] philhellenism abroad continued to focus its attacks on Ottoman rule. There is nothing in English remotely resembling the Greek author Ion Dragoumis's *Blood of Martyrs and Heroes*, which glorified the guerrilla struggles of the Greek bands against the Bulgarians. The discrepancy between the attitude toward the Macedonian struggle within Greece and that of philhellenes abroad can be seen in the response to the death of Pavlos Melas, a leading figure in the Macedonian struggle. All Greece mourned Melas, indeed, Dakin wrote that on the announcement of his death: "All work stopped—just as eighty years earlier on the occasion of Byron's death at Missalonghi; everyone walked around mournfully in the streets and squares; and the church bells tolled the passing of a national hero" (*Greek Struggle in Macedonia* 191). Melas remains a revered figure in Greece. Yet, to my knowledge, his name appears just once in British or American philhellenic literature of the period, in the decidedly second-rate composition by Ronald Burrows: "Red the blood's that flowed for Hellas, / Varatassis died and Melas" (Glasgow 161).

Although the Greeks and Bulgarians would be at odds, and often at war, during much of the first half of the twentieth century, the Bulgarians never became the villains of philhellenic literature. That role was reserved for the Turks, the Germans, and the Communists. The Bulgarians may have been a threat to Greece, but they were never a threat to Western civilization as it was conceived in France, Britain, or America. And since the intellectuals in those countries transposed their concerns about Western civilization onto Greece, there was no place for the Bulgarian problem in most Western writing about Greece.

The main effect of the diffusion of philhellenic sentiment among various Balkan peoples was that the number of true, or "narrow" philhellenes, never a large number, was reduced even further. Allen Upward claimed, "Philhellenism has been confined to a small number of enthusiasts" (*East End of Europe* 80). The challenge of the Gladstonian extension of philhellenic rhetoric did not cause a new reevaluation or reappraisal of the literary construction of Greece. If anything, the attempted appropriation of the Byronic mantle led authors to cling even more firmly to the Byronic tradition and so served to further discourage any reconsideration of the magic force of philhellenic legend. Whether that stance was a wise decision politically might be open to debate. From an aesthetic point of view, however, it encouraged the perception that the springs of inspiration had indeed run dry in Greece.

The first significant change in the romance of Greek liberation occurred in Justin McCarthy's *Maid of Athens* (1883), published less than a decade after the Bulgarian agitation. The heroine is "an English girl, who was born in Athens, and has always lived there with her mother. She's pretty and clever and above all a Greek patriot and all that, and the English there have taken it into their heads to call her the Maid of Athens, I am told" (I.8). Her name, appropriately enough, is Athena, and the reader first encounters her on the Acropolis in front of the Parthenon. The hero is Kelvin Cleveland, a philhellenic Englishman who had first arrived in Greece with "a fever mood of Hellenic enthusiasm" that he described as "a rapture blended of an impossible past and an unattainable present." "I, too, felt myself a Greek; I, too, knew that I must have been a Greek; I must have worshipped my mother Athens under Pericles, and visited Socrates in prison. But I was also full of heroic thoughts . . . of the great unfinished struggle for Greek independence; and I longed for a renewal of that struggle, with my own chivalric form, to be sure, as a volunteer in the midst of it" (I.13). The romantic triangle is completed by Constantine Margarites, an aspiring but deceitful young Greek politician.

Athena becomes engaged to marry the Greek Constantine in order to further her philhellenic dreams of a Greater Greece. The announcement prompts the following outburst from Sir Thomas Vale, an Englishman visiting Athens: "Marry a Greek! Oh no, no; surely not; that would never do— quite impossible, I should say. A charming young English lady marry a Greek! Will no young Englishman intervene?" (III.15). Vale is presented as something of a Turkophile, so his feelings should not be instantly taken as the sentiment of the author. But in the end, of course, the English heroine, does indeed marry her Western suitor.

In McCarthy's version of the Greek romance, the Greek female has been dropped from the story in favor of an English female, although one born in Greece. Yet the only difference between Athena and earlier Greek heroines is her nationality; in all other respects she retains the position as the personification of modern Greece (see I.66, where Athena is described as "some sort of Macaria sacrificing herself for Athens," and I.77, where Athena says that she thought of herself as Myrrha, the Greek slave in Byron's *Sardanapalus*). Despite Sir Thomas Vale's objection about the joining of an Englishwoman with a Greek man, that is *not* the motivating factor behind the author's decision to alter his heroine's ethnicity. Western girls had rarely married Greeks in the Greek romances. Rather, the change from Greek to English female ensures that the Western hero will marry a Western woman. In short, McCarthy's new formulation of the romance raises, for the first time, nagging questions about the place of the Greek female in the European family. It is hard not to link McCarthy's reservations about Greek ethnicity, which are so clearly implied in his shift of the heroine's nationality, and the emergence of the conception of the Balkans, which had occurred just a decade or so earlier. When the choice was simply between the West or Turkey, Greeks were invariably associated with the West. But after 1876, Greece was conceptually incorporated into a predominantly Slavic region, and the issue of its place in the West became, even for some philhellenes, less self-evident.

The confusion caused by the new geographical configuration is apparent in McCarthy's book. The title, *Maid of Athens*, points directly back to Byron and the philhellenic tradition. But the manner in which McCarthy constructs his version of the Greek romance could well be called Fallmerayer's revenge. The German scholar had argued that the modern Greeks were really Slavs, and he certainly would have reveled in the fact that a prominent philhellene like McCarthy now had enough questions about the racial background of contemporary Greeks to employ an English heroine.

McCarthy was not the only writer who had doubts about the Greek female's place in the established romance of liberation. In *Like Another Helen* (1900), George Horton's American philhellene expresses reservations about how the beautiful Cretan Panayotta would fit into Boston society (see chap. 4). In his *A Fair Brigand* (1897), Kyriakoula, the sister of a mountain klepht who is called a "cross between a wild rose and a tigress" (71), stabs her former lover in the middle of a fashionable party at the end of the book. Her similarity to her lawless brother implies that she, like the heroine of *Like Another Helen*, is innately too wild for civilized society. Kyriakoula would seem to be a Greek who has the passion and fire of the "Eastern" female, yet she is never unequivocally Greek. One description of her ends, "these *Albanian* women are perfect devils when they get started" (79, my italics; she is also called an Albanian on 329). The American heroes, or rather antiheroes, in both of these novels are also deeply flawed. The philhellene in *Like Another Helen* is a young cad, and the self-absorbed archaeologist in *A Fair Brigand* only marries the Greek girl who saved his life because he cannot find another means of escape. But there are no such extenuating circumstances in Horton's *The Monk's Treasure* (1905), in which Horton's image of a "modern Nausicaa" (42), whose pose seemed "as though it had been carved out of Pentelic marble by some pupil of Phidias" (44) and who is descended from refugees of the massacre on Scio, turns out to be an Italian in origin, a fact that helps to justify her natural superiority to the other islanders, her rejection of her Greek fiancé, and her suitability for life in America.[29] A scholar in *The Monk's Treasure* declares, "I am not of those who hold with Professor Fallmerayer that the Greeks are *all* Slavonians" (126, my italics). The dilemma for Horton, McCarthy, and other philhellenes was to recognize who were the Greeks and who were the Slavonians or, in the case of Kyriakoula in *A Fair Brigand*, the Albanians. At times, it seemed this was so difficult that it was easier and safer to import a heroine from the West.[30]

It is important to stress that McCarthy, like Horton, had an impeccable reputation as a philhellene.[31] McCarthy's name appears in the list of the London Greek Committee members from 1879 to 1881. He visited Greece more than once and wrote some poems on classical Greek themes in *Serapion and Other Poems*. His novel openly espoused Greece's claim to Thessaly,

Epirus, Crete, and other areas and presented active measures to ensure those claims as noble and heroic. The oddity is that it expressed a philhellenism without either a Greek hero or a Greek heroine. Mr. Vlachos's explanation as to why so many foreigners in Athens enlist in the cause of Greece points out the disjunction that occurs when the heroine in the romance is herself no longer Greek: "Did not all your great men busy themselves about Greek independence? . . . Besides, in this case it is not Greece alone: there is the beautiful English girl" (I.137–38).

There was no consensus about the cultural identity of the Greek female among English and American authors at the end of the nineteenth century. While McCarthy and Horton seemed uncertain about her European status, in Anthony Hope's *Phroso*, Edmonds's *Amygdala*, and Bohun Lynch's *Glamour*, Greek women are "married" into the European family just as they had been in previous decades. About the Otherness or Easternness of the Greek male there was general unanimity. When a Greek male left the homosocial world of the klephtic band, it seems that he immediately became as much a sexual threat to both Greek and Western women as a Turk.

The main Greek character in McCarthy's *Maid of Athens* has taken the place of the Turk in the romantic triangle. McCarthy, again apparently building on the arguments of Fallmerayer, justified his negative portrayal of Constantine by stressing his mixed "Levantine" background ("There is a difference, after all, between Greek and Levantine," I.2). An English character says of Constantine: "His morality clearly was not our morality; his code of honour was not our code of honour" (III.65). The real Greeks in McCarthy's book are men from the islands (I.80) or the klephts of the mountains (II.189–95), who are still pure in blood and ethnic spirit.[32] In *Glamour: A Tale of Modern Greece* (1912), Bohun Lynch distinguished between the Greeks of Athens, who are a "mongrel, mongering race" (55) and the Ypsiladiotes, a mountain people "all nobly made and beautiful" who are "living in what is, after all, Europe, but so remote from any modern influence that they believe—actually, positively, openly believe—that satyrs sweep down upon them in night time" (169–70).

After 1883, three basic versions of the Greek romance would exist side by side. One would replicate the Byronic original in which a Turk, or later a German, would appear as the embodiment of tyranny. Greece would be personified by a beautiful Greek female with Praxitelean features, and the hero would be a Western philhellene with Byronic dreams. This construction appears in such works as Edmonds's *Amygdala: A Tale of the Greek Revolution* (1894), Lafayette McClaws's *Maid of Athens* (1904), Horton's *Like Another Helen* (1900), Demetra Vaka Brown's *Grasp of the Sultan* (1917) and *In Pawn to a Throne* (1919), and Hocking's *Tommy and the Maid of Athens* (1917).

In the second version of the romance, the Greek female remains the romantic heroine, but a Greek male replaces the Turk as the sexual threat. In Lynch's *Glamour*, the villain, as in McCarthy, is one of the mixed and corrupted Greek politicians from the city of Athens, who tries to force the beautiful village girl Chrysoula into marriage.[33] The equation between the Greek male and the Turk is particularly evident in Anthony Hope's *Phroso* (1894), which is set on a Greek island still under Ottoman control. The hero, Lord Wheatley, whose friends attribute his journey to the island of Neopalia to the fact that he has "been reading old Byron again" (24), must first save Euphrosyne from her treacherous cousin Constantine and then from the clutches of the Turkish governor, Mouraki Pasha. In neither book is liberation from Turkish rule a major part of the plot, although it remains in the background of both. Lynch made several references to the fighting in Macedonia and the hero's desire to participate in it (65–67, 207–8), while Hope referred to Mouraki Pasha's tyranny of the islanders (228, 249).

The third group followed McCarthy's lead and imported a Western female into Greece, such as the Italian heroine of Horton's *The Monk's Treasure*. Richard Harding Davis's comic play *The Galloper*, set during the war of 1897, expressed philhellenic sentiments but included two American women serving as Red Cross nurses. Jane Aiken Hodge's *Greek Wedding* (1970), set during the Greek War of Independence, had an American girl with strong philhellenic sentiments, who must first be rescued from a harem in Constantinople and then from the fortress of a Greek pirate by a countryman of Lord Byron. As there neither is a Greek in the wedding ceremony nor is the event held in Greece proper, Hodge's title might baffle a reader who did not realize that philhellenic writing no longer needed Greeks. The Byronic backdrop of political philhellenism gave romance in Greece a "spell" or "glamour," even if there were no integral connection between romance and politics. In Stephen Crane's *Active Service* (1899), set during the war of 1897, the hero muses, "War and love—war and Margery—were in conjunction—both in Greece—and he could tilt with one lance at both gods" (*Works* 3.157). But philhellenism and the fight against the Turks are totally extraneous to the plot; neither the American heroine, Margery; her father, the archaeologist; nor the hero, Rufus Coleman, are involved with the political fortunes of Greece nor even possess strong philhellenic sentiments. Yet, as Crane was aware, one needed only to say, "War and love . . . were in conjunction—both in Greece," and the reader would supply a whole set of Byronic dreams to the words on his page.

In only a few novels and stories do Greek heroines marry Greeks, such as Edmonds's "Daughter of Crete" (1891) and Mayo's *Daughter of the Klephts* (1897). In both cases, as the titles clearly reveal, the focus is on the Greek females while their male counterparts remain in the background.[34]

It is significant, and perhaps not surprising, that the first updated version of the romance of liberation in which a Greek man appears as the central hero, *A Man of Athens* (1916), whose very title inverts the gender of the phrase "Maid of Athens," was written by a writer of Greek descent, Julia Dragoumis.

Although Western women began to be leading characters in some novels set in Greece after 1883, such as McCarthy's *Maid of Athens*, Crane's *Active Service*, Richard Harding Davis's *Princess Aline*, and Benson's *Limitations*, one does not find anything like the examination of the experience of the American or English girl in Italy that was so prevalent in the last quarter of the nineteenth century. Near the end of Henry James's *Portrait of a Lady*, Isabel Archer's relations to the ruins of Rome are described: "She had long before this taken old Rome into her confidence, for in a world of ruins the ruin of her own happiness seemed a less unnatural catastrophe. . . . She had become deeply, tenderly acquainted with Rome; it interfused and moderated her passion. But she had grown to think of it chiefly as a place where people suffered" (551). We are told that, on a trip to the Levant during "an interval that we are not closely concerned with her" (345), Isabel had "a thousand uses for her sense of the romantic, which was more active than it had been. I do not allude to the impulse it received as she gazed at the Pyramids in the course of an excursion from Cairo, or as she stood among the broken columns of the Acropolis and fixed her eyes upon the point designated to her as the strait of Salamis, deep and memorable as those emotions had remained" (351). Athens was always deep and memorable; it was also almost always off stage.

In George Gissing's *Emancipated*, the heroine, Miriam, like Isabel Archer, makes a trip to Greece "during an interval when we are not closely concerned with her." She might very well have a reverie about beauty at a classical temple, for Gissing's other character who makes an off-stage visit to Athens, Reardon in *New Grub Street*, recounts such an experience (369–70). But for Miriam, as for Isabel, "the name of Italy signified perilous enticement, and she was beginning to feel it" (204). In George Eliot's *Middlemarch*, Mr. Brooke has an album with pictures of memorable moments of his visit to Greece in his youth (22). But, once again, it is Italy and Rome that widen Dorothea Brooke's horizons. We sometimes hear of people traveling to Greece in novels by major writers, but we never see them there, and it is somewhat remarkable how little the place matters in their books. Some authors who traveled to Greece never published creative work based on that experience. In 1888, Edith Wharton took a cruise in the Aegean for four months, which, she says in her autobiography, *A Backward Glance*, was "the greatest step forward in my making" and left her with "inexhaustible memories" (98). Yet unlike her travels in Italy, she never used her memories of this journey through the Greek islands in her fiction.[35] Greece was not, as Lambropoulos put it, hospitable to the "bourgeois interiority" necessary for novels (57).

Where Rome conjured thoughts of decline and the passage of time, Athens was often associated with Winckelmann's serenity and grandeur. Richard Jenkyns noted, "There are very few [nineteenth-century] novels actually set in ancient Greece, and those insignificant. Lytton left *Pausanias the Spartan* unfinished, while Landor's *Pericles and Aspasia*, a collection of imaginary letters, merely illustrates why the novelists kept clear of Hellas. It is less a novel than a succession of moral reflections; Landor sees the Greeks not as real people but as heroic figures on a bas-relief" (79). This perception carried over to the classical places. As Leontis observed, for some authors the "incarnation of an eternal and universal beauty on the site of the Acropolis brings the viewer to 'the revelation of the divine'" (51).[36] Tom Carlingford, the hero of Benson's *Limitations*, says of his trip to Olympia: "For the first time in my life I feel fully sane. . . . I have seen perfection and I know what it means" (80). This has a predictable result: "So he gave himself up heart and soul to his religion. . . . he sat in the Dionysiac theatre and read Aristophanes; he spelt out shorter inscriptions with reverence; he walked to Eleusis by the Sacred Way; he sat an hour on the barrow of Marathon that holds the bones of the Greeks who conquered the Persians and died in victory. If this is to be mad, it is a pleasant thing to be mad, but it is a form of madness which is the outcome of youth and enthusiasm, and possibly genius." (83).

But where Isabel Archer could take Rome "into her confidence," on the Acropolis Tom Carlingford says that he "can only look and wonder" (78). The hero of Richard Harding Davis's *Princess Aline* (1895) tells a first-time visitor to Athens: "You are coming now, Miss Morris . . . into a land where one restores his lost illusions. Anyone who wants to get back his belief in beautiful things should do it here" (113). This consists, of course, in being overwhelmed by the beauty and serenity of the Acropolis. Where the ruins of Rome acted as a door to one's inner feelings, Greek ruins were thought to lead one away from the individual to abstract concepts, which was hardly amenable to bourgeois interiority. Benson's *Limitations*, like Gissing's *New Grub Street*, explores the psychological dilemma of an artist who has to balance an attraction to the purity of classical Greek art with the need to work and live in the modern world. Still, in Benson as in Gissing, Greece is where one comes "face to face with perfection" (*Limitations* 83), while England is where one struggles with the consequences of that vision.

Yet classical sites, with their fallen columns and marble pieces, also conjured up notions other than perfection, grandeur, and serenity.[37] In 1785, fifteen years after the revolt of 1770, Henry Home, Lord Kames, stated that Greek ruins had a political significance that made them inappropriate to imitate in English gardens. According to Home, Gothic ruins, operating in a manner similar to the Colosseum at Rome, exhibited "the triumph of time over strength; a melancholy, but not unpleasant thought: a Grecian ruin suggests rather the triumph of barbarity over taste; a gloomy and discouraging thought" (II.350). Home does not indicate whose barbarity was responsible for the gloomy and discouraging thoughts inspired by Greek ruins—Roman, Byzantine, or Turkish—but the latter would certainly have been present in a number of minds after the failure of the recent uprising.

Classical sites continued to convey a contemporary political meaning throughout the nineteenth century. Chateaubriand remarked of his visit to Greece: "Travellers who are content to visit civilized Europe are extremely fortunate: they penetrate not into those regions where the heart is wounded at every step; where living ruins every moment divert attention from the ruins of stone and marble. In vain would you give full scope in Greece to the illusion of the imagination: the mournful truth necessarily pursues you" (175). William Cullen Bryant made the following observation after a visit to the Acropolis around the middle of the nineteenth century: "In looking at these remains, one can hardly help asking oneself whether the Greeks of that early period, which produced works of art weaving such a stamp of calm greatness and employing such a fine harmony of the intellectual faculties, were not of a different character than the Greeks of the present day" (*Letters from the East* 219). Musings at the Colosseum rarely became occasions for inquiries into the ethnological origin of the Italians.

Greek ruins had, of course, been a central element in philhellenic art from the beginning; one need only recall the ancient column behind the bound Greek woman in the frontispiece to Choiseul-Gouffier's book. Throughout the nineteenth century Greek ruins continued to be linked to ideas about modern Greek freedom, as in Karl Krazeisen's painting of the War of Independence, *Greeks Fighting among Classical Ruins*, and Delacroix's *Greece Expiring on the Ruins of Missolonghi*; the opening set of "a temple in ruins and some columns prostrate and broken" in Deering's *Marco Bozzaris* (1851); and Cale Young Rice's poem of 1912, "In a Greek Temple (during the First Balkan War)."

As the leading classical site, the Acropolis was also the preeminent place to dream of modern Greek freedom. The front of the Parthenon is the backdrop for the opening soliloquy about Greek freedom in Mordecai Noah's *Greek Captive* (1823) and Disraeli's *Rise of Iskander* (1831). Robert Underwood Johnson's 1886 poem "Apostrophe to Greece: Inscribed to the Greek People on the Seventy-Fifth Anniversary of Their Independence" is subtitled "From the Parthenon," and it includes a note saying that it was on the steps of Athena's temple that the author began composing the lines (93).

Given the identification between Greece and the heroine of the romance of liberation, the sight of the Parthenon and the Acropolis often leads a philhellenic hero to think about the living Greek "virgin," who now personifies the country. For example, when the hero of Lynch's *Glamour* makes a midnight visit to the Acropolis, he thinks, "Of all the emotions at the call of beauty, that derived from such a moment must stand out alone. Something, varying in explicitness according to personality, something far above yearning for power of expression floods the heart at such a time." Yet John Strellie does not remain in a state of reverie or sublime wonder, for he notes that "through it all as a setting to my mood, emphasising all the loveliness before me, was the recollection of the girl at Kephissia" (31–32). In Demetra Vaka Brown's *Grasp of the Sultan*, a daughter of "ever-rising, ever-struggling Crete" (275) is rescued from the sultan's harem in Constantinople by an Englishman and brought to Athens: "And here, within sight of the Parthenon, she is freed from Musulman shackles—she is a living emblem of Greater Greece," and she is fittingly paired with the eternal emblem of classical Greece visible above the city (275). In the romance of liberation, the Acropolis is, like Greece itself, both politicized and, by its identification with the heroine, feminized.

If one judges simply by the number of pages written, the modern Greek struggle for freedom was somewhat less inhospitable to fiction than the Greece of Winckelmann, especially in the last decades of the century. Yet the Grèce de Byron was hardly more amenable to the bourgeois interiority necessary for Bildungsromans or stories of inner growth than the classical bas-relief. For the politicization of Greek ruins and their surroundings, like the escape into the divine sphere, moved the focus away from the individual and his or her own psychology toward partisan external concerns. With the exception of Brailsford's *Broom of the War God*, which chronicles the disillusionment of a philhellenic volunteer, the aim of most philhellenic novels was to celebrate the Byronic past and keep its spirit alive. Further, the magic force of Byronic legend tended to make both real and fictional philhellenes less interested in and less aware of how modern Greece might alter them and more interested in how they might assist in altering the fate of the modern Greeks. McCarthy's hero, who claimed, "I, too, felt myself a Greek," longs for a renewal "of the great unfinished struggle for Greek independence . . . with my own chivalric form, to be sure, in the midst of it" (I.13). When the philhellene T. S. Hutchinson arrived in Greece at the start of the First Balkan War, he remarked, "I am expecting to be a Greek as soon as I get a uniform" (53). No one in the fiction of Henry James, as far as I can recall, ends up thinking not of what Italy did for them, but of what they did or could do for Italy. Byron, viewed in England and America as both the poet of Greece and the hero of Greece, set a different precedent for the land across the Ionian sea. "Athens," said Z. D. Ferriman, "is the only foreign city which has reared statues to Englishmen" (*Greece and the Greeks* 163). One was to Byron, the other to Gladstone.

The first fictional character in English who, like Isabel Archer in Rome, would become deeply and tenderly acquainted with Greece, who would take

Greek ruins "into her confidence," who would let them "interfuse and moderate her passion" did not appear until Susan Glaspell's *Fugitive's Return* was published in 1929. By then, the Asia Minor Disaster of 1922 had occurred, and the broken columns and marble fragments had begun to acquire a different, tragic significance, one that was more hospitable to bourgeois interiority. In the years before that "great catastrophe," for those actual or armchair visitors who were not lost in clouds of divine glory, Greek ruins suggested the triumph of barbarity over taste. And it was not only Greek ruins that carried such political meaning but also the villages and villagers that one passed on the way to the classical sites.

6

Politicized Pans

After the "rebirth" of Greece in 1833, the Western world began to look for signs of the promised revitalization that had been so confidently assumed in earlier philhellenic literature. In 1897, Lewis Sergeant curtly summed up the European view: "The Greeks of today stand in this special relation to the rest of Europe, that their condition is regarded as a state of probation" (*New Greece* 41). From 1833 until 1900, philhellenes and Turkophiles fought over the degree of progress in Greece just as an earlier generation had traded words over the nature of the Athenian democracy.[1] Murray's *Handbook for Travellers in Greece* for 1872 stated that one of the main reasons for a trip to Greece was to judge the country's progress: "A journey in Greece is full of interest for a traveler of every character, except indeed for a mere idler or man of pleasure. There the politician may contemplate for himself the condition and progress of a people of illustrious origin, and richly endowed by Nature, which, after a servitude of centuries, has again taken its place among nations; there can he best form an accurate opinion on that most important question, the present state and future destinies of the Levant" (1). Shelley had said, "We are all Greeks," and if Greece were to be a mirror into which the West could look and see its own sense of "Greekness," then it had to become more like Europe and America.[2]

Toward the end of the nineteenth century, however, intellectuals in Britain and America began to turn away from "the Victorian view of science and advancement as a sign of progress" (Hynes, *Edwardian Turn of Mind* 31). In opposition to the perceived ugliness and emptiness of modern urban life, a pastoral ideal once again found favor. The new life of post-Christian man, according to Edward Carpenter in *Civilisation: Its Cause and Cure* (1889), would be essentially a return to pre-Christian customs:

> The meaning of the old religions will come back to him. On the high tops once more gathering he will celebrate with naked dances the glory of the human form and the great procession of the stars, or greet the bright horn of the young moon which now after a hundred

centuries comes back laden with such wondrous associations— . . .
once more in sacred groves will he reunite the passion and the delight
of human love with his deepest feelings of the sanctity and beauty of
Nature; or in the open, standing uncovered to the Sun, will adore the
emblem of everlasting splendour which shines within. (46–47)

As at the end of the eighteenth century, a hundred years later the ancient
Greeks again occupied a special place in the pastoral vogue. For many
thinkers of European descent the ancient Greek world still represented their
collective, lost, bucolic past. The importance of Greek antiquity in this
desire to return to nature is supported by Samuel Hynes's observation that
"Pan is a particularly prominent figure" in the late Victorian and Edwardian
periods (*Edwardian Turn of Mind* 146).[3] Oscar Wilde put the idea succinctly
in his poem "Pan: Double Villanelle":

> O goat-foot God of Arcady!
> This modern world is grey and old,
> And what remains to us of thee? . . .
>
> Then blow some trumpet loud and free,
> And give thine oaten pipe away,
> Ah, leave the hills of Arcady!
> The modern world has need of Thee!
>
> (*Complete Poetry* 121–22)

But Hynes noted that modern appearances of Pan were not always "in
forms that would be recognizable to the Greeks; Barrie, someone had said,
had robbed Pan to pay Peter, and other Edwardian Pans were similarly domesticated" (146).[4] Nor was it necessary to meet the Greek god on his native
ground of Arcadia. One could meet him in the English countryside, as in
Saki's "The Music on the Hill" and Meredith's poem "The Woods of West-
ermain," or in America, as in Kipling's "Pan in Vermont." Those who
looked in the Mediterranean usually went to Italy, as in E. M. Forster's
"Story of a Panic." As Kenneth Churchill observed, in the years after 1870
"if what was needed to rejuvenate industrial society was a return to the
essence of paganism, then Italy was the place to establish contact" (165). A
character in H. D.'s novel *Asphodel* states the connection between Greek
gods and Italian soil at the turn of the century quite simply: "We had
Greece, having Italy" (111). Many other travelers, both real and imaginary,
had the same feeling.

The case of Norman Douglas is instructive. In his book about the Sorren-
tine peninsula, *Siren Land* (1911), Douglas wrote:

many of us would do well to *mediterraneanize* ourselves for a season, to quicken those ethnic roots from which has sprung so much of what is best in our natures. To dream in Siren land, pursuing the moods and memories as they shift in labyrinthine mazes, like shadows on a wood-land path in June; to stroll among the hills and fill the mind with new images upon which to browse at leisure, casting off outworn weeds of thought with the painless ease of a serpent and unperplexing, inciden-tally, some of those "questions of the day" of which the daily papers nevertheless know nothing—this is an antidote for many ills. (28)

Douglas presented the benefits of southern Italy as a place of such repose in *Siren Land, Old Calabria* (1915), and the novel *South Wind* (1917). In all of these books, a key reason the region provided an antidote to what Douglas termed "the spiritual blunting or anaesthesia" of northern European life (*Siren Land* 151) was that it still manifested traces of its classical Greek her-itage. In a passage that echoed his Romantic predecessors, Douglas discussed the relation between ancient Greek civilization and its natural surroundings: "And the Greeks? The idea that we entered into the world tainted from birth, that feeling of duty unfulfilled which is rooted in the doctrine of sin and has hindered millions from enjoying life in a rational and plenary manner—all this was alien to their mode of thought. A healthy man is naturally blithe, and the so-called joy of life of the ancient Greeks is simply the appropriate reac-tion of the body to its surroundings" (*Siren Land* 151).

Such eloquent thoughts and musings eluded Douglas in the Greek heart-land. In 1920, he traveled to Athens on a commission from the Greek gov-ernment, which had paid him 300 English pounds to compose a book about Greece. After an uncongenial visit prompted an early return, he complained, "I have tried to write an article about Greece. Two pages in the better part of a week. They read like a Board-School exercise" (Holloway 286).[5] A second visit with his friend and would-be collaborator Edward Hutton in 1926 was no more successful. Douglas told Hutton, "I cannot write a book about Greece; if I could I should have written it long ago" (Holloway 347). Even with Hutton sending him a *rédaction* of each chapter to fill out, Douglas eventually withdrew from the project, and Hutton published *A Glimpse of Greece* (1928) on his own. In 1929, almost ten years after he had received pay-ment, Douglas finally published a very slender Greek book of around fifty pages, *One Day*.

Why was it so difficult to Mediterraneanize in Greece? A large part of the reason was that through the middle of the 1920s, modern Greece was a highly politicized space in the minds of English and Americans, where one pondered the present state and future destiny of Greece and the Levant. At around the same time that Wilde composed "Pan," Robert Underwood

Johnson claimed that the modern world had need of Greece for a very different reason:

> Then Hellas! scorn the sneer
> Of kings who will not hear
>   Their people's moaning voice
> More deaf than shore to sea!
>   The world hath need of Thee— . . .
>
> Troy was, but Athens is
> The World's and Liberty's
>   Nor ever less shall be!
>   ("Apostrophe to Greece" 101–2)

Even Pans seen on Greek soil were politicized.[6] One of the few appearances of Pan in Greece written by a major writer dealt specifically with "the tough old riddle of the modern Greek and his position in the world today."

Virginia Woolf's early story "A Dialogue on Mount Pentelicus," unpublished until 1987, begins when a party of six English visitors have just finished a trip up Mount Pentelicus near Athens and started their descent. Woolf had made such a journey during her stay in Athens in 1906 (*Passionate Apprentice* 326–27). "Tourists," we are informed, is not how the group would refer to themselves. "Germans are tourists and Frenchmen are tourists but Englishmen are Greeks. Such was the sense of their discourse, and we must take their word for it that it was very good sense indeed" (*Complete Shorter Fiction* 63).[7] While at the top of the mountain, they feel themselves "charged on each side by tremendous presences," but they are a bit put off by their attempt to speak to their guides in the classical language: "the fact that Greek words spoken on Greek soil were misunderstood by Greeks destroys at a blow the whole population of Greece" (64). During a rest near a stream they commence the "dialogue" of the title. It ranges "over many subjects—over birds and foxes, and whether turpentine is good in wine . . . and over so sinking and surging like the flight of an eagle through mid-air dropped at last upon the tough old riddle of the modern Greek and his position in the world today. Some, of optimistic nature[,] claimed for him a present, some less credulous but still sanguine expected a future, and others with generous imagination recalled a past" (65, brackets in original).

An exchange occurs between one speaker, who maintains that ancient Greece had "died as the day dies here in Greece, completely" (65), and another, who claims that the English idea of the ancient Greeks is simply an illusion. But after these initial speeches, the dialogue is interrupted by an Orthodox monk carrying a load of wood. He was "large and finely made, and had the nose and brow of a Greek statue. It was true that he wore a beard and his hair was long, and there was every reason to think him both dirty and illiterate. But as he stood there, suspended, with open eyes, a fantastic—pathetic—hope shot through the minds of some who saw him that his was one of those original figures" (67). But, unfortunately, it is "no longer in the power of the English mind . . . to see fur grow upon smooth ears and cloven hoofs where there are ten separate toes. It is their power to see something different from that, and perhaps, who knows?, something finer" (67). What the English tourists did see was the light in the monk's eye (perhaps an echo of Byron's comment about "the fire still sparkling in each eye" in a modern Greek?), which "pierced through much, and went like an arrow drawing a golden chain through ages and races till the shapes of men and women and the sky and the trees rose up on either side of its passage and stretched in a solid and continuous avenue from one end of time to the other" (68). Even the man who had argued against the continuity of the Greeks now answers the monk's greeting "as a Greek to a Greek and if Cambridge disavowed the relationship the slopes of Pentelicus and the olive groves of Mendeli confirmed it" (68).

Woolf's affirmation of a link, however fragile, between the ancient and modern Greeks in this story is a bit surprising. In her journal of her visit in 1906 she had written, "I take some pains to put old Greece on my right hand & new Greece on my left & nothing I say of one shall apply to the other. The justice of that division has been proved etymologically, & ethnologically,—*indeed* & I daresay I could go on proving it through all the arts & sciences, but these shall be sufficient" (*Passionate Apprentice* 340). She also remarked, "Modern Greece is so flimsy & fragile, that it goes to pieces entirely when confronted with the roughest fragment of the old. But there is very little of it, & if you choose you may see exactly what the Greeks of the 5th century saw" (324), and "the people of Athens are, of course, no more Athenians than I am" (328). How Woolf would have reconciled these statements with the solid and unbroken avenue of the Greek race in her story need not detain us here.[8] We can be content with the fact that her story of an encounter with a Pan figure in Greece did not provide an antidote to the many ills of the modern world but offered instead a new insight into the position of the modern Greek in that world.

For if one made contact with "the essence of paganism" in Greece, that was routinely offered as proof that the Greeks were still the Greeks and enlisted to support Greece's national aspirations. In the introduction to his translation of the stories of Argyris Eftaliotis, *Tales from the Isles of Greece* (1897), W. H. D. Rouse, invoking the cultural icon of the period, claimed, "Out on the [Greek] hills Pan is not yet dead" (xi). He returned to this idea at the end of the introduction where he said, "With all around so untouched by what is ugly in modern life," one could "half expect to hear Pan piping down there in the glen" (xv). But, while "there is something Homeric still lingering about rural Greece," there is something Byronic as well. For "it is not so long since blind Homers trudged the country-side, and in return for a welcome, sang the heroic ballads of olden days; only now no Troy was their theme, but the struggle of Greece for freedom against the Turk" (ix).

This is not at all surprising, as interest in Greek liberation had always centered on the link between the ancient and modern Greeks. In one of the first book-length studies of modern Greek folklore in English, *Customs and Lore of the Modern Greeks* (1892), the poet Rennell Rodd justified the topic by declaring that the present Greeks can help Mediterraneanize the West: "There lives a people who seem to have preserved, in manner and look, that old-world freshness of *our* dreams, who still live the natural life with little heed or knowledge of the world beyond" the village (x–xi, my italics). But, as with Rouse, that statement has political implications: "A people which has retained through inevitable transformations so much that it is directly traceable to the Hellenic fountain head, must therefore be looked upon as the genuine representatives of those whose languages they still speak and whose name they still assume" (*Customs and Lore* 204). However, Rodd's book, like Edward Grosvenor's *The Permanence of the Greek Type* (1897), should not be read simply as propaganda for the Greek cause. Just as, according to Michael Herzfeld, Greek scholars used folklore to construct a "cultural continuity in defense of their national identity" (4), foreign philhellenes constructed a cultural continuity in Greece to defend *their* individual identity in the face of the dehumanization in the modern world. The way for Rodd to save his own dreams was to assist the cause of the Greeks.

Although the interest in the customs of rural Greece and the relation of those practices to the classical past had a broad cultural impetus, most of those who introduced modern Greek folklore and village life to an English audience in the last quarter of the nineteenth century were literary philhellenes, like the novelists Elizabeth Edmonds ("Quaint Customs of Rural Greece" and "Superstitions in Greece," 1892), Isabella Fyvie Mayo ("Patriot Songs of the Greeks," 1897), and George Horton (*In Argolis*, 1902). They all, in their various ways, would agree with what was stated forthrightly in the introduction to Lucy Garnett's *Greek Folk Songs from the Turkish Provinces of Greece* (1885): "We hope that such study will have not only speculative and scientific, but practical and political results in exciting sympathy, and gaining aid, for that reconstitution of Hellas which is still unachieved, and the fulfillment yet of Shelley's prophetic vision in the first year of the War of Independence (1821)—'Another Athens shall arise'" (66).[9] An encounter with Pan in Italy was an antidote for a civilization that "makes a man unhappy and unhealthy" (Douglas, *South Wind* 346). An encounter with Pan in Greece, on the other hand, could lead to a quotation from *Hellas* or "The Isles of Greece." As Thackeray said, it was dangerous ground. Woolf was not simply recounting a meeting with one modern Greek in her story "A Dialogue on Mount Pentelicus" but engaging with a touristic convention that had become firmly established in the previous decades. In 1849, for example, Walter Colton published an account of a conversation in Athens that was "quite intellectual, as usually happens on such occasions; it ran on the present condition and future prospects of Greece and embraced many glowing predictions" (292).

While the study of modern Greek folklore and customs was offered as an "excavation" of the beliefs of antiquity, there was no place for the Dionysian ecstasy found in Nietzsche's *The Birth of Tragedy* nor the violent origins ascribed to some Greek rites by J. G. Frazer and the Cambridge anthropologists in most accounts of late nineteenth-century village life. The Greeks were, on the whole, portrayed as less primitive than the Italians, and certainly than the Etruscans, because, as the descendants however far removed of the founders of civilization, they had to be "refined" primitives.[10] In the caves of southern Italy, Douglas could "step outside and beyond the decent Hellenic civilization" to prehistoric beliefs (*Siren Land* 178). The inhabitants of Greek villages, on the other hand, were generally offered as the living representatives of fifth-century Hellenic civilization, reincarnations of Owenson's Ida who sang, in the place of Pindaric odes, folk songs of antique derivation.

Of a Greek in a Parisian drawing room, Proust remarked: "What we seek in vain to embrace in the shy young Greek is the figure admired long ago on the side of a vase" (3.255). On Greek soil, however, authors often had more success finding those admired figures in the Greeks whom they met. In 1853, C. C. Felton stopped for a night at Delphi at a home where a girl was preparing for her wedding: "Statho, the future bride, is a dark-eyed, comely damsel, looking, in her Parnassian costume, like a bas-relief on the Parthenon,—so statuesque is she in her attitude and the flow of her drapery" (*Familiar Letters* 285). In her story "The Only Son of His Mother," Julia Dragoumis wrote, "In the islands, it is still possible to meet in the flesh the prototypes of Praxiteles, Myron, and Polycletus" (*Tales of a Greek Island* 233).[11] In Hocking's novel *Tommy and the Maid of Athens* (1917), "the almost classical features" and "the finely chiseled nostrils" of the heroine lead the English hero to ponder not of the sublimity of the caryatids, but her features rather "made him think of Byron's poem" "Maid of Athens" (50). If the Greeks were simply generic primitives, one might not be able to distinguish them from Albanians, Bulgarians, or, even worse, Turks. The "classical features" found by philhellenes in the faces of the modern Greeks situated the Greeks in the world of Byron as much as in that of Homer. In fact, the interest in rural Greece among philhellenic writers appeared simultaneously with and as a response to the Bulgarian agitation and the new geographical construction of southeastern Europe. It was one strategy used to preserve the special status of the Greeks.

peasants

Paradoxically, in order to substantiate the link between the ancient and modern Greeks, philhellenes like Rodd disinherited the vast majority of the Greek population. Rodd claimed, "It is in the folk of the mountains and the upper air, living their changeless life apart, with their tanned faun-like features, and the laughing look in their clear brown eyes under the matted hair, that the link with the old world is closest" (*Customs and Lore* 81; notice how his rural Greeks even look like Pans).[12] While Rodd's book, like many other studies of Greek customs, "proved" that the folk in the mountains were closely connected to the ancient worthies, it also supported the position, found in several novels of the late nineteenth century, that the Greeks of Athens and the larger towns who had abandoned those customs were a mongrel race, which might best be called Levantine and considered no better than Turks. In 1859, Bayard Taylor claimed, "Not one fifth of the present population can with justice be called Greeks" (262). In an article of 1909, Bohun Lynch said, "We [Westerners] must withhold our respect from the mass [of the Greek people], and reserve it for only two or three component groups" ("Some Sidelights on Modern Greece" 385). Three years later, in his novel *Glamour*, he revised the romance of liberation to depict a foreign philhellene saving an Ypsaliote woman "of a purer stock than most of the Greeks" (167) from a mongrel Athenian. He goes on to say that these imagined Ypsaliotes "are absolutely untouched by modern influences" and continue to celebrate ancient "festivals in honour of Pan" (172, 234).[13]

In the twentieth century, much would be written in English about the struggles between Greek and Greek, such as the controversies between Royalists and Venizelists during World War I, the civil war between the Right and the Left after World War II, and the years of the military junta from 1967 to 1974. But it is important to remember that the tendency to split the country into "true" Greeks and "false" Greeks arose not from an examination of internal Greek politics but from an external distinction imposed from abroad. The growing population of Athens in the late nineteenth century came from rural villages with which they kept strong family ties. Even today, a family in Athens often identifies itself by its village of origin, and Athenians have never been considered less "Greek" by their Greek rural relatives.[14] The division between "true" rural and "false" urban and the urge to save village "Greeks" from city "non-Greeks" grew from a Western desire to find as direct a link as possible with antiquity. But that framework, when it was applied to real dissension in Greece, distorted the picture of Greek politics abroad for almost a century.

Largely missing from late Victorian and Edwardian descriptions of Greece is the claustrophobic, realistic depiction of village life that can be found in the stories and novels of the late nineteenth-century Greek author Alexandros Papadiamantis, to mention only the most prominent example. Papadiamantis's novel *The Murderess* (1903), for example, tells the story of a grandmother on the island of Skiathos who goes on a mission to kill little girls in order to remove the pain and torment they and their families will have to face as they grow up in a place where many of the young men leave to find their fortune elsewhere. The fact that Papadiamantis, who is now regarded as one of the most important prose writers of his generation, was completely passed over by Elizabeth Edmonds and W. H. D. Rouse in favor of Drosinis and Eftaliotis, whose view of village life was more benign, speaks volumes about the politics and ideology of nineteenth-century translations from modern Greek. Edmonds did translate Gregory Xenopoulos's *The Stepmother: A Tale of Modern Athens* (1897), and she wrote in the introduction that the "author had written several longer novels in the realistic style, and upon my making strictures upon one which he kindly sent me, he most eloquently and warmly defended himself in a long letter, which declared his admiration of Zola as his master. His most recent stories, however, are not open to any such criticism" (7). Edmonds clearly did not want realism in Greece and probably in England as well, and she was not going to translate nor compose it (see her *Amygdala*). Neil Wynn William offered a corrective and realistic look in *Greek Peasant Stories* (1899) and his novel *The Bayonet that Came Home: A Vanity of Modern Greece* (1896). His tale "The Story of a Grecian Boy" tells how a child's pet lamb is taken first by klephts and then by soldiers, who despite the fact that they have orders to restore it to its youthful owner, slaughter it in front of the boy. But William was a lonely voice, hampered by a rather wooden prose style, and had no influence on other authors.[15]

Rouse summed up the prevalent attitude about rural Greece and its people: "The charm of these sunny lands, and their people so merry and lighthearted, attracts the thoughts to them again and again" (introduction to Eftaliotis, xv). Certainly tragedies strike the villagers in tales written in English, as in Horton's *Aphroessa* and Dragoumis's "Vasilis," and in the stories of Eftaliotis and Xenopoulos translated from the Greek. At times there are strange, unexplained phenomena, like Nereids or vampires, subjects in keeping with the contemporary rejection of science and interest in the mysterious and paranormal, which, among other things, led Yeats to the seances of Madame Blavatsky.[16] In most of these works, however, Greece possesses the therapeutic qualities for foreigners often found in Italy. It too is a place where those from a cold and straitlaced world can find "a refuge from materialism" (Wright 23) or "a return to the essence of paganism" (Kenneth Churchill 165). Julia Dragoumis's aptly named story "North and South," which recounts how a stay on the island of Poros leads an American woman toward happiness, hardly differs in kind from such Italian tales as E. M. Forster's *A Room with a View* or Elizabeth von Arnim's *The Enchanted April*.[17] And Horton opens *Aphroessa* (1897), a narrative poem about the encounter of a village shepherd and a Nereid, with his Western narrator addressing the people on Poros:

Here on this innocent Aegean isle,
Whose mountains look on blooming Argolis,
Will I take refuge from the world awhile—
There is no other spot so sweet as this.

(2)

At the end of Lynch's *Glamour*, the English hero, John Strellie, dwelling on a Greek island with the Greek girl whom he had saved from an evil Athenian "Levantine" and then married, has found that escape from civilization so often sought in writing of the period: "Here at Philotion, among the vineyards or out on the desolate headland, modern existence, I think, with its hopelessly entangled principles, its ludicrous ideas of right and wrong falls into perspective. For in the wilds a man may live; and is not eaten up by vain regrets" (314).

Still, underlying the majority of these depictions of rural Greece as an idyllic retreat was a desire to comment, at times directly and other times indirectly, on what Woolf had called "the tough old riddle of the place of the modern Greek in the world today." In the late nineteenth century, as at the beginning of the same century, politics played a central role in the manner in which the local inhabitants were perceived. Upon his arrival in Greece, John Strellie had expressed a desire to go and fight with a Greek band in Macedonia. Even as he begins his description of his island idyll, Strellie says of the Greek klepht who had helped him rescue the beautiful Chrysoula, "for him there is always Macedonia as a playground—always war again" (314). In addition to their idyllic depictions of rural Greek life, both Dragoumis (*A Man of Athens*) and Horton (*Like Another Helen*) wrote philhellenic novels about Greeks fighting for liberation. For English or Americans who really wanted to take refuge from the world for a while, Italy was a better destination since there one could find traces of the pagan vitality without the politicized baggage of the Greece of Byron, in which there was always war again. In the introduction to a volume entitled *A Sheaf of Greek Folk Songs*, Countess Cesaresco reflected the politicized perception of Greek rural life when she wrote: "Folk poetry is the work of the peasant and the peasant is rarely political. In Greece he is political: when he took to the mountain fastnesses to fight the battle of his race he became political to an intense degree, but politics is still his passion when he is simply hoeing and sowing" (xxiv).

Because of the persistence of modern Greece as a politicized space, the Western perception of the land and its people was less open to change than that of the ancient Greeks, and a different kind of Hellenism arose at the end of the nineteenth century. In 1897, Gilbert Murray wrote, "The 'serene and classical' Greek of Winckelmann and Goethe did good service in his day, though we now feel him to be a phantom. He has been survived, especially in the painters and poets, by an aesthetic and fleshly Greek in fine raiment, an abstract Pagan who lives to be contrasted with an equally abstract early Christian and Puritan, and to be glorified or mishandled according to the sentiments of his critic. . . . He would pass, perhaps, as a 'Graeculus' of the Decadence" (*History of Greek Literature* iv). Although the move to more fleshly Greeks had begun with the French writers Baudelaire and Gautier, the great apostle of aesthetic Hellenism in the English speaking world was Walter Pater. For him, "not the fruit of experience, but experience itself, is the end. A counted number of pulses only is given to us. . . . To burn always with this hard, gem-like flame, to maintain this ecstasy, is success in life" (*Renaissance* 219). This concern with individual perceptions and pleasures complete with "strange dyes, strange colours," and "curious odours" (219) led to a new interest in the Hellenistic and late Roman periods, epochs when, as Pater suggested in *Marius the Epicurean* (1885), life was more personal, luxurious, and open to Eastern influence.[18] As Richard Jenkyns said, "The Hellenism of the decadents languishes in an atmosphere swimming with oriental odours" (297). The turn to a languid sensuality might also be called the Ottomanization of antiquity. This aspect of decadence exhibited itself more openly in France than in England, for after 1890 French writers produced a number of works about ancient Greek courtesans and prostitutes, the most important being Pierre Louÿs's *Chansons de Bilitis* (1894) and *Aphrodite* (1896), as well as Fernand Nief's *Phryne La Courtesan* (1905) and Prosper Castanier's *Les Amants des Lesbos* (1900). Louÿs's work resembles and draws on such Oriental writing as Flaubert's *Salammbo* (1862) and Pierre Loti's *Aziyade* (1879). Louÿs, who never visited Greece, found inspirations for his ancient Greek novels during trips to Algeria.[19]

There could not, of course, be a similar Ottomanization of modern Greece, so there was no modern Graeculus of the decadence. The philhellenic desire to redeem more Greeks from Turkish rule required that the Greeks be defined in opposition to the Turks and, by extension, Oriental sensuality. From the revolt of 1770, modern Greece was portrayed as a victim of Turkish lust and vice. Throughout the nineteenth century and the first decades of the twentieth, modern Greek women continued to be portrayed in the tradition of the chaste and austere, if also natural and pagan, Ida.[20] In her novel *In the Shadow of Islam* (1911), Demetra Vaka Brown portrays the Greek Elpis as immune to the erotic allure of the Orient, which briefly enthralls the visiting American, Millicent Grey. "The primitive woman" is "in you," Elpis tells Millicent, and "Orkhan Effendi is just the man to awake that primitive woman in you,—and who would defend you against him?" (116). The answer, of course, is Elpis, who, being Greek, has complete control of the primitive woman within her. Modern Greek men, if they were not actually deceitful Levantines, were generally poor, brave, and quite willing to let the foreigner have the Greek heroine.[21]

While the conception of ancient Greece could be broadened and ener-
gized by new ideas and directions, the conception of modern Greece, because of the way in which it was politicized, could not take part in any of
these developments. Nothing demonstrates this as clearly as the fact that in
the 1890s, the years during which the French were writing novels about
ancient Greek sexuality, English and American authors composed philhellenic novels, short stories, and poems about the Greek War of Independence, in which there is hardly a trace of a fleshly Greek or a hetaira to
be found.

Perhaps for the same reason, one finds a surprising dearth of references to
homosexuality, among foreigners or Greeks, in nineteenth-century writing
about modern Greece.[22] Certainly some travelers went to Greece after 1833
because of the homosexual associations of the classical past. Two of the most
famous were Natalie Clifford Barney and Renée Vivien, who in 1904 journeyed to Lesbos, an island still held by the Turks, in the hopes of starting a
new Sapphic circle.[23] But if any, like James Merrill some fifty years later,
went to Athens "to follow the faun incarnate in this or that young man" in a
culture where, according to Merrill, a soldier, "like nine out of ten from his
class and culture, would count himself lucky to catch a permissive male
lover," they did not write about it (*A Different Person* 191, 192). Although
homosexuality could be referred to as Greek love, at the end of the nineteenth century it was more readily found, like almost everything else
"Greek," in Italy. Kenneth Churchill noted that an "atmosphere of homosexuality . . . pervades the literary treatment of Italians, at least until [D. H.]
Lawrence" (121).[24] The avoidance of homosexuality might, as with Oriental
sensuality generally, stem from the fact that, although it was an ancient
Greek trait in the Western mind, it could also be associated with contemporary Oriental or Ottoman life. In 1812, when Greece was still the East, Byron
found male lovers in Greece, but, at the end of the century, André Gide and
Oscar Wilde sought partners in Algiers, not Athens.[25]

The first novel in English to use Greece's homosexual associations in a
contemporary Greek setting was Ronald Firbank's *Inclinations* (1916), in the
first part of which Geraldine O'Brookomore, whose inclinations give the
book its title, travels to Greece with young Mabel Collins, a pair who might
have been loosely modeled on Barney and Vivien.[26] Other foreign women of
similar inclinations show up in Greece. For example, on the ship they meet
Miss Arne, who is on her "way to Greece to study Lysistrata" (238). Since
there are no significant Greek characters in the novel, we have no indication
if the inclinations of the foreigners are shared by the natives. O'Brookomore's hopes of creating a Sapphic garden in Greece with Mabel are foiled
when the girl elopes with Count Pastorelli, a persistent satyr, who follows
them around from place to place. Still, *Inclinations* broke ground in writing
about Sapphic love in the country of Sappho at a time when one could do so

only guardedly. Firbank did not break ground in writing about the sexuality of modern Greek men, however. He imported his satyr from Italy.

E. M. Forster's short story about contact with the essence of paganism in the Peloponnesus, "The Road from Colonus" (1905), was rather unusual for its time in that it made no mention of "the tough old puzzle of the modern Greek and his position in the world today." Mr. Lucas, the leading character in the tale, had "caught the fever of Hellenism" forty years earlier, "and all his life he had felt that if he could but visit that land, he would not have lived in vain. But Athens had been dusty, Delphi wet, Thermopylae flat, and he had listened with amazement and cynicism to the rapturous exclamations of his companions. Greece was like England: it was a man who was growing old. . . . Yet Greece had done something for him, though he did not know it. It had made him discontented, and there are stirrings of life in discontentment" (127). Riding ahead of his party, he finds a spring in a hollow tree with a powerful presiding spirit, and his one desire now is, like Oedipus, to remain near the hallowed ground. "To Mr. Lucas, who in a brief span of time, discovered not only Greece, but England and all the world and life, there seemed nothing ludicrous in the desire to hang within the tree another votive offering—a little model of an entire man" (130). His daughter and the other English travelers physically force him to leave the spot. Mr. Lucas feels that he has missed the "supreme event . . . which would transfigure the face of the world" (137). Later, we find such an event did occur when the sacred tree demolished the local inn during a storm on the very night Mr. Lucas had wanted to stay there. Back in England, he becomes just an irritable old man.

"The Road from Colonus" has affinities to Forster's early Italian stories, "The Story of a Panic" and "Albergo Empedocle," with one great exception.[27] As Furbank observed, "'The Road from Colonus' was the story of the chance of salvation lost, as 'The Story of a Panic' was the chance of salvation taken" (I.103). This is not a coincidence. Forster visited Greece on a group tour for archaeologists and classical language students in 1903. Furbank, Forster's biographer, wrote of that journey that the writer "came overprepared to many of the famous sights, and they made no impression. Marathon was no more than a view, and 'Aegina by moonlight did not come off'" (I.102). The whole visit does not appear to have come off, for years later Forster wrote in a letter to Christopher Isherwood: "Do I know Greece well? I should hope so. I was there in 1903 and have not been there since. I got tuned up by a modern Greek who stole another archaeologist's coat before we landed, and said I had given it to him" (*Selected Letters* II.118).[28] Something of Forster's own impressions almost certainly show up in his novel *Maurice* (written in 1914 but published posthumously in 1971), in which Clive Durham, like Forster a Cambridge man, catches the fever of Hellenism and visits Athens. Sitting in the theater of Dionysus, he thinks:

"Here dwelt his gods. . . . But he saw only a dying light and dead land. He uttered no prayer, believed in no deity, and knew the past was devoid of meaning like the present, and a refuge for cowards" (116).[29] Like Norman Douglas, Forster found it easier to Mediterraneanize in Italy, which he called "the beautiful country where they say 'yes'" and "the place where things happen" (Furbank I.96).

In Forster's case, the avoidance of the political question of the modern Greek was itself a political decision. From his first contact with Greece in 1903, Forster, to use the words of Woolf, kept old Greece on his right hand and new Greece on his left. He argued that the spirit of the classical age had departed from the modern country. In "Cnidus" (1904), he described a visit to an important Greek city on the coast of southern Asia Minor:[30]

> But I did see the home of the Goddess who has made Cnidus famous to us . . . that Demeter of Cnidus, whom we hold in the British museum now. She was there at that moment, warm and comfortable in the little access room of hers between the Ephesian room and the Archaic room. . . .
>
> I am not going to turn sentimental, and pity the exiled Demeter and declare her sorrowful eyes are straining for the scarped rock, and the twin harbours, and Triopia, and the sea. She is doing nothing of the sort. . . . And if, as I believe, she is alive, she must know that she has come among people who love her, for all they are so weak-chested and anaemic and feeble-kneed, and who pay such prosaic homage as they can. (*Abinger Harvest* 175–76)

The return of antiquities taken from Greece had been the subject of debate since Byron excoriated Lord Elgin in *The Curse of Minerva*. Forster's comment about the Demeter of Cnidus must be read in the context of that debate, for the statue is a symbol of Hellenism, which, according to Forster, now belonged in England.

Another article Forster wrote after his trip to Greece, "Gemistus Pletho" (1905), briefly told the life of the famous Greek philosopher who lived at Mistra in the early fifteenth century and desired to return to the worship of the old pagan gods.[31] Forster recounted how Gemistus came to Italy in 1439 for the Council of Florence and caused a revival of the study of Plato in the Italian city. Gemistus went back to Mistra and died only three years before the city was taken by the Turks. Forster notes that Gemistus "did not see that the revival had really taken place in Italy; that Greece is just a spirit which can appear, not only at any time, but also in any land" (*Abinger Harvest* 186–87). Gemistus became both a symbol and an artifact in the transition of Greek culture from Greece to Italy, for in 1465 his body was taken from Mistra by Sigismundo Malatesta and buried in the Tempio at Rimini. Forster concluded, "The Renaissance can point to many a career which is greater, but to none which is so strangely symbolical" (191).

The view that the spirit of Greece had been transferred to England appeared in the writings of others who, like Forster, combined the fever of Hellenism with opposition to Greece's national aspirations. Near the end of his poem "At Delphi," the Turkophile Alfred Austin had the Castalian fountain say:

> Though the Muses may have left
> Tempe's glen and Delphi's cleft,
> Wanderer! they have only gone
> Hence to murmuring Albion. . . .
> There the Muses prompt the strain,
> There they renovate my reign;
> There you wilt not call in vain,
>   "Apollo! Apollo! Apollo!"
>   (*Lyrical Poems* 214)

Austin does not appear to have cared about Turkey qua Turkey; he held to the old Tory policy that a strong Ottoman Empire was needed to preserve British imperial interests. But Forster, like Marmaduke Pickthall, was more of a Romantic Orientalist, for in the later essay "Salute to the Orient," he offered a prayer "that the East may be delivered from Europe the known and Russia the unknown, and may remain the East" (*Abinger Harvest* 269).[32]

Forster's defense of the Orient stemmed in part from what he saw as a fundamental difference in outlook between East and West in the area of personal relations. In his diary for December 24, 1906, Forster noted that his Indian friend Syed Ross Masood "gives up his duties for his friend—which is civilisation. Though as he remarks, 'Hence the confusion of Oriental states. To them personal relations come first'" (Furbank I.145). Forster paraphrased Masood's comment in "Salute to the Orient" when he said that a "personal relationship is most important" for the Oriental (*Abinger Harvest* 273). In this respect Forster, who declared that he would rather betray his country than a friend, saw himself as more Oriental than Western, as did Masood, who once told Forster "in you I see an oriental with an oriental view *in most things*" (Furbank I.194). Forster, like Disraeli, identified with the Orient, and the two authors both created characters who wanted to fight for the preservation of the Ottoman Empire. In Forster's posthumously published "Arctic Summer," when the main character, Cyril, hears about the Italian invasion of Libya in 1911, he wants to go to Tripoli and help the Turks, stating simply, "Those Italians have got to be smashed" (193).

If the Italians had to be smashed, then so did philhellenism, for it provided the ideological structure used to challenge the continued existence of the Ottoman Empire. "Cnidus" and "Gemistus Pletho" both offer an implicit if indirect challenge to that abiding part of the political consciousness by denying a connection between the ancient and modern Greeks.[33] It was an understated and subtle approach, much less direct than the French Romantic Orientalist Pierre Loti produced in *Turquie Agonisante* (1913), but one that Forster perhaps thought would be more effective with a public still attracted to the magic force of Byronic legend.

Before the Great War, in the politicized environment of modern Greece, those who wrote reveries set on Greek ground, as Forster did in "The Road from Colonus," were not always simply ignoring the puzzle of the modern Greek but often intentionally avoiding it. They tried to read Sophocles without noticing the contemporary world around them, as did certain Hellenists during the Greek War of Independence.[34] One wonders whether the destruction of the sacred site at the end of "The Road from Colonus," like the transfer of the statue of Demeter from Cnidus, suggested that the Greek spirit can no longer be found in the land where it originated.

In the autumn of 1912, Serbia, Bulgaria, Montenegro, and Greece joined forces and nearly drove the Turks from Europe. Just three weeks after hostilities commenced, Greek troops entered Thessaloniki. By the time the Turks signed an armistice with the Balkan allies, the Greek flag flew over Ioannina in Epirus, and the Greek navy had taken possession of almost all of the Turkish-held islands in the Aegean. Greece had nearly doubled in size and population. It was a startling triumph for all of the Balkan nations, but for the Greeks, who had suffered a humiliating defeat in 1897, it was especially sweet.

With the Turkish bear badly wounded if not slain, the Balkan allies almost immediately fell to fighting over the bear's skin. The Second Balkan War began on June 29, 1913, when the Bulgarians, who felt that their territorial acquisitions were not commensurate with their burden on the battlefield, attacked the Serbs and Greeks in Macedonia. The offensive went badly, and both the Turks and the Romanians took advantage of the concentration of Bulgarian forces on its western border to advance on other fronts. The result was a disaster for Bulgaria. It gained no ground in Macedonia, lost more territory on the Aegean coast, ceded fertile land in the Danube basin to Romania, and, perhaps most galling of all, gave the city of Adrianople and other areas won in the First Balkan War back to Turkey.

For the Greeks, the Second Balkan War was another triumph. They extended their reach another hundred miles eastward from Thessaloniki. Constantinople was now only two hundred miles away from troops serving under the Greek flag.[35] But if it were a new day for the Greek armed forces, it was also another opportunity for old rhetoric.

A comparison of 1897 with 1912–1913 reveals an odd inverse proportion between the number of Greeks freed from Turkish rule and the amount of philhellenic poetry and fiction written in English. In the 1890s, philhellenic literature had reached a level not seen since the War of Independence, but the only practical result of the conflict was that the Cretans achieved a semiautonomous status under the sultan. In the Balkan Wars, the Greeks had enormous success in expanding the Greek state, but the output of philhellenic writing barely surpassed the attention given to the Cretan revolt in the 1860s. Timing was certainly a factor, since by the middle of 1914 the eyes of the world were drawn to the possibility of a general European war. Looking back later, some writers would view the Balkan Wars not as the liberation of the Balkans but rather as a prelude to the Great War.[36] Still, the lack of literature about modern Greece in 1912 and 1913 strikes one as a bit odd, because the years from 1906 until 1920 were a busy time for philhellenic organizations and publications. The announced aim of the *Hellenic Herald*, published in London from November 1906 until May 1912, was to "give an exhaustive account of the various movements and affairs—political, racial, and social—in the Near East; and to set forth with clearness the Greek claims in the Balkan peninsula. In addition . . . a portion of each number will be given over to literary matters—more particularly to modern Greek literature" (Dec. 1906, p. 1). A literary section was included in an avowedly partisan political journal to show that the modern Greeks were the cultural descendents of ancient Greece and to set them apart from the other Balkan nationalities. The Anglo-Hellenic League was formed in 1913 to support the cause of Greater Greece in England. Its counterpart in America, the American Hellenic Society, started in 1916. In the forefront of this new wave of philhellenism on both sides of the Atlantic were professors of classics. The only author of note in the reformed Anglo-Hellenic League of 1912, which included the prominent scholars Ronald Burrows and Gilbert Murray, was Maurice Hewlett; no author of similar stature appears on the rolls of the American Hellenic Society. Writers, especially the avant-garde, which had been the soul of the philhellenic movement in the 1820s, were replaced in the 1910s by academics.

In 1912, some foreign philhellenes again packed their Byrons and went to fight so that more Greeks might be free. T. S. Hutchinson, a veteran of the U.S. Civil War who made the journey from New York, gave an account of the make-up and experience of the philhellenic foreign legion in the siege of Ioannina in *An American Volunteer under the Greek Flag* (1913). Hutchinson rehearsed all of the nostrums of nineteenth-century philhellenism. The Turk was of "no value to civilization. Humanity and modern progress demand his retirement to Asia" (26). To Greece, on the other hand, "we owe . . . everything that our modern civilization represents" (67), and "the same spirit of these old heroes had descended to the Greeks of today" (80). He provided a glowing account of the klephts in their "fantastic and beautiful costumes" (112). "They are not desperate, independent outlaws as some people have pictured them" but freedom fighters like the klephts of old (113).

The ships that carried Hutchinson and the other philhellenes to Greece were far from empty. They were packed with emigrant Greeks returning home to fight for their motherland. Some, as Dragoumis says in *A Man of Athens*, had "not even been taught their own language, but they are Greeks all the same" (363; see also Vaka Brown's *In Pawn to a Throne* 120–21). The fight to free Greeks became more ethnic around 1912 because fewer foreigners chose to involve themselves, although philhellenic rhetoric still proclaimed the Greek cause as a means to regenerate all of the Western world.

The most noteworthy philhellenic voice of the Balkan Wars was James Elroy Flecker, who had gone to the Levant to serve in the British mission in Smyrna in 1909, then met and married his own "maid of Athens" in 1910.[37] In "Ode to the Glory of Greece: A Fragment," Flecker is visited by the shades of Byron and Shelley in a dream after the first Greek victories. Shelley, referring to Flecker as the "inheritor," instructs his successor:

> "Go thou to Athens, go to Salonica,
> Go thou to Yannina beside the lake . . .
> Cry, 'The Olympians wake!'
> And cry, 'O Towers of Hellas built anew by rhyme,
> Star-woven to my Amphionic lyre,
> Stand you in steel for ever,
> And from your lofty lanterns sweeping the dim hills
>   and the nocturnal sea
> Pour out the fire of Hellas, the everlasting fire!'"
>   (*Collected Poems* 243)

Byron and Shelley were the Amphions whose verse had begun the rebuilding of Hellas, and another English poet, Flecker, would make new towers arise. Despite, or maybe because of, the fact that Flecker had been to Greece and had married a Greek, he still saw the country through the medium of Romantic philhellenism.

At the end of the poem Flecker wrote, "if no Pheidias with marble towers / Grace our new Athens" and if modern Greek poets are gentler in tone than Aeschylus:

> Yet still victorious Hellas, thou hast heard
> Those ancient voices thundering to arms
>   (246)

The victory in the Balkan Wars was not the fulfillment of the philhellenic legacy, as Flecker made clear in another poem, "A Sacred Dialogue (Christmas 1912)." At the opening, Christ says:

Peace and good will the world may sing
But we shall talk of war!

How fare my armies of the north!
(*Collected Poems* 212)

The bishop of Jerusalem answers, "They wait victorious peace, / All the high forts of Macedonia / Fly the proud flag of Greece." Christ then asks about Constantinople and the Church of St. Sophia. The bishop sighs: "Ah, it still wants redeeming!" Christ laments, "Still waits—five hundred years, and still / My soldiers wait—so long?" (213). The note following the poem says that it was "originally written for Christmas, 1912, and referring to the first Balkan war, this poem contains in the last speech of Christ words that read like a prophecy of events that may occur very soon (December, 1914)" (215). The mantle of philhellenism could pass relatively intact from Byron and Shelley through Swinburne to Flecker because the dream that Greece might still be free was still potent.[38]

But, just as Greek emigrants returning to aid their native country were re-placing foreign philhellenes on the battlefield, writers of Greek descent also began to emerge as the literary champions of Greece, including John Mavro-gordato (*Letters from Greece*), D. J. Cassavetti (*Hellas and the Balkan Wars*), and Demetra Vaka Brown (*A Child of the Orient*). The most interesting effort from this group was Julia Dragoumis's novel *A Man of Athens*, published in Boston in 1916. Dragoumis was not the first person of Greek descent to write a version of the romance of Greek liberation in English; Demetra Vaka Brown's *In the Shadow of Islam* had appeared in 1911. But Dragoumis was the first to firmly place a Greek male in the role usually assigned to a foreign philhellenic hero, one Metro Philippides, a young professor of archaeology at the University of Athens. He was born in a humble family on the island of Poros and orphaned young; at their first meeting the heroine notices "that his wrists were large, betraying peasant origin" (11). At the opening of the book, however, he has just returned from Paris, where he earned his doctorate. Dragoumis lessens Metro's Westernization in France by making archaeology his field of study; he is a real Greek in search of the "real" Greeks.

Like so many philhellenic stories, the novel opens on the Acropolis. Metro sees Theodora Douka, who, although she comes from an aristocratic Con-stantinople family, seems "like some statues of Artemis of the fourth cen-tury; not at all a Byzantine type" (35). Theodora, the last descendant of an imperial family, is the personification of Greece, and the first part of the novel depicts a struggle for her by representatives of "old Greeks" and "new Greeks." On one side is her father, an old-style, upper-class Phanariot of the Byzantine type, who insists that she marry someone of her own class. On the other is the orphan from Poros who, through talent and hard work, has made his way in the world.

Theodora marries the young professor, but their union is difficult at first. Her father refuses to acknowledge the couple, and she remains somewhat emotionally aloof from her new husband. In the last section, the First Balkan War starts, and Metro and all of his friends leave for the front. "This is a war of liberation," says one. "This is to set free all our brothers who are enslaved" (352). Earlier, one of the young men had said, "The heroes of 1821 are all dead and buried" (300), but the war reveals that the heroic spirit is very much alive. Dragoumis separates the "rescue" and marriage of Theodora from the war of liberation but uses Metro's participation in the fighting to solidify his place as the new Greek man. The novel ends with the return of Metro, who was presumed dead, after the fall of Ioannina. Theodora and Metro come to a new, fuller understanding, which is presented as symbolic of a new, expanded Greece.

A Man of Athens can be read as the first real Greek appropriation of the Greek romance in English. With the exception of one elderly French professor, all of the characters are Greek, and, for almost the first time in a novel written in English, one listens to realistic Greek characters discussing Greek problems. While Dragoumis's most striking innovation is to make the hero a Greek, her most radical might be placing the focus on the kind of future Greece will have. Since she separates the marriage of Theodora from the war, Metro's initial function is not to rescue Theodora from the Turks or some other enemy, something he never has to do, but to "rescue" her from her "old Greek" past and prod her to have a new vision of the country. Earlier versions of the romance of liberation often ended with the departure of the heroine from Greece and the question of the future of the country in limbo. Of course, what Dragoumis offers her American readers sounds a great deal like the Americanization of Greece. Metro might be a familiar figure in the land where Horatio Alger wrote, but the orphan of a poor Greek fisherman at the turn of the century lived in a different world. Whether Dragoumis, a Greek emigrant to America, desired the Americanization of Greece or was simply playing to her intended American readership is an open question. The book was written, after all, not to make Greeks rethink the direction of their country but to garner support for Greece in America by arguing that Greece was not simply changing but doing so in a way recognizable to Americans.

Dragoumis may have hoped that by modifying the well-known formula of the romance, she could rehabilitate the perception of Greek men abroad. She seems to have failed. No one would try to replicate her strategy of appropriating the romance of liberation for a Greek hero in the coming decades. And her book was less well known than those of her fellow Greek author Demetra Vaka Brown, who was more successful in promoting the cause of Greece by consistently employing Greek heroines in the traditional philhellenic manner in her novels *In the Shadow of Islam, The Grasp of the Sultan,* and *In Pawn to a Throne.*

Dragoumis's novel closes at the end of the First Balkan War. The title of Cale Young Rice's poem is "In a Greek Temple (during the First Balkan War)." Flecker's poems were also written during the First Balkan War; he wrote nothing about the subsequent fight with the Bulgarians. Philhellenic writing had always focused on the confrontations with the Turks, and the Balkan Wars were no exception. After the Turks were beaten at Ioannina, literary philhellenes waited for the final battle for Constantinople. Conflicts with the Bulgarians simply did not matter.

The victory of 1912 had no more effect on writing about Greece than the defeat of 1897. A clear sign of the discouraging state of philhellenic literature, whether of the narrowly Greek or the wider Balkan variety, was that, for literary history, the most famous and, sadly, perhaps the most innovative work relating to the Balkan Wars was probably the Futurist Filippo Tommaso Marinetti's poem "The Siege of Adrianople." Wyndham Lewis was present when Marinetti gave a public reading of the work. Marinetti, said Lewis, "had been at Adrianople, when there was a siege. He wanted to imitate the noise of bombardment. It was a poetic declamation which was packed to the muzzle with what he called 'le rage Balkanique.' . . . it was a matter of astonishment what Marinetti could do with his unaided voice. He certainly made an extraordinary amount of noise. A day attack upon the Western front, with all the 'heavies' hammering together, was nothing to it" (*Blasting and Bombadiering* 33). A text of the "Bombardement d'Andrinople" published in Lista's *Marinetti et le Futurisme* bears out Lewis's remarks, well over half the words of the poem are the onomatopoetic *zang, toumb,* and *taratata* (44). Marinetti may have reduced the Balkan Wars to "an extraordinary amount of noise," but he provided no clue as to how to infuse that noise with some new meaning.

In 1897, writers had, on the whole, kept faith with what Brailsford had termed "the bright aims of Hellenism" even as they found fault with philhellenes or Greeks for failing to uphold those ideals. But at the beginning of the twentieth century, some writers started a serious assault on the Romantic tradition underlying the philhellenic tradition and, by extension, philhellenism itself. One warning shot was fired in the preface to *Arms and the Man* (1898), where Shaw remarked how a critic complained that his depiction of the Bulgarians would set back the cause of freedom in the Balkans. But, Shaw said, "the real issue between the critic and myself" was "whether the political and religious idealism which had inspired Gladstone to call for the rescue of those Balkan principalities from the despotism of the Turk, and converted miserably enslaved provinces into hopeful and gallant little States, will survive the general onslaught on idealism which is implicit, and indeed, explicit, in *Arms and the Man* and the naturalist plays of the modern school. For my part, I hope not; for idealism, which is only a flattering name for romance in politics and morals, is as obnoxious to me as romance in ethics and religion" (*Complete Prefaces* I.50). Shaw recognized that the quarrel was not about the politics of the Balkan states but with certain invalid preconceptions, which had caused his audience to view the Balkans in a certain way. He thought that that ideological construct could not withstand a searching critique from "modern" drama.

Still, as Shaw surely knew, behind Gladstone's Balkans stood Byron's Greece. *Arms and the Man* is, in fact, more an attack on Romantic Byronism than on Gladstonian principles, for Raina asserts that "our heroic ideas" come from reading Byron and Pushkin, not the Bulgarian pamphlets of the Liberal leader. One wonders whether Shaw, consciously or unconsciously, chose to avoid Byron by speaking of Gladstone in the preface, just as he avoided Greece by setting the action in Bulgaria.

Another warning was sounded in Ford Madox Ford's essay "Little States and Great Nations" in May 1909. Greece, Ford said, "because she was once the fair field of heroes, poets, and wise men, has been artificially turned into a kind of Yellowstone Park, into a reserve where strange races quarrel futilely in a territory that appears not to be worth commercial exploitation. Greece, indeed, we may say, is the ironic tribute that Europe pays to the Arts of peace" (357). Ford echoed, perhaps unintentionally, an idea that had first appeared in Mary Shelley's *The Last Man* eighty years earlier and that would often be heard in the next decade: Greece had become a place of endless— and futile—struggles to be free.[39]

Unlike Shaw, Ford lamented the passing of the heroic ideals and the fact that England had lost its place as the home "of Humanitarian ideals," a place that "sent Byron to Greece" and "gave hospitality to Mazzini, to Cavour, to Garibaldi" (358). He provided a reason for this development in another piece published later in the same year, "The Passing of the Great Figure," where he said, "For the time being and until others arise the great Victorian figures were the last of the priests" (104). Ford here acknowledged the end of an era, for it was not simply that the Victorian age had great figures but also, as Beckson noted, "the Victorians were notable for their hero-worship" (286; he points particularly to Carlyle's *On Heroes and Hero-worship*). Ford argued that, in the modern age, "the conditions of everyday life and thought have changed so entirely that we very much doubt whether a Ruskin or a Gladstone would to-day find any kind of widespread dominion" (104). The present, Ford said, was a time of "innumerable shades of opinion, each shade finding its expression and contributing to the obscuring of the issues." He continued:

And this produces in the public mind a weariness, a confusion that leads in the end to something amounting almost to indifference. Thus, supposing that Mr. Gladstone should nowadays call attention to the misrule in Macedonia, he might very well find a tendency upon the part of the public to say that the Macedonians are one of the weak races of the world, and that the sooner and the more efficiently they are stamped out the better it will be for a world which was already growing over-populated. Or—this is still more likely—he might find that the public mind was utterly unable to make the effort to interest itself at all in the matter of Macedonia. (105)

Like Shaw, Ford employed Gladstone's wider philhellenism as a prime example of a way of thinking that no longer existed. But, while the road to understanding Macedonia, an important part of Ford's "reserve where strange races quarrel futilely," lay through Greece and Byron, Ford, like Shaw, confined himself in the passage above to Macedonia and Gladstone. It is as though the two writers were sparring with the magic force of legend, trying to gauge how strong it still was.

A more direct challenge was sounded in T. E. Hulme's "Romanticism and Classicism," a lecture given in 1911. Hulme declared, "After a hundred years of romanticism, we are in for a classical revival" (59). That may at first sound like good news to philhellenes, but he means a *neo*classical revival. In an ominous note for the fate of Byronic philhellenism, Hulme said that contemporary conservative critics in France held that "romanticism made their revolution, so they hate romanticism," as "romanticism in both England and France is associated with political views" (60). The central premise of Romanticism, according to Hulme, is that "man is by nature good . . . an infinite reservoir of possibilities, and if you can so rearrange society by the destruction of oppressive order then these possibilities will have a chance and you will get Progress." Classicism, on the other hand, holds that "man is an extraordinary fixed and limited animal whose nature is absolutely constant. It is only by tradition and organization that anything decent can be got out of him" (61).

Hulme's aesthetic idea of ancient Greeks, not surprisingly, was the exact opposite of the "fleshly" Greeks presented by Pater. As Cassandra Laity, in a discussion of Hulme's masculinization of the Greek past, observed, "The Romanticism of Swinburne, Shelley, and Byron was defined as 'feminine,' 'damp,' and 'vague'; Classicism, which formed the model for Imagism, 'dry,' 'hard,' 'virile,' and 'exact.'" (2–3). In Hulme's aesthetics, the Greece of Homer appeared to be in opposition to the Greece of Byron, and a logical corollary, one that Hulme does not state directly, would be that, to paraphrase Woolf, one should keep old Greece on the right hand with Imagism and new Greece on the left with Romanticism.

Echoing the sentiment of Hulme, in his essay "The Function of Criticism" (1919), T. S. Eliot stated simply that the difference between classicism and Romanticism "seems . . . rather the difference between the complete and the fragmentary, the adult and the immature, the orderly and the chaotic" (*Selected Essays* 70). As M. H. Abrams observed, "Many of the chief figures of the Modernist movement—including, in England and America, Hulme, Pound, and Eliot—identified themselves as explicitly counter-Romantic" (427).[40] The Western construction of modern Greece, obviously, was closely tied to Romanticism, indeed one might say that it had been built upon it. If in his poem "September 1913," Yeats could write, "Romantic Ireland's dead and gone, / Its with O'Leary in the grave," what would a modern poet say about the Romantic Greece of Byron, a historical and literary precursor for Yeats's Romantic Ireland? Not surprisingly, the end of the Grèce de Byron, therefore, could be employed as a symbol of the death of Romanticism.

It soon was—in a short piece of fiction in the *Harvard Monthly* by the young John Dos Passos entitled "The Honor of the Klepht," which appeared, fittingly, just five months before the start of the Great War. The story begins with a familiar ring: a youthful leader of a band of klephts arrives at his village to find that the Turks have carried away his beloved Louka. He organizes a night attack on the Turkish camp to rescue her. All goes well until he finds Louka in a Turkish tent, dressed in silks, and seated on a divan beside the pasha. The young Greek flees the scene, cutting his way through Turkish soldiers, only to fling himself from a cliff, yelling "Louka is dead." The romance of liberation, as well as the idea of a feminized Greece, which needed to be rescued, had finally been subverted, and so was a way of writing that had lasted at least since the publication of *The Giaour* more than a century earlier. This was not the last time that "klepht" would appear in a title, and versions of the romance of liberation would continue to appear throughout the twentieth century. But the hollowness of the literary convention had been exposed.

Dos Passos had visited Greece in the winter of 1912,[41] but his story is more an engagement with literary history than with anything that he saw on his journey. The theme of many of Dos Passos's undergraduate stories is Romantic disillusionment in general; in "The Almeh," his first story in the *Harvard Monthly*, he deconstructed Romantic Orientalism in a similar fashion. "The Honor of the Klepht" is remarkable not because it is terribly insightful nor clever, but rather because it took so long for someone to write such a revision. Nor did Dos Passos's story have wide influence on other writers; few knew of its existence. While "The Honor of the Klepht" demonstrated that Byron's Greece was moribund, it did not indicate what kind of Greek would replace the young klepht in Western literature.

Clearly, the onslaught of modern literature that Shaw had predicted in 1898 had hardly touched English and American attitudes toward modern

Greece by the first months of 1914. If people wrote about modern Greece, it was generally within the Byronic tradition. Through the end of the Balkan Wars, it remained as if in a sealed compartment, seemingly immune to the innovations in thought and art around it. It would take more than an onslaught of naturalistic plays or the declaration of a new classicist era to end the Greece of Byron. It would take a catastrophe on a grand scale.

III

THE END OF
AMBROSIA & BRIGANDS
(1914–1939)

7

Constantinople, Our Star

On April 25, 1915, Denis Browne wrote a long letter to Edward Marsh concerning the passing and burial of Rupert Brooke, who had died of a fever on a British hospital ship in the Aegean. Brooke and Browne were among the British troops sent to the Aegean to take part in the assault on Gallipoli, which the British and French hoped would force open the Hellespont and Dardanelles, cause Turkey to sue for peace, and bring a speedy conclusion to the First World War. Browne described Brooke's gravesite on the island of Skyros:

> We buried him the same evening in the olive grove I mentioned before—one of the loveliest places on this earth, with grey-green olives round him, one weeping above his head; the ground covered with flowering sage, bluish grey & smelling more delicious than any flowers I know. . . . Think of it all under a clouded moon, with the three mountains around & behind us, and all those divine scents everywhere. We lined his grave with all the flowers we could find, & Quilter set a wreath of olives on the coffin. . . .
>
> Freyberg, Oc, and I, Charles and Cleg stayed behind and covered the grave with great pieces of marble which were lying about everywhere. Of the cross at the head you know [it was white wood with Brooke's name in black letters]. . . . On the back of it our Greek interpreter, a man picked up by Oc at Lemnos, wrote in pencil:

> ἐνθαδε κεῖται
> ὁδοῦλος τοῦ θεοῦ
> ἀνθυπολοχαγὸς τοῦ
> Ἀγγλικοῦ ναυτικοῦ
> ἀποθανὼν ὑπὲρ τῆς
> ἀπελευθέρωσεως τῆς
> Κων-πόλεως ἀπὸ
> τῶν Τουρκῶν.

It was quite spontaneous, and, don't you think, apt. (*Letters of Rupert Brooke* 685–86)

Geoffrey Keynes, Brooke's friend and editor, translated the passage in a note as "here lies the servant of God, sublieutenant of the British navy, who died for the deliverance of Constantinople from the Turks" (686).

If Brooke's funeral had been a simple and hurried affair carried out by men who had to embark for the beaches of Gallipoli at 6:00 A.M. the next morning, Browne's description of the event was a carefully crafted attempt at myth making. The detailed account of the natural abundance around the gravesite intentionally calls to mind Brooke's involvement with the "neopagans."[1] Neopaganism was at least partly based on a desire to return to a pastoral Greek way of life, an impression Browne strengthens by those "great pieces of marble," scattered remnants of antiquity, which add a touch of Winckelmann to a grove of Theocritus. Those slabs also contain a bit of irony, as during his life Brooke had found his version of pastoral "Greece" in Polynesia, not on the shores of the Mediterranean.

After the poet's English friends had established a classical Brooke, the Greek interpreter, we are informed, took a pencil and created another Brooke, a philhellene who died fighting to free Constantinople. In Browne's text, it reads as a touching, spontaneous act by the only Greek present. Curiously, although the Greek wrote in his native language on a wooden cross with a pencil in the middle of the night, Browne could give a precise transcription of the Greek text in his letter. Was there some discussion, either at the graveside or earlier, about what should be written in Greek on the cross? If so, was the Greek interpreter serving mainly as a translator rather than as an author? To whom were these words really directed?

Not to the local Greeks, one assumes. The message in pencil on painted white wood would be hard to read immediately after it was written and was probably illegible within days. Both the marble fragments and the interpreter's message on the cross were intended, to use the words of Henry James, to link Brooke, "like Byron, for consecration in the final romance, with the islands of Greece" ("Rupert Brooke" 749). The language and the author of the lines on the cross provided the bona fides that the Greeks thought of Brooke as a philhellenic hero, a somewhat dubious proposition. In his *Roumeli* (1962), Patrick Leigh Fermor reported that the inhabitants of Skyros were not sure of who Brooke was although they were "proud of his presence" on the island (174).[2] The Greeks, who would not join the war on the side of the Allies until 1917, had serious misgivings about the liberation of Constantinople by an expeditionary force whose stated goal was to leave the Golden City in the hands of the Russians.[3] The Byronization of Brooke was an exclusively English enterprise, a kind of philhellenism without Greeks.[4]

Given the aura of Byron that had pervaded writing about modern Greece, it was perhaps too much to ask a group of aspiring young authors not to associate a fellow poet who had died of a fever on the eve of an assault against the Turks with the hero of Missolonghi. Yet, as Robert Liddell soberly observed, the link between the "poet of England" and a Greek isle seems more than a bit anomalous: "For any other poet it [Skyros] would be a most fortunate place of burial—not perhaps for Rupert Brooke, as it makes his most famous poem a little silly. Can we think of this corner of Skyros as forever Rugby?" (*Aegean Greece* 29). It is, of course, ironic that Byron and Brooke died in the service of opposing causes. Byron went to Greece to struggle against the political order and cultural values of which Britain was a part, while Brooke died in the service and was posthumously offered to the British public as the prime representative of, to use the phrase of Kipling, "all we have and are." If Brooke had perished on the Western front, or any place other than the Aegean, it is fairly safe to assume that no one would have attempted to make him the new Byron. But on Skyros, with Missolonghi just beyond the horizon, it was almost impossible to think sanely. In D. M. Thomas's novel *Lady with a Laptop* (1997), the hero notes, "Later the Greeks made a marble tomb [for Brooke on Skyros], and on it there's his famous sonnet which starts 'If I should die, think only this of me. That there's some corner of a foreign field that is forever England'" (212). Skyros *could* become forever Rugby.

In the same month that Brooke died, Wyndham Lewis published a piece in the avant-garde journal *Blast* entitled "Constantinople Our Star," which began: "That Russia will get Constantinople should be the prayer of every good artist in Europe. And more, immediately, if the Turks succeeded in beating off the Allies' attack, it would be a personal calamity to those interested in the Arts" (11). Some of the benefits of a Russian Constantinople would be "probably the best Shakespeare Theatre in the world at this gate of the East" along with such amenities as "week-end bungalows in Babylon," a "long white 'independents' exhibition on the shores of the Bosphorus," and "endless varieties of Cafes, Gaming-houses, Casinos, and Cinemas" (11). The rest of this satirical sketch focused on the lack of "an organized intellectual life" in England and the wretched English sense of humor. In this piece, Lewis ridiculed the inflated rhetoric surrounding the contemporary Gallipoli campaign, a campaign that in turn exploited the millennarian dreams about Constantinople and the long-held philhellenic belief about a revival of the classical Greeks.

Lewis may not have been serious when he concluded: "Let us keep our eyes fixed on Constantinople" (11). But others were, and that included, not counting Russians, Bulgarians, and Serbs, nearly every Greek and foreign philhellene.[5] These latter two groups certainly were not praying that Russia should gain control of the Golden City. The liberation of Constantinople from the Turks had always been the ultimate goal of "the great unfinished struggle for Greek independence" (McCarthy I.13). In 1830, two years before the treaty establishing the Greek state was signed, Charles MacFarlane depicted a Greek in Constantinople yearning for freedom in *The Armenians: A Tale of Constantinople*. In 1883, Elizabeth Edmonds wrote in her poem "Fair Athenae" that Greece's "love-longing eyes forever turn toward Constantinople." Throughout nineteenth-century writing in English about Greece, Constantinople was indeed "our star."[6]

In Mary Shelley's *Last Man*, the sign of Greek victory was to be the planting of "the Grecian standard on the height of St. Sophia" (194), and the restoration of the famous church became a symbol not only of the liberation of the city but also of the regeneration of the Greek race and, by extension, Western civilization. In a curious case of historical amnesia, the fate of the center of the Orthodox faith, which had closed Plato's academy in 529 CE, became a sacred cause for those who had caught the fever of Hellenism by reading that same Plato. In "The Present Position of the Greek Nation" (1879), Edward Augustus Freeman said, "The hearth and home of the Greek nation is the Church of Saint Sophia. Till the worship of the Eastern Church again goes up within its walls in the tongue of Chrysostom and Photios, the Greek nation must still be looked on as strangers and pilgrims in its own land" (3). Prior to the Greek defeat in the Greco-Turkish War of 1920–1922, "no modern Greek ever dreamed of reconstituting Athens as the permanent capital of the Greek world. . . . Not to the Parthenon of Athens, but to Santa Sophia in Constantinople did his mingled emotions of religious and political greatness yearn with a burning zeal" (Morgenthau, *I Was Sent to Athens* 11).

Such statements presented something of an ideological dilemma for philhellenes, as the Acropolis also had a claim to be the hearth and home of the "real" Greek race, and its liberation was to have ended the period in which Greeks were strangers in their own land. In 1912, Joseph Conrad wrote: "I cannot imagine that most democratic of kingdoms desiring a capital other than Athens—the very cradle of democracy, matchless in the wonders of its life and vicissitudes of its history" ("Future of Constantinople" 149). In her novel *The Grasp of the Sultan*, Demetra Vaka Brown attempted to address this problem. Athens, says a Greek patriot in Constantinople, "is without soul. It is Greece in body, in form; but the soul is here. When that is free, the Acropolis will come to life—not before" (189). In Compton Mackenzie's *South Wind of Love* (1937), set during World War I, the main character, a fictional representation of the author, suggests that Constantinople and parts of Asia Minor were crucial to the long-awaited Greek resurrection: "If the Turks are driven out of Europe and pushed back into the interior of Asia where they belong, and whence they should never have been allowed to emerge, why then Greece can be her complete self again" (805). Greece's true self, for Mackenzie and other foreign philhellenes, was the pagan past, and they sought a revival of classical rather than Byzantine civilization. How a Greek Constantinople would revive the Hellenism of Athens was never clearly addressed. Most philhellenes simply accepted the logic, or illogic, that the way to bring life back to the Parthenon lay through Constantinople and St. Sophia.[7]

In the first two decades of the twentieth century, Vaka Brown, a native of Constantinople, transferred the romance of Greek liberation to the Golden Horn with her novels *The First Secretary* (1907), *In the Shadow of Islam* (1911), and *The Grasp of the Sultan* (1917), all of which are set in Constantinople before the beginning of the Balkan Wars.[8] The last of the three is the more traditional philhellenic romance, in which an English hero, in this case a tutor to the sons of the sultan, rescues a Greek from the Turkish ruler's harem. The woman is a Cretan who as a baby had somehow survived a fall from cliffs when her mother had committed suicide to escape Turkish soldiers. Once again, the Greek female personifies the nation; a Greek who has dedicated himself to the national struggle describes the heroine: "She is Greece—the noblest part—the daughter of ever-rising, ever-struggling Crete" (275). Her liberation is taken by the same patriot as symbolic of the fate of the Golden City: "And here, within sight of the Parthenon, she is freed from Musulman shackles—she is a living emblem of Greater Greece— a forerunner of the destiny which is Constantinople's some day" (298). At the end of the book, however, the living emblem of Greater Greece is on her way to France and has agreed to marry her British rescuer, which makes her fate resemble that of the Elgin marbles. But as with other versions of the romance, Vaka Brown is more interested in exciting sentiment for the cause than working out the details.[9]

In the Shadow of Islam is a more interesting version of the Greek romance, in part because it speaks directly about a historical development within Turkey that threatened the Hellenic dreams of a Greek Constantinople. In his novel *Paul Patoff* (1888), F. Marion Crawford has a resident of the Ottoman capital tell his American visitors: "To you Franks we are a nation of robbers, murderers and thieves, we are the Turkey of Byron, always thirsting for blood, spilling it senselessly, and crying out for more" (231). In 1908, however, a movement called the Young Turks took power, forced Sultan Abdul Hamid to abdicate the following year, and promised that it would enact constitutional reforms, which would bring the Ottoman lands into the "modern" world. In reaction to this news, as George Burgin put it in a fictional exposé of the Young Turks, *The Man Behind* (1923), "Sanguine but inexperienced Englishmen immediately announced that Turkey was about to cast off the fatalism of the ages and reform itself" (235). In reality, according to Burgin, the Young Turks were the worst of the Ottomans and "ruffians of the deepest dye" (114).[10] In Barry Unsworth's more recent novels, *Pascali's Island* (1980) and *The Rage of the Vulture* (1982), the events of 1908 were depicted as the end of the Ottoman era, but this was rarely the case in fiction written in the first two decades of the twentieth century.

Vaka Brown's novel appeared at a time of debate in the West over the real intentions and designs of the Young Turks, and her purpose, like Burgin's, was to show that the Turks were incapable of reform. The major Turkish character, the Oxford-educated Orkhan, is introduced as "a dreamer and an idealist. He had believed that all those in the cause of Young Turkey had, like him, one aim, the making of Turkey into a country just to all her subjects" (96). But when faced with the reality of such principles, Orkhan reveals himself to be a despotic Oriental who cannot conceive of equality for non-Turks or freedom for women. Orkhan asserts, "Turks and Turks alone must rule" (226), and "the mere fact that he wanted a woman was sufficient reason that she should become his" (165). The controlling motif for Turkish oppression remains sexual domination, and Vaka Brown's use of an American heroine, Millicent Grey, and her abduction into a harem is no doubt intended to bring the "truth" about the Young Turks forcefully home to her American audience.

Although not a Greek, Millicent has the requisite Praxitelean features of a heroine of the romance of liberation (1). She falls for the combination of Orkhan's Western idealism and Eastern allure during a visit to an aunt in Constantinople. She is able to come to her senses and refuse Orkhan's proposal of marriage with the help of her Greek friend Elpis, just as American readers of the novel are helped to see through the Young Turks with the aid of the Greek author, Vaka Brown.

Vaka Brown's view of Greek men in this book is strikingly negative. Elpis tells Millicent that she will never marry because the available Greeks are "burned-out lamps," "and those that are not burned-out are smoking. Every beautiful emotion which God has given them to cultivate through life, is forced and wasted in ten years. . . . That is why we are the race we are today. We inherit the hellenic dreams which have kept our race alive for so many centuries, in spite of conquests, but we do not receive our fathers' strength to turn dreams into action" (118; see also 200–201). Her own brother is a "lukewarm Greek" through much of the book, although near the end he dies in an attempt to rescue the abducted Millicent from the palace harem.

If English-speaking audiences were presented with a Greek woman offering a positive view of Greek men by Julia Dragoumis, then with Demetra Vaka Brown that same audience heard an insider present a rather severe catalogue of their faults. The difference between the two writers might have something to do with their personal experiences. Vaka Brown not only wrote a version of the romance of liberation, she lived one. In her autobiography, she says that her move to America, where she met and married Kenneth Brown, was made to avoid an arranged marriage, referred to as "the usual fate of a Greek girl . . . and the worst thing that could befall one" (*Child of the Orient* 195).[11] Vaka Brown, a Greek patriot who championed the cause of Greater Greece in all of her works, had serious disagreements with the social structure of her own people. Like her heroine Elpis, she rejected marriage into what she saw as a dissipated patriarchal society. Yet in presenting her critique of Greek society to an American audience, she, unlike Dragoumis, could be accused of perpetuating a negative stereotype of the Greek male.

With the Greek victories in the Balkan Wars, the recovery of Constantinople changed from a vague dream to an actual possibility. Conrad mused whether "I have lived long enough to see the end of the Eastern question which has dogged my footsteps from my very cradle?" (*Collected Letters* 5.124). The anticipation was heightened by an old legend. The assassination of the Greek king, George I, in Thessaloniki in March 1912 brought his son Constantine to the throne. When John Dos Passos visited Constantinople in 1921, a Greek told him: "You know the legend [about the city], a Constantine built it, a Constantine lost it, and a Constantine will regain it" (*Orient Express* 22). In 1915, while traveling through a still-neutral Greece, John Reed reported that a Greek soldier said: "Sure we want to go to war! We conquer Constantinople. Our king—he is named Constantine, and once Constantinople was Greek! You remember? We will go back to Constantinople with Constantine" (14).

But before the Greeks could follow their king into Constantinople, the Allies landed at Gallipoli in their own attempt to triumphantly recover the city from Islam. As the troops arrived on the peninsula, Prime Minister Herbert Henry Asquith declared that the success of the campaign would signify "the death knell of Ottoman domination, not only in Europe, but in Asia. The mastery of the Dardanelles will pass into other hands. The cross will replace the crescent on the minaret of St. Sophia" (*The Dardanelles* 160). In Ernest Raymond's novel *Tell England* (1922), the young heroes are initially disappointed to learn they will be sent to Gallipoli rather than to France. Their colonel, invoking the Trojan War, Marathon, and Byron's swim across the Hellespont (195), concludes his justification of the expedition: "I say the Gallipoli campaign is a new Crusade. . . . It's the Cross against the Crescent again, my lads. By Jove, it's splendid, perfectly splendid! And an English cross, too!" (196–97).[12] Philhellenic language had already been extended to cover the other Christian peoples of the Balkans. In 1915, by reason of the same geographical contiguity that had led to the Byronization of Brooke, that rhetoric also covered patriotic young Englishmen in the service of their homeland.

Gallipoli eventually found a place not in the literary tradition of philhellenism but rather within what Samuel Hynes has called the myth of the

Great War—that "a generation of innocent young men, their heads full of
high abstractions like Honour, Glory, and England, went off to war to make a
world safe for democracy. They were slaughtered in stupid battles planned
by stupid generals. They were shocked, disillusioned, and embittered by
their own war experience, and saw that the real enemies were not Germans,
but the old men who had lied to them. They rejected the values of the society
that had sent them to the war, and in doing so separated themselves from the
past and from their cultural inheritance." (*War Imagined* xii). One of the first
novels in English to express this viewpoint was A. P. Herbert's *The Secret
Battle* (1919), in which the hero serves with distinction at Gallipoli before
being shot for desertion in France.

Near the beginning of *The Secret Battle*, the troops are "threading a
placid way between the deceitful Aegean islands. Harry loved them because
they wore so green and inviting an aspect, and again I did not undeceive him
and tell him how parched and austere, how barren of comfortable grass and
shade he would find them on closer acquaintance" (12). The isles of Greece
themselves are presented as complicit in a "romantic, imaginative outlook,"
which will not survive careful scrutiny nor the experience of battle (15). The
link between the adjectives "romantic" and "Romantic" can at times be ten-
uous, but the deceitful Greek islands certainly put both meanings into play,
since romance and Romanticism were part of the cultural heritage from
which the "myth of the war" desired to separate itself. That most of the
philhellenes of the Greek War of Independence had experienced a similar
disenchantment after their experience of war was ignored. At the end of the
nineteenth century, the fight for Greek freedom had become one of the inherited myths connected with the "high abstractions" told by the "old
men." In Raymond's *Tell England*, Doe, who would die at Helles, remarks,
"The romantic genius of Britain is beginning to see the contour of Gallipoli
invested with a mist of sadness, and presenting an appearance like a mirage
of lost illusions" (269–70). Within that mirage of illusions were names and
words such as Marathon, Byron, classical ideals, glory, and progress. The
last of these had been closely associated with the concept of the regeneration
of the ancient Greeks after 1770 in particular and through Romanticism in
general. But, as Paul Fussell remarked, the Great War "reversed the idea of
progress" (*Great War and Modern Memory* 21). A passage from Jack Bennett's novel *Gallipoli* (1981) illustrates the contrast of the "old" and the
"modern" perspective of the campaign on "classic ground": "'Over there is
Lemnos! Lemnos, Gray, and on those very mountains you're looking at now,
why, more than two thousand years ago, the Trojan War was fought. Think
of the mighty warriors who have fought in this area—Achilles, Nestor,
Ulysses, Hector!' 'And we're still fighting here in 1915,' murmured Lieu-
tenant Gray. 'We haven't learned much, have we, sir?'" (200). What was
learned in the Great War would have an enormous impact on how Lieu-

tenant Gray and his generation would respond to the Greece of Byron in the years after the war.

If the contour of Gallipoli was soon viewed within a mirage of lost illusions, that mirage did not immediately extend to the contours of wartime Greece. "Perhaps the last thing forgotten about the war will be that the King of Greece was called Tino," Compton Mackenzie wrote in *First Athenian Memories* (33). The Greek king's nickname was indeed well known, even by Marcel's butler in Proust's *In Search of Lost Time*: "Our butler, for instance, if the King of Greece was mentioned, was able, thanks to the newspapers, to say like the Kaiser Wilhelm: 'Tino?'" (648). But that knowledge hardly ranked among the things that most people remembered about the years of conflict; neither Paul Fussell nor Samuel Hynes ever mention Constantine in their magisterial books about the cultural legacy of the Great War.[13] With respect to writing in English about Greece during the war, however, Mackenzie was largely correct. The focus was not on armies and battles but rather on the confrontation between the pro-Allied Prime Minister Eleftherios Venizelos and King Constantine, who favored maintaining Greece's neutrality.[14]

When the Great War began, Venizelos urged the Greeks to ally themselves with the British and French. King Constantine and Army Chief of Staff Ioannis Metaxas were a bit more cautious. Unlike Venizelos, they thought that the Germans had a good chance for victory and, if Greece chose the wrong side, it could expect to lose territory to both Turkey and Bulgaria. Another major disagreement was that Venizelos appeared ready to cede some of eastern Macedonia for promised territory in Asia Minor. The king found such a deal decidedly less appealing. And, almost from the beginning of the conflict, Britain and France, on the rather specious grounds that they were two of Greece's guarantors, violated Greek sovereignty with impunity, eventually occupying the second city of the country, Thessaloniki, and sending troops into Athens itself. Yet, Venizelos tacitly supported the Allies and encouraged them to land in Thessaloniki even as he informed them that, in the event, he would have to lodge a formal protest.

In addition, the king had shown himself to be a rather inept constitutional monarch at a time when the country had a dynamic elected leader. In 1915, Constantine forced Venizelos to resign, but in the following election the prime minister was returned to office with a substantial majority. Yet just months later, the king asked for Venizelos's resignation again. The king may have truly believed that the prime minister's pro-Allied policy placed Greece in jeopardy, but such open disregard for the will of the people was bound to cause trouble. Venizelos and his party boycotted the next election as a protest, which led to a government with a secure base in Parliament but not in the country.

In September 1916, the Greek commander in eastern Macedonia surrendered the town of Kavala to the Germans. It is unclear precisely why this event occurred, but the Germans could certainly point to the fact that there were British and French troops all over Greece. For Greeks, the matter was viewed differently, for with the Germans came the hated Bulgarians. The king and the army officers who had opposed Venizelos in order to keep, they had said, the Bulgarians out of Macedonia, had just handed it over without a fight. Venizelos, who may have been waiting for such an excuse, left Athens for Crete to declare a rival provisional government.

Venizelos was not instantly recognized by the Allies as the legitimate ruler of Greece, although he received various kinds of assistance. As relations between King Constantine and the Allies worsened, it would have been logical for the Greek king to seek support in the other camp. Whether he did or not, in June 1917 the British and French moved troops into Athens, forced the king to abdicate and leave for exile, and restored Venizelos to power in the Greek capital. Greece, which already had some Venizelist regiments fighting with the Allies on the Salonica front, now officially joined the war on the Allied side.

Greeks were genuinely divided between Constantine and Venizelos. In his novel *Argo* (1936, tr. 1951), the Greek author George Theotokas said of the political division in Greece: "There were National Venizelists and Nationalist anti-Venizelists, Marxist Venizelists and anti-Venizelist Marxists. And it was a thousand times easier for a Venizelist Nationalist to reach an understanding with a Venizelist Marxist than with an anti-Venizelist Nationalist. There were men who believed deeply in a republic and yet became fanatical monarchists to revenge themselves on Venizelos; and vice versa" (287).

No such split existed among English, French, and American writers, who were nearly unanimously enthusiastic Venizelists. So popular was Venizelos in England after 1916 that the scholar P. N. Ure warned his audience, "we can not be pro-Venizelos and anti-Greek" (6). The enthusiasm for Venizelos in countries opposed to Germany was entirely predictable, since Constantine, whose queen was a member of the German royal family, was perceived to favor the Central Powers in the war. But philhellenic Venizelism ran deeper than the simple adage that the enemy of my enemy is my friend. The strong liberal tradition of philhellenism had always been rather uncomfortable with a king in regenerated Greece. Athens was sacred as the fount of world liberty and representative government. The Greek king, because he was a king, had almost as much chance as the Turks to gain favor with English and American philhellenes. In *Greek Salad* (1935), Kenneth Matthews said that his friend Gresham "was a Venizelist. But he was not a Venizelist for the same reason that a Greek or even an interested Englishman was a Venizelist. Gresham hated monarchy; he had, as it were, an *a priori* hatred of it" (157).[15] The philhellenic societies in Britain, France, and America operated as propaganda machines for Venizelos, since, in their eyes, they were defending the "real"

Greeks from the "non-Greeks."[16] The division between "pure" Greeks and "mixed" Greeks, so prevalent in late nineteenth-century literature, now entered Greek domestic politics and was used almost exclusively for the benefit of Venizelos.

Indeed, Venizelos had been hailed, to use the phrase in Robert Byron's *The Byzantine Achievement*, as "the one living undegenerate descendant of Pericles" even before the war (2). The first publication of the Anglo-Hellenic League, founded in December 1913 "to remind the English world of the continuity of the Hellenic race and language; of the merit of modern Greek literature; of the undying elements in national character; and the extraordinary public spirit displayed by the Hellenes during the vicissitudes of the last hundred years," claimed that the organization would be nonpartisan in Greek and English politics (2). Yet shortly thereafter, one of its leading members, R. M. Burrows, stated, "Venizelos is curiously like the bust of Pericles by Cresilos in the British Museum" (*New Greece* 7–8).[17]

It is not surprising then, that Burrows viewed Constantine's abdication and Venizelos's return to Athens as "a dramatic moment,—a glorious moment—for us Philhellenes, who have had so much hard fighting to do" (*Annual Meeting of the Anglo-Hellenic League* 16). Not to be outdone by their British counterparts, the American Hellenic Society published two poems by Edith M. Thomas, one entitled "Who Shall Save Hellas?" (the answer was Venizelos) and another about the departure of King Constantine called "The Freedom of Greece Has Come Once More" (in Ferriman, *Greece— and Tomorrow* 51–52).

Philhellenic writers wrapped Venizelos in the magic force of Byronic legend. On the title page of his book *Venizelos* (1920), Richard Boardman quoted from "The Isles of Greece." Venizelos was often depicted as a "Cretan klepht" for his role in the Cretan uprising of 1897.[18] In the face of numerous Venizelist books, including those by novelists Vincent Seligman (*The Victory of Venizelos*, 1920) and Demetra Vaka Brown (*Constantine: King and Traitor* and *In the Heart of German Intrigue*), the king found only one notable English or American philhellene to speak up for him, Paxton Hibben, an American with ties to Greenwich Village radicals who served on the editorial board of the *New Masses* in the 1920s.[19] In *Constantine I and the Greek People* (1920), Hibben attempted to employ traditional philhellenic arguments by asserting that the Greek king was "more democratic, perhaps, than any monarch of his day" (6) and that Venizelos's faction was supported by "elements to a certain extent not even Greek" (8). But a monarch could hardly seem more democratic than the new Pericles and a half-Danish king with a German wife more Greek than a Cretan klepht. Hibben himself accurately predicted what would come from the pens of his fellow writers: "They will blackguard Constantine like a pickpocket and advertise Venizelos as an angel from heaven" (viii).

If during the War of Independence philhellenes viewed "the cause of Greece" as "the cause of Europe," then during World War I British intelligence agents in the country, nearly all of whom had caught Hellenic fever, could view the cause of Greece as the "cause of the Entente" and foster dreams of careers as little Byrons. J. C. Lawson wrote of his work in intelligence during the war that "it fell into my lot to play a conscious part in the fashioning of Modern Greek history" (2). Lawson reported how he dreamed of creating a "greater Aegean Republic" cut loose from mainland Greece, comprising a region "wherein alone survives a pure strain of old Greek blood; a little world belonging to neither West nor to East, enjoying freedom, yet not coveting progress as the Western world interprets it" (151).[20] Greece was still an area where some Westerners thought that they could actively seek their imagined "perfect state," even in the midst of the universal carnage.

The fiction in English written about the Great War in Greece usually depict the adventures of little Byrons who, with "maids of Athens" by their sides, save Greece from the new barbarian, the Teutonic Constantine, and assist the patriot, Venizelos. In Joseph Hocking's *Tommy and the Maid of Athens* (1917), a British captain helps a patriotic Greek girl prevent the betrayal of the country to the Germans or, to use the words of the Greek heroine, to prevent "Greece being made a slave state to a nation of savages" (93). The captain found "something romantic" about the tales of a modern "Maid of Athens," "something that fitted with his ideas of the old Greek capital" (36). Eventually, the magic force of Byronic legend takes over the hero's mind: "John Penrose ceased to be a soldier who had come to Athens to discover the enemies' plan; the spirit of mystery, of romance which pervaded everything had caused him to forget" (95). That same spirit appears to have pervaded the mind of the author, for Hocking depicts an Athens that fitted with his notions of Byron. Vaka Brown's *In Pawn to a Throne* (1919), dedicated to Eleftherios Venizelos, has a similar plot with an American hero who helps a Greek girl foil Constantine's attempt to become an absolute monarch in the land that gave the world freedom (153; see pp. 68–70). Julia Dragoumis's novel about the Balkan Wars, *A Man of Athens* (1916), was also pro-Venizelist (see pp. 177–79).

The most famous, and most prolific, of both little Byrons and literary philhellenes of the day without question was Compton Mackenzie. With *Sinister Street* and *Guy and Pauline*, Mackenzie was already a bestselling author before he was sent to the Aegean in 1915 in the intelligence service. In the late 1920s and 1930s, he wrote his memoirs of the war, which appeared as *Gallipoli Memories*, *Greek Memories*, *First Athenian Memories*, and *Aegean Memories*.

Mackenzie, like Lawson, was still firmly in the grasp of Byronic legend. "Little did I guess at this date," he wrote, "how much of the Greek history I had learned in school would with myself as one of the protagonists be repeated nearly two thousand years later" (*First Athenian Memories* 68). Like other English philhellenes, he stood firmly with Venizelos, to whom a Greek in *First Athenian Memories* refers as "the greatest man Greece has known since the days of Marathon and Salamis" (52). On his first visit to Athens, Mackenzie met a young Greek woman who pleaded the cause of Venizelos and Greater Greece. He imagined that he "was listening to Pallas Athene herself pleading before Zeus the cause of her beloved Greeks. While she stood there, that glorious young woman, delivering a tirade against the oppressors of her country, I was thinking what a heroine of romance she would make" (*First Athenian Memories* 50). Mackenzie's picture of a female Greece pleading her case before an English Zeus gives pause and suggests that the tendency to feminize and victimize Greece had not diminished at all from the time of the War of Independence.

Mackenzie briefly presents the Venizelist position in his 1919 novel *Sylvia and Michael*, in which a Greek-American volunteer kills a Royalist Greek officer who had betrayed western Thrace to the Bulgarians (773–75). It also surfaces at times in his secret service novels *Extremes Meet* (1928) and *Three Couriers* (1929), both of which, like Hocking's *Maid of Athens*, center on intercepting communications between the German kaiser and the Greek king. But his most extended fictional depiction of wartime Greece occurs in *South Wind of Love* (1937), part of the semiautobiographical series called *The Four Winds of Love*. The hero, John Ogilvie, holds the same sentiments about Greece and Venizelos as his creator. For Ogilvie, the sight of the Acropolis has "the quality of the most intimate experience with a woman whom he had loved for a long while but whom time and place had never agreed to surrender to his arms" (395). His love of Greece leads him to become an active supporter of Venizelos, who in the book embodies the philhellenic dream of a Greater Greece. He also becomes the fiancé of a maid of Athens, suitably named Zoe, who inspires him to recite Byron's poem. Ogilvie loses his maid of Athens when the Germans torpedo the ship on which she was traveling to Athens to buy her wedding dress. This romanticized ending solves the complication that the eighteen-year-old Zoe seems in reality a poor match for an accomplished English playwright approaching middle age. Ogilvie's love of Zoe, admiration for Greece, and zeal for Venizelos suffer no disillusionment in the course of the novel; his fiercest criticism is reserved for the ineptitude and narrow-mindedness of the British military bureaucracy. As he prepares to depart from Greece, Ogilvie asks another Greek maiden, whose brother had been killed on the Macedonian front: "May not patriotism be a false god when we worship it with human sacrifices like a Moloch"? (804). She replies:

> You only wonder that now because you are weak after your illness, and heavy at heart from your loss. Surely when we sacrifice to patriotism

we sacrifice to the best part of ourselves. What is patriotism except an ideal conception of a country which expresses all that is best of the individuals who together make it a nation? . . . When I think of Leo lying dead at Doiran I do not think of my brother as the boy with whom I played and laughed through childhood, I think of him as a fragment of Hellas won back from the barbarians who have been defiling her for centuries. Without war she would now be dead. (804–6)

No expression of "the myth of the Great War" nor deconstruction of the "big words" can be found in this passage. Given that *South Wind of Love* was written after Robert Graves's *Good-Bye to All That*, Siegfried Sassoon's *Memoirs of a Fox-Hunting Man*, Robert Aldington's *Death of a Hero*, and Ernest Hemingway's *A Farewell to Arms*, one can read Mackenzie's book as an attempt at a revision of earlier accounts of the war. And Mackenzie specifically uses Greece and a Greek maiden in his response. At one point in Mackenzie's novel, someone asks the hero: "What would Byron sing of Greece today?" (393). The answer that Mackenzie's book provides, one must think intentionally, is just a slightly different version of the Maid of Athens legend along with the scarcely modified sentiments of *Childe Harold* and *The Giaour*. It was as if the Great War had changed nothing at all.

Proust found a more subtle and probing literary use for the confrontation between Venizelos and Constantine, one that, again, reveals the direction that English and American authors did not take. Although the two Greek leaders appear only briefly in the last volume of *In Search of Lost Time, Time Regained*, they represent another version of the central conflict between aristocracy and bourgeoisie so important to the novel.[21] King Constantine, of course, is aligned with the aristocratic Guermantes, especially baron de Charlus, who tells Marcel that, like most other royal figures, the Greek king shares both his pro-Germanism and his homosexual tastes: "I knew Constantine of Greece very well indeed when he was diadoch, he is a splendid man. I always thought that the Emperor Nicholas had a great affection for him. Of course I mean to imply nothing dishonourable. Princess Christian used to talk openly about it, but she is a terrible scandalmonger. As for the Tsar of the Bulgars, he is an out-and-out nancy and a monstrous liar, but very intelligent, a remarkable man. He likes me very much" (120–21). The baron is "in the tradition of Talleyrand and the Congress of Vienna" (87), and it was that very tradition that had provided Constantine's father with the Greek throne. But as Charlus's nephew says, "The age of the Congress of Vienna is dead and gone" (6:88), and the social upstarts, like the Verdurins and Brichot, are waiting for "the hour of Venizelos to strike" (6:120; see also Madame Verdurin's comments on 6:47). Proust created something more illuminating than a collision between a Greek patriot and a tyrannical barbarian; he employed the confrontation between leaders in Greece as a metaphor for the changes in politics and society at home in France.

One of the last and most innovative of the Byronic romances in English from the period of the war is Vita Sackville-West's *Challenge*; the novel was written from May 1918 to November 1919 but not printed until 1924. The book is a roman à clef about the author's tempestuous affair with Violet Trefusis grafted onto a tale of a rebellion of a Greek island, Aphros, from Herakleion, a fictitious Greek state that has won its independence from mainland Greece.[22] Sackville-West had never been to Greece before she wrote *Challenge*, so the Greek setting of the story was chosen, at least in part, to suggest the veiled lesbian love behind the affair of the cousins Julian and Eve, members of a prominent English merchant family in the Levant. Eve eventually betrays Julian and his attachment to the cause of liberty for the island of Aphros because she does not want to share her lover with anyone or anything.

In his introduction to the 1974 edition, Nigel Nicolson dismissed the political plot with the comment that "a young Byronic Englishman is not likely to have seduced the loyalty of a bunch of Greek islanders from their parent state" (10). This was, however, exactly what a number of young Byronic Englishmen, such as Mackenzie and Lawson, were attempting to do during the war. The rebellion in *Challenge* can be read as a reflection of the division between Constantine's preeminence on the mainland and Venizelos's control of Crete and the islands in 1916–1917. In fact, the territories of Greece and Herakleion in the novel reflect the actual geographic division between the areas of the Royalists and Venizelists.

The history of the fictitious Herakleion is, however, suspiciously like the history of modern Greece; independence was declared in 1826 and the first premier "after the secession from Greece" died in 1831, just like the first president of Greece (60–61). On an ideological level, then, the freedom of Herakleion from Greece might be read as the liberation of the modern Greek state from the burden of its Greek past. Whether Sackville-West intended such a reading is not made clear in the text. But the central theme of the novel is the desire to be rid of all oppression and constrictions, whether political, social, or sexual.

Challenge is, as far as I know, the first romance of liberation that deconstructs the idea of Greek irredentism. A Tory Englishman in the novel scoffs: "free peoples. Too many, too many." He adds that Herakleion, already broken away from Greece, is now "not even a chip. Only a chip of a chip." To which his companion says that the island of Aphros "wants to be a chip of a chip of a chip" (53). Ironically, the book was finished at a time when the author's husband, Harold Nicolson, was advising the British government to create a Greater Greece after the war.[23] Ironically again, where J. C. Lawson advocated an Aegean republic because only there "alone survives a pure strain of old Greek blood," Aphros and its neighboring islands are "ancestrally more Italian than Greek, for the archipelago of Hagios Zacharie had, centuries before, been swamped by the settlements of colonizing Genoese" (71) and speak their own Italianate Greek patois. It is fitting that one of the last romances of Greek liberation written before the Asia Minor Disaster of 1922 depicts an attempt to fracture rather than unify the Greek world. But the struggle for freedom in the novel is still not depicted ironically; rather, it is noble even in failure. *Challenge* is still a romance of liberation and its hero, as Nicolson observed, "a young Byronic Englishman."

The battlefield might have been absent from most books about wartime Greece, but the country had its share of troops and fighting. The second largest Allied army was centered at the Greek city of Salonica, or Thessaloniki. Curiously, however, the word *Greece* is rarely found in titles, nor does it figure prominently in the texts of books written by veterans of the army of the Orient. By their own accounts, they served in "Salonica" or "Macedonia"; see Seligman's *The Salonica Side-Show* and *Macedonian Musings*, H. Collinson Owen's *Salonica and After*, Lake's *In Salonica with Our Army*, Day's *Macedonian Memories*, and Macleod's *Macedonian Measures*. The inhabitants of the region are often referred to as "Macedonians," who are detached from the conflict and "did not seem to mind what happened, one way or another" (Isabel Hutton 49). That Macedonia was not considered an integral part of Greece is made clear by Harold Lake's comment: "I do not want to ask whether Macedonia should be returned to Greece or left in the hands of some other power. I have no suggestions to make about boundary lines or treaties after the war" (274). During the Great War, the region around Thessaloniki appeared, at least to Hugh MacDiarmid, as "a Greece that is not yet Helas [sic]" (*Letters* 14).

Unlike Gallipoli, the Macedonian campaign did not find a significant place in literature in English about the war; writers, even those who served there, seemed to accept that the enterprise was something of a sideshow to France. Vincent Seligman said of his service in the quartermaster corps of the army of the Orient that "in every way [his] adventures were unsatisfactory and unromantic" (*Salonica Side-Show* 115).[24] The only significant English artistic works inspired by the Salonica front were the paintings of camp life in the Sandham Memorial Chapel in Burghclere by Stanley Spencer. Hynes noted that the "spirit of the paintings is comradeship, kindness, caring, and love, and in the landscapes there is a kind of pastoral innocence, as though news of the death of landscape on the Western front had not yet reached the outskirts of Macedonia" (*War Imagined* 461).

Few Greeks would see the Macedonian campaign in that light, especially after 1924. Stratis Myrivilis's *Life in the Tomb*, whose first edition appeared in that year, is, according to its translator, "the single most successful and most widely read novel in Greece since the Great War" (Bien xiii). In outlook and subject matter, it resembles *A Farewell to Arms, All Quiet on the Western Front,* and *Parade's End,* books of the late 1920s that defined, if they did not create, our current memory of the Great War. Since Myrivilis was not translated into English until 1977, he had little impact on how the war in Greece was perceived by those abroad.

The most interesting piece of fiction in English from the Salonica front is probably Richard Harding Davis's last short story, "The Deserter" (1917), in which three American reporters covering the Macedonian front dissuade an American serving in the British ambulance corps from deserting and going home.[25] Their main argument is that the deserter, an aspiring author, would not be able to write about his experiences in the war because of public shame at his desertion. The deserter, hungry and half-frozen, suggests that warm, well-fed men cannot understand his situation. In the end, he reluctantly returns to the front, telling the reporters they can all go to hell (733). Davis raised questions about the role of honor and service while still upholding them. Now, when such famous American novels about the war as Dos Passos's *Three Soldiers,* e. e. cummings's *The Enormous Room,* and Hemingway's *A Farewell to Arms* all have deserters as heroes, Davis's story reads like one of the last, failed attempts by one of the old men to salvage some of the prewar values. Whether Davis himself thought that it would be easier to salvage them in a classic land far from the Western front, in hindsight it seems appropriate that he set his story where the death of landscape and civilization had not yet, in foreign eyes, found its way.

On October 17, 1918, the *Daily Telegraph* published on its front page a translation by Rudyard Kipling of the Greek national anthem, originally written during the Greek War of Independence by Dionysios Solomos. The beginning and ending are given below:

> We knew thee of old,
>   Oh divinely restored,
> By the light of thine eyes
>   And the light of the Sword.
>
> From the graves of our slain
>   Shall thy valour prevail
> As we greet thee again—
>   Hail Liberty! Hail! . . .
>
> Yet, behold now thy sons
>   With impetuous breath
> Go forth to the fight
>   Seeking Freedom or Death.

> From the graves of our slain
> Shall thy valour prevail
> As we greet thee again
> Hail, Liberty, Hail!
>
> (*Verse* 93–94)

It is surely one of the oddest pieces in the Kipling corpus. And the timing, at first glance, seems rather strange. Why was Kipling translating Solomos in the last months of the Great War?

The poem was part of an effort by philhellenes to attract attention to Greece and its territorial ambitions before and after the Versailles conference.[26] From 1915 to 1922 the number of philhellenic pamphlets and articles produced was surpassed in quantity only during the Greek War of Independence. The Anglo-Hellenic League alone printed fifty-two pamphlets, while the American Hellenic Society added another eighteen. Nearly all of them echoed the language of the previous century. In an essay of 1921 entitled "The Resurrection of Greece, 1821–1921," Harold Spender asserted that the present war in Asia Minor was "only one act in the great drama of Greek emancipation which began precisely one hundred years ago" (152). The first publication of the American Hellenic Society announced, "The day is at hand when Hellas will take the part that by right belongs to it in that struggle for grand ideals pursued by noble nations of the world" (in Gauvin xi). Edith Thomas encouraged Greek Americans to do their part by reminding them in verse that there "still resides in you / A Klephtic spark that can be blown again" (Ferriman, *Greece—and Tomorrow* 52). Beaumont reported to the *Daily Telegraph* from the frontlines in Asia Minor in 1921: "The Greeks are always Greeks. These of today are the same as the Greeks of old. In fighting their hereditary ancestors they seem to have caught the spirit of their ancestors" (*Greek Campaign in Asia Minor* 13). And T. P. O'Connor, a member of Parliament for Ireland, stated: "One thing is by this time settled in the mind of all Europe, that, so far as Europe is concerned, there is no policy for the Turks but the old Gladstone policy of driving them out of Europe, bag and baggage" (introduction to *Greece before the Conference* xxii).

Looking back on the postwar years in 1939, T. S. Eliot noted that the "period immediately following the war is often spoken of as a time of disillusionment: in some ways and for some people it was rather a period of illusions" (*Criterion*, vol. 18, p. 271). For philhellenes, it was clearly a time of illusions from the prewar era. The possible resurrection of Greece once again filled a psychic need for some in Western Europe during a period of stress, and the activity of philhellenes for Greater Greece was in part a desire to find hope and promise in a world that seemed lost. As Bourdon put it, "If, on the morrow of the fall of Turkey, the Greeks of Constantinople had again possession of St. Sophia, which belongs to them, a great sign would suddenly illumine the black sky with light and the oriental problem would have been simplified" (23).[27]

Kipling's translation of the Greek national anthem was, then, a translation of several kinds. It was, at the basic level, a translation into English of a text from the time of the Greek War of Independence. It was also an attempt to "translate" the philhellenic spirit of that time to the twentieth century, as well as to suggest that the regeneration of Greece, and by extension civilization itself, were finally at hand. And it was an assertion that the prewar, nineteenth-century world still existed; the very language of the translation tries to make such a case with its consistent archaisms ("light of thine eye," "behold now thy sons"). Kipling's own involvement in the enterprise was itself part of the Romantic association of Greek freedom and English poetry. Kipling had never been previously connected with the cause of Greece, but as one of England's most popular writers, his translation would honor the spirit of Byron and generate attention. That the conservative Kipling, who had close ties to the Tories, made the translation shows how far the Greek cause had drifted from its liberal/radical origins.

Kipling may have been flattered to be asked by Demetrius Caclamanos, the Greek minister in London, to be a "new Byron" for a day.[28] Yet certain phrases of the poem suggest that Kipling might have felt a kinship to the philhellenic enterprise, like "behold thy sons" and "the graves of our slain." Kipling's only son had been killed at the battle of Loos in 1915, and two years later he was appointed to the Imperial War Graves Commission, where he "remained a member for eighteen years, and was responsible for every inscription used by it" (Birkenhead 272). Kipling was one of those to whom Hynes has referred as "monument-makers" (*A War Imagined* 279); he, like the middlebrow writers discussed by Bracco, sought a meaning and continuity after the war that resisted the ironic interpretation of the "modernists" (3). Philhellenic writers, as the passages above demonstrate, also resisted an ironic interpretation of the conflict just past. However it came about, the connection between Kipling and the Greek national anthem was in many ways a perfect fit—one of the old men speaking up for one of the old causes.

The old men made the peace. Venizelos succeeded beyond expectations in achieving Greater Greece. By the Treaty of Sèvres in 1920, Greece obtained territory in western Thrace and Asia Minor, while Greek troops entered Smyrna, Adrianople, and even Constantinople itself as part of the Allied Military Occupation. Charles Woods wrote in the *Fortnightly Review* in 1920 that the Hellenic kingdom "now stands to secure, in proportion to its size, practically as great if not greater, territorial advantages than any other country engaged in the war" (57). Clearly, part of Greece's success at the conferences was due to the fact that it had, however belatedly, entered the conflict on the winning side. Yet the Greeks were also rewarded for being Greeks, because, as Vincent Seligman said in 1919, "the debt we owe to the priceless civilization of Ancient Greece is immense" (*Salonica Side-Show* 49). In paying that debt and in aiding the Greeks in the final chapter of their regeneration, the West would also fulfill, to use the words of Valentine Chirol in 1919, "one of the great opportunities for the betterment of the world" (32). Or, as Anthony Gibbs sardonically put it, "The statesmen of the world, feeling some slight changes were necessary, if for no other reason than to avoid the uncomfortable conclusion that a few million dead had been unintelligently disposed of, presented the city [Smyrna] with some surrounding acres to our friends the Greeks" (14).

In 1888, the novelist F. Marion Crawford had proleptically written of the Turks: "It was not possible . . . that such men could ever be really conquered. They might be driven from the capital of the East by overwhelming force, but they would soon rally in greater numbers on the Asiatic shore" (*Paul Patoff* 34–35). In 1919, the Turks were driven from the capital of the East by the Allies and, in the next year, from much of the coast of Asia Minor by the Greeks. As many scholars and diplomats realized at the time, the allocation of Smyrna to Greece was economically impractical and potentially dangerous. The American Commission on the Peace reported: "To give her [Greece] a foothold upon the mainland would invite immediate trouble. Greece would press her claim for more territory; Turkey would feel that her new boundaries were run so as to give her a great handicap at the very start. The harbor at Smyrna has been for centuries an outlet for products of the central Anatolian valleys and upland" (Gelfand 254). The trouble started immediately, for on the very day that Greek troops landed in Smyrna on May 15, 1919, riots broke out in the city, which left about 400 Turks and 100 Greeks dead.[29] As the American commission predicted, the Greek forces, harassed by bands of Turkish irregulars, pressed for a larger and more defensible boundary. Within a year, Greece was at war with the nationalist Turks under the leadership of Mustafa Kemal, one of the first wars to begin after the conclusion of the war to end all wars.

"Now I do not doubt that M. Venizelos is a statesman of great capabilities, but who says that the Greeks are so particularly eager to have him?" Baron de Charlus asks Marcel (*In Search of Lost Time* 6:120). The answer, as Proust knew when he wrote the passage, was that the Greeks were not particularly eager to have the new Pericles at the helm. In the elections of November 1920, a Royalist majority was returned to the Greek Parliament. Venizelos left the country, and King Constantine was recalled to the throne by a popular plebiscite. Winston Churchill, a minister in the British government at the time, later said in his history of the First World War that the "return of Constantine . . . dissolved all Allied loyalties to Greece and cancelled all but legal obligations. In England, the feeling was not resentment, but a total extinction of sympathy or even interest." Churchill, who had misgivings about the

Greek presence in Smyrna, further commented: "For the sake of Venizelos much had to be endured, for the sake of Constantine, nothing" (*World Crisis* 4:388).[30] Britain, France, and Italy suspended all financial assistance to Greece after the return of Constantine, which hampered the ability of the Greeks to pursue the war against the Turks. In *West to North*, Compton Mackenzie has his fictional alter ego, John Ogilvie, say: "I was one of those who helped to create the notion that after the war we should be grateful to the Greeks for what they did. But because they brought back their king we are treating them like naughty children. I think they're mad to reject Venizelos, but that doesn't justify refusing them support against the Turkish Nationalists in Asia Minor" (147). The recall of King Constantine to power posed a problem for philhellenes, since so many of them, like Mackenzie, had demonized him as an enemy of Greece and Western civilization. Still, most supporters of a Greater Greece, including Mackenzie, did not turn against the idea of Greater Greece when Venizelos left office.[31]

Mackenzie's suggestion that public opinion went against the Greeks reveals how far his philhellenism was out of touch with the spirit of the time. In *West to North*, Ogilvie laments, "It is a bitter thought for a man to discover that the whole of his energy during the war was a waste of his own time and of his country's money. And that's what my years in Greece will be seeming to me if we allow the Greeks to be thrown out of Asia Minor and Eastern Thrace" (361). Mackenzie, amazingly, somehow failed to realize that nearly everyone who had returned from France had already discovered that they had wasted their energy during the war. They were quite willing for Greece to lose Asia Minor and eastern Thrace as long as it did not involve them. In the autumn of 1922, when Turkish forces confronted British troops at the Hellespont, it seemed as if Britain would be drawn into the Aegean conflict. The prevailing opinion at home was expressed by the *Daily Mail* in a banner headline on September 18, "STOP THIS NEW WAR" and in A. A. Milne's letter to the *Daily News* on October 4, 1922, where he wrote: "They have almost brought it off, the War to End Peace, for which they have been striving for three years . . . our chosen statesmen, sitting round a table; the same old statesmen; each with his war memories thick upon him" (quoted in Furbank 2.112).[32] The fact that Lloyd George's government had brought Britain to the brink of war contributed heavily to its defeat in the elections held the following month.

In 1927, T. S. Eliot remarked, "We have been for nine years reminded, by the facts and fancies of the press, of the growth of the spirit of nationalism, of the greater number of nationalities, and the multiplicity of the reasons which all these nations have for failing to get on with each other. Instead of few 'oppressed minorities,' the oppressed minorities seem to be almost in a majority, instead of a few potential Sarajevos, we seem to have dozens. . . . Not how Europe can be 'freed,' but how Europe can be organized, is the question of the day" (*Criterion*, vol. 6, p. 97). In his novel *A People Betrayed*, Alfred Döblin agreed that there were now dozens of potential Sarajevos. "Meanwhile the many small nations and states floundered about, especially those who had just been called to life by the fourteen points. With what savagery these homunculi carried on. . . . The Czechs did battle with the Poles over the mining areas of Cziezyn, the Yugoslavs and the Rumanians [*sic*] demanded the same region of Banat. Wonderful old Venizelos was enchanted by Constantinople and Asia Minor and wanted to have them, plus Cyprus, Thrace, and Northern Epirus, they all seemed so Greek to him, and after all he was the only Greek at the Conference and he ought to know" (623). In this passage we hear what Paul Fussell has termed the dominant tone of the world, and literature, after the Great War—irony. James Joyce, master ironist, punctured the political aspirations of the small nations, Byronic philhellenism, and Romantic nationalism in general, with just six words in *Finnegans Wake*: "Meed of anthems, here we pant" (41). His words depend upon, and underscore, how Byron's "Maid of Athens" had become a metaphor for liberal nineteenth-century nationalism.

A. A. Milne did not oppose Greek irredentism in Asia Minor because he was at heart pro-Turkish; he was rather, like most of his generation, antiwar. The Greco-Turkish War of 1920–1922 was the first conflict of Greeks against Turks since the War of Independence began in 1821 in which, it seems, no battalion of foreign philhellenes fought beside the Greek army. The entire notion of volunteering to fight for the liberation of Greeks in Asia Minor had changed by the end of the Great War. For the same reason, no writer of note under the age of thirty composed a poem in the manner of Flecker's "Ode to the Glory of Greece," written less than a decade earlier. If someone had, it would not have escaped the prevailing sense of irony.

The Greeks initially had success against the Turks; by August 1921 they had advanced to within forty miles of the Turkish capital of Ankara. There they reached the limit of their energy and resources. The Greek army made a short retreat to winter lines, and the two combatants uneasily faced one another for a year while various attempts were made to end the conflict by diplomatic means. On August 26, 1922, Kemal and the Turks launched an offensive against the southern flank of the Greeks. After a day of stiff resistance, the Greek forces simply dissolved and ran for the Aegean coast. The Turkish army covered the 200 miles to the Mediterranean shore in about two weeks.[33]

On September 9, the Turks entered the city of Smyrna. For a few days there was relative calm. On September 13, the Armenian quarter was set ablaze. When the smoke cleared, the Armenian, Greek, and European sections of the city had been destroyed. Dakin estimates around 25,000 Greeks and Armenians were killed (*Unification of Greece* 236). Another 200,000 were crammed by the shore without food or water, hoping that they might somehow find a means of escape. The majority of these were eventually trans-ported to Greece, never to see their homes again.[34] "Hellenic Smyrna was dead. Christian Smyrna, too, one of the great ancient Christian foundations of Asia Minor, was dead. The phoenix that was to rise from these ashes was a Turkish Izmir purged of two thousand and more years of history" (Michael Llewellyn Smith, 311). With Smyrna, the dream of a regenerated Greece with a liberated Constantinople was also purged. Greece lost more than the territory it had gained by the Treaty of Sèvres. It also lost what had been an integral part of its national identity at home and abroad.

Eileen Gregory suggested that modernists such as Eliot and Pound saw the Great War within a paradigm of the Trojan War and with Aeschylus's *Oresteia*, especially *Agamemnon*, as the central text. It was, she said, "the story of the aftermath of a devastating war, in which military violence and sacrifice of innocence are brought home with the hero" (23). If the years between 1918 and 1922, during which the Greeks seemed about to realize their dreams of a Greater Greece centered in Constantinople, appeared to sepa-rate modern Greece from the wasteland of modernity in France and Eng-land, then the retreat of the Greek army and the million and a half Greek refugees streaming across Asia Minor and eastern Thrace to escape the vic-torious Turkish army in the summer and autumn of 1922 brought Greece squarely into that barren landscape. As one journalist covering the evacua-tion of the Greeks from eastern Thrace put it: "All day I have been passing them, dirty, tired, unshaven, wind-bitten soldiers hiking along the trails across the brown, rolling, barren Thracian countryside. No bands, no relief organizations, no leave areas, nothing but lice, dirty blankets, and mosquitoes at night. They are the last of the glory that was Greece. This is the end of their second siege of Troy" (*Dateline: Toronto* 245). Ernest Hemingway, in this dispatch to the *Toronto Star*, inserted the Greek retreat into the contem-porary Aeschylean paradigm of the war. The disaster in Asia Minor was not only the end of the second siege of Troy, it became, quite literally as we shall see, the last event of the world *In Our Time*.

8

On the Quai at Smyrna

In 1966, just four years before his death, John Dos Passos published *The Best Times*, "an informal memoir." In the book, he gave a vivid account of an incident that he says occurred when he was in Constantinople during the summer of 1921 to report on the war between the Greeks and the Turks. His description of the event takes up half of the space that he devotes to his stay in the city:

> A grubby little war was going on in Asia Minor. Our Admiral Bristol was trying to make what sense he could of a senseless business. I remember relinquishing my prejudice against brass hats enough to think highly of Admiral Bristol. He felt if the news could only be published in the American newspapers somebody might try to do something to stop it. I managed to get aboard a destroyer he sent off with a batch of correspondents to interview the refugees.
>
> One port on the Sea of Marmara was crowded to the waterline with desperate Greeks, men, women, and children, whose villages had been burned by the Turks. Another was stuffed with Turks in the same plight, only it was the Greeks who had done the raping and maiming and murdering. They all begged to be taken aboard. At any moment they expected the enemy to march in and finish the massacre. The irony was that the Greeks and Turks and their pathetic women and crying children all looked so much alike it would have taken a linguistic expert to tell them apart.
>
> The skipper didn't have the orders and there wasn't room anyway on a World War I destroyer, so we had to leave them to their fate. We sat with pale faces in the wardroom while the narrow ship lurched through the cross seas at twenty-five knots on the way back to Constant. It was not only the pitching and tossing that had turned our stomachs. (91–92)

Dos Passos never took such a trip. The meticulous diary of the American high commissioner in Constantinople from 1919 to 1947, Admiral Mark Lambert Bristol, contained the following paragraph in the entry for July 20, 1921:[1]

> Mr. John R. Dos Passos, an American press representative, called by appointment. He is here writing stories for the New York Tribune and for the Metropolitan Magazine. He said he would like to go to Anatolia, to Angora, and I told him I would assist him in any way possible. However, I suggested he stay here for a while and become oriented. He quite agreed to this idea and then stated that he was thinking of going to Rodosto where the refugees from Ismidt are now located. I told him that I thought it would be better for him to go to Ismidt where these refugees came from and get a proper background for a visit to Rodosto. Also to Yalova and Guemlik where the Greeks had murdered and burned the Turkish villages; and then visit these refugees where they are now located in and around Constantinople. I suggested that he might then write one story bringing out the savagery of both the Greeks and the Turks against each other. Mr. Dos Passos liked this idea.

Dos Passos could not have seen the refugees huddled on the shore awaiting rescue, since, as Bristol's comments clearly indicate, the refugees had already been removed from their villages. The admiral suggested that Dos Passos visit the ruined villages before interviewing the refugees, which would have made a much less dramatic tale than the one that Dos Passos eventually wrote.

There is no evidence that Dos Passos ever made the visits that Bristol recommended. They certainly do not occur in the reports that he filed in 1921 nor in the travelogue of his trip based on those dispatches from the Near East, *Orient Express*, published in 1927. It appears that Dos Passos constructed the account of the boat trip in his memoirs of 1966 from his conversation with Admiral Bristol in 1921.[2] Why did Dos Passos invent such an incident?

The answer, in a single word, is Hemingway, who had gone to Constantinople about a year after Dos Passos to cover the end of the Greco-Turkish War. Indeed, a reader asked to identify the author of the passage in *The Best Times* would probably, and justifiably, respond, "Hemingway." As Herbert Schneidau said, "Hemingway made ironic laconism a salient feature of his art" (187), and the same technique is central to the account of the boat trip in *The Best Times*. In Dos Passos's *Orient Express*, the language of a passage in which a Greek archbishop announces to a group of foreign correspondents that the Greek population has been given just three days to leave the city of Samsoun contains just a touch of irony without laconism:

The archbishop's full lips are at the rim of his tiny coffee-cup. He drinks quickly and meticulously. In one's mind beyond the red plush a vision of dark crowds crawling inland over sunshriveled hills. The women were crying and wailing in the streets of Samsoun, says the officer. The news must be sent out, continues the archbishop; the world must know the barbarity of the Turks; America must know. A telegram to the President of the United States must be sent off. Again in one's mind beyond the red plush, and the polished phrases of official telegrams, the roads at night under the terrible bloodorange moon of Asia, and the wind of the defiles blowing dust among the huddled women, stinging the dark attentive eyes of children, and far off on the heat-baked hills a sound of horsemen. (13–14)

Notice the ornate and vague adjectives throughout the passage, such as "sunshriveled hills," "bloodorange moon," "dark crowds," and "huddled women." These are absent from the account of the boat trip in *The Best Times*, as they are from the following paragraph from Hemingway's story "On the Quai at Smyrna" from the volume *In Our Time* (1930):

The Greeks were nice chaps too. When they evacuated they had all their baggage animals they couldn't take off with them so they just broke their forelegs and dumped them into the shallow water. All those mules with their forelegs broken pushed over into the shallow water. It was all a pleasant business. My word yes a pleasant business. (12)

Dos Passos signals the dominant status of Hemingway's text for writing in English about events in postwar Asia Minor by implying that he had experienced Hemingway's version of the Greco-Turkish War a year before Hemingway ever set foot in Constantinople.

In his book about the Asia Minor Disaster in Greek fiction, Thomas Doulis wrote that the "Greco-Turkish War of 1920–1922 was important only for Turkey and Greece. Though it may have changed somewhat the power structures of the Balkans, the Near East, and the Eastern Mediterranean, this effect had little more than local significance. For the two nations in question, however, the war was of decisive importance" (2). The last sentence is undoubtedly true. The first needs qualification, if not rejection. Doulis himself went on to say, "The events of 1922 have entered the English language as the 'Asia Minor Disaster,' a phrase used interchangeably with 'the Smyrna Disaster'" (3). The Smyrna Disaster is the first event in modern Greek history after the Greek War of Independence to have a secure place in English literature and language; the text that canonized it was Hemingway's "On the Quai at Smyrna." And, as the passage from Dos Passos above suggests, in English the phrase *the Smyrna Disaster* referred not simply to a historical event but also to a style of writing and a particular postwar perspective.

If the literary world still, to borrow the words of Philip Gibbs, "knows the tragedy of Smyrna, the burning of that fair city" and "the cry of agony that went out to sea above the fire" (*Little Novels of Nowadays* 63), it is because *In Our Time* holds an important place in the study of modern fiction. Just as the Greece of Byron resonated in subsequent writing, so has the Smyrna of Hemingway. In his novel *Blood Dance* (1993) James William Brown had the heroine describe the scene at the harbor of Smyrna:

> And there was screaming. As if the people wailed and keened for
> Smyrna which was dying. It tore from thousands of throats as the
> people stretched their hands to the departing ships.
> And screamed. (36–37)

The passage clearly evokes the opening of "On the Quai at Smyrna": "The strange thing was, he said, how they screamed at midnight. I do not know why they screamed at that time. We were in the harbor and they were all on the pier and at midnight they started screaming. We used to turn the searchlight on to quiet them. That always did the trick" (11). Even the dispatches that Hemingway wrote for the *Toronto Star* in 1922 have become part of the canon of writing about the war. In *A Byzantine Journey* (1995), for example, John Ash ended a brief account of the Greco-Turkish War of 1920–1922 with a single quotation designed to encapsulate the experience of the refugees, explaining that we "can gain some idea of the situation in Bithynia from firsthand accounts in nearby Thrace, written for the *Toronto Star* by a young reporter named Ernest Hemingway" (91).

The Colossus of Maroussi, a key book in the construction of post-Byronic Greece, also acknowledged the central position of Hemingway's brief story. Henry Miller asserted:

> The Smyrna affair, which far outweighs the horrors of the First
> World War or even the present one, has been somehow soft-pedaled
> and almost expunged from the memory of present day man. The pe-
> culiar horror which clings to this catastrophe is due not alone to the
> savagery and barbarism of the Turks but to the supine acquiescence of
> the big powers. It was one of the few shocks the modern world has
> suffered. . . . And so long as human beings can sit and watch with
> hands folded while their fellow-men are tortured and butchered so
> long will civilization be a hollow mockery, a wordy phantom sus-
> pended like a mirage above a sea of murdered carcasses. (172–73)

The "wordy" phantom suspended over Miller's passage, as it was suspended over both Dos Passos's boat trip in *The Best Times* and the quotation from Brown's novel above, is Hemingway's story, right down to the sea of floating carcasses: "You remember the harbor. There were plenty of nice things floating around in it. That was the only time in my life I got so I dreamed about things" ("On the Quai at Smyrna" 12).[3] Miller, however, added an admonitory message not found in Hemingway's text. The point of "On the Quai at Smyrna," as well as *In Our Time* as a whole, is that civilization really has become a hollow mockery. Or, as Edward Whittemore later put it in his novel *Nile Shadows* (1983), "Meaning, sir? *Meaning*? Pardon me, sir, but in a world at war you're actually looking for *meaning*?" (63). Who could be better used to make the point than the descendants of the creators of civilization, the Greeks, coming home from their second Trojan War?

"On the Quai at Smyrna," first added to the text of *In Our Time* in 1930 as "An Introduction by the Author," was not given its current title until 1938.[4] But the Greek defeat in Asia Minor had a crucial role in the text of *In Our Time* through its various mutations from the appearance of the vignettes or "interchapters" without the short stories in the 1923 *in our time* to the edition of 1930 with the description of the harbor at Smyrna. E. R. Hagemann, observing that the events in the vignettes can be dated between 1914 and 1923, said that Hemingway "has reconstruct[ed] a decade . . . the Great War and its aftermath," which Hagemann called "*the* experience of his [Hemingway's] generation" (52). Robert Slabey concurred, stating that there were two major sequences in the vignettes, "World War I and the Greco-Turkish War" (77). In his first volume, therefore, Hemingway stressed the two events that opened and closed the critical decade of his generation. The message to be gleaned from the book was, as Hagemann observed, that "there is no peace *In Our Time*" (79), a sentiment Hemingway also expressed in his poem "They All Made Peace—What Is Peace?" about the Lausanne conference that followed the Greek defeat in Asia Minor.

T. S. Eliot once wrote: "Only from about the year 1926 did the features of the post-war world clearly begin to emerge—and not only in the sphere of politics" (*Criterion*, vol. 18, p. 271). Hemingway suggested that the features of the postwar world came into view a few years earlier, with the retreat of the Greeks from Asia Minor. Edward Whittemore, undoubtedly influenced by Hemingway's formulation, also thought that the Asia Minor catastrophe, and particularly the destruction of Smyrna, opened a new era. In the first volume of *Jerusalem Quintet, Sinai Tapestry* (1977), he wrote: "Right at the beginning of the new century, that's when it was. Right after the world of the Strongbows and Wallensteins had died in the First World War. It couldn't survive the anonymous machine guns, their world, and the faceless tanks and the poison gas that killed brave men and cowards equally, the strong and the weak all the same, the good and the bad all together so that it no longer mattered who you were, what you were. Yes their world died and we had to have a new one and we got it, we got our new century in 1918 and Smyrna was its very first act, the prelude to everything" (279–80). This passage is the best argument that I know for the reason that a piece eventually called "On the Quai at Smyrna" could, in 1930, serve as a fitting introduction, a "prelude to everything," for a volume of stories entitled *In Our Time*.

Why did Hemingway, who spent less than two weeks in Constantinople in the autumn of 1922 and who did not see the destruction of Smyrna, grant such a prominent position to the Greco-Turkish War almost from the outset?[5] What Hemingway saw and heard on his trip to the Near East validated his own experience of the war in Italy. Samuel Hynes noted that at the end of the Great War, "the soldier was seen as a victim," and "if entire armies could be imagined composed of such victims—if indeed every army was an army of martyrs—then Victory too must fade from the story, and become only a long catastrophe, with neither significant action nor direction, a violence that was neither fought nor won, but only endured" (*War Imagined* 215). In Hemingway's writing about the Greco-Turkish War, nearly everyone is a victim, from the Turkish cart driver senselessly murdered by Greek troops in Thrace, to the Greeks slaughtered by the Turks on the quay at Smyrna, to the animals mutilated and thrown into the bay by the Greeks. In his accounts, we are not given significant action nor direction, simply endured violence.

One of the prime characteristics of the Asia Minor Disaster in English writing was the elision of national identities. In a dispatch from the front, Hemingway reported that the landlady in a fleabag hotel in Adrianople saw no difference in the various ethnicities in the region:

> "I won't care when the Turks come," Madame Marie said, sitting her great bulk down at a table and scratching her chin.
> "Why not?"
> "They're all the same. The Greeks and the Turks and the Bulgars. They're all the same." She accepted a glass of wine. "I've seen them all. They've all had Karagatch."
> "Who are the best?" I asked.
> "Nobody. They're all the same."
>
> (*Dateline: Toronto* 251)

Dos Passos, in the passage that opened this chapter, said the various refugees "looked so much alike it would take a linguistic expert to tell them apart." The Greeks, Turks, and Bulgars, of course, *could* tell one another apart, and to them the differences were quite meaningful. But for Hemingway and Dos Passos, the key to understanding the postwar Near East ran through the Western front. When every soldier and every civilian could be seen as a victim, national identities seemed insignificant. Anthony Gibbs described the arrival of Greek troops in Smyrna as a mirror image of the destruction of the city by the Turks in 1922: "The Greeks seized the opportunity to get rid of their age-old oppressors by the simple process of bayonetting as many of them as could be induced to submit to the operation and pushing them off the quayside into the sea" (14).

The people with the most to lose by the elision of nationality were the Greeks, who for more than a century had had a special place in the eyes of the West. Clare Sheridan, another journalist in Constantinople in the autumn of 1922, reported that the Turkish leader, Hamid Bey, told her: "The Acropolis cost the Turks a great deal. Public opinion always went to the Greeks on account of the Acropolis" (*West and East* 162). The Great War leveled such distinctions; after 1918, as Madame Marie said, the victims were "all the same."

Hemingway appears to have viewed the Greek defeat as a quintessential Great War scenario, such as he had portrayed in his 1922 poem "To Good Guys Dead":

> They sucked us in;
> King and country,
> Christ Almighty
> And the rest.
> Patriotism,
> Democracy,
> Honor—
> Words and phrases.
> They either bitched us or killed us.
> (*Complete Poems* 47)

According to Hemingway, the Greek soldiers "were thoroughly fed up and becoming conscious that they were going into battle to die doing a cat's paw job" (*Dateline: Toronto* 233). In a dispatch entitled "The Greek Revolt," a Captain Wittal tells Hemingway that the "Greek soldiers were first-class fighting men. . . . I believe they would have captured Angora and ended the war if they had not been betrayed" by their officers and government (*Dateline: Toronto* 244). The dying narrator of "The Snows of Kilimanjaro" echoes that sentiment when he recalls that the Greeks "made the attack with the newly arrived Constantine officers, that did not know a goddamned thing, and the artillery had fired into the troops and the British observer had cried like a child" (16).[6] Hemingway said near the end of "The Greek Revolt": "That is the story of the Greek army's betrayal by King Constantine. And that is the reason the revolution in Athens was not just a fake as many people have claimed. It was the rising of an army that had been betrayed against the man who had betrayed it" (*Dateline: Toronto* 245). The crucial decade reconstructed in *In Our Time* ends chronologically with the execution of the cabi-

net ministers responsible for the defeat of the Greek army, the ultimate revenge of all the armies of "young" who had been betrayed by the "old men"
at home.[7] Hemingway was not the only one whose attention was caught by
the treatment of the Greek political leaders; Kenneth Matthews noted, "The
executions shocked Europe; it was considered a dangerous precedent that
soldiers should come back from a war and shoot the people who had crimi-
nally caused it" (*Greek Salad* 162- 63). But in *In Our Time* even the revenge of
the soldiers became hollow, since it entailed shooting an old man with typhus:
"They tried to hold him up against the wall but he sat down in a puddle of
water. The other five stood quietly against the wall. Finally the officer told the
soldiers it was not good trying to make him stand up. When they fired the first
volley he was sitting in water with his head on his knees" (51). This subtly
connected the minister with the description of the corpses floating in the
water at Smyrna that, after 1930, opened the volume.

What Hemingway failed to stress was that the revolution in Greece in November 1922, which led to the second abdication and exile of King Constantine in addition to the execution of six ministers of the Royalist government,
was led by a group of Venizelist officers. It was not really a Great War scenario, a "rising of an army against the man who had betrayed it," but, as
Clogg noted, a raising of the stakes in the "venomous feud" between the
Venizelists and the Royalists (*Concise History of Greece* 101).[8] The Greek
king in the "Envoi" of *In Our Time*, who "the revolutionary committee . . .
would not allow to go outside the palace grounds" and who thought that "the
great thing in this sort of affair is not to be shot oneself" (157), is Constantine's eldest son, George II. George took his father's place in November 1922
only to be forced to abdicate and leave the country himself in December 1923
after the failure of a Royalist coup against the revolutionary committee of
Venizelist officers. Venizelos, who returned to Greece and became prime
minister again in 1928, exchanged roles with King George II in 1935. After
the Royalist party won the election of 1932, the Venizelists attempted coups
of their own in 1933 and 1935. Venizelos was forced to leave Greece again
after the last of these, which led to the restoration of King George II after
twelve years abroad. Viewed from within Greek history, the execution of
ministers in 1922 was not a generational struggle of an army of the young
versus the old men at home. It was not even the end of the story but rather
one more move in a bitter partisan dispute that continued throughout the
period between the wars.

For Hemingway, though, Smyrna was not a "Greek" event but a symbol
of the world in "our" time. As part of this strategy, as Jeffrey Meyers said,
Hemingway "deliberately excluded all the political background of the
Greco-Turkish War and objectively reported only the immediate event in
order to achieve a concentration and intensity of focus—a spotlight rather
than a stage" (26). One could, and Greek writers certainly did, position

Smyrna and the Asia Minor Disaster within a specifically Greek political and historical framework. In the preface to the translation of Ilias Venezis's *Aeolia*, one of the first Greek books about life in Ionia to be translated into English (1949), Lawrence Durrell said that the "waters of Smyrna were choked with dead bodies. . . . But it is more than the injustice, the cruelty, the madness of the episode that sticks in the mind of the modern Greek. It is also a sense of the lost richness, a lost peace of mind." "If he is an exile," Durrell remarked, "he returns again and again to Anatolia in his dreams" (v). Venezis's novel carefully recalled the life in Anatolia that was lost and then covered the evacuation in very few pages. The narrator in Stratis Myrivilis's *The Mermaid Madonna* says of the refugees: "The odd thing was, however, that for all the readiness with which they described the blessings they had left behind, it was difficult to get anything out of them about the atrocities they had survived. When they undertook to relate such things, their eyes became veiled and their tongues twisted in knots" (16). Many Greek writers also found their tongues twisted in knots when confronting the horrors of the disaster and like Myrivilis's refugees "skimmed rapidly over details of this kind" (17). Foreign eyes were drawn to the very things from which Greeks had to turn their faces.

The Smyrna of Hemingway is precisely about the injustice, cruelty, and madness on the quay, because it stands for, to use the words of Clare Sheridan, "all the suppurating sores of Europe." The phrase *the Smyrna Disaster* entered the English language, as Doulis said, but mainly as a representative sign for "our" postwar condition, not as an event in the history of Greece.

Hemingway's use of Smyrna as a symbol of postwar chaos resembles that of Eliot's in *The Waste Land*.[9] In the notes to the poem, Eliot said that a major theme of part 5, and so by extension the work as a whole, is "the present decay of Eastern Europe." One of the Eastern "Europeans" of the poem appears in the third section, "The Fire Sermon":

> Unreal City
> Under the brown fog of a winter noon
> Mr. Eugenides, the Smyrna merchant
> Unshaven, with a pocket full of currants
> C.i.f. London: documents at sight,
> Asked me in demotic French
> To luncheon at the Cannon Street Hotel
> Followed by a weekend at the Metropole.
> (61)

Eugenides means "well-born" in Greek, a description that clashes with the appearance of the man as "unshaven, with a pocket full of currants." But the irony of the name runs deeper. For an argument was made that the Greeks of

Asia Minor should be part of the Greek nation because they were the last direct descendants of ancient Greeks. In his novel *Enter the Greek* (1926), which ends with the destruction of Smyrna in 1922, Anthony Gibbs echoed these claims: "The Smyrna Greeks are very nearly a pure strain. The Athenian is a mixed breed. . . . But the Greeks of Smyrna, cut off by foreign domination from intermarriage with any but the Armenian and Israelite, both of which races they detest and are a little afraid of, have contrived to keep themselves Greek. In Smyrna every lady is an Aphrodite and every man an Apollo" (24). And the hero's father in the novel is a Smyrniot by the name of Euxenophilos, which has the Homeric meaning of "good friend to strangers." Despite this name and lineage, however, his son feels he is just a "dago" in England.

Eugenides' profession might also cast doubt on his connection to the classical past. In a contribution on Greece for *The Balkans* (1915), Arnold Toynbee said that the "name of Greece has two entirely different associations in our minds. Sometimes it calls up a wonderful literature enshrined in a 'dead' language; and exquisite works of vanished art recovered by the spade, at other times it is connected with the currant-trade returns quoted in the financial pages of our newspapers" (163). And the currant trade, whether conducted by Greeks, Turks, or emigrant Italians, was thought to be a profession for "Levantines" and "mixed breeds" rather than a career for Apollos and Aphrodites. Eugenides' business might be a way of signaling to which of the "two entirely different associations" of Greece he belongs.

The full political significance of Eugenides in the poem stems from the fact that the Greek comes from Smyrna, one of what Eliot termed "dozens of potential Sarajevos" created by the Versailles conference. Eliot completed "The Fire Sermon" before the catastrophe at Smyrna, so he could use ironic humor to puncture "Romantic" reasons to assist the Greeks. After the event, Hemingway could dismiss such philhellenic rhetoric out of hand.

For Hemingway's generation, the Smyrna Disaster was a potent symbol of the fate of a "botched civilization," to use Pound's phrase, so potent that the single word *Smyrna* or a brief reference to the disaster conjured up both banal violence and deep irony. Dos Passos included the following headline in newsreel 38 of *1919*: "ORDERED TO ALLOW ALL GREEKS TO DIE" (*USA* 701). The last line of e. e. cummings's *XLI Poems* (1925) reads, "but Hassan chuckles seeing the Greeks breathe)" (*Complete Poems* 119).[10] Given the common connection between the Trojan War and the Asia Minor Disaster, it is hard not to see an intended allusion to the disaster at Smyrna in the following lines at the end of Pound's Canto XXIII.

> And that was when Troy was down, all right,
>   superbo Ilion . . .
> And they were sailing along

Sitting in the stern-sheets,
Under the lee of an island
And the wind drifting off from the island.
"Tet, tet . . .
        what is it?" said Anchises.
"Tethnéké," said the helmsman, "I think they
Are howling because Adonis died virgin."
"Huh! Tet . . ." said Anchises,
      "well, they've made a bloody mess of that city."
                              (*Cantos* 109)

The shared elements in Canto XXIII, "On the Quai at Smyrna," and Hemingway's other writing about the Asia Minor Disaster are striking, such as the references to the Trojan War, the screaming onshore, even the language: "I had the wind up when we came in that morning. . . . We were going to come in, run along the pier, let go the front and rear anchors and then shell the Turkish quarter of the town. They would have blown us out of the water, but we would have blown the town simply to hell. . . . It would have been a hell of a mess" ("On the Quai at Smyrna" 12).[11] Pound had written the lines above before Hemingway composed "On the Quai at Smyrna," but the two authors had taken a walking tour together in early 1923 after Hemingway had returned from his trip to Constantinople. One cannot be sure who has influenced whom, but what Pound's lines along with the passages from cummings and Eliot reveal is that Smyrna was already being used as an allusion for the state of the world in our time by modernists before Hemingway took it over for himself. He may have been drawn to use it for that very reason.

In his poem "Hypocrite Auteur," Archibald MacLeish stated:

A world ends when its metaphor is dead.

An age becomes an age, all else beside,
When sensuous poets in their pride invent
Emblems for the soul's content
That speak the meanings men will never know
But man-imagined images can show:
It perishes when those images, though seen,
No longer mean.

                           (415)

If one of the metaphors for the nineteenth-century Romantic world, which believed in the possibility of human progress, was the revival of the Greeks and all of the high-minded concepts they represented in the English and American imagination, then the death of the Greeks could be used to signal the expiration of that world. MacLeish himself began "Invocation to the Social Muse" (1932) with the line: "Señora, it is true, the Greeks are dead." The death of the "Greeks" functioned in modernism to mark the end of one and the beginning of another era,[12] and the demise of the philhellenic legacy was employed to this end also, as by Joyce in the phrase "meed of anthems, here we pant." A number of modernists, like Hemingway and Dos Passos, used the fate of the modern Greeks in Asia Minor as a metonym for the state of the world after the war. By inserting references to the Greek defeat of 1922, however briefly, into modernist works, these writers ensured not just that the fate of Smyrna and the collapse of Greece's territorial aspirations would not be forgotten but also that the meaning of its fate was caught up in what might be called the postwar "end of meaning."

Just as Byron was not the only one to write about a Greek revival, Hemingway was not the only one to write about the horror of Smyrna. Hemingway's perspective did not differ greatly in outlook from most of the others, just as Byron's verses about a Greek revival in the first decades of the nineteenth century were hardly unique in sentiment. A number of descriptions came from journalists who, unlike Hemingway, witnessed part of the evacuation from Smyrna. One such account came from Clare Sheridan, who Hemingway once described as a reporter who "smiled her way into many interviews" (*Dateline: Toronto* 256). Sheridan, Hemingway surely knew, had seen "the filthy water that was stagnant and stinking with rotten corpses of men and beasts" (*West and East* 150).[13]

In *West and East* (1923), Sheridan tried to give a wide picture of "after-war conditions" throughout Europe, an overview of the world in our time from Ireland to Turkey. She summed up her opinion: "Everything I have ever believed in is shattered, and has been replaced by nothing very tangible" (vii, xi). Like Eliot, she considered Smyrna an example of the problems to come: "I saw in these refugees not the victims of the Turks, but of the Allied political situation. I had visions of Lloyd George leaning over a map on a big table in a comfortable conference chamber, and pencil in hand deciding that Smyrna should be handed over to the Greeks. The Smyrna debacle is not the only one in store. Europe is full of suppurating sores ready to burst, each one caused by needless post-war politics" (156–57). She also provided a gendered assessment of the disaster and war. Looking upon the refugees at Smyrna, she remarked: "To men there is a certain satisfaction in fighting, and death is sometimes easier than life. But the fate of women and children is tragic beyond the conception of statesmen" (157).[14] She seems not to have recognized that few of the male writers who had taken part in the Great War had come away with any sense of satisfaction from the fighting.[15]

For Sheridan, one problem was the complete randomness of human behavior. Turks did "murderous things one moment, they would be tender the next. A Turk would stone a man to death in the water, and then throw himself upon a fallen child and protect it with his body from being trampled at the gate. The Turks were no worse than any other and not so bad as they might have been" (155). Or, in her mind, as bad as the Greeks.

Sheridan saw the Greek civilians as "victims of their own people, of the Greek army that had devastated the interior, who had burned and destroyed everything" (176). She had a more positive view of the Turks, in part because she was attracted to their Orientalism; in describing Mustafa Kemal, in the course of four pages she noted "the Oriental in him," his "Oriental graciousness," and his "perfect Oriental manners" (142–46).[16] If we can believe Harold Nicolson, she was attracted to Kemal himself. Nicolson wrote his wife, Vita Sackville-West, that Sheridan was "having an affair with Kemal Ataturk" (Lees-Milne 1.192).

Philip Gibbs, a prolific English "popular" novelist, had observed the "horror of the quayside at Smyrna" and heard the "cry of agony which chilled the soul of the world," which he wrote about in a chapter of *Little Novels of Nowadays* (4, 261).[17] As his title suggests, Gibbs, like Hemingway, wanted to provide a picture of the postwar world in our time. Unlike Hemingway, Gibbs provided a programmatic introduction for the reader:

> The stories in this book are connected by a thread of plot which I have
> followed from London to Moscow and beyond through other cities.
> It is a thread woven by the three ugly sisters of fate in the wake of war,
> and fastened round the necks of men and women so that they can
> hardly escape from the wreckage of hopes in the life of Europe. . . .
> Civilization itself is threatened, or, at least in the minds of many men
> and women there is a sense of impending downfall. . . . A new world is
> coming, with desperate problems and many dangers. My idea in writ-
> ing them was to put them in the form of little novels . . . the thoughts
> and moods and hopes of Europe as I have seen it lately. (v, viii)

This passage equally serves as a comment on *In Our Time* and *The Waste Land*.

Gibbs attempted to paint a broad picture of the European situation by setting his stories in a wide variety of Western and Eastern locales. "Miss Smith of Smyrna" is the second story. The heroine is a wealthy, aging British woman who has spent a lifetime spreading civilized values through hospitals and schools as a kind of "Queen Victoria of the East." She realizes that the Greek army will evacuate Asia Minor and goes to Athens to appeal to King Constantine to remove all of the Greek women and children in the area in order to prevent a massacre. She fails and dies with her schoolchildren when the Turks set fire to the building. But the real culprits, according to Miss

Smith, are the architects "of the preposterous treaty," which will cause "a great tragedy hereabouts" (48). In exasperation, she asks a British journalist, "Are the British forces coming to defend this unhappy population when the Greek army is routed, or before?" He answers, "Our people are for peace, and sick of war" (57). Miss Smith also learns that there is no peace in our time.[18]

West and East, Little Novels of Nowadays, and *In Our Time* share a large perspective, but the methods and styles of the first two and Hemingway's book are quite different. Sheridan and Gibbs tried to put as much as they could in their volumes, and their presentation, while stressing the horror of what they saw, lacked biting irony. At one point Gibbs asked, "Are modern novelists and story writers to go on recording the little love tales of highly strung ladies and introspective men" and leave the terrible condition of the world "on one side because it frightens them? Or they find them too big for their imagination?" (viii). But Gibbs, on the evidence of his own book, had only the language and structure of those same little love tales to employ in telling of the collapse of the world, so his stories do not offer a new approach to writing about the postwar era. Hemingway's language is as stripped down as his selection of material, and it is laced with the ironic temperament of the times. It is Hemingway's style that stands out, and that style made Smyrna and the Asia Minor Disaster part of literature.

Some years after the disaster, a few attempts were made to place Smyrna within the Byronic literary inheritance. Philhellenic writing had survived defeats in the past, and there were some writers who had not yet realized that the Great War had changed the perception of Greek wars of liberation. One such author, as we have already seen, was Compton Mackenzie. At the end of *West to North* (1940), the fifth and final volume of his *Four Winds of Love* series, Mackenzie sent his hero back to "Mileto," a city on the Asia Minor coast, to help in the evacuation of Greek refugees. It is one of the least interesting passages in the series, due largely, one suspects, to the fact that Mackenzie had no personal experience of the event upon which to draw. It simply provided John Ogilvie with another chance to voice pro-Greek sentiments and rant at the failure of the British to back their allies with force: "I'm in a state of depression about the small nations. The Greek debacle has dealt me a tragic blow" (408). Mackenzie attempted to reclaim Smyrna for the philhellenic tradition by placing it within a nineteenth-century, rather than a postwar, paradigm. For example, he consistently relied on Disraeli's policy of supporting the Turks to explain the debacle, and he charged the Labour party with Tory notions of the Levant: "But one might have known," his hero laments, "that the pro-Turkish party in England would be too strong for Lloyd George" (322).[19]

Anthony Gibbs's *Enter the Greek* (1926) is a more curious Smyrna novel. For most of the novel, Tony Sutherland, the son of an English mother and a

Greek Smyrniote father, tries to hide his Greek heritage as he pursues a career as a successful playwright in London. Only at the end, during a stay on the French Riviera, does his "race memory" return, as well as literary tastes from his youth, linking Romantic writing and the fight for Greek freedom: "There came to mock him a vision of himself as the world's perfect lover, as something a little nineteenth century—as Percy Bysshe, as Charles Algernon, as Byron—Byron . . . Byron. . . . The Turks were coming down on Smyrna" (271).

Sutherland has a yacht take him to Smyrna, now in flames and with "a massacre on the quays" (287). The captain refuses to approach shore, so Sutherland takes off his clothes and swims to join his compatriots in death. We are, it seems, meant to approve Tony's Byronic end, but, aside from the awakening in Tony of "race memory," it has no practical purpose. For literary history, however, it is fitting that a hero who is a little nineteenth century, who admires Shelley, Swinburne, and Byron—philhellenic writers all—dies at Smyrna, where the idea of Greek regeneration went up in flames.

It was possible to view Smyrna and the entire Asia Minor war as something other than a disaster; the Turks always have. For them, the day of the critical Greek defeat in Asia Minor was called *büyük gün*, the great day, and the war is called the War of Independence. As far as I am aware, it was not until 1952, when Ann Bridge (Mary O'Malley) published her novel *The Dark Moment*, that the Turkish victory entered English literature as a great day.[20] If, as Doulis noted, Smyrna entered the English language as a "disaster," it was not simply because the English and American writers saw events in the Aegean area only through the eyes of the Greeks. It was also, and perhaps mainly, due to the fact that the death and defeat of the Greeks validated their postwar ideas about war and nationalism. Smyrna could only be "the first act" of the new age if it were looked at from the side of the losers.

The Turkish romance of liberation in fiction differs curiously from its Greek counterpart. In both Bridge's *The Dark Moment* and Catherine Gavin's *The House of War* (1970), American women fall in love with the heroic Mustafa Kemal, the leader of the Turkish army and effective head of the Turkish state. Kemal is depicted as a fitting mate for a Western woman; he is certainly not the sensuous Oriental nor lustful Turk of earlier novels. In both novels, Kemal is not simply winning a war but embarking on a project to "turn a primitive oriental country into a *twentieth* century one" (*Dark Moment* 337). Although Bridge conceded, "Smyrna was an ugly business" (233), *The Dark Moment* celebrated the fortitude of the Turks in overcoming both the Greek threat to their national sovereignty and their Ottoman past. Neither Western heroine can marry Kemal at the end; the fragile Turkish state demands that its leader not have a foreign wife.

Gavin's *House of War* places the conventions of the Greek romance of liberation side by side with her heroine's involvement with Mustafa Kemal.

Evelyn Anderson, left by her estranged journalist husband, Jeff, in Ankara, becomes the lover of Kemal. Jeff, on assignment in Constantinople, renews a relationship with a Greek from Smyrna with the Byronic name of Leila—she is a cabaret singer and Jeff has taught her to sing "Maid of Athens," which is quoted several times in the text (136–37, 209). Leila is killed as Jeff attempts to take her from Smyrna during the disaster. She is stabbed not by a Turk but by an uncle who wants to use her transit pass. Both Gavin's and Bridge's novels were published after the Second World War, when relations between Mediterranean men and Western women were far more common than in the decades before the conflict. It is worth noting that in neither book is there even a suggestion of a relationship between a Turkish woman and a foreign man. Gavin depicts King Constantine as a fool and his generals as inept. The one Greek whom Kemal loathes and slightly fears is, of course, Venizelos (36). But unlike the Turks, who let their leader take them into the twentieth century, the Greeks sent their great man into exile. Still, there are no novels in which an English or American woman falls in love with the great Cretan. Modern Greece was still female, but modern Turkey, when it finally came to be considered, took a male form.

In a key moment between Evelyn and Kemal, the American woman speaks of the support for the Greeks abroad: "You're up against a whole century of prejudice. Ever since the British got excited about the Greek War of Independence, they've thought of the Greeks as heroes, like Hector and Achilles." Kemal responds: "While we were what their Lord Bryce called us—'the unspeakable Turk.'"

> "I wouldn't know about Lord Bryce," said Evelyn, "but I know you can't buck Lord Byron. He's the one who put it into immortal poetry.
>
> > *The isles of Greece, the isles of Greece,*
> > *Where burning Sappho loved and sung,*
> > *Where grew the arts of war and peace,*
> > *Where Delos rose and Phoebus sprung.*
>
> That's it you see. That's what all the Philhellenes are crazy for."
> (38–39)

Lord Byron is that with which both Kemal and Gavin, with her pro-Turkish perspective, perceive they have to contend. As late as 1970, it still seemed necessary to "buck Lord Byron."

For writing about modern Greece after 1922, Smyrna was indeed, as Edward Whittemore said, "the first act, the prelude to everything." In the story "On the Balcony," Patrick White commented that an aging woman "unconsciously . . . divided her life into Before and After the Catastrophe. Her world, the real tangible world, had ceased with Smyrna, and the best she could do was chase back a melancholy reflection of reality on to the face of life" (123). It was precisely the opposite for writing about Greece in English; authors were finally confronted with "the real tangible world" now that the pretense was gone that somehow, when one ventured into the world of modern Greece, one entered the era of 1821. The disaster became a benchmark in later literature to situate readers in a post-Romantic Greece.

In Louis MacNeice's poem "The Island," "the time-worn baker / Burnt out of Smyrna, smokes his hubble-bubble" (*Collected Poems* 306). MacNeice may be giving us details of a real baker; there were a million and a half refugees in Greece after 1925, and in certain areas they made up more than half of the population. But he is also placing his baker, and the Greek island of Ikaria that he visits, in a historical chronology, which we as readers are supposed to understand. Significantly, the baker is the only Greek on the island identified in such historical terms. The "slim and silent girl" who "gathers salt from the sea crags" and the "tall woman" who "strides out of Homer over the pine-needles, mule droppings, / Holding a distaff" may appear close to the baker in the text, but they are outside the contemporary geography and history that includes the "time-worn" baker (306). All MacNeice needed were the words "burnt out of Smyrna" to bring the "real tangible world" of postdisaster Greece into his poem.

Smyrna is the first event, chronologically, in novels such as Vaka Brown's *Blood Dance* and Edmund Keeley's *The Libation*. Hero Pavloussis in Patrick White's *The Vivisector* commences the story of her life by saying simply: "After the Catastrophe—at Smyrna—we escaped to Chios" (294). Hero, like the characters in the other books mentioned, does not attempt to describe the prelapsarian world in Anatolia. "Smyrna" functions as "year 1" of a new age.[21]

It is hard to imagine a more anticlimactic event than the centenary of Byron's death at Missolonghi in 1924. The following passage from a speech upon the occasion by Demetrius Caclamanos in London underscores the oddity of the ceremonies: "I think that this audience will be pleased to hear that in addition to the Commemoration Celebrations, it is proposed that one of the small towns around Athens, in the progress of construction for establishing Greeks from Asia Minor, should be named after Byron. It will be called 'Byronea.' Its streets will be named after Byron's friends—Thomas Moore, John Murray, Hobhouse, Shelley, Trelawny, and it is only too natural to think that there will also be a 'Maid of Athens' street" (8). The man who had dreamed that Greece might be free now would be honored by giving his name to a town full of those forced from their homes by the Turks. Irony, as Fussell said, was the dominant mode of expression after the Great War.

The Greece of Byron, as it had been understood for a century, had effectively come to an end two years earlier. As if in recognition of the end of an era, the Anglo-Hellenic League managed to publish but a single pamphlet in 1924 and, after another slender issue the following year, ceased publication altogether. Greece, which was still coping with the aftermath of a domestic revolution and the assimilation of a million and a half refugees, was understandably distracted and exhausted. Harold Spender reported to the Anglo-Hellenic League after his visit to Greece for the official ceremony in Missolonghi, "The Byron centenary was the cause of political demonstrations" in the Balkans, but many weary British would not have greeted those remarks with enthusiasm.

That weariness was clearly revealed in the number of English and American authors who passed over the Byron centenary in silence. Spender (*Byron and Greece*) and Harold Nicolson (*Byron: The Last Journey*), two prewar philhellenes, published volumes honoring the event. Nicolson began with a revisionary note: "I have discarded the legend that Byron went to Greece inspired solely by philhellenic enthusiasms, or that his sojourn in Missalonghi was anything but a succession of humiliating failures." After that note of caution, Nicolson went on to assert that, if "Byron accomplished nothing at Missalonghi but his own suicide . . . by that single act of heroism he secured the liberation of Greece" (ix). And the dedication of the book to Eletherios Venizelos demonstrates clearly that Nicolson's attitudes were formed before the disaster.[22]

If Greece needed time to assimilate the defeat of the army and the arrival of the refugees, then literature also needed time to assimilate the end of Greek regeneration and to rethink the place of Byron in the canon. Anthony Hecht perceptively noted that when "in 1989 Paul Muldoon came to make his selection of Byron's poetry for the volume *The Essential Byron*, he included none of the poetry that had been admired by Byron's contemporaries, and focused instead on what we might call 'the modern Byron.'" He went on, correctly, to say that W. H. Auden "defined this 'modern Byron' for us" (172).

Surveying Byron's oeuvre, Auden commented that, after "*Beppo, The Vision of Judgment*, and *Don Juan*, and what is left of lasting value? A few lyrics, though none as good as Moore's, two adequate satires, though inferior to Pope and Dryden, 'Darkness,' a fine piece of blank verse marred by some false sentiment, a few charming occasional pieces, half a dozen lines from *Childe Harold*, half a dozen lines from *Cain*, and that is all" ("Don Juan" 394). As Hecht observed, this excludes nearly all of the works that made the poet famous in the nineteenth century, particularly *Childe Harold*, the Oriental Tales (172), and, of course, most of the passages that had made Byron the poet of Greece.

Auden's Byron was closer in spirit to Pope and Dryden than to Romantics like Keats and Shelley. In 1938, Auden asserted that Byron's "distinctive contribution to English poetry was to be, not the defiant thunder of the rebel angel, but the speaking voice of the tolerant man-about-town" ("George Gordon Byron" 489). This is the Byron whom Auden addresses in "Letter to Lord Byron" in *Letters from Iceland* (1937). Auden said, "I want a form that's large enough to swim in / And talk on any subject that I choose," but Byron's connection to Greece is not a topic in the poem, although political views come in at the end of part 2, where, four stanzas apart, Auden wrote that "suggestions have been made that" Hitler would have appealed to the Romantic poet "as being the true heir to the Byronic" but also that Byron "might indeed / Have walked in the United Front with Gide" (*Collected Poems* 94–95). As Richard Davenport-Hines noted, Auden did not start writing to Byron until the European world faced a series of crises: in March the Germans retook the Rhineland; in May the Italians annexed Ethiopia; and in July the Spanish War began (160). Auden may have felt the need to talk to the poet who "tamed the Dragon by his intervention" as he himself wrestled with how he should react to news from Spain and elsewhere, for he points out that he and Byron lived in different ages: "In modern warfare, though it's just as gory, / There isn't any individual glory" (94). Auden may have wanted to recreate Byron as a "man about town" to justify his own behavior in that year of crisis.

The modern Byron did not transport easily to Greece. One need only look at a poem of Auden's friend and collaborator on *Letters from Iceland*, Louis MacNeice, written after a visit to Missolonghi. "Cock o' the North" begins as a satirical ballad, which promises to rewrite the Byron myth:

> Bad Lord Byron went to the firing, helmet and dogs and all,
> He rode and he swam and swam and he rode but now he rode for a fall;
> Twang the lyre and rattle the lexicon, Marathon, Harrow and all,
> Lame George Gordon broke the cordon, nobody broke his fall.
>
> (*Collected Poems* 291)

MacNeice depicted Byron's stay in Greece in 1824 as a series of humiliating and inept episodes in a tone that at times sounded a bit like Byron's own letters, and he proceeded to blast at the "sugary lies" that "the golden age is coming back." But one is not quite sure whether, at the end of the section, the line "Spring and Greece and glory—and Easter too—are coming" (291) and the refrain "Christos aneste" are part of the sugary lies or an indication that Byron's sacrifice somehow changed these satirical notes to heroic.

The second section offered perhaps the most accurate description of Missolonghi in English poetry. It opened: "The flattest place, it seems, in Hellas. A bad dream" (292). MacNeice claimed that you "would never guess

/ From Greece who Veeron was," but he did not effectively explore this theme, and some of the verse seems uninspired ("And miles behind, away, / Byron while shooting a duck felt groping in his liver / The flames of Six Mile Bottom," 292). The last two sections, which dealt with the poet's death, strengthened the analogies to the fates of Meleager and Christ. This development tended to reverse the deconstruction of the Byron myth in the first two sections. It is never quite clear what the connection between Meleager and Byron is supposed to signify, beyond geographical contiguity in western Greece. The Scottish dialect in the last section hardly helps matters, as in these lines:

> I flew like a bumblin' moth to the lure
> O' the gutterin' lamp o' Hellas.
>
> (294)

D. B. Moore said of this part that, though some of it is "clever," it "lacks conviction," and "as poetry it remains pedestrian" (154). The same could be said for the poem as a whole.

One reason for that might be that MacNeice himself, like his poem, was caught between the two versions of Byron. On the one hand, he had collaborated with Auden on a new poetic movement within England, one that contributed to the creation of the new Byron. On the other hand, he had been appointed director of the British Institute in Athens in 1950 because, according to his biographer Jon Stallworthy, "who could be more appropriate—given Byron's place in modern Greek mythology—than a well-known British poet with a classical education?" (376). It might have been hard to deconstruct the Byronic myth with Missolonghi so near.

Byron did not disappear from English and American writing about Greece in the years after the war. Visitors were still quoting his poems in travel books,[23] And novels with a foreign philhellene in the happy hunting ground of adventure saving a Greek girl from a barbarian still appeared with some regularity. But after the Great War and the catastrophe in Asia Minor, it had no place in the changed circumstances of the eastern Mediterranean nor in the modern mentality of Western writers. It could exist only as an anachronism. In Dora Bradford's *Greek Fire* (1935), an English heroine is kidnapped by brigands driving a car from Marathon to Athens, as if the fateful Dilessi tragedy in 1870 could be reenacted in the 1930s. Denis Meadows's *The Greek Virgin* (1947) had to resort to a fictional island where Greeks could still rebel against the oppression of a Turkish pasha who, the author carefully noted, is not a friend of Kemal and Turkey. A space for the romance of liberation would reappear in the years of the Second World War and the Greek Civil War (1939–1949), when foreign philhellenes with their maids of Athens could confront Nazis or Communists, such as in Mary Richmond's *Maid of Athens* (1948) or Winston Graham's *Greek Fire* (1957).

By then, however, literature had embraced a different idea of Greece. The Greek defeat in 1922 created, for the first time, a clear divide between the attitude of modern authors, here used broadly to include not only Hemingway and Dos Passos but also Susan Glaspell, Christopher Isherwood, William Plomer, Henry Miller, Lawrence Durrell, Louis MacNeice, Patrick White, James Merrill, and John Fowles, and popular or middlebrow writers. The Greece of Byron, although it continued to appear in such works as Jan Roberts's *The Judas Sheep* (1975), in which an American philhellene with an updated maid of Athens opposes the military dictatorship in Greece in 1971, was now consigned to the latter category. Those writers determined, as Pound said, to "make it new" turned away from the Byronic legacy, in part, perhaps, to separate themselves from the legacy of Romanticism and also from the popular books with their conventional, middle-class values.

Still, a new perception of Greece was slow to emerge in English and American literature. One problem for Greece was that modernism was a cultural movement based in and on the concept of cities, particularly London, Paris, New York, and Berlin.[24] Modern Greece, with a reputation as a rural Arcadia and with strong Romantic associations, never became an important site of modernism. In the 1920s it passed from being dangerous ground to a forgotten land. Only at the end of that decade would authors begin to explore it again.

9

A Hard Place to Write About

"The golden ages of ambrosia and brigandage are past." In 1935, Kenneth Matthews, with some exaggeration, announced the end of both the Greece of Homer and the Greece of Byron (*Greek Salad* 98). The "last klepht" became a common theme in the years after the war. For example, on a road in Arcadia in 1939, Dorothy Ratcliffe met a grandly dressed Greek. "Are you the last of the Klephts?" she asked. "No, Kyria," he answered, "it is you motorists who are the Klephts today, but unlike the Klephts of yore who robbed the rich so that they might give to the poor, your passing by does not benefit the poor" (99).[1] Ratcliffe learned, to her disappointment, that the last klepht had died about twenty years earlier, just as the Great War ended.

A new conception of Greece, one not based on classical or Romantic texts, required some contact with the country and its people. Between the wars, at the time that Paul Fussell in *Abroad* declared that the Mediterranean was in vogue, Greece, to use E. M. Forster's comment about Cavafy, was "at a slight angle to the universe." For Americans, Greece was the lost country for both the Lost Generation and the generation after that. Eliot, cummings, Fitzgerald, Hemingway, Moore, and Robert Lowell never saw the Acropolis. Faulkner spent two weeks in Greece in 1957; Pound and Langston Hughes visited briefly in 1965; and Elizabeth Bishop took a cruise in Greek waters in 1979. Edith Wharton sailed the eastern Mediterranean in 1926, yet the only work inspired by that trip was the story set in Crusader Cyprus, "Dieu d'Amour" (1928).

Greece had only slightly more literary travelers from Britain in the 1920s and 1930s. Of Corfu, now one of Greece's most popular destinations, William Plomer wrote in 1933: "Visitors to the island are not numerous, although it lies on the direct route between Brindisi and Athens, and this is perhaps because nothing is done to attract them" (*Child of Queen Victoria* 151). In *Illyrian Spring* (1935) by Ann Bridge (Mary O'Malley), the heroine plans to go to Greece but leaves the boat on the Dalmatian coast. "Greece for me is like the end of the rainbow," she says, "It's become a sort of bogey, a mirage" (336).

Greece became a bit of a bogey for those who went as well. Upon his return to England in 1951, Louis MacNeice averred: "Having lived in Athens for a year and a half, I find it a hard place to write about" (Coulton 115). So did H.D., the only noteworthy American poet to stand on Greek soil between the wars and the author of numerous poems with classical Greek settings and themes. Barbara Guest, in her biography of H.D., suggested that there is a feeling of "estrangement" in the poet's letters and notes about a trip to Greece in 1920: "There is no spontaneous reaction to the setting of her poetic inspiration" (124). The visits of Arnold Bennett and Norman Douglas led to two rather forgettable works (*Mediterranean Scenes* [1928] and *One Day* [1929]), while neither Osbert Sitwell, Sacheverell Sitwell, nor Evelyn Waugh offered any fresh perspectives.[2] With the "Auden generation"— Christopher Isherwood, Louis MacNeice, Stephen Spender, John Lehmann, and William Plomer—the situation improved, but only Plomer published works about modern Greece before the Second World War.

One reason that "the cult of heliotropy," to use Fussell's phrase, missed modern Greece in the 1920s may have been that the country seemed permeated by a sense of loss and tragedy, the knowledge that, as a popular song later announced, the Golden City was "Istanbul not Constantinople."[3] The heroine of French Strother's novel *Maid of Athens* (1932) tells how refugees from the Pontus were relocated in Macedonia, an area where walnuts did not grow wild: "These poor people looked and looked, and not a nut could they find. They could not understand it. Who ever heard of woods that had no walnuts in them? There were always walnuts in Pontus! How could one get on in a country that had no walnuts? They were almost in despair. Gathering walnuts in the fall was something they had always done, and they felt lost when they could not find them" (188). In the decade after Smyrna, English and American writers in search of the Mediterranean experience, like the Pontic refugees, could not find what they were looking for in Greece. They turned to the French Riviera, Italy, Spain, and even Dalmatia.

Several authors tried to recuperate the events of 1922–1923 as a boon for Greece and to extend the nineteenth-century narrative of modern Greek regeneration. Francis Yeats-Brown declared, "Greece had received a revivifying blood transfusion [from the refugees] after her defeat in Asia Minor, and today Athens is a city of 800,000 people, with a great future" (305). Henry Morgenthau asserted, "The flight of the Greeks from Asia Minor was the birth pangs of the Greek republic. Out of their bitter tribulations has arisen a new nation, welded by suffering into a closer bond of union, and destined, I believe, to revive in great measure the ancient glories of that rocky land where Western civilization was born" (*I Was Sent to Athens* [1929] 5).

Not everyone agreed with Morgenthau that the Asia Minor Disaster would lead to the regeneration of Hellas. But most concurred that, in their modern tragedy, the Greeks had approached the *pathei mathos*, "learning by suffering," prominent in Attic tragic drama. For the Greek, Morgenthau went on to observe, "Tragedy has been another familiar fact of life down through all the ages of his history. He has been acutely conscious of it but has never yielded to despair" (300). Up until 1922, the unfortunate events of modern Greek history, such as the suicide of the Suliot women, the massacre at Scio in 1822, and the explosion of the Arkadi monastery on Crete in 1866, had been placed in a narrative of national rebirth, as Thermopylaes on the way to a final victory. With the end of the idea of progress and the hope to expand Greek territory, the defeat of 1922 was perceived through the prism of ancient tragic drama, as a modern version of, for example, Euripides' *The Trojan Women* with an entire nation as the cast. Modern Greece had always been what Lawrence Durrell said of Epidaurus in his poem "At Epidaurus": "a theatre where redemption was enacted." But the nature of that redemption changed drastically after 1922; it became personal rather than public or political.

The idea of modern Greece as the orchestra of a tragic theater would recur often in discussions of modern Greece, especially concerning the Greek Civil War in the late 1940s and the military junta from 1967 to 1974.[4] Rex Warner's novel *Men of Stones* (1950) used a performance of *King Lear* by leftists in a detention camp in the time of the civil war as a metaphor for the state of the country, and Edmund Keeley's *The Libation* (1958) updated Aeschylus's *Oresteia* with the recent history of modern Greece as a background. This motif could, of course, also be employed when other nations were forced to turn inward and examine moments of national failure. Vaclav Havel recently said of the state of the Czech republic: "However unpleasant and stressful and even dangerous what we are going through may be, it can also be a force for good, because it can call for a catharsis, the intended outcome of a Greek tragedy" (46). Yet the notion that tragedy was a "familiar fact of [Greek] life through all the ages of history" has been especially prevalent in twentieth-century constructions of Greece. And tragedy became a familiar element in writing about Greece only after Smyrna.

Greek stories of loss and exile after the Asia Minor Disaster could provide an example, and at times a catharsis, to an audience of foreign observers.[5] Glaspell remembered the refugees: "To see the Greek peasants come ashore that night in Salonica was to respect the fortitude of human nature. These were people who had for ten days been massed on the waterfront at Smyrna. They had seen their homes burn, and their husbands taken by the Turks. Children had seen their mother[s] killed, and mothers had lost their children" ("Dwellers on Parnassus" 199). She left with a "respect for the fortitude of human nature," despite the fact that "this exodus was their destruction." French Strother wrote in his novel *Maid of Athens*: "They've all experienced tragedy, individually and as a nation. . . . But you never see a

Greek who despairs. Look at old Theodora, here, that keeps house for me. Saw her husband and five children murdered before her eyes in Smyrna six years ago, and God knows what they did to her. She is as relentless as the furies in her hate, but she isn't broken, and she isn't afraid of life" (13–14). In 1981, the Australian novelist Patrick White, in a description of a toilet that refused to be flushed, employed the tragic paradigm for all close encounters with modern Greece by foreigners: "Any true Grecophile will understand when I say that the unsinkable condom and the smell of shit which precede the moment of illumination make it more rewarding when it happens" (*Flaws in the Glass* 157).

White also said, "Most Greek eyes wear an expression of fatality, as though brooding over disaster, personal, historic, and those still in store for them" (*Flaws in the Glass* 101). But, he added, "Greek fatality is also my own, and why I was drawn to Greece from a distance, and one Greek in particular" (118). Greece was no longer, as it had been for a century, "the last shred of happy hunting-ground for the adventurous" (Munro 528). In the endurance of and catharsis after defeat, it became a land where a foreigner could go to overcome personal loss or to confront one's own fatalism. To quote Durrell's "At Epidaurus" again: "Here we can carry our own small death / With the resignation of place and identity" (97). In 1836, celebrating a "Birthday in Scio" in verse, John Pierpont had remembered the struggles of the War of Independence. But in 1963, May Sarton's "Birthday on the Acropolis" engendered different thoughts and a different Greece. The fifth and last section reads:

> On my fiftieth birthday I met the archaic smile
> It was the right year
> To confront
> The smile beyond suffering,
> As intimate and suffused
> As a wave's curve
> Just before it breaks.
>
> Evanescence held still;
> Change stated in external terms
> Aloof, Absolute:
> The criterion before us.
>
> On my fiftieth birthday
> I suffered from the archaic smile.
>   (*Collected Poems* 259)

Survival also figured prominently in James Merrill's "After Greece" (1962), which concluded:

The first glass I down
To the last time
I ate and drank in that old world. May I
Also survive its meanings, and my own.
(*Selected Poems* 63)

As Conchis put it in Fowles's *Magus*, "Greece is like a mirror. It makes you suffer. Then you learn" (99). Such was the scenario in the most significant American novel with a Greek setting written in the 1920s, Susan Glaspell's *Fugitive's Return* (1929). Where an encounter with the ruins of Greece in E. F. Benson's *Limitations* (1896) had sent the hero home unhappy and impatient with the limitations of the modern world, in Glaspell's novel the antique surroundings allow one to come to "know oneself" and one's place in society. The heroine is an American woman who, after the death of her child and a divorce from her husband, suffers from complete aphasia and memory loss. Speechless, she manages to travel alone to Delphi under an assumed name, that of her sister's friend Myra Freeman (a surname with obvious symbolism). When the season at Delphi ends and the hotel closes, "Myra" stays on in the only house located within the sacred sanctuary, "a setting for the ultimate drama" (248). Communing with the spirit of the place and the local population, particularly a Greek woman, Stamula, who she assists in weaving, she recovers both her speech and her old identity as Irma Lee Schraeder.

Glaspell's heroine, like Glaspell herself, found a seamless web between the ancient and modern Greeks. Irma muses that "those years in Delphi had been as if taken into something else" (90). Glaspell described her first encounter with the slopes of Parnassus: "It was as if we had come upon another world—their world, a hidden place where has been maintained a way of life through centuries of change. And Greece herself is not unlike that" ("Dwellers on Parnassus" 199). Glaspell worried that the incursion of Western materialism would ruin the world of the Greek village: "What our lives have become is now destroying this way of life that was in Greece before Homer was in Greece" (199). In *Fugitive's Return*, however, the American heroine, who has recovered her sense of self at Delphi, steps in to ensure that the ancient ways of the Greeks, which demand the death of a young Greek rape victim, are subverted.

Andreas, an attractive young man, had some years earlier raped Constantina, a dwarflike shepherd girl. Rather than marry Constantina as custom demanded, Andreas served time in prison, which only increased the shame of Constantina in the village. When Andreas asks a pretty refugee from Constantinople, Theodora, to marry him, Constantina kills the young man by dropping a rock from the ancient stadium on his head. The village turns on Constantina, except for Irma and her friend Stamula. The two devise a plan in which Irma will take the young Greek girl to America. Irma becomes in

Delphi not simply a new woman, but a "New Woman" of the kind that had been familiar in fiction from the 1890s.[6] She may well be the first fictional foreign New Woman to experience Greece, and her defiance of the village's tradition ensures that she can never return. Greece, to quote Durrell once again, offered "the discovery of yourself" (*Prospero's Cell* 11), but the realization of that discovery often entailed a departure from the Hellenic world. Irma is one of the first characters in literature to undergo this cycle.

Glaspell had gone to Greece in 1922 at the urging of her companion and collaborator in the Provincetown Players, George Cram Cook. Cook had from boyhood a dream of an Apollonian Greece similar to that offered by Winckelmann, according to Glaspell in her book about him, *The Road to the Temple* (1927). The two lived mainly at Delphi and the Parnassian village of Agoryianni until Cook's death in 1924, an experience that made Glaspell the first major writer since Byron and Lear to have an extensive, firsthand experience of Greek village life. Glaspell buried Cook in the Greek cemetery at Delphi in 1924 and then returned to the United States. Veronica Makowsky suggested, plausibly, that Glaspell had reservations about her life in Greece, reservations that Cook did not care to hear (99–100). Further, even in her admiring memoir of her life with Cook in Greece in *The Road to the Temple*, Glaspell presented examples of Cook's increasingly erratic behavior. The most prominent manifestation was, of course, the desire to live on the slopes of Parnassus, hardly the touristic site in 1922 that it has become today. Indeed, if Cook had had access to a hospital, he might not have died.

In *Fugitive's Return*, Cook's view of the continuing spiritual power of Delphi and the virtues of village life, sentiments that Glaspell repeatedly puts in the mouth of Cook in *The Road to the Temple*, are combined with Glaspell's own awareness of gender inequities in Greek society, and as Makowsky noted, in her relationship with Cook. Irma finds in the spirit of the place something as "pure and strong as the Castalian [spring] itself" (*Fugitive's Return* 252) and a correlation between the ruined temple of Apollo and the "temple that was her own heart" (316). Yet within that temple of her own heart, Glaspell and her heroine both learn that women need to be able to "know themselves" and not simply be constructed by societal roles. It is this tension that makes *Fugitive's Return* one of the most interesting novels set in Greece before World War II.

In Glaspell's story "The Faithless Shepherd" (1926), the hero begins and ends the action by attempting to trace out the letters of the name Dionysus.[7] It is a presence absent from *Fugitive's Return*, although the name Dionysus appears several times in the text. Irma's awakening is decidedly Apollonian in nature; even her love for the archaeologist John Knight has an ethereal character to it. Irma certainly did not leave colder climes to find a sexual awakening in the sun nor to escape the strictures of "civilized society" in the manner of the heroine of D. H. Lawrence's story "Sun" (1925). Rather, like the trip that the heroine of May Sarton's *Joanna and Ulysses* (1963) makes to the Greek island of Santorini, Irma's journey prepares her to reenter civilized society after a personal crisis. In the 1920s, Italy was still the site to search for Pan. And Irma, unlike Lawrence's heroine, has no romantic nor erotic connection to a Mediterranean man. When Irma needs a love interest, one appears from over the sea.

French Strother's *Maid of Athens* (1932) in subject matter if not in style presents the reverse journey from *Fugitive's Return*. A Greek woman leaves Greece to marry an American and have a career on the world stage, learns more about her true self, and then returns to her homeland. Strother's title signals that he is rewriting the romance of liberation in the post–Smyrna age, and his book holds some interest as the first treatment of the fate of the Greek woman after she marries the Western hero and departs for life abroad.

Thea Milo, Strother's heroine, is a refugee from Smyrna and an actress who has gained renown playing the lead in ancient tragedies; she escaped the destruction of her city by portraying Cassandra. Her dreams of a career on the stage are threatened when her family arranges a match with a rich, but physically unappealing, merchant named Akopoulos. In this version of the Maid of Athens, the liberation becomes personal rather than national. Hearing of her family's plans, Thea declares: "I must be free! I must live! I must be happy!" (49). All heroines of the romance had made such pronouncements, but Thea's fate is no longer tied to that of her nation.

Thea escapes on her wedding night with the help of a young American diplomat, Tim Johnson. The two later marry and live in Paris, where Thea continues to act. She scores a success in a production of *Antigone*, but it soon becomes clear that the Smyrna refugee can only successfully perform in Greek tragedies, as if there is some intrinsic connection between her own life and the plots of Attic drama. The couple move to America, where Thea discovers that "Greece alone had been understanding; Greece alone she had understood; and now Greece, her spiritual home, was locked against her" (269). Eventually she returns to Greece to see her dying father and to be killed by her brother, who had vowed to take her life for not staying with the man her family had chosen for her.

Strother's ideological perspective also reverses that of Glaspell. Where *Fugitive's Return* depicts a woman coming into consciousness and becoming a New Woman, *Maid of Athens* is a diatribe against sexual equality and careers for women. An American woman, asked whether her sex should have careers, responds, "Of course I do, when a career is all they can get. But careers for their own sake, no! They don't bring what women really want" (176). Strother's book, at the basic level, is an attack on the New Woman, and it is intriguing that he uses a Greek heroine to make his point.

In *Maid of Athens*, liberation turns out to be a false illusion, a viewpoint never voiced before the defeat of 1922, the end of the dream of Greater

Greece, and the recovery of Constantinople. But the world had changed after Smyrna, and a Greek girl who had exclaimed, "I must be free!" could now find that she did not really want freedom at all. The failure of Thea's marriage, as well as Strother's often-repeated axiom that like must marry like, raises the question whether Strother wants to reposition, or even remove, the Greeks from the European family.

Since the Second World War, the writer who has most consistently linked modern Greece with the tragic experience of Smyrna is Patrick White, winner of the Nobel Prize in 1973. For example, his stories "A Glass of Tea" and "An Evening at Sissy Kamara's" are both variations of the Meleager story in which the existence of household objects carried from Smyrna are interconnected with the emotional and physical well-being of the characters.[8] White "married" into a refugee family, since his companion of forty years, Manoli Lascaris, was from a family from Asia Minor (see *Flaws in the Glass* 100–102), and this may explain why White returned to it so often in his work.

Although the Greek characters in White's fiction are survivors, they rarely if ever gain the kind of illumination or peace of Glaspell's Irma Lee Schraeder. In White's novel *The Aunt's Story* (1948), a Greek tells a new acquaintance, "Greeks are happiest dying. . . . Their memorials do not reflect this fatality. All Greek monuments suggest a continuity of life. The theatre at Epidaurus, you have seen it, and Sounion? Pure life. But the Greeks are born to die" (102). In *The Vivisector* (1970), Hero Pavlousis, a Smyrna refugee who married her husband for money, tells an Australian artist: "I was not completely healed, not completely, until Cosmas took me to Perialos. That is an island off the coast of Asia Minor. It is an island of saints and miracles" (297). But in a typical White twist, when Hero takes the artist, now her lover, to this sacred island, her healing is called into question: "Do we come all this way for—nothing? Yes of course we do; it is not so extraordinary. Cosmas would have warned you this hermit—who is dead, or gone—was a filthy old man" (355). She concludes: "It was I who was foolish enough to believe in the idea of regeneration," and the artist himself leaves the holy island with an "unregenerate soul" (353). In the early nineteenth century, the regeneration of the Greeks was interconnected with a new age of freedom and happiness. In White, the failure of the Greek rebirth serves as a fitting metaphor for the fate of the individual in the modern world.

Osbert Lancaster, in his comic characterization of lovers of Greece, remarked that, in addition to a large group of enthusiastic admirers of the classical past, there are also "a few angry and aggressive little figures, quarreling violently among themselves and on the worst possible terms with the classical party below, following the dynamic form of Robert Byron bearing a banner with a strange device on which is inscribed the single word 'Byzantium'" (7). In the late 1920s, Robert Byron began an ambitious project to build an entirely new conception of modern Greece, which eschewed the Greeces of both Homer and the earlier Byron; in the words of Robert Byron, the one of "hexameters and lifeless stones" and the other of "abstract freedom, or the hatred of infidel misgovernment," which he termed, respectively, cultural and political philhellenism. "What then is real Philhellenism?" he asked. A "higher form than the Philhellenism of reconstruction; a Philhellenism not of the mind, but of the soul" (*Byzantine Achievement* 21–22) or, simply put, a Greece of Byzantium. Of the Byzantine Empire he asserted: "Spiritually, it is doubtful whether there has ever existed, over so long a period of time, so large a proportion of men and women, under one government, deeply and sincerely anxious to maintain communion with God at all moments of their lives" (37). Echoing earlier nineteenth-century rhetoric, he suggested that the example of Byzantium might open up potentialities "in which may lie the future of Europe, and the future of the earth" (22–23).

Byron's starting point in *The Byzantine Achievement* (1929) is, once again, Smyrna: "The intention of this book was originally to present a history of the Eastern Mediterranean between 1919 and 1923. But it became immediately apparent, upon a second and protracted exploration of the Greek seaboard in 1926, that to portray events of those years without previous investigation of their historical foundations, was equivalent to offering the public the last act of a play without the first. The fault now committed, the offer of the first without the last, is, I hope, the lesser" (ix). Notice again the dramatic reference; if the last act ended at 1923, the play was undoubtedly a tragedy.

Byzantium, according to Byron, has a special importance for understanding the postwar world in search of order and structure: "In the whole of European history, no moment offers more relevant comparison to our own than that in which Christianity became the state religion of the Roman Empire. A new civilisation was then born, the nature and achievement of which have remained unintelligible in the centuries of Triumphant Reason that have followed its extinction" (6). Byron's move here is not unlike that of other modernist writers, who attempted to go back before the rise of secular liberalism and triumphant reason to find an older, more secure, ideological anchor. Around the same time that Byron confessed an attachment to the Greek Orthodox empire of the East, T. S. Eliot was proclaiming that he was a Royalist in politics and an Anglo-Catholic in faith. Where Robert Byron differed was that he alone among English and American writers turned to the medieval Greek world as the road to salvation. Eliot could point to the company of such Catholic converts as Evelyn Waugh. In fact, Byron created his own schism between the churches of East and West. Paul Fussell noted, "Byron's quarrel with Waugh dates from Autumn, 1930, when Waugh chose to be received into the Roman Catholic Church, an act of hostility, as Byron conceived it, to his own Byzantinism" (*Abroad* 82).

Although after 1922 "political philhellenism was finally discredited," Lord Byron maintained his position as first philhellene. The spiritual essence of Greece, according to Robert Byron, is contained in the word *Romiosyne*, a word often translated as "Greekness" but which has a Byzantine (literally "Roman") rather than a classical derivation. He says that the meaning of this word "eludes the comprehension of man" but then goes on to add, "[Lord] Byron knew it" (*Byzantine Achievement* 21).[9] Near the end of *The Byzantine Achievement*, Robert Byron declared that the Byzantine tradition was still alive in Greece because it had been kindled, among other places, in "the craggy fastnesses of honorable brigands" (311), those same honorable brigands who, others claimed, had kept the ancient Greek tradition of freedom alive. Despite his rejection of political philhellenism as an idea, he seems to have been too drawn to the magic force of legend to place it in the same trash heap where he put Edward Gibbon and the degenerate view of Byzantium, and he attempted to appropriate Lord Byron for his Greece of Byzantium.

If partisans of the Greece of Homer had the Acropolis and those of the Greece of Byron had Missolonghi, Robert Byron's sacred ground was the peninsula of Mount Athos, which contained twenty monasteries and various lesser religious establishments of the Orthodox church. Byron claims the holy mountain as "one fragment, one living, articulate community of my chosen past" (*Station* 39) and a "station of a faith where all the years have stopped" (256). Byron wrote about this holy spot in his book *The Station: Athos, Treasures and Men* (1931), the first noteworthy travel book about Greece since Edward Lear's *Journal of a Landscape Painter* (1851). Like Lear, Byron dealt with a region on the margins of Greece proper; Mount Athos is an autonomous area that is not part of the Greek state. Neither the "haunted, holy ground" of Athens, the sunny Cycladic isles, nor the Peloponnesus had called forth a travel book in English of real literary merit since Childe Harold left Aegean shores.

As Paul Fussell remarked, part of the great charm of *The Station* lies in "the disparity between the monks' proclaimed spirituality and their readiness to cheat their visitors" (*Abroad* 85).[10] In spite of Byron's assertion that he had been "translated" to another dimension wholly different from other places on earth, "back into that mysterious, immaterial *regnum* from which the mind cast loose with the Renaissance" (*Station* 54), he seemed to be surrounded by figures quite familiar to readers—those nasty Greek degenerates called "Levantines." The venality of the monks is balanced, however, by Byron's own boorishness and his apparent lack of interest in the spiritual life of the monasteries. When an elderly monk refused to let Byron and his friend use a telephone, "we gradually forced the gesticulating old man up a flight of stairs till we stood upon a landing. 'Now,' we said like a trio of Chicago gangsters, 'where is it?'" (230). Later, Byron and one of his companions were invited to a feast at the monastery of Xeropotamou. After the food, "coffee, accompanied by a light sweet wine in lieu of port, was handed in the other room, till it was time for the momentous service, which was to last all night, to begin. Did we wish to come to the church, or to sleep? Sleep, we thought" (236). Byron attempted to sleep until two in the morning, but sleep would not come. So he got up and went to the church and was "transfixed" by the "rhythm of chant and paces. . . . Once and again, a hundred and a thousand times, the *Kyrie eleison*, in limitless plurality, beginning deep and hushed, mounted the scale with presage of impending triumph—to die off and begin again" (238). Why did this rabid Byzantinist not plan to go to the momentous service from the start? Why, in the text, is the only description of a service on the Holy Mountain dependent on the fact that Byron could not sleep? It is the collision of Byron's vision of Byzantium with both the reality of life on Mount Athos and his own crass behavior that makes *The Station* so refreshingly unique. Sacheverell Sitwell clearly had his friend Byron and his book in mind when he referred to the enthusiastic partisans of Byzantium, "most of whom, it can be said, had they been alive in it would have grumbled and complained incessantly at the conditions prevailing in their ideal world" (*Roumanian Journey* 91).

Byron sparked a Byzantine renaissance in England; Sitwell noted that in the 1930s "all serious minded undergraduates from Oxford and Cambridge" wanted to repair to Mount Athos "with that enthusiasm which carried their grandfathers to go to Rome and Florence. To that extent have the canons of taste changed the directions in which they face" (*Roumanian Journey* 93). But for some reason it hardly touched writing about modern Greece. His influence is most keenly felt in writing about the Byzantine heritage outside of Greece. In recent years, the poet John Ash has published *A Byzantine Journey* (1995), an account of his travels in Anatolia, and William Dalrymple has offered *From the Holy Mountain: A Journey in the Shadow of Byzantium* (1997), in which, after a brief beginning at Mount Athos, he goes down the eastern shore of the Mediterranean from Constantinople to Egypt. Neither Byzantine journey, significantly, takes the author to the modern Greek state. Rebecca West's massive book about Yugoslavia, *Black Lamb and Grey Falcon* (1941), which Robert Kaplan called "the century's greatest travel book" (3), owes a direct debt to Byron's revision of the Byzantine era. West acknowledged this in the following note in the bibliography about *The Byzantine Achievement*: "The author, whose death by enemy action all his friends and readers must deplore, wrote this when he was under twenty-five, and it is a remarkable effort. It forms a wholesome corrective to the nonsense that used to be talked about the decadence of Byzantium" (1155).

Yet West attempted to undercut Byron's central premise that the modern Greeks are a living link to the medieval past. Rather, she asserted that her own pet Balkan people, the Serbs, who had been "among the last to achieve order and gentleness are the last legatees of the Byzantine Empire in its law and magnificence" (1149). To add insult to injury, she employed the concept of Byzantine decadence, Byron's own *bête noir*, to justify her disinheriting the Greeks from the Byzantine legacy. Of emperor John Cantacuzenos, who in West's eyes forfeited the mantle of Byzantium, she wrote: "That detestable man was one of those men who are the price a civilisation pays in its decay for the achievements of its prime" (881). During his reign, "the Byzantine Empire was a masterless land, where weeds that grew spread to all neighboring fields and smothered all profitable crops" (881). The hope for civilization at that moment passed from the decadent Cantacuzenos and his Byzantines to the younger, more vibrant Serbs under the energetic Stephen Dushan. This was a twist that Byron could not have foreseen.

Byron's Byzantinism influenced other works, such as Sitwell's *Roumanian Journey* (1938) and Rose Macaulay's novel *The Towers of Trebizond* (1956). There is no reference to Byron or *The Byzantine Achievement* in Macaulay's published letters, but her use of Byzantine Trebizond as a sacred spot and a positive symbol surely owe something to Byron's revisonist history. Near the end of the book, she wrote: "Still, the towers of Trebizond, the fabled city, shimmer on a far horizon, gated and walled and held in a luminous enchantment" (288).[11] Both *Black Lamb and Grey Falcon* and *The Towers of Trebizond* are major books by major writers. There is no work of similar stature in fiction or nonfiction that employs Byron's revised Byzantium in a Greek setting. In *Labels* (1930), Evelyn Waugh declined to describe the Byzantine mosaics at Dafni because he would be treading "on Robert Byron's ground" (150). Perhaps that explains it. But one cannot help thinking that the idea of "Greece" in the minds of the West was not Byzantine. It was easier to carry Robert Byron's banner in other lands.

In 1974, the poet James Merrill told a story of how he had once met a young Belgian on the Brindisi-Patras ferry who requested a ride to Athens. On the way, "he asked if I knew the Greek poet Cavafy. When I said yes, he lit up: 'Well, it's with *him* that I shall be staying the next few days in Athens'" ("Marvelous Poet" 17). Merrill had to tell his companion that Constantine Cavafy had been dead for decades and besides had never lived in Athens. Yet Merrill certainly realized that, the counterfeit Cavafy aside, there was a deep truth in what the Belgian had said. Through a misinterpretation that because Cavafy wrote in Greek, then Athens must be "Alexandria," many have carried copies of the Alexandrian poet in their pockets to find the "Greece of Cavafy." Merrill himself was one of those who had spent more than a few days "staying with Cavafy" in Athens. For example, Merrill's poem "Days of 1964," which is about passion in an Athenian setting, directly evokes a series of poems by Cavafy, including "Days of 1896," "Days of 1902," and "Days of 1903."[12]

W. H. Auden, who first encountered Cavafy in the late 1920s through E. M. Forster and his Oxford professor, R. M. Dawkins, declared that the Greek poet's themes were "love, art, and politics in the original Greek sense" (ix).[13] For those who "stayed with Cavafy" in Athens, the chief attraction was verse on the first theme. Auden went on to say, "Cavafy was a homosexual, and his erotic poems make no attempt to conceal that fact," and the "erotic world he depicts is one of casual pickups and short-lived affairs. Love, there, is rarely more than physical passion, and when tenderer emotions do exist, they are almost always one-sided. At the same time, he refuses to pretend that his memories of sensual pleasure are unhappy or spoiled by feelings of guilt" (ix). Cavafy's "Days of 1908" is an example of such a poem:

> He was out of work that year,
> so he lived off card games,
> backgammon, and borrowed money.
>
> He was offered a job at three pounds a month
> in a small stationery store,
> but he turned it down without the slightest hesitation.
> It wasn't suitable. It wasn't the right pay for him,
> a reasonably educated young man, twenty-five years old. . . .
>
> His clothes were a terrible mess.
> He always wore the same suit,
> a very faded cinnamon-brown suit.
>
> O summer days of nineteen hundred and eight,
> from your perspective
> the cinnamon-brown suit was tastefully excluded.
>
> Your perspective has preserved him
> as he was when he took off, threw off,
> those unworthy clothes, that mended underwear,
> and stood stark naked, impeccably handsome, a miracle—
> his hair uncombed, swept back,
> his limbs a little tanned
> from his morning nakedness at the baths and at the beach.
>   (tr. Keeley and Sherrard 177–78)

In his autobiography, Merrill remarked that his yearly trips to Greece were driven by a desire for such casual pickups and short-lived assignations with social inferiors such as those about which Cavafy had written:

> The soldier on the dance floor, like nine out of ten of his class and culture, would count himself lucky to catch a permissive male lover,

one who wouldn't appear in the yitoniá [neighborhood] making a scene.
No reflection on the dancer's masculinity. Girls weren't easy to come by
in 1959, outside of marriage or the brothel; and who on a military wage
of thirty shoeshines a month could afford either one? . . . That the
dancing soldier hoped one day to marry and raise a family struck me as
the best news yet. More than the barriers of language and background,
it seemed to ensure our never going overboard in Greece. David and I
could follow with no harm to him the faun incarnate in this or that
young man, and without losing ourselves. (*Different Person* 191–92)

Cavafy offered not simply a series of casual erotic affairs but also a decadent city in which to pursue them. In "The Tomb of Iasis," he ended an epigraph for a young hedonist in Hellenistic times as follows:[14]

But from being considered so often a Narcissus and Hermes,
excess wore me out, killed me. Traveler,
if you're an Alexandrian, you won't blame me.
You know the pace of our life—its fever, its unsurpassable sensuality.
                                                    (tr. Keeley and Sherrard 76)

Athens, as a literary, urban Greek setting began as an "Alexandrian"
world. In John Fowles's *The Magus*, Nicholas recounts an encounter with his
old girlfriend in a hotel room in Piraeus:

I felt no attraction and no tenderness for her; no real interest in the
breakup of her long relationship with the boor of an Australian pilot;
simply the complex, ambiguous sadness of the darkening room. The
light had drained out of the sky, it became rapid dusk. All the treach-
eries of modern love seemed beautiful, and I had my great secret, safe,
locked away. It was Greece again, the Alexandrian Greece of Cavafy;
there were only degrees of aesthetic pleasure; of beauty in decadence.
Morality was a North European lie. (249)

In a rundown bar in Thessaloniki, the narrator of Francis King's story
"The Vultures" experienced "little sense of vice or squalor. Perhaps it is only
guilt in search of pleasure that produces that sense; and guilt, though so terrible a reality to the ancient Greeks, is fortunately almost unknown to their
descendants" (*So Hurt and Humiliated* 158).[15] Under the banner of Cavafy,
the fleshly Greeks of Pater and the aesthetics of the 1890s first appeared in
literary constructions of modern Athens. The modern movement, as far as
writers were concerned, came to Greece from the East not the West. And the
Levantines of Athens became, if not real Greeks, true Alexandrians.

The first person to follow the faun incarnate in Athens with Cavafy in his pocket also wrote the first poem in English dedicated to the Greek poet. William Plomer, like Auden, had learned about Cavafy from Forster. In "To the Greek Poet C. P. Cavafy on His Ποιηματα (1908–1914)" from his volume *The Five-fold Screen* (1932), Plomer situated the poems of Cavafy in a Greek rather than an Egyptian setting:

> Your temple is built, without the least pretense,
> On that antique foundation-stone, good sense,
> A curious music fills its colonnades,
> And Attic sunbeams stripe the lofty shades
>
> (57)

Since in Plomer's poem Attic sunbeams stripe the shades of Cavafy's temple, it makes sense that Plomer headed to Athens to worship in it.

Plomer's biographer, Peter Alexander, noted, "Greece had long had an attraction for English homosexuals" before Plomer arrived in 1931 (367), but that attraction had not surfaced in any significant way in published descriptions of modern Greece. Evelyn Waugh wrote in a letter to a friend in 1927 from Athens, where he was staying with Alastair Graham, a prototype for Sebastian in *Brideshead Revisited*, that "the flat is usually full of Dago youths called by such heroic names as Miltiades or Agamemnon with blue chins and greasy clothes who sleep with the English colony for 25 drachmas a night" (Hastings 147–48). But, despite the comic potential of such youths, Waugh did not mention them in his first novel, *Decline and Fall* (1928), in which the only reminiscence of his trip to Greece is the description of a villa on Corfu. Nor did he mention them in *Labels* (1930), his account of a Mediterranean tour in 1929, during which he spent two days in Athens with his gay friends Graham and Mark Ogilvie-Grant. In that book, he said only that Graham had "a house filled with mechanical singing birds and eikons," as if it were a setting for Yeats's "Sailing to Byzantium" (149). Only much later, in *Brideshead Revisited* (1945), does Waugh suggest that Athens was a haven for European homosexuals in the interwar period (174–75, 349–50). Gay modern Greece first appeared on the page in the early 1930s with the poems and stories of Plomer and a Kenneth Matthews novel, *Aleko* (1934).[16]

Plomer's debt to Cavafy can be seen in two poems and most of the stories he wrote about Greece. In the poems, a first person narrator records a passing moment of sensual and tender pleasure, which, according to Auden, was a trademark of the Alexandrian. "Three Pinks" depicts two lovers who awaken after a night of passion to greet the dawn that will separate them. The first published version of the poem reads:

We'll observe through the dry and timeless air of Attica
In which there is no nostalgia
The pepper-tree garden where last night by the full moon
An old woman disturbed our intimacy
To sell us three pinks with long stems.

(Five-fold Screen 51)[17]

"Another Country" begins with a direct evocation of Cavafy's poem "The City": "Let us go to another country, / Not yours or mine, / And start again." But the speaker then asserts:

> *This* is that other country
> We two populate,
> Land of a brief and brilliant
> Aurora, noon and night,
> The stratosphere of love
> From which we must descend,
>
> And leaving this rare country
> Must each to his own
> Return alone.
>
> (Collected Poems 67)

In both of these poems, since English does not have gender terminations as does Greek, the gender of the lover is left uncertain. This is not the case in the stories "Local Colour," "The Island," and "Nausicaa" (*Child of Queen Victoria and Other Stories* 1933), where two males are clearly paired together. Curiously, however, in all of these stories the pairs consist of two Greeks; even in "Nausicaa," in which a young Corfiote boatman is seduced by a visitor from abroad, the "foreigner" is a Greek from Alexandria (perhaps another nod to Cavafy). Alexander plausibly suggested that in this story Plomer critiqued his own behavior toward the Greeks with whom he became involved (174), which makes the change in nationality of the predatory tourist even more unsettling. Did Plomer think that homosexuality would be more palatable to an English audience if the participants were exclusively Greek? Or did he simply want a cover to write about his own experiences? If Plomer took advantage of Greeks during his stay in Athens, he also took advantage of them in his fiction, by removing the Western tourists who created the market for Greek youths.

Plomer's Greece is filled with decadent men, as if the fleshly ancient Greeks of Pater had to wait until the disaster to appear in modern Athens. In a letter to Stephen Spender, Plomer asserted: "England is a land of male women, Greece is a land of female men" (Alexander 168).[18] That is certainly the way he presented them in fiction. In "Local Colour," Madame Stroutho-kámelos discovers that her husband was "a little too Greek in his nature for her taste," but she publicly asserts that members of the younger generation "are manly and patriotic. I think there is great hope for the future" (*Child of Queen Victoria* 222, 225). When she takes the two young English visitors to a local restaurant so that "they can see a bit of the *real* Greece" (229), the country boys act a bit too effeminate for her liking. After one of the boys, referred to as Lilac Shirt because of his attire, has danced "a little too intimately" with his partner, then "embraced him and kissed him on the mouth," his fellows respond with a rousing cheer (233). Madame Strouthokámelos becomes appalled. "'They have forgotten themselves,' she said in a tone of disgust," (234), although, as with her husband, the boys could simply be remembering their Greek nature. "I think while you are in Greece you ought to do as the Greeks do" (223), their matronly hostess had advised her guests when they left for lunch, and we as readers are certain that the two Englishmen, particularly the one who has a copy of Proust's *Sodome et Gomorrhe* in his pocket, intend to do just that. Plomer's Greek companions, like Cavafy's erotic partners, were social inferiors who were often bought, and this certainly had some effect on his view of Greek men. Still, it is significant that in Plomer's gay construction of Greece, it was still a decidedly effeminate space.[19]

Cavafy wrote little about the great classical past, and those in search of the Greece of Cavafy followed suit. "There are other things in Athens besides the Parthenon," Plomer wrote in his *Autobiography* (275), and with that comment he summarily dispensed with the classical past. In Christopher Isherwood's *Down There on a Visit* (1962), Ambrose expresses the same attitude toward the classical past when he asks Christopher: "You've never been in Athens before, have you? Then I suppose you *ought* to see the Acropolis. I always think it's a good thing to get *that* over, as soon as possible" (72). Political philhellenism also held no interest for Plomer: "Greece was for the time being a republic. I forget why if I knew" (*Autobiography* 280). Greece, it seems, was simply a decadent, sensual Disneyland where, to use the words of James Merrill, one could "follow the faun incarnate" as one pleased.

Still, Plomer, like Robert Byron, was caught by the magic force of Byronic Greece. He wrote a poem about the Greek War of Independence entitled "The Young Klepht" at a time when the age of brigands had passed. In his autobiography, he related how on Corfu he read "a great deal about the War of Independence" and saw a "painting of the Suliot women about to throw themselves over a precipice rather than fall into the clutches of Ali Pacha," which inspired him to write a biography of Ali Pasha called *Ali the Lion*. Yet this endeavor itself suggests that, for Plomer, Byronic Greece had become history rather than a living legacy in which a young phihellene could still take part.

The "Athens of Cavafy" has had an enduring literary importance, as its appearance in Merrill and Fowles attests.[20] But it has not had the wide influence or circulation of the Greece of Byron. Part of the reason was undoubtedly that the heterosexual world was not going to embrace a conception of Greece, the birthplace of Western civilization, as the site of transient assignations, often homosexual. But the problem probably went a bit deeper. Athens was simply not Alexandria. Plomer's construction of Athens was no worse than any other Western construction that had appeared in the previous hundred or so years, but it depended, as did his ability to go to bed with boors, on bad lighting (see Alexander 168). In good lighting, and Athens has remarkable natural light, the landscape was simply wrong for a Cavafian setting. One can just as easily create a Cavafian London, New York, or Berlin, and many writers have.[21] There was nothing recognizably Greek in Plomer's Athens of Cavafy except that the available boys spoke Greek. Of all modern Greek poets, Cavafy has, I believe, the largest following among readers of poetry outside of Greece. But for English and American poets who write about modern Greece, the shadow of George Seferis looms larger. Rex Warner spoke for the generation that encountered Greece from 1946 to 1955 when he said that George Seferis, "more than any other writer, has been able to express . . . the detail and clarity of the Greek scene" ("Where Shall John Go?" 300).

A different spirit invests the homoerotic utopia that Ambrose attempts to build on the island of St. Gregory in the "Ambrose" section of Christopher Isherwood's *Down There on a Visit* (1962), a fictionalized version of the author's actual stay on the island of St. Nicholas in the summer of 1933.[22] At one point, Ambrose remembers how, right before his abrupt departure from Cambridge, he had "discovered Ronald Firbank, and I couldn't put it down" (111). This suggests an alternative comic, or perhaps more precisely "camp," gay tradition. Ambrose's island seems to intentionally suggest a male version of Miss O'Brookomore's lesbian garden of delights in Firbank's *Inclinations*. Both of these prospective Edens never flower, and they begin to fail when they are "invaded" by the other sex. In Isherwood, Maria plays the role of the Italian count in Firbank, seducing Ambrose's young charges from his noble vision. The books of Firbank and Isherwood are also linked by the fact that, before 1970, they are two of only a handful of books that conceive of Greece as a predominantly comic space.

Ambrose's island is hardly an Arcadian paradise. It is full of strange, prickly grass, brackish water that sours the stomach, hordes of flies, and enormous rats. Isherwood is undoubtedly suggesting that the only place where one might conceivably build a gay utopia must be a space so uninhabitable and unappealing that heterosexuals would not want to live there. The foreign contingent drinks to excess. This might explain why, in a world created for homosexuals, the two sexual acts clearly related are the heterosexual union of Maria and Waldemar and Theo's rape of a chicken later served for lunch.

The Greek boys are Dionysiac fauns taken to extreme. They are "swinishly dirty, inhumanly destructive and altogether on the side of the forces of disorder" (*Down There on a Visit* 106). When they are late with the boat, Geoffrey acidly comments, "They were *screwing*. They were screwing somebody or something. Each other, most likely" (90). The older Greek workmen on the island are scarcely better. They routinely dynamite the house that they are building for Ambrose. "Ambrose tells this with pride—possessive pride. He feels that he owns these people—their charm, their unreliability, their madness; everything about them. And, in a sense, he does, since it is he who is interpreting them to us. In a sense, this place is merely the projection of his will" (92). "The forces of disorder" are, then, not entirely natural to the island but part of the creation of a rich Englishman who, for whatever reason, wanted the Greeks on his island to act like the satyrs in the depiction of a Bacchic revel on a Greek vase.

William Plomer began his story "Local Colour" by remarking: "Upon certain kinds of Nordics the effect of living in Mediterranean countries is the reverse of bracing. The freedom, warmth, and glamour of their surroundings begin to sap their intellectual and artistic activity and ambition. While constantly talking about what they are going to accomplish, they do or make nothing, and at last discover that in gaining liberty and sunshine they have lost purpose and vigor" (*Child of Queen Victoria* 219). Fowles called this condition the "Aegean Blues" (foreword to *The Magus* 8). In gaining complete liberty and sunshine, Christopher loses his ability to structure his life, as the group as a whole loses its ability to decide anything. Anarchy and the forces of disorder eventually take over the pen and paper. While in Berlin, Isherwood noted, "I wrote a novel about England. Here, I want to get on with my novel about Berlin; but already I know that I shan't. All I can possibly write nowadays is this diary, because, here, one can only write about this place" (*Down There on a Visit* 97). But later, looking back at the diary, Isherwood found that the "handwriting of all these last short entries is big and straggly and, at the end of the lines, it tends to collapse, like playing cards fallen on top of each other. Obviously, it was done when I was very drunk" (129). He found in the end that the island was a hard place about which to write, especially while he was on it.

In Isherwood's geography, St. Gregory and Greece were not the Berlin he left and the London to which he will return; they offered a non-urban and, from a literary perspective, nonmodernist interlude between the political oppression of Hitler and the social oppression of London. "I couldn't care less, here, about classical Greece; I feel far more remote from it than I ever do in Northern Europe. But Northern Europe is becoming remote, too; quite shockingly so. . . . There may easily be war with Hitler this year, or next. I say this and believe it, but somehow I no longer quite care" (96–97). Still, many of the social tensions in the larger world emerged on this small island away from everything. For example, after one altercation, Christopher asked Waldemar, "Since when did you join the Brownshirts?" (128).

Down There on a Visit was not published until 1962. Although Isherwood used the journal he kept during his stay in Greece in 1933, he wrote much of the Greek section of the book later. If it had appeared in the 1930s, the "Ambrose" section of *Down There on a Visit* would have been one of the most innovative constructions of Greece between the wars. One suspects that the strong Dionysiac strain in Isherwood's Greece owes something to the influence of Henry Miller and Nikos Kazantzakis. In fact, Isherwood might be playing with the image of Kazantzakis's Zorba and creating a kind of "camp" Zorba with Aleko, who "wore a gaudy striped shirt, mechanic's overalls, and long, elegantly pointed shoes. A flower was stuck in behind his left ear. The fingernail on the little finger of his left hand had been allowed to grow nearly a half an inch long. 'That's the fashion in Athens just now,' Ambrose told me" (75). He held a fascination for the new arrivals to Greece: "He must have been aware of this, for he behaved with a self-conscious swagger, though he pretended to take little notice of us" (75). Whether such influence affected the composition of Isherwood's book might be debated, but that it affected the reception of the book is beyond doubt. By 1962, his satyrs were familiar figures on Greek soil, and Isherwood appeared to be riding a wave.

As the 1930s came to an end, a new modern Greece had still not emerged in English writing. From 1929 to 1934, authors had experimented with tragic Greece, the Byzantine legacy, and Cavafian Athens, and these ideas have all to some degree been subsumed into what we now think of as "Greece." But none of them gained a wide following, especially in the years that followed. The drought in writing about Greece from 1935 to 1939 was just as bad as the one that had lasted from 1924 to 1929. [23]

In August 1940, Lawrence Durrell wrote Henry Miller a letter that included the "story of the Cocks of Attica." One summer night on the Acropolis, George Katsimbalis

> threw back his head, clapped the crook of his stock into his wounded arm, and sent out the most blood-curdling clarion I have ever heard. Cock-a-doodle-doo. It echoed all over the city. . . . We were so shocked that we were struck dumb. And while we were still looking at each other in the darkness, lo, from the distance silvery clear in the darkness a cock drowsily answered—then another, then another. This drove K. wild. Squaring himself, like a bird ready to fly into space, and flapping his coat tails, he set up a terrific scream—and the echoes multiplied. . . . The whole night was alive with cockcrows— all Athens, all Attica, all Greece, it seemed, until I almost imagined you being woken at your desk late in New York to hear these terrific

silvery peals: Katsimbaline cockcrow in Athens. (*Colossus of Maroussi* 243–44)

Miller added Durrell's letter as an epigraph to his book on Greece, published in 1941. From then on, the Katsimbaline cockcrow continued to resound, first in America and then on the other side of the Atlantic. It was muted a bit by the Second World War, but after 1945 nearly everyone had heard it before he or she went to Greece. Those cocks, the world would discover, announced the reappearance of Dionysus in Greece.

CONCLUSION

A New Kind of Byronism

But Athens for me was Katsimbalis, Seferis, Antoniou,

New friends for merry places.

John Waller, *Kiss of Stars*

So wrote Waller in his poem "Spring in Athens" dated April 1945. A new note strikes one immediately. Athens had been many things over the years—haunted, holy ground for Byron, an irritation to Thackeray, a haven of decadence for Plomer—but the violet-crowned city had never, in a poem in English, been summed up by three Greek males treated as peers. In his *Views of Attica* (1950), Rex Warner's first chapter took the reader to the wine bar Psaras, where the author was found drinking with these same three men (28). For both Waller and Warner, the geographical center of Greece had shifted from the Acropolis, Marathon, or Missolonghi to the tavernas and cafes of Athens. Greece was no longer predominantly a visual experience, the sights of the sites, but an aural one; both authors made a point of telling us that listening to Greeks, or at least these three Greeks, had a significant place in their construction of Greece. Something, clearly, had changed since 1935.

Waller pointed to the main reason for this shift when he spoke of Katsimbalis "calling to the cocks from the Acropolis, / Roaring through nightfall" (27), which did not take place when Waller was in Athens in the spring of 1945 but in 1940, and the event was memorialized in *The Colossus of Maroussi*. This event became an emblem of new writing about Greece; Patrick Leigh Fermor, for example, referred to it directly in *Mani* (1958, 123–24). By including an incident with links to Miller and Durrell, Waller, like Leigh Fermor and Warner, was signaling that he wanted to be considered within a particular line of writing about Greece, a "movement," for lack of a better term, that was still too new in 1945 to be called a tradition. And he counts on the fact that these names, Katsimbalis, Seferis, and Antoniou, are not wholly unfamiliar. His readers already met them in Henry Miller's Greek book, *The Colossus of Maroussi* (1941).

The narrator of Edmund Keeley's novel *The Gold-Hatted Lover* (1961) has also read *The Colossus of Maroussi*; he makes a reference to Miller's visit to Phaestos and the presence of his name in the guest book at the Minoan site (105; see *Colossus of Maroussi* 163). What this reference really does, however, is to inscribe *The Gold-Hatted Lover* beside the works of Waller, Warner, and Leigh Fermor in the guest book, as it were, of *The Colossus of Maroussi*. The desire was widespread.[1] John Fowles mentioned only one contemporary book about Greece in the preface to the revised edition of *The Magus*. When Fowles was teaching on Spetses in 1951, he ran down to the harbor to pay his respects to "Henry Miller's Colossus of Maroussi Katsimbalis" (8).

Louis MacNeice also recognized the prominence of *The Colossus of Maroussi*, although he was hardly happy about it. In 1959, he began his review of Kevin Andrews's *The Flight of Ikaros*: "Many Europeans and Americans visiting Greece fall so in love with the country that they gush into print and give a one-sided picture. *The Colossus of Maroussi* by Henry Miller, though some of its gush is good, suggests that Greece is a never-never land where Miller can become Peter Pan. . . . Now comes Kevin Andrews to redress the balance" (*Selected Prose* 217). Andrews wrote a good book, but *The Flight of Ikaros* hardly redressed the balance, as the numerous references to Miller by other writers demonstrate.

Miller's *Colossus of Maroussi* and Lawrence Durrell's *Prospero's Cell* (1945), along with the Greek poems in Durrell's volume *A Private Country* (1943), invented a new modern Greece, as Edmund Keeley has shown.[2] Their books had an almost immediate impact. Durrell wrote to his editor and fellow poet, Anne Ridler, in 1946, "I'm afraid we've had a bad influence Henry and I's [*sic*] books about Greece. It is becoming a cult. In the last few weeks the number of poets who are compiling anthologies called SALUTE TO GREECE has risen" (*Spirit of Place* 84). The change reflected more than just volume. In 1954, Stephen Spender spoke of "this new philhellenism which has grown up during and since the war" as "a rediscovery of a classical by way of modern Greece," precisely the reverse of Romanticism's attempt to rediscover within the modern Greeks their ancient heritage ("Brilliant Athens and Us" 77). His list of new philhellenes includes Leigh Fermor, Durrell, Bernard Spencer, Francis King, Rex Warner, Osbert Lancaster, and the painter John Craxton. "In common with the American writer Henry Miller," Spender added, "they think of Katsimbalis . . . as their Virgilian guide to modern Athens. He seems to stand in the central square of Athens like one of the gigantic stone lions over the entrance to the ancient ruins of Mycenae" (78).[3] "In common with . . . Henry Miller" is a bit misleading, since Miller's book essentially created Katsimbalis as the guide to modern

Greece. Even Durrell's most important contribution to the Katsimbalis myth, the story of the cocks, was published in *The Colossus of Maroussi*. It is the main reason that writers wanted their works inscribed in the guest book of that volume rather than in Durrell's *Prospero's Cell* or *Reflections on a Marine Venus*.[4]

The Colossus of Maroussi is itself like one of those Katsimbaline monologues it memorializes—it too attacks from all sides at once, tosses things in the air only to catch them many pages later, and contradicts itself often in a wandering, boustrophedontic logic in which Miller delights. Still, it is possible to pick out of what MacNeice called Miller's "gush" several key ideas central to the formation of a new view of Greece.

First and foremost, Greece is a Dionysian place.[5] Greeks were now viewed, as Rex Warner put it in 1950, as "a race knowing excess, knowing intoxication of all kinds" (*Views of Attica* 16). On the Sacred Way to Eleusis, Miller related, "I was on the point of madness several times. I actually did start running up the hillside only to stop midway, terror-stricken, wondering what had taken possession of me" (44).[6] For Miller, this was one of the "marvelous things" that "happen to one in Greece—marvelous *good* things that can happen no where else on earth" (15). At one point, when discussing the terrain on the island of Corfu, Miller asserted, "All Greece is diademed with such antinomian spots; it is perhaps the explanation for the fact that Greece has emancipated itself as a country, a nation, a people, in order to continue as a luminous carrefour of a changing humanity" (21–22). One aspect of a Dionysian madness in which everyone acts on impulse is that there can be no organization of either society or life. In *Reflections on a Marine Venus*, Durrell recorded the following conversation with Manoli the fisherman:

> "You are English. They never see things before they happen. The English are very slow."
> "And what about the Greeks?"
> "The Greeks are fast . . . piff . . . paff . . . They decide."
> "But each one decides differently."
> "That is individualism."
> "But it leads to chaos."
> "We like chaos." (49)

The madness and chaos of Greece put Miller in touch with the elemental world as opposed to the "abstract, dehumanized world" built "out of the ashes of illusory materialism" of America and France (237).[7] In *Prospero's Cell*, Durrell said: "You will think it strange to have come from England to this fine Grecian promontory where our only company can be rock, air, sky—and all the elementals" (13). About a half century earlier, the antidote to a sick Western civilization had been Greek villages, which exuded a combination of pastoral values and the Apollonian sublime, juxtaposing modern civilization with real civilization, as it were. As Robert Kaplan observed, Durrell and Miller offered a new Greece "linked to an enjoyment of the physical senses that bordered on annihilation" (250). It is this Greece to which a character in Israel Horovitz's play *The Good Parts* (1983) refers when she says, "You're in Greece, remember. There's no need to be embarrassed about anything in Greece. Anything. Ever" (41). As Charmian Clift pointedly observed in *Peel Me a Lotus* (1959), this foreign idea of Greece had deleterious consequences for the Greeks. Every year, the country was awash with visitors who "absolve[d] themselves from all responsibility, all control, all moral laws, all sense of duty" (128). Their justification was that they were simply being "Greek."[8]

This should have a slightly familiar ring. Contact with the "classic" soil of Italy had played somewhat the same role in the fiction of writers such as E. M. Forster and D. H. Lawrence. For Victorian and Edwardian writers, Italy had been the place where "the marvelous *good* things happen." It is not a coincidence that early in Durrell's *Prospero's Cell*, N. defends Lawrence's "grasp of place" or that near the end Count D. says, "It's thirsty work talking like a Norman Douglas character" (15, 125). The two passages serve as bookends for a literature of place, *Italian* place, upon which Durrell drew for his Corfu book.[9] One might say that, despite the gush of the prose, all Miller and Durrell really did was see Pan in Greece. What is surprising is how liberating this "Italianizing" of Greece became for foreign authors. It was, to a significant degree, old wine drunk from a new bottle. But it really was a "new" Greece, one that had not been written about before, and it set a lot of pens in motion.

As if to underline the point that one could see Pan in Greece, Durrell's first book with a Greek setting was a novel entitled *Panic Spring* (1937), which Durrell's biographer, Ian MacNiven, said, "owes almost nothing to Henry Miller but a good deal to Norman Douglas and Aldous Huxley. The evocation of the island scenes are reminiscent of *South Wind*" (142). In *Prospero's Cell*, Count D. points out that, although Corfu has received the report of Pan's death, "in our modern pantheon we have a creature whose resemblance to Pan is not, I think, fortuitous. He is, as you know, the *kallikanzaros*. He is the house sprite, a little cloven-hoofed satyr with pointed ears, who is responsible for turning milk sour, for leaving doors unlocked, and for causing mischief of every kind" (105). In *Reflections on a Marine Venus*, Durrell wrote, "Rhodes, like the rest of Greece, has clung to its belief in Pan" (101).[10] On Nicholas Urfe's first visit to the Villa Bourani in Fowles's *The Magus*, he is confronted by a bronze statue with an enormous phallus. "'You know what it is?' . . . 'Pan?' 'A Priapus'" (84). In 1931, Isabel Anderson lamented that her greatest disappointment upon leaving Greece was that "I did not see Pan or hear his distant flute" (173). She was just a decade too early.

Miller did not catch sight of a Pan; he met a contemporary Dionysus in the flesh, a high priest of madness and chaos. That is why George Katsimbalis is a colossus and the Vergilian guide to modern Greece. Miller said that Katsimbalis "didn't believe in moderation nor good sense nor anything that was inhibitory. He believed in going the whole hog and then taking your punishment." While he was physically restricted as a result of war wounds, he could still "galvanize the dead with his talk" (30). Katsimbalis told Miller he refused to write because he is "an extemporaneous fellow," and "the best stories are those you don't want to preserve. If you have any arrière pensée the story is ruined" (66). Extemporaneity, for Miller, provided a key to human happiness. When the happiest man alive, as Miller called himself in *The Tropic of Cancer*, meets an even happier man alive, he must be colossal.

Katsimbalis was the ur-model for a new "masculine personification" of Greece, as the Katsimbaline figure Manoli was called in George Johnston and Charmian Clift's novel *The Sponge Divers* (1955, 183). The Greek seaman is "*pure* Greek, the essence of it," because he is a fanatic "about life. About living. He takes life in both hands and eats it as if it were a piece of meat" (183, 52). The American poet Kenneth Hanson described his encounter with this new Greek male in his poem "Take It from Me": "Greeks never fill up the tank, he said / so I pushed the car uphill / around a mountain curve at midnight." Hanson concluded:

> But look at it my way.
> Here was a new geography
> a mind where anything that grows
> grows by a kind of tour de force
> requiring only unconditional surrender.
> Here was the pure perfection of an art.
> Nothing like it in the British Museum.
> (*Distance Anywhere* 16–17)

James Merrill had one of these new Greeks phrase it as follows in his poem "Kostas Tympakianákis":

> Take me with you when you sail next week,
> You'll see a different cosmos through the eyes of a Greek.
> (*Selected Poems* 149)

The "new geography," the "different cosmos," of a masculine Greece, extemporaneous with no *arrière pensée*, was first charted by Miller after he met Katsimbalis. To put it another way, Katsimbalis was already Zorba before Kazantzakis wrote his novel in Greek. Greek women, on the other hand, played a small part in both Miller's *Colossus of Maroussi* and the works of the new philhellenism generally.[11] In her recent poem "Last Visit to Greece," Rachel Hadas wrote that the Greek language "had three genders, it was true, / but only one mattered. What was new / was how I saw this world as one of men" (5). The Greece of the new philhellenes basically had only one gender that mattered as well; the writers were mainly men, as were all of the names on Spender's list of new philhellenes, and their prime subject was the Greek male. Women were not central to this new geography of Greece.

The absence of sex and, for the most part, the female of the species, from the Dionysian world of *The Colossus of Maroussi* is puzzling, particularly since Miller constructed it. From the text, as Eisner noted, one might think that Miller was celibate for his six months in Greece (195). Peter Levi, however, reported, that when, in a cafe in Athens, Miller found that the poets Odysseus Elytis and Nikos Gatsos knew of his books, he "became so excited he wanted a brothel. 'Elytis and I do not know much about those things. We will introduce you to Mr. Katsimbalis. He will know'" (*Hill of Kronos* 140). But if there was no sex in *The Colossus of Maroussi*, there was a kind of romance, for Miller was mesmerized by Katsimbalis's stories, and some of the language of romantic thralldom creeps into Miller's admiration of the garrulous Greek. No other Western male author, including gay authors, has so submitted in print to the dominance of a Greek man.[12] To be sure, Miller viewed Katsimbalis as an alter ego. As Miller noted, Katsimbalis "talked about himself because he was the most interesting person he knew. I admire that quality very much—I have a little bit of it myself" (28). Still, Miller left no doubt in his text that he was, as it were, a Dr. Watson to Katsimbalis's Sherlock Holmes. *The Colossus of Maroussi* remains unique in English and American literature for its celebration of Katsimbalis and other Greek intellectuals. Greek males were generally depicted with an animal physicality while intellectual and emotional sophistication remained with the foreign observer. In the first and only issue of *Greek Horizons*, Derek Patmore said, "The modern Greek character has much of the lovable child" (59), and the "childlike Greek" became a common theme. In *The Sponge Divers*, the Australian narrator explained to a woman who has had sex with Manoli that she can expect no sentimental attention from the "masculine personification of Greece" since he lacks any interior life. "That's his real world, and he lives in it like a child. . . . It isn't complicated in the way that we are complicated, it doesn't have the threads connecting it to any interior mechanisms" (183). A touch of condescension can even be found in statements of Durrell like "the Greek is a terrible fellow. Mercuric, noisy, voluble and proud—was there ever such a conjunction of qualities locked in a human breast? Only the Irishman could match him for intractability, for rowdy feckless generosity" (*Reflections on a Marine Venus* 41). Miller's book is one of the few exceptions where the Greek characters possess superior abilities in both mind and body.

If Katsimbalis provided Miller with a new Greece, then Miller in turn created a version of Katsimbalis that the real man felt compelled to emulate. Whereas in the 1850s a visit to Teresa Macri, the "Maid of Athens," was part of any tour of Athens, in the 1950s literary travelers penciled in a trip to hear Katsimbalis, "the liveliest talker and most fantastic raconteur in Greece," according to John Lehmann (*Ample Proposition* 68). Miller's effect on Katsimbalis can be seen as early as 1940. Durrell wrote his old companion from the Villa Seurat:

> For a week after getting news of you or a letter from you he [Katsimbalis] is quite unquenchably not himself. You seem to stand in some relation of a half-analyst because he develops this mock-colossus, like a mock-turtle out of nowhere. Then he begins to stagger and lurch and boast and swear; and every story he says: "I forgot to tell Miller that one." Or, "Miller would have enjoyed that one, eh?" Some of his stories are so manifestly neither funny, elevating, or even commonly humane, that one winces for him and wonders why. But he goes on roaring and washing the air with his long flat dead-looking hands, trying to carve a mythical personality for himself from the rubbish of language. (*Durrell-Miller Letters* 134)

Still, Durrell ended by saying that "he is the truest Greek I know," and Katsimbalis remained the living embodiment of the true Greek throughout the 1950s. John Lehmann's description of Katsimbalis on a boat from Athens to Poros, "like an archaic statue dressed up in modern clothing for a lark" and "roaring to the wind and the waves and the uncomprehending, rather scared young sailors" appears to imitate a scene on a boat on page 63 of Miller's book, but we cannot be sure if it is Lehmann, Katsimbalis, or both who are trying to recreate the earlier incident (*Ample Proposition* 68).[13] Greece in English and American literature was never the same after Durrell and Miller met Katsimbalis in Athens in the autumn of 1939, but neither was Katsimbalis.

Miller's trip to Greece in 1939 was a symptom as much as a cause of a rethinking of the geography of the Mediterranean. In George Johnston's novel *Clean Straw for Nothing* (1969), a character remarks: "Italy, alas, is spoiling. . . . Even in the south. . . . Now one must go farther afield, I am afraid. Greece is the place, I think. Greece is still possible" (139). Miller commented, "Greece is *still* a sacred precinct" (15, my italics). Landscape was a crucial element in the explanation as to why Greece was still a sacred precinct, for it produced the condition that made Pans possible—"We are the children of our landscape," Durrell said in *Justine*, "it dictates behavior and thought in the measure to which we are responsive to it" (41). He began his

chapter on the history of Corfu with the comment, "Under the formal pag-
eant of events which we have dignified by our interest, the land changes very
little, and the structure of the basic self of man hardly at all" (59). In his discussion of the new philhellenism, Stephen Spender said that it "opens on to
the 'eternal Greece' not through politics, but through the landscape and the
people, and through modern Greek poetry" ("Brilliant Athens and Us" 78).
The point is supported by numerous titles and subtitles of works by the new
philhellenes, such as Durrell's *Prospero's Cell: A Guide to the Landscape and
Manners of the Island of Corfu* and *Reflections on a Marine Venus: A Guide to
the Landscape of Rhodes*; Osbert Lancaster's *Classical Landscape with Figures*;
Rex Warner's *Views of Attica and Its Surroundings*; and John Lehmann's
poem "Greek Landscape with Figures."

As Eisner noted, ideas about the effect of the Greek climate in these works
hardly differ from the "Rationalist/Romantic melody of landscape as meaning," which had appeared at the end of the eighteenth century (195). Landscape had, of course, always been an important consideration in the construction of Greece. Arnold Bennett in 1928 repeated the old nostrum about
the role of the environment in the creation of the Greek miracle: "The Greek
landscape was classical before Greek literature and architecture and sculpture. It is the origin of the Greek spirit" (30). One can compare such sentiment to Fowles's musing, "Perhaps ancient Greece was only the effect of a
landscape and a light on a sensitive people" ("Behind *The Magus*" 62).

But the terrain of the new philhellenism was decidedly different from, almost the opposite of, the Greek landscape of Romantic Hellenism. In 1806,
Chateaubriand found that in Greece "a suavity, a softness, a repose pervade
all nature. . . . In the native land of the Muses, Nature suggests no wild deviations, she tends, on the contrary, to dispose the mind to the love of the uniform and the harmonious" (67). His Greek environment was a reflection of
the presiding deity of the day, Apollo.

Over a hundred years later, however, the landscape of Greece was perceived to be full of wild deviations, as if the trees themselves responded to the
reappearance of Dionysus on Greek soil. At the beginning of *Prospero's Cell*,
Durrell said: "All the way across Italy you find yourself moving through a
landscape severely domesticated—each valley laid out after an architect's
pattern, brilliantly lighted, human" (11). Greece, Durrell went on, by contrast you approach "as one might enter a dark crystal; the form of things becomes irregular, refracted" (11). The olive tree is never pruned: "Prolix in its
freedom therefore the olive takes strange shapes" (94).[14] According to Leigh
Fermor, the scenery of the island of Hydra "is violent and dionysiac" ("Background of Nikos Ghika" 42). John Fowles told how he fell instantly in love
"with what I have come to call *agria Ellada*, or wild Greece" ("Greece" 71).
In 1970, Storm Jameson remarked that what is unique about Greece is not
"only the light, nakedly clear, but the hardness. Greece has the hardness—

not of stone, which can soften—but of marble" (*Journey from the North* 2:366). The wildness and hardness of the Greek landscape functioned as both an objective correlative for the psychological freedom of the individual and as a facilitator for shedding restraints placed upon him by society. It was this wildness that made Greece special and unique. "Other countries may offer you discoveries in manners or lore or landscape," Durrell said at the opening of *Prospero's Cell*. "Greece offers you something harder—the discovery of yourself" (11). In Greece, Fermor suggested, "Nature becomes supernatural; the frontier between the physical and the metaphysical is confounded" (*Mani* 288).

A key feature in the search for the primitive in Italy from 1870 through the writings of D. H. Lawrence in the 1920s had been the romanticizing of the Etruscans as a pre-Roman, peace-loving, natural people, a view made possible because little was known about the Etruscans. Miller and Durrell also celebrated the primitive in Greece; in their different ways they were as little interested in the Periclean glory that was Greece as Lawrence had been in the Augustan grandeur that was Rome. Back before Pericles, however, were the Mycenaeans, perceived, after Schliemann's excavations at Mycenae, as a rather bloodthirsty and matter-of-fact crew. Miller said that the Mycenaean fortress of Tiryns "smells of cruelty, barbarism, suspicion, isolation," and he added that the quiet at Mycenae today resembles "the exhaustion of a cruel and intelligent monster which has been bled to death" (85). These were hardly a people on which one could build an idyllic vision of life. But, with the excavations of Arthur Evans at Knossos, one could now go back before the Mycenaeans to the Minoans, about whom even less was known than the Etruscans. In what Lawrence referred to in a poem as "the Minoan distance," the Minoans became a pre-Greek, peace-loving, natural people—or, to put it another way, Etruscans on Greek soil.[15] Osbert Lancaster called the Minoans "a race of happy little extroverts unshadowed by the inhibiting preoccupation with the future life which so troubled the contemporary Egyptians and were quite unconcerned with the intellectual problems which engaged the fascinated attention of the Classical Greeks" (203–5). The hero of Keeley's *The Gold-Hatted Lover* sees Knossos as an "unembarrassed monument to the pleasures of the flesh" (79). At the Minoan site of Knossos, Henry Miller went into more detail:

> Knossos in all its manifestations suggests the splendor and sanity and opulence of a powerful and peaceful people. It is gay—gay, healthful, sanitary, salubrious. . . . The religious note seems to be graciously diminished; women played an important, equal role in the affairs of this people; a spirit of play is markedly noticeable. In short, the prevailing note is one of joy. One feels that man lived to live, that he was not plagued by thoughts of a life beyond . . . that he was religious in the

only way becoming to man, by making the most of everything that comes to hand, by extracting the utmost from every passing minute. Knossos was worldly in the best sense of the word. (121–22)

Katsimbalis, it appears, was not only a modern Dionysus but also a modern Minoan.

It would be wrong to underestimate the impact of the Minoans on the new pastoral perception of a primitive Greece, even for Durrell on Corfu. In a letter to George Wilkinson in 1934, Durrell informed his friend, "Nancy is rabid to examine the traces of early Byzantine paintings down the coast of Greece, while I am mad to get to Knossos and examine the traces of a Minoan civilization, of which by this time I'm quite sure, my ancestors were a part. . . . They were sturdy and lustful, and had a vital art of their own, which owes practically nothing to the huge contemporary civilizations around it" (*Spirit of Place* 29). Soon after the Second World War, Durrell was at work on a "Minoan" novel, *Cefalù*.[16] In his poem "Greek Excavations" (1942) Bernard Spencer claimed:

> Peering for coin or confident bust
> Or vase in bloom with swiftness of horses,
> My mind was never turned the way
> Of the classic of the just and unjust,
> I was looking for things which have a date
>   (20)

But the new philhellenes were not looking for things that had a date, they were in search of a place that had no dates, that was outside of time. They were trying, as Spencer said in "Aegean Islands, 1940–41," to find "elements in a happiness / More distant now than any date like '40, / A.D. or B.C., ever can express" (19). Those elements of happiness, when they had to be placed in a chronology, were placed before history began. Durrell's "In Arcadia" (1940) suggested that "Greece" existed even before the Greeks arrived. The poem opens with the arrival of the Dorians in Greece, bringing fire and a "brute art":

> Rain fell, tasting of the sky,
> Trees grew, composing a grammar,
> The river, the river you see was brought down
> By force of prayer on this fertile floor.
>
> Now small skills; the fingers laid upon
> The nostrils of flutes, the speech of women
> Whose tutors were the birds; who singing
> Now civilized their children with the kiss.
>   (*Collected Poems* 88)

The effect of the rain, trees, and birds could still be felt in the 1930s when this was written, since the poem concludes that there might be "Something dead out by the river: / but it seems less than a nightingale ago" (89). Even with the substitution of Dionysus for Apollo, such sentiments were, to use Eisner's phrase again, little more than the "Rationalist/Romantic melody of landscape as meaning" recycled.

The writing of the new philhellenism, however, was much more than that, because, as Spender said, it drew not only upon "the landscape and people" but also on "modern Greek poetry." Spender might simply have named George Seferis as the Greek poet of the new philhellenism. His only Greek rivals in influence were Katsimbalis and the painter Ghika.[17] Three of the names on Spender's list of new philhellenes were involved in early translations of Seferis. Bernard Spencer and Lawrence Durrell teamed with Nanos Valaoritis on *The King of Asine and Other Poems* (1948), and Rex Warner brought out another collection in 1960. In the 1940s, Durrell penned the poem "Letter to Seferis the Greek"; in the 1950s Spender dedicated "The Messenger" to Seferis; and in the 1960s C. Day-Lewis wrote "The Room" in homage to the same Greek writer. Peter Levi said, "It is amazing how much I understood, how early from George Seferis" (*Hill of Kronos* 34). He added that there "is a sense in which he virtually invented modern Greek, both as prose and verse" (34). More to the point, for Levi, as for Miller, Durrell, Fermor, and Spencer, there is a sense in which Seferis created modern Greece.

Miller admitted that he knew "his [Seferis's] work only from translation, but even if I had never read his poetry I would say this is the man who is destined to transmit the flame" (46).[18] The statement is not quite as prescient as it might first seem. For, just as it was Miller who caused literary travelers to look for Katsimbalis in Athens, it was Miller again who ensured that those same literary travelers were reading Seferis.

Miller, like Winckelmann, linked the "spirit of eternality which is everywhere in Greece" to the fact that the landscape does not change. Miller did not adduce, as Arnold Bennett had, the classical sublime created by the German thinker but claimed instead that this idea was "embedded in the poems" of George Seferiades, whose "pen name is Seferis." Miller then recalled

> going with Seferiades one afternoon to look at a piece of land on which he thought he might build himself a bungalow. There was nothing extraordinary about the place—it was even a bit shabby and forlorn, I might say. Or rather it *was*, at first sight. I never had a chance to consolidate my first fleeting impression; it changed under my eyes as he led me about like an electrified jelly-fish from spot to spot, rhapsodizing on herbs, flowers, shrubs, rocks, clay, slopes, declivities, coves, inlets, and so on. . . . His native flexibility was responding to the cosmic laws of curvature and finitude. He had ceased

going out in all directions; his lines were making the encircling movement of embrace. He had begun to ripen into the universal poet—by
passionately rooting himself in the soil of his people. Wherever there
is life today in Greek art it is based on this Antaean gesture, this passion which transmits itself from heart to feet, creating strong roots
which transform the body into a tree of potent beauty. (*Colossus of
Maroussi* 46–47)

Miller also depicted Katsimbalis as rooted in the Greek landscape; in fact,
Miller concluded his book with the colossus in an Antaean gesture of picking
a flower in an Attic field (240–41).[19] But with the appearance of a selection of
Seferis's poetry in *The King of Asine*, translated by Durrell, Spencer, and
Valaoritis, the example of Seferis was available for imitation. This volume, as
Avi Sharon has shown, was part of a concerted effort on the part of Spencer,
Durrell, Lehmann, and others to create a reputation for Seferis outside of
Greece.[20] Katsimbalis might sit astride the entrance to the "new geography"
of Greece like one of the lions of Mycenae, but the poems of Seferis were
there to be pondered, translated, and transported to England. Durrell,
Spencer, Warner, Sherrard, Keeley, and Levi are only a few of the writers
who included translating Seferis as part of their Greek experience. While the
extemporaneous fellow now speaks only in the pages of Miller for most English and American readers, Seferis stands firmly at the center of a canon of
modern Greek verse, which any real lover of modern Greece must learn to
confront in the original, like the poems of Homer for classical enthusiasts.

In his Nobel Prize speech, Seferis asserted that the present Greeks have a
kinship with the ancient Greeks because they have been formed by the same
geological features, because they are in effect children of the same landscape.
Seferis explored the use of landscape as a connecting link in the Greek experience in his poems, such as the twelfth section of *Mythistorima* (1935):

Bottle in the Sea

three rocks, a few burnt pines, a solitary chapel
and farther above
the same landscape repeated starts again:
three rocks in the shape of a gate-way, rusted,
a few burnt pines, black and yellow,
and a square hut buried in whitewash;
and still farther above, many times over,
the same landscape recurs level after level
to the horizon, to the twilight sky.
Here we moored the ship to splice the broken oars,
To drink water and to sleep.

The sea that embittered us is deep and unexplored
and unfolds a boundless calm.
Here among the pebbles we found a coin
and threw dice for it.
The youngest won it and disappeared.

We set out again with out broken oars.

(tr. Keeley and Sherrard 31)

Edmund Keeley suggested that in *Mythistorima*, as Seferis "attempts to carry the reader to the level of myth, the level of timeless universalities, he wins sympathy and belief by convincingly representing the present reality sustaining the myth—a contemporary Greek reality always" (*Modern Greek Poetry* 54). Keeley went on to observe that this strategy resembles to a degree the "mythical method" that Eliot coined in his review of Joyce's *Ulysses*, in which myth is used "'to give a shape and a significance to the immense panorama of futility and anarchy which is contemporary history' by using the mythology of Homer to manipulate 'a continuous parallel between contemporaneity and antiquity'" (74). Leigh Fermor said something similar to this when he remarked that Ghika extracted "a logic from the disorder" composed of the "convulsions of planes, angles, circles, cylinders, polygons, polyhydra" on the island of Hydra ("Background of Nikos Ghika" 30). Eliot asserted that the mythical method was "a serious step toward making the modern world possible for art" (*Selected Essays* 177). It was certainly a major step toward making modern Greece possible for foreign artists. Durrell suggested that the mythical method was almost a natural phenomenon in Corfu: "In this landscape observed objects still retain a kind of mythological form— so that though we are separated from Ulysses by hundreds of years in time, yet we dwell in his shadow" (*Prospero's Cell* 59). In *Reflections on a Marine Venus*, he used the term *historical present* for the sense of observed objects retaining in the present their mythical force. In her autobiography, Storm Jameson concurred: "I suppose that one reason for the stubborn persistence in us of Greece . . . is that, in this light scarred country, one is able, no, forced to impose a myth on reality" (2:369).[21]

As Keeley cautioned, Seferis can only be said to use the example of Joyce and Eliot in a general way, as a "kindred spirit" (*Modern Greek Poetry* 77).[22] But that was enough. To Durrell, as to Warner, Spender, and Lehmann, Seferis wrote verse that could be viewed within a framework that was familiar to them—it was giving back to them a modernism they had learned from Eliot. This may well have had a role in Durrell's warning to Seferis in 1944, "We are having trouble translating you so that you don't sound like Eliot."[23] Seferis, Katsimbalis, and Ghika provided a way into modern Greece because they were perceived to be both Greek and "modernist," different and yet familiar. But even if to some degree this was a vicarious celebration by West-erners of their own practices by praising those traits in Greeks, even if it could be viewed as a form of intellectual colonialism, it caused a break-through in writing about Greece. In the late 1940s and 1950s, some writers may have been attracted to the concept of a Greece connected to the mythical method of modernism and a "Greek Eliot," because it appeared to offer them one of the last modernist spots in a literary world slipping into the in-determinacy of postmodernism after the Second World War.

A crucial ingredient in Seferis's poetry was what Keeley called his insis-tence on "the contemporary Greek reality always," a characteristic he shared with the painter Ghika, the poet Odysseus Elytis, and other Greek artists. Miller presented a blueprint for the new encounter with Greece, although he might not have accomplished it to the same degree as Durrell did in *Pros-pero's Cell*. In Greece, he asserted: "Everything is delineated, sculptured, etched. Even the waste lands have an eternal cast about them. You see every-thing in its uniqueness—*a* man sitting on *a* road under *a* tree: *a* donkey climbing *a* path near *a* mountain: *a* ship in *a* harbor in *a* sea of turquoise: *a* table in *a* terrace beneath *a* cloud. And so on. Whatever you look at you see as if for the first time" (146). In *Reflections on a Marine Venus*, Durrell said, "We have learned to see Greece with inner eyes—not as a collection of bat-tered vestiges left over from cultures long since abandoned, but as some-thing ever-present and ever-renewed: the symbol married to the prime—so that a cypress tree, a mask, an orange, a plough were extended beyond them-selves into an eternity they enjoyed only with the furniture of all good poetry" (179). In Don DeLillo's *The Names*, Owen states: "Correctness of detail. This is what the light provides. Look to small things for your joy, your truth. This is the Greek specific" (26). The goal of the writer is now to some-how get that uniqueness, that correctness of detail, on the page, to know the "natural history of a sacred place," as Durrell put it in "To Argos," and to offer a text analogous to what anthropologists would term "thick descrip-tion." That phrase accurately fits the writing of Durrell in *Prospero's Cell and Reflections of a Marine Venus* and even more precisely the work of Leigh Fermor, who told the reader that his goal was "to attack the country at cer-tain points and penetrate, as far as my abilities went, in depth" (*Mani* x). In *Prospero's Cell*, for example, Durrell carefully recorded the seasonal changes in his island home: "You wake one morning in the late autumn and notice that the tone of everything has changed; the sky shines more deeply pearl, and the sun rises like a ball of blood—for the peaks of the Albanian hills are touched with snow. The sea has become leaden and sluggish and the olive a deep platinum grey. Fires smoke in the villages, and the breath of Maria as she passes with her sheep to the headland, is faintly white upon the air" (45–46). Bernard Spencer strove for precision of description in the poem "Aegean Islands, 1940–41":

> To sun one's bones beside the
> Explosive crushed-blue, nostril-opening sea
> (The weaving sea, splintered with sails and foam,
> Familiar of famous and deserted harbors,
> Of coins with dolphins on and fallen pillars).
>
> (19)

Miller did not say that one could now look at Greece as if he were seeing it for the first time because the classical and Byronic preconceptions had been laid aside. But the fact that those constructions of Greece were no longer potent was a major factor in permitting English and American visitors to "see" Greece anew. It is worth noting that Miller and Durrell encountered Greece with less literary baggage about the country than most of their contemporaries. Seferis once praised Miller as "the first man I admired for not having any classical preparation on going to Greece. . . . There is such a freshness about him" (in Keeley, *Modern Greek Poetry* 200). Robert Liddell lamented to George Seferis that his university training in the classics interfered with his understanding of modern Greece, while Durrell, who never finished university, "starts with an innocent eye" and "has no means of knowing that Homer is more considerable than Erotokritos [a medieval poem from Crete]."[24]

Even the best of the poems that Durrell wrote on Corfu lack the "spirit of eternality" and historical depth one finds later in the verse he wrote after Seferis had "greatly influenced" him, as Kenneth Young recognized as early as 1950 (58). In Durrell's early Greek poems the discovery of one's self tends to overpower the natural history of the place. But the powerful poems that began to appear in late 1939, like "At Epidaurus," "In Arcadia," "To Argos," and "At Corinth," concern an individual contemplating myth with the help of a charged Greek setting. In "To Argos," despite the fact that the roads have been "identified now by scholars":

> Only the shepherd in his cowl
> Who walks upon them really knows
> The natural history of a sacred place;
> Takes like a text of stone
> A familiar cloud-shape or fortress,
> Pointing at what is mutually seen,
> His dark eyes wearing the crowsfoot.
>
> (*Collected Poems* 105)

All of Durrell's and Bernard Spencer's longer Greek poems from the early war period employ a kind of Antaean gesture to evoke the eternality that is everywhere in Greece.[25] But a fundamental difference separates the

work of Seferis from the writings of foreign philhellenes. At the end of Durrell's poems there is often a clear recuperative moment with a pastoral aura,
involving some sort of "discovery of yourself," as in "At Epidaurus":

> Then smile, my dear, above the holy wands,
> Make the indefinite gesture of the hands,
> Unlocking this world which is not our world.
> The somnambulists walk again in the north
> With the long black rifles, to bring us answers.
> Useless a morality for slaves, useless
> The shouting at echoes to silence them.
> Most useless inhabitants of the kind blue air,
> Four ragged travellers in Homer.
> All causes end in the great Because.
>
> *(Collected Poems* 98)

The Greek world of Seferis is bleaker and less secure. Here is the final section
of *Mythistorima*:

> Here end the works of the sea, the works of love.
> Those who will some day live here where we end—
> should the blood happen to darken in their memory and overflow—
> let them not forget us, the weak souls among the asphodels,
> let them turn the heads of the victims towards Erebus:
>
> We who had nothing will teach them peace.
>
> (tr. Keeley and Sherrard 59)

The first person plural in Seferis's poem opens out to include the entire
Greek nation. That same first person plural appears in Durrell's poem
above, but it refers to expatriates in Greece, removed from the larger world.[26]
The difference between the two writers is highlighted in "Letter to Seferis
the Greek," where Durrell wrote:

> O my friend, history with all her compromises
> Cannot disturb the circuit made by this,
> Alone in the house, a single candle burning
> Upon a table in the whole of Greece.
>
> *(Collected Poems* 102)[27]

Any perceptive reading of Seferis instantly reveals that "history with all
her compromises" did disturb the private circuit Durrell attempted to carve
out in Greece; indeed, the perspective offered by Durrell is one to which, in

my view, Seferis would never assent. In the opening of the second section of Seferis's *Mythistorima*, the poet literally grappled with the Greek past:

I woke with this marble head in my hands;
it exhausts my elbows and I don't know where to put it down.
It was falling into the dream as I was coming out of the dream
so our life became one and it will be very difficult for it to disunite again.

(tr. Keeley and Sherrard 7)

In *Journey to the Morea*, Kazantzakis wrote, "For a foreigner the pilgrimage to Greece is simple, it happens without any great convulsion; his mind, liberated from sentimental entanglements, leaps on to discuss the essence of Greece. But for a Greek, this pilgrimage is fraught with hopes and fears, with distress and painful comparison" (8). One can take issue with how easily a foreigner can discuss the essence of Greece, but the visitor is prone to depict the pilgrimage to find Greece in literature as a relatively straightforward endeavor. Greeks like Seferis render that same journey as exceedingly difficult.

The Greek newspaper *Kathimerini* for May 13, 1998, carried an article entitled "Zorba, the Quintessential Greek, Is Still Controversial." The article called Zorba an "icon of the modern Greek since Michalis Cacoyannis filmed *Zorba the Greek* in 1964" and reported that the face of Anthony Quinn, who played Zorba in the movie, "became identified with the modern Greeks almost as much as the Parthenon was the symbol of the glory that was Ancient Greece." Robert Kaplan said, "The Greek myth was born out of movement in twentieth-century literature that was eventually crystallized in one of history's most memorable films" (249). No one can dispute that the picture of Anthony Quinn, dancing the *zeïmbekiko*, popularized the perception of a Dionysian Greece.[28] Surprisingly, the evidence suggests that Kazantzakis's novel *Zorba* had little to do with creating the new Greece nor much influence on any of the writers involved in the enterprise. In 1964, Patrick Anderson thought that it was strange that Henry Miller did not mention Kazantzakis in *The Colossus of Maroussi* (10–11). Miller, who did not know Greek, could not have read either Kazantzakis's novel nor his epic *The Odyssey* in English until more than a decade after the publication of the book about his trip to Greece. Still, Anderson has a point. *Zorba* appeared in an English translation in 1952 and was known well enough that *Holiday Magazine* asked Kazantzakis, called in the periodical "Greece's foremost novelist," to write an article about the Greek islands in 1954. Why did Spender not mention Kazantzakis in his article delineating the new philhellenism, "Brilliant Athens and Us"? Why did no one mention *Zorba*?

Peter Levi told the following tale of a visit to Athens in 1963: "Late at night, as café after café closed down, everyone in Athens who was still awake homed in on the same few tables, and conversations mingled. A film producer I had never met was wandering around looking for someone, anyone, to write an English script for a film called *Zorba the Greek*. We all refused, no one liked Kazantzakis" (*Hill of Kronos* 29). Neither Levi nor anyone else, so far as I am aware, has revealed why no one liked Kazantzakis, but the statement appears to be sound. In the 1950s and early 1960s, when nearly everyone was carrying *The Colossus of Maroussi* and invoking the name of Seferis, no English or American writer of note went to "stay with Zorba in Greece." From one point of view, Zorba was simply Katsimbalis dressed up as a peasant, and one might have expected those who were enamored of the colossus of Maroussi to find his rural alter ego somewhat appealing. It might have been that when a real Dionysus was available as a guide to Greece, one did not need to turn to a fictional one. Zorba did not replace Katsimbalis as the masculine personification of a new Greece until the middle of the 1960s.

Greece was available as an alternative to Italy in the late 1930s because the Smyrna Disaster had depoliticized its soil and its Pans. Spender noted in 1954 that a "revealing aspect of this rediscovered love of Greece is that it has nothing to do with current Greek politics. . . . Their [the new philhellenes'] passion for the country is unpolitical. It implies a recognition of the fact that the politics of foreign countries are more complex than they appeared in the thirties. This mood of refusal to judge Greek politics, or even to take them into account, is probably as characteristic of the 1950s as taboos about Spain are a hang-over from the 1930s" ("Brilliant Athens and Us" 78). The refusal to take account of Greek politics began earlier than 1950. The first and only issue of *Greek Horizons* (1946), a magazine featuring the work of British expatriates in Greece and published in Athens, announced in the midst of a civil war: "This quarterly will not be political. It aims rather at describing the natural beauties, customs, and the varied progress the modern Greeks have made in the arts" (2).[29] The struggle of West against East to free the Greeks was over, and after the Great War those who wanted to revolutionize the world sought Moscow not Athens. Without the quotations from Byron, without maids of Athens who needed rescue, without the dream of regeneration, Greece could be a sunny Mediterranean place where one could rid oneself of Western inhibitions. On the boat to Greece Miller met people of several Mediterranean nationalities: "The Turk aroused my antipathies at once. He had a mania for logic which infuriated me. It was a bad logic too. And like the others, all of whom I violently disagreed with, I found in him an expression of the American spirit at its worst. Progress was their obsession" (6). Here the concept of progress, so closely tied to the construction of modern Greece for decades, has been transferred to the Turk, whose race throughout the nineteenth century was thought to be impervious to progress.

Further, in the late 1930s another Italy was also needed because Italy, under Mussolini, had itself become a politicized place for visitors. Thomas

Mann signaled that in his story "Mario and the Magician" (1929), in which a vacationing German family is confronted by Fascists on the beach. And Spain had erupted in civil war by the middle of the decade. Ironically, when the impending war politicized nearly all places in Europe and many elsewhere, Greece, because the disaster had depoliticized it, was available as a pastoral retreat—"a private country," as Durrell called the book that contained many of his early Greek poems. It was certainly no longer the political country it once had been. "Left to his own resources," Miller wrote, "man always begins again the Greek way—a few goats or sheep, a rude hut, a patch of crops, a clump of olives, a running stream, a flute" (170). Durrell has Father Nicholas phrase it a bit differently: "What more does a man want than an olive tree, a native island, and [a] woman from his own place?" (*Prospero's Cell* 19). Greece was now envisioned as an escape from the quotidian world; Miller described the boat from Athens to Corfu as gliding in "more than a Greek atmosphere—it was poetic and of no time or place actually known to man" (24).[30]

Olivia Manning's *Friends and Heroes* (1965), set in Athens in 1940–1941, contained a revealing discussion between Alan Frewell and Guy Pringle:

> Alan talked for some time about the Greeks and the countryside: "an idyllic, unspoilt countryside." Guy, interested in the more practical aspects of Greek life, here broke in to ask if by "unspoilt" Alan did not mean undeveloped, and by "idyllic," simply that conditions had not changed since the days of the Ottoman empire. How was it possible to enjoy the beauty of a country when the inhabitants lived in privation and misery?

"'I've seen a great deal of the country,' Alan responded. 'I have not noticed that the people are unhappy'" (658). When Alan is asked whether Greece is "happy under a dictatorship," he laughs. "'You *could* call it a dictatorship, but a very benevolent one. . . . Before Metaxas took over there'd been an attempt to impose a modern political system on what was virtually a primitive society. The result was chaos.'" Guy responds: "'You prefer the peasants to remain in picturesque poverty, I suppose?'" To which Alan answers: "'I prefer that they remain as they are: courteous, generous, honourable, and courageous'" (658–59). Like Manning's Alan Frewell, most of the new philhellenes did not draw attention to whether the Greeks were unhappy under the dictatorship of General Ioannis Metaxas, which lasted from August 4, 1936, until Greece's entry into the Second World War, or whether there were political prisoners in Greece. "'I'm sure I don't know,'" Alan says in Manning's novel. "'There may be, but if people are intent on making a nuisance of themselves, then prison is the best place for them'" (659–60). Neither of the protagonists gets the better of the other in this exchange, since the leftist,

Guy Pringle, has his own set of ideological preconceptions, which impede his vision of the country around him.

The Colossus of Maroussi, Prospero's Cell, and Reflections on a Marine Venus are not deeply concerned with Greek politics either. Miller and Durrell surely knew that Greece was under a dictatorship in 1939, but they did not allow that to affect their view of it as a sacred precinct. Miller briefly met a political exile during a trip to Spetses, but he never tells us what the man had done to deserve his sentence (65–66). Durrell made only the briefest mention of the political problems that brought Metaxas to power in 1936 in his first novel, Panic Spring (9–10).[31] Bernard Spencer, in his poem "Salonika (June 1940)," began: "My end of Europe is at war." He concluded that he would "shut . . . if I could, out of harm's way" the whole of bright life he witnessed in the Greek city. "The dancing, the bathing, the order of the market, and as day / Cools into the night, boys playing in the square; / Island boats and lemon-peel tang and the timeless café crowd, / And the outcry of dice on wood" (21). Who could tell from this description that Greeks lacked political freedom when Spencer wrote the poem? Of those who wrote about Greece in the late 1930s, only Bert Birtles clearly connected the Metaxas regime with authoritarian governments elsewhere in Europe, and he dedicated his book Exiles in the Aegean (1938) to "the brave Greek victims of Fascist terror in prison and in exile."[32] Ironically, Greece could be the sacred precinct for the new philhellenes in part because the political liberty of the Greeks was no longer a central concern. The real "Greece," as Miller and Durrell conceived it at the start of the Second World War, was one of personal discovery, not of political action.

This helps to explain the rather bizarre fact that the great majority of the texts written by the new philhellenes in the 1950s did not depict the terrible years of the Nazi occupation and the Greek Civil War, a struggle between bands of Communist guerrillas and the right-wing government supported by Britain and America, with the same defining sense of tragedy that imbued the Asia Minor Disaster. In Views of Attica (1950), Rex Warner offered this disclaimer for his book. "It is by no means to attempt any kind of description of the civil war in Greece. I shall be chiefly concerned with sights and sounds. Violence, savagery, poverty, irreconcilable hatreds are not part of my theme, yet it is only too true they exist." It was not that he was ignorant of the conflict, he added, but his book aspired to recount "other aspects of the scene which are real and will be, I hope, more permanent" (36–37). The sights and sounds of Greece could, in fact, be the civil war, as Kevin Andrews's The Flight of Ikaros: Travels in Greece during a Civil War (1959) demonstrated. Andrews's book stands out for the fact that, almost alone of the books of the 1950s, it did not attempt to separate the sights and sounds of Greece from its politics and did not present the view that the strife in Greece was any less crucial than the landscape. But where Durrell presented a journey to Greece that ended with the "discovery of yourself" in *Prospero's Cell*, Andrews recorded a journey to find the self that ended in the discovery of Greece. Not many of his generation made that trip.

Most of the other writers, even those who served in the eastern Mediterranean during the Second World War, had a reaction about the war in Greece and its aftermath similar to that of John Fowles:

> All my generation had been dazzled by the exploits of a celebrated band of odd men who had fought beside the brave Greek resistance from 1939 to 1945. The aura of these contemporary Xans and Paddys somehow gilded our dream of those other handsome, dashing, and divine *andarte* and their women friends who once lived on Mount Olympus. We knew we couldn't rival them; my generation just missed fighting in the Nazi war and the bout of world belligerence in Korea, Malaysia, and so on that followed. We read all those glamorous exploits in Crete rather as the suburbs today read of the flamboyant goings-on in Hollywood. All that was somehow not quite credible, belonging less to real life—or certainly our own real lives—than to fiction. It allowed us to nibble and float in lotus land, but not to live where we really were. ("Behind *The Magus*" 69)

The Greek resistance to the Nazi occupation was viewed as a kind of heroic age, a return to the Greece of Byron. C. M. Woodhouse, one of the British officers who worked with the Greek resistance, later wrote: "Every experience of the 1820s was repeated, including torture, betrayal, and attempted murder, but also including loyalty, generosity and heroic self-sacrifice. The very names were the same, even if they were only pseudonymous: Odysseus, Kolokotronis, Botsaris, Karaiskakis, even Byron—all were there again in the 1940s" (*Philhellenes* 168). Patrick Leigh Fermor, who parachuted into occupied Crete during the war, recalled, "The people we lived among were mountaineers, shepherds, and villagers living high above the plains and cities in circumstances which exactly tallied with the life and background of the klephts in revolt at any point in the past few hundred years" (*Roumeli* 126). But after the war, that Byronic world was considered, as Fowles said, "not quite credible, belonging less to real life," and it was quickly relegated to the past. A klephtic past was hardly credible to Woodhouse, author of the best fiction written about Greece during the war, the sadly neglected collection *One Omen*. These stories are a grimly realistic picture of working with the resistance in Greece, in which the "brigand" clothes of some of the guerrillas are referred to as "romantic relics of an unreal past that had perhaps never lived" (18). The quick disappearance of the Byronic tradition after a brief resuscitation during World War II may have occurred because, as Woodhouse suggested:

Nothing comparable to the progressive causes of the 1820s—Catholic emancipation, parliamentary reform, republicanism, utilitarianism, evangelicanism, abolition of slavery, freedom of trade unions, education for the working class, and so on—existed in the 1940s to be merged with the philhellenism in a "protest movement." . . . The desire to liberate the Greeks from the Nazis was not, as the desire to liberate them from the Ottoman empire had been, part of a complex of radical ideas. It was in fact singularly free of ideology. (*Philhellenes* 169)

The desire to keep Greece out of the Communist bloc was also fairly free of ideological discussion in Western writing and certainly not part of a complex of radical ideas. None of the new philhellenes, however liberal, championed a leftist victory in the Greek Civil War. Once again, foreigners found unanimity on an issue that was deeply divisive among the Greeks themselves. Just as all of the versions of the romance of Greek liberation were Venizelist in the First World War, so all of the versions of the romance of liberation set during the civil war, such as Mary Richmond's *Maid of Athens* (1948), Winston Graham's *Greek Fire* (1957), and Helen MacInnes's *Decision at Delphi* (1962), are anti-Communist in sentiment.

What was new was the desire of so many of the new philhellenes to leave politics out of their experience of Greece, a reaction that partly stemmed from the fact that, by the 1940s, politics was part of a Byronic Greece associated with both Romanticism and "popular" writing. The "new philhellenism," as Fowles suggested, portrayed Greece as the new lotus land. The wheel had come full circle from the early nineteenth century. In 1872, Murray's *Handbook for Travellers in Greece* suggested that travelers to the country could "form an accurate opinion of the important question, the present state and future destiny of the Levant." By the 1950s, the lotus eaters went to Greece to avoid such worldly concerns.

As a result, the books about the wars in Greece during the 1940s did not make a large impact on the postwar idea of Greece in the English and American mind. Andrews's *The Flight of Ikaros* has had admirers, to be sure, but nowhere near the number of readers or the importance as the books of Miller and Durrell.[33] John Waller, for example, visited Athens in the spring of 1945 while on active duty, but his poem "Spring in Athens" celebrated evenings with Katsimbalis, Seferis, and Antoniou, as if his Athens were hardly different from the city Miller left in December 1939. Many writers turned their heads away from the civil war as Warner had, at least in print. In *Reflections on a Marine Venus*, Durrell alluded briefly to the problems in Greece during his stay on Rhodes from 1945 to 1947, when Manoli the fisherman says of the Communists: "They come to deliver us from poverty. God knows we need that. But they will end in enslaving us with other evils. God knows we don't want that"; but he did so mainly to indicate that no such political strife interrupted his enjoyment of Rhodes (50). Leigh Fermor knew as much about the civil war as anyone, but in *Mani* he made only a passing reference to the fighting in the 1940s (18–19). From his "private invasions of Greece," he stated in the preface, he would leave out "anything which had not filled me with interest, curiosity, pleasure, or excitement" (xi, x). Politics, apparently, was one of those things.[34]

A curious irony, then, lay at the heart of the work of Spender's new philhellenes. "Whatever you look at you see for the first time," Miller proclaimed, and there was an effort to put that advice into practice in descriptions of the landscape and people. On the other hand, Greek politics were not quite credible or real to these foreign observers, to paraphrase Fowles, and since their goal was to portray their Greek reality, politics were largely left out. Louis MacNeice appeared to take aim at the prevalent attitude of his literary colleagues in the third section of "The Island" in which a visitor, "gorged" on a Greek meal, settles down to take an August siesta:

> Here, he feels, is peace,
> The world is not after all a shambles
>
> And, granted there is no God, there are gods at least, at least in Greece,
>   And begins to drowse; but his dreams are troubled
> By the sawmill noises of cicadas, on and on—Will they never cease?
>
>   Were he to count a thousand, a hundred
> Thousand sheep, they would all be scraggy and stare at him with the stare
>   Of refugees, outraged and sullen, . . .
>
> And there are prisoners really, here in the hills, who do not agree
>   To sign for their freedom, whether in doubt of
> Such freedom or having forgotten or never having known what it
>   meant to be free.
>
>   (*Collected Poems* 306–7)

Yet even in this poem there seems to be a recuperation and reaffirmation for, in the fourth section, after asking, "But where is their island of wind and oil? / Where the slow concord of an island?" MacNeice concluded that one can find it in the light of the Greek sun, which can soothe one even in sleep, and he suggested there might be something to what Durrell called "islomania" after all:

> The round of dark has a lip of light,
> The dams of sleep are large with daybreak,
> Sleeping cocks are primed to crow
> While blood may hear, in ear's despite,

The sun's wheels turning in the night
Which drowns and feeds, reproves and heartens.
                    (308)

When politics mattered in the English and American construction of
Greece, the country was routinely personified as female. Greece gained a
masculine personification abroad when political concerns were not taken
into account. This suggests that there was still a problem in coming to terms
with the enduring dichotomy of Greece.

"The best books in English about Greece, as a personal discovery, are by
Patrick Leigh Fermor, Lawrence Durrell, Henry Miller, Kevin Andrews,
Dilys Powell. They have something in common, which I take to be Greek reality, not just a similar temperament, though most of them have been a close
friend of at least one of the others, and a quality of the same generation
marks them all" (Levi, *Hill of Kronos* 9). As a canon, this list is open to some
revision; Robert Eisner suggested that Charmian Clift's *Mermaid Singing*
(1956) and *Peel Me a Lotus* (1959) deserve consideration (229). One thing
that all of these books have in common, which gives them the sense of Greek
reality, is that they all are or purport to be nonfiction. In what V. S. Pritchett
called "the candor of Greek light" (141), the discovery of the self seemed unsuited to the shadows of fiction's ambiguity. In Greece, Miller said, "The
light penetrates directly to the soul, opens the doors and windows of the
heart, makes one naked, exposed, isolated in a metaphysical bliss which
makes everything clear without being known. No analysis can go on in this
light" (*Colossus of Maroussi* 45).[35] Such a view made the country as inhospitable to the bourgeois interiority of the novel as had the idea of the classical
sublime. The story of Italy as a personal discovery was often, if not predominantly, told in novels. But then Italy, especially places like Rome, Florence,
and Venice, was granted a murkier atmosphere and a Renaissance past. The
first novel of Greece as a "personal discovery" of which most readers would
think would probably be James Merrill's *The (Diblos) Notebook* (1965), a
fictional account of his visit to the island of Poros with Kimon Friar, or
Fowles's *The Magus* (1966), both of which appeared just before the idea of
Greece as lotus land was challenged by the military coup of 1967.

   With Miller, of course, the distinction between fiction and nonfiction
might not be appropriate; nearly all of his work is about the life of Henry
Miller. But it is worth noting that while the story of Miller in Paris, narrated
in *Tropic of Cancer*, has generally been recognized as a novel, the account of
Miller in Greece in *The Colossus of Maroussi* has consistently been placed in
the category of nonfiction. Readers and critics have determined that whatever Paris might be, Greece should be real. Durrell might seem a better example of the need for "the real" in writing about Greece. One might reasonably

argue that Durrell could not write fiction set in Greece, adducing *Panic Spring*, *Cefalú*, and the Athenian sections of *Tunc* and *Numquam* as proof. Durrell's most engaging fictional places were the urban, decadent cities of London (*The Black Book*), Alexandria, and Avignon. Things are actually not quite so clear, however. Durrell's Greek island books might not be autobiographical fiction, but they are certainly fictional autobiography, for Durrell was actually in Paris for many of the dates in *Prospero's Cell* and invented at least one main character, Gideon, for *Reflections on a Marine Venus*.[36] George Johnston's autobiographical novel about his life on Hydra in the 1950s, *Clean Straw for Nothing* (1969), is truer in "the correctness of detail" than either of Durrell's books.

The canon offered by Levi erased the novels about Greece as a personal discovery written in the early 1960s, including George Johnston's *Closer to the Sun* (1960); Charmian Clift's *Honour's Mimic* (1964), in my view her best book about the Greek experience; and Edmund Keeley's *The Gold-Hatted Lover* (1961). *Closer to the Sun* and *The Gold-Hatted Lover* both invoke Henry Miller as a precursor and attempt to critique the new Greece under the microscope of fiction's probing lenses. The specific merits of these works can be argued elsewhere, but they have at least partly been ignored because of the kind of fictional project in which they were engaged. Fiction qua fiction did not have to deconstruct Greece as a personal discovery—Johnston's and Clift's *The Sponge Divers* did not nor, on stage or screen, did Willy Russell's *Shirley Valentine* (1988).[37] As Fowles said in *The Magus*: "Greece is like a mirror. It makes you suffer. Then you learn" (99). His novel in fact fits this pattern, for while we may not agree on what Nicholas Urfe has learned or discovered about himself during the novel, we think that the problem is not with the mirror but with the reflection.[38] Interestingly, while both *The Magus*, with its illusory psychological permutations of the god game, and Merrill's *The (Diblos) Notebook*, with its device of replicating the jottings and crossed-out lines of a provisional text, have narrative styles that are influenced by the new trends of postmodern fiction, the Greek setting in both books is still enveloped in something like the mythical method of modernism.[39] Six years before the publication of *The Magus*, however, the characters of Johnston's *Closer to the Sun* discuss the problem of the "flawing of the mirror" (294); personal discovery in Greece might itself be a fiction.

In *Closer to the Sun*, an Australian family moves to the Greek island of Silenos to learn "something about the light and shadow on the rocks against the sky, the true taste of water, the rhythm of the seasons, the value of simplicity" (48). In the course of the novel, that project is threatened by an invasion of crass outsiders, the lure of money, and infidelity. The heroine says near the end, "Everybody thinks we're escaping from something by living here, and really this is where you find that there isn't any escape at all, not from anything, not yourself" (167). That has the typical Durrellian ring to it, except that such sentiments are balanced by statements that, by living on Silenos, the main characters have simply "lost [their] way" and have "to find it again" (275); in the end they have learned no more in lotus land than Odysseus's sailors did among the lotus eaters.[40] The sexual awakening that Kate has with a handsome, faunlike Frenchman does not lead to a happy return home to her husband in the manner of *Shirley Valentine*, but rather it threatens everything that she really cares about in her life. As the hero of Johnston's other novel about life on Hydra, *Clean Straw for Nothing*, is told, "You simply cannot cut yourselves off on a little island, as you have done, for all these years. Not without reckoning cost. Life becomes altogether too claustrophobic. Even incestuous. In the long run fatally destructive" (141). When one turns to Charmian Clift's *Mermaid Singing* and *Peel Me a Lotus*, rather cheerful memoirs of Clift's life with Johnston on Kalymnos and Hydra, one realizes that in the new Greece nonfiction is really Sophoclean, the world as the authors think it should be, while fiction is Euripidean, men and women as they really are.

In Clift's *Honour's Mimic*, Kate, an Australian woman married to an Englishman, is sent to stay with her sister-in-law on a Greek island after a suicide attempt. When she arrives, her brother-in-law tells her that her sister "has found it difficult . . . to adjust her romantic expectations to the reality of this poor and primitive place" (13). Kate's romantic expectations are different, but they also cannot survive the reality of life on a remote Greek island. She has an affair with a sponge diver but in the end realizes that they both must return to the worlds in which they lived before they met. This again sounds, minus the suicide attempt, much like the plot of *Shirley Valentine*. But in this case the sponge diver is a crude, sleazy, rather lazy fellow, more "Levantine" than "Greek," and Kate's jealous brother-in-law rapes her when he finds out. Early in the novel, Kate is said to have a predilection for slumming, and the reader is left to wonder if Kate's love affair with Fotis is a growth experience—*the* event that reconciles her to life—or simply an attraction to Greek lowlife. The Greek setting is not emphasized in this work; in fact the island and its inhabitants are depicted as rather dull, savage, and claustrophobic. The novel ends when, as her Greek lover departs on a sponge boat, a woman in the market spits on Kate and the boys throw stones at her, hardly a fitting end to an island idyll.

The narrator of Keeley's *The Gold-Hatted Lover*, an American diplomat stationed in Greece, takes an old college friend and his wife on a holiday to Crete with a beautiful Greek woman as a guide. She offers many of the standard lines about American visitors: they are "cold" and "ashamed of showing their emotions" (87). The married American has an affair with the guide, while his wife takes up with the narrator. As the reunited married couple leave for America together at the end, the narrator imagines they will be "pleased to be back in their own little world after such a trying and dangerous excursion into unknown territory, and who could argue that it wasn't for the best?" (235). On the last page of the novel, the narrator has retreated at night to the temple at Sounion where "none of the proper responses were aroused: no sense of imminent death, no final illuminations, no hint of tragic joy that one might feel in swan-diving over that cliff towards the black sea. . . . the only tangible emotion I felt was a sort of comic despair over having felt nothing at all, over having failed so miserably when the moment for the grand gesture—or at least for a grand thrill—finally came" (243). He concludes that he had not "loved hard enough." But Greece, or the idea of Greece as a place where one manages to have the grand thrill, has also failed the hero. None of the novels that subverted the idea of Greece as a personal discovery has received much notice. Nonfiction seemed better suited to the candor of Greek light.

> "What were you doing in Greece?"
> "Being happy." He turned his handsome face to her and smiled.
> "Just being happy. But unfortunately"—he sighed—"happiness does not last." (King, "Kind," in *So Hurt and Humiliated* 66)

If Greece was a paradise, then the inevitable fall from the garden had to occur. In *Prospero's Cell* and *The Colossus of Maroussi*, the loss of paradise was caused by World War II. The Germans were snakes on a biblical scale, so the end of paradise became especially poignant; in 1941 Durrell felt "the loss of Greece like an amputation" (*Prospero's Cell* 131). In *Reflections on a Marine Venus*, paradise ended with the termination of Durrell's position with the British Military Administration of the Dodecanese islands in 1947. In the decade after the war, ironically, the snakes became the very people who carried the books of Durrell and Miller under their arms. Leigh Fermor noted, "An old Athenian aware of the havoc that tourism has spread in Spain and France and Italy, laments that this gregarious passion, which destroys the object of its love, should have chosen Greece as its most recent, most beautiful, perhaps most fragile victim. . . . Greece is suffering its most dangerous invasion since the time of Xerxes" (*Roumeli* 117–18).

Throughout the 1950s and 1960s, the "real" Greece kept getting pushed by tourists into remoter mountains and islands. Leigh Fermor said in the preface of *Mani* that his project was "to situate and describe the present day Greeks of the mountains in relation to their habitat and history; to seek them out in those regions where bad communications and remoteness have left this ancient relationship, comparatively speaking, undisturbed" (x). This argument has both logic and illogic, for by writing about regions like the Mani, Leigh Fermor ensured that the tourist hordes would disturb life there. In "Matapan" (1943) Durrell began:

Unrevisited perhaps forever
Southward from the capes of smoke
Where past and present to the waters are one
And the peninsula's end points out
Three fingers down the night
                              (*Collected Poems* 116)

Durrell never returned to Cape Matapan, the southernmost point of mainland Greece, but Leigh Fermor traveled there in *Mani*, as did Robert Liddell
in *The Morea* (127). It became harder and harder to find the unvisited and unwritten place in Greece; William Travis went as far as the small island of
Symi just off the Turkish coast (*Bus Stop Symi*, 1970). Even the region in
Greece called *ta agrafa*, literally, the unwritten places, has been written
about, most recently in Tim Salmon's *The Unwritten Places* (1995) and Patricia Storace's chapter "The Unwritten" in *Dinner with Persephone* (1996).

   The unwritten places in Greece in English and American literature actually have been the cities of Athens and Thessaloniki. The comparison with
Egypt is instructive. More than three-quarters of the books in English about
Egypt focus on the urban centers of Cairo or Alexandria. Foreign authors
can find something Egyptian about Cairo but not, apparently, anything
Greek about Athens. Few books center on expatriate life in Athens and use
the city as a character with various moods represented by its geographical regions. One that does, however, is Olivia Manning's *Friends and Heroes* (1965),
which describes life in the city during 1940–1941, just before the German invasion. Another is Francis King's *The Firewalkers* (1956; published under
the pseudonym Frank Caulfield), which is about the good life among expatriates in Athens in the early 1950s.[41] King was a gay author greatly influenced
by the idea of a Cavafian Athens, and he employed the decadent hedonism
found earlier in the work of William Plomer in both *The Firewalkers* and *The
Man on the Rock* (1957), a fictional autobiography of one of the handsome,
young, kept men. Thessaloniki has gained a presence in writing in English
with Keeley's *The Libation* (1958) and *School for Pagan Lovers* (1993).[42]

Writing in 1981, Peter Levi suggested that the Greece of Durrell and Miller,
that is, Greece as a personal discovery, "was hardly born in 1930, and in the
last ten years has been transformed" (9). The military coup of 1967 in
Greece certainly marked a breaking point in the narrative of Levi's *Hill of
Kronos*—the snakes in paradise in this case being homegrown. The coup
clearly altered the landscape of Greece; the junta that ruled for the next
seven years ended, or at the least interrupted, the new philhellenism and
caused a repoliticization of Greece as a place on the map. Once again, Greece
became part of a complex of radical ideas when foreign opposition to the

Greek dictatorship became associated with, among other things, student rebellions in Europe and America, the movement against the Vietnam War, and
reaction to the Soviet invasion of Czechoslovakia.

Lawrence Ferlinghetti, one of the San Francisco Beat poets, embodied
the renewed links between desire for freedom in Greece and opposition to
political and social oppression elsewhere. His poem "Forty Odd Questions
for the Greek Regime and One Cry for Freedom" (first read at a benefit for
the Greek Resistance on April 20, 1972) suggested that the coup destroyed
the new Greece of Durrell and Miller when it asked the questions: "Where
is Katsimbalis Where Zorba Who stole Euripides?" and "Why can't we sail
the Isles of Greece and forget everything?" (*Open Eye, Open Heart* 109).
Spender's new philhellenes of the 1950s themselves contributed to the re-
examination of the place of Greece by putting aside their refusal to comment about Greek politics. Osbert Lancaster, for example, penned a poem
entitled "On not going to Greece, Easter, 1968" and steadfastly declined to
set foot in the country until after the collapse of the junta in 1974.[43] In a
work entitled simply "Political Poem" (1970), Kenneth Hanson reached
back to a potent name not heard in writing about Greece for several decades:
"Now in spite of the censorship / Greeks by the sea / or sitting on stones.
Are flexing their muscles / and dreaming a new Marathon" (*Uncorrected
Word* 14). In "After the Countercoup That Failed" (1970), Hanson used an
allusion to Yeats's "The Fish" to inject politics into what would have been
an idyllic seaside scene:

> What will the fishermen in Kalamáki
> do but spread their nets
> as yellow as the sun
> beside the sea, blue as the sky
> and name the colonels one by one
> until the colonels' names
> are bitter on the tongue?
>   (*Uncorrected Word* 12)

Seferis became an overtly political figure within Greece during the last
years of his life. His famous statement against the junta in March 1969 and
his superb poem of protest, "The Cats of St. Nicholas," ensured that after
his death in 1971, which was itself a political event within Greece, foreigners could never again engage with Seferis without taking account of Greek
politics.[44]

The Greek coup not only politicized Greece and Seferis abroad but also
Henry Miller and his Greek book. Ferlinghetti invoked the totemic moment
of the new philhellenism when he asked: "Can you still hear the cocks
of Athens from the Acropolis?" (111). Kay Boyle's "A Poem for the Stu-

dents of Greece," commemorating the uprising against the junta at the Polytechnic University in Athens in the autumn of 1973, included the following passage:

"I am thinking of that age to come," Henry Miller
Wrote for those who have closed their windows, their doors,
"When men will fight and kill for God . . . when food
Will be forgotten. . . . I am thinking of a world
Of men and women with dynamos between their legs,
A world of natural fury, passion, action, drama, madness, dreams."

(155)

In place of Seferis, the poet of Spender's new philhellenism, Boyle invoked Yannis Ritsos as the "poet of Greece, poet of prison, poet of house arrest" (156). It was because he was placed in detention in 1967 by the junta and then kept under house arrest from 1968 to 1974 that Ritsos became the poet of Greece for Boyle in 1973. Ritsos had been the leading poet of the Greek Left for decades, but his name was not often heard in English writing about Greece before the coup of 1967.[45]

There is a specific moment, within the period of the dictatorship, that I think symbolizes the end of the Greece of the new philhellenes. In 1972, the American author Mary Lee Settle went to Kos because it was cheap and she was trying to finish a book on seventeenth-century England; as she noted, it was always good to get some distance from the subject. "Wild packs of adolescent boys" roamed the area near her house, but they smiled at her, because, as she later discovered, her friend Vangeli had threatened them if they did not behave (*Turkish Reflections* 5). As soon as Vangeli left the island for a holiday in Athens, however, the situation changed: "The first large stone hit me in the back. I ran to my house, with stones being thrown at me from behind, got into the door, locked it behind me" (6). She decided to take the ferry across to the Turkish city of Bodrun as soon as she could. "The Greeks were terrible to me," she said as she got off the boat, "I have come for the protection of the Turks. . . . When what I said got around, as I knew it would, they welcomed me as if I were their long-lost sister" (7, 8). Settle stayed in Bodrun for three years and in 1977 published her novel about the Turkish city, *Blood Tie*, which won the National Book Award. By 1972, Greece was politically unappealing and spoiling, but Turkey—Turkey was still possible.

The politicization of Greece in foreign eyes did not end when the junta lost power in 1974. In Don DeLillo's *The Names*, the main character sounds a note not stressed in the years before the junta: "You realize the trouble with Greece, Greece is strategically located." To which his Greek companion replies simply, "We have noticed" (236). From the political point of view, Greece had been strategically located throughout the 1950s and the early 1960s. But from the literary perspective, Greece, as the place where one went to escape into "antinomian spots," could not be situated strategically in the international world. In a telling moment that places *The Names* in the post-Arcadian, post-Millerian, and postmodern Greece created by the junta, the main character says: "I think I'd feel at home with the Minoans. . . . They weren't subject to overwhelming awe. They didn't take things that seriously." His estranged wife replies:

> "Don't go too far. . . . There's the Minotaur, the labyrinth. Darker things. Beneath the lilies and antelopes and blue monkeys."
> "I don't see it at all."
> "Where have you looked?"
> "Only at the frescoes in Athens. Reproductions in books. Nature was a delight to them, not an angry god-like force."
> "A dig in north-central Crete has turned up signs of human sacrifice. No one is saying much." . . .
> "A Minoan site?"
> "All the usual signs. . . . Human sacrifice isn't new to Greece."
> "But not Minoans."
> "Not Minoans. They'll be arguing for years."
>
> (84)

Rachel Hadas also signaled that she had entered a post-Arcadian and postmodern Greece in the opening of "Last Visit to Greece" (1988):

> I had the labels ready with their essence:
> Add water, serve. Light, language, beauty, sea,
> body, etcetera, etcetera. Time.
> In honesty I had to change the tune:
> Queasiness, boredom, and misogyny.
>
> (5)

In addition, beginning in the 1960s, the image of Greece in writing in English began to be extended and complicated by the work of authors of Greek ancestry of the diaspora; in America alone, modern Greece and its past have been explored in Harry Mark Petrakis's novel of the Greek War of Independence, *The Hour of the Bell* (1976), Theodore Vrettos's revisionist look at the removal of the Elgin marbles in *Lord Elgin's Lady* (1982), the poems of Greek-born Olga Broumas starting with the volume *Beginning with O* (1977), and Catherine Temma Davidson's *The Priest Fainted* (1998), to name just a few works. They bring a different perspective to the encounter with Greece; one could say they offer the reader an entirely new country.

Many years after Seferis first met Durrell in Athens in 1939, he was asked to contribute an essay on Durrell's Greek poems. In a draft of that essay, written in French and now in the Gennadius Archive in Athens, Seferis, like Spender, noted that Durrell, Miller, and Spencer had exhibited a new kind of enthusiasm for the modern Greeks and a new interest in the Greek landscape not present in the work of earlier writers. The name he gave to their enterprise was "une nouvelle sort de Byronisme." This new kind of Byronism was meant, of course, to be the death of the old Byronism and, consequently, the end of Byron as a guide to modern Greece. Seferis apparently had no other term by which to denote this new direction in writing about modern Greece, so the very movement that finally superseded the Greece of Byron, by the use of the term *new Byronism*, still had the shadow of Byron attached to it.

There were, not surprisingly, several attempts to appropriate the famous first philhellene for the new kind of Byronism. In "At Corinth" (1940) Durrell invoked the spirit of Byron in his personal discovery in Greece:

> My skill is in words only:
> To tell you, writing this home,
> That we, whose blood was sweetened once
> By Byron or his elders in the magic,
> Entered the circle safely.
>
> (*Collected Poems* 87)

Durrell's magic circle here was hardly Byronic in the traditional sense in which the philhellenic journeys to Greece are supposed to help reform both Greece and the world. It was this latter kind of Byronism that had led Durrell, then "young, serviceable, and English," to consider enlisting in the Greek army in the autumn of 1939.[46] In "At Corinth," Durrell coopts Byron for the magic of Greece as a private circle, as opposed to the politicized "magic force of legend" so prominent in English writing in the century after Byron's death. Patrick Anderson entitled a chapter in his book *Dolphin Days* (1964) "Missalonghi: The Pleasures of Youth," and he portrayed Byron in Greece as the forerunner of contemporary lotus eaters. More recently, Stephen Minta, in *On a Voiceless Shore: Byron in Greece* (1997), spoke of Byron's "fascination with life beyond the boundary"; the "imagined Greece of Byron's youth was almost all extraordinary, a wild place, always on the edge" (151, 51). "What was original about Byron," Minta also said, "was that he found in Greece not a paradise of monuments, as many did, but a land of sensation, of sun, sea, and sky; a place of mountains, a rough physicality of sunburn and dust" (70). Such elements can in fact be found in Byron, and Minta cannot be faulted for reminding us about them. But this is a Byron who resembles Henry Miller and Lawrence Durrell, and before Miller and Durrell, hardly anyone paid any attention to this aspect of Byron's Greek experience.

John Lehmann was close to the mark in his poem "The Road to Rhamnous" when he said, "The way we came, we seemed to have left the map / Somewhere beyond Marathon" (*Collected Poems* 123). The map to Marathon had been written by Byron. The writers who provided directions for those going beyond were Miller and Durrell. Yet the name that Seferis gave to the place that they discovered was the new Byronism. With Missolonghi so near, it was still almost impossible to think sanely about Greece.

NOTES

Introduction

1. Vesna Goldsworthy's useful investigation of British attitudes about the Balkans, *Inventing Ruritania*, was published after this manuscript had been completed.

Chapter 1

1. See Finlay, *History of Greece* 5:250–57.

2. The author quickly went on to say, "Their first attacks discovered the womanly spirit by which they were inspired," indicating that the Greeks fell short of expectations in the West from the very beginning; see the comments of Constantine 172. On the reaction in the West to Orloff's arrival, see Constantine 168–72, Augustinos 146 and Terence Spencer 184–86.

3. Even in the midst of the Greek War of Independence, the most famous American philhellene, Samuel Gridley Howe, saw Greek freedom as a cause larger than Greece itself: "The Independence of Greece is not to release her children alone from the thralldom of the Turks, but it will open the door for the advance of liberty, of civilization, and of Christianity in the East" (*Historical Sketch of the Greek Revolution* xxx). As late as 1852, Edward Masson, an old philhellene, wrote: "The regeneration of Greece and the establishment of the Hellenic Kingdom are destined to exert a powerful influence, social and religious, as well as literary, on the rest of the world" (12–13).

4. As Jusdanis noted, the only other people who could "relate their own national imaginings to the core of European identity" were the Zionists (14). On the enduring yet different cultural significations of Hebraism and Hellenism in modern Europe generally, see Lambropoulos.

5. See St. Clair, *That Greece Might Still Be Free* 19–20. On the growth of a Western identity among the Greek intelligentsia in the late eighteenth century, see Jusdanis 17–30.

6. Augustinos noted that Catherine wanted to "use him [Voltaire] as a propagandist to promote her image in Europe" (141).

7. See Jusdanis 26–27.

8. Terence Spencer analyzed traces of philhellenic sentiment in English literature from the time of Shakespeare but agreed that interest in the modern Greeks and their regeneration increased in importance after 1770 (189). On philhellenism in Italian literature, see Persico; in German literature, see Quack-Eustathiades; and in French literature and art, see Canat, Tabaki-Iona, Athanassoglou-Kalmyer, and Augustinos.

9. On Chateaubriand's philhellenism and its influence, see Canat, *L'Hellénisme des Romantiques* 1:37–64, Malakis 63–73, and Augustinos 175–227.

10. *Anastasius* recounts the life and travels of a young Greek in the Levant from the 1770s to the 1790s. Early in the novel, the hero is compelled to adopt the Muslim faith in order to save his life, an act that alienates him from his Greek family and community. The work is more of a fictional story of Oriental life and travel than a philhellenic manifesto like *Woman; or, Ida of Athens or Hyperion*. Still, certain passages reflect the philhellenic thought of the time, such as the statement that the "complexion of the modern Greek may receive a different cast from different surrounding objects: The core is still the same as in the days of Pericles" (I.85) and the hero's comment that "the very noblest of the Greeks . . . is daily exposed to the insults of the meanest Turk. Were it not for my principles, I would rather be a Turkish porter than a Greek prince" (I.83). *Anastasius* was widely read and often cited by philhellenic authors, including Mary Shelley, *Collected Tales and Stories* 379 and Bulwer 76.

11. Sydney Owenson directly attested to Winckelmann's role in shaping ideas about Greece when she said in a note, "According to Winkleman [*sic*], the native Grecian countenance is distinguished by the calm and serenity of its features, and by its expression of benevolence and genius" (II.267). Winckelmann's most important scholarly work was the *Geschichte der Kunst der Ältertums* (1764), but his most influential was the early pamphlet of 1755, *Gedanken über die Nachahmung der griechischen Werke in der Mahlerey und Bildhauer-Kunst*, first translated by Henry Fuseli in *Reflections on the Painting and Sculpture of the Greeks* (1765). On Winckelmann's life and thought, see the first chapter of Eliza Butler's *Tyranny of Greece over Germany* and Wolfgang Leppman's biography. On Winckelmann's influence, see Stern 78–117, John Buxton 1–24, Constantine 104–27, and Ferris 16–51.

12. Thomas Seymour commented in 1888, "Living in the midst of the same surroundings, with the same climate, the same needs, and the same occupations, the Greeks have retained many of the peculiarities of their ancestors" (63). On the special qualities of the Greek landscape, see also the remarks of Flaubert in *Notes de Voyages* (II.137–38).

13. Malcolm Kelsall and Wallace (135–36) have also discussed the implications of philhellenism and Orientalism in Owenson's novel.

14. The early travel accounts of modern Greece have been the subject of several excellent books in recent years, among them Angelomatis-Tsougarakis, Augustinos, and Constantine. Along the way, travelers used modern Greek customs to interpret classical texts; see esp. Constantine 155–56. On the generally negative view of the modern Greeks, see Angelomatis-Tsougarakis 86–88.

15. In *Horae Ionicae* (1809), his narrative poem about a journey through the Ionian islands, W. R. Wright used Guys in a similar fashion. Referring to lines about a musical shepherd ("He sings the warlike deeds of other times; / Or wildly modulates to simple lays / His reed—the Doric reed of ancient days," 45), he added the following note: "The modern Greeks still retain a variety of traditional stories, which they derive from classical antiquity; their national dance they pretend had its origins in the days of Theseus and consider it as emblematical of that hero's adventures in the labyrinth; and the strain which accompanies it, is said to be the lamentation of Ariadne, deserted by him on Naxos. See the interesting work of M. Guys" (45). On Guys and his work, see Augustinos 147–57 and Constantine 147–67. English readers could also turn to Frederick Douglas's *Essay on Certain Points of Resemblance between the Ancient and Modern Greek* (1813).

16. At the beginning of his notes about Athens in *Childe Harold* II, Byron chided Owenson for her lack of real knowledge of Greece: "Before I say anything about a city, of which every body, traveller or not, has thought it necessary to say something, I will request Miss Owenson, when next she borrows an Athenian for her four volumes, to have the goodness to marry her to somebody more of a gentleman than a 'Disdar Aga'" (*CPW* II, p. 199). Byron's criticism is both playful and skillful, for Ida actually marries into one of the two noblest Greek families (the other is Ida's own), while her brief forced and unconsummated connection to the aga was never a real union.

17. Tsigakou noted "The majority of artists, influenced by the conventions of the day, depicted Greek scenery in a Claudian diffused half-light that tended to blur forms until they seemed part of the very irridescence of the atmosphere. But in Greece there are no mists, no half-tones" (28). Of depictions of the Acropolis, she added, "Again and again, . . . what one sees are fairy-land views bathed in a haze of golden light—a visual cliche of the golden age" (29).

18. See Eisner 77–78.

19. The rustic world of Greece among the ruins also provided a positive alternative to England in *Childe Harold's Pilgrimage*. Harold "through sin's labyrinth had run" (I.5.37) and leaves his own land "sore sick at heart" (I.6.46). He finds solace for his personal disquiet among the ancient ruins:

> He that is lonely hither let him roam,
> And gaze complacent on congenial earth.
> Greece is no lightsome land of social mirth;
> But he whom Sadness sootheth may abide,
> And scarce regret the region of his birth,
> When wandering slow by Delphi's sacred side,
> Or gazing o'er the plains where the Greek and Persian died.
>
> (II.92.866–72)

But unlike Owenson, Byron did not suggest that contact with the modern Greeks aids in a moral rejuvenation.

20. See the books on Victorian Hellenism by DeLaura, Richard Jenkyns, and Turner. Hellenism, like philhellenism, was complex and had numerous manifestations; on the differences between Matthew Arnold and Walter Pater see, e.g., DeLaura 171–81. A number of prominent English intellectuals of the nineteenth century, notably Arnold, stressed "the common position within the [Viconian] cycle of nations of Periclean Athens and contemporary Britain" and viewed ancient Greek civilization as "an immediately relevant point of departure for comprehending contemporary Victorian intellectual and spiritual perplexities" (Turner 28). Since in this conceptual framework, Britain was the reincarnation of ancient Athens, modern Greece and its situation held no particular importance. With the notable exceptions of Swinburne and Gladstone, few of the prominent Victorian Hellenists treated in the books of DeLaura, Turner, or Jenkyns concerned themselves with modern Greece and its politics, and so they fall outside of the scope of this study.

21. On the relation between *The Revolt of Islam* and the French Revolution, see Duff, esp. 154–61.

22. At Cambridge, E. F. Benson "threw himself with joy into the arms of the pagan Greeks, with their tolerance, their admiration of the beautiful, their psychological maturity" (Masters 95). It was at least partly a desire to recover that past that led Benson to write novels about the Greek War of Independence in the late 1890s, as it led fellow author Allen Upward to go to Crete as a volunteer in 1897 (see his autobiography, *Some Personalities* 136–49). A belief in the classical ideal also played a central role in the creation of Compton Mackenzie's philhellenism (see *Greece in My Life* 1–19).

23. Shelley's transcendental Hellenism also figured prominently in *Hellas*, the play he wrote in 1821 to encourage support for the Greek War of Independence. On the tension between Shelley's idealist Hellenism and contemporary politics in that work, see Kipperman, Wallace 196–205, and Ferris 108–33. On Chateaubriand's "subjective response to Greece," which was based on an attraction to the classical ideal and also led to expressions of philhellenism, see Augustinos 226. On Chateaubriand's reaction to the Greek Revolution, see Koukou 53–62.

24. On the political interests of those drawn to philhellenism, see Woodhouse, *The Philhellenes* 159. On how the cause of Greece was considered suspect by many because of the radicalism of the English philhellenes, see St. Clair, *That Greece Might Still Be Free* 145–47. The Literary Association of the Friends of Poland, formed in the early 1830s to support the movement for Polish independence, included numerous people who had been prominent in the London Greek Committee a few years earlier, such as Thomas Campbell, John Bowring, and John Cam Hobhouse (see Gleason 119–120).

25. During the Greek War of Independence, the English government tolerated and occasionally assisted the activities of certain philhellenes and philhellenic groups as a counterweight to Russian or French influence in Greece in the event of a Greek victory. But such support stemmed more from a desire to control their activities than to see Greece achieve liberty (see St. Clair, *That Greece Might Still Be Free* 132–37, and Penn 657–60).

26. In the introduction to *An Autumn in Greece*, Henry Bulwer speculated on Greece's fate under various protectors and concluded: "The old aristocratic powers of Europe would never allow the modern flag of America to be hoisted in their face, and wave from the shores of the Peloponnesus. So connecting a link between the independence of the New and the Old World would cause every crowned head to shake; and there is not a tyrant but would see, in the annihilation of Turkish despotism, the approaching insecurity of his own" (10). Yet Bulwer, like the anonymous author of the letter to George Canning printed at the end of *An Autumn in Greece*, argued that, since the "positive existence" of the Greeks was threatened by the unlimited tyranny of the Turks, "The cause of Greece should be separated from that of all nations, or parts of nations, who have contended for any particular form of government" (6). Bulwer's two statements indicate how liberal philhellenism was viewed as a threat to European governments at the same time that it privileged Western culture and government over those considered Eastern. For the long-established association of the Turks with tyranny, see Norman Daniel, *Islam and the West* 11.

27. See St. Clair, *That Greece Might Still Be Free* 244–62.

28. See also Athanassoglou-Kalmyer on the iconography of Leonidas in late eighteenth- and early nineteenth-century France (38–65).

29. See Marilyn Butler's discussion of the development of a "left-wing cult of the classical" by Shelley, Peacock, Keats, and Leigh Hunt in England as a balance to the conservative classicism of the Germans, which was admired and championed by Coleridge (*Romantics, Rebels and Reactionaries* 121). Butler suggested that Byron and Shelley located their "revolutionary" poems in the East to remove them from the partisanship of European politics: "Merely by adding a second theatre of war Byron implies that liberty is a universal ideal. The enemy is not Napoleon, who is England's enemy; it is tyranny" (118). The choice of Greece as a setting increased the universal idealism of the message. I cannot agree with Richard Jenkyns, who said, "Christians and pagans, radicals and conservatives could all feel eager for the independence of Greece" (15). In England, as in France, philhellenism was closely associated with the radicals and liberals (on the French situation, see Athanassoglou-Kalmyer 10).

30. Dennis Porter observed that, in contrast to Flaubert, "whatever their quarrels with their fatherlands, both Byron and Stendhal remain firm in their commitment to 'Western civilization' as embodied in the tradition of Greece, Rome, and Renaissance Italy" (181).

31. On the differing views of the East in *The Persians* and *The Bacchae*, see Said 56–57. The early nineteenth-century cultural battle between Hellenism and Orientalism can also be seen in Keats's *Hyperion*. Alan Bewell noted that in the poem Keats, by depicting the Titans with Egyptian features, "radically transformed the meaning of the war between the Titans and the Classical Gods: the war was restructured along an east-west axis, less as a theogony within a single culture than as an international event, a confrontation of the gods of Europe and those of the Orient" (224). Both Hellenists and Orientalists saw a confrontation on an East-West axis but differed on which side was to win. On the emergence of

the concept of Europe during the eighteenth-century Enlightenment and the use of the East as an alter ego in that development, see Chabod 82–121 and Hay 117–27.

The tension between the intra- and extra-European goals of early nineteenth-century liberals and radicals explains how so many authors of philhellenic works also composed Oriental writings, e.g., Thomas Moore, Walter Savage Landor, P. B. Shelley, and Byron himself (*The Island*). On the place of Romantic Orientalism in the cultural politics of the time, see Sharuffin, although I find his analysis of the Turkish Tales problematic. The celebrated leap of the Suliot women to escape from the hands of the Turks in 1803 at least suggests that the end of *The Siege of Corinth*, when Minotti sets fire to the powder magazine, is not simply an example of the futility of action.

32. On a Crusading view toward the East by the West, see Said 59–72. On Thomas Hughes's anti-Muslim sentiment, see also St. Clair, *That Greece Might Still Be Free* 59, and Charles Brinsley Sheridan's response to Hughes's *Address to the People of England in the Cause of the Greeks* in *Thoughts on the Greek Revolution*. Sheridan objected to the notion that "the present struggle is an attempt to drive the Turk out of Europe" (1). As a liberal European, Sheridan could not countenance such out-and-out bigotry. On the other hand, Sheridan went on to express the hope that Christianity would spread throughout the East.

33. "Philhellènisme religieux," as Canat called it (*Renaissance* 11), was much stronger in France, where the country's traditional role as the defender of the Levantine Catholics kept the Crusading sentiment alive (see France's involvement in the dispute between Catholics and Orthodox about the holy places in Jerusalem in the 1850s, an issue that hardly attracted attention in England and America). So, for example, in Stendhal's *Armance* a young royalist nobleman goes to Greece to fight as a philhellene (chap. 31), an unlikely event in England. Yet religious philhellenism never gained a firm hold in Catholic countries because the clergy viewed the Greek Orthodox as schismatics (see Athanassoglou-Kalmyer 24–25 and Malakis 12–13).

A few poets writing in English were inspired solely or primarily by religion rather than the classics or the idea of liberty, yet the slender section of only five poems entitled "Poems on the Spiritual Emancipation of Greece" in the anthology *The Greek Revolution and the American Muse* (ed. Raizis and Papas) shows how uncommon that attitude really was.

34. On Shelley's portrayal of Mahmud and Islam in *Hellas*, see Wallace (202–4) and Ferris (130–33).

35. See also Agnes Strickland, whose hero conflates a Crusading outlook with the classical past when he vows that "the stain / Of Pagan [i.e., in this context, Muslim] worship shall no more profane / A Grecian temple" (22–23).

36. Marilyn Butler said of Byron's *The Giaour* that "the story 'proves' Turkish rule ethically unacceptable to civilized westerners, without showing the Christian church in a more favorable light" ("Orientalism of Byron's *Giaour*" 91). Such an attitude aligns the poem with one of the major premises of literary philhellenism. On the connection between the ancient Greeks and both political and sex-

ual freedom, see Butler, *Romantics, Rebels and Reactionaries* 128–37. For the connection between the Greeks and homosexuality, see Eliza Butler on Winckelmann (13, 29–33) and Crompton on Byron (esp. 86–96). Toward the end of Heinse's novel, Ardinghello becomes involved in plotting an insurrection against Turkish rule, linking the notion of rebellion and free love.

37. Nigel Leask deals more fully with the imperialist implications of a Greek revival in the works of Byron and Shelley in *British Romantic Writers and the East*, esp. 13–37 and 103–33.

38. On this, see St. Clair, *That Greece Might Still Be Free* 197.

39. On Voltaire's reaction to the defeat of 1770, see Terence Spencer 187–88 and Augustinos 145.

40. Parga, a town on the western coast of mainland Greece, came under British control at the same time as the Ionian islands at the end of the Napoleonic Wars. In 1819, the British Government decided that it was not tenable to hold Parga and sold it to the Ottoman empire. This decision was criticized in several philhellenic writings, notably the anonymous narrative poem *Parga*. On this see the articles of Nielsen and Cochrane. Wright's poem was written before the British held Parga, but when the inhabitants of the town, like the Suliotes, had a reputation for their opposition to Turkish rule.

41. Lear also mentioned the story of the Suliot women in *Journal of a Landscape Painter in Albania and Illyria* (346–47).

Chapter 2

1. See St. Clair, *That Greece Might Still Be Free* 330–31.

2. In 1893, R. A. H. Bickford-Smith suggested that, in England, the "Grèce de Byron" actually had a wider following than its classical counterpart: "The dilletanti introduced her [Greece] to the upper ten [percent of the population]," but it was Byron who was responsible for making the country "known and loved by the great poetry reading middle class" (*Greece under King George* 341). On Byron's reputation among French philhellenes, see Tabaki-Iona 23–45.

3. See St. Clair, *That Greece Might Still Be Free* 176, 337.

4. On the career of Edward Trelawny, see the biography by St. Clair, whose first sentence reads: "Some of his admirers still cling to the belief that Trelawny merely exaggerated his stories at the margin for the sake of effect; but this is too charitable a judgement [*sic*]" (1). Trelawny was not the model for the hero of *The Corsair*, as he was fond of telling people, since he did not even meet Byron until 1822.

5. See Eisner 110–11.

6. See Terence Spencer 259–94 and W. C. Brown, "Byron and English Interest in the Near East."

7. About ten years before Byron went to Greece for the first time, Richard Polwhele also expressed the same sentiment in the lines: "Majestic Athens! Who thy ruins pil'd / In aweful heaps surveys, nor drops a tear?" (12). One should also

compare Byron's "'Tis Greece, but living Greece no more" with Charles Kelsall's "Athens, yet no more Athens!" (9).

8. See Dakin, *Unification of Greece* 20–23; Walter Savage Landor gave an account of Rhigas's life and work in the dialogue between Maurocordato and Colocotroni in *Imaginary Conversations* (*Complete Works* 8:186–87).

9. Barthélemy's novel of 1789, in which the hero travels through ancient Greece from 363 to 337 BCE, was one of the most popular and influential works of late eighteenth-century Hellenism. See the remarks of Stern 13–15.

10. For example, in *Philhellenika*, Masson translated poems by Alexander Soutzos, who was trained in Europe and brought Western poetical and aesthetic ideas back to Greece. On Soutzos, see Beaton 37–38. The propaganda purpose of Masson's translation work was made clear at the outset: "The object of this small volume . . . is to promote, among classical scholars, a more intimate acquaintance with the existing language and literature, as well as the social condition, of regenerated Greece" (1).

11. As Leask noted, in these passages Byron seemed to subtly advocate British rule in Greece (23). Yet in other places of *Childe Harold* (e.g., *CPW* II, pp. 201, 202), Byron appeared to take a different position as he attacked the cynicism of the European powers, which made liberty in Greece a pawn in the foreign affairs of the Holy Alliance (see the comments of McGann, *Beauty of Inflections* 260–62). As chapter 1 has argued, Byron's ambiguity about Greece's future was not unique. Like many European liberals, Byron wanted Greek independence to undermine Western monarchies at the same time that he thought those Western monarchies preferable to the perceived despotism of the East.

12. McGann's discussion of the context of "The Isles of Greece" in *Beauty of Inflections* (271–86) is especially useful, although I am not in full agreement with his conclusion that the poet has succeeded in composing "a song on behalf of freedom which escapes incorporation by the Age of Cant" (286).

13. Raizis used the term *Byronic philhellenism* to refer to an interest in Greece that went beyond "broken columns" and the restoration of antiquity to include the customs and lives of "living Greeks" ("Aspects of Byronic Philhellenism" 129–30).

14. *The Giaour* is deeply indebted to the literary tradition of the Oriental Tale (on the nature and popularity of the genre in eighteenth-century England, see Conant). As Wiener has shown, Byron drew heavily upon William Beckford's *Vathek*. Yet by setting his tale in Greece in the 1770s, Byron politicized many of his borrowings from Beckford and others in a strikingly new way. To give one example, Byron took the phrase "accursed giaour" directly from Beckford (see Wiener 95–103). But in Beckford's work, the caliph Vathek uses it to refer to a pesky Hindu magician with a dark skin. The phrase added an authentic touch to Beckford's novel, and the confrontation between the caliph and the magician certainly contains an important racial dimension, but it carries no overt historical or religious significance in the cultural confrontation between East and West. In *The Giaour*, however, when Hassan says: "'Tis he, well met in any hour / Lost Leila's love—Accursed Giaour!" (618–19), the location of Byron's tale in what was for a

Western audience a recognizable classical past and recognizable recent politics charges the words with all of the ideological baggage of the hope of the revival of Greece and liberty as well as the Crusades. Byron and, to a degree, Owenson, were, as far as I am aware, the first English writers to fuse the genre of the Oriental Tale with the desire to reclaim ancient Greece. This makes his work different in character from other English Oriental Tales, like Southey's *Thalaba*, Landor's *Gebir*, Moore's *Lalla Rookh*, or Beckford's *Vathek*. Byron's construction of the Oriental Tale was a model for others, notably Thomas Hope in *Anastasius*. Marilyn Butler pointed out that Greece was a more suitable political setting for Byron, since the Spanish resistance to the French was "rightist, Catholic, and ideologically uncongenial" ("Orientalism of Byron's *Giaour*" 79). The Greek Revolution was, to a large degree, ideologically uncongenial as well, but because it was situated on the borders of Europe and was seen through classical lenses, the discrepancies between the Greeks and Western liberalism were overlooked.

15. On the fad of Greek dress in France in the 1820s, see Athanassoglou-Kalmyer 11. For England, with a focus on Trelawny, see the article by Collcutt.

16. See St. Clair, *That Greece Might Still Be Free* 171, 239–40.

17. Marilyn Butler reiterated Byron's role in creating the image of the klephts in the West when she said of Byron's Eastern Tales, "Their political contribution was to familiarize a British (and, rapidly, a European) readership with the idea that the fight within Greece would not be led by 'respectable leaders' . . . but by the bandits" ("Orientalism of Byron's *Giaour*" 91).

18. In a letter to Hobhouse about the incident, Byron said that the pirates asked their prisoners about the foreigners at Colonna, and "one of the Greeks knew *me*, and they were preparing to attack us, when seeing my Albanians and conjecturing there were others in the vicinity, they were seized with a panic and marched off" (*BLJ* 2.31).

19. Levinson, drawing upon the accounts of Themistocles in Herodotus and Plutarch, called him "a famously ambiguous hero" and suggested that the ancient Athenian represents both "the epitome of Greece's greatness and perhaps an expression of her fatal weakness" (120). The historical "facts of Themistocles's career are double-edged," but I cannot agree with Levinson that early nineteenth-century liberals concerned themselves with such historical accuracy. The evidence suggests that Themistocles was perceived as a hero of liberty and was used in the opening of *The Giaour* and elsewhere as a signal of the gap between past and present rather than to deconstruct admired antiquity. The suggestion that Themistocles might not be considered one of the "unforgotten brave" seems doubtful in the context of the time when the poem was written. In Choiseul-Gouffier's famous frontispiece (see chap. 3), a chained Greece is "surrounded by the sepulchral monuments in honour of the great men who had *championed her liberty*" (my italics), and the second name on the list is Themistocles. Further, Chateaubriand ended his account of a visit to the site of the battle of Salamis: "The waves, raised by the evening breeze, broke against the beach and expired at my feet; I walked for some time along the shore of that sea which bathed the tomb of Themistocles: and in all probability I was at this moment the only person in

Greece that called to mind this great man" (*Travels in Greece* 129). In his discussion of the battle of Salamis and the supposed discovery of Themistocles' tomb at Munychia by the French consul Fauvel (who was also undoubtedly Byron's source about Themistocles' resting place), Chateaubriand never alluded to the Athenian politician's checkered career after the Persian Wars (129, 155–56). Nor could Themistocles in these passages stand as an example for the rise and fall of Napoleon, since Chateaubriand wrote in 1806. After the demise of Napoleon, the Greek hero of Charles MacFarlane's novel *The Armenians: A Tale of Constantinople* (1830) still unambiguously invokes Themistocles and Leonidas in the following passage: "May Hellas again be free—may the arms of a Themistocles or a Leonidas again prepare the way for the arts and the dynamism of a Pericles" (I.29). Further, one must keep in mind that Themistocles was a partisan figure in the debate about Athenian liberty in the early nineteenth century, and criticism of him would place a writer on the conservative side of that debate, where Byron would probably not situate himself.

20. McGann suggested just such a critical reading in *The Beauty of Inflections*, when he said that the radical split in the poem's two viewpoints "reflects, and interprets, the European understanding of the Levant between 1770–1813. The interpretation which Byron produces is a critical one. The European understanding is self-deluded and helpless, and Byron's own exposure to this failed understanding is represented as the vision of a one-eyed man in the kingdom of the blind" (263). However attractive this may be for understanding Byron's real intent, it does not accurately represent how philhellenic readers responded to *The Giaour*.

21. McGann said that "at the level of political allegory," Leila represents the land over which the Turks and Venetians have been fighting for centuries and to which neither can have any complete claim" (*Fiery Dust* 156; see also Sharuffin 254–63). Byron was certainly skeptical of the West's interest in Greek freedom and perhaps also of the Giaour's interest in Leila. But to suggest that in the early nineteenth century the West's interest in Greece, as symbolized by the Venetians, could be equated with Hassan and Turkish tyranny, a familiar theme at the time, cuts, I think, too much against the historical context in which Byron wrote. While neither the Turks nor the Venetians might have a "complete" claim to Greece, a major point of philhellenic literature was that the Greeks themselves had a claim on the West. They were not viewed as having a similar claim upon the Turks.

22. See Norman Daniel 11. The point is made quite clearly in *The Corsair* by Zuleika, another female slave in a harem, when she says, "I felt—I feel—love dwells with—the free" (II.502). The idea is important for all of Byron's Oriental Tales.

23. On the parallels between love and politics in the poem, see Gleckner 105–6. I do not agree with Leask's argument that "Leila, as the symbolic embodiment of the Hellenic values underlying European civilization, can find representational space only as a beautiful corpse or as a phantom which returns near the end of the poem to exacerbate the Giaour's remorse" (33). "The symbolic embodiment of Hellenic values" could, and often was, portrayed as a living being in Byron's day, as in *Woman; or, Ida of Athens*, a book the poet had read. Byron's portrayal of Greece as a female corpse might have been designed to generate interest

in and action on behalf of a Greek revival rather than simply to suggest the impossibility of regeneration.

24. Andrew Rutherford, among others, has argued that the poem celebrates "the outlaw, the rebel, the renegade, the Ishmaelite, the bold bad man" (43). But this necessitates placing the hero outside of the historic and geographic context of the tale, as outlaws in general and not the Greek bands that Byron's former follower, Dervish, joined. The Giaour of the poem occupies an anomalous region of Greece and, by extension, an anomalous position in Western thinking about Greece. Further, the fact that Byron's Tales, particularly *The Corsair*, were admired by those engaged in the struggle for the collective rights of workers in nineteenth-century England indicates that they were not read as encomia of "bold bad men" but as stories of people concerned about liberty and social justice. See Manning 206–7 and David Erdman's "Byron and Revolt in England" and "Byron and the Genteel Reformers."

25. Sheridan's volume was a translation of a collection of texts first published by M. C. Fauriel in *Chantes Populaires de la Grèce Moderne* (on this book, see Canat, *L'Hellénisme des Romantiques* I.238–45).

26. See for example the characterization of Odysseus in Mrs. Vaughan's drama *The Grecians* (1824) and the conversation among Odysseus, Tersitza, Akrive, and Trelawny in Landor's *Imaginary Conversations* (1829).

27. A similar illustration, perhaps influenced by the one in Choiseul-Gouffier's book, appeared as the frontispiece to A. Corai [Korais]'s *Appel aux Grecs*, first published in Greek in 1801 and reprinted in French in 1821. See Athanassoglou-Kalmyer 92.

28. *Theopha; or, Memoirs of a Greek Slave as Related by Her Lover, Envoy from the Court of France to the Sublime Porte*, a book printed in London in 1798, reads much like a retelling of Prévost's story.

29. On the sexual triangle of a white man saving a brown woman from a brown man as a paradigm for the European view of colonization, see Spivak 297. For another use of this model with regard to Byron's *Giaour*, see Meyer 670–77. Meyer reads *The Giaour* as a colonial enterprise and makes consistent analogies between Egypt and Greece, which, in my view, do not hold up well. The inhabitants of Egypt never looked to France for succor, and the French invasion was clearly a colonial aggression. The Greeks did in fact want to be rescued from the Turks and some made it known that they would rather be subjects of the czar than of the sultan. Meyer overlooked Greek desires, which caused both the revolt of 1770 and the Greek War of Independence in 1821, desires that provide a historical context for the poem, to preserve his reading of the work. Leask approached the same error when he said, "The world of *The Giaour* is a world suppressed under the (modern) sign of imperialism" (30). Byron, who translated Rhigas's famous song, knew very well who was suppressing whom in the Greece of 1809–1811, and it was not the modern sign of imperialism, unless Leask meant by that the Ottomans. I prefer Marilyn Butler's formulation that "the story of the *Giaour* 'proves' Turkish rule ethically unacceptable to civilized westerners, without showing the Christian character in a more favorable light" ("Orientalism of Byron's *Giaour*" 91).

30. On the ambiguity of the sexual politics of the Tales, see Leask 25–33, 38–54 and the article of Christensen. Like Leask (15), I find Daniel Watkins's reading of the Tales as critiques of English social structure too far removed from the actual Eastern settings of the poems to be convincing. Byron himself offered another variant of the romance in *Sardanapalus*, in which the patriotic Greek slave girl Myrrha is devoted to her royal master. The drama, however, is set in the ancient past, and neither Byron nor any other author offers a similar scenario involving a modern Greek girl who is devoted to her Turkish lord. The title of Madame D——'s novel, *Les Amours d'un Turc et d'une Grecque: Épisode de la Guerre de 1821*, is more sensational than accurate, since the "Turk" turns out to be a young man of *Greek* birth who, through his love for the heroine, returns to his true heritage.

31. On Shelley's use of Byron's Tales, particularly *The Corsair*, in *The Revolt of Islam*, see Robinson 65–68. On the differences between the Greeces of Byron and Shelley, see Wallace 4–5.

32. Like Owenson's Ida, the heroine in Mary Shelley's story "Euphrasia" is a "scholar" who "improvised patriotic songs" (*Collected Tales and Stories* 302). In *Amygdala: A Tale of the Greek Revolution* (1894) by Elizabeth Edmonds, a young English philhellene on a reconnaissance mission in Attica meets two sisters, Irene and Neroula, who represent the Greek and the Eastern female. Irene, a fair blonde, is devoted to the Greek cause and strikes the young man as a model for "'Athena sad'—grieving over the ruin and misery of her beloved city" (65). Neroula, with dark hair and a dark complexion, possesses a sensual nature and has more in common with the Oriental female. After Irene's death in the Greek War of Independence, Gerard keeps his promise to marry Neroula, but he continues to paint portraits of Athena with the face of Irene. Briseis, the Greek heroine in William Black's novel of that name, is called "too august somehow, too serene and remote" (27) as if she embodies the ideal of a classical statue.

It is worth noting that, at the end of *The Lustful Turk*, an anonymous 1828 pornographic novel set in Algeria in which two Englishwomen become enamored with the sensuality of their Oriental captor, it is a Grecian girl who castrates the novel's Algerian hero and then kills herself (140). This is in keeping with the prevalent thinking about Greek women at the time of the war of independence. Against my interpretation, Wallace said, "Greece and the east were associated with uninhibited erotic beauty" (126). It is true, as she said, that Byron's Tales depict a "world of primitive values of love, violence and revenge, a world in which eastern passion is more important than western decorum" (126). But, with the exception of the Turkish Gulnare in *The Corsair*, it is men who represent those Eastern passions, and certainly not Greek women.

33. In the preface to his novel *Hypatia*, Charles Kingsley provided a racial theory for the effeminacy of the Christians in the Levant: Western Christianity had "some infusion of healthier blood into a world drained and tainted by Rome" (xii). The Christians of Egypt and Syria, on the other hand, were "effeminate, over civilized, exhausted by centuries during which no fresh blood came to renew the stock" (xv). Kingsley did not include the Greeks in his indictment (in his view they had received an "infusion" from the Goths in late antiquity), but he certainly

presented a negative picture of Orthodoxy and its monks, one that could easily be extended to the Greeks.

34. The most notable exception is John Baldwin Buckstone's *Maid of Athens* (1824), in which the Greek Demetrius and the English Madeline, with the help of philhellenic Lord Byron, are able to marry against the wishes of her father, who prefers a Swede. Although a Greek does end up marrying an Englishwoman in this play, he does so only through the good offices of Byron, who stands as a champion of freedom of choice in both politics and love.

35. This refers not only to fictional Greek women; see Celine Donald's *Adventures of a Greek Lady, the Adopted Daughter of the Late Queen Caroline, Written by Herself* (1849). In the novels of Black, Collins, and Jewsbury, the Greek descent of the heroines is one of the factors employed to signal their difference from their English neighbors. The motif also appears in Mayo's *Daughter of the Klephts*, in which the heroine, taken to England and orphaned as a child, functions perfectly well in her new environment but remains slightly different from her peers. There, however, is no such discussion about the place of Greek men in England. They simply do not belong.

36. See also Pashley, who says that when Cretans took up arms, they "shrunk from the caresses of their wives, as from a pollution, which would most probably be punished by their falling in the next engagement" (II.175, n. 32). And in the anonymous narrative poem *Parga* (1819), the father of the heroine, Haidee, forbids her to marry the hero, Marcarius, until Parga is liberated from the Turks. The pair of lovers are able to marry after the father's death.

37. One of Landor's *Imaginary Conversations* opens with Tersitza asking her brother, "What have I done that the stranger [Trelawny] should liken me to the idols of antiquity?" (*Complete Works* VIII.204); she adds later that she "is desirous not to be thought an idol" (*Complete Works* VIII.206).

Chapter 3

1. See St. Clair, *That Greece Might Still Be Free* 169.

2. On this, see Marchand III.1204–6.

3. On Stanhope and his activities in Greece, see St. Clair, *That Greece Might Still Be Free* 186–94; Koumarianou 115–22; and, more favorably, Rosen 144–63.

4. Millingen became a target for philhellenes when, after he was captured by the Turks, he agreed to serve as a physician for them (see St. Clair, *That Greece Might Still Be Free* 236–37 and Woodhouse, *Philhellenes* 149). He went on to become a devoted Turkophile; he lived for many years in Constantinople and repudiated both his own and Byron's philhellenism. In 1918, Lord Eversley, in "Some Reminiscences: Lord Byron and Dr. Millingen," still argued that Millingen was an outright liar.

5. See St. Clair, *That Greece Might Still Be Free* 126–28.

6. On the iconography of Delacroix's painting, see Athanassoglou-Kalmyer 87–100.

7. On the life of Teresa Macri, see the two articles by C. G. Brouzas. The mentions of Mrs. Black in travel narratives are too numerous to be listed here, but see Willis 240–42, Stephens 56, Prime 217, Baird 369–70, Eames 139, and even the posthumous mention by Joseph Moore 248.

8. On the second of the two plays, see Droulia 220.

9. See also William Black's *Briseis* (1896), in which the heroine says that she had "also been a maid of Athens" (2) and translates the phrase *zoe mou, sas agapo* (73). Near the end of the book, she returns to Athens, where the hero comes in search of her. In the final paragraph, Athens has arrayed herself "in her bridal robes of silver and white," but Briseis will also leave Greece for England after her nuptials (317). John Colquhar's *Zoe: An Athenian Tale* (1824), a romance set in antiquity, appears to be an attempt to translate Byron's Romantic-era Maid of Athens into the past. The heroine, brought up in a small village, wins the noble Alcibiades by her beauty and "her artlessness, her pure feelings, her taste so unlike her situation. . . . She possessed a simple naivete" (33).

10. Trelawny's account of Byron in Greece in *Recollections of the Last Days of Byron and Shelley*, which was less flattering, did not appear until 1858. Yet Trelawny's criticism of Byron did not extend to the cause of the Greeks. Rather, he tried to represent that he was the real hero of the philhellenes. The fact that these early eyewitness accounts lauded Byron did not mean that the authors were equally complimentary of one another. See especially Rosen's analysis of how Parry used Byron to attack Stanhope (185–218).

11. St. Clair suggested that Edward Blacquiere cajoled and conned Byron into going to Greece, and "the London Greek Committee were not really interested in him [Byron] at all but only in the publicity value of his name" (*That Greece Might Still Be Free* 167).

12. Philhellenism did not have a major impact in France until 1825, and "much of the stimulus for the upsurge . . . can be attributed to the story of Lord Byron's pilgrimage and his death at Missalonghi" (St. Clair, *That Greece Might Still Be Free* 267). Byron's involvement in the Greek struggle had the same effect in America and England.

13. Nineteenth-century English philhellenes faced a peculiar dilemma during the Crimean War, during which the Greeks sympathized with the Russians. This caused the British and French to send troops into Athens to keep the country out of the conflict. For most British, however, the Crimean War was not seen through the lenses of the Greek War of Independence. Rather, as Palmerston told Lord Clarendon, the goal was "not so much to keep the Sultan and Musulmans in Turkey as to keep the Russians out of Turkey (quoted in Palmer, *Banner of Battle* 237). John Bright, in a letter of 1854 opposing the war, said that England was "not only at war with Russia, but with all the Christian population of the Turkish empire," and he questioned a policy founded on the "perpetual maintenance of the most immoral and filthy of all despotism over one of the fairest portions of the earth." He added: "Our love for civilization, when we subject Greeks and Christians to the Turks, is a sham" (15; see also Gladstone's pseudonymous 1956 article, "War and Peace"). For his sentiments, Bright lost his parliamentary seat in

the election of 1857 and was burned in effigy. On Byronism in America, see Leonard, esp. p. 2.

14. See, for example, Robert Harding Lawrence's *Graecia Nova! A Plea for Sympathy with Modern Greece* (1875), which concludes with the poem "Missalonghi! (The Death of Lord Byron)" (he also includes a Shelleyan effort entitled, not surprisingly, "Ode to Liberty"); the anonymous "Byron in Greece" in the *Temple Bar* during the border crisis in 1881; "Lord Byron in the Greek Revolution" by Frank Sanborn in *Scribner's Magazine* in September 1897; "Lord Byron in the Greek Revolution" in *Chamber's Journal* by George Pignatorre in 1913; and the pamphlet *Some English Philhellenes: Lord Byron* by Z. D. Ferriman, which was published in 1920 by the philhellenic Anglo-Hellenic League.

15. On Byron's reputation among reformers in England, see the articles by Erdman and the book by Philip Collins.

16. One could even desire to be the Byron of the Arabs. Wilfred Scaven Blunt wrote in *The Secret History of the English Occupation of Egypt* (1895): "My wife, Lady Anne Blunt, who accompanied me on all these [Oriental] travels, was the granddaughter of our great national poet, Lord Byron, and so was the inheritor, in some sort, of sympathy in the cause of freedom in the East. . . . it seemed to us, in the presence of the events of 1881–82 that to champion the cause of Arabian liberty could be as worthy an endeavor as had been that for which Byron had died" (2). This stretched somewhat the Europe-versus-Asia rhetoric found in Byron's own work. On Blunt's "Byron complex" see Tetrault, "Heirs to Virtue: Byron, Gobineau, Blunt."

17. For example, in *Rambles and Studies in Greece*, J. P. Mahaffy lamented the neglect of Byron, saying that it was "a bad sign" about contemporary European culture that "the love of modern poets has weaned them [readers] from the study of one not less great in most respects, but far greater in one at least . . . in that burning enthusiasm for a national cause, in that red hot passion for liberty which, even when misapplied, or wasted upon unworthy objects, is ever of the noblest and most stirring instinct of man" (190–91).

18. In *Byronism and the Victorians*, Elfenbein noted that the influence of Byron's work and life went beyond literature and politics to "fashion, social manners, erotic experience, and gender roles" (8). One of the merits of Elfenbein's study is that it shows how much of a draw Byronism still was in Victorian times and how British upper- and middle-class readers devised a Byron very different from that of radicals like Mazzini—a point demonstrated by the infrequent mention of Greece in the work.

19. St. Clair said to Leicester Stanhope "perhaps belongs the doubtful credit of being the only man who went to Greece during the war whose political ideas were not modified by the experience" (*That Greece Might Still Be Free* 185).

20. Raizis, who did important work on American philhellenic writing during the 1820s and 1830s as coeditor of *The Greek Revolution and the American Muse* and in his study, with Alexander Papas, *American Poets and the Greek Revolution*, used the term *Byronic philhellenism* to characterize the period ("Aspects of Literary Philhellenism" 130). He added: "The literary expression of that [philhellenic]

sentiment owes much more to cultural, and especially Byronic philhellenism, than what has hitherto been acknowledged by scholars." See also Raizis and Papas, *American Poets* 12–17, on the immense impact of Byron on American philhellenic writing of the 1820s.

21. Landor's philhellenism has never received the attention it deserves nor has the relationship of the philhellenic poems "Regeneration" and "To Corinth" with the more famous *Hellenics* been explored.

22. I lay upon the solemn plain
    And by the funeral mound,
Where those who died not there in vain,
    Their place of sleep had found.
Twas silent where the free blood gushed,
    When Persia came arrayed—
So many a voice had there been hushed,
    So many a footstep stayed.

I slumbered on the lonely spot,
    So sanctified by Death—
I slumbered—but my rest was not
    As theirs who lay beneath.
For on my dreams, that shadowy hour,
    they rose—the chainless dead—
All armed they spring, in joy, in power
    Up from their grassy bed.

                    (*Poetical Works* 274)

23. See the comments of Raizis and Papas on classical sentimentalism in American philhellenic poetry (*American Poets*, esp. 45, but also 37–51 generally).

24. On Krazeisen's painting, see Tsigakou 52–53. Garber (91–101) discusses the Orientalism of Delacroix's *Combat du giaour et du pacha* without mentioning that the picture was painted during the War of Independence and was first shown with *La Gréce sur les ruines de Missolonghi* during an exhibition to raise money for the Greeks in July 1826; see Athanassoglou-Kalmyer (91).

25. Shelley's "The Evil Eye," a story of Epirot klephts and Maniote corsairs, is set in Greece before the War of Independence but includes a pirate raid on Scio (Chios), which evokes the great tragedy of the revolution.

26. For example, in Landor's dialogue between Maurocordato and Colocotroni, a discussion is held as to whether the Greek troops should be equipped with bows and arrows in order to ensure a renewable supply of ammunition, a suggestion first made, according to Landor, by Benjamin Franklin to the American revolutionary army (*Complete Works* VIII.189–92).

27. See St. Clair, *That Greece Might Still Be Free* 80–81.

28. See also L. E. L.'s [Letitia Elizabeth Landon] "The Ionian Captive," Lydia Huntley Sigourney's "The Martyr of Scio," William Cullen Bryant's "The Massacre at Scio," Bradfield's "The Maid of Scio," Snowden's *The Maid of Scio: A Tale of Modern Greece*, and Strickland's *Demetrius*.

29. Mordecai Noah explained his use of Ali in a play about the Greek War of Independence in the preface as follows: "I have taken the liberty of transferring Ali Pacha from Joannina to Athens being a more extended field of operation and quite convenient, and have also made him an enemy of the Greeks, which he truly was, as his rebellion and hostility to the Sublime Porte were the only motives which induced him to favor the Greek cause" (iii).

30. The American playwright John Howard Payne wrote two dramas concerned with the Greek struggle for freedom, *Ali Pacha; or, The Signet Ring* (1825) and *Oswaldi of Athens* (1831), both of which feature Ali as "the terrible Turk," who lusts after a Greek captive. Ali Pasha also appears as the villain in Henry Galley Knight's narrative poem "Phrosyne" in *Eastern Sketches in Verse* (1830). In France, Ali was the villain in the dramas *Les Martyrs de Souli* by Nepomucene Louis Lamercier (1825) and *Youli; ou, Les Suliotes* by Franconi and Henri (1830) and the narrative poem *Ali Pacha et Vasiliki* by Prosper Poitevin (1835).

31. Garnett's *Reine Canziani* is the only novel about the Greek War of Independence written in the 1820s of which I am aware. The great majority of prose written in English offered itself as nonfiction, even if, as with the anonymous *Scenes in the Morea; or, A Sketch of the Life of Demetrius Argyri*, it may well have been fiction. One slight short story was written on the same theme as *The Giaour*, "An Athenian Adventure" in *The Stanley Tales* by Ambrose Marten. Marten, like Charles MacFarlane in *The Armenians: A Tale of Constantinople* (1830) places philhellenic sentiment in the mouths of some characters but sets the story before the beginning of the revolution.

Cedric Hentschel has said that in *Vier Erzählungen der Geschichte des jetzigne Griechenlands* (1826), the German poet Friedrich Wilhelm Waiblinger "blended the traditions of Byron and Hölderlin" ("Byron and Germany" 66). One reason that French and German writers may have felt Byron's shadow a bit less than writers in English is that they also had other significant influences in their own languages, like Hölderlin, Chateaubriand, and later Hugo. The only work in English about modern Greece other than Byron that had significant impact in the 1820s was Hope's *Anastasius*, and R. R. Madden wrote a three-volume novel called *The Mussulman* (1830), which blends Byron and Hope. But *The Mussulman* takes place outside of Greece and the War of Independence.

32. Southey was a liberal in the 1790s but became progressively more conservative in the nineteenth century, like Coleridge and Wordsworth: see Woodring 67–69; Marilyn Butler, *Romantics, Rebels and Reactionaries* 144–45; and, at greater length, Curry's biography of Southey 11–42. Curry discusses the disagreements between Southey and Byron on 68–70.

33. In France, according to Malakis, during the early years of the Greek Revolution, "the salons were divided into two camps; the question of the day was 'êtes vous Grecs, êtes vous Turcs?'" (12). But by 1824, "everyone was 'Greek,' and the 'Turks,' if there were any, were forced to be silent" (13). This should not be taken as a sign that in France philhellenism had transcended party politics, for, as Athanassoglou-Kalmyer said, by 1825, "The Greek cause had become almost entirely an appanage of the liberal opposition" (10–11). The "Turks" were keeping silent.

34. See Penn 363–71 and Rosen, who noted that the success of the appeal of the London Greek Committee was to a degree determined "by a division in society that can only be described as ideological in character" (243). On the British attitude toward Russia for most of the nineteenth century, see Gleason.

35. There were serious disagreements among the philhellenes on the nature of a projected government for Greece, which were often lost within the larger ideological division of Tories/conservatives and liberals/radicals. On the different conceptions of the Greek government offered by Blacquiere and Stanhope, see Rosen 125–84.

36. On the failure of the loan and its contribution to the decline of the philhellenic spirit in England, see Penn 654–57 and Rosen 265–88. It was in the context of a discussion of this loan and the material that it should have purchased that Finlay remarked: "It was by those who called themselves Philhellenes in England and America that Greece was most injured" (6:433; see also 434–35). The money raised and sent to Greece was also misused. Henry Bulwer, sent to Greece as one of the commissioners of the second installment of the loan, told his readers what the great sum had accomplished: "Nothing!—except support of a faction, which has lavished the public treasure in procuring itself partisans, and in converting an enthusiastic peasantry into mercenary soldiers" (12–13).

37. Henry Bradfield's *The Atheniad*, a long poem on the failed campaign to attack Athens in 1827, came closest to satirizing the efforts of the Greeks in the war. In a second philhellenic book published later in the same year, Bradfield explained that "In the Atheniad, it was my object to describe the existing errors of the Greeks, more in the indulgence of playful humor than in anger; . . . the incidents related in the present volume will tend to remove an impression which seems to have been excited by my former poem. I am too much devoted to the interests of Greece to originate this supposition, save in those who are strangers to me, and should be sorry if I were, directly or indirectly, the means of adding to the misfortunes of an oppressed people." (*Tales of the Cyclades* iii–iv). So much for a declaration of artistic freedom.

38. See also Raizis and Papas, *American Poets* 21–23.

39. Congress backed away from recognizing the Greek government and sending official representatives to Greece because such intervention would have jeopardized the recently announced Monroe Doctrine about European interference in the Americas (see Larrabee 69–72). America did, however, produce the philhellenic movement's greatest success. The American relief efforts of 1827 and 1828, in which food and clothing were sent to noncombatants, were according to St. Clair, "the first and last time the vast reserves of enthusiasm, sacrifice, and good will which the name of Greece aroused throughout Western Christendom were mobilized in a manner which was wholly and intrinsically good, and the measures carried through with intelligence and efficiency. At last the slogans of philhellenism were put into practice and it was found that the slogans were not needed" (*That Greece Might Still Be Free* 335–36). The slogans may not have been needed, but as the anthology of American verse about the Greek War of Independence by Raizis and Papas reveals on every page, the poets continued to use them with frequency.

40. Willis went on to say, "The convulsions of Europe may soon leave her to herself; and the slipper of the Turk and the hand of the Christian, once lifted from her neck, she will rise, and stand there among the imperishable temples, once more *free!*" (II.20).

41. Richard Monckton Milnes wrote a poem for "young Mavromikali," one of the assassins of the first president of Greece, Capodistrias, in 1829, in which Milnes calls the young murderer "the new Harmodius" (158; the poem appears on 159–60); Alexander Cochrane lauded the same event in his narrative poem *The Morea* (126–37); and Edward Masson translated Alexander Suzzo's [Soutsos] "Soliloquy of George Mavromichali" and "Capodistris" in *Philhellenika*. But these are rather rare examples of interest in Greek domestic politics. And Masson, Suzzo's translator, repudiated the poet's negative view of Capodistrias in his introduction (16–18).

42. See the comments of Monckton Milnes 151–54. Lewis Sergeant wrote, "The true character of Hellenism reveals itself wherever Greeks have enjoyed a few generations of free social life" (*New Greece* 59). He based his remark on the observation of Greeks in London, Paris, and other Western cities, since, in his view, the Greeks in Greece had still not been blessed with a few generations of free social life.

43. In the introduction to the 1994 edition of *The Last Man*, Paley said that one of the novel's main themes is the "failure of the imagination" (xi).

Chapter 4

1. For antiquity see Richard Jenkyns and Vickery; on Schliemann's excavations, see Kenner 42–44. For Italy, see Pemble, Kenneth Churchill, Van Wyck Brooks, *Dream of Arcadia*, and Nathalia Wright.

2. George Gissing's novella *Sleeping Fires* (1895) opens in Athens, where the hero has just spent the winter. But at the end he calls Greece a "mere fairy land; to us of the north an escape for rest amid scenes we hardly believe real. . . . Who cares to know the modern names of the mountains? Who thinks of the people who dwell among them? . . . I, whose life is now to begin, must shake off this sorcery of Athens, and remember it only as a delightful dream" (210).

3. The same is true of the following books, or sections of books, of poems about travel to Greece in the later nineteenth century: George Savage-Armstrong's *Garland from Greece*, Elizabeth Edmonds's *Hesperas*, and Lloyd Mifflin's *Castalian Days*.

4. When Nathaniel Parker Willis first approached Greece by ship, *Childe Harold's Pilgrimage* laid "open on my knee at the Second Canto, describing our position, even to the hour" (245). On a visit to Marathon, Jane Eames was all but overcome with emotion: "How many times I ejaculated, 'Oh, the glorious land of Greece!' And even while I ate my lunch, I broke out a dozen times with: 'The mountains look on Marathon / And Marathon looks on the sea'" (125). Travelers who might not be aware of the appropriate Byronic quotation were assisted by

guidebooks like Murray's *Handbook for Travellers in Greece*, which told the visitor to Acrocorinth, "On this spot the traveler will recall Byron's 'Siege of Corinth' with renewed interest" and provided a lengthy excerpt (162). Fitz-Greene Halleck's poem "Marco Bozzaris" was often quoted by American travelers (e.g., Eames 142 and Ward 262–71). But since Halleck's verses were themselves an example of Romantic Byronism, they served to increase rather than decrease the hold of the Grèce de Byron on the American mind.

5. Tsigakou said that "the main attraction of the plates of Edward Lear's *Journal of a Landscape Painter in Albania and Illyria*, published in 1851, is the artist's genuine sensitivity in conveying the historical association of each particular site connected with the recent events in Greece," a comment that could be extended to some of Lear's paintings of classical sites (70). Tsigakou also noted that much of Lear's work was tinged with the Romantic philhellenism of earlier decades.

6. Two major American poets traveled to Greece. William Cullen Bryant, the author of about a half dozen philhellenic poems during the War of Independence (e.g., "The Greek Partizan," "The Greek Amazon," "The Massacre at Scio," and "The Greek Boy"), went to the Levant as a correspondent for the New York *Evening Post* in 1852–1853. Greece was described in one brief chapter of the book based upon these columns, *Letters from the East* (1869), in which Bryant observed, "The remains of ancient art, which are to be seen in Athens, have the character of the surrounding scenery—repose and harmony" (218; see also Larrabee 266–67). In short, the poet found those very qualities of Romantic Hellenism that had made him so interested in the Greek Revolution decades earlier. Herman Melville journeyed through the East in 1856 and 1857 (Larrabee 273–82), and his "The Attic Landscape," "The Parthenon," and "The Archipelago" show the influence of the Romantic Hellenism of Winckelmann, while his poem "Syra" describes the Greek islanders as free from the ills of American materialism. The last work is slightly at odds with the following passage from his journal: "Contrast between the Greek isles & those of the Polynesian archipelago. The former have lost their virginity. The latter are fresh as their first creation. The former look worn, and are meagre, like life after enthusiasm is gone" (*Journals* 72). One might say that this is more a comment on the young Melville, who traveled in the Pacific, and the older, disillusioned Melville, who came to the Levant. Still, if Melville had developed this contrast in published poetry or prose, it might have provided a new perspective for viewing Greece in English writing, one that was more readily available on the European Continent. For example, Gautier in *Constantinople* suggested that modern Greece is "wasted by its production of masterpieces and genius and heroism" (33), and Gérard de Nerval approached Greece as "un fils d'un siècle douteur" (II.255).

7. In contrast, see the depth, development, and debate in nineteenth-century literature about Renaissance Italy in Bullen and in Fraser.

8. See Chew 255–72. In the second half of the nineteenth century, Byron's verse was unfavorably compared to Wordsworth and the emerging reputations of Shelley and Keats. In 1896, the critic George Saintsbury said, "Counter-jumpers like Thackeray's own Pogson worshipped the 'noble poet' [Byron]; beings of a no-

bler stripe like Tennyson thought they worshipped him, but if they were going to become men of affairs forgot all about him; if they were to be poets they took to Shelley and Keats as models, not to him" (Grierson 30). Americans were more admiring of Byron; see Leonard, esp. the first chapter.

9. Even Walter Savage Landor's "A Modern Greek Idyll" (1854), a poem about the domestic relations of a Greek mother and her three sons, was rooted in the period of the Greek War of Independence. In a note, Landor said he found the story in M. C. Fauriel's *Chantes Populaires de la Grèce*, a two-volume work published in 1824–1825 to show the preservation of Hellenic culture among the modern Greeks. In 1854, the novelist Elizabeth Gaskell also called attention to Fauriel's book in an article for the magazine *Household Words*. Writers continued to focus on the period between 1770 and 1830 in the decades after 1870; see, for example, Gilbert Murray's *Mesolonghi Capta* (1877) and Elizabeth Edmonds's poem "Rhigas" (*Hesperas*, 1889).

10. The exception is Collins's *The Albanian*, which recounts how an Italian philhellene joined the cause, fell in love with his "Helen," and died in the siege of Missolonghi.

11. Requier also made the obligatory connection between a ruined temple and a captive female. When his heroine finds herself a captive in the Turkish leader's tent, it happens to be situated on the ruins of a temple to Diana. She gets possession of a knife and threatens to commit suicide on the altar:

> Upon this altar I rear my form—
> This fragmentary relic of a grace,
> Which as a deity my sires adored.
> A voluntary victim, here I stand.
> (183)

12. Edward Lear's most recent biographer, Peter Levi, says of *Journal of a Landscape Painter in Albania and Illyria*: "There was nothing Greek about it except for the idea, the name, the excitement of modern Greece, which was still an image of revolutionary liberty and pure mountains" (117).

13. At one point, Lear thought of a "huge work (if I can *do* all Greece—) of the Morea and all together" (quoted in Levi 113). But he could not do it, and all that appeared were *Journal of a Landscape Painter in Albania and Illyria*, *Views of the Seven Ionian Islands*, and *The Cretan Journal* (published posthumously in 1984, but which Lear had begun to revise for publication before his death; see Rowena Fowler in the introduction to *The Cretan Journal* 15–17). These books give the impression of Lear circling around the land of "grace and detail" without ever attempting a book on Attica and the Peloponnesus.

14. See Raizis, "Aspects of Byronic Philhellenism" (138–39), who observed that in the decades after the Greek Revolution the "combined and collective circulation" of the verse of the 1820s "was enormous." In 1852, for example, Edward Masson reprinted his poem of 1824, "The Rising of Hellas," without any changes

to indicate the success of the revolution (e.g., "Each fair Muse, by Freedom led, / Resumes her haunts of yore, nor glow to see, / Through ages still reborn, thy glories yet to be," *Philhellenika* 53).

15. See Dakin, *Unification of Greece* 111–12.

16. See Howe's *Appeal* and *Cretan Refugees*. Julia Ward Howe provided an account of Howe's visit to Athens in *From the Oak to the Olive*. See Juin, *Victor Hugo* II.578–79, for the public response of that famous philhellene of *Les Orientales* to the Cretan revolt.

17. See Marcoglou 93–98. On the American William Stillman in Crete, see Marcoglou 82–92.

18. Frank Lentricchia discussed Stedman's role in the "genteel tradition" of American poetry in *Modernist Quartet* 59–60 and 79–80.

19. On Shelley's importance for Swinburne, see the articles by David Riede and Terry Meyers.

20. Thackeray advised readers who "loved the 'Arabian Nights' in their youth," [to] "book themselves on board one of the Peninsular and Oriental vessels, and try one *dip* into Constantinople or Smyrna" (326–27).

21. Alexander Kinglake also noted "an almost universal and unbroken testimony against the character of the people whose ancestors invented Virtue" (66). He added that many Greeks preferred "groaning under the Turkish yoke" in Smyrna to "the honour of 'being the only true source of legitimate power' in their own land." But, like many of the time, he concluded his criticism by stating: "For myself I love the race: in spite of their vices, and even in spite of their meanesses [*sic*], I remember the blood that is in them, and still love the Greeks" (66).

22. Thomas Wyse, the British minister in Athens in the 1860s, was harsher in his opinion of Otho: "A more honorable, high-minded ruler . . . might have made them [the Greeks] the light and the hope of the East" (15). On the other hand, George Horton, the American ambassador to Greece in the 1890s, presented a positive view of Otho in his novel *Constantine* (172).

23. See also Skene's poem "The Greek Slave" (1843) and the play of the same name by Edward Fitzball (1851). Browning's poem was put to music in 1874 by J. W. Hobbs, as was a poem by Miss Pardoe with the same title by Henry Allen in the 1840s. See also Pardoe's *The Romance of the Harem* (1839), whose heroine is a Greek slave from Chios who escaped the massacre, and the chapter entitled "The Greek Slave" in Frederick Marryat's novel *The Pasha of Many Tales* (1836). The idea of the Greek slave was also kept alive by the appearance of "slave narratives," such as Kelch's *Turkish Barbarity: An Affecting Narrative of the Unparalleled Sufferings of Mrs. Sophia Mazro, a Greek Lady of Missalonghi* (1828), *The Personal Sufferings of J. Stefanini* (1829), and *The Greek Exile: A Narrative of the Captivity and Escape of Christophoros Plato Castanis during the Massacre on Scio by the Turks. Written by Himself* (1845), as well as by such books as Franz Hoffman's, *The Greek Slave* (1870) and Frederick Millingen's *Slavery in Turkey: The Sultan's Harem* (1870).

The feminization of Greece was employed in political pamphlets. A manifesto against British policy during the Crimean War appeared with the title *A Grecian*

Lady's Complaint on the Protection Offered for Turkey (1854) by G. L., and a publication of the London Greek Committee in 1880 was called *Greece Abandoned; or, Three Years of Diplomacy on the Eastern Question.*

24. On Fallmerayer and the reaction to his thesis, see Herzfeld 75–96. MacFarlane's *The Armenians* (1830) spoke against the "political troglodytes" who "ransack their brains for proofs that the Hellenes of the present day are not descendants of the ancients" (I.33). In George Horton's *The Monk's Treasure* (1905), the hero declared, "I am not of those who hold with Professor Fallmerayer that all Greeks are Slavonians" (126) and William Miller said that by 1905 Fallmerayer's theory was "as dead as its author" (*Greek Life in Town and Country* 2). See also the comments of Lewis Sergeant in *New Greece*, where he concluded that Fallmerayer "seems to have been the victim of a reaction against the Philhellenic movement of his time" (225), and C. C. Felton's criticism of Fallmerayer in *Greece, Ancient and Modern* 312–15. On the basically negative view of the modern Greeks in the early nineteenth century, see Angelomatis-Tsougarakis 86–88.

25. This was the view presented by Demetra Vaka Brown in her philhellenic novel *Bribed to be Born*, posthumously published in 1951. A patriotic Greek woman from Constantinople says of Disraeli's power: "Had he used it for the good of the world, even we here might not be living under the Turkish yoke. The Jew, Disraeli, the prime minister. No one will ever know what was behind that masklike face. Even when he laughed, there was in the depths of his dark, burning eyes the reflection of all the suffering of the Jewish race. . . . And I dared say to him: 'If only England had thought of the good of the world after the Crimean War, and not the narrow British viewpoint, Constantinople would not be what it is, and we, the subject races of Turkey, might have some benefit of civilization.' He made no answer, yet his glowing eyes seemed to say: 'You talk of the misery of subject races of the Turk. What of my people, forever persecuted, everywhere in fear of their lives?'" (45).

26. The only English poem of which I am aware that deals with life on the Ionian islands is Skene's lesser effort "Revenge of the Zantiote Maiden." Frances Maclellan's *Sketches of Corfu* (1835) offered a rather bucolic picture of the life and lore of the ordinary people. Letitia Elizabeth Landon visited the area in the 1830s and wrote several short efforts about the landscape, e.g., "Corfu." Two chapters of Bulwer Lytton's novel *Zanoni* are set on one of the Ionian islands, but they contain no authentic local color. See James Tetreault, "This Violent Passion: Gobineau and Greece," for a discussion of the French author's encounter with Greece. In Germany, Hermann von Pückler-Muskau published *Südostlicher Bildersal—Griechischen Leiden* (1840), of which Hentschel said: "In presenting an unvarnished image of contemporary Greece, Puckler-Muskau began to free the German spirit from that 'tyranny of Greece' which had originated with Winckelmann" (70).

27. About's novel appeared in a translation in England in 1862, in a version done by C. F. L. Wraxall, which was reissued in 1881. It was first released in America in 1861 in a translation by Mary Booth, and the preface to that edition states that six different translations of the book had been offered to American

publishers since the announcement of Booth's version. New translations appeared in both England and America in 1897.

28. In the introduction to an English translation of *The King of the Mountains* (1902), Andrew Lang said of Greek brigands and the tragedy at Dilessi: "On the whole subject, Great Britain has very little right to throw the first stone at Hellas," and he argued that conditions in Greece a few decades earlier were no different from those in the Scotland of Rob Roy. "Greece was not abnormal, she was just belated—that was all" (viii-ix). In English, therefore, even the introduction to About's novel takes exception to the book's point of view. Other writers had positive views of Greek brigands. In 1864, C. C. Felton was delighted to be invited to a "klephtic feast" by a man who had been "for eleven years a klepht, or robber, on Mount Olympus" and called the occasion "the most classical and Homeric thing that has come from past ages" (*Greece, Ancient and Modern* II.268). Interest in the klephts in the West is further demonstrated by Dreyfus's 1883 comedy *Le Klephte*, in which a group of French characters discuss whether *klepht* is a pleasing word to the ear. In 1858, Charles Asselineau's *Mon Cousin Don Quixote: Physiognomie d'un philhellène*, did to the philhellenic volunteers what About had done to the klephts.

29. In these poems, as well as in prose writings, the sacred names of Marathon, Salamis, and Thermopylae were often invoked. For example, on March 13, 1897, Gladstone said that Greece was "a Power representing the race that fought the battles of Thermopylae and Salamis and hurled the hordes of Asia back from European shores" (*Eastern Crisis* 12). In his satirical poem "Our Learned Philhellenes," H. D. Traill made fun of the way poets invoked the classical past in support of modern Greece in 1897:

> For if Sparta that resolute nation,
> Stood fast in Thermopylae's gorge,
> What's that but a clear demonstration
> That Crete should belong to King George.
>
> (506)

See also Richard Vasey's *Psiloriti: A Dramatic Poem Illustrative of Life under the Turk in Crete* (1896).

30. One of the French offerings from this time was de Vogüé's *Vangheli: La Vie Orientale* (1901).

31. The number of books and articles about the Greek Revolution published during the war of 1897 is staggering; a sampling includes Mayo's novel and her two articles; Frank Sanborn's "Lord Byron and the Greek Revolution"; Benson's two novels on the theme; and Allison's history of the War of Independence. In his translation of stories by Argyris Eftaliotis, entitled *Tales from the Isles of Greece*, W. H. D. Rouse said that until recently there were still village "Homers" in Greece "only now no Troy is their theme, but the struggle of Greece for freedom against the Turk" (ix). He also said, "One or two of the sketches in the original work have been omitted, and their place has been taken by three others given at the end, dealing with the days of the War of Independence" (v).

32. Bettina Knapp has argued that Crane's *Active Service* was meant to be a parody of Richard Harding Davis-like romances, which partly explains why its tone is so different from Crane's previous works (109–20). But, as Michael Robertson noted, "the claim rings hollow" (1). Robertson's suggestion that the book is a confrontation between the "new" world emerging in the 1890s and an older, more genteel society has some merit but still does not account for the reasons that Crane makes such a bad job of it. D. A. Boxley's article argued for the connection between the "dark," enticing Nora and the East and examines how the Eastern female can be emasculating for a Western male, a common theme also found in, for example, Hichens's *In the Wilderness*. Boxley argued that, in *Active Service*, Crane both replicated and deconstructed the prevalent idea of the Orient, but I do not agree that the text can bear that interpretation. My point is simply that Crane was not alone in somehow losing his skills when writing about Greece.

33. The coverage of the war by writers at home (e.g., Diplomaticus) and reporters in the field (e.g., Steevens) was occasionally critical, if not hostile, to the Greeks. Clive Bigham prefaced his account by saying, "It is, of course, extremely difficult to avoid sympathizing with the troops one accompanies," and most of the reporters who viewed the war from the Turkish side, like Bigham (*With the Turkish Army in Thessaly*), Steevens (*With the Conquering Turk*), and Ellis Ashland Barret (*Battlefields of Thessaly*), were more sympathetic to the Turks than to the Greeks. But the poets, fiction writers, and volunteers who were drawn to the war were, at least initially, overwhelmingly philhellenic in outlook (in addition to Brailsford's novel, see "Experiences and Reminiscences of Jock Herbert"). Even Traill, who satirized English philhellenes, did not take a stand against the Greeks themselves.

Chapter 5

1. See Shannon, *Gladstone and the Bulgarian Agitation* 22.

2. On the Bulgarian agitation in Britain, see Seton-Watson; Harris; Shannon, *Gladstone and the Bulgarian Agitation*; Milman; and Saab. On the same period from the Greek side, see Kofos.

3. See also Gladstone's distinction between slavery in archaic Greece and Ottoman despotism: "The song of Homer witnesses that the mild slavery of the heroic age took away half the manhood of a man. But the slavery (for that is what it really was) imposed by the Ottoman Turk, not only substituting will for law, but mutilating the sacred structure of the family, and clothing the excesses of tyrannical power with the awful sanction of religion, was such as to take away even half the remaining virtue of a slave" ("Hellenic Factor" 7).

4. Stillman, perceiving a causal link between the rebellions on Crete and in Herzegovina, went on to say, "The Cretan insurrection made the Herzegovinian revolt practicable and possible" (*Herzegovina and the Late Uprising* 6).

5. How dependent the perception of the Balkan struggle for freedom after 1876 was on the conception of wider philhellenism can be illustrated by two books

published in the early years of the twentieth century. Arthur Howden Smith's *Fighting the Turk in the Balkans: An American's Adventures with the Macedonian Revolutionaries* (1908) opened by asserting that "romance has in large measure passed" from everyday life in America and Europe (1). This American descendant of Childe Harold went on to say: "To those who have not visited them, the Balkans are a shadow-land of mystery; to those who know them they become even more mysterious, for as one begins to fancy he has peered under the veil, he finds himself caught in its meshes, and the spell of the land has him in thrall. You become, in a sense, part of the spell, and of the mystery and glamour of the whole" (2). Smith did not say precisely what the "spell" entailed, but it clearly was related to the magic force of Byronic legend, which had enveloped Greece and was now extending its geographical range. In fact, the first part of Smith's title, *Fighting the Turk in the Balkans*, which emphasized against whom he was fighting even before one knew for whom he was fighting, intentionally evoked the philhellenic legacy. Smith was a wider Romantic Byronist, who attempted to fulfill his yearnings for romance by carrying a rifle in a band of Bulgarians from Macedonia. Another one was the young Joyce Cary, who served in a Red Cross unit with the Montenegrin army in 1912 during the First Balkan War. Cary once said, "I had a certain romantic enthusiasm for the cause of Montenegro, in short I was young and eager for any sort of adventure" (8). During the First Balkan War of 1912–1913, the French poet Fernand Hauser published *Les Balkaniques* (1913), whose title looked back to the philhellenic sentiment of Victor Hugo's *Les Orientales* while at the same time updating the geographical terminology to reflect the new conditions of southeastern Europe. Hauser was so tied to the philhellenic language of the past that he was unable to convey or analyze the changes that had occurred in the Balkans since the late 1870s. *Les Balkaniques* was hopelessly out of date within the year it appeared, for the Second Balkan War of 1912–1913, in which the Balkan Christians squared off against one another, rendered the construction of wider philhellenism not just obsolete, but absurd. In reality, Hauser's vision was outdated from the start; it was drawn more from Hugo and literary philhellenism than from the twentieth-century context. The majority of wider philhellenic verse suffered from the same flaw; *Les Balkaniques* is simply, in terms of quantity, the most egregious example.

6. For a fuller discussion of Disraeli's speech on this occasion, see Saab 44.

7. Ironically, after all the difficulties with the Greek loan in the 1820s, one of the reasons for the British public's turn against the Turks was the Ottoman default on a loan (see Milman 27).

8. On Morris's involvement with the Bulgarian agitation, see Thompson 202–25.

9. As Saab said, the Bulgarian agitation offered a means for cooperation among "disparate groups": "Given the fact that the Nonconformists, the High Churchmen, the secular working-class radicals, and the agricultural laborers represented distinct and even opposing communities, it would have been extremely difficult for them to coalesce around an issue internal to England. What was needed was a symbolic grievance; a cause that would allow them to protest religious intolerance, the persecution of Christianity, and the corruption and unre-

sponsiveness of government, without ever having to deal with cases familiar enough to bring out their deep and well-founded disagreements" (63; for further discussion see 46–63). But Gladstone and the established Liberals were, to a fair extent, able to direct the movement once they decided to join the fray.

10. See Nelson 135–36.

11. Shannon said that Gladstone had "a sense of embarrassment" when his name was mentioned as a possible sovereign for Greece after the abdication of Otho in 1863: "He was in the false position of enjoying a spurious reputation for political philhellenism stemming from misconceptions about his Homerology and for the fortunate non-publication of his report as High Commissioner in 1859. Gladstone played no part in the initiative [to return the Ionian islands to Greece] in 1862" (*Gladstone* 475). The reputation for philhellenism was not completely spurious, though; Gladstone had spoken out in favor of Greece during the Don Pacifico debate in 1851 (see Shannon, *Gladstone* 222–23) and in 1856 had written an article, "War and Peace," to which he had attached only his initials, which advocated a Greek empire in the Near East. But there would be far fewer "Gladstone streets" in Greek towns if the Greeks had known what Gladstone had written concerning the Ionian islands. Saab had some interesting comments on the trips to the eastern Mediterranean of Disraeli and Gladstone and how their varied reactions to the land provided insight into their Eastern policies (9–10).

12. Some even used the differences between East and West found in early nineteenth-century philhellenic rhetoric to argue openly for British imperialism. So, for example, the novelist and poet Maurice Baring, noting how the questions "India for the Indians" and "Egypt for the Egyptians" were cognates of "Turkey for the Turks," asked in his volume *Letters from the Near East* (1913): "Is it possible to graft on to Oriental habits the modes of thought, the system and the forms of government of the West?" (15). Baring did not offer a final and complete negative, but he thought that it would take centuries, not decades, and concluded that benign Western rule was the best for which the East could hope (18), since how "can progress ever be a reality in Moslem countries unless the Mohammedan religion is changed out of all recognition?" (20). In the true Gladstonian tradition, however, he was far more receptive to "Bulgaria for the Bulgars," "Serbia for the Serbs," and "Greece for the Greeks." For Baring, "Oriental habits" apparently began on the other side of the Bosporus.

13. On the emergence of the terms *Romantic* and *Romanticism* in the second half of the nineteenth century to refer to a period of English literary history, see Welleck (esp. 15–16), Whalley (esp. 246–56), and Rieder (esp. 28–30). The incorporation of Byron into the mainstream provoked a reaction from Swinburne, who in 1865 published an essay that had helped to renew interest in the poet (see Chew 257–58). His criticism of Byron in the later essay "Wordsworth and Byron" was at least partly a response to Matthew Arnold's praise of the work of those two poets over the verse of Shelley. But it was also, I think, a challenge to Arnold's reading of Byron as more reformist than revolutionary. In "Wordsworth and Byron," Swinburne said, "On the day when it shall become accepted as a canon of criticism that the political work and the political opinions of a poet are to weigh nothing in the

balance that suspends his reputation—on that day the fame of Byron will fly up and vanish in the air," and he added, "We find little really living or really perma- . nent in the works of Byron which has not in it some direct or indirect touch of political emotion" (*Complete Works* 14.166). Swinburne wrote this at a time when Arnold and others were in fact fitting Byron and Shelley into the canon by lessening the poets' political emotions.

14. Jean Moorcroft Wilson, in *I Was Once an English Poet: A Biography of William Watson*, said that when Watson referred to "Shelley's 'foes,' " "he meant those who admired him for his revolutionary thought more than his lyricism. Watson believed that Shelley's greatness had been misinterpreted and it lay with his lyrical not his political achievements" (105).

15. On the Armenian massacres of the 1890s, see W. T. Stead's *The Haunting Horrors of Armenia* (1897), which uses a quotation from *The Purple East* as an epigraph.

16. The same problem occurs in the majority of verse written during the Bulgarian agitation. They are mostly satires, often doggerel in quality, about the inaction of British leadership, such as *The Devil's Visit to Bulgaria and Other Lands*. Even Swinburne's *Ballad of Bulgarie*, which satirizes Gladstone and the Liberals, falls into this category. The focus in nearly all works of this kind is English domestic politics instead of the Bulgarians and their aspirations, demonstrating the lack of a significant emotional connection between the Bulgarians and their British supporters.

17. See Todorova's essay "The Balkans: From Discovery to Invention" and Goldsworthy's recent *Inventing Ruritania*. Jelavich's "British Travelers in the Balkans" surveys early British travel writing about the area.

18. See Abbott, *Tale of a Tour of Macedonia*, who says that to a Turkish official "Christian and Greek are convertible terms" (60).

19. See, for example, Emile Lavalaye's *Balkan Peninsula* (1887), William Miller's *Balkans* (1903), W. V. Herbert's *By-Paths in the Balkans* (1906), John Fraser's *Pictures from the Balkans* (1912), Edith Durham's *Burden of the Balkans* (1905), and Winifred Gordon's *Woman in the Balkans* (1916). See also Saki's story "The Lost Sanjak," in which a man is put to death because he does not know where the Sanjak of Novibazar is. The story is discussed by Goldsworthy 117–125.

20. On the idea of Eastern Europe as a half-civilized/half-savage space, see Wolff. On the change from the Renaissance conception of the North/South division of Europe to an East/West division during the Enlightenment, see esp. 4–8.

21. See Wolff 1–2.

22. Surveying American literature at the turn of the century, Van Wyck Brooks commented that "in scores of other crude romances . . . dealing with court-intrigue in imaginary countries in the Balkans,—Graustark, Asturnia, Scarvania, Waleria, and others, big bold Americans humbled effete Europeans, as America had humbled Spain in 1898" (*Confident Years* 142). Goldsworthy has done an excellent job mapping the imaginary Balkans in British writing, and I regret that I was not able to read her book until after my own manuscript had been

submitted. On p. 30 of his novel, Upward referred to the "Balkiad Atrocities," which "furnished a theme for the scathing eloquence of the greatest of living orators." Despite that eloquence and the public outcry, this was one of the few references to the Bulgarian agitation in English. For more on Upward, who assisted the Greeks in Crete in 1897 and in Macedonia in 1908, his spiritual and mystical books *The New Word* (1907) and *The Divine Mystery* (1915), and their influence on Ezra Pound, see the articles by Knox and by Moody. In France, on the other hand, Pierre D'Éspignot published *Avant le Massacre: Roman Macédonien* in 1902, which, like Turgenev's early novel *On the Eve* (1859), presented the Bulgarians in a positive light.

23. On pp. 42–43, Moore wrote a rather poor poem for a Greek girl whose father died fighting in Macedonia ("And the dear one of my race / who gavest thy life that Greece might grow / Strong, and regain her lost domain"). A book by George Demetrius in a series for children, *I Was Once a Boy in Greece* (1913), revealed how the picture of Greece as a politicized space was offered to the youngest American readers: "And when I say Greece, I mean more particularly Macedonia, for that was where I was born, in a village inside the Turkish frontier [so the author was not really a Greek national at all]. But we are all Greeks in Southern Macedonia, Greek in thought, language, customs, Greek in our hope for, love of, and belief in the Greece that never dies" (1).

24. See Dakin, *Greek Struggle in Macedonia* 51.

25. The Turkophile Marmaduke Pickthall went so far as to appropriate the classical past for the Turks. He said, "Classical illusions flourish in the atmosphere of Turkey rather than that of modern Greece. . . . The Turks preserve the old Greek's love of beauty for its own sake;—his delight in seaside vistas, colonnades, white temples, solemn cypress groves; his clear poetic gaze at love and death; whereas the modern Greek's romance is simply money" (quoted in Freemantle 220).

26. On the fighting in Macedonia in the early years of the twentieth century, see Dakin, *Greek Struggle in Macedonia*.

27. There were some attempts to use the traditional British Russophobia to combat "Pan-Slavism." Lewis Sergeant commented in *New Greece*: "If there is a single Englishman who is not convinced of the real importance of Greece to Europe—which of necessity implies the duty of Europe to take every opportunity of strengthening the Greek kingdom . . . he would do well to sit down before a map of Europe, to blot out the name of Greece, and to substitute for it 'Turkey,' or 'Slavonia,' or one of the letters of the Russian empire. . . . For Panslavonianism has been set up in rivalry to Philhellenism" (2, 4). But since Russophobia was no longer as potent as it had been at midcentury, this was not effective.

28. See Dakin, *Greek Struggle in Macedonia* 118–19.

29. Karanikas observed that as "the novel nears its melodramatic end, the Greeks turn more villainous and the Ango-Saxons more noble. Reference also turns more ethnic, with Walter cited as 'the American' and Spiro, for example, as 'the jealous Greek' or just 'the Greek'" (52). He also said that the heroine's "true identity . . . allows her to depart from her status as a Greek peasant girl" (53). This

is an understatement, since her newfound identity actually allows her to depart from her status as a Greek altogether.

30. In George Henty's novel *In Greek Waters*, a ship of philhellenic English volunteers becomes so disenchanted with the Greeks after their arrival in the Aegean that they decide on a mission of rescuing refugees from both sides. Some of the young Englishmen are puzzled when a group of Greek women who have been saved from the massacre on Scio "don't seem as delighted as one would expect at getting out of the hands of the Turks" (291). A man with experience in the Levant explains, "As to their being sold as slaves, I do not suppose they view it at all in the same way we do. . . . To us it is an abominable thing that a Greek woman or child should be a slave to the heathen Turk. I am only pointing out to you that from their point of view there is nothing so terrible in their lot" (292, 293). To the Greeks of Chios, Henty's character continues, slavery in a Turkish house would be preferable to trying to make one's way in the world as a shopgirl or laundress. But two Englishwomen who are also rescued from the slave market are relieved that they are saved from "the most awful of fates" (407). Henty, more critical of the modern Greeks than McCarthy or Horton, strikes at the very heart of the romance of Greek liberation by suggesting that the Greek female, or rather the mostly Albanian and Suliot female, is really so different from a Western woman that she would prefer not to be rescued from Turkish slavery. At the end of the book, predictably, the young English hero marries one of the two Englishwomen who he saved from an Eastern harem.

31. Horton was "strongly pro-Greek" (Karanikas 38). His philhellenism was recognized by the American Greek community, for *Athene*, an important Greek-American journal published in Chicago, said in an issue commemorating Horton, "The time will come when the people of Greece will honor their Horton, their 'kyr Giorgos,' . . . by erecting a monument to him in some secluded spot near his beloved Acropolis" (Karanikas 38). It has not happened yet.

32. The Western-educated Greek villain in Anthony Hope's *Phroso* has been "freed by scepticism learned in the West to practice crimes the East had taught him" (203). Constantine is also the only resident of Neopalia who does not believe in the traditional power of the island's patron, St. Tryphon, and tells lies with his hand on the saint's icon. In Black's *Briseis*, the villain who tries to blackmail the heroine is a Greek of "the degenerate Hellenic type" (197).

33. See also the installment in Filbert Patton's [Burt Standish] Dick Merriwell series for children, *Dick Merriwell in Greece; or, The Maid of Athens*, in which two American boys, after quoting Byron on the Acropolis, rescue a maid of Athens from her Greek uncle and cousin so that she can marry her English sweetheart.

34. In Benson's *The Capsina*, the heroine of the title is an Amazon who dies unmarried. The Greek man who she loves, the hero of *The Vintage*, is married to a woman rescued from a Turkish harem, but she does not have a significant presence in either book.

35. In the "False Dawn" section of Wharton's *Old New York*, the hero took a ship to Piraeus and "plunged into pure romance, and the tourist became a Giaour." With good results, for "it was the East which had made him a new Lewis

Raycie" (41). In the story, though, we only observe this new Lewis Raycie in Italy and New York; we are not given a picture of him being "made" in the East. After a second cruise in the Aegean in 1926, Wharton wrote a story set in Cyprus during the Crusader period entitled "Dieu d'Amour" (see R. W. B. Lewis 468–70) but nothing that dealt with contemporary Greece. Wharton's diary from her first journey has recently been discovered and published by Claudine Lesage as *The Cruise of the Vanadis*.

36. This effect occurs, for example, in Richard Watson Gilder's poem "The Parthenon by Moonlight" and Reardon's contact with a world "beyond the human sphere, bathed in divine light" in Gissing's *New Grub Street* (370).

37. Leontis's comment that "the Acropolis becomes for the viewer a place where the highest aesthetic values of Western culture escape the ravages of time and limitation of 'local and nationalist color' that obstruct modern incarnations" is only half right (51). She overlooked the fact that for a fair number of foreigners the Acropolis was a symbol of modern Greece's national aspirations and struggles, and this perspective appears frequently in English and American writing. It poses a central dilemma for her theoretical construction of the relation between Western travelers and Greece in the nineteenth century.

Chapter 6

1. In 1879, D. W. Dilke said, "The progress that Greece has made during the last fifty years has been more than satisfactory, it has been astonishing—almost miraculous" (*Papers of the Greek Committee*, no. 2, p. 11). Lewis Sergeant titled one of his books *Greece in the Nineteenth Century: A Record of Hellenic Emancipation and Progress, 1821–1897*. A more cautious S. G. W. Benjamin wrote, "Although Greece has failed to make that degree of progress that was expected of her, still she has advanced considerably, for which she should have full credit" (229). Arguing for the other side, Diplomaticus asserted: "For seventy years Greece has been a spoiled child. She has played ducks and drakes with her resources. She has not even civilised the land given her in 1830 and enlarged in 1886" (780). Still, despite the fact that what Mazzini termed "the sacred word of progress" was the measuring stick of the success of the Greek state, the idea of the Greeks as "noble savages" living the natural life still appeared in some works, such as Melville's "Syra," in which the island is described as "Primitive, such an island resort / As heartless Homer might have known" (*Complete Poems* 250).

2. See Leontis's discussion of how the Acropolis "becomes a place of homecoming set apart, quite literally, from home" (47; also 45–52).

3. See also Merivale's comment that from 1890 to 1926 "there [was] an astonishing resurgence in the Pan motif" (vii).

4. Some of the modern devotees of the Pan cult were also rather tame. D. H. Lawrence described the neopagan Rupert Brooke, leader of a fervid back-to-nature sect, as "a Greek God under a Japanese Sunshade, reading poetry in his pajamas, at Grantchester, at Grantchester, where the river goes" (Delany xvi). A

sinister Pan did, as Merivale has shown, play a role in several late Victorian and Edwardian horror stories (154–80), but Hynes's remarks about the yearning for the rural and Pan's place in that desire generally ring true.

5. Douglas complained bitterly about the condition of lodgings and food in Greece, as well as the habits of the people; see Holloway 279–80. But conditions were no better in Calabria. According to Holloway, Douglas faced the rigors and difficulties of a stay in Calabria at age sixty-four because of his affection for the area, "for only love, or something nearly as powerful, could have made the sacrifice worth it" (403). Douglas did not have that kind of feeling for Greece.

6. In Margaret Sherwood's story "Pan and the Crusader," set in the Middle Ages, a Greek island has the kind of pastoral, nonpolitical significance that it usually lacks when the setting is contemporary. It was easier, apparently, to envision a meeting with Pan in Greece in the remote past than it was in the present day.

7. See Leontis's discussion of the story on 107–12, especially her comments on the irony and detachment of the narrator's voice. But I must take issue with her comment that the claim that "the modern Greek offers the traveler access to Hellenism" was new and revisionary when Woolf wrote. Further, Leontis overlooked the fact that for a considerable number of Westerners, the statement "I, too, am a Greek" led them to identify with the modern Greeks as well as the ancients (see McCarthy I.13).

8. In Woolf's novel *Jacob's Room*, the main character, in a letter to England during a stay in Greece, echoes the sentiment that the Mediterranean provides an antidote to the world of industrialism: "I intend to come to Greece every year so long as I live. It is the only chance that I can see of protecting oneself from civilization" (146). Yet in Athens, Jacob begins to find contact with ancient ruins on the Acropolis wearing ("the sight of Hymettus, Pentelicus, Lycabettus on one side and the sea on the other, as one stands in the Parthenon at sunset, the sky pink feathered, the plain all colours, the marble tawny in one's eyes, is thus oppressive," 149). One must keep in mind that, although Jacob's visit to Greece occurs before the beginning of World War I, *Jacob's Room* is a postwar book with a postwar outlook. In fact, the first quote can stand for Greece in the imagination of the prewar traveler, while the second is the postwar reaction to that prewar image.

9. In the introduction to a volume of translations by Elizabeth Edmonds, *Greek Lays, Idylls, Legends* (1885), Matthew Jenkyns stated that the book would inform a generation of readers "who have not had their sympathies awakened by the daring deeds of the Hellenes" in the revolutionary period and arouse within that generation philhellenic sympathy "by presenting a few sketches calculated to show that the modern Greeks are not the degenerate race some Turkophiles have represented them to be" (1). Some earlier writers had placed Greek folklore within a framework of the progress of the Greeks. During the years of British rule in the Ionian islands, the Greeks were often viewed within an imperial discourse that validated their colonized status. Tertius Kendrick, who wrote two rather fanciful books on Greek folk practices in the 1820s (*The Kako-damon; or, The Cavern of Anti-Paros*, 1825, and *The Travellers: A Tale Illustrative of the Manners, Customs, and Superstitions of Modern Greece* 1825), commented in 1822 on the "almost

hottentot customs of the peasantry" on Corfu and its sister islands, which were "a striking proof of their masters' character; and furnish an unequivocal demonstration of their neglect in exercizing all humane and generous principles toward an emancipation from ignorance and wretchedness" (*Ionian Islands* vii). Walter Goodisson, his contemporary, made similar observations in *A Historical and Topographical Essay upon the Islands of Cephalonia, Corfu, Leucadia, Ithaca, and Zante* (203). For both authors, the advent of the British would bring "progress" to the Greek villagers and an end to "hottentot customs." In *The Ionian Islands in Relation to Greece* (1859), written at a time of debate as to whether the islands should be given to Greece, John Dunn Gardner said that "the renown of the ancient inhabitants has blinded Europe to the demerits of the modern race" (27), that the Ionian islands have "nothing to do with Homer" (12), and that Greeks were more like Orientals and "should not be dealt with as Englishmen" (10). He also lamented that "Byron did a great mischief by encouraging philhellenism," which has become "a thorough vice and a nuisance" (43, 44).

10. On Ouida's use of the Etruscan past "to evoke the graceful and joyous response to life" in *In Maremma* (1882), see Kenneth Churchill 163. One reason for the utopian portrayal of Etruscan life was that little was known about these people beyond the banquet scenes in Etruscan tombs. So the Etruscan period was viewed as a pre-Roman idyll and the people as the perfect primitives before the militarized invasion of the descendants of Romulus and Remus.

11. See also Woolf's comment about the Greek monk who had "the nose and brow of a Greek statue" (*Complete Shorter Fiction* 67) and Horton's hero, Spiridon, in *Aphroessa*, who has the features of Narcissus because he could claim blood that "has trickled down the years" (*Poems of an Exile* 193). Emilie Barrington was amazed to find a Greek "urchin" in Olympia who had "the face of the Hermes of Praxiteles" (123).

12. J. Theodore Bent felt that real Greeks could now only be found in the Aegean islands (vi–vii): "These islands, especially the smaller ones, offer unusual facilities for the study of the manners and the customs of the Greeks as they are, with a view to comparing them to the Greeks as they were. The mainland of Greece has been overrun with barbarian tribes" (vii).

13. Lynch's ambivalence about the modern Greeks can be seen in his conflicting statements about the Ypsaliotes. On the one hand, they are "of a purer stock than most of the Greeks" (167) and "they're original" (172); on the other, their genealogy is "a hopeless problem. Of course, they are not Greeks in the Athenian sense, nor Arnauts, nor Turks, nor Bulgars. For all we can tell they come from the Caucasus—for they're nobly made and beautiful—or they may be a remnant of an old time—who can say?" (172). The Ypsaliotes are either a remnant of the classical Greeks or a remnant of the original Indo-Europeans, and the confusion at least in part reflects Lynch's doubts about the modern Greeks.

14. For example, in Drosinis's *Amaryllis*, translated by Elizabeth Edmonds in 1891, the "rural" Greek girl with whom the sophisticated Athenian youth falls in love on a visit to his ancestral village turns out to be his equal in status and wealth; in fact, the two families are old friends, and the perceived gap between the maid

and her "citified" lover was an error on the part of the youth. But this kind of elision of the boundaries between urban and rural Greeks is usually absent from works written by English or American authors, who tend to magnify rather than elide the differences between Athens and the villages.

15. In a series of letters reprinted at the end of his volume *Tales and Sketches of Modern Greece*, William discussed domestic problems in modern Greece and their cause. Given the absence of good government and the lack of a decent press, he wrote, "What wonder then, that with an illiterate, half-starved public spirit, the Greeks should sometimes place party before country?" (77). He also criticized the treatment of women, citing it as a sign that "it is not so very long ago the Turks were master" (67). Of the Greek peasant he said: "He is said to be the degenerate descendant of a great race. Of his body he proves it a lie. . . . With close-cropped hair, or dark shady looks, he resembles no one so much as himself, and but rarely approaches the classical type of virile beauty met with in a sculpture by Phidias" (61). Despite such remarks, William wanted the English to support reforms in Greece, and his knowledge and interest in the land suggested a deep attraction for the place and its people. William appears to be a philhellene who is wholly concerned with the present Greek state, which makes him rather unique in the 1890s.

16. See Hynes, *Edwardian Turn of Mind* 132–49.

17. Horton's novel *Constantine: A Tale of Greece under King Otho* (1896), which told the history of a local madman, also began with the description of an idyllic island by a Western narrator: "The effect upon the sensibilities of a few days residence in Poros is peculiar. One is so shut off for the time being from the vastness of the world . . . that the passage outward through the little strait seems like the emergence from time into eternity" (7). Horton also offered a happy picture of Greek village life in *The Tempting of Father Anthony*, in which a teenager attempts to become a saint against the wishes of his parents. The same elegiac picture of rural Greece can be found in Rennell Rodd's "In Arcadia" and "The Keynote" (which concludes, "A Shepherd's crook, a coat of fleece, / A grazing flock,—the sense of peace, / The long sweet silence,—this is Greece!" *Violet Crown* 4); in Ernest Myers's "Arcadia" ("But now amid the oak of Arcady / Pan passed me"); and in Elizabeth Edmonds's *The History of a Church Mouse* (1892) and several poems in her volume of verse *Hesperas*. The final story of Julia Dragoumis's *Tales of a Greek Island*, which described a character's departure from the island of Poros, is fittingly entitled "The End of the Fairy Tale," for despite some tragedies, the island is portrayed as a pastoral retreat.

18. On Pater and Hellenism, see DeLaura 177; Richard Jenkyns 52–59, 252–61, 293–97; and Turner 68–74.

19. The model for the courtesan in Louÿs's *Chansons de Bilitis* was apparently a sixteen-year-old Algerian prostitute named Meriem ben Atala (see Clive 105–6).

20. See, for example, the description of Chrysoula in the chapter entitled "The Little Golden One" in Lynch's *Glamour*. The Turkophile Marmaduke Pickthall, who announced his conversion to Islam in 1917, attempted to subvert this image of Greek women in his short story "A Matter of Taste," in which a

Levantine girl of Greek descent and English nationality is portrayed "abounding in soft gestures and alluring glances" (*As Others See Us* 139). Her marriage to an Englishman, Stanley Jackson, does not, as happens in philhellenic literature, raise her up to Western European status but rather reduces him to the level of a gross Levantine. At the end of the story, a former friend says of Jackson: "He's just a dago! . . . Whoever would have thought that a decent Englishman could change skin like that?" (153). On one level, the story attacks English females ("There is one thing English girls are bad at—that is love. They think too much of themselves," 153), who through their ineptness at love render Englishmen susceptible to the alluring but coarse charms of Levantine women. Pickthall's sympathies can be clearly seen by comparing "A Matter of Taste" to his novel *Veiled Women*. Where Jackson becomes a "dago" by marrying a Levantine Greek, the English heroine of *Veiled Women* learns lessons about the nature of womanhood by marrying a Turk and joining his harem.

21. In Dora Bradford's novel *Greek Fire* (1935), a rather eligible suitor of the English heroine, Angel, is tortured by the brigands who capture the two of them, leaving him with no thumbs. As Bradford is not writing *Jane Eyre*, a mutilated man is clearly no match for her heroine—certainly not a mutilated Greek. The mutilation, I would argue, is itself symbolic of the Western conception of the place of the Greek male who is not a brigand.

22. On the association between Hellenism and homosexuality in late Victorian England, see Richard Jenkyns 280–93 and Dowling.

23. See Jay 72–73.

24. See also Richard Jenkyns, who wrote that, for the Victorians, "ancient Greece had produced the literary treatments of homosexuality and Italy was where it was practiced in the present day. In either case the imagination dwelt upon the Mediterranean world" (291).

25. For Byron, see Crompton 107–57. For Gide and Wilde, see Delay 388–98 and Ellmann 429–30.

26. See Brophy 366.

27. On Forster's Italian writings, see Kenneth Churchill 176–79, Merivale 181–86, and Papazoglou 77–80, 94–97, 102–19.

28. In the same letter to Isherwood, Forster said that the Greek poet C. P. Cavafy once told him, "Never forget about the Greeks that we are bankrupt. That is the difference between us and the ancient Greeks, and my dear Forster, between us and yourselves" (*Selected Letters* II.118). Whether Cavafy ever said this or not, it accurately reflects Forster's opinion of the gap between the ancient and modern Greeks and his belief that the ancient Greek spirit could now be found in England.

29. On this trip, Clive experiences a conversion from homosexuality and platonic love to heterosexuality. He writes to Maurice, "Against my will I have become normal. I cannot help it" (116). On the irony of this turn of events in the land of Greek love, see, with a discussion of previous views, Papazoglou 179–82. Papazoglou's reading of Clive's sexual conversion—that "the artificiality of Clive's Hellenism . . . could not survive the confrontation with what Forster thought to be

the true spirit of Hellenism represented . . . by the physical surroundings and the reality of the country itself"—seems a bit odd, given that contemporary Greece never appeared to represent the true spirit of Hellenism for Forster. Since earlier, in "The Road from Colonus," Greece was the land where the chance of salvation was lost, it seems perfectly appropriate for Clive to experience what, in the novel, seems another lost chance at salvation. Put simply, for Forster, Greece was not amenable to the saving "eternal moments," which occur in Italy.

30. At one point in "Cnidus," Papazoglou and others have seen an epiphany, "a manifestation of [a god's] presence in the world" (64). I am less certain about this, for I think the passage sounds slightly ironic; see Roessel, "Live Orientals and Dead Greeks" 55–57. In either interpretation, the "eternal moment" is quickly broken.

31. Forster wrote an earlier, fictional account of Malatesta's journey for Pletho's body entitled "The Tomb of Pletone," which was reprinted in *Arctic Summer and Other Stories*. In this version, Malatesta openly proclaims, "We will bring Italy to Greece" (98; see also his comment that Greece will rise from the dead and flower in Italy, 114). Greece, on the other hand, is called a "dead country" (109; see also the description of Aphrodite's island of Cerigo as a "dead island" with not even a column remaining from the goddess's temple). I cannot agree with Papazoglou, who sees in the line "Greece may slumber but she never dies," which is repeated by several characters, a possibility of a revival in Greece itself (67). At no point is it asserted that Greece's regeneration will take place on Greek soil, while the entire plot of the story concerns an attempt to make "Greece" awake in Italy.

32. On Pickthall's far more aggressive and direct defense of the Turkish national and territorial aspirations from 1911 to 1922, see Freemantle. Still, when Pickthall eventually wrote a novel about the politics of the period from 1908 through the Balkan Wars from a Turkish point of view (*Early Hours*), he avoided vituperative attacks on the modern Greeks. Pickthall once used the depiction of Greece as a woman in an attempt to undermine sympathy for Greece in England. He wrote about the accounts of massacres in the English press: "The rumors current in the West are due to the reports of Armenians, Greeks and other Levantines—mostly women" (Freemantle 200).

33. See Roessel, "Live Orientals and Dead Greeks" 52–53 and n. 27.

34. Another visitor who confessed a lack of interest in the contemporary Greek world and its politics was Isadora Duncan. Of her family's stay in the Greek capital in 1904, she wrote, "We were completely self-sufficient in our Clan. We did not mingle with the inhabitants of Athens. Even when we heard one day from the peasants that the King of Greece had ridden out to see our temple, we remained unimpressed. For we were living under the reign of other kings, Agamemnon, Menelaus, and Priam," and she remembered their "effort to reach over two thousand years to beauty not perhaps understood by us" (128, 133). For Duncan, "Greece" and "modern" seem to have been opposing terms, and she and her family steadfastly wore classical tunics to show it.

35. See Dakin, *Unification of Greece* 90–100.

36. The Balkan Wars appear in this way in Virginia Woolf's *Jacob's Room* (160, 175) and *The Years* (201, 220); see Roessel, "The Significance of Constantinople in *Orlando*." Some responses to the Balkan Wars focused more on opposition to Turkey than on support for Greece or any single Balkan nation; see, for example, the 1912 section of Maurice Baring's *Letters from the Near East*. Another supporter, surprisingly, was Ezra Pound, not generally thought of as someone in the camp of Gladstone. Pound asserted, "The disgrace to Europe is not that Turkey is about to be driven from Europe, but that she has not long since been driven out" ("The Black Crusade" 108). But Gladstone would have been shocked at Pound's reasoning: "If Oriental despotism is not lock, stock and barrel, of one matter with the industrial tyrannies of Europe to what is it allied. . . . If we cannot break the ring in our own countries, the next best thing is to see it broken elsewhere." Consequently, he concluded: "Uncivilized Montenegrins, Servians, decadent Greeks, pestilent Bulgarians, I wish you well, and I pray you conserve your ideal of freedom better than men have done in my own 'free' country or in constitutional England" (108). This was an attempt to inject into "wider" philhellenism, which had been comfortably Christian and middle class, a new kind of revolutionary meaning. It was, as much of Pound's thinking, idiosyncratic, and while Pound probably meant the adjectives "uncivilized," "decadent," and "pestilent" as complimentary, the Balkan peoples were probably not pleased. They were not, at this stage, interested in defining themselves against England or America.

37. See Hodgson 163–65.

38. The American Cale Young Rice also evoked many of the traditional elements of Byronic philhellenism in his poem "In a Greek Temple (during the First Balkan War)." Like Hutchinson, he expressed hope that the victory would bring about a regeneration within the present Greek population of the character and traits of old Hellas: "While cries that Mitylene / Is taken come again, / I gaze upon this shrine you reared / And think how you were men!" (*Collected Plays and Poems* 437). He returns to this thought at the end of the piece, which echoes the final couplet of Byron's "The Isles of Greece": "O Life, fill up again your cup / For such a race to drain!"

39. On this development, see Roessel, "'Mr. Eugenides, the Smyrna Merchant' and Post-War Politics in *The Waste Land*" and "'The Repeat in History': Canto 26 and Greece's Asia Minor Disaster."

40. Abrams went on to add, "From any comprehensive view of their basic premises and literary practice, it seems to me that in this judgment they were manifestly right" (427; see also Quinones 187–90). This view has been challenged by some critics, notably Harold Bloom (*Ringers in the Tower*) and George Bornstein (*Transformation of Romanticism in Yeats, Eliot and Stevens*), who for the most part view the modernists as post-Romantics. While I personally am more inclined to the position of Abrams and Quinones, for my purpose it is sufficient that, whatever their actual literary practice, the modernists, as Abrams put it, "identified

themselves as, explicitly, counter-Romantic." The perception of modern Greece was colored by that stance.

41. See Carr 44–45.

Chapter 7

1. On Brooke and the neopagans, see Delany, esp. 37–62.

2. Leigh Fermor reported the account of a visitor to Brooke's tomb, who met a local shepherd. The shepherd said that "*o Broukis* used to wander about the woods [of the island] in silence, the very picture of an old-fashioned English gentleman."

> "What did he look like?"
> "Magnificent, Sir," the shepherd answered. "Tall, dignified, flowing hair, burning eyes, and a long white beard." (*Roumeli* 175)

3. On the offer of Constantinople to the Russians, see Clogg, *Concise History of Greece* 87 and Fromkin 127.

4. On the Byronization of Brooke, see also Delany 211. At the dedication of the statue of Brooke on Skyros, nearly every speaker mentioned Byron. See, for example, *Hommage à Rupert Brooke* 21, 38.

5. Mansell said, "Never did the city inspire so much rivalry as in its last years as an imperial capital" (374); see also Coolidge. The nagging question of what should be done with the city appeared in the title of numerous books, among them the anonymous *Constantinople: Its Past, Present and Future* (1853); Dwight's *Constantinople and Its Problems* (1901); Leonard Woolf's *Future of Constantinople* (1917); and Shotwell's *Short History of the Question of Constantinople and the Straits* (1922).

6. Several works written at the end of the nineteenth century about the fall of Constantinople encouraged the idea that the city should be redeemed, for example, Neale's novel *Theodora Phrantza* (1857); C. R. Eaglestone's *Siege of Constantinople: A Historical Romance* (1878); and C. L. Johnstone's *Conquest of Constantinople* (1898), which has a section entitled "Greece in 1829 by Alphonse Lamartine."

7. This mirrors a fundamental dichotomy between the words *Romios* and *Hellene* within the Greek tradition itself (see Leigh Fermor, *Roumeli* 96–142), but one that has little effect on the history of philhellenism. The Byzantine heritage, which Leigh Fermor associated with Romios, was largely seen as Levantine until Robert Byron championed it in the late 1920s and 1930s (see chap. 9).

8. *The First Secretary*, Vaka Brown's first effort, has a young official at the American legation helping a Circassian woman escape from a Turkish harem but without the explicit connection to the Greek aspirations for Constantinople that appear in the other novels. On her career, see Kenneth Brown's article and Karanikas 53–60.

9. Vaka Brown's most interesting twist on the romance of liberation is that the heroine of *The Grasp of the Sultan* has, with the Turkish ruler, had a child, who es-

capes with his mother. The idea that the loss of virginity did not taint the honor of the heroine is unique to the genre, although Vaka Brown stresses that the Greek woman did not have sex with the sultan after the birth of her son.

10. In *Letters from the East*, the novelist Maurice Baring says that "in reality there is no such thing as Young Turks: there are only Turks and foreigners" (31) and that the attitude was that "if there is to be any order in this country the Turk must be top dog. Whether he be young or old is a question of detail" (67). E. F. Benson depicted the Young Turks as simply more depraved and murderous versions of the Old Turks in *Crescent and Iron Cross*. On the other side, Marmaduke Pickthall, in his novel *The Early Hours*, depicts the Young Turks as a continuation of the Muslim legacy from the Ottomans.

11. In her book *In the Heart of German Intrigue*, Vaka Brown begins by saying, "then I married an American, and began to have a career—one I owed absolutely to my American husband, to American encouragement, and the American public" (2).

12. Allusions to the Trojan War were common in the writings of those who served in Gallipoli and Macedonia; for example, see Brooke's fragment with the lines "And Priam and his fifty sons / Wake all amazed and hear the guns / And shake for Troy again" (*Poetical Works* 205). Mention of Byron was also fairly ubiquitous, such as A. Griffin Tapp's refusal to describe the scenes of his voyage to Salonika because "are they not written in two books of the chronicle of Childe Harold?" (13) and Isabel Hutton's musing, as she passed near Missolonghi, on what Byron would think of submarine warfare (130).

13. Fussell mentions Venizelos in passing in connection to a passage in David Jones's *In Parenthesis*, where Signaler Oliver tells John Ball about "the Greek Venizelos" (154).

14. On Greek politics during World War I see Clogg, *Concise History of Greece* 86–99; Michael Llewellyn Smith 35–61; and Dakin, *Unification of Greece* 201–20.

15. Max Beerbohm, a committed Royalist, let his ideas about monarchy color his reaction to the possibility that King Constantine might be deposed again in 1922: "One refuses to believe this morning's *Tribune* that the throne of Constantine is [in] danger because the Greeks haven't lost their inveterate habit of running at the first sight of a fez on their classic horizon. 'Dash down yon cup of Samian wine,' by all means, but the throne of Constantine shall never be tampered with" (*Letters* 136). But the party of Gresham far outnumbered the party of Beerbohm. In their first publication in 1918, the American Hellenic Society announced, "Upon the departure of King Constantine and his courtiers, all apostles of Pan-German ideas, the Greek people are once again in an atmosphere purely Greek" (introduction to Gauvin ix). Demetra Vaka Brown dismissed the king as a man who was "not a Greek by blood, and lacks the cultivation to be a Philhellene" (*In Pawn to a Throne* 120). In Mackenzie's *South Wind of Love*, Venizelos represented the true Greek spirit, while Constantine and the Royalists were "quite content with a tinpot Balkan court" (382).

16. See also Clogg, *Politics and the Academy* 2.

17. During the Balkan Wars, Burrows published his poem "Song of the Hellenes to Veniselos the Cretan," which began:

> Veniselos! Veniselos!
> Do not fail us! Do not fail us!
> Now is come to thee the hour
> To show forth thy master power.
> Lord of all Hellenic men,
> Make our country great again.
> (quoted in Clogg, *Politics and the Academy* 1)

18. See Gibbons 24 and Chester 54. Venizelos himself contributed to this notion. At the Versailles conference, he told Stephen Bonsal: "While you were studying at Heidelberg and Bonn, I was hiding from the Turkish zaptiehs in the mountain caves of my native Crete. For months I never saw a book" (175).

19. Other Venizelist books include those by Gibbons, Price, Ure, and Trowbridge. Katapodes published a set of anti-Venizelist essays in England in 1917, but he and Hibben were lonely voices. On attempts to manipulate foreign opinion about domestic Greek politics, see Kitsikis 163–292.

20. Basil Thomson in *The Allied Secret Service in Greece* complained that agents inspired by the "example of Byron and the philhellenes in Greece" had distorted and even falsified intelligence reports to assist Venizelos (15).

21. On this, see Sprinker, esp. 5–6.

22. On the autobiographical aspects of the novel, see Nigel Nicolson 145–81 and Glendinning 92–113. Nicolson suggested that Aphros stood for Sackville-West's husband, Harold Nicolson, and he viewed Julian's conflict as one between love and duty.

23. On Nicolson's philhellenic sympathies, see Lees-Milne I.111–12.

24. A significant poet who did serve in the army of the Orient, Hugh MacDiarmid, considered arranging a volume to "fill a gap in the Soldier Poet's series published by Erskine MacDonald, which so far has mainly concentrated on the Western front and at all events has not included anything from Salonika. I suggest calling it A Voice from Macedonia" (*Letters* 24). The book never materialized. According to his biographer, MacDiarmid "wondered whether the paucity of poetry [on the Salonica front] was due to the monotonously grim routine of death by disease—as opposed to the horrific drama of death in the trenches—but rejected this explanation" (Bold 91).

25. Other literary works set in Salonica are Mackenzie's novel *Extremes Meet*, A. Griffin Tapp's *Stories of Salonica and the New Crusade*, and Macleod's volume of verse, *Macedonian Measures*.

26. See also Goldstein, "Great Britain and Greater Greece." Philhellenes also produced poems to support the cause. In 1919, F. Noel Byron published *Athenian Days*, which contained in the traditional philhellenic vein such poems as "Spirit of Greece" and "Marathon by Night." In 1921, William Palmer weighed in with his long poem *The Philhellenes*.

27. On the St. Sophia restoration movement and its problems, see Goldstein, "Holy Wisdom and British Foreign Policy."

28. Thomas Pinney, commenting on a letter that Kipling wrote to Caclamanos, the Greek minister in England, said that the translation of the Greek national anthem "was made apparently at the request of Caclamanos: an entry in CK's [Mrs. Kipling's] diary, October 1918, says 'Rud writing his Greek Nat. Anthem for Greek Minister.'" Pinney reported that Kipling later received a gold coin from the era of Alexander the Great from the Greek government for his effort (*Letters of Rudyard Kipling* 4:514).

29. See Michael Llewellyn Smith 90–91. Arnold Toynbee, who visited Greek-occupied Asia Minor in 1921, said, "The Greeks and the Turks appeared in unfamiliar roles. The Greeks have shown the same inability as the Turks for governing a mixed population" (*Western Question* vii). Yet not everyone saw the Greeks and Turks in unfamiliar roles, as Toynbee found out when he was forced to resign from the Korais Chair of Modern Greek Studies at King's College for his negative accounts of Greek actions in Asia Minor in 1919 and 1920. For the story of Toynbee and the Korais chair, see Clogg, *Politics and the Academy*, esp. 53–102.

30. On British policy toward Greece at this time, see Churchill, *World Crisis* 388–90. On the philhellenic sentiment of Lloyd George, which complicated British policy, see Churchill's comments on 391 and the article by Montgomery. On the short, unhappy reign of Constantine's second son, Alexander, which lasted from 1917 until his death in 1922 from the bite of a pet monkey, see Michael Llewellyn Smith 58, 136–38, 156–58.

31. The Venizelist philhellenes, while they still supported Greece during the Greco-Turkish War, would later blame Constantine for the defeat in Asia Minor. For example, in his novel *The Labyrinth*, Cecil Roberts has a Cretan say of Venizelos: "He got us Smyrna, but that fool, Constantine, lost it for us by trampling too much on Turkish toes" (78).

32. On what is called the "Chanak crisis," when British and Turkish troops faced each other at the Hellespont in the autumn of 1922 and how close Britain came to war, see Winston Churchill, *World Crisis* 4:409–37. For E. M. Forster's response to the prospect of a war between Britain and Turkey in 1922, see Roessel, "Live Orientals and Dead Greeks."

33. On the Greek defeat in Asia Minor, see Michael Llewellyn Smith 266–311; Dakin, *Unification of Greece* 231–37; and Fromkin 540–57.

34. Clogg puts the figure killed in Smyrna at 30,000; see *Concise History of Greece* 97. On the destruction of Smyrna, see Housepian.

Chapter 8

1. Papers of Mark Lambert Bristol, box 3, in the Manuscript Collection of the Library of Congress, Washington, D.C.

2. Dos Passos has the character Anne Comfort in *Chosen Country* (1951) take a similar boat trip, but in this case "even being right there she couldn't feel their plight the way she had felt the plight of the French and the Belgians and the East

Side Jews; she couldn't feel it really: it was too awful and she didn't know the language" (240). For more on Dos Passos and the Asia Minor Disaster, see Roessel, "Rewriting Reminiscences."

3. Hemingway's description of Smyrna also floats like a wordy phantom over the account of the disaster in Edward Whittemore's *Sinai Tapestry* (1977). Whittemore included passages such as:

> People were pushed off the quay to drown. Others jumped in to commit suicide. Still others swam out to the ships.
> The English poured scalding water on the swimmers.
>
> (299)

In a sentence that sums up the meaning of "Smyrna" in English and American literature from 1920 to 1930, he approvingly quoted an American schoolteacher: "Some people here were guilty of unauthorized acts of humanity" (302).

4. On the stages of composition of *In Our Time*, see Hagemann, "A Collation, with Commentary, of the Five Texts of the Chapters in Hemingway's *In Our Time*" 443–58. On the date of composition of "On the Quai at Smyrna," see the article by Paul Smith. On the way that Hemingway honed his style of laconic irony in the interchapters of *In Our Time*, see Fenton 229–36. The vignettes that concern the war in Asia Minor comprise chap. 2, chap. 5, and "Envoi."

5. For Hemingway's stay in Constantinople, during much of which he was sick with malaria, see Reynolds 71–78. In the story "On the Quai at Smyrna," readers are led to conceive that a nameless narrator is telling the story through the author. In *Death in the Afternoon* (1932), however, Hemingway implies that he saw the mules that were pushed into the harbor at Smyrna when he says that the action of the Greeks in Smyrna initially made him think he would not like bullfights because of the suffering of the animals (11).

6. In another passage from "The Snows of Kilimanjaro," Hemingway presents the evacuation of the Greek refugees from Thrace as part of a Great War scenario in which the old men send others to die: "Nansen's secretary asking the old man if it were snow and the old man looking at it and saying, No, that's not snow. It's too early for snow. . . . But it was snow all right and he sent them on into it when he evolved the exchange of population. And it was snow they tramped along in until they died that winter" (6–7).

7. In a letter to Ezra Pound, Hemingway tersely explained the connection between the Greek vignettes: "The refugees leave Thrace, due to the Greek ministers, who are shot" (*Selected Letters* 92). On the confrontation between young and old in the years after the war, see Hynes, *War Imagined* 384, and as a motif in the work of Pound and Eliot, see Bush 267–74.

8. In "The Greek Revolt" (*Dateline: Toronto* 244–45) Hemingway briefly explained that the Royalist officers who replaced the Venizelist officers in 1920 were responsible for the defeat, but that explanation is absent from "The Snows of Kilimanjaro," where the officers are simply called "Constantine officers" without any indication of what that might mean. Even after the revolution, according to Hem-

ingway, the soldiers wanted to fight but were sold out by the government in Athens; see *Dateline: Toronto* 245. On the revolution in Greece led by Venizelist officers after the defeat and return of the army from Asia Minor, which led to the second abdication of King Constantine and the execution of six ministers of the Royalist government, see Michael Llewellyn Smith 312–29. On the continued rivalry between the Venizelists and Royalists in the years between the wars, see, among others, Clogg, *Concise History of Greece* 107–19.

9. On this passage of *The Waste Land* and the Asia Minor Disaster, see Roessel "'Mr. Eugenides, the Smyrna Merchant' and Post-War Politics in *The Waste Land*."

10. Hemingway ended the poem "They All Want Peace—What Is Peace?" with the lines: "And the Greek Patriarch / What about the Greek Patriarch?" (*Complete Poems* 64). Mackenzie provided a gloss to the lines when he explained that when the Turks entered Smyrna they "nailed the Greek archbishop to the doors of the Cathedral, and pulled out his beard" (*My Life and Times* 5.240). Hemingway felt that his readers would get the message that he wanted without the gloss. If readers did not know what exactly had happened to the Greek archbishop, they would know about the recent deaths of the Greeks. At the beginning of act 3 of William Saroyan's play *Love's Old Sweet Song*, a refugee from Smyrna says that he wants to return to the city, to which his son observes that his father "is *still* fighting the Turks" (115, my italics).

11. For more on this passage and other possible references to Asia Minor in Pound, see Roessel, "'The Repeat in History.'"

12. For example, John Dos Passos originally intended *Three Soldiers* to have the title *The Sack of Corinth*, and by employing the sack of the Greek city by the Romans in 146 BCE as a palimpsest for the Great War, he suggested that the world from 1914 to 1918 was a mirror image of the defeat of the Greek world by the Romans in the second century BCE. Independently of Dos Passos, and with greater depth, H. D. also used the sack of Corinth as a palimpsest for the Great War in her novel *Palimpsest* (1926). On this, see Gregory 59–66.

13. Their journalistic competition, especially at the Lausanne conference, where Sheridan snagged the only personal interview with Mussolini, might have been the reason that Hemingway later would imply in *Death in the Afternoon* that he, too, had been at Smyrna.

14. Clare Sheridan noted the "cases of childbirth on the quay, amid the crippled and blind and very aged who were trying to get away" (*West and East* 152), a detail that also appears in "On the Quai at Smyrna." But she does not mention the screaming that opens Hemingway's account.

15. George Horton, a prewar philhellene and author of such novels as *Like Another Helen* and *The Monk's Treasure*, was the American consul in Smyrna in 1922. His account of the destruction of the city's Christian population and heritage, *The Blight on Asia*, appeared in 1926. Horton lamented a "hardening of hearts that seems to have developed in the days since Gladstone—a less exalted and more shifty state of mind. This is partly due to the fact that men's sensibilities have been blunted by the Great War, and also in large measure a result of that materialism which is engulfing our civilization" (14). But in the rest of

the book, Horton reverted to the philhellenic and anti-Turkish rhetoric of an earlier age.

16. Some years later, she called Turkey "a beacon-light of the Oriental Renaissance" (*Turkish Kaleidoscope* 223). Greece was described as "dead, as all nations must die that have reached the height of self-expression" (*West and East* 164; see also her comments in *The Naked Truth* 305).

17. On Gibbs's career in the war and postwar years, see Hynes, *War Imagined* 183–88. Hynes noted, "Gibbs was not a [Wilfred] Owen or a Hemingway, but he had come to something like their sense of what was real in the world of war" (285). Gibbs's view of the catastrophe in Asia Minor did not differ greatly from Hemingway's; he just did not write about it as well.

18. Gibbs also included an account of the destruction of Smyrna in his novel *Cities of Refuge* (1936), which closely resembles "On the Quai at Smyrna" (115–17). It opens with two men on a British ship "watching and listening to the horror." It then continues, "On the quayside were crowds of Greeks and Armenians. They seemed to be running about. Their figures were dark against the glare of the fire. Screams of terror came from them, bloodcurdling across the water." The hero wants to do something, but his companion replies, "The World War was quite enough for one man's lifetime. I can't say I'm lusting for another" (116).

19. In the final volume of *The Four Winds of Love*, *North Wind of Love*, Ogilvie reiterated his Venizelist sympathies during the rebellion of Crete's Republicans against Kondylis and the Royalists (201). The book ends with Ogilvie marrying a "maid of Athens" from the fictional island of Lipsia, who had fallen in love with him twenty years earlier.

20. In Anne Duffield's *Stamboul Love* (1934), an Englishwoman marries one of Kemal's lieutenants, only to find him quickly "conforming to type." At the end of the book Beatrice flees from her Turkish husband with the help of her English lover, replicating the romance of liberation in a novel about the Young Turks by Vaka Brown. Dennis Wheatley's *Eunuch of Stamboul* (1935) has a similar plot with a more overt political message: a group of unreformed Ottomans plans to overthrow Kemal and recapture Thessaloniki. Marmaduke Pickthall's *The Early Hours* presented the Young Turks as the inheritors of the Ottoman legacy.

21. For 1923 as the beginning of a new era, see also Robert Byron's introduction to *The Byzantine Achievement* and Ash xiv. Female refugees from Smyrna appear as the heroines in French Strother's *Maid of Athens* (1932), Mary Richmond's *Maid of Athens* (1948), and Winston Graham's *Greek Fire* (1957). The first sixty-seven pages of Dora Bradford's novel *Greek Fire* provide a graphic description of the destruction of Smyrna, which is rather extraneous to the main "brigand" plot that follows.

22. Spender held to the view that Greece, both as a place and as a subject, transformed and ennobled Byron: "Wherever he touched on Greece, his mood was transformed." Greece turned the "satyr" into an "angel" (3).

23. For example, see Ratcliffe 9, Hunter 19, and Lancaster 88.

24. See Bradbury, esp. 96.

Chapter 9

1. In John Cousins's novel *The Secret Valleys* (1950), three friends who return to Crete to find a Greek guerrilla discover that he is now the last klepht in the mountains, and with his death we are to understand the end of an era. His daughter escapes from the police and a vengeful uncle with the help of one of the young Englishmen and, when last seen, is on her way to England with her admirer.

2. Greece makes a brief appearance in Osbert Sitwell's story "That Flesh Was Heir to . . . ," in which an English tourist spreads the plague wherever she goes. Sacheverell Sitwell wrote a poem about a visit to Mycenae called "Agamemnon's Tomb" (*Collected Poems* 457–65). But neither produced a book about Greece nearly as good as Sacheverell Sitwell's *Roumanian Journey*, a minor classic of its kind. In *Labels*, Waugh described brief visits to Athens and Crete (148–56, 135–38). Eisner found a fresh perspective in Waugh's brief account of his stay in Greece, which runs ten pages (*Labels* 148–58). It is true that Waugh did not simply go to the Mediterranean to gush at the sights, but neither had Twain more than fifty years earlier, and on the whole Twain's account is more interesting.

3. Eisner's explanation is that "by 1932 the country was bankrupt. It took a pretty serious tourist to go there" (178–79). But France was bankrupt after the First World War, and everyone went there because it was cheap. Something deeper, I believe, was at work.

4. See, among others, Winston Churchill's "The Greek Tragedy" in vol. 4 of *The World Crisis*; Cosmetatos, *The Tragedy of Greece* (1928); Byford-Jones, *Greek Trilogy* (1946); and Tsoucalis, *Greek Tragedy, 1821–1965* (1969). The title of this last book suggests that all of modern Greek history has been tragic. There is certainly a connection between the "tragic" view of Greece and efforts in the 1920s to revive, with performances of tragedy, the festivals of the ancient Greeks, such as the poet Angelos Sikelianos's Delphic Festivals in 1927 and 1930. Both, I would suggest, found some degree of impetus in the Smyrna Disaster.

5. In 1923, George Cram Cook told the villagers of Delphi, "We will take the plays that are in your lives and put them on up there. Too long that old theatre has wanted for the people of Delphi to return!" (Glaspell, *Road to the Temple* 312).

6. On the New Woman, see Hynes, *Edwardian Turn of Mind* 172–211, and Jane Eldredge Miller's *Rebel Women*. On Glaspell and feminism in general, see Makowsky.

7. Although the name of Dionysus appears in "The Faithless Shepherd," his spirit is largely missing from that work. The story, about a shepherd who joins a band of brigands preying upon the flocks, equates Dionysus with moments when "delight was too sharp" and with "ecstasy he did not quite know how to bear" (89). But these moments are, according to the story, reveries in nature that seem to have more to do with the Apollonian setting of the tale at Delphi than with Dionysian revelry.

8. See also his stories "On the Balcony" and "Being Kind to Titina," in which the disaster also features prominently. In addition to appearing in *The Vivisector*, a

refugee from Asia Minor also figures in *The Twyborn Affair*. A few of White's Greek stories deal with suffering but do not use Smyrna, like "The Full Belly," which is about famine during the German occupation, and "The Woman Who Was Not Allowed to Keep Cats." On the tragic perspective in White's work generally, see McCulloch.

9. See *The Byzantine Achievement* 21–22. *Romiosyne* remains a word over which to argue, but the best discussion of it in English, to my mind, remains Leigh Fermor's chapter "The Helleno-Romaic Dilemma and a Side-Track to Crete" in *Roumeli* 96–147.

10. On Robert Byron as a travel writer, see Fussell, *Abroad* 79–112.

11. Macaulay acknowledged that "there is no denying that Trapezuntines, like most Byzantines, did behave corruptly and cruelly and coldly very often, and like most empires they deserved to go under, but not so deeply under as Trebizond has gone, becoming Trabzon, with a dark squalid beach, and full of those who do not know the past, or that there ever was Trebizond or a Greek empire, and women all muffled up and hiding their faces, and the Byzantine churches mostly turned into mosques, or broken up, or used for army stores and things" (81). Here she replicates to some degree the early philhellenic rhetoric—that the period of Turkish domination was a complete break with the past and the end of the previous civilization.

12. On Merrill and Cavafy, see Yenser 114–17.

13. On Forster and Cavafy's initial reception in England, see Pinchin, *Alexandria Still* 98–111, and Bien, "Cavafy's Homosexuality and His Reputation outside Greece" 198–203.

14. On Cavafy's "sensual city," see Keeley, *Cavafy's Alexandria* 43–74.

15. A decadent Greece was a central element in the novels and stories of King (e.g., *The Dark Glasses* and *The Firewalkers*). King explored the territory of "Levantine" Greece most thoroughly in his novel *The Man on the Rock* (1957), the fictional autobiography of an attractive young Greek man who is picked up by a foreigner.

16. *Aleko* (1934) tells the story of an English teacher at a school on Spetses whose infatuation with a Greek pupil leads to the termination of his contract and the end of his marriage. The teacher realizes that Aleko's physical beauty does not reflect inner sublimity or emotional depth. His awakening to his homosexuality is, however, tied to the Greek setting of the story: "I have no illusions about Aleko. The glory of young limbs is for the rock and island, for the wild nature of which it is a part" (69). The book caused a scandal and has become rather hard to find.

17. Plomer later revised this poem, and in his *Collected Poems* this stanza reads:

> See, in the exsiccate light of Attica
> The pepper-tree garden where last night by full moon
> An old woman disturbed our intimacy
> To sell us three pinks with long stems.
>
> (66)

I find the first version more Cavafian in spirit and have cited that in the text.

18. The one manly Greek in Plomer appears in the poem "The Philhellene." In this piece, a rich American woman takes up with a Greek man whose "favorite tense, is the Present Erotic." After the Greek gets a hold of all her money and leaves her, she wanders around Athens in a dazed state. Plomer may be alluding to his own relationship with the sailor Niko, who Plomer described as a tender little lamb until Niko robbed him and left him with a case of gonorrhea.

19. The Greek from Alexandria in "Nausicaa" is a dandy, while the people of Corfu are so "decadent" that "one is not prepared for the degree of degeneration as that in which they live and move" (*Child of Queen Victoria* 149–50).

20. Christopher Brennan's novel *Massacre of Innocents* (1967) makes an explicit connection between Alexandria and Greece. The book opens with the narrator on a boat between Alexandria and Athens pondering a passage of Cavafy.

21. Christopher Isherwood went to Berlin, he tells us, because he "couldn't relax sexually with a member of his own class and nation. He needed working class foreigners" (*Christopher and His Kind* 10; see also the comments of Fussell, *Abroad* 115–16). See also Mark Doty's collection of poems, *My Alexandria*, which brings the atmosphere of the Greek poet to New York. Isherwood never mentioned Cavafy in *Down There on a Visit*, but it seems likely that he knew of the Greek poet. Plomer and Isherwood became friends in 1929 and met in London in 1932—after Plomer's trip to Athens but before Isherwood's stay on the Greek island of St. Gregory in 1933. The tone of Isherwood's account, however, owes little to Cavafy and more, as I have suggested, to Firbank.

22. A briefer, more autobiographical, version of Isherwood's sojourn in Greece with Francis Turvill-Petre, the original for the fictional Ambrose, appears in *Christopher and His Kind* 107–12. Stephen Spender visited Turvill-Petre on St. Gregory in 1936 and described what he saw there in a letter to Isherwood; see *Letters to Christopher* 114–17.

23. As Roger Hinks asked when he arrived in Greece to work at the British Council in the early 1950s, "As the Hellas of the Philhellenes—Byronic Greece—is bankrupt, and the Byzantine Greece has always been publicly suspect—even to English Levant-fanciers like Robert Byron, what can we put in their place? How can we give Greece a new look?" Hinks suggested a "Mannerist Greece" of "the empty centre, the distilled perspective, and the lurid lighting" (194). Greece was acquiring its new look even as Hinks posed his question.

Conclusion

1. See also Lancaster 63. In *The Children of Thetis*, Christopher Kininmouth (214–16) does not cite *The Colossus of Maroussi*, but, as Avi Sharon informed me, took Durrell's concept of the "heraldic universe" almost wholesale from its pages; see *Colossus of Maroussi* 95–97. See also the mention of Katsimbalis as "the best-known figure in Athens" in King's *Firewalkers* (9). See also Durrell's reference to Katsimbalis in his poem "Mythology":

All of my favorite characters have been
Out of all proportion
Some living in villas by railways
Some like Katsimbalis heard but seldom seem.
                    (*Collected Poems* 115)

2. See *Inventing Paradise: The Greek Journey 1937–47* (1999). The point was made as early as 1950 by Kenneth Young, who said, "In the last twenty years, artists and writers have skipped the enchantments of France and Italy, and have gone purposefully to Greece. They have 'discovered' Greece—or, more accurately, rediscovered it" (53). The first writers whom he adduces to show the emergence of a new Greece free from inhibitions are Durrell and Miller.

In *Inventing Paradise*, Keeley described in detail the friendship and interrelations among Miller, Durrell, Seferis, and Katsimbalis in Greece during 1939, and those who want to follow that story further should look at that volume. Keeley also made extensive use of Miller's notebook of his trip to Greece, which was published in 1973 as *First Impressions of Greece*. Since that work appeared beyond the boundaries of this study, and Keeley has discussed at length the differences between the notebook and *The Colossus of Maroussi*, I have refrained from going over that ground again here.

3. Philip Sherrard, one of those involved in the creation of a "new Greece," has also called attention to the central role of Katsimbalis in the discovery of a "living Greece"; see 68–69.

4. Lancaster, for example, used a quotation from Durrell's poem "To Argos" as an epigraph for his chapter on the Argolid (111) and later referred to *Prospero's Cell*; also see the mention of Durrell in Martin Sherman's play *A Madhouse in Goa* (9). But specific references to Durrell are far fewer than those to Miller. Durrell's Greece, one should note, is much tamer than that of Miller. One reason for this might be Durrell's decision to promote silence as one of the dominant, if not *the* dominant, aspects of Greek island life. The opening epigraph of *Prospero's Cell* from *The Tempest* reads, "No tongue: all eyes: be silent," and silence is an important presence throughout the book. "At such moments we never speak," Durrell wrote of himself and his wife. Durrell's choice of silence as the hallmark of his Corfu was, I believe, largely literary in origin. His friend Miller had depicted Greece as a world of noise and conversation, and he wanted to offer something different. It was Durrell, after all, who wrote Miller the letter about Katsimbalis calling the cocks, but those sorts of loud, extemporaneous episodes are largely absent from *Prospero's Cell* and *Reflections on a Marine Venus*.

5. The word *Dionysiac* began to show up more often in writing about Greece after 1940. For example, in 1946, Derek Patmore said that the men dancing in a taverna on Aegina "seemed entirely unself-conscious and rapt in what was almost a dionysiac pleasure" ("Notes in a Greek Journal" 285). See also Leigh Fermor's comment that the landscape of Hydra is "violent and Dionysiac" ("Background of Nikos Ghika" 42).

6. On the madness Miller found in Greece, see also the comments of Katsimbalis in Miller's book about Yannopoulos, a poet "greater than your Walt Whitman and all the American poets combined. He was a madman, yes, like all great Greek fellows." Yannopoulos, Katsimbalis went on to say, "became so intoxicated with the Greek language, the Greek philosophy, the Greek sky, the Greek mountains, the Greek sea, the Greek vegetables, even, that he killed himself." Katsimbalis then concluded: "He wasn't crazy—he was *mad*. There's a difference. . . . He was out of proportion" (67–68).

7. Charmian Clift also contrasted life on Hydra with "the rat-race of modern commercialism" in *Peel Me a Lotus* 19.

8. Osbert Lancaster remarked that after the Second World War, "a new contingent . . . arrived, easily to be distinguished from the other [classical or Byzantine enthusiasts] by the erratic and seemingly purposeless nature of their course and by the fact that they are entirely unencumbered by guide-books or intellectual impedimenta of any sort" (7–8).

9. See also Fowles's remarks on the influence of Lawrence on *The Magus* in "Behind *The Magus*" 72.

10. In *Children of Thetis*, Christopher Kininmouth asserted that "on islands one expects to see Pan" (14). In 1994, Fiona Pitt-Keithley went in search of Pan in the Mediterranean in *The Pan Principle* but reported that the Greeks were the least priapic men she found.

11. In *Inventing Paradise* 139–52, Keeley has a short but interesting discussion of Greek women in *The Colossus of Maroussi*. Melina Mercouri played a female "Zorba" character as a prostitute in the film *Never on Sunday* (1960), but female Zorbas were rather rare in literature (one appears in Keeley's novel *The Gold-Hatted Lover*). Usually, both Greeks and foreigners would have sex with foreign women in Greece, as in Merrill's *The (Diblos) Notebook*, where the foreign narrator and his Greek acquaintances share a Scandinavian woman during a drunken orgy.

12. In Christopher Brennan's novel *The Massacre of the Innocents*, for example, the gay narrator says that with Greek youths he could be "physically dominated, but not, in any way, mentally so" (106).

13. Louis MacNeice, according to Stallworthy, was put off by the flamboyance of Katsimbalis and his mock-Katsimbalis act (391).

14. Miller made somewhat the same point about domestication versus wildness when he said that, unlike the Greek, the Frenchman "puts walls around his talk, as he does around his garden: he puts limits about everything in order to feel at home," but a Greek "has not walls around him: he gives and takes without stint" (32, 36). See also the comparison between Italian and Greek olive trees in Warner, *Views of Attica* 10; and see Lancaster 9–10 on landscape generally.

15. The pastoral picture of the Minoans was already in place by the late 1920s, for Waugh was certainly playing with it when he mentioned the "barbarities of Minoan culture" and presented the Minoans as if they were variants of the bloody Mycenaeans (*Labels* 136–37). On the attitude toward the Minoans in English writing in the 1940s, see also Cecil Day-Lewis's poem "Statuette: Late Minoan."

16. In Durrell's *Cefalú*, also published as *The Dark Labyrinth*, a group of tourists finds itself lost in a cave labyrinth in the east of Greece; each meets the Minotaur in his or her own way. After the initial Cretan setting, the story becomes highly allegorical, but at least two of the characters find their way back to a land before time began.

17. For example, in his poem "A Kind of a Philhellene," written in the early 1950s, John Fowles remarked on English-speaking expatriates who found the "essence of Greece" in the poetry of Seferis, the paintings of Ghika, and whatever Katsimbalis "said last week" (*Poems* 13). It was Miller's book that had guided these foreigners to Seferis, Ghika, and Katsimbalis. On Ghika, see *The Colossus of Maroussi* 52 and the essays on the painter by Spender and Fermor in *Ghika: Paintings, Drawings, Sculptures*. John Lehmann said that he learned about the Greek poets Seferis, Odysseus Elytis, and Angelos Sikelianos "owing to a chance meeting with Demetrios Capetanakis at Cambridge during 1940–41" and that Capetanakis provided translations of these poets for Lehmann's journal *New Writing* (*Ample Proposition* 58; see also Young's mention of Capetanakis, 56–57). But neither Durrell, Miller, nor Spender mention Capetanakis, and his influence does not appear to be extensive nor lasting. Further, when Lehmann traveled to Greece in 1946, he met Katsimbalis, with whom he visited Seferis on Poros; he then went to see Ghika at Hydra. He also had a chance meeting with Sikelianos in a taverna, but he never mentioned meeting Elytis, although he said that when he arrived in Athens in 1946, he quoted from Elytis's "The Age of Blue Memory" (*Ample Proposition* 59). He took, in essence, the Miller tour of Greek intellectuals. In the first stanza of the poem "A Spring Wind" from 1945, Bernard Spencer said:

> Upon this table
> Elytis's poems lie
> Uttering the tangle of the sea, the "breathing caves"
> And the fling of the Aegean waves.
>
> (48)

One is struck by the passage in part because it is rather rare to find the poet Odysseus Elytis, who won the Nobel Prize in 1979, invoked by an English or American writer before 1960. In the fourth stanza, "haunted Seferis, smiling, playing with beads" makes an appearance. That is not surprising at all. If a Greek writer received mention, it was usually Seferis.

18. For a discussion of what the Greek-less Miller might have known about Seferis's poetry, see Keeley, *Inventing Paradise* 60–70.

19. For more on this, see Keeley, *Inventing Paradise* 54–55.

20. I am grateful to Sharon for letting me see this paper before publication and for pointing me to Stephen Spender's essay "Brilliant Athens and Us."

21. The painter John Craxton asserted that "some painters can make their reality out of myth. By going to Greece I was trying to make a myth out of reality" (7).

22. See Keeley's discussion about how Seferis "has been particularly vulnerable to the prejudices of his English-speaking interpreters" in *Modern Greek Poetry*

68–86, as well as his perspective on a related prejudice, for some of the same reasons, for viewing Elytis as the "poet of the Aegean" (131–48).

23. This letter, dated March 29, 1944, is now in the George Seferis Archive in the Gennadius Library, Athens. Speaking of Seferis, Peter Levi said, "As a poet he belongs undoubtedly to the modern movement; he knew and loved the work of Laforgue before he ever met Eliot; but there is a directness in his poems unique in Europe, I think. Yeats is hysterical and Eliot is obscure by comparison" (*Hill of Kronos* 34).

24. The letter is dated November 26, 1941, and is now in the George Seferis Archive, Gennadius Library, Athens.

25. This is also true of John Lehmann's poems "The Road to Rhamnous" and "Greek Landscape with Figures" and Craxton's comments that he was drawn to paint "certain features of landscape, and a human identity in it, an inhabited landscape if you like, which were like tokens for Greece" (6). See also Francis King's comment that tourists should not go to Greece primarily for the ancient sites but for "its unparalleled landscape and its unparalleled people" (*Introducing Greece* 31).

26. The last lines of Durrell's "To Argos"—"The hyssop and the vinegar have lost their meaning, / And this is what breaks the heart"—seem to suggest a more problematic ending for "we the endowed who pass here/ With the assurance of visitors in rugs" who "Can raise from the menhir no ghost/ By the cold sound English idioms" (106). But as Keeley points out in *Inventing Paradise* (120–21), the despair is only for those who look for their meaning in the landscape and not in the living beings around them. For the fate of the English "well endowed" in Greece depends on whether they understand that "Our true parenthood rests with the eagle / We recognize him turning over his vaults" and in the shepherd with "dark eyes wearing the crowsfoot." As one of the English who had learned this lesson, it seems to me, Durrell suggested that he had, again, entered a sacred circle.

27. Elsewhere in his poem "Letter to Seferis the Greek," Durrell reprised the idea that life in Greece focuses on the personal and private: "can one say that / Any response is enough for those / Who have a woman, an island and a tree?" (*Collected Poems* 101).

28. On the difference between the film and the book, see Bien, *Nikos Kazantzakis: Novelist* 11–12. In his article "Greece Today," Kazantzakis presented Zorba as a talker like Katsimbalis: "He used to talk and talk, and when words could no longer encompass what he wanted to say, he would jump up and begin to dance" (70). The film, by making the dancing visual, diminished the fact that the Greece of Katsimbalis and of Zorba was like a siren song—a charm of words.

29. Durrell opened *Bitter Lemons*, a book about Cyprus during the EOKA uprising, with a similar statement: "This is not a political book, but simply an impressionistic study of the moods and atmospheres of Cyprus during the troubled years 1953–6." Durrell went on to say that he had concentrated on individuals, not policies, because he wanted to keep the book "free from the smaller contempts, in the hope that it would remain readable long after the current misunderstandings have been resolved as they must sooner or later" (11). No one would have tried to write a book about the "moods and impressions" of Spain from 1935

to 1939 or about Nazi Germany without acknowledging that politics was a crucial factor in the equation. One could, it seems, look at the Greek world with a "long" view that was beyond political concerns.

30. Gore Vidal said of the first group of American artists and writers to visit Rome after World War II: "Rome was strange to all of us. For one thing, Italy had been sealed off not only by war but by fascism. Since the early thirties, few English or American artists knew Italy well" (150). Greek islands function as places outside of the "real world" and even the world of the narrative in Storm Jameson's *One Ulysses Too Many* (1958; see, e.g., 39–41) and Durrell's *Justine* (1957).

31. Keeley commented that as "far as one can gather from his travel writing and his letters, Durrell's view of Greek politics was never very broad or deep, and though he celebrated the courage and vigor of the Greeks' resistance to the Italian invasion in 1941, he subsequently appears to have shared something of the superficial cynicism of those Western observers who could not fathom or were uninterested in penetrating the complexities of a political landscape that often seemed alien to them in the conflicting passions it occasioned, especially in times of crisis" (*Inventing Paradise* 229–30). In *First Impressions of Greece*, Miller identified the political exile he met on Spetses as Seferis's brother-in-law Constantine Tsatsos; see Keeley, *Inventing Paradise* 90–91.

32. Birtles, a committed leftist, had a different view of Seferis. Noting Seferis's "studied air of intellectual evasion" and his "unwillingness to see the Fascist implications" of Eliot's poetry, he predicted the poet would support "some form of retrograde authoritarianism" (88). One hopes that Birtles lived long enough to read Seferis's denunciation of the Greek junta in 1969.

33. For nonfictional works from the periods of the Second World War and the Greek Civil War, see Eisner 199–215; for fiction see Karanikas 227–42. What was written generally recalled the Byronic tradition of liberation from the previous century. Glenway Westcott's *Apartment in Athens* depicted the sufferings of the Athenians under the brutal Nazi occupation, but see Karanikas on its "total lack of ethnicity" (236). Cherakis's *Hand of Alexander*, Sedgewick's *Tell Sparta*, and Mary Richmond's *Maid of Athens* are all variations on the romance of liberation. George Weller's *Crack in the Column* is the most politically sophisticated in this vein, but it too invoked the Greek War of Independence with an epigraph from the famous American philhellene Samuel Gridley Howe. Winston Graham's *Greek Fire* offered a Greek romance of liberation in which the role of the Turks is taken by the Communists.

34. In *An Affair of the Heart*, Dilys Powell divided her narrative into sections entitled "First Sight," "Estrangement," "Reconciliation," and "Ever After." "First Sight" provided a brief account of a prewar idyll in Greece with her archaeologist husband with some similarities to *Prospero's Cell*; it ended with his death in 1936. At first one might think that "Estrangement" was an attempt to come to terms with this loss, but it turns out to be a disenchantment with Greece in 1945 because politics and the civil war have come between her and the Greece of her memory. She departed thinking it might be "time for me to get Greece out of my blood" (55). Her next visit went better. There were still hardships, but in her

touchstone village of Perachora "the war is over. Nobody speaks of it any more. . . . now they go back to their old ways, now they concern themselves with today and tomorrow. They grow old, they die, but they are the same" (146)—as if that were what they were *not* doing in 1945. Because the old ways have returned, Powell can once again find the Greece she loved. What estranged her from Greece, it seems, was a period in which she could not avoid Greek politics and could not pretend that it did not affect her relationships with the people of the country.

35. The idea appears in fiction as well. Everything "seems to be stripped away by this light, stripped away to bare bones," says Kate in Johnston's novel *Closer to the Sun*. "You see people all the way through, as if they're transparent almost. And you see yourself the same way" (167).

36. See MacNiven 166–214 for Durrell's whereabouts in 1937 and 1938; and on the character of Gideon, see 306 and 722 n. 2.

37. Johnston's *The Cyprian Woman* (1955), which uses Aphrodite instead of Dionysus as the presiding deity in a Greece of the libido, also does not deconstruct the efficacy of personal discovery in Greece.

38. Thomas Fisher plausibly suggests that at the end of *The Magus* readers are asked to "decide whether Nicholas has grown adequately from his experiences on Phraxos, or if he is even capable of growth" (61). What the novel does not ask us to decide is whether the experiences on Phraxos do in fact promote personal growth; that seems to be assumed.

39. See, for example, Nicholas Urfe's description in *The Magus* of his first encounter with "the stripping-to-essentials" sunlight and with the "Circe-like quality of Greece; the quality that makes it unique. In England we live in a very muted, calm, domesticated relationship with what remains of our natural landscape and its soft northern light; in Greece landscape and light are so beautiful, so all-present, so intense, so wild, that the relationship is immediately love-hatred, one of passion" (49). In Merrill's novel, Orson offers the following toast: "I give you the light of Greece. . . . Once you have had your vision no lesser world is tolerable" (*The [Diblos] Notebook* 113), and that sentiment about the hold of the place on the characters runs throughout the book.

40. In *Clean Straw for Nothing*, the narrator muses on his personal and professional failure: "Is it the island that has done this to us? Or only ourselves? I don't think we can find redemption here. It must be elsewhere" (145). Perhaps Johnston is the only one who could ask this question because he spent a decade on a Greek island with only a six-month hiatus in England.

41. Barry Unsworth's first novel, *The Greeks Have a Word for It* (1967), provided a look at the several kinds of English and Americans who came to Athens in the early 1960s. The book is something of an apprentice work and has never been reprinted.

42. Thessaloniki was the setting for Daniel Nash's novel, *My Son Is in the Mountains* (1955), which is based loosely on the killing of the journalist George Polk (on which see Keeley, *The Salonika Bay Murder*).

43. Charmian Clift also spoke out strongly against the junta in her article "The Voices of Greece" (*Being Alone with Oneself* 33–36). Clift, who lived in

Greece for ten years, never indicated such an interest in Greek politics in *Mermaid Singing*, *Peel Me a Lotus*, or *Honour's Mimic*, but something like the coup of 1967 had not occurred during Clift's stay in Greece.

44. On Seferis's declaration against the junta in March 1969, see Levi, *Hill of Kronos* 151–53, who provides the full text of the statement in English. The aging Katsimbalis's star may have faded a bit at this time because of his sympathy with, if not his support for, the military government; see Levi 140.

45. In the introduction to of a collection of poems by Ritsos published in England, *Selected Poems* translated by Nikos Strangos (1974), Peter Bien remarked "how extraordinary" it was "that Yannis Ritsos, who for decades was acknowledged inside Greece as one of the undeniably major figures of her literary revival . . . should be so new to the English-speaking world" (11; in 1971 Strangos had translated a smaller selection of Ritsos's work from 1968 to 1970). Bien does not consider that the English-speaking world might be more ready to accept Ritsos because of the new interest in the Greek political situation. The early 1970s saw the real emergence of translations of Ritsos in English; in addition to the translations by Strangos, Amy Mims brought out a translation called *Eighteen Short Songs of the Bitter Motherland*. A collection of poems published in the United States in 1969, *Romiossini and Other Poems*, translated by Georgakas and Paidoussi, explicitly made the connection between Ritsos's detention and the appearance of the book; the introduction includes a request that the reader write to the U.S. State Department demanding Ritsos's release, for a "poet's life might be saved." I would not want to push the point, however, since the first volumes in English of the work of Odysseus Elytis also began to appear in the early 1970s, and Elytis could not be described as the poet of prison and house arrest. Still, the coup does seem to have had an effect on the dominance of Seferis as "the poet of Greece." A description of Ritsos's career up to 1973, including his detention in a camp from 1948 to 1952 and his subsequent imprisonment by the junta in 1967, which was changed a year later to house arrest, can be found, among other places, in Bien's introduction to Ritsos's *Selected Poems*.

46. See Durrell's poem "Byron," written in 1944 during the Second World War; Ian MacNiven correctly noted that a "deliberate ambiguity" in the first person pronoun serves to conflate the present and past poets (273). But writing from the "headquarters of a war" like the one to which he referred in the poem, Durrell communed with a Byronic spirit far different from the one invoked in "At Corinth" within the magic circle. He was, rather, looking back to the Byron of Missolonghi for solidarity in a time of war and disenchantment.

BIBLIOGRAPHY

Abbott, G. F. *Tale of a Tour of Macedonia*. London: Edward Arnold, 1903.
———. *Turkey, Greece, and the Great Powers*. London: Robert Scott, 1916.
———, ed. *Greece in Evolution*. London: Fisher Unwin, 1909.
About, Edmond. *La Grèce contemporaine*. Translated as *Greece and the Greeks of the Present Day*. London: Hamilton Adams, 1855.
———. *Le roi des montagnes*. Paris: Librairie de L. Hachette, 1857. Citations in the text are from *The King of the Mountains*. Tr. R. Davey. New York: P. F. Collier, 1902.
Abrams, M. H. *Natural Supernaturalism: Tradition and Revolution in Romantic Literature*. New York: Norton, 1971.
Alexander, Peter. *William Plomer*. Oxford: Oxford University Press, 1989.
Allut, Mélanie. *Les adieux du klephte*. Paris: Grius, 1831.
Anderson, Isabel. *A Yacht in the Mediterranean Seas*. Boston: Marshall Jones, 1931.
Anderson, Patrick. *Dolphin Days: A Writer's Notebook of Mediterranean Pleasures*. New York: Dutton, 1964.
Andrews, Kevin. *The Flight of Ikaros: Travels in Greece during a Civil War*. 1959. Reprint, London: Penguin, 1984.
Angelomatis-Tsougarakis, Helen. *The Eve of the Greek Revival: British Travelers' Perception of Early Nineteenth Century Greece*. London: Routledge, 1990.
An Appeal for a New Nation. By the author of "Mainoc." London: B. M. Pickering, 1876.
Arnold, Matthew. "Byron." In *Poetry and Criticism of Matthew Arnold*, 347–62. Ed. A. Dwight Cullen. Boston: Houghton Mifflin, 1961.
———. *The Poems of Matthew Arnold*, 2d ed. Ed. Kenneth Allott and Miriam Allott. London: Longmans, 1979.
Ash, John. *A Byzantine Journey*. New York: Random House, 1995.
Asselineau, Charles. *Mon cousin Don Quixote: Physiognomie d'un philhelléne*. Paris: Poulet, 1858.
Athanasia die schönen Griechen aus Samos. Leipzig: Rein'sche Buchandlung, 1829.
Athanassoglou-Kalmyer, Nina. *French Images of the Greek War of Independence, 1821–1830*. New Haven, Conn.: Yale University Press, 1989.
Auden, W. H. *Collected Poems*. Ed. Edward Mendelson. New York: Vintage, 1991.

Auden, W. H. "Don Juan." In *The Dyer's Hand and Other Essays*, 386–402. New York: Random House, 1962.

———. "George Gordon Byron." In *Prose*, vol. 1, 487–89. Ed. Edward Mendelson. Princeton, N.J.: Princeton University Press, 1996.

———. Introduction to *The Collected Poems of C. P. Cavafy*, vii–xv. Tr. Rae Dalven. 1961. Reprint, New York: Harcourt Brace Jovanovich, 1968.

———, with Louis MacNeice. *Letters from Iceland*. 1937. Reprint, New York: Random House, 1969.

Augustinos, Olga. *French Odysseys: Greece in French Travel Writing from the Renaissance to the Romantic Era*. Baltimore: Johns Hopkins University Press, 1994.

Austin, Alfred. *The Autobiography of Alfred Austin*. 2 vols. London: Macmillan, 1911.

———. *Lyrical Poems*. London: Macmillan, 1896.

Baird, Henry. *Modern Greece: A Narrative of Residence and Travel in that Country*. New York: Harper, 1856.

Baring, Maurice. *Letters from the Near East, 1909 and 1912*. London: Smith, Elder, 1913.

Barrington, Emilie Isabel. *Through Greece and Dalmatia*. London: Adam and Charles Black, 1912.

Barrows, Samuel. *The Isles and Shrines of Greece*. London: S. Low, 1898.

Barthélemy, Jean Jacques. *Voyages du jeune Anacharsis en Grèce*. 4 vols. 1788. Translated as *Travels of Anacharsis the Younger in Greece*. 6 vols. London, 1817.

Bartlett, Ellis Ashland. *Battlefields of Thessaly*. London: John Murray, 1897.

Baxter, W. E. *New Greece*. Edinburgh: Morrison and Gibbs, 1879.

Bayard, William. *Address to the Committee of the Greek Fund of the City of New York*. New York, 1825.

Beaton, Roderick. *An Introduction to Modern Greek Literature*. Oxford: Oxford University Press, 1994.

Beckford, William. *Vathek*. 1786. Reprint, New York: John Day, 1928.

Beckson, Karl. *London in the 1890s: A Cultural History*. New York: Norton, 1992.

Beerbohm, Max. *The Letters of Max Beerbohm*. Ed. Rupert Hart-Davis. London: John Murray, 1988.

Benjamin, S. G. W. *The Turk and the Greek; or, Creeds, Races, Society, and Scenery in Turkey, Greece, and the Isles of Greece*. New York: Hurd and Houghton, 1867.

Bennett, Arnold. *Mediterranean Scenes*. London: Cassell, 1928.

Bennett, Jack. *Gallipoli*. New York: St. Martin's, 1981.

Benson, E. F. *As We Were: A Victorian Peepshow*. London: Longmans, Green, 1933.

———. *The Capsina*. New York: Harper, 1899.

———. *Crescent and Iron Cross*. London: Hodder and Stoughton, 1918.

———. *Limitations*. New York: Harper, 1896.

———. *The Princess Sophia*. London: Heineman, 1900.

———. *The Vintage: A Romance of the Greek War of Independence*. 1898. Reprint, London: Heineman, 1912.

Bent, J. Theodore. *The Cyclades; or, Life among the Insular Greeks*. London: Longmans, Green, 1885.

Bernard, Henry. *The Shade of the Balkans*. London: David Nutt, 1904.

Bewell, Alan. "The Political Implications of Keats's Classicist Aesthetics." *Studies in Romanticism* 25.2 (1986): 220–29.

Bickford-Smith, R. A. H. *Cretan Sketches*. London: Richard Bentley, 1898.

———. *Greece under King George*. London: Richard Bentley, 1893.

Bien, Peter. "Cavafy's Homosexuality and His Reputation outside Greece." *Journal of Modern Greek Studies* 8 (1990): 197–212.

———. *Nikos Kazantzakis: Novelist*. Bristol: Bristol Classical Press, 1989.

Bigham, Clive. *With the Turkish Army in Thessaly*. London: Macmillan, 1897.

Bikelas, Demetrios. *Loukis Laras: Reminiscences of a Chiote Merchant during the War of Independence*. Tr. John Gennadius. London: Macmillan, 1883.

———. *Tales from the Aegean*. Tr. Leonard Opdycke. Chicago: McClurg, 1894.

Birkenhead, Frederick Winston Furneaux Smith, Lord. *Rudyard Kipling*. New York: Random House, 1978.

Birtles, Bert. *Exiles in the Aegean: A Personal Narrative of Greek Travel and Politics*. London: Victor Gollancz, 1938.

Blacquiere, Edward. *Narrative of a Second Visit to Greece, including Facts Connected with the Last Days of Lord Byron*. London: Whittaker, 1825.

Black, William. *Briseis*. London: Simpson, Low, Marston, 1896.

Blake, Robert. *Disraeli*. London: Eyre and Spottiswoode, 1966.

———. *Disraeli's Grand Tour*. London: Weidenfeld & Nicolson, 1982.

Bloom, Harold. *The Ringers in the Tower: Studies in the Romantic Tradition*. Chicago: University of Chicago Press, 1971.

Blunt, Wilfred Scaven. *The Secret History of the English Occupation of Egypt*. 1895. Reprint, New York: Knopf, 1922.

Bois, Jules. "De la Grèce antique à la Grèce nouvelle." L'Hellénisme (Nov. 1910): 589–620.

Bold, Alan. *MacDiarmid*. London: John Murray, 1988.

Bonsal, Stephen. *Suitors and Suppliants: The Little Nations at the Versailles Conference*. New York: Prentice Hall, 1946.

Bornstein, George. *The Transformation of Romanticism in Yeats, Eliot and Stevens*. Chicago: University of Chicago Press, 1976.

Bourdon, Georges. "The Policy of Victory in the East and Its Results." In *Hellas and Unredeemed Hellenism*, 1–32. New York: Publications of the American Hellenic Society, 1920.

Boxley, D. A. "Whipping the Turks: Stephen Crane's Orientalism." *American Literary Realism* 31 (1998): 1–11.

Boyle, Kay. *Collected Poems of Kay Boyle*. Port Townsend, Wash.: Copper Canyon Press, 1992.

Bracco, Rosa Maria. *Merchants of Hope: British Middlebrow Writers and the First World War, 1919–1939*. Providence, R.I.: Berg, 1993.

Bradbury, Malcolm. "The Cities of Modernism." In *Modernism, 1890–1930*, 95–103. Ed. Malcolm Bradbury and James McFarlane. New York: Penguin, 1975.

Bradfield, Henry J. *The Atheniad*. London: Marsh and Miller, 1830.

———. *Tales of the Cyclades*. London: William Kidd, 1830.

Bradford, Dora. *Greek Fire: A Tale of the Levant*. London: George Harrap, 1935.

Brailsford, Henry Noel. *The Broom of the War God*. New York: D. Appleton, 1898.

Brennan, Christopher. *The Massacre of the Innocents*. London: Hart-Davis, 1967.

Bright, John. "The Letter of John Bright, Esq., M.P., on the War." London: F. G. Cash, 1854. Reprinted in *The Crimean War: Pro and Con*, 1–16. New York: Garland, 1973.

Brooke, Rupert. *Letters of Rupert Brooke*. Ed. Geoffrey Keynes. London: Faber and Faber, 1968.

———. *The Poetical Works of Rupert Brooke*. Ed. Geoffrey Keynes. London: Faber and Faber, 1946.

Brooks, James Gordon. *The Rivals of Este and Other Poems*. New York: Harper, 1829.

Brooks, Van Wyck. *The Confident Years: 1885–1913*. New York: Dutton, 1955.

———. *The Dream of Arcadia: American Writers in Italy*. New York: Dutton, 1958.

Brophy, Brigid. *Prancing Novelist: A Defense of Fiction in the Form of a Critical Biography in Praise of Ronald Firbank*. New York: Barnes and Noble, 1973.

Broumas, Olga. *Beginning with O*. New Haven, Conn.: Yale University Press, 1977.

Brouzas, C. G. "Byron's Maid of Athens: Her Family and Surroundings." West Virginia University Bulletin, *Philological Papers* 7 (June 1949): 1–65.

———. "Teresa Macri: The Maid of Athens." West Virginia University Bulletin, *Philological Papers* 5 (May 1947): 1–31.

Brown, Demetra Vaka. *Bribed to be Born*. New York: Exposition Press, 1951.

———. *A Child of the Orient*. Boston: Houghton Mifflin, 1914.

———. *Constantine: King and Traitor*. New York: John Lane, 1918.

———, with Kenneth Brown. *The First Secretary*. New York: B. W. Dodge, 1907.

———. *The Grasp of the Sultan*. New York: Cassell, 1917.

———. *The Heart of the Balkans*. Boston: Houghton Mifflin, 1916.

———. *In the Heart of German Intrigue*. Boston: Houghton Mifflin, 1918.

———, with Kenneth Brown. *In Pawn to a Throne*. New York: John Lane, 1919.

———. *In the Shadow of Islam*. Boston: Houghton Mifflin, 1911.

———, with Aristides Phoutides. *Modern Greek Stories*. New York: Duffield, 1920.

Brown, James William. *Blood Dance*. New York: Harcourt Brace Jovanovich, 1993.

Brown, Kenneth. "Demetra Vaka." *Athene* 9 (1948): 16.

Brown, W. C. "Byron and English Interest in the Near East." *Studies in Philology* 34 (1937): 55–64.

———. "The Popularity of Travel Books about the Near East." *Philological Quarterly* 15 (1936): 70–80.

Browning, Elizabeth Barrett. *Poetical Works of Elizabeth Barrett Browning*. New York: Macmillan, 1899.

Bryant, William Cullen. *Letters from the East*. New York: Putnam, 1869.

———. *The Poetical Works of William Cullen Bryant*. 2 vols. Ed. Parke Godwin. 1883. Reprint, New York: Russell & Russell, 1967.

Buckstone, John Baldwin. *The Revolt of the Greeks; or, The Maid of Athens*. 1824. Reprint, London: Dicks Plays, 1887.

Bullen, J. B. *The Myth of the Renaissance in Nineteenth-Century Literature*. Oxford: Oxford University Press, 1994.

Bulwer, Henry. *An Autumn in Greece*. London: John Ebers, 1826.

Bunce, Oliver Bell. "Marco Bozzaris: The Grecian Hero." Manuscript in the Widener Library at Harvard University with the note "produced in 1849."

Burges, George. *The Son of Erin; or, The Cause of the Greeks: A Play in Five Acts*. London: J. Miller, 1823.

Burgin, G. B. *The Man Behind: A Turkish Romance*. London: Hutchinson, 1923.

Burrows, Ronald. *Annual Meeting of the Anglo-Hellenic League, Thursday July 15, 1917*. London: Publications of the Anglo-Hellenic League, 1917.

———. *The New Greece*. London: Publications of the Anglo-Hellenic League, 1914.

———. "Philhellenism in England and France." *Contemporary Review* (Feb. 1916): 161–64.

———. "The Unity of the Greek Race." *Contemporary Review* (Feb. 1919): 153–64.

Bush, Ronald. *The Genesis of Ezra Pound's Cantos*. Princeton, N.J.: Princeton University Press, 1976.

Butler, Eliza M. *The Tyranny of Greece over Germany*. 1935. Reprint, Boston: Beacon Press, 1958.

Butler, Marilyn. "The Orientalism of Byron's *Giaour*." In *Byron and the Limits of Fiction*, 78–96. Ed. B. Beatty and V. Newey. Liverpool: University of Liverpool, 1988.

———. *Romantics, Rebels and Reactionaries*. Oxford: Oxford University Press, 1981.

Buxton, John. *The Grecian Taste*. New York: Barnes and Noble, 1978.

Buxton, Noel Edward. *With the Bulgarian Staff*. New York: Macmillan, 1913.

Buxton, Noel Edward, and Charles R. Buxton. *The War and the Balkans*. London: G. Allen Unwin, 1915.

———. "The Macedonian Crisis." In *Macedonia 1903*, 1–8. London: Publications of the Balkan Committee.

Buzzard, James. "The Uses of Romanticism: Byron and the Victorian Continental Tour." *Victorian Studies* 35 (1991): 29–49.

Byford-Jones, Wilfred. *Greek Trilogy: Resistance, Liberation, Revolution*. London: Hutchinson, 1946.

Byron, F. Noel. *Athenian Days*. London, 1919.

Byron, George Gordon, Lord. *Byron's Letters and Journals*. 12 vols. Ed. Leslie Marchand. Cambridge, Mass.: Harvard University Press, 1973–1982.

———. *The Complete Miscellaneous Prose*. Ed. Andrew Nicholson. Oxford: Oxford University Press, 1991.

Byron, George Gordon, Lord. *The Complete Poetical Works.* 7 vols. Ed. Jerome McGann. Oxford: Oxford University Press, 1977–1993.

"Byron in Greece." *Temple Bar* (May 1881): 101–8.

Byron, Robert. *The Byzantine Achievement.* London: Routledge,1929.

———. *The Station: Athos, Treasures and Men.* 1931. Reprint, New York: Century, 1984.

Caclamanos, D. "Byron and Greece." *Hellenic Herald* (Aug. 1909): 150–53; (Sept. 1909): 162–64; and (Oct.–Nov. 1909): 178–82.

———. *The Centenary of Byron's Death: Two Addresses Delivered by Demetrius Caclamenos.* London, 1924.

Campbell, Thomas. *The Complete Poetical Works.* Ed. J. Logie Robertson. London: Henry Frowde, 1907.

Canat, Rene. *L'Hellénisme des romantiques.* 3 vols. Paris: Marcel Dider, 1951–1955.

———. *La renaissance de la Grèce antique (1820–1850).* Paris: Hachette, 1911.

Carlisle, George William Frederick, Earl of. *The Last of the Greeks; or, The Fall of Constantinople.* London: J. Ridgeway, 1828.

Carlyle, Joseph Dacre. *Poems, Suggested Chiefly by Scenes in Asia-Minor, Syria, and Greece.* London: W. Bulmer, 1805.

Carpenter, Edward. *Civilisation: Its Cause and Cure.* 1889. Reprint, London: Swan Sonnenschein, 1891.

Carr, Virginia Spencer. *John Dos Passos.* Garden City, N.Y.: Doubleday, 1989.

Cartwright, Joseph. *The Insurrection in Candia and the Public Press.* New Orleans, 1866.

Cary, Joyce. *The Memoir of the Bobotes.* 1960. Reprint, London: Michael Joseph, 1964.

Cassavetes, Cécile. *Anthea: A Story of the Greek War of Independence.* London: Cassell, 1891.

Cassavetti, D. J. *Hellas and the Balkan Wars.* London: Fisher Unwin, 1914.

Castanier, Prosper. *Les amants des Lesbos.* Paris: Librairie L. Borel, 1900.

———. *Le fleur de Cythere: Roman antique.* Paris: A. Charles, 1899.

Castanis, Christophoros. *The Greek Exile: A Narrative of the Captivity and Escape of Christophoros Plato Castanis during the Massacre on Scio by the Turks. Written by Himself.* Philadelphia: Lippincott, 1851.

The Cause of Greece, the Cause of Europe. Translated from the German. London: James Ridgeway, 1821.

Cavafy, C. P. *Collected Poems*, rev. ed. Tr. Edmund Keeley and Philip Sherrard. Princeton, N.J.: Princeton University Press, 1992.

Chabod, Federico. *Storia dell'Idea d'Europa.* Bari: Edititori Laterza, 1965.

Chateaubriand, François-René. *Itinéraire de Jérusalem à Paris.* 1811. Tr. Frederic Schoberl as *Travels in Greece, Palestine, Egypt and the Barbary during the Years 1806 and 1807.* New York: Van Winkle and Wiley, 1814.

———. *Note sur la Grèce.* Paris: Le Nomant, 1825.

Chatfield, Robert. *An Appeal to the British Public in the Cause of the Persecuted Greeks.* London: John Hatchard and Sons, 1822.

Cherakis, George. *The Hand of Alexander.* New York: FSG, 1950.

Chester, S. B. *The Life of Venizelos*. London: Constable, 1921.

Chew, Samuel. *Byron in England*. London: John Murray, 1925.

Chirol, Valentine. "Islam and the Future of Constantinople." *Fortnightly Review* (Jan. 1, 1919): 37.

Choiseul-Gouffier, Marie Gabriel Auguste Florent. *Voyage pittoresque de la Grèce*. Paris: Tilliard, 1782.

Christensen, Jerome. "Perversion, Parody, and Cultural Hegemony: Lord Byron's Oriental Tales." *South Atlantic Quarterly* 88.3 (1989): 569–604.

Churchill, Kenneth. *Italy and English Literature 1764–1930*. London: Macmillan, 1980.

Churchill, Winston. "The Iron Curtain." In *Blood, Soil, Tears, and Sweat: The Speeches of Winston Churchill*, 295–308. Ed. D. Cannadine. Boston: Houghton Mifflin, 1989.

———. *The World Crisis: The Aftermath*, vol. 4. London: Thornton Butterworth, 1929.

Clift, Charmian. *Being Alone with Oneself: Essays 1968–69*. Ed. by Nadia Wheatley. North Ryde, New South Wales, Australia: Angus and Robertson, 1991.

———. *Honour's Mimic*. London: Hutchinson, 1964.

———. *Mermaid Singing*. London: Michael Joseph, 1956.

———. *Peel Me a Lotus*. London: Hutchinson, 1959.

Cline, Myrtle. *American Attitudes toward the Greek War of Independence, 1821–1828*. Atlanta, Ga.: Higgin McArthur, 1930.

Clive, H. P. *Pierre Louÿs: A Biography*. Oxford: Oxford University Press, 1978.

Clogg, Richard. *A Concise History of Greece*. Cambridge: Cambridge University Press, 1979.

———. *Politics and the Academy: Arnold Toynbee and the Koraes Chair*. London: Frank Cass, 1986.

———. *A Short History of Modern Greece*. 2d ed. Cambridge: Cambridge University Press, 1986.

Cochrane, Alexander Baillie. *The Morea*. London: Sanders and Otley, 1840.

Cochrane, Peter. "The Sale of Parge and the Isles of Greece." *Keats-Shelley Review* 14 (2000): 42–51.

Collcut, Cathleen. "Costume for a Corsair: Trelawny and the Greeks." *Costume* 27 (1993): 26–34.

Collins, C. J. *The Albanian: A Tale of Modern Greece*. London: W. Strange, 1844.

Collins, Edward. *The Vivien Romance*. New York: Harper and Row, 1870.

Collins, Philip. *Thomas Cooper, the Chartist: Byron and the Poets of the Poor*. Nottingham, England: Nottingham Byron Lecture, 1967.

Colquhar, John. *Zoe: An Athenian Tale*. Edinburgh: Archibald Constable, 1824.

Colton, Walter. *A Visit to Constantinople and Athens*. Dublin: James McGlashen, 1849.

Colvin, Sidney. *Memories and Notes of Persons and Places: 1852–1912*. New York: Scribner's, 1921.

Conant, Mary Pike. *The Oriental Tale in Eighteenth-Century England*. New York: Columbia University Press, 1908.

Conrad, Joseph. *Collected Letters*, vol. 5. Ed. Frederick Karl and Laurence Davis. Cambridge: Cambridge University Press, 1996.

————. "The Future of Constantinople." In *Collected Edition of the Works of Joseph Conrad*, vol. 21, 149–54. London: J. M. Dent, 1963.

Constantine, David. *Early Greek Travelers and the Hellenic Ideal*. Cambridge: Cambridge University Press, 1984.

Constantinople: Its Past, Present and Future. London: Moulston and Stoneman, 1853.

Coolidge, Archibald Cary. "Claimants to Constantinople." In *Three Peace Conferences of the Nineteenth Century*, 73–93. Ed. W. R. Thayer and R. Willard. Cambridge, Mass.: Harvard University Press, 1917.

Cosmetatos, S. P. *The Tragedy of Greece*. London: Kegan Paul, 1928.

Coulton, Barbara. *Louis MacNeice and the BBC*. London: Faber and Faber, 1980.

Coupland, Reginald. *Wilberforce*. Oxford: Oxford University Press, 1923.

Cousins, John. *Secret Valleys*. London: Jonathan Cape, 1950.

Cox, Samuel. *A Buckeye Abroad; or, Wanderings in Europe and the Orient*. Columbus, Ohio: Follet, Foster, 1852.

Crane, Stephen. *Collected Works*. 10 vols. Ed. Fredson Bowers. Charlottesville: University of Virginia Press, 1969–1975.

Crawford, F. Marion. *Constantinople*. London: Macmillan, 1896.

————. *Paul Patoff*. Boston: Houghton Mifflin, 1888.

Craxton, John. *Paintings and Drawings, 1941–1966*. London: Whitechapel Gallery, 1973.

Credulity John. London: James Blanchard, 1877.

Creswell, Henry. *A Modern Greek Heroine*. 3 vols. London: Hurst and Blackett, 1880.

Croly, George. *Poetical Works*. 2 vols. London: Colburn & Bentley, 1830.

Crompton, Louis. *Byron and Greek Love*. Berkeley: University of California Press, 1985.

cummings, e. e. *Complete Poems: 1904–1962*. Ed. George J. Firmage. New York: Liveright, 1994.

————. *XLI Poems*. New York: Dial, 1925.

Curry, Kenneth. *Southey*. London: Routledge & Kegan Paul, 1975.

Cuyler, Theodore L. *From the Nile to Norway and Homeward*. New York: Robert Carter, 1882.

D——, Madame. *Les amours d'un Turc et d'une Grecque: Épisode de la guerre de 1821*. 5 vols. Paris: Kleffer, 1822.

Dakin, Douglas. *The Greek Struggle in Macedonia, 1897–1913*. Thessaloniki: Institute for Balkan Studies, 1966.

————. *The Unification of Greece, 1770–1923*. London: Ernst and Benn, 1972.

Dalrymple, William. *From the Holy Mountain: A Journey in the Shadow of Byzantium*. London: HarperCollins, 1997.

Daniel, Henry John. *The Bride of Scio, Songs of the Heart, and Other Poems*. Truro, Mass.: E. Heard, 1842.

Daniel, Norman. *Islam and the West: The Making of an Image*. Edinburgh: University of Edinburgh Press, 1960.

The Dardanelles: Their Story and Significance in the Great War. London: Andrew Melrose, 1915.

Davenport-Hines, Richard. *Auden*. New York: Pantheon, 1995.

Davidson, Catherine Temma. *The Priest Fainted*. New York: Henry Holt, 1998.

Davis, Richard Harding. *Farces*. New York: Scribner's, 1906.

———. *From Gallegher to the Deserter: The Best Short Stories of Richard Harding Davis*. New York: Scribner's, 1922.

———. *The Princess Aline*. New York: Harper, 1895.

———. *With the French in France and Salonica*. New York: Scribner's, 1916.

———. "With the Greek Soldiers." *Harper's* (Nov. 1897): 813–31.

———. *A Year from a Reporter's Notebook*. New York: Harper, 1898.

Day, H. C. *Macedonian Memories*. London: Heath Cranston, 1930.

Day-Lewis, Cecil. *Collected Poems*. Stanford, Calif.: Stanford University Press, 1992.

Deering, Nathaniel. *Bozzaris*. Portland, Maine: J. S. Baily, 1851.

[DeKay, James Ellsworth]. *Sketches of Turkey in 1831 and 1832, by an American*. New York: Harper, 1833.

Delany, Paul. *The Neopagans*. New York: Free Press, 1987.

DeLaura, David. *Hebrew and Hellene in Victorian England*. Austin: University of Texas Press, 1969.

Delavigne, Casimir. *Messénienne sur Lord Byron*. Paris: Ladvocat, 1824. Trans. as *Messenian on Lord Byron* by G. H. Poppleton. Marseilles: Ricard, 1824.

Delay, Jean. *The Youth of André Gide*. Tr. J. Guicharnard. Chicago: University of Chicago Press, 1963.

DeLillo, Don. *The Names*. New York: Knopf, 1982.

Delves-Broughton, V. "Baptism, Marriage, and Funerals in Greece." *Newberry House Magazine* (Aug. 1893): 165–72.

———. "Easter-Tide in Greece." *Newberry House Magazine* (Apr. 1892): 416–20.

Demetrius, George. *I Was Once a Boy in Greece*. Boston: Lothrop, Lear and Stephens, 1913.

Deschamps, Gaston. *La Grèce d'aujourd'hui*. 2d ed. Paris: Armand Colin, 1897.

D'Éspignot, Pierre. *Avant la massacre: Roman Macédonien*. Paris: Charpentier, 1902.

D'Estournelle, P. "The Superstitions of Modern Greece." *Nineteenth Century* (Apr. 1882): 586–605.

de Vere, Aubrey. *Picturesque Sketches in Greece and Turkey*. 2 vols. London: Richard Bentley, 1850.

———. *Poetical Works*. 6 vols. London: K. Paul, Trench, 1884–1898.

The Devil's Visit to Bulgaria and Other Lands. Brighton: W. Junior, 1876.

de Vogüé, Melchior. *Vangheli: La vie orientale*. Paris: Librairie L. Borel, 1901.

De Windt, Henry. *Through Savage Europe*. Philadelphia: Lippincott, 1907.

Dickens, Charles. "Something about Crete." *All the Year Round* (Dec. 24, 1864): 460–65.

Dilke, Charles. *The Eastern Question*. London: Robert Bush, 1878.

Diplomaticus. "The Case against Greece." *Fortnightly Review* (May 1897): 772–81.

Disraeli, Benjamin [Lord Beaconsfield]. *Letters*, vol 1. Ed. J. A. W. Gunn. Toronto: University of Toronto Press, 1982.

———. *Works*. 20 vols. London: M. Walter Dunne, 1906.

Dixon, William Hepworth. *Azamoglan, a Tragedy: An Incident in the Greek Revolution*. London: Simpkins & Marshall, 1845.

Döblin, Alfred. *A People Betrayed. November 1918: A German Revolution*. Tr. John E. Woods. New York: Fromm, 1983.

Doin, Sophie. *Cornelie*. Paris: Desanges, 1826.

Dominois, Adele. *Alais; ou, La vierge de Ténédos*. Paris: Pigoreau, Roumestant, Leterier, 1826.

Donald, Celine Stephano. *Adventures of a Greek Lady, the Adopted Daughter of Late Queen Caroline, Written by Herself*. 2 vols. London: Henry Colburn, 1849.

Dos Passos, John. "The Almeh." *Harvard Monthly* (July 1913): 172–79.

———. *The Best Times*. New York: New American Library, 1966.

———. *Chosen Country*. Boston: Houghton Mifflin, 1951.

———. "The Honor of a Klepht." *Harvard Monthly* (Feb. 1914): 158–63.

———. *Orient Express*. New York: Harper, 1927.

———. *U.S.A.* 1937. Reprint, New York: Literary Classics of America, 1996.

Doty, Mark. *My Alexandria*. Urbana: University of Illinois Press, 1993.

Douglas, Frederick Sylvester North. *An Essay Concerning Certain Points of Resemblance between the Ancient and Modern Greek*. London: John Murray, 1813.

Douglas, John A. *The Redemption of St. Sophia*. London: Faith Press, 1919.

Douglas, Norman. *One Day*. 1929. Reprinted in *Three of Them*. London: Chatto and Windus, 1930.

———. *Siren Land*. 1911. Reprint, New York: Penguin, 1983.

———. *South Wind*. 1917. Reprint, New York: Modern Library, 1925.

Doulis, Thomas. *Disaster and Fiction: Modern Greek Writers and the Asia Minor Disaster of 1922*. Berkeley: University of California Press, 1977.

Dowling, Linda. *Hellenism and Homosexuality in Victorian Oxford*. Ithaca, N.Y.: Cornell University Press, 1994.

Doyle, Francis H. *Return of the Gods and Other Poems*. London: Macmillan, 1883.

Dragoumis, Ion. *The Blood of Martyrs and Heroes* (in Greek). Athens, 1907.

Dragoumis, Julia. *A Man of Athens*. Boston: Houghton Mifflin, 1916.

———. *Tales of a Greek Island*. London: Constable, 1912.

———. *Under Greek Skies*. New York: Dutton, 1913.

Dreyfus, Abraham. *Le klephte*. Paris: Calmann Levy, 1858.

Driault, Edouard. *La grande idée: La renaissance de l'Hellénisme*. Paris: Librairie Felix Alcan, 1920.

Drosinis, George. *Amaryllis*. Tr. Elizabeth Edmonds. London: Fisher Unwin, 1891.

———. *The Herb of Love*. Tr. Elizabeth Edmonds. London: Fisher Unwin, 1893.

Droulia, Loukia. *Philhellénisme: Ouvrages inspirées par la guerre del l'indépendance grecque 1821–1833*. Athens: Centre de recherches neo-Helleniques, 1974.

Ducange, Victor. *Thélène; ou, L'amour de la guerre grecque*. 4 vols. Paris: Pollet, 1824.

Duff, David. *Romance and Revolution: Shelley and the Politics of a Genre*. Cambridge: Cambridge University Press, 1994.

Duffield, Anne. *Grecian Rhapsody*. London: Cassell, 1938.

———. *Stamboul Love*. New York: Knopf, 1934.

Duncan, Isadora. *My Life*. New York: Boni and Liveright, 1927.

Durham, Edith. *The Burden of the Balkans*. London: Nelson, 1905.

———. *Twenty Years of the Balkan Tangle*. New York: Putnam's, 1920.

Durrell, Lawrence. *Bitter Lemons*. London: Faber and Faber, 1957.

———. *Cefalú*. London: Poetry Editions, 1947.

———. *Collected Poems 1931–1974*. London: Faber and Faber, 1985.

———. *The Durrell-Miller Letters*. Ed. Ian S. MacNiven. New York: New Directions, 1980.

———. *Justine*. London: Faber and Faber, 1957.

———. *A Private Country, Poems*. London: Faber and Faber, 1943.

———. *Prospero's Cell*. 1945. Reprint, New York: Penguin, 1978.

———. *Reflections on a Marine Venus*. 1953. Reprint, New York: Penguin, 1978.

———. *Spirit of Place: Letters and Essays on Travel*. Ed. Alan Thomas. New York: Dutton, 1969.

——— [as Charles Norden]. *Panic Spring*. London: Faber and Faber, 1937.

Dwight, Henry Otis. *Constantinople and Its Problems*. New York: Revell, 1901.

Dwight, Sereno Edwards. *The Greek Revolution: An Address Delivered at Park Street Church, Boston*. Boston: Crocker and Brewster, 1824.

Eaglestone, C. R. *The Siege of Constantinople: A Historical Romance*. London: Sydenham, 1878.

Eames, Jane. *The Budget Closed*. Boston: Ticknor and Fields, 1860.

Earle, Pliny. *Marathon and Other Poems*. Philadelphia: H. Perkins, 1841.

The Eastern Ogre; or, St. George to the Rescue! London: 1876.

Edgeworth, Maria. *Helen*. 1834. Reprint, London: Richard Bentley, 1850.

Edmonds, Elizabeth. *Amygdala: A Tale of the Greek Revolution*. London: Bell, 1894.

———. "A Daugher of Crete" *Newberry House Magazine* (Mar. 1891): 310–19.

———. *Fair Athens*. London: Remington, 1881.

———. *Greek Lays, Idylls, Legends, Etc.* London: Teubner, 1885.

———. *Hesperas*. London: Kegan Paul, 1883.

———. *The History of a Church Mouse*. London: Lawrence and Bullen, 1892.

———. "Quaint Customs of Rural Greece." *Eastern and Western Review* (July 1892): 115–22.

———. *Rhigas Pheraios: The Protomartyr of Greek Independence*. London: Longmans, 1889.

———. "Scenes from Greek Life I: Chyrsanthos. From the Greek of Andreas Karkavitsos." *Eastern and Western Review* (Aug. 1892): 235–40.

———. "Superstitions in Greece." *Eastern and Western Review* (Nov. 1892): 521–27.

Eisner, Robert. *Travelers to an Antique Land: The History and Literature of Travel to Greece*. Ann Arbor: University of Michigan Press, 1991.

Elfenbein, Andrew. *Byronism and the Victorians*. Cambridge: Cambridge University Press, 1994.

Eliot, George. *Letters*. 7 vols. Ed. Gordon S. Haight. New Haven, Conn.: Yale University Press, 1954–1955.

———. *Middlemarch*. Ed. David Carroll. Oxford: Oxford World's Classics, 1988.

Eliot, T. S. *Collected Poems: 1909–1962*. New York: Harcourt Brace Jovanovich, 1963.

———. *Selected Essays*. Ed. Frank Kermode. New York: Harcourt Brace Jovanovich, 1975.

Ellmann, Richard. *Oscar Wilde*. New York: Knopf, 1988.

Elton, C. A. "Byron in Greece." In *The Tribute: A Collection of Miscellaneous and Unpublished Poems by Various Authors*, 315–19. Ed. Lord Northampton. London: J. Murray and H. Lindsell, 1837.

Eftaliotis, Argyris. *Tales from the Isles of Greece: Being Sketches of Modern Greek Peasant Life by Argyris Eftaliotis*. Tr. W. H. D. Rouse. London: J. M. Dent, 1897.

Erdman, David. "Byron and the Genteel Reformers." *PMLA* (1941): 1065–94.

———. "Byron and the Revolt in England." *Science and Society* 11 (1947): 234–38.

Esher, Reginald, Viscount. *Ionicus: The Life and Letters of William Cory*. London: John Murray, 1923.

Eversley, Lord. "Some Reminiscences: Lord Byron and Dr. Millingen." *Cornhill Magazine* (Nov. 1918): 471–82.

Fallmerayer, Jacob. *Geschichte der Habinsel Morea*. Stuttgart and Tubingen: J. G. Cotta, 1830.

Fauriel, M. C. *Chantes populaire de la Grèce moderne*. 2 vols. Paris: Dondey-Dupré, 1824–1825.

Felton, C. C. *Familiar Letters from Europe*. Boston: Ticknor and Fields, 1865.

———. *Greece, Ancient and Modern*. 2 vols. Boston: Ticknor and Fields, 1867.

Fenton, Charles. *The Apprenticeship of Ernest Hemingway: The Early Years*. New York: FSG, 1954.

Ferlinghetti, Lawrence. *Open Eye, Open Heart*. New York: New Directions, 1973.

Fermor, Patrick Leigh. "The Background of Nikos Ghika." In *Ghika: Paintings, Drawings, Sculptures*, 25–44. London: Lund Humphries, 1964.

———. *Mani*. 1958. Reprint, New York: Penguin, 1984.

———. *Roumeli: Travels in Northern Greece*. New York: Viking, 1964.

Ferriman, Z. D. *Greece and the Greeks*. New York: James Pott, 1910.

———. *Greece—and Tomorrow*. Publications of the American Hellenic Society, 1918.

———. *Greeks, Bulgars, and English Opinion*. London: Bonner, 1913.

———. *Some English Philhellenes. No. 8: Lord Byron*. London: Publications of the Anglo-Hellenic League, 1920.

Ferris, David. *Silent Urns: Romanticism, Hellenism, Modernity*. Stanford, Calif.: Stanford University Press, 2000.

Finlay, George. *A History of Greece*. 7 vols. 1877. Reprint, New York: AMS Press, 1970.

Finnemore, John. *Foray and Fight: Being the Story of the Remarkable Adventures of an Englishman and an American in Macedonia*. London: W. R. Chambers, 1906.

Firbank, Ronald. *Inclinations*. 1916. Reprinted in *The Complete Ronald Firbank*. London: Duckworth, 1961.

Fisher, Thomas. *Understanding John Fowles*. Columbia: University of South Carolina Press, 1994.

Fitzball, Edward. *The Greek Slave*. London: S. French, 1851.

Flaubert, Gustave. *Bouvard and Pécuchet*. Tr. T. W. Earp and G. W. Steiner. New York: New Directions, 1954.

———. *Notes de voyages*. 2 vols. In *Oeuvres complètes de Gustave Flaubert*. Paris: Louis Conard, 1910.

———. "Portrait of Lord Byron." In *Early Works of Flaubert*, 3–4. Tr. Robert Griffin. Lincoln: University of Nebraska Press, 1991.

Flecker, James Elroy. *The Collected Poems of James Elroy Flecker*. Ed. J. C. Squire. New York: Doubleday, Page, 1916.

———. *Complete Prose*. London: G. Bell, 1920.

Ford, Ford Madox [as F. M. Hueffer]. "Little States and Great Nations." *English Review* (May 1909): 355–56.

———. "The Passing of the Great Figure." *English Review* (Dec. 1909): 101–10.

Forster, E. M. *Abinger Harvest*. 1936. Reprint, New York: Harcourt Brace Jovanovich, 1964.

———. *Arctic Summer and Other Tales*. London: Edward Arnold, 1980.

———. *Collected Tales*. 1928. Reprint, New York: Knopf, 1951.

———. *The Life to Come and Other Stories*. Ed. O. Stallybrass. London: Edward Arnold, 1971.

———. *Maurice*. New York: Norton, 1971.

———. *A Room with a View*. 1908. Reprint, New York: Vintage, 1960.

———. *The Selected Letters of E. M. Forster*, vol. 2. Ed. P. N. Furbank and Mary Lago. London: Collins, 1985.

Fotheringham, David Ross, ed. and trans. *War Songs of the Greeks and Other Poems*. London: George Bell, 1907.

Fowles, John. "Behind *The Magus*." In *Wormholes: Essays and Occasional Writings*, 56–66. New York: Henry Holt, 1998.

———. "Greece." In *Wormholes*, 68–72. New York: Henry Holt, 1998.

———. *The Magus*. 1966. Rev. ed. London: Jonathan Cape, 1977.

———. *Poems*. New York: Ecco Press, 1973.

Frappa, Jean-José. *A Salonique sous l'oeil des deux*. Paris: Flammarion, 1917.

Fraser, Hilary. *The Victorians and Renaissance Italy*. Oxford: Basil Blackwell, 1992.

Fraser, John Fisher. *Pictures from the Balkans*. London: Cassell, 1912.

Freeman, Edward Augustus. *Historical Essays*, 3d ser., 2d ed. London and New York: Macmillan, 1892.

———. "The Present Position of the Greek Nation. *Panhellenic Review* 1.1 (Mar. 1879): 2–9.

Freemantle, Ann. *Loyal Enemy: The Life of Marmaduke Pickthall*. London: Hutchinson, 1938.

Fromkin, David. *A Peace to End All Peace: Creating the Modern Middle East, 1914–1922*. New York: Henry Holt, 1989.

Frost, Robert. *Complete Poems, Prose & Plays*. Ed. R. Poirier and M. Richardson. New York: Library of America, 1995.

Furbank, P. N. *E. M. Forster: A Life*. New York: Harcourt Brace Jovanovich, 1978.

Fussell, Paul. *Abroad: British Literary Traveling between the Wars*. Oxford: Oxford University Press, 1980.

———. *The Great War and Modern Memory*. Oxford: Oxford University Press, 1975.

Gamba, Count Pietro. *A Narrative of Byron's Last Journey to Greece*. London: John Murray, 1825.

Garber, Frederick. *Self, Text, and Romantic Irony: The Example of Byron*. Princeton, N.J.: Princeton University Presss, 1988.

Gardner, John Dunn. *The Ionian Islands in Relation to Greece*. London: J. Ridgway, 1859.

Garnett, Catherine Grace. *Reine Canziani*. London: Hurst, Robinson, 1825.

Garnett, Lucy. *Greek Folk Songs from the Turkish Provinces of Greece*. London: Eliot Stock, 1885.

Garston, Edgar. *Greece Revisited and Sketches of Lower Egypt in 1840*. London: Sanders and Otley, 1842.

Gaskell, Elizabeth. "Modern Greek Songs." 1854. Reprinted in *Works of Mrs. Gaskell*, vol. 3. New York: AMS Press, 1972.

Gautier, Theophile. *Constantinople*. 1853. Tr. Robert Howe Gould. Reprint, New York: Henry Holt, 1875.

Gauvin, Auguste. *The Greek Question*. Tr. Carroll Brown. New York: Publications of the American Hellenic Society, 1918.

Gavin, Catherine. *The House of War*. New York: William and Morrow, 1970.

Gelfand, L. E. *The Inquiry: American Preparation for Peace, 1917–1919*. New Haven, Conn.: Yale University Press, 1963.

Gibbons, Herbert Adams. *Venizelos*. New York: Houghton Mifflin, 1920.

Gibbs, Anthony. *Enter the Greek*. New York: Harper, 1926.

Gibbs, Philip. *Cities of Refuge*. Garden City, N.Y.: Doubleday, Doran, 1937.

———. *Little Novels of Nowadays*. New York: George Doran, 1924.

Gifford, Edward. *A Short Visit to the Ionian Islands, Athens, and the Morea*. London: John Murray, 1837.

Gilder, Richard Watson. *The Poems of Richard Watson Gilder*. Boston: Houghton Mifflin, 1908.

Ginsberg, Allen. *Collected Poems: 1947–1980*. New York, Harper and Row, 1984.

Gissing, George. *By the Ionian Sea: Notes of a Ramble in South Italy*. 1901. Reprint, Evanston, Ill.: Northwestern University Press, 1996.

———. *Collected Letters*. 8 vols. Ed. P. F. Matheisen, A. C. Young, and P. Coustillas. Athens: Ohio University Press, 1990–1996.

———. *The Emancipated*. Ed. P. Coustillas. Cranbury, N.J.: Associated Universities Press, 1977.

Gissing, George. *New Grub Street*. Oxford: Oxford World's Classics, 1993.

————. *Sleeping Fires*. New York: D. Appleton, 1895.

Gladstone, William Ewart. *The Bulgarian Horrors and the Question of the East*. London: John Murray, 1876.

————. *The Eastern Crisis: A Letter to the Duke of Westminster, K. G.* London: John Murray, 1897.

————. "Greece and the Treaty of Berlin." *Nineteenth Century* (June 1879): 121–34.

————. "The Hellenic Factor in the Eastern Question." *Contemporary Review* (Dec. 1876): 1–27.

————. *Lessons in Massacre*. London: John Murray, 1877.

————. "The Macedonian Question." *Publications of the Balkan Committee*, no. 15, p. 4.

————. "Montenegro: A Sketch." *Nineteenth Century* (May 1877): 360–79.

————. "The Peace to Come." *Nineteenth Century* (Feb. 1878): 209–22.

———— [as W. E. G.]. "War and Peace." *Gentleman's Magazine* (July 1856): 141–55.

Glasgow, George. *Ronald Burrows: A Memoir*. London: Nisbet, 1924.

Glaspell, Susan. "Dwellers on Parnassus." *New Republic* (Jan. 17, 1923): 198–200.

————. "The Faithless Shepherd." *Cornhill Magazine* 60 (Jan. 1926): 51–71.

————. *Fugitive's Return*. New York: Frederick Stokes, 1929.

————. *The Road to the Temple*. New York: Frederick Stokes, 1927.

Gleason, John Howes. *The Genesis of Russophobia*. Cambridge, Mass.: Harvard University Press, 1950.

Gleckner, Robert. *Byron and the Ruins of Paradise*. Baltimore: Johns Hopkins University Press, 1962.

Glendinning, Victoria. *Vita: A Biography of Vita Sackville-West*. New York: Knopf, 1983.

Gobineau, Arthur de. *Au royaume des Hellénes*. 1878. Reprint, Paris: Maurice Nordeau, 1993.

————. *Souvenirs de voyage: Céphalonie, Naxie, et Terre-Neuve*. Paris: Henri Plon, 1872.

Goldstein, Erik. "Great Britain and Greater Greece 1917–1920." *Historical Journal* 32 (1989): 339–56.

————. "Holy Wisdom and British Foreign Policy 1918–1922: The St. Sophia Redemption Agitation." *Byzantine and Modern Greek Studies* 15 (1991): 36–64.

Goldsworthy, Vesna. *Inventing Ruritania: The Imperialism of the Imagination*. New Haven, Conn.: Yale University Press, 1998.

Goodisson, William. *A Historical and Topographical Essay upon the Islands of Cephalonia, Corfu, Leucadia, Ithaca, and Zante*. London: Thomas and George Underwood, 1822.

Gordon, Winifred. *A Woman in the Balkans*. New York: Dodd Mead, 1916.

Gosse, Edmund. *The Life of Algernon Charles Swinburne*. New York: Macmillan, 1917.

Graham, Thomas, tr. *Barba Tassi, the Greek Patriot: A Romance*. London: Bentley, 1850.

Graham, Winston. *Greek Fire*. London: Hodder and Stoughton, 1957.

Greece Abandoned; or, Three Years of Diplomacy on the Greek Question. London: Publication of the Greek Committee, 1880.

Greek Campaign in Asia Minor: Telegraphs of the Correspondents of the World Press. Athens: 1921.

Green, Philip James. *Sketches of the War in Greece*. London: Thomas Hurst, 1827.

Gregory, Eileen. *H. D. and Hellenism*. Cambridge: Cambridge University Press, 1997.

Grierson, Herbert J. C. "Lord Byron, Arnold and Swinburne." *Proceedings of the British Academy* 9 (1920): 431–61.

Grosvenor, Edwin A. *The Permanence of the Greek Type*. Cambridge, Mass.: Charles Hamilton, 1897.

Guest, Barbara. *Herself Defined: A Life of H. D.* Garden City, N.Y.: Doubleday, 1984.

Guillard, Nicholas Francois. *Miltiade à Marathon*. [Libretto by Jean Baptiste Le Moyne]. Paris: Roullet, 1797 or 1799.

Guys, Pierre-Augustin. *Voyage littéraire de la Grèce; ou Lettres sur les Grecs anciennes et modernes, avec un paralèle de leur moeurs*. 1771. Translated as *Sentimental Journey through Greece*. Dublin: J. Milliken, 1773.

H. D. [Hilda Doolittle]. *Asphodel*. Ed. Robert Spoo. Durham, N.C.: Duke University Press, 1992.

Hadas, Rachel. *Halfway Down the Hall: New and Selected Poems*. Hanover, N.H.: Wesleyan University Press, 1998.

Hagemann, E. R. "A Collation, with Commentary, of the Five Texts of the Chapters in Hemingway's *In Our Time*." In *Critical Essays on Ernest Hemingway's* In Our Time, 38–51. Ed. Michael Reynolds. Boston: G. K. Hall, 1983.

———. "'Only Let the Story End as Soon as Possible': Time and History in Ernest Hemingway's *In Our Time*." In *Critical Essays on Hemingway's* In Our Time, 52–60. Ed. Michael Reynolds. Boston: G. K. Hall, 1983.

Halleck, Fitz-Greene. *Poetical Writings*. Ed. James Grant Wilson. 1869. Reprint, New York: AMS Press, 1969.

A Handbook for Travellers in Greece. 4th ed. London: John Murray, 1872.

Hanson, Kenneth O. *The Distance Anywhere*. Seattle: University of Washington Press, 1967.

———. *Saronikos and Other Poems*. Portland, Ore.: Press-22, 1970.

———. *The Uncorrected Word*. Middletown, Conn.: Wesleyan University Press, 1973.

Harris, David. *Britain and the Bulgarian Horrors of 1876*. Chicago: University of Chicago Press, 1939.

Harrison, James. *Greek Vignettes*. Boston: Houghton Osgood, 1878.

Hastings, Selena. *Evelyn Waugh: A Biography*. Boston: Houghton Mifflin, 1994.

Hatfield, Henry. *Aesthetic Paganism in German Literature: From Winckelmann to the Death of Goethe*. Cambridge, Mass.: Harvard University Press, 1964.

Hauser, Fernand. *Les Balkaniques: Poèmes*. Paris, 1913.

Havel, Vaclav. "The State of the Country." *New York Review of Books* (Mar. 5, 1998): 42–46.

Hawthorne, Nathaniel. *Novels*. Ed. Milicent Bell. New York: Library of America, 1983.

Hay, Denys. *Europe: The Emergence of an Idea*. Edinburgh: University of Edinburgh, 1968.

Haygarth, William. *Greece: A Poem in Three Parts*. London: W. Bulmer, 1814.

Hecht, Anthony. *The Hidden Law: The Poetry of W. H. Auden*. Cambridge, Mass.: Harvard University Press, 1993.

Heckstall-Smith, Anthony. *Greek Tragedy, 1941*. New York: Norton, 1961.

Heidenstam, Charles de. *L'Orpheline d'Argos: Épisode de la révolution grecque*. 3 vols. Paris: G. A. Dentu, 1830.

Heinse, Wilhelm. *Ardinghello und die glückseligen Inseln*. Berlin: W. J. Morlinns, 1785.

Hemans, Felicia. *Poetical Works*. Philadelphia: Grigg and Elliot, 1847.

Hemingway, Ernest. *Complete Poems*. Ed. Nicholas Gerogiannis. Lincoln: University of Nebraska Press, 1992.

———. *Dateline: Toronto*. Ed. William White. New York: Scribner's, 1985.

———. *Death in the Afternoon*. 1932. Reprint, New York: Scribner's Classics Edition, 1999.

———. *A Farewell to Arms*. New York: Scribner's, 1929.

———. *In Our Time*. 1930. Reprint, New York: Scribner's, 1970.

———. *Selected Letters, 1917–1961*. Ed. Carlos Baker. New York: Scribner's, 1981.

———. *The Snows of Kilimanjaro and Other Stories*. 1936. Reprint, New York: Scribner's, 1970.

Henry, W. M. *The Corsair's Bride, Scio, and Other Poems*. London: Sanders and Otley, 1840.

Hentschel, Cedric. "Byron and Germany." In *Byron's Political and Cultural Influence in Nineteenth-Century Europe*, 59–60. Ed. Paul Graham Trueblood. London: Macmillan, 1981.

Henty, George. *In Greek Waters: A Story of the War of Independence*. New York: Scribner's, 1892.

Herbert, A. P. *The Secret Battle*. New York: Knopf, 1919.

Herbert, Jock. "Experiences and Reminiscences of Jock Herbert." *Goodwill* (Sept. 1898): 204–6.

Herbert, W. V. *By-Paths in the Balkans*. London: Chapman Hall, 1906.

Herzfeld, Michael. *Ours Once More: Folklore, Ideology, and the Making of Modern Greece*. Austin: University of Texas Press, 1982.

Hibben, Paxton. *Constantine I and the Greek People*. New York: Century, 1920.

Hichens, R. S. *In the Wilderness*. New York: Frederick Stokes, 1917.

Hill, George. *The Ruins of Athens, Titiania's Banquet, A Mask, and Other Poems*. Boston: Otis, Broaders, 1839.

Hinks, Roger. *The Gymnasium of the Mind: The Journals of Roger Hinks*. Ed. John Goldsworth. Salisbury, Wiltshire, England: Michael Russell, 1984.

Hobhouse, John Cam. *Journey to Albania and Other Provinces of Turkey*. 2 vols. 1813. Reprint, Philadelphia: John Carey, 1817.

Hocking, Joseph. *Tommy and the Maid of Athens*. London: Hodder and Stoughton, 1917.

Hodge, Jane Aiken. *Greek Wedding*. London: Hodder and Stoughton, 1970.

Hodgson, Geraldine. *The Life of James Elroy Flecker*. Boston: Houghton Mifflin, 1925.

Hölderlin, Friedrich. *Hyperion*. Tr. Willard Trask. New York: Frederick Ungar, 1965.

Holland, Henry. *Travels in the Ionian Islands, Albania, Thessaly, Macedonia, Etc., during the Years 1812 and 1813*. London: Longman, Hurst, Rees, Orne and Browne, 1815.

Holloway, Mark. *Norman Douglas*. London: Secker and Warburg, 1976.

Home, Henry Lord Kames. *Elements of Criticism*. 2 vols. Boston: Samuel Etheridge, 1796.

Hommage à Rupert Brooke et la poesie immortelle. Athens: Hestia, 1931.

Hope, Anthony. *Phroso*. New York: F. A. Stokes, 1897.

Hope, Thomas. *Anastasius; or, Memories of a Greek*. 3 vols. London: John Murray, 1819.

Hopper, Sidney. *Greek Earth*. London: Michael Joseph, 1939.

Horovitz, Israel. *The Good Parts*. New York: Samuel French, 1983.

Horton, George. *Aphroessa: A Legend of Argolis and Other Poems*. London: Fisher and Unwin, 1897.

———. *The Blight on Asia*. Indianapolis: Bobbs-Merrill, 1926.

———. *Constantine: A Tale of Greece under King Otho*. London: Fisher and Unwin, 1896.

———. *A Fair Brigand*. New York: Herbert Stone, 1899.

———. *Home of the Nymphs and Vampires: The Isles of Greece*. Indianapolis: Bobbs-Merrill, 1929.

———. *Like Another Helen*. Indianapolis: Bobbs-Merrill, 1900.

———. *The Monk's Treaure*. New York: A. L. Burt, 1905.

———. *Poems of an Exile*. Indianapolis: Bobbs-Merill, 1931.

———. *The Tempting of Father Anthony*. Chicago: McClurg, 1901.

Housepian, Marjorie. *The Smyrna Affair*. New York: Harcourt Brace Jovanovich, 1971.

Howe, Julia Ward. *From the Oak to the Olive*. Boston: Lee and Shepherd, 1868.

Howe, Samuel Gridley. *An Appeal to the People of the United States to Relieve from Starvation the Women and Children of the Greeks of the Island of Crete*. Boston: Rand and Avery, 1867.

———. *The Cretan Refugees and Their American Helpers*. Boston: Lee and Shepherd, 1868.

———. *A Historical Sketch of the Greek Revolution*. New York: Gallagher and White, 1828.

———. "A Modern Greek." *New England Magazine* (Sept. 1831): 240–45.

Hughes, Thomas. *An Address to the People of England in the Cause of the Greeks.* London: Simpkin and Marshall, 1822.

———. *Travels in Greece and Albania*, 2d ed. 2 vols. London: Henry Colburn and Richard Bentley, 1830.

Hugo, Victor. *Oeuvres poètiques.* 4 vols. Ed. P. Albouy. Paris: Gallimard, 1964.

Hulme, T. E. *The Collected Works of T. E. Hulme.* Ed. Karen Csengaria. Oxford: Oxford University Press, 1994.

Hunter, Isabel. *This Is Greece.* London: Evans, 1947.

Hutchinson, T. S. *An American Volunteer under the Greek Flag at Bezani.* Nashville, Tenn.: Greek American Publishing, 1913.

Hutton, Edward. *A Glimpse of Greece.* New York: Macmillan, 1928.

Hutton, Isabel. *With a Woman's Unit in Serbia, Salonica, and Sebastopol.* London: Williams and Norgate, 1928.

Hynes, Samuel. *The Edwardian Turn of Mind.* Princeton, N.J.: Princeton University Press, 1968.

———. *A War Imagined: The First World War and English Culture.* 1990. Reprint, London: Pimlico, 1992.

Ioannides. *Das Mädchen aus Zante.* Bamberg und Murzburg: Goebhardtischen Buchandlungen, 1822.

L'Ipsariote; ou, La Grèce vengée. 2 vols. Paris: Bollard, 1825.

Isherwood, Christopher. *Christopher and His Kind.* New York: Simon and Schuster, 1976.

———. *Down There on a Visit.* New York: Simon and Schuster, 1962.

James, Henry. *The Portrait of a Lady.* 1881. Ed. Nicola Bradbury. Reprint, Oxford: Oxford World's Classics, 1995.

———. "Rupert Brooke." In *Literary Criticism*, vol. 1, 747–69. Ed. Leon Edel. New York: Library of America, 1984.

Jameson, Storm. *The Journey from the North: An Autobiography*, vol. 2. London: Collins and Harvill, 1970.

———. *One Ulysses Too Many.* New York: Harper, 1958.

Jay, Karla. *The Amazon and the Page: Natalie Clifford Barney and Renée Vivien.* Bloomington: Indiana University Press, 1988.

Jebb, R. C. *Modern Greece.* London: Macmillan, 1880.

Jelavich, Barbara. "British Travelers in the Balkans." *Slavonic Review* 23 (June 1955): 396–413.

Jenkyns, Richard. *The Victorians and Ancient Greece.* Cambridge, Mass.: Harvard University Press, 1980.

Jenkins, Romilly. *The Dilessi Murders.* London: Longmans, 1961.

Jerome, Jerome K. *My Life and Times.* New York and London: Harper, 1926.

Jewsbury, Geraldine. *Zoe.* 1845. Reprint, New York: Garland, 1975.

Johnson, Robert Underwood. *Collected Poems, 1881–1919.* New Haven, Conn.: Yale University Press, 1920.

Johnston, George. *Clean Straw for Nothing.* London: Collins, 1969.

———. *Closer to the Sun.* New York: Morrow, 1960.

Johnston, George. *The Cyprian Woman*. London: Collins, 1955.

———, and Charmian Clift. *The Sponge Divers*. London: Collins, 1958.

———. *The Strong Man of Piraeus and Other Stories*. New York: Penguin, 1984.

Johnstone, C. L. *The Conquest of Constantinople*. London: Kegan Paul, 1898.

Juin, Hubert. *Victor Hugo*. 3 vols. Paris: Flammarion, 1980–1986.

Jusdanis, Gregory. *Belated Modernity and Aesthetic Culture: Inventing National Literature*. Minneapolis: University of Minnesota Press, 1991.

Kaplan, Robert. *Balkan Ghosts*. New York: St. Martin's, 1993.

Karanikas, Alexander. *Hellenes and Hellions: Modern Greek Characters in American Literature*. Urbana: University of Illinois Press, 1981.

Kasasis, Neocles. *Greece and Bulgaria in the Nineteenth and Twentieth Centuries: An Open Letter to Sir Charles Dilke*. London: Ballantyne, 1907.

Katapodes, P. *The Voice of Greece: Pamphlets Supporting King Constantine*. London, 1917.

Kazantzakis, Nikos. "Greece Today." *Holiday* (June 1956): 46–57ff.

———. *Journey to the Morea*. Tr. F. A. Reed. New York: Simon and Schuster, 1965.

———. *Zorba the Greek*. Tr. Carl Wildman. New York: Simon and Schuster, 1952.

Keeley, Edmund. *Cavafy's Alexandria*. 1976. Reprint, Princeton, N.J.: Princeton University Press, 1996.

———. *The Gold-Hatted Lover*. New York: Little, Brown, 1961.

———. *The Imposter*. Garden City, N.Y.: Doubleday, 1970.

———. *Inventing Paradise: The Greek Journey 1937–1947*. New York: FSG, 1999.

———. *The Libation*. New York: Scribner's, 1958.

———. *Modern Greek Poetry: Voice and Myth*. Princeton, N.J.: Princeton University Press, 1983.

———. *The Salonika Bay Murder: Cold War Politics and the Polk Affair*. Princeton, N.J.: Princeton University Press, 1989.

———. *School for Pagan Lovers*. New Brunswick, N.J.: Rutgers University Press, 1993.

Kelch, M. *Turkish Barbarity: An Affecting Narrative of the Unparalleled Sufferings of Mrs. Sophia Mazro, a Greek Lady of Missalonghi*. Providence, R.I.: G. C. Jennings, 1828.

Kelsall, Charles. *A Letter from Athens*. London: T. Beasley, 1812.

Kelsall, Malcolm. "Reading Orientalism: *Woman or Ida of Athens*." *Review of National Literatures and World Report* 1 (1998): 11–20.

Kendrick, Tertius. *The Ionian Islands*. London: James Haldane, 1822.

———. *The Kako-damon; or, The Cavern of Anti-Paros*. London: C. S. Arnold, 1825.

———. *The Travellers: A Tale Illustrative of the Manners, Customs, and Superstitions of Modern Greece*. 3 vols. London: C. S. Arnold, 1825.

Kenner, Hugh. *The Pound Era*. Berkeley: University of California Press, 1971.

King, Francis. *The Dark Glasses*. London: Longmans Green, 1954.

———. *The Man on the Rock*. New York: Pantheon, 1957.

King, Francis. *So Hurt and Humiliated and Other Stories*. London: Longmans Green, 1959.

———. *Yesterday Came Slowly: An Autobiography*. London: Constable, 1993.

——— [as Frank Caulfield]. *The Firewalkers*. 1956. Reprint, London: GMP Publishers, 1985.

———, ed. *Introducing Greece*. London: Methuen, 1956.

Kinglake, Alexander. *Eothen*. 1844. Reprint, Lincoln: University of Nebraska Press, 1970.

Kingsley, Charles. *Hypatia*. Reprinted in *The Works of Charles Kingsley*, vol. 9. London: Macmillan, 1902.

Kininmouth, Christopher. *The Children of Thetis*. London: John Lehmann, 1950.

Kipling, Rudyard. *The Letters of Rudyard Kipling*, vol. 4. Ed. Thomas Pinney. Iowa City: University of Iowa Press, 1999.

———. *Rudyard Kipling's Verse, 1885–1926*. Garden City, N.Y.: Doubleday, 1931.

Kipperman, Mark. "History and Ideality: The Politics of Shelley's *Hellas*." *Studies in Romanticism* 30.2 (1991): 147–68.

Kitsikis, Dimitri. *Propagande et pressions en politique internationale: La Grèce et ses revendications à la conférence de la paix (1919–1920)*. Paris: Presses universitaires de France, 1963.

Knapp, Bettina. *Stephen Crane*. New York: Ungar, 1987.

Knight, Henry Galley. *Eastern Sketches in Verse*. London: John Murray, 1830.

Knox, Bryant. "Allen Upward and Ezra Pound." *Paideuma* 3 (1974): 71–83.

Kofos, Evangelis. *Greece and the Eastern Question, 1875–1878*. Thessaloniki: Institute for Balkan Studies, 1975.

Kotsageorgi, Xanthippi. "British Travelers in the Early Nineteenth Century on Greece and the Greeks." *Balkan Studies* 33 (1992): 209–21.

Koukou, Helen. "The 'Note on Greece' (Note sur la Grèce) by Francois René de Chateaubriand." *Europäischer Philhellenismus*, 2:53–62. Ed. Evangelos Konstantinou. Berlin: Peter Lang, 1992.

Koumarianou, Catirina. "British Philhellenism and the Greek Press (1824)." *Europäischer Philhellenismus*, 3:115–22. Ed. Evangelos Konstantinou. Berlin: Peter Lang, 1994.

Koumoulides, John, ed. *Greece in Transition: Essays in the History of Modern Greece, 1821–1977*. London: Zeno, 1977.

Kyrias, Gerasimos. *Captured by Brigands: A Story of Modern Greece*. London: Relifious Tract Society, 1901.

[L., G.] *A Grecian Lady's Complaint on the Protection Offered for Turkey*. London: Home's Library, 1854.

Laity, Cassandra. *H. D. and the Victorian Fin de Siecle*. Cambridge: Cambridge University Press, 1996.

Lake, Harold. *In Salonica with Our Army*. London: Andrew Melrose, 1918.

Lamartine, Alphonse Marie Louis de. *Voyage en Orient*. 1835. Translated as *A Pilgrimage to the Holy Land*. 1838. Reprint, Delmar, N.Y.: Scholar's Facsimiles and Reprints, 1978.

Lambropoulos, Vassili. *The Rise of Eurocentrism*. Princeton, N.J.: Princeton University Press, 1992.

Lancaster, Osbert. *Classical Landscape with Figures*. 1947. Reprint, London: John Murray, 1975.

Landon, Letitia Elizabeth [L. E. L.]. *Works*. 2 vols. Philadelphia: Jesper Hardy, 1850.

Landor, Walter Savage. *The Complete Works of Walter Savage Landor*. 16 vols. London: Chapman and Hall, 1925–1938.

———. *Poetical Works of Walter Savage Landor*. 3 vols. Ed. Stephen Wheeler. Oxford: Oxford University Press, 1937.

Lang, Andrew. *Poetical Works*. 4 vols. Ed. Mrs. Lang. London: Longman, Green, 1923.

Larrabee, Steven. *Greece Observed: The American Experience of Greece, 1775–1865*. New York: New York University Press, 1957.

Lavalaye, Emile. *The Balkan Peninsula*. Tr. Mrs. Thorpe. London: Fisher Unwin, 1887.

Lawrence, Robert Harding. *Graecia Nova! A Plea for Sympathy with Modern Greece*. London: Clayton, 1875.

Lawson, J. C. *Tales of Aegean Intrigue*. London: Chatto and Windus, 1920.

Lear, Edward. *The Cretan Journal*. Ed. Rowena Fowler. Athens and Dedham: Denise Harvey, 1984.

———. *Edward Lear in the Levant*. Ed. Susan Hyman. London: John Murray, 1988.

———. *Journal of a Landscape Painter in Albania and Illyria*. 1851. Reprint, London: Richard Bentley, 1852.

———. *Selected Letters*. Ed. Vivien Noakes. Oxford: Oxford University Press, 1988.

———. *Views of the Seven Ionian Islands*. London: Edward Lear, 1863.

Leask, Nigel. *British Romantic Writers and the East*. Cambridge: Cambridge University Press, 1992.

Lees-Milne, James. *Harold Nicolson: A Biography*. 2 vols. London: Chatto and Windus, 1980–1982.

Lehmann, John. *The Ample Proposition: Autobiography III*. London: Eyre and Spottiswoode, 1966.

———. *Collected Poems: 1930–1963*. London: Eyre and Spottiswoode, 1963.

Lemercier, Népomucène-Louis. *Les martyrs de Souli*. Paris: Urbain Canel, 1825.

Lentricchia, Frank. *Modernist Quartet*. Cambridge: Cambridge University Press, 1994.

Leonard, William. *Byron and Byronism in America*. Boston: Nicholl's Press, 1905.

Leontis, Artemis. *Topographies of Hellenism*. Ithaca, N.Y.: Cornell University Press, 1995.

Leppman, Wolfgang. *Winckelmann*. New York: Knopf, 1970.

Letter from a Grecian Traveler, Respecting the Intended Cession of Parga, by England, to the Porte. London: Sherwood, Neely, and James, 1819.

Levi, Peter. *Edward Lear: A Biography*. London: Macmillan, 1995.

Levi, Peter. *The Hill of Kronos*. 1981. Reprint, London: HarperCollins, 1991.

Levin, Harry. *The Broken Column: A Study in Romantic Hellenism*. Cambridge, Mass.: Harvard University Press, 1931.

Levinson, Marjorie. *The Romantic Fragment Poem*. Chapel Hill: University of North Carolina Press, 1986.

Lew, Joseph. "The Necessary Orientalist? *The Giaour* and Nineteenth-Century Imperialist Misogyny." In *Romanticism, Race, and Imperial Culture, 1780–1834*, 179–202. Ed. A. Richardson and S. Hofkosh. Bloomington: Indiana University Press, 1988.

Lewis, R. W. B. *Edith Wharton: A Biography*. New York: Harper and Row, 1975.

Lewis, Wyndham. *Blasting and Bombadiering*. 1937. Reprint, London: John Calder, 1982.

———. "Constantinople Our Star." *Blast* 2 (July 1915): 11.

Liddell, Robert. *Aegean Greece*. London: Jonathan Cape, 1954.

———. *The Morea*. London: Jonathan Cape, 1958.

Linklater, Andro. *Compton MacKenzie: A Life*. London: Chatto and Windus, 1987.

Lista, Giovanni. *Marinetti et le futurisme*. Lausanne: L'Age d'Homme, 1977.

Lohde, Clarissa. *Auf Klassichen Boden: Roman aus Zeit Konig Otto's*. Berlin: Eugen Grosser, 1882.

Loti, Pierre. *Aziyadé*. Paris: Callman Levy, 1879.

———. *La Turquie agonisante*. Paris: Callman Levy, 1913.

Louÿs, Pierre. *Aphrodite*. 1896. Tr. Willis Parker. New York: Three Sirens Press, 1932.

———. *Les chansons de Bilitis*. 1894. Ed. J.-P. Goujon. Paris: Gallimard, 1990.

The Lustful Turk. 1828. Reprint, London: W. H. Allen, 1985.

Lynch, Bohun. *Glamour: A Tale of Modern Greece*. London: John Murray, 1912.

———. "Some Sidelights on Modern Greece." *English Review* (May 1909): 385–93.

Macaulay, Rose. *The Towers of Trebizond*. 1956. Reprint, London: Collins, 1965.

MacDiarmid, Hugh. *The Letters of Hugh MacDiarmid*. Ed. Alan Bold. Athens: University of Georgia Press, 1984.

MacFarlane, Charles. *The Armenians: A Tale of Constantinople*. 3 vols. London: Sanders and Otley, 1830.

———. *Turkey and Its Destiny*. London: J. Murray, 1850.

MacGill, Stevenson. *Nacnud: A Tale of Asia Minor*. Edinburgh: Neill, 1840.

MacInnis, Helen. *Decision at Delphi*. New York: Harcourt, Brace, Jovanovich, 1960.

Mack Smith, Dennis. *Mazzini*. New Haven, Conn.: Yale University Press, 1994.

Mackenzie, Compton. *Aegean Memories*. London: Chatto and Windus, 1940.

———. *Extremes Meet*. Garden City, N.Y.: Doubleday, 1928.

———. *First Athenian Memories*. London: Cassell, 1931.

———. *Gallipoli Memories*. London: Cassell, 1929.

———. *Greece in My Life*. London: Chatto and Windus, 1960.

———. *Greek Memories*. London: Constable, 1932.

Mackenzie, Compton. *My Life and Times*. 10 vols. London: Chatto and Windus, 1963–1971.

———. *North Wind of Love*. London: Chatto and Windus, 1944–1945.

———. *South Wind of Love*. London: Rich and Cowan, 1937.

———. *Sylvia and Michael*. 1919. Reprinted in *The Life and Adventures of Sylvia Scarlett*. London: Martin Secker, 1933.

———. *Three Couriers*. London: Cassell, 1929.

———. *West to North*. London: Chatto and Windus, 1940.

Mackenzie, Georgiana M. M., and Alice P. Irby. *Travels in the Slavonic Provinces of Turkey-in-Europe*. 1866. Reprint, New York: Arno, 1971.

MacLeish, Archibald. *Collected Poems 1917–1982*. Boston: Houghton Mifflin, 1985.

Maclellan, Frances. *Sketches of Corfu*. London: Smith Elder, 1835.

Macleod, John. *Macedonian Measures, and Others*. Cambridge: Cambridge University Press, 1919.

MacNeice, Louis. *Collected Poems*. Ed. E. R. Dodds. New York: Oxford University Press, 1967.

———. *Selected Prose of Louis MacNeice*. Ed. Alan Heuser. Oxford: Oxford University Press, 1900.

MacNiven, Ian. *Lawrence Durrell: A Biography*. London: Faber and Faber, 1998.

Madden, R. R. *The Mussulman*. 3 vols. Henry Colburn and Richard Bentley, 1830.

Madeleine, Jacques. *Le sourire d'Hellas*. Paris: 1899.

Mahaffy, J. P. *Rambles and Studies in Greece*, 3d ed. London: Macmillan, 1887.

Makdisi, Saree. "Versions of the East: Byron, Shelley and the Orient." In *Romanticism, Race, and Imperialist Culture, 1780–1830*, 203–36. Ed. A Richardson and S. Hofksoh. Bloomington: Indiana University Press, 1988.

Makowsky, Veronica. *Susan Glaspell's Century of American Women*. Oxford: Oxford University Press, 1993.

Malakis, Emile. *French Travelers in Greece (1770–1820): An Early Phase of French Philhellenism*. Philadelphia: 1925.

Manatt, J. Irving. *Aegean Days*. Boston: Houghton Mifflin, 1914.

Mango, Cyril. "Byzantium and Romantic Hellenism." *Journal of the Warburg and Courtauld Institutes* 28 (1965): 29–43.

Mann, A. J., and William Wood. *The Salonika Front*. London: A. G. Black, 1920.

Manning, Olivia. *Friends and Heroes*. 1965. Reprinted in *The Balkan Trilogy*. New York: Penguin, 1981, 589–918.

Manning, Peter. *Reading Romantics*. Oxford: Oxford University Press, 1990.

Mansell, Philip. *Constantinople: City of the World's Desire*. New York: St. Martin's Press, 1996.

Mansfield, Charlotte. *Flowers of the Wind*. London: Elkin Matthews, 1898.

Marchand, Leslie. *Byron: A Biography*. 3 vols. New York: Knopf, 1957.

Marcoglou, Emmanuel. *The American Interest in the Cretan Revolution*. Athens: National Center for Social Research, 1971.

Marden, Phillip S. *Greece and the Aegean Islands*. Boston: Houghton Mifflin, 1907.

Marryat, Frederick. *The Pasha of Many Tales*. London: George Routledge, 1836.

Marten, Ambrose. *The Stanley Tales*. London. W. Morgan, 1826.

Masson, Edward. *Philhellenika; or, Poetic Translations*. Edinburgh: Johnstone and Hunter, 1852.

Masters, Brian. *The Life of E. F. Benson*. London: Chatto and Windus, 1991.

Matthews, Kenneth. *Aleko*. London: Peter Davies, 1934.

———. *Greek Salad*. London: Peter Davies, 1935.

Mavrogordato, John. *Letters from Greece Concerning the War of the Balkan Allies, 1912–1913*. London: Secker, 1914.

Mayo, Isabella Fyvie. "Athens Arisen." *Osborne* (Apr. 1897): 274–77.

———. *A Daughter of the Klephts*. London: W. & R. Chambers, 1897.

———. "The Last of the Klephts: A Glimpse of the Greek War of Independence." *Leisure Hour* (Apr. 1897): 361–68.

———. "Patriot Songs of the Greeks." *Good Words* (May 1897): 275–78.

Mazzini, Joseph. "Byron and Goethe." In *The Life and Work of Joseph Mazzini*, vol. 6, 61–94. London: Smith and Elder, 1908.

McCarthy, Justin. *Maid of Athens*. 3 vols. London: Chatto and Windus, 1883.

McCulloch. A. M. *A Tragic Vision: The Novels of Patrick White*. St. Lucia, Queensland, Australia: University of Queensland Press, 1983.

McGann, Jerome. *The Beauty of Inflections*. Oxford: Oxford University Press, 1985.

———. *Fiery Dust: Byron's Poetic Development*. Chicago: University of Chicago Press, 1968.

———. *The Romantic Ideology*. Chicago: University of Chicago Press, 1983.

McLaws, Lafayette [Emily Lafayette]. *Maid of Athens*. Boston: Little, Brown, 1906.

Meadows, Dennis. *The Greek Virgin*. London: Andrew Melrose, 1947.

Melville, Herman. *Complete Poems*. Ed. H. P. Vincent. Chicago: Packard, 1947.

———. *Journals*. Chicago: Northwestern University Press and the Newberry Library, 1989.

Merivale, Patricia. *Pan the Goat God*. Cambridge, Mass.: Harvard University Press, 1969.

Merrill, James. *A Different Person*. New York: Knopf, 1993.

———. *The (Diblos) Notebook*. 1965. Reprint, Normal, Ill.: Dalkey Archive Press, 1994.

———. "Marvelous Poet." *New York Review of Books* (July 15, 1975): 12–17.

———. *Selected Poems, 1945–1985*. New York: Knopf, 1992.

Meyer, Eric. "'I Know Thee Not, I Loathe Thy Race': Romantic Orientalism in the Eye of the Other." *ELH* 58.3 (1991): 657–700.

Meyers, Jeffrey. "Hemingway's Second War: The Greco-Turkish Conflict of 1920–1922." *Modern Fiction Studies* 30 (1984): 25–36.

Meyers, Terry. "Swinburne, Shelley, and *Songs before Sunrise*." In *The Whole Music of Passion: New Essays on Swinburne*, 40–51. Ed. R. Rooksby and N. Shrimpton. Brookfield, Vt.: Scholar Press, 1994.

Mifflin, Lloyd. *Castalian Days*. London: Henry Frowde, 1906.

———. *The Slopes of Helicon and Other Poems*. Boston: Estes and Lauriat, 1898.

Mill, John Stuart. "Grote's History of Greece." In *The Collected Works of John Stuart Mill*, vol. 11, 291–306. Ed. J. M. Robson. Toronto: University of Toronto Press, 1978.

Miller, Henry, *The Colossus of Maroussi*. New York: New Directions, 1941.

———. *First Impressions of Greece*. Santa Barbara, Calif., Capua Press, 1973.

Miller, Jane Eldredge. *Rebel Women: Feminism, Modernism, and the Edwardian Novel*. Chicago: University of Chicago Press, 1997.

Miller, William A. *The Balkans*. New York: Putnam's, 1903.

———. *Greek Life in Town and Country*. London: George Newnes, 1905.

Millingen, Frederick. *Slavery in Turkey: The Sultan's Harem*. London: Stafford, 1870.

Millingen, Julius. *Memoirs of the Affairs of Greece*. London: John Rodwell, 1831.

Milman, Richard. *Britain and the Eastern Question*. Oxford: Oxford University Press, 1979.

Milnes, Richard Monckton. *Memorials of a Tour in Greece, Chiefly Poetical*. London: Edward Moxon, 1834.

Minta, Stephen. *On a Voiceless Shore: Byron in Greece*. New York: Henry Holt, 1997.

Montgomery, A. E. "Lloyd George and the Greek Question, 1918–1922." In *Lloyd George: Twelve Essays*, 257–84. Ed. A. J. P. Taylor. New York: Athenaeum, 1971.

Moody, A. D. "Pound's Allen Upward." *Paideuma* 4 (1975): 55–70.

Moore, D. B. *The Poetry of Louis MacNeice*. Leicester, England: University of Leicester Press, 1972.

Moore, Joseph. *Outlying Europe and the Nearer Orient*. Philadelphia: Lippincott, 1880.

Moore, Mabel. *Days in Hellas*. London: Heinemann, 1909.

Moore, Thomas. *Poetical Works*. Ed. A. C. Godley. 1929. Reprint, New York: AMS Press, 1979.

Morgenthau, Henry. *I Was Sent to Athens*. Garden City, N.Y.: Doubleday, Doran, 1929.

———. *Secrets of the Bosphorus*. London: Hutchinson, 1918.

Morier, David. *Photo the Suliote*. 3 vols. London: L. Booth, 1857.

Morris, William. *News from Nowhere and Other Writings*. Ed. Clive Wilmer. New York: Penguin, 1993.

Mott, Valentine. *Travels in Europe and the East*. New York: Harper, 1842.

Mowrer, Paul Scott. *Balkanized Europe*. New York: Dutton, 1921.

Munro, Hector Herbert [Saki]. *Complete Works*. New York: Doubleday, 1976.

Murphy, Arthur. *The Grecian Daughter*. London: W. Griffin, 1772.

Murray, Gilbert G. A. *Gobi; or, Shamo*. London: Longmans, 1889.

———. *A History of Greek Literature*. 1897. Reprint, New York: Frederick Ungar, 1967.

———. *Mesolonghi Capta*. Oxford: B. H. Blackwell, 1877.

Myers, Ernest. *Gathered Poems*. London: Macmillan, 1904.

Myrivilis, Stratis. *Life in the Tomb*. Tr. Peter Bien. Hanover, N.H.: University Press of New England, 1977.

Myrivilis, Stratis. *The Mermaid Madonna*. Tr. Abbott Rick. London: Hutchinson, 1959.

Nash, Daniel. *My Son Is in the Mountains*. London: Jonathan Cape, 1955.

Neale, John Mason. *Theodora Phrantza*. London: Society for Promoting Christian Knowledge, 1857.

Nelson, James. *Sir William Watson*. New York: Twayne, 1966.

Nerval, Gérard de [Gérard Labrunie]. *Voyage en Orient*. 1851. Reprinted in *Oeuvres complètes*, vol. 2. Ed. J. Guillaume and C. Pichois. Paris: Gallimard, 1984.

Nevinson, Henry. *Scenes in the Thirty Day War between Greece and Turkey*. London: J. M. Dent, 1898.

Nicolson, Harold. *Byron: The Last Journey*. London: Constable, 1924.

Nicolson, Nigel. *Portrait of a Marriage*. New York: Athenaeum, 1973.

Nief, Fernand. *Phryne, la courtesan*. Paris: P. Douville, 1905.

Nielsen, Joergen Erik. "Parga: A Tale Attributed to Byron." *English Studies* 50 (1969): 397–405.

Noah, Mordecai. *The Captive; or, The Fall of Athens*. New York : E. Murden, 1822.

Norman, Henry. "The Wreck of Greece." *Scribner's* (Oct. 1897): 399–426.

O'Malley, Mary [Ann Bridge]. *The Dark Moment*. New York: Macmillan, 1952.

———. *Illyrian Spring*. New York: Little, Brown, 1935.

———. *Singing Waters*. London: Chatto and Windus, 1945.

Owenson, H. C. *Salonica and After*. London: Hodder and Stoughton, 1919.

Owenson, Sydney. *Woman; or, Ida of Athens*. 4 vols. London: Longman, Hurst, Reeve, and Orne, 1809.

Paley, Morton. "Introduction." In *The Last Man* by Mary Shelley, vii–xxiii. Oxford: Oxford University Press, 1994.

Palgrave, W. C. *Essays on the Eastern Question*. London: Macmillan, 1872.

Palmer, Alan Warwick. *The Banner of Battle: The Story of the Crimean War*. New York: St. Martin's, 1987.

———. *The Gardeners of Salonica*. New York: Simon and Schuster, 1965.

Palmer, Frederick. *Going to War in Greece*. New York: R. H. Russell, 1897.

Palmer, William Kimberley. *The Philhellenes*. Chicopee, Mass.: 1921.

Papadiamantis, Alexandros. *The Murderess*. 1903. Tr. Peter Levi. New York: Writers and Readers, 1983.

Papazoglou, Dimitra. *The Fever of Hellenism: The Influence of Ancient Greece in the Work of E. M. Forster*. Athens: University of Athens, 1995.

Papers of the Greek Committee. No. 2. Report of the banquet at Liverpool, June 5th, 1879. London: Greek Committee, 1879.

Pardoe, Miss. *The Romance of the Harem*. 3 vols. London: Henry Colburn, 1839.

Parga, A Poem. London: Gold and Northhouse, 1819.

Parry, William. *The Last Days of Lord Byron*. London: Knight and Lacy, 1825.

Partridge, Lucy. *Costanza of Mistra: A Tale of Modern Greece*. London: Whittaker, 1839.

Pashley, Robert. *Travels in Crete*. 2 vols. London: John Murray, 1837.

Pater, Walter. "Diaphaneitè." In *Miscellaneous Studies*, 249–54. 1895. Reprint, London: Macmillan, 1920.

Pater, Walter. *Marius the Epicurean: His Sensations and Ideas*. London: Macmillan, 1885.

———. *The Renaissance. Walter Pater: Three Major Texts*. Ed. William Buckler. New York: New York University Press, 1986.

Patmore, Derek. "Notes in a Greek Journal." *Yale Review* 36 (Dec. 1946): 278–86.

———. "Pages from a Greek Journal." *Greek Horizons* 1 (1946): 57–62.

Payne, John Howard. *Ali Pacha; or, The Signet Ring*. New York: E. Murden, 1823.

Peel, Edmund. *An Appeal to Europe on Behalf of Greece and Other Poems*. Isle of Wight: J. Hill, 1829.

Pemble, John. *The Mediterranean Passion: The Victorians in the South*. Oxford: Oxford University Press, 1987.

Penn, Virginia. "Philhellenism in England." *Slavonic Review* 14.41–42 (1936): 363–71, 647–60.

Percival, James Gates. *The Poetical Works*. 2 vols. Boston: Ticknor and Fields, 1859.

Persico, Elena. *Letteratura filellenica Italiana, 1787–1870*. Rome: Boudi, 1920.

Petrakis, Harry Mark. *The Hour of the Bell*. Garden City, N.Y.: Doubleday, 1976.

Pettifer, James. *The Greeks: The Land and People since the War*. New York: Viking, 1993.

Pfeiffer, Emily. *Flowers of the Night*. London: Turner and Ludgate, 1899.

———. *Flying Leaves from East and West*. London: Field and Tuer, 1885.

Philips, W. Allison. *The War of Independence in Greece*. New York: Scribner's, 1897.

Pickthall, Marmaduke. *As Others See Us*. London: W. Collins' Sons, 1922.

———. *The Early Hours*. London: W. Collins' Sons, 1921.

———. *The House of Islam*. London: Methuen, 1906.

———. *Oriental Encounters*. London: W. Collins' Sons, 1918.

———. *Veiled Women*. London: Eveleigh Nash, 1913.

Pierpont, John. *Airs of Palestine and Other Poems*. Boston: James Munro, 1840.

Pignatorre, George. "Lord Byron in the Greek Revolution." *Chamber's Journal* (Feb. 1913): 122–25.

Pinchin, Jane Lagoudis. *Alexandria Still: The City in the Work of Cavafy, Forster and Durrell*. Princeton, N.J. Princeton University Press, 1977.

Pitt-Keithley, Fiona. *The Pan Principle*. London: Sinclair Stevenson, 1994.

Plomer, William. *Ali the Lion*. London: Jonathan Cape, 1936.

———. *The Autobiography of William Plomer*. London: Jonathan Cape, 1975.

———. *Collected Poems*. London: Jonathan Cape, 1973.

———. *The Diamond of Jannina*. London: Jonathan Cape, 1970.

———. *The Five-fold Screen*. London: Hogarth, 1932.

———. "The Island: An Afternoon in the Life of Costa Zappaglou." In *A Child of Queen Victoria and Other Stories*, 205–16. London: Jonathan Cape, 1933.

———. "Local Colour." In *A Child of Queen Victoria and Other Stories*, 219–34. London: Jonathan Cape, 1933.

———. "Nausicaa." In *A Child of Queen Victoria and Other Stories*, 147–79. London: Jonathan Cape, 1933.

Polwhele, Richard. *Grecian Prospects*. London: Cadella and Davis, 1799.

Polybius. *Greece before the Conference*. London: Methuen, 1919.

Porter, Dennis *Haunted Journeys: Desire and Transgression in European Travel Writing*. Princeton, N.J.: Princeton University Press, 1994.

Porter, James. *Observations on the Religion, Law, Government, and Manners of the Turks*, 2d ed. London: J. Nourse, 1771.

Postlethwaite, Edward. *Letters from Greece*. London: J. C. Hotten, 1868.

Potter, Bob. *Greek Tragedy*. Bromley (Kent): Solidarity, 1968.

Pound, Ezra. "The Black Crusade." *New Age* 12.5 (Nov. 21, 1912): 116. Reprinted in *Poetry and Prose: Contributions to Periodicals*, vol. 1, 110. Ed. L. Baechler, A. W. Litz, and J. Longenbach. New York: Garland, 1991.

———. *The Cantos*. New York: New Directions, 1995.

Powell, Dilys. *An Affair of the Heart*. 1957. Reprint, Athens: Efstathiades, 1983.

Prévost, Antoine-François. *Un histoire d'une Grecque moderne*. 1740. Translated in 1741 as *The Story of a Fair Greek of Yester-Year*. Reprint, Potomac, Md.: Scripta Humanistica, 1984.

Price, G. Ward. *The Story of the Salonica Army*. New York: Edward Clarke, 1918.

Price, W. Crawford. *Venizelos and the War*. London: Simpkins, Marshall, 1917.

Prime, Samuel I. *Travels in Europe and the East*. 2 vols. New York: Harper, 1855.

Pritchett, V. S. "Journey in Greece." 1961. Reprinted in *At Home and Abroad*, 140–54. San Francisco: North Point Press, 1989.

Proust, Marcel. *In Search of Lost Times*. 6 vols. Tr. C. K. Scott Moncrief and Terence Kilmartin. New York: Modern Library, 1992.

Pückler-Muskau, Hermann von. *Südostlicher Bildersal—Griechischen Leiden*. 3 vols. Stuttgart: Hallberger'sche Verlagshandlung, 1840.

Quack-Eustathiades, Regina. *De deutsche Philhellenismus während des grieschischen Freiheitskampfes (1821–1827)*. Munich: D. Oldenbourg, 1984.

Quinones, Ricardo. *Mapping Literary Modernism*. Princeton, N.J.: Princeton University Press, 1985.

Raizis, Marius Byron. "Aspects of Byronic Philhellenism." In *Lord Byron: Byronism—Liberalism—Philhellenism*, 127–42. Ed. M. B. Raizis. Athens: Proceedings of the Fourteenth International Byron Symposium, 1988.

Raizis, Marius Byron, and Alexander Papas. *American Poets and the Greek Revolution*. Thessaloniki: Institute for Balkan Studies, 1972.

———, eds. *The Greek Revolution and the American Muse*. Thessaloniki: Institute for Balkan Studies, 1972.

Ratcliffe, Dorothy Una. *News of Persephone*. London: Eyre and Spottiswoode, 1939.

Rathbone, A. B. *Turkey and the Victims of Its Bad Faith and Its Mis-Government*. London: J. G. Taylor, 1875.

Raymond, Ernest. *Tell England: A Study in a Generation*. New York: George Doran, 1922.

Reed, John. *War in Eastern Europe*. New York: Scribner's, 1916.

Requier, Julius Augustus. *Marco Bozzaris: Poems*. Philadelphia: Lippincott, 1860.

Reynolds, Michael. *Hemingway: The Paris Years*. Oxford: Basil Blackwell, 1989.

Rice, Cale Young. *Collected Plays and Poems*. New York: Doubleday, 1915.

Richmond, Mary. *Maid of Athens*. London: Wright and Brown, 1948.

Riede, David. "Swinburne and Romantic Authority." In *The Whole Music of Passion: New Essays on Swinburne*, 22–39. Ed. R. Rooksby and N. Shrimpton. Brookfield, Vt.: Scholar Press, 1994.

Rieder, John. "Wordsworth and Romanticism in the Academy." In *At the Limits of Romanticism: Essays in Cultural, Feminist and Materialist Criticism*, 21–39. Ed. M. A. Favret and M. J. Watson. Bloomington: Indiana University Press, 1994.

Ritsos, Yannis. *Eighteen Short Songs of the Bitter Motherland*. Tr. Amy Mims. St. Paul: North Central Press, 1974.

———. *Gestures and Other Poems, 1968–1970*. Tr. Nikos Strangos. London: Cape Goliard, 1971.

———. *Romiossini and Other Poems*. Tr. D. Georgakas and E. Paidoussi. Madison, Wis.: Quixote Press, 1969.

———. *Selected Poems*. Tr. Nikos Strangos. London: Penguin, 1974.

Rives, Hallie Ermine. *The Castaway*. Indianapolis: Bobbs-Merrill, 1904.

Roberts, Cecil. *The Labyrinth*. Garden City, N.Y.: Doubleday, 1944.

Roberts, Jan. *The Judas Sheep*. 1975. Reprint, New York: Bantam Books, 1976.

Roberts, Jennifer Tolbert. *Athens on Trial*. Princeton, N.J.: Princeton University Press, 1994.

Robertson, Michael. "The Cultural Work of *Active Service*." *American Literary Realism* 28.2 (1996): 1–10.

Robinson, Charles. *Shelley and Byron: The Snake and the Eagle Wreathed in Flight*. Baltimore: Johns Hopkins University Press, 1976.

Rodd, Rennell. *The Customs and Lore of the Modern Greeks*. London: David Scott, 1892.

———. *The Violet Crown*, 2d ed. London: Edward Arnold, 1913.

———, ed. *The Englishman in Greece*. Oxford: Oxford University Press, 1910.

Roessel, David. "Live Orientals and Dead Greeks: E. M. Forster's Response to the Chanak Crisis." *Twentieth Century Literature* 36 (1990): 43–60.

———. "'Mr. Eugenides, the Smyrna Merchant' and Post-War Politics in *The Waste Land*." *Journal of Modern Literature* 16 (1988): 171–76.

———. "'The Repeat in History': Canto 26 and Greece's Asia Minor Disaster." *Twentieth Century Literature* 34 (1988): 180–90.

———. "Rewriting Reminiscences: Hemingway, Dos Passos and the Greco-Turkish War of 1920–22." In *Hellenism and the U.S.: Constructions / Deconstructions*, 33–40. Ed. Savas Patislides. Thessaloniki: Aristotle University, 1994.

———. "The Significance of Constantinople in *Orlando*." *Papers on Language and Literature* 28 (1992): 398–416.

Rose, W. Kinnarid. *With the Greeks in Thessaly*. London: Methuen, 1897.

Rosen, F. *Bentham, Byron and Greece: Constitutionalism, Nationalism, and Early Liberal Political Thought*. Oxford: Oxford University Press, 1992.

Rostand, Edmond. *Pour la Grèce*. Paris: Charpentier, 1897.

Rouse, W. H. D. "Folklore: First Fruits from Lesbos." *Folklore* 7 (1896): 142–49.

Rouse, W. H. D. "Folklore from the Sporades." *Folklore* 10 (1899): 150–85.
———. "Presidential Address." *Folklore* 16 (1905): 14–26.
Ruddick, William. "Byron in England." In *Byron in Nineteenth Century Europe*, 25–47. Ed. Paul Graham Trueblood. London: Methuen, 1981.
Ruskin, John. *The Works of John Ruskin*, vol. 5. Ed. E. T. Cook and A. Wedderbrun. London: George Allen, 1904.
Russell, Willy. *Shirley Valentine*. New York: Samuel French, 1988.
Rutherford, Andrew. Byron: *A Critical Study*. Stanford, Calif.: Stanford University Press, 1961.
Saab, Ann Pottinger. *Reluctant Icon: Gladstone, Bulgaria, and the Working Classes, 1856–1878*. Cambridge, Mass.: Harvard University Press, 1991.
Sackville-West, Vita. *Challenge*. 1924. Reprint, London: William Collins, 1974.
Said, Edward. *Orientalism*. New York: Pantheon, 1978.
St. Clair, William. *That Greece Might Still Be Free: The Philhellenes in the War of Independence*. Oxford: Oxford University Press, 1972.
———. *Trelawny*. London: J. Murray, 1977.
Salmon, Tim. *The Unwritten Places*. Athens: Lykavettos Press, 1995.
Samuelson, James. *Greece: Her Present Condition and Recent Progress*. London: Sampson Low, Marston, 1894.
Sanborn, Frank. "Lord Byron in the Greek Revolution." *Scribner's Magazine* (Sept. 1897): 345–59.
Sandiford, K. P. "Gladstone and Europe." In *The Gladstonian Turn of Mind*, 177–96. Ed. Bruce Kinzer. Toronto: University of Toronto Press, 1985.
Saroyan, William. *Love's Old Sweet Song*. New York: French, 1940.
Sarton, May. *Collected Poems: 1930–1993*. New York: Norton, 1993.
———. *Joanna and Ulysses*. New York: Norton, 1963.
Savage-Armstrong, George Francis. *A Garland from Greece*. London: Longmans, Green, 1882.
Scenes in the Morea; or, A Sketch of the Life of Demetrius Argyri. London: Sherwood, Jones, 1824.
Schneidau, Herbert. *Waking Giants: The Presence of the Past in Modernism*. Oxford: Oxford University Press, 1991.
Scrivener, Michael. *Radical Shelley*. Princeton, N.J.: Princeton University Press, 1982.
Sedgwick, Alexander C. *Tell Sparta*. Boston: Houghton Mifflin, 1945.
Seferis, George. *Collected Poems*. Tr. Edmund Keeley and Philip Sherrard. Princeton, N.J.: Princeton University Press, 1981.
———. *The King of Asine and Other Poems*. Tr. Lawrence Durrell, Bernard Spencer, and Nanos Valaoritis. London: Lehmann, 1948.
———. *Poems*. Tr. Rex Warner. London: Bodley Head, 1960.
Seligman, Vincent J. *Bank Holiday*. London: Longmans, 1934.
———. *Macedonian Musings*. London: Allen and Unwin, 1918.
———. *The Salonica Side-Show*. London: Allen and Unwin, 1919.
———. *The Victory of Venizelos: A Study in Greek Politics*. London: Allen and Unwin, 1920.

Sergeant, Lewis. *Greece in the Nineteenth Century: A Record of Hellenic Emancipation and Progress*. London: T. Fisher Unwin, 1897.

———. *New Greece*. London: Cassell Petter & Gilpin, 1878.

Sétier, M. *L'Athénienne; ou, Les Français en Grèce*. Paris: Sanson, 1826.

Seton-Watson, R. W. *Disraeli, Gladstone and the Eastern Question*. London: Macmillan, 1935.

Settle, Mary Lee. *Blood Tie*. 1977. Reprint, New York: Scribner's, 1986.

———. *Turkish Reflections: A Biography of a Place*. New York: Simon and Schuster, 1991.

Seymour, Thomas. "Life and Travel in Modern Greece." *Scribner's* (July 1888): 46–63.

Shannon, R. T. *Gladstone*, vol. 1. London: Hamish Hamilton, 1982.

———. *Gladstone and the Bulgarian Agitation*. London: Thomas Nelson, 1963.

Sharon, Avi. "New Friends for New Places: England Rediscovers Greece." *Arion* 8.2 (2000): 42–62.

Sharuffin, Mohammed. *Islam and Romantic Orientalism: Literary Encounters with the East*. New York: I. B. Tauris, 1991.

Shaw, George Bernard. *Collected Plays*. 7 vols. London: Bodley Head, 1971.

———. *The Complete Prefaces*. 2 vols. Ed. Dan Laurence and Daniel Leary. London: Allen Lane/Penguin, 1993.

A Sheaf of Greek Folk Songs. Gleaned by an Old Philhellene. Oxford: Basil Blackwell, 1922.

Shelley, Mary. *Collected Tales and Stories*. Ed. Charles Robinson. Baltimore: Johns Hopkins University Press, 1976.

———. *The Last Man*. 1826. Ed. Morton Paley. Reprint, Oxford: Oxford World's Classics, 1994.

Shelley, Percy Bysshe. *Letters of P. B. Shelley*. 2 vols. Ed. Frederick Jones. Oxford: Oxford University Press, 1964.

———. *The Revolt of Islam: The Complete Poetical Works*, vol. 2. Ed. Neville Rogers. Oxford: Oxford University Press, 1975.

———. *Shelley's Prose and Poetry*. Ed. Donald Reiman and Sharon Powers. New York: Norton, 1977.

Sheridan, Charles Brinsley. *Songs of the Modern Greeks*. London: Longman, Hurst, Rees, and Orne, 1825.

———. *Thoughts on the Greek Revolution*. London: John Murray, 1822.

Sheridan, Clare. *The Naked Truth*. New York: Harper, 1928.

———. *Turkish Kaleidoscope*. London: Duckworth, 1928.

———. *West and East*. New York: Boni and Liveright, 1923.

Sherman, Martin. *A Madhouse in Goa*. Chalbury, Oxon, England: Amber Lane Press, 1989.

Sherrard, Philip. "The Light and the Blood." *Arion*, 3d ser., 7 (1999): 61–71.

Sherwood, Margaret. "Pan and the Crusader." *Atlantic Monthly* (Aug. 1910): 145–64.

Shotwell, James. *A Short History of the Question of Constantinople and the Straits*. New York: American Association for International Conciliation, 1922.

Sitwell, Osbert. "That Flesh Was Heir to . . ." In *Collected Stories*, 7–50. New York: Harper, 1953.

Sitwell, Sacheverell. *Collected Poems of Sacheverell Sitwell*. London: Duckworth, 1936. Reprint, New York: AMS Press, 1976.

———. *Roumanian Journey*. 1938. Reprint, Oxford: Oxford University Press, 1992.

Skene, Felicia. *The Isles of Greece and Other Poems*. Edinburgh: Grant, 1843.

Slabey, Robert M. "The Structure of *In Our Time*." In *Critical Essays on Hemingway's "In Our Time,"* 76–87. Ed. Michael Reynolds. Boston: G. K. Hall, 1983.

Slade, Adolphus. *Records of Travel in Turkey, Greece, & C.* 2 vols. London: Sanders and Otley, 1833.

Smith, Arthur Howden. *Fighting the Turk in the Balkans: An American's Adventures with the Macedonian Revolutionaries*. New York: Putnam's Sons, 1908.

Smith, Michael Llewellyn. *Ionian Vision*. London: Allen Lane, 1973.

Smith, Paul. "The Bloody Typewriter and the Burning Snakes." In *Hemingway: Essays of Reassessment*, 80–90. Ed. F. Scafella. New York: Oxford University Press.

Snider, Denton J. *A Walk in Hellas; or, The Old and the New*. St. Louis: 1881.

Snowden, Eleanor. *The Maid of Scio: A Tale of Modern Greece*. London: Whittaker, 1830.

Spencer, Bernard. *Collected Poems*. Ed. Roger Bowen. Oxford: Oxford University Press, 1981.

Spencer, Edward. *Travels in European Turkey*. London: Coburn, 1851.

Spencer, Terence. *Fair Greece, Sad Relic*. London: Weidenfield and Nicolson, 1954.

Spender, Harold. *Byron and Greece*. London: John Murray, 1924.

———. "Never Again." *Publications of the Balkan Committee* [London], no. 17 (1912): 29–39.

———. "The Resurrection of Greece, 1821–1921." *Contemporary Review* (Aug. 1921): 152–59.

Spender, Stephen. "Brilliant Athens and Us." *Encounter* (Jan. 1954): 77–80.

———. *Collected Poems: 1928–1985*. Oxford: Oxford University Press, 1987.

———. "Ghika." In *Ghika: Paintings, Drawings, Sculptures*, 22–24. London: Lund Humphries, 1964.

———. *Letters to Christopher: Stephen Spender's Letters to Christopher Isherwood, 1929–1939*. Ed. Lee Bartlett. Santa Barbara, Calif.: Black Sparrow Press, 1980.

Spivak, Gayatri. "Can the Subaltern Speak?" In *Marxism and the Interpretation of Cultures*, 271–313. Ed. C. Nelson and L. Grossberg. Urbana: University of Illinois Press, 1988.

Sprinker, Michael. *History and Ideology in Proust*. Cambridge: Cambridge University Press, 1994.

Stallworthy, Jon. *Louis MacNeice*. New York: Norton, 1995.

Standish, Burt [Filbert Pattison]. *Dick Merriwell in Greece; or, The Maid of Athens*. New York: Street & Smith, 1905.

Stanhope, Leicester. *Greece in 1823 and 1824*. London: Sherwood, Pope and Gilbert, 1825.

Stead, W. T. *The Haunting Horrors of Armenia*. London: Review of Reviews, 1896.

Stebbing, E. P. *At the Serbian Front in Macedonia*. London: John Lane, 1917.

Stedman, Edmund Clarence. *Poetical Works*. Boston: Houghton Mifflin, 1901.

Steevens, G. W. "What Happened in Thessaly." *Blackwood's Magazine* (July 1897): 146–60.

———. *With the Conquering Turk*. London: William Blackwood, 1897.

Stefanini, J. *The Personal Sufferings of J. Stefanini*. New York: Vanderpool and Cole, 1829.

Stephens, John L. *Incidents of Travel in Greece, Turkey, Russia and Poland*. 2 vols. London: Richard Bentley, 1839.

Stern, B. H. *The Rise of Romantic Hellenism in English Literature, 1732–1786*. 1940. Reprint, New York: Octagon Books, 1969.

Stillman, William J. *An American Consul in a Cretan War*. Ed. George Arnakis. Austin: Center for Neo-Hellenic Studies, 1966. A revised edition of *The Cretan Insurrection of 1866–7–8*. New York: Henry Holt, 1874.

———. *Articles and Despatches from Crete*. Ed. George Arnakis. Austin: Center for Neo-Hellenic Studies, 1976.

———. *Herzegovina and the Late Uprising*. London: Longman Green, 1877.

Stoddard, R. H. *The Poems of R. H. Stoddard*. New York: Scribner's, 1880.

Storace, Patricia. *Dinner with Persephone*. New York: Pantheon, 1996.

Strickland, Agnes. *Demetrius: A Tale of Modern Greece*. London: James Frazer, 1833.

Strother, French. *Maid of Athens*. Garden City, N.Y.: Doubleday, 1932.

Stuart, James, and Revett, Nicholas. *The Antiquities of Athens*. 4 vols. 1762–1816.

Swinburne, Algernon Charles. *The Ballad of Bulgarie*. London: privately printed, 1893 (a copy can be found in the British Library).

———. *The Complete Works of Algernon Charles Swinburne*. 20 vols. Ed. E. Gosse and T. J. Wise. London: Heinemann, 1925–1927.

———. *The Swinburne Letters*, vol. 4. Ed. Cecil Lang. New Haven Conn.: Yale University Press, 1960.

Symonds, John Addington. *Sketches and Studies in Italy and Greece*. 3 vols. London: John Murray, 1910.

Tabaki-Iona, Frederiki. *Poésie philhellénique et périodique del la restauration*. Athens: Societes des Archives Helleniques, 1993.

Tapp, Arthur Griffin. *Stories of Salonica and the New Crusade*. London: Drane's, 1922.

Taylor, Bayard. *Travels in Greece and Russia: With an Excursion to Crete*. New York: Putnam, 1859.

Temple, Sir Grenville. *Travels in Greeece, Turkey, and the Mediterranean*. 2 vols. London: Sanders and Otley, 1843.

Tennyson, Alfred. *Poems of Alfred Tennyson*. 3 vols. 2d ed. Ed. Christopher Ricks. Berkeley: University of California Press, 1987.

Tetrault, James. "Heirs to Virtue: Byron, Gobineau, Blunt." In *Lord Byron: Byronism—Liberalism—Philhellenism*, 53–65. Ed. Marius Byron Raizis. Athens: Proceedings of the Fourteenth International Byron Symposium, 1988.

———. "This Violent Passion: Gobineau and Greece." *Modern Greek Studies Yearbook 8* (1992): 57–74.

Thackeray, William Makepeace. *Notes of a Journey from Cornhill to Grand Cairo*. 1846. Reprinted in *The Works of William Makepeace Thackeray*, vol. 21. New York: Scribner's, 1904.

Theotokas, George. *Argo*. Tr. E. Margaret Brooke and Ares Tsatsopoulos. London: Methuen, 1951.

Les Thermopyles: Tragédie de circonstances. Paris: Didot le Jeune, 1791.

Thery, E. "Modern Greece as She Is and as She Should Be." *Hellenic Herald* (Apr. 1907): 81–86.

Thomas, D. M. *Lady with a Laptop*. New York: Carroll and Graf, 1997.

Thomas, Hugh. *The Spanish Civil War*. New York: Harper's, 1961.

Thompson, E. P. *William Morris: Romantic to Revolutionary*. 1955. Reprint, New York: Pantheon, 1977.

Thomson, Basil. *The Allied Secret Service in Greece*. London: Hutchinson, 1931.

Thorn, Michael. *Tennyson*. New York: St. Martin's, 1993.

Todorova, Maria. "The Balkans: From Discovery to Invention." *Slavic Review* 53 (1994): 453–82.

Toynbee, Arnold. "Greece." In *The Balkans*, 163–250. Ed. Neville Forbes et al. Oxford: Oxford University Press, 1915.

———. *The Western Question in Greece and Turkey*. Boston: Houghton Mifflin, 1920.

Traill, H. D. "Our Learned Philhellenes." *Fortnightly Review* (Apr. 1897): 504–12.

Trappman, A. H. *The Greeks Triumphant*. London: Forster Grier, 1915.

Trask, Katerina. "Hands Off." *Review of Reviews* (Apr. 1897): 481.

Travis, William. *Bus Stop Symi*. London: Rapp and Whiting, 1970.

Trelawny, Edward. *Records of Shelley, Byron and the Author*. 1878. Ed. David Wright. Reprint, Hammondsworth, Middlesex, England: Penguin, 1973. An early version of this work first appeared in 1858 as *Recollections of the Last Days of Byron and Shelley*.

Trollope, Anthony. *The Bertrams*. 1859. Reprint, Oxford: Oxford World's Classics, 1991.

Trowbridge, Breck. *Venizelos: An Opportunity and the Man*. New York: Society of American Philhellenes, 1918.

Tsigakou, Fani-Maria. *The Rediscovery of Greece: Travelers and Painters of the Romantic Era*. London: Thames and Hudson, 1981.

Tsoucalas, Constantine. *Greek Tragedy*. London: Penguin, 1969.

Turner, Frank. *The Greek Heritage in Victorian Britain*. New Haven, Conn.: Yale University Press, 1981.

Twain, Mark. *The Innocents Abroad: Roughing It*. Ed. Guy Cardwell. New York: Library of America, 1984.

Unsworth, Barry. *The Greeks Have a Word for It*. London: Hutchinson, 1967.

Unsworth, Barry. *Pascali's Island*. 1980. Reprint, New York: Norton, 1997.
————. *The Rage of the Vulture*. 1982. Reprint, New York: Norton, 1997.
Upward, Allen. "Bankrupt Turkey." *Forum* 44 (1910): 513–24.
————. *The East End of Europe*. London: J. Murray, 1908.
————. *The Prince of Balkistan*. Philadelphia: Lippincott, 1895.
————. *Some Personalities*. London: John Murray, 1921.
Ure, P. N. *Venizelos and His Fellow Countrymen*. London: Publications of the Anglo-Hellenic League, 1917.
Urquhart, David. *The Spirit of the East, Illustrated in a Journal of Travels through Roumeli during an Eventful Period*. 2 vols. London: Henry Colburn, 1838.
Vasey, Richard. *Psiloriti: A Dramatic Poem Illustrative of Life under the Turk in Crete*. Bradford, England: Thomas Brown, 1896.
Vasov, Ivan. *Under the Yoke*. 1893. Reprint, London: Heinemann, 1902.
Venezis, Ilias. *Aeolia*. Tr. E. D. Scott-Kilvert. London: W. Campion, 1949.
Verne, Jules. *The Complete Twenty-Thousand Leagues under the Sea*. Tr. Emmanuel Mickel. Bloomington: Indiana University Press, 1991.
Verney, F. "Songs and Legends of the Modern Greeks." *Contemporary Review* (Dec. 1875): 96–113.
Vickery, John. *The Literary Impact of the Golden Bough*. Princeton, N.J.: Princeton University Press, 1973.
Vidal, Gore. *Palimpsest: A Memoir*. New York: Random House, 1995.
Voltaire, François-Marie Arouet de. *Oeuvres complètes*. Paris: Garnier Frères, 1877–85.
Vrettos, Theodore. *Lord Elgin's Lady*. Boston: Little, Brown, 1982.
Waiblinger, Friedrich Wilhelm. *Vier Erzählungen aus der Geschichte des jetzigen Griechenlands*. Ludwigsburg: C. F. Nast, 1826.
Walkerdine, W. E. *Ode of Triumph: November 1912*. Cambridge: W. Heffer, 1913.
Wallace, Jennifer. *Shelley and Greece*. New York: St. Martin's, 1997.
Waller, John. *The Kiss of Stars*. London: Heinemann, 1948.
Walsh, Douglas. *With the Serbs in Macedonia*. London: John Lane, 1920.
War in Greece. London: James Ridgeway, 1821.
Ward, Aaron. *Around the Pyramids*. New York: Carleton, 1863.
Warner, Rex. *Men of Stones*. London: Bodley Head, 1950.
————. *Views of Attica and Its Surroundings*. London: John Lehmann, 1950.
————. "Where Shall John Go? XV Greece." *Horizon* 17 (1948): 295–300.
Watkins, Daniel. *Social Relations in Byron's Eastern Tales*. Cranbury, N.J.: Associated University Presses, 1987.
Watson, William. *The Hope of the World and Other Poems*. London: John Lane, 1898.
————. *Poems of William Watson*. 2 vols. London: John Lane, 1912.
————. *The Purple East: A Series of Sonnets on England's Desertion of Armenia*. Chicago: Stone and Kimball, 1896.
————. *The Year of Shame*. London: John Lane, 1897.
Waugh, Evelyn. *Brideshead Revisited*. 1945. Reprint, London: Penguin, 1962.
————. *Labels: A Mediterranean Journey*. 1930. Reprint, London: Duckworth, 1974.

Webb, Timothy, ed. *English Romantic Hellenism*. Manchester: University of Manchester Press, 1982.

Webster, Daniel. *Mr. Webster's Speech on the Greek Revolution*. Washington, D.C.: John Mecham, 1824.

Welleck, René. "The Concept of 'Romanticism' in Literary History." *Comparative Literature* 1 (1949): 1–23.

Weller, George. *A Crack in the Column*. New York: Random House, 1949.

West, Rebecca. *Black Lamb and Grey Falcon*. 1941. New York: Penguin, 1982.

Westcott, Glenway. *Apartment in Athens*. New York: Harper, 1945.

Whalley, George. "England/Romantic-Romanticism." In *"Romantic" and Its Cognates*, 157–262. Ed. Hans Eichner. Toronto: University of Toronto Press, 1972.

Wharton, Edith. *A Backward Glance*. 1933. Reprint, New York: Scribner's, 1964.

———. *The Cruise of the Vanadis*. Ed. Claudine Lesage. Amiens: Sterne, 1992.

———. "Dieu d'amour." In *Certain People*, 102–40. New York: D. Appleton, 1930.

———. *Old New York*. 1924. Reprint, New York: Scribner's 1995.

———. "Roman Fever." In *The Collected Short Stories of Edith Wharton Vol. 2*, *833–43*. Ed. R. W. B. Lewis. New York: Scribner's, 1968.

Wheatley, Dennis. *The Eunuch of Stamboul*. Boston: Little, Brown, 1935.

White, Patrick. *The Aunt's Story*. New York: Viking, 1948.

———. "Being Kind to Titina." In *The Burnt Ones*, 185–205. London: Spottiswoode and Eyre, 1966.

———. "An Evening at Sissy Kamara's." In *The Burnt Ones*, 134–50. London: Spottiswoode and Eyre, 1966.

———. "The Full Belly." In *The Cockatoos: Shorter Novels and Stories*, 95–119. London: Jonathan Cape, 1974.

———. *Flaws in the Glass*. 1981. Reprint, New York: Penguin, 1983.

———. "A Glass of Tea." In *The Burnt Ones*, 88–111. London: Spottiswoode and Eyre, 1966.

———. "Greece—My Other Country." In *Patrick White Speaks*, 133–36. Sydney: Primavera Press, 1989.

———. "On the Balcony." In *Patrick White: Selected Writings*, 123–33. Ed. Alan Lawson. Queensland, Australia: University of Queensland, 1997.

———. *The Vivisector*. New York: Viking, 1970.

———. "The Woman Who Wasn't Allowed to Keep Cats." In *The Burnt Ones*, 240–82. London: Spottiswoode and Eyre, 1964.

Whittemore, Edward. *Jerusalem Poker*. New York: Holt, Rinehart and Winston, 1978.

———. *Nile Shadows*. New York: Holt, Rinehart and Winston, 1983.

———. *Sinai Tapestry*. New York: Holt, Rinehart and Winston, 1977.

Whittier, John Greenleaf. *Poetical Works*. Ed. H. H. Waggoner. Boston: Houghton Mifflin, 1975.

Wiener, Harold. "Byron and the East: Literary Sources of the Turkish Tales." In *Nineteenth-Century Studies*, 89–129. Ed. H. Davis, W. C. Devane, and R. C. Bald. Ithaca, N.Y.: Cornell University Press, 1940.

Wilde, Oscar. *Complete Poetry*. Ed. Isobel Murray. Oxford: Oxford University Press, 1997.

William, Neil Wynn. *The Bayonet that Came Home: A Vanity of Modern Greece*. London: Edward Arnold, 1896.

———. *Greek Peasant Stories; or, Gleams and Glooms of Grecian Colour*. London: Digby, Long, 1899.

———. *Tales and Sketches of Modern Greece*. London: Bedford, 1894.

Willis, Nathaniel Parker. *Pencillings by the Way*. London: John Macrone, 1935.

Wilson, J. M. *I Was Once an English Poet: A Biography of William Watson*. London: Cecil Woolf, 1981.

Winckelmann, Johann J. *Gedanken über die Nachahmung der griechischen Werke in der Mahlerey und Bildhaur-Kunst*. Tr. Henry Fuseli in *Reflections on the Painting and Sculpture of the Greeks*. Glasgow: 1765.

Wolff, Larry. *Inventing Eastern Europe*. Stanford, Calif.: Stanford University Press, 1994.

Woodberry, George. *The Flight and Other Poems*. New York: Macmillan, 1914.

Woodhouse, C. M. "English Literary Philhellenism." In *Europäischer Philhellenismus*, 2:112–19. Ed. Evangelos Konstantinou. Berlin: Peter Lang, 1992.

———. *One Omen*. London: Hutchinson, 1950.

———. *The Philhellenes*. London: Hodder and Stoughton, 1969.

Woodring, Carl. *Politics in English Romantic Poetry*. Cambridge, Mass.: Harvard University Press, 1970.

Woods, Charles. "The Turkish Treaty" *Fortnightly Review* (July 1, 1920): 57.

Woolf, Leonard. *The Future of Constantinople*. London: Allen and Unwin, 1917.

Woolf, Virginia. *The Complete Shorter Fiction*, rev. ed. Ed. Susan Dick. London: Hogarth, 1989.

———. *Jacob's Room*. 1922. Reprint, New York: Harcourt Brace Jovanovich, 1960.

———. *A Passionate Apprentice: The Early Journals 1897–1906*. Ed. Mitchell Leaska. New York: Harcourt Brace Jovanovich, 1990.

———. *The Years*. London: Hogarth, 1937.

Woolsey, Theodore. "The Powers and the Greco-Turkish War." *Forum* (July 1897): 513–22.

Wright, Nathalia. *American Novelists in Italy*. Philadelphia: University of Pennsylvania Press, 1965.

Wright, W. R. *Horae Ionicae: A Poem Descriptive of the Ionian Islands and Part of the Adjacent Coast of Greece*, 2d ed. London: James Cawthorn, 1811.

Wyse, Thomas. *Impressions of Greece*. London: Hurst and Blackett, 1871.

Xenopoulos, Gregory. *The Stepmother: A Tale of Modern Athens*. Tr. Elizabeth Edmonds. London: John Lane, 1897.

Xenos, Stephanos. *Andronike: A Heroine of the Greek Revolution*. Tr. E. A. Grosvenor. Boston: Robert, 1897.

Yeats, William Butler. *The Poems of William Butler Yeats*. Ed. Richard Finneran. New York: Macmillan, 1983.

Yeats-Brown, Francis. *The Bloody Years*. New York: Viking, 1942.

Yenser, Stephen. *The Consuming Myth: The Poetry of James Merrill*. Cambridge, Mass.: Harvard University Press, 1987.

Young, Kenneth. "The Contemporary Greek Influence on English Writers." *Life and Letters* 64 (Jan. 1950): 53–64.

INDEX

379